THE PHILOSOPHY OF
HANS-GEORG GADAMER

THE LIBRARY OF LIVING PHILOSOPHERS

PAUL ARTHUR SCHILPP, FOUNDER AND EDITOR 1939–1981
LEWIS EDWIN HAHN, EDITOR 1981–

Paul Arthur Schilpp, Editor
THE PHILOSOPHY OF JOHN DEWEY (1939, 1971, 1989)
THE PHILOSOPHY OF GEORGE SANTAYANA (1940, 1951)
THE PHILOSOPHY OF ALFRED NORTH WHITEHEAD (1941, 1951)
THE PHILOSOPHY OF G.E. MOORE (1942, 1971)
THE PHILOSOPHY OF BERTRAND RUSSELL (1944, 1971)
THE PHILOSOPHY OF ERNST CASSIRER (1949)
ALBERT EINSTEIN: PHILOSOPHER-SCIENTIST (1949, 1970)
THE PHILOSOPHY OF SARVEPALLI RADHAKRISHNAN (1952)
THE PHILOSOPHY OF KARL JASPERS (1957; AUG. ED., 1981)
THE PHILOSOPHY OF C.D. BROAD (1959)
THE PHILOSOPHY OF RUDOLF CARNAP (1963)
THE PHILOSOPHY OF C.I. LEWIS (1968)
THE PHILOSOPHY OF KARL POPPER (1974)
THE PHILOSOPHY OF BRAND BLANSHARD (1980)
THE PHILOSOPHY OF JEAN-PAUL SARTRE (1981)

Paul Arthur Schilpp and Maurice Friedman, Editors
THE PHILOSOPHY OF MARTIN BUBER (1967)

Paul Arthur Schilpp and Lewis Edwin Hahn, Editors
THE PHILOSOPHY OF GABRIEL MARCEL (1984)
THE PHILOSOPHY OF W.V. QUINE (1986)
THE PHILOSOPHY OF GEORG HENRIK VON WRIGHT (1989)

Lewis Edwin Hahn, Editor
THE PHILOSOPHY OF CHARLES HARTSHORNE (1991)
THE PHILOSOPHY OF A.J. AYER (1992)
THE PHILOSOPHY OF PAUL RICOEUR (1995)
THE PHILOSOPHY OF PAUL WEISS (1995)
THE PHILOSOPHY OF HANS-GEORG GADAMER (1997)

In Preparation:
Lewis Edwin Hahn, Editor
THE PHILOSOPHY OF RODERICK M. CHISHOLM
THE PHILOSOPHY OF DONALD DAVIDSON
THE PHILOSOPHY OF SIR PETER F. STRAWSON
THE PHILOSOPHY OF JÜRGEN HABERMAS
THE PHILOSOPHY OF SEYYED HOSSEIN NASR

Hans-Georg Gadamer

THE LIBRARY OF LIVING PHILOSOPHERS
VOLUME XXIV

THE PHILOSOPHY OF

HANS-GEORG GADAMER

EDITED BY

LEWIS EDWIN HAHN

SOUTHERN ILLINOIS UNIVERSITY AT CARBONDALE

1997

CHICAGO AND LA SALLE, ILLINOIS • OPEN COURT • ESTABLISHED 1887

THE PHILOSOPHY OF HANS-GEORG GADAMER

Open Court Publishing Company is a division of Carus Publishing Company.

Printed and bound in the United States of America.

Library of Congress Cataloging-in-Publication Data

Gadamer, Hans Georg, 1900-
    The philosophy of Hans-Georg Gadamer / edited by Lewis Edwin Hahn.
        p.   cm. — (The Library of living philosophers ; v. 24)
    Includes bibliographical references and index.
    ISBN 0-8126-9341-8 (cloth : alk. paper). — ISBN 0-8126-9342-6
(paper : alk. paper)
       1. Gadamer, Hans Georg, 1900– . 2. Philosophy.
   3. Hermeneutics.   I. Hahn, Lewis Edwin, 1908– . II. Title.
   III. Series.
   B3248.G34G34   1997
   193—dc21   96-48164
                                                   CIP

The Library of Living Philosophers is published under the sponsorship of Southern Illinois University at Carbondale.

GENERAL INTRODUCTION
TO
THE LIBRARY OF LIVING PHILOSOPHERS

Founded in 1938 by Professor Paul Arthur Schilpp and edited by him until July 1981, when the present writer became editor, the Library of Living Philosophers is devoted to critical analysis and discussion of some of the world's greatest living philosophers. The format for the series provides for setting up in each volume a dialogue between the critics and the great philosopher. The aim is not refutation or confrontation but rather fruitful joining of issues and improved understanding of the positions and issues involved. That is, the goal is not overcoming those who differ from us philosophically but interacting creatively with them.

The basic idea for the series, according to Professor Schilpp's general introduction to each of the earlier volumes, came from the late F. C. S. Schiller, who declared in his essay on "Must Philosophers Disagree?" (in *Must Philosophers Disagree?* London: Macmillan, 1934) that the greatest obstacle to fruitful discussion in philosophy is "the curious etiquette which apparently taboos the asking of questions about a philosopher's meaning while he is alive." The "interminable controversies which fill the histories of philosophy," in Schiller's opinion, "could have been ended at once by asking the living philosophers a few searching questions." And while he may have been overly optimistic about ending "interminable controversies" in this way, it seems clear that directing searching questions to great philosophers about what they really mean or how they think certain difficulties in their philosophy can be resolved while they are still alive can produce far greater clarity of understanding and more fruitful philosophizing than might otherwise be had.

And to Paul Arthur Schilpp's undying credit, he acted on this basic thought in launching in 1938 the Library of Living Philosophers. It is planned that each volume in the Library of Living Philosophers include preferably an intellectual autobiography by the principal philosopher or an authorized biography as well as a bibliography of that thinker's publications, a series of expository and critical essays written by leading exponents and opponents of the philosopher's thought, and the philosopher's replies to the interpretations and queries in these articles. The intellectual autobiographies usually shed a great deal of light on both how the philosophies of the great thinkers developed and the major philosophical movements and issues of their time; and many of our great philosophers seek to orient their outlook not merely to their contemporaries but also to what they find most important in earlier philosophers. The bibliography will help provide ready access to the featured scholar's writings and thought.

With this format in mind, the Library expects to publish at more or less regular intervals a volume on one of the world's greater living philosophers.

In accordance with past practice, the editor has deemed it desirable to secure the services of an Advisory Board of philosophers to aid him in the selection of subjects of future volumes. The names of eight prominent American philosophers who have agreed to serve appear on the page following the Founder's General Introduction. To each of them the editor is most grateful.

Future volumes in this series will appear in as rapid succession as is feasible in view of the scholarly nature of this library. The next volume in the series will be devoted to the philosophy of Roderick M. Chisholm, and it will be followed by ones on Donald Davidson and Sir Peter F. Strawson.

Volumes are also projected on Jürgen Habermas and Seyyed Hossein Nasr.

Throughout its career, since its founding in 1938, the Library of Living Philosophers, because of its scholarly nature, has never been self-supporting. We acknowledge gratefully that the generosity of the Edward C. Hegeler Foundation has made possible the publication of many volumes, but for support of future volumes additional funds are needed. On 20 February 1979 the Board of Trustees of Southern Illinois University contractually assumed sponsorship of the Library, which is therefore no longer separately incorporated. Gifts specifically designated for the Library, however, may be made through the Southern Illinois University Foundation, and inasmuch as the latter is a tax-exempt institution, such gifts are tax-deductible.

LEWIS E. HAHN
EDITOR

DEPARTMENT OF PHILOSOPHY
SOUTHERN ILLINOIS UNIVERSITY AT CARBONDALE

FOUNDER'S GENERAL INTRODUCTION*
TO
THE LIBRARY OF LIVING PHILOSOPHERS

According to the late F. C. S. Schiller, the greatest obstacle to fruitful discussion in philosophy is "the curious etiquette which apparently taboos the asking of questions about a philosopher's meaning while he is alive." The "interminable controversies which fill the histories of philosophy," he goes on to say, "could have been ended at once by asking the living philosophers a few searching questions."

The confident optimism of this last remark undoubtedly goes too far. Living thinkers have often been asked "a few searching questions," but their answers have not stopped "interminable controversies" about their real meaning. It is nonetheless true that there would be far greater clarity of understanding than is now often the case if more such searching questions had been directed to great thinkers while they were still alive.

This, at any rate, is the basic thought behind the present undertaking. The volumes of the Library of Living Philosophers can in no sense take the place of the major writings of great and original thinkers. Students who would know the philosophies of such men as John Dewey, George Santayana, Alfred North Whitehead, G. E. Moore, Bertrand Russell, Ernst Cassirer, Karl Jaspers, Rudolf Carnap, Martin Buber, et al., will still need to read the writings of these men. There is no substitute for first-hand contact with the original thought of the philosopher himself. Least of all does this Library pretend to be such a substitute. The Library in fact will spare neither effort nor expense in offering to the student the best possible guide to the published writings of a given thinker. We shall attempt to meet this aim by providing at the end of each volume in our series as nearly complete a bibliography of the published work of the philosopher in question as possible. Nor should one overlook the fact that essays in each volume cannot but finally lead to this same goal. The interpretative and critical discussions of the various phases of a great thinker's work and, most of all, the reply of the thinker himself, are bound to lead the reader to the works of the philosopher himself.

---

*This General Introduction sets forth in the founder's words the underlying conception of the Library. L.E.H.

At the same time, there is no denying that different experts find different ideas in the writings of the same philosopher. This is as true of the appreciative interpreter and grateful disciple as it is of the critical opponent. Nor can it be denied that such differences of reading and of interpretation on the part of other experts often leave the neophyte aghast before the whole maze of widely varying and even opposing interpretations. Who is right and whose interpretation shall he accept? When the doctors disagree among themselves, what is the poor student to do? If, in desperation, he decides that all of the interpreters are probably wrong and that the only thing for him to do is to go back to the original writings of the philosopher himself and then make his own decision—uninfluenced (as if this were possible) by the interpretation of anyone else—the result is not that he has actually come to the meaning of the original philosopher himself, but rather that he has set up one more interpretation, which may differ to a greater or lesser degree from the interpretations already existing. It is clear that in this direction lies chaos, just the kind of chaos which Schiller has so graphically and inimitably described.[1]

It is curious that until now no way of escaping this difficulty has been seriously considered. It has not occurred to students of philosophy that one effective way of meeting the problem at least partially is to put these varying interpretations and critiques before the philosopher while he is still alive and to ask him to act at one and the same time as both defendant and judge. If the world's greatest living philosophers can be induced to cooperate in an enterprise whereby their own work can, at least to some extent, be saved from becoming merely "desiccated lecture-fodder," which on the one hand "provides innocuous sustenance for ruminant professors," and on the other hand gives an opportunity to such ruminants and their understudies to "speculate safely, endlessly, and fruitlessly, about what a philosopher must have meant" (Schiller), they will have taken a long step toward making their intentions more clearly comprehensible.

With this in mind, the Library of Living Philosophers expects to publish at more or less regular intervals a volume on each of the greater among the world's living philosophers. In each case it will be the purpose of the editor of the Library to bring together in the volume the interpretations and criticisms of a wide range of that particular thinker's scholarly contemporaries, each of whom will be given a free hand to discuss the specific phase of the thinker's work that has been assigned to him. All contributed essays will finally be submitted to the philosopher with whose work and thought they are concerned, for his careful perusal and reply. And, although it would be expecting too much to imagine that the philosopher's reply will be able to stop all differences of interpretation and of critique, this should at least serve the purpose of stopping certain of the

---

1. In his essay "Must Philosophers Disagree?" in the volume of the same title (London: Macmillan, 1934), from which the above quotations were taken.

grosser and more general kinds of misinterpretations. If no further gain than this were to come from the present and projected volumes of this Library, it would seem to be fully justified.

In carrying out this principal purpose of the Library, the editor announces that (as far as is humanly possible) each volume will contain the following elements:

First, an intellectual autobiography of the thinker whenever this can be secured; in any case an authoritative and authorized biography;

Second, a series of expository and critical articles written by the leading exponents and opponents of the philosopher's thought;

Third, the reply to the critics and commentators by the philosopher himself; and

Fourth, a bibliography of writings of the philosopher to provide a ready instrument to give access to his writings and thought.

PAUL ARTHUR SCHILPP
FOUNDER AND EDITOR, 1939–1981

DEPARTMENT OF PHILOSOPHY
SOUTHERN ILLINOIS UNIVERSITY AT CARBONDALE

ADVISORY BOARD

ACKNOWLEDGMENTS

The editor hereby gratefully acknowledges his obligation and sincere gratitude to all the publishers of Hans-Georg Gadamer's books and publications for their kind and uniform courtesy in permitting us to quote—sometimes at some length—from Professor Gadamer.

Editor's Note: I sadly report that our colleague Thomas S. Kuhn died 17 June 1996 after a lengthy bout with cancer. He and we had been looking forward with keen anticipation to an LLP volume on him and having it blocked is a great loss for the world of philosophy and the sciences.

LEWIS E. HAHN
3 OCTOBER 1996

#Added to Board after the subject of this volume was chosen.

TABLE OF CONTENTS

FRONTISPIECE   iv

GENERAL INTRODUCTION TO THE LIBRARY OF LIVING
        PHILOSOPHERS   vii

FOUNDER'S GENERAL INTRODUCTION TO THE LIBRARY OF LIVING
        PHILOSOPHERS   ix

ACKNOWLEDGMENTS   xii

PREFACE   xvii

PART ONE: INTELLECTUAL AUTOBIOGRAPHY OF HANS-GEORG
        GADAMER   1

SAMPLE OF GADAMER'S HANDWRITING WITH GERMAN TEXT AND
        ENGLISH TRANSLATION   2

REFLECTIONS ON MY PHILOSOPHICAL JOURNEY   3

FOREWORD TO THE ESSAYS AND REPLIES BY HANS-GEORG GADAMER   64

PART TWO: DESCRIPTIVE AND CRITICAL ESSAYS ON THE
        PHILOSOPHY OF HANS-GEORG GADAMER, WITH REPLIES   65

1. KARL-OTTO APEL: Regulative Ideas or Truth-Happening?: An
      Attempt to Answer the Question of the Conditions of the
      Possibility of Valid Understanding   67
      REPLY TO KARL-OTTO APEL   95

2. RODERICK M. CHISHOLM: Gadamer and Realism: Reaching an
      Understanding   99
      REPLY TO RODERICK M. CHISHOLM   109

3. DAVID C. HOY: Post-Cartesian Interpretation: Hans-Georg
   Gadamer and Donald Davidson 111
   REPLY TO DAVID C. HOY 129

4. JOAN STAMBAUGH: Gadamer on the Beautiful 131
   REPLY TO JOAN STAMBAUGH 135

5. DONALD PHILLIP VERENE: Gadamer and Vico on *Sensus
   Communis* and the Tradition of Humane Knowledge 137
   REPLY TO DONALD PHILLIP VERENE 154

6. JEAN GRONDIN: Gadamer on Humanism 157
   REPLY TO JEAN GRONDIN 171

7. GEORGE R. LUCAS, JR.: Philosophy, Its History, and
   Hermeneutics 173
   REPLY TO GEORGE R. LUCAS, JR. 190

8. HERTA NAGL-DOCEKAL: Towards a New Theory of the
   Historical Sciences: The Relevance of *Truth and Method* 193
   REPLY TO HERTA NAGL-DOCEKAL 205

9. STANLEY H. ROSEN: Horizontverschmelzung 207
   REPLY TO STANLEY H. ROSEN 219

10. ROBERT SOKOLOWSKI: Gadamer's Theory of Hermeneutics 223
    REPLY TO ROBERT SOKOLOWSKI 235

11. ROBERT R. SULLIVAN: Gadamer's Early and Distinctively
    Political Hermeneutics 237
    REPLY TO ROBERT R. SULLIVAN 256

12. FRANCIS J. AMBROSIO: The Figure of Socrates in Gadamer's
    Philosophical Hermeneutics 259
    REPLY TO FRANCIS J. AMBROSIO 274

13. DAVID DETMER: Gadamer's Critique of the Enlightenment 275
    REPLY TO DAVID DETMER 287

14. ROBERT J. DOSTAL: Gadamer's Continuous Challenge:
    Heidegger's Plato Interpretation 289
    REPLY TO ROBERT J. DOSTAL 308

15. GRAEME NICHOLSON: Truth in Metaphysics and in
    Hermeneutics 309
    REPLY TO GRAEME NICHOLSON 321

16. THOMAS M. ALEXANDER: Eros and Understanding: Gadamer's
    Aesthetic Ontology of the Community 323
    REPLY TO THOMAS M. ALEXANDER 346

17. G. B. MADISON: Hermeneutics' Claim to Universality   349
    REPLY TO G. B. MADISON   366

18. CARL PAGE: Historicistic Finitude and Philosophical
    Hermeneutics   369
    REPLY TO CARL PAGE   385

19. JAMES RISSER: The Voice of the Other in Gadamer's
    Hermeneutics   389
    REPLY TO JAMES RISSER   403

20. D. WYATT AIKEN: Hermeneia: An Anatomy of History and
    Ab-wesenheit   405
    REPLY TO D. WYATT AIKEN   420

21. DONALD DAVIDSON: Gadamer and Plato's *Philebus*   421
    REPLY TO DONALD DAVIDSON   433

22. DIANE P. MICHELFELDER: Gadamer on Heidegger on Art   437
    REPLY TO DIANE P. MICHELFELDER   457

23. BJØRN T. RAMBERG: The Source of the Subjective   459
    REPLY TO BJØRN T. RAMBERG   472

24. JOHN SALLIS: Rereading the *Timaeus:* The Memorial Power of
    Discourse   475
    REPLY TO JOHN SALLIS   482

25. DENNIS J. SCHMIDT: Putting Oneself in Words . . .   483
    REPLY TO DENNIS J. SCHMIDT   496

26. ROBIN MAY SCHOTT: Gender, Nazism, and Hermeneutics   499
    REPLY TO ROBIN MAY SCHOTT   508

27. P. CHRISTOPHER SMITH: The I-Thou Encounter *(Begegnung)* in
    Gadamer's Reception of Heidegger   509
    REPLY TO P. CHRISTOPHER SMITH   526

28. RICHARD E. PALMER: Ritual, Rightness, and Truth in Two Late
    Works of Hans-Georg Gadamer   529
    REPLY TO RICHARD E. PALMER   548

29. THOMAS PRUFER: A Thought or Two on Gadamer's Plato   549
    REPLY TO THOMAS PRUFER   552

PART THREE: BIBLIOGRAPHY OF HANS-GEORG
              GADAMER   555

INDEX   603

PREFACE

Hans-Georg Gadamer, currently emeritus but still active at the University of Heidelberg, is clearly one of the greatest exponents or interpreters of hermeneutics of our time. He is, moreover, a master of hermeneutic praxis who stresses dialogue. Hermeneutics for him, as he states in his autobiography in this volume, "is above all a practice, the art of understanding and of making something understood by someone else. It is the heart of all education that seeks to teach how to philosophize." A further essential part of his teaching, as he reports in his autobiography, is that "it is the context of problems surrounding the indissoluble connection between thinking and speaking which compels hermeneutics to become philosophy." Yet another major emphasis of his outlook is that at a time when many leading philosophers took as their model of reasonability the perfection of logical understanding specific to mathematics and the physical sciences Gadamer defended the model of a kind of Aristotelian practical reason stemming from poetry, the arts, and the humanities.

The two main foci of his work have been Greek philosophy, especially Plato, and hermeneutics; but as this volume makes clear, his interests range afar, and he is broadly learned in other figures in the history of philosophy. For example, Kant's *Critique of Judgment* played a decisive role in his work, and in his response to one of his critics (Ambrosio) he declares that Kant's example taught him what the Socratic wisdom basically was: namely, "to leave questions open and to keep them open." He adds that this "is not skepticism but originates from the spiritual need for freedom." Our volume also clarifies his complex relation to another key figure, Heidegger, going from discipleship to a position of his own. And in the volume we find illuminating references to dozens of other figures. In his written work, his interpretation of poetic and philosophical texts, he covers a span of themes from Plato to Heidegger, from the Pre-Socratics to the poetry of Rilke and technology.

Plato, however, is for him the major philosopher, and with reference to him, he thinks the major task is not just to criticize him but to philosophize with him. Perhaps Gadamer's greatest contribution is that he has helped us to find words to push forward, extend, and light up the horizons of communication.

I am grateful to Professor Gadamer and his twenty-nine critics for making this volume possible. And special thanks are due Professor Richard E. Palmer, who translated Gadamer's intellectual autobiography, compiled his bibliography, and helped in a variety of other ways. Special thanks are also due Professors Matthias Lütkehermölle and Dennis J. Schmidt for translating Gadamer's response to his critics. In addition my warm thanks go to Dr. Ralf Sommermeier for his translation of Professor Apel's essay from the German. I am grateful also for the friendly counsel of Professors Darrel E. Christensen and George L. Kline.

Unfortunately, one of our contributors, Professor Thomas Prufer, who was helpful in various ways in the early stages of this volume, did not live to see his essay in print along with Gadamer's response.

I also regret to report belatedly the death of Sir Karl Popper, one of our most popular Library of Living Philosophers subjects, on 17 September 1994 at the age of 92.

The support, encouragement, and cooperation of our publisher, Open Court Publishing Company, especially M. Blouke Carus, David R. Steele, and Kerri Mommer, both facilitate my work and make it more enjoyable. And I am most grateful for continued support, understanding, and encouragement from the administration of Southern Illinois University.

As always, moreover, my grateful appreciation goes to the staff of Morris Library, especially people like Angela Rubin and David V. Koch, for help in a variety of ways. My warm gratitude also goes to Claudia Roseberry, Vernis Shownes, and the Philosophy Department secretariat for help with many projects, and to Sharon R. Langrand I give special thanks for help with manuscripts and proofs and with keeping our lines of communication open.

Finally, for warm support, stimulation, and counsel I am deeply grateful to my pluralistic colleagues whose resourcefulness and diversity in a common cause never cease to amaze me.

LEWIS EDWIN HAHN
EDITOR

DEPARTMENT OF PHILOSOPHY
SOUTHERN ILLINOIS UNIVERSITY AT CARBONDALE
JANUARY 1996

PART ONE

INTELLECTUAL AUTOBIOGRAPHY OF HANS-GEORG GADAMER

First Part of Early Version of *Wahrheit und Methode* (ca. 1956)

Translation

It is not just a requirement for logical self-clarification that links the human sciences [*Geisteswissenschaften*] with philosophy. Rather, the so-called *Geisteswissenschaften* [humanities and social sciences] pose a problem for philosophy itself: What one has to say and what can be said, about the laying of their logical and epistemological foundations and on behalf of their scholarly/scientific independence vis-a-vis the natural sciences, still remains far behind what the *Geisteswissenschaften* are and what they can signify for philosophy. It can be nothing—or everything. Nothing, if they are viewed as only an incomplete realization of the idea of science. For this is at one with the idea of a "scientific philosophy" that is measured by the completely developed form of this idea as found in the mathematical sciences of nature, which means one understands it [philosophy] as a tool of these sciences.

German Text of First Part of Early Version of Wahrheit und Methode (ca. 1956)

Es ist nicht nur ein Bedürfnis logischer Selbstklärung, das die Geisteswissenschaften mit der Philosophie verbindet. Vielmehr stellen die sog. Geisteswissenschaften für die Philosophie selbst ein Problem: Was man zu ihrer logischen, erkenntnistheoretischen Grundlegung und zur Begründung ihrer wissenschaftlichen Selbständigkeit gegenüber den Naturwissenschaften gesagt hat und sagen kann, bleibt weit hinter dem zurück, was die Geisteswissenschaften sind und was sie der Philosophie bedeuten. Es kann nichts - oder alles sein. Nichts, wenn sie nur als eine unvollkommene Verwirklichung der Idee der Wissenschaft angesehen werden. Denn in eins damit wird sich auch die Idee der »wissenschaftlichen Philosophie« an der vollkommenen Ausprägung dieser Wissenschaftsidee, die in den mathematischen Naturwissenschaften vorliegt, messen, d.h. aber, sich lediglich als ein Organon dieser Wissenschaften verstehen.

Translated from the German by Richard E. Palmer. [The beginning pages of this early draft have recently been published in the *Dilthey-Jahrbuch*. See Hans-Georg Gadamer, "*Wahrheit und Methode*: Der Anfang der Urfassung (ca. 1956)," ed. Jean Grondin and Hans-Ulrich Lessing, *Dilthey-Jahrbuch für Philosophie und Geschichte der Geisteswissenschaften*, 8 (1992–93): 131–40. *Trans.*]

Hans-Georg Gadamer
(b. February 11, 1900)

REFLECTIONS
ON MY
PHILOSOPHICAL JOURNEY

PART I: 1918–1968[1]

When, in 1918, with the First World War in its last year, I was graduated from the Holy Spirit *Gymnasium* in Breslau and enrolled in the Breslau University, I had no idea, as I looked around, that my path would eventually lead into the field of philosophy.[2]

My father was a researcher in the natural sciences, and was basically averse to all book knowledge, although his own knowledge of Horace was excellent. During my childhood he sought in a variety of ways to interest me in the natural sciences, and I must say he was quite disappointed at his lack of success. Of course, the fact that I liked what he called those "chattering professors" [*"Schwätzprofessoren"*] was clear from the beginning. Still, he let me have my way, although for the rest of his life he remained unhappy about my choice.

My studies in those days were like the first adventures in a long Odyssey. A whole range of things enticed me and I tasted many of them; and if, in the end, it was the philosophical interest that gained the upper hand, rather than my genuine interest in the study of literature, history, or art history, this was really less a turning away from one of these and towards the others so much as it was a gradual pressing further and further on into the discipline of scholarly work as such. In the confusion which the First World War and its end had brought to the whole German scene, to try to mold oneself unquestioningly into the surviving tradition was simply no longer possible. And the perplexity we were experiencing was in itself already an impetus to philosophical questioning.

In philosophy, too, it was obvious that merely accepting and continuing what the older generation had accomplished was no longer feasible for us in the

---

Translated from the German by Richard E. Palmer.

younger generation. In the First World War's grisly trench warfare and heavy-artillery battles for position, the Neo-Kantianism which had up to then been accorded a truly worldwide acceptance, though not undisputed, was just as thoroughly defeated as was the proud cultural consciousness of that liberal age, with its faith in scientifically based progress. In a disoriented world, we who were young at that time were searching for a new orientation. In our search we were limited, in practice, to the intra-German scene, where bitterness, mania for innovation, poverty, hopelessness, and yet also the unbroken will to live, all competed with each other in the youth of the time. Expressionism was the reigning force in life as well as art at that time, and while the natural sciences continued their upswing—with the Einsteinian theory of relativity in particular causing a great deal of discussion—still, in those areas of study and research conditioned by world view, namely writing and scholarship, truly a mood of catastrophe was spreading more and more, and was bringing about a break with the old traditions. *Der Zusammenbruch des deutschen Idealismus* [The Collapse of German Idealism], an oft-cited book of that time by Paul Ernst,[3] was one side of the new "mood of the times" [*Zeitgefühl*]—the academic side. The other and far more encompassing side of this *Zeitgefühl* found its expression in the sensational success of Oswald Spengler's *The Decline of the West*.[4] This "romance," as I think it must be called, made up partly of scholarship and mostly of world-historical fantasy, was "much admired, much reviled," but in the end it would seem to be just as much the inscription of a world-historical mood of pessimism as it was a genuine putting in question of the modern faith in progress and its proud ideal of proficiency and "accomplishing things." In this situation it is hardly surprising that a completely second-rate book of the times had a truly revolutionary effect on me: Theodor Lessing's *Europa und Asien* [Europe and Asia]. This book, based on the wisdom of the East, put the totality of European accomplishment-oriented thinking in question. Regrettably, in a later and still more chaotic time, Lessing was assassinated by German nationalists. In any case, for the first time in my experience the all-encompassing horizon which I had grown into through birth, education, schooling, and, indeed, the whole world around me, was relativized. And so for me something like *thinking* began.

Of course, a number of significant authors had already given me a certain first introduction to thinking. I remember the powerful impression which Thomas Mann's *Betrachtungen eines Unpolitischen* [Observations of an Unpolitical Person] made on me during my final year of high school. His fanciful but enthusiastic opposition between art and life as it was expressed in "Tonio Kröger" also touched me deeply, and I remember being enchanted by the melancholy tone of Hermann Hesse's early novels. My first introduction to the art of conceptual thinking, on the other hand, came from Richard Hönigswald, whose chiseled dialectic elegantly, although a little monotonously, defended the transcendental-idealistic position of Neo-Kantianism against all psychologism. I very faithfully took down his lecture course, "Basic Questions in the Theory of Knowledge," word for word in shorthand and then translated it into longhand. My two notebooks containing this lecture course have since been donated to the Hönigswald Archive in Würzburg, which was brought into being by Hans Wagner. In any case, these lectures offered me a good introduction to transcendental philosophy. So when in 1919 I came to Marburg I already had a fair preparation in transcendental philosophy.

In Marburg I was soon confronted with new academic experiences. Unlike the universities in the large cities, the "small" universities of that time still led a real academic life—a "life of ideas" as Humboldt meant that phrase—and in the philosophical faculty there was in every area and with every professor a "circle," so one was soon drawn in several directions toward a variety of interests. At that time the critique of historical theology following in the footsteps of Karl Barth's *Commentary on the Letter to the Romans* [1919] was just beginning in Marburg, a critique which was later to become the so-called "dialectical theology." Among more and more young people in those days, there was sharp criticism of the "methodologism" of the Neo-Kantian school, and over against this, there was acclaim for Husserl's art of phenomenological description. But it was "life-philosophy," above all—behind which stood the European event of Friedrich Nietzsche—that was taking hold of our whole feeling for life. And of course the problem of historical relativism connected with this preoccupied the minds of many young people, whose discussion of it related especially to the works of Wilhelm Dilthey[5] and Ernst Troeltsch.[6]

In addition to these theological and philosophical developments, it was about that time that the influence of the circle around the poet Stefan George, in particular, began to penetrate into the general academic world, and it should be remarked that the extremely effective and fascinating books of Friedrich Gundolf brought a new artistic sensitivity into the scholarly interaction with poetry. Overall, everything that came out of the George circle—Gundolf's books as well as the Nietzsche book of Ernst Bertram, Wolters's skillful pamphlet rhetoric, Salin's crystalline delicacy, and finally, Erich von Kahler's exceptionally explicit declamatory attack on Max Weber's famous speech on "Science as a Profession"—amounted to a single great provocation. These were the voices of a strongly held critique of the culture. And I had the feeling that, in this case, in contrast to similar tones of protest from other sides—which, in light of my being a typically dissatisfied beginning student, also gained a certain hearing from me—there was definitely something to it. A certain power seemed to stand behind these often monotonous declamations. The fact that a poet like George could, with the magical sound of his verse and the force of his person, exercise such a powerful formative effect on human beings remained a nagging question for many thoughtful persons, and represented a never completely forgotten corrective to the play with concepts I was encountering in my philosophical study.

I myself simply could not ignore the fact that the experience of art had something to do with philosophy. Philosophers in the German Romantic period, right up to the end of the idealistic era, held that art was the true instrument of philosophy, if not its superior adversary, and they found in this truth their all-encompassing task. Indeed, the price that the university philosophy of the post-Hegelian era had to pay for its failure to recognize this truth—was barrenness. The same thing also held and holds for Neo-Kantianism, and indeed it applies also to positivism right up to the present day new positivism. In my view then, and it remains my view, the task of reclaiming this truth about the relevance of art to philosophy is something our historical heritage has assigned to us.

But certainly the task of appealing to the truth of art against the doubt which an historical relativism had already attached to the conceptual truth claims of philosophy was not an easy one. The experience of art constitutes a kind of evidence which is both too strong and at the same time not strong enough. It is too strong in the sense that probably no one would venture to extend their faith in scientific progress to the heights of art and try, for instance, to see in Shakespeare an advance over Sophocles, or in Michelangelo an advance beyond Phidias. On the other hand, the evidence of art is also too weak in the sense that the artwork withholds the very truth that it embodies and prevents it from becoming conceptually precise. In any case, by the time I was in Marburg, the form that the cultural education—of the aesthetic consciousness as well as of historical consciousness—had degenerated into the study of "world views." This did not mean, of course, that either art or the encounter with the historical tradition of thought had lost their fascination. On the contrary, the assertions of art, like those of the great philosophers, raised a claim to truth then more than ever, confused but unavoidable, which would not allow itself to be neutralized by any Kantian "history of problems," nor to be subordinated to the rules of rigorous scientific exactitude and methodical progress.

Rather, the claim to truth at that time, under the influence of a new reception of Kierkegaard in Germany, called itself "existential." Existentialism dealt with a truth which was supposed to be demonstrated not so much in terms of universally held propositions or knowledge as rather in the immediacy of one's own experience and in the absolute unsubstitutability of one's own existence. Dostoevsky, above all others, seemed to us to have known about this. The red Piper volumes of the Dostoyevskian novels flamed on every writing desk. The letters of van Gogh and Kierkegaard's *Either-Or*, which he wrote against Hegel, beckoned to us, and of course behind all the boldness and riskiness of our existential engagement—as a still scarcely visible threat to the romantic traditionalism of our culture—stood the gigantic form of Friedrich Nietzsche with his ecstatic critique of everything, including all the illusions of self-consciousness. Where, we wondered, was a thinker whose philosophical power was adequate to the powerful initiatives put forward by Nietzsche?

The new feeling that had arisen in that time was causing new ground to be broken also in the Marburg School of philosophy.[7] Paul Natorp, the brilliant methodologist of the Marburg School, who in his older days sought with muse-like enthusiasm to penetrate into the mystical unsayability of the primordially concrete left behind lasting impressions. Natorp conjured up not only Plato and Dostoyevsky but Beethoven and Rabindranath Tagore, and also the mystical tradition from Plotinus and Meister Eckhart up to the Quakers. And no less impressive was the daemonism of Max Scheler, who, as guest lecturer in Marburg, demonstrated his penetrating phenomenological gifts, which had directed him into very new, unexpected fields of exploration. And also there was the cool acuteness with which Nicolai Hartmann, a thinker and teacher of imposing perseverance, sought to strip away his own idealistic past through critical argumentation. When I wrote my Plato dissertation and in 1922 received my doctorate far too young, I stood under the influence of Nicolai Hartmann, above all, who had come out in opposition to Natorp's system-oriented, idealistic style.

We also lived in the expectation of a new philosophical orientation, which was particularly tied to the dark, magical word, "phenomenology." But when Husserl himself, who with all his analytical genius and inexhaustible descriptive patience that continuously pressed on for final evidence, had envisioned no better philosophical support than a Neo-Kantian transcendental idealism, where was help for thinking to come from? Heidegger brought it. Some followers built their interpretation of Marx on Heidegger, others their interpretation of Freud on Heidegger, and all of us, in the end, our interpretation of what Nietzsche was. I myself suddenly realized from Heidegger that we could only "fetch back" [*"wiederholen,"* repeat] the philosophizing of the Greeks once we had forfeited that *fundamentum inconcussum* of philosophy on the basis of which Hegel had written his story of philosophy and the Neo-Kantians their history of problems—namely, *self-consciousness*.

From that point on I had a glimpse of what I wanted—and obviously it had nothing to do with the idea of a new, all-encompassing system. For I had not forgotten Kierkegaard's critique of Hegel. In my early essay, "On the Idea of System in Philosophy," written for the Festschrift celebrating Natorp's seventieth birthday,[8] I attempted to refute the new idea that philosophy can be reduced to basic experiences that carry human existence and that philosophy can be explained somewhere beyond all historicism. Although a document of my immaturity, this essay also gave evidence of my new involvement with Heidegger and the inspiration he had already become for me. Because this essay appeared in 1924, it has sometimes been interpreted as an anticipation of Heidegger's turn against transcendental idealism—an interpretation which I think is completely wrong. As a matter of fact, the three months in the summer of 1923 that I was in Freiburg studying with Heidegger would in themselves scarcely have led me to this "inspiration" if there were not all sorts of things already in place and ready to receive it. Certainly Heidegger was the one who permitted me to have the necessary distance from the work of my two other Marburg teachers: Natorp's construction of encompassing systems, and the naive objectivism of Hartmann's categorial research. That essay, at that point, was of course quite impertinent stuff. As I came to know more, I began to remain silent. In fact, at the time of my habilitation in 1928, I could present as philosophical publications in addition to my habilitation, only one other, equally impertinent publication, from 1923, on Hartmann's *Metaphysik der Erkenntnis,* published in *Logos.*[9] I had in the meantime, however, been studying classical philology, and I was later able to develop from my entry paper in the philological seminar of Paul Friedländer, namely, "The Aristotelian *Protreptikos* and Aristotelian Ethics from the Standpoint of their Developmental History," an essay which Richard Heinze accepted for publication in *Hermes.*[10] It was a critique of Werner Jaeger. The success of this essay gained me recognition in philological circles—even though I professed to be a student of Heidegger.

What was it that so attracted me and others to Heidegger? At the time, of course, I could not tell you. Today I would put it as follows: In Heidegger the development of thought in the philosophical tradition came to life because it was understood as answers to real questions. The disclosure of the history of the motivation of these philosophical questions lent to them a certain inevitability. And questions that are understood cannot simply pass into one's stock of knowledge. They become one's own questions.

Indeed, it had also been the claim of the Neo-Kantian "history of problems" approach to recognize in those problems one's own questions. But their claim to fetch back these supertemporal, "eternal" problems in ever new systematic contexts was not shown to be correct, and these "identical" problems actually were purloined with full naïveté from the building materials of Neo-Kantian and German Idealist philosophy. The objection lodged by historical relativist skepticism against such supposed supertemporality is persuasive, I think, and simply cannot be gainsaid. Only when I learned from Heidegger how to bring historical thinking into the recovering of our own questions, did this make the old questions of the tradition understandable and so alive that they became our own questions. What I am describing here I would today call the fundamental experience in hermeneutics.

Above all, it was the intensity with which Heidegger evoked Greek philosophy that worked on us like a magical spell. The fact that such a spell was more a counterexample than an example of what his own questioning was intending was something we were scarcely aware of at the time. Heidegger's *Destruktion* of Greek metaphysics was concerned, however, not just with the consciousness-based idealism of the modern age, but likewise with its origins in Greek metaphysics. Heidegger's "destruction" and radical critique also called into question the Christian character of theology as well as the scientific character of philoso phy. What a contrast to the bloodless academic philosophizing of the time, which moved within an alienated Kantian or Hegelian language and attempted once again either to bring transcendental idealism to perfection or else to overcome it! Suddenly Plato and Aristotle appeared as co-conspirators and comrades in arms to everyone who had found that the playing around with systems in academic philosophy had become obsolete—even in the form of that open system of problems, categories, and values, on the basis of which both the phenomenological research into essences [*Wesenforschung*], the history of problems, or the analysis of categories understood themselves. From the Greeks one could learn that thinking in philosophy does not, in order to be responsible, have to adopt as system-guiding the thought that there must be a final grounding for philosophy in a highest principle; on the contrary, it stands always under the guiding thought that it must be based on primordial world experience, achieved through the conceptual and intuitive power of the language in which we live. The secret of the Platonic dialogues, it seems to me, is that they teach us this.

Among German Plato scholars at that time it was Julius Stenzel whose work pointed in a direction similar to my own. Taking note of the aporiae of self-consciousness in which both idealism and its critics found themselves trapped, Stenzel observed in the Greeks the "restraining of subjectivity."[11] This occurred to me, likewise, and even before Heidegger began to teach me, as being a superiority of the Greeks, yet it is a puzzling superiority in which out of self-forgetful surrender they abandoned themselves in boundless innocence to the passion of thinking.

Already very early, and on the same basis, I had taken an interest in Hegel, so far as I understood him, and precisely because I only understood him that far. Above all, his *Logic* possessed, for me, really something of Greek innocence, and the genial, but unfortunately poorly edited, *Lectures on the History of Philosophy,* provided a bridge to a nonhistorical but truly speculative understanding of Platonic and Aristotelian thinking.

What was most important for me, however, I learned from Heidegger. And it was, above all, in the first seminar in which I participated, in 1923, when Heidegger was still in Freiburg, on the Sixth Book of the *Nicomachean Ethics.* At that time, *"phronēsis,"* the virtue of "practical reason," that *"allo eidos gnōseōs,"* that "other form of cognition," was for me truly a magical word. Certainly, it was an immediate provocation to me when Heidegger one day analyzed the demarcation between *techne* and *phronēis* and then in reference to the sentence, *"phronēseōs de ouk esti lēthē"*[12] (in practical reason there is no forgetting), explained, "That is conscience!" But this bit of spontaneous pedagogical exaggeration focussed on a decisive point, by means of which Heidegger himself was preparing for his new posing of the being-question later in *Being and Time.* One thinks, in this connection, of terms like *"Gewissen-Habenwollen"*—"the will-to-have-conscience"—in *Being and Time* §54ff.

What was by no means clear to me at the time was that Heidegger's remark also could be understood in a completely different way, namely as also a covert critique of the Greeks. Then this saying means that only as a thought whose certainty of knowledge was unthreatened by any forgetting was Greek thought able to think the nonprimordial, the only apparently human phenomenon of conscience. —For me, in any case, Heidegger's provocative remark stimulated me to make alien questions my own and at the same time made me aware of the anticipation within concepts [*Vorgreiflichkeit*].

The second essential point I gained from Heidegger's instruction was one which Heidegger demonstrated to me from Aristotle's text (in some private encounters), namely how untenable the alleged "realism" of Aristotle was, and that Aristotle stood on the same ground of the *logos* which Plato had prepared in his discipleship to Socrates. Many years later—following a paper given in one of my seminars—Heidegger discussed with us the fact that the new common ground in the *logos,* and thereby in dialectical philosophizing, between Plato and Aristotle not only supports Aristotle's doctrine of the categories but also enables one to sort out the differences between *dynamis* and *energeia.*[13]

What I have described above was, in reality, my first introduction to the universality of hermeneutics.

This was of course not clear to me at the time. Only slowly did it dawn on me that the Aristotle that had been strongly pressed on us by Heidegger, an Aristotle whose conceptual precision was filled to the limit with intuition and experience, did not at all itself express the new thinking. Heidegger followed the principle put forward in Plato's "The Sophist," that one should make the dialogical opponent stronger, so well that Heidegger almost appeared like an *Aristotle redivivus* [Aristotle brought back to life], an Aristotle who through the power of intuition and the boldness of his original conceptuality cast a spell over everyone. Nevertheless, the identification, to which Heidegger's interpretations forced us, posed a powerful challenge to me personally. I was acutely aware that my diverse studies up to that time, studies which had ranged through many areas, literature and art history, and even my studies in the field of ancient philosophy, in which I had written my dissertation, were of no use to me in coming to grips with this challenge. So I began a new and systematically laid out study of classical philology under the direction of Paul Friedländer, a plan of study in which, along with the Greek philosophers, the radiant figure of Pindar, who had been put in a new light by the then new edition of Hölderlin, attracted me above all— not to mention ancient rhetoric, whose complementary function to philosophy dawned on me then and has accompanied me in the development of my philosophical hermeneutics. All things considered, I feel strongly indebted to these studies because they made the strong identification with Aristotle, to which Heidegger had invited us, ever more difficult on my part. For the more or less conscious leitmotif of all my studies was: In becoming aware of the otherness of the

Greeks to be at the same time loyal to them, to discover truths in their being-other that have perhaps been covered over but that perhaps were still today operative and unmastered. In Heidegger's interpretation of the Greeks, however, lay a problem that especially in the works after *Being and Time* [1927] kept bothering me. Certainly it was possible in terms of Heidegger's purposes at that time to contrast the existential concept of "*Dasein*" with "the merely at hand" [*Vorhandenheit,* just being objectively "on hand"] as its counterconcept and extremist derivation without differentiating between this Greek understanding of being and the "concept of object in the natural sciences." But there lay in this for me a strong provocation to test the validity of this point in Heidegger, and from this stimulus I went so far as to immerse myself for a time in studying the Aristotelian concept of nature and the rise of modern science, above all in Galileo.

Of course, the hermeneutical situation which I took as a starting point was given through the shattering of the idealistic and romantic search for a restoration of unity. The claim to be able to integrate even the empirical sciences of modern times into the unity of philosophical sciences, a claim which found its expression in the concept of "speculative physics" (a journal carried this name!) was simply unfulfillable. Any new effort at an integrative claim obviously could not be a repeat of that earlier, failed attempt. However, in order to know more clearly the reasons for this impossibility, the concept of science in modern times must, for its part, present a sharper profile, and the Greek concept of "science" based on the concept of purpose must do so as well, a concept which German Idealism had undertaken to renew. It is self-evident that Kant's *Critique of Judgment,* in particular its critique of "teleological judgment," becomes significant in connection with this problem, and a number of my students have undertaken to work this out further.

For the history of Greek science is apparently quite different from the history of modern science. Plato has already succeeded in joining together the path of enlightenment, that is, the path of free research and rational explanations of the world, with the traditional world of Greek religion and traditional Greek view of life. Plato and Aristotle, not Democritus, held sway over the history of science in late antiquity, and this was by no means a history of scientific decline. Specialized science [*Fachwissenschaft*], as we now call it, did not in Hellenistic times have to defend itself against philosophy and its prejudices, but rather received its emancipation *by means of* Greek philosophy, through the *Timaios* and Aristotelian philosophy of nature, as I tried to show in a paper titled "Is there Matter?" (1973).[14] Actually, even the counterproject of Galileian and Newtonian physics remains conditioned by Greek philosophy. My study on "Ancient Atomic Theory" (1935) is the only piece from this study-circle that I published at that time.[15] It should help to correct the childish preference which modern science has held for the great unknown figure of Democritus. I should also add that this does not in the least detract from the greatness of Democritus.

But of course Plato was at the center of my studies. My first Plato book, *Plato's Dialectical Ethics*,[16] based on my habilitation thesis, was an Aristotle book that got stuck, because my starting-point was actually Aristotle's two treatises on "pleasure" in the *Nicomachean Ethics* (Book H: 10–13 and Book K: 1–5). However, the problem is scarcely solvable if one takes a genetic approach, so I argued that the problem should be posed in a phenomenological way. Even though I could not "explain" this juxtaposition historically-genetically, I wanted, if possible, to demonstrate that it could be justified anyway. But this could not be done without relating both treatises to the Platonic *Philebus;* and so it was with this intention that I undertook a phenomenological interpretation of this dialogue. In those days I was not yet able to appreciate the universal significance of the *Philebus* for the Platonic view of numbers and, in general, for the problem of the relationship of idea and "reality."[17] Rather, the two things I had in mind both had to do with method: first, to understand the function of Platonic dialectic from a phenomenology of the dialogue, and second, to explain the teaching about pleasure and its forms of appearance from a phenomenological analysis of real phenomena found in life. The phenomenological art of description which I had tried to learn from Husserl (in Freiburg 1923) and also from Heidegger was supposed to yield an interpretation of ancient texts that was oriented "to the things themselves." It had relative success and received some recognition, of course not from the specialized historians, who indeed always live in the delusion that it is trivial to understand what is simply there. What should be investigated, they think, is what lies behind it. So Hans Leisegang in his review of current Plato research in 1932 for *Archiv für Geschichte der Philosophie* thrust my work aside with a disdainful reference to a sentence from my introduction: "Its relationship to historical criticism is then already a positive one, if such criticism—taking the view that no progress is going to be made from our interpretation—finds that what is said in our interpretation [of what the text says] is self-evident."[18] In reality, however, I was well grounded in classical philology. I had in the mid-twenties pursued a rigorous course of studies to become certified as a classical philologist and passed a state exam in it in 1927. I was habilitated in philosophy very soon thereafter (1928/29). What is at issue here is a contrast in methodological standpoints which I undertook to clarify later through my hermeneutical analyses—obviously without success according to all those who are not ready for the work of reflection but can only regard one's research as "positive" if something new is produced (even if it remains as "un-understood" as the old that it replaced).

Nevertheless, it was a successful start. As a teacher of philosophy I learned new things every semester. In those days, even under the poverty-stricken conditions of a foundation-supported scholar or commissioned and authorized teacher [*Lehrbeauftrager*], my teaching could be completely in line with my own research plans. So I entered into Plato's thought ever more deeply. In this connection, I was greatly helped by working with Jakob Klein in the area of mathematics and number theory. It was in those times that Klein's classical treatise, "Greek Logistics and the Rise of Algebra" (1936) was first published. I certainly will not claim that these mathematics-oriented studies of mine, which extended over a decade, reflected in any meaningful way the horror drama of the events of that time. At most they did so indirectly in that in light of the situation after 1933 I purposely abandoned a larger study of the Sophistic and Platonic doctrines of the state, although I did publish two partial aspects of it: "Plato and the Poets" (1934) and "Plato's Educational State" (1942).[19]

Each of these essays has its story. The first little piece developed an interpretation of the *Republic* by which I still stand today as the only correct one: that the Platonic ideal state presents a conscious utopia which has more to do with Jonathan Swift than with "political science."[20] My publication of this essay in 1934 also documents my position vis-à-vis National Socialism with the motto placed at the beginning: "Whoever philosophizes will not be in agreement with the conceptions of the times." As a quotation from Goethe it was indeed well masked, as it was in continuity with Goethe's characterization of the Platonic writings. But if one does not want to make a martyr of oneself or voluntarily choose emigration, such a motto can nevertheless convey a certain emphasis to the understanding reader in a time of enforced conformity, an affirmation of one's own identity—similar to Karl Reinhardt's inscription at the end of the preface to his book on the Greek tragedian Sophocles: "In January and September 1933." Indeed, from that time on the fact that one strenuously avoided politically relevant themes (and publication in journals outside one's special field altogether) was in accord with the same law of self-preservation. It remains true even to this day that a state which, in philosophical questions, designates a single "doctrine" about the state as "correct," must know that its best people will move into other fields where they will not be censured by politicians—which in effect means by laymen. In this case, it makes no difference whether they are black or red, no outcry can change anything. So I continued my work unnoticed and found gifted students, among whom I would like to mention here Walter Schulz, Karlheinz Volkmann-Schluck, and Arthur Henkel. Fortunately, in those days the policies of national-socialistic politics, in preparation for war in the East, somewhat moderated their pressure on the universities, and so my academic opportunities, which for years had been nil, improved. After ten years working in Marburg as a *Dozent,* I finally attained the long-desired rank of professor at Marburg in the spring of 1937.[21] In 1938, an offer of a chair in classical philology at Halle came, and shortly thereafter I received a call to the philosophical ordinariate in Leipzig, which confronted me with new tasks.

The second piece, "Plato's Educational State," was written as a kind of alibi. It was already during the war. A professor of the Hannover Institute of Technology [*Technische Hochschule*] by the name of Osenberg had persuaded Hitler of

the decisive role of science in the war effort and through this was given full powers to preserve and cultivate the natural sciences, and in particular to further
develop talented younger people. This so-called Osenberg-action saved the lives
of many young researchers. It aroused the envy of scholars in the humanities and
social sciences, until finally a clever Party member came up with the proposal of
a "parallel action." This was an idea whose inventiveness would have done honor
to Robert Musil![22] It went under the label, *"der Einsatz der Geisteswissenschaften für den Krieg"*—"dedicating the humanities and social sciences to
the war effort." The fact that what it had to do with in reality was the dedication
of the war effort to the humanities and social sciences—and nothing else,
really—was hard to miss. In order to avoid getting entangled in some cooperative project in the philosophical sector of this effort, where such wonderful
themes as "The Jews and Philosophy" or "The German Element in Philosophy"
were surfacing, I emigrated into classical philology. There everything was very
mannerly, and under the protection of Helmut Berve an interesting collective
work titled *The Heritage of Antiquity* was created which after the war one could
find in an unchanged second edition. My contribution to it, "Plato's Educational
State," carried further my earlier study, "Plato and the Poets," and also pointed in
the direction of some of my more recent studies with its last words, *"die Zahl
und das Sein"*—"number and being."

The only monograph I submitted for publication during the whole era of the
"Third Reich" was *People and History in the Thinking of Herder* (1942).[23] In
this study, what I principally tried to work out was the role of the concept of
power in Herder's historical thinking. Of course, the study avoided every hint of
relevance to the present. Nevertheless, it still offended some people, above all
those who had made themselves heard on similar themes and who believed that
a little more sychronization, working together, "toeing the line" [*"Gleichschal-
tung"*], was not to be avoided. There is a particular reason why I am fond of this
work. I had dealt with this theme for the first time in a lecture given in French to
French officers in a prisoners of war camp. In the question period and discussion
afterwards I said that an empire that extends itself beyond measure, beyond
moderation, is *"auprès de sa chute"*—"near its fall." The French officers looked
at each other meaningfully and understood. (I sometimes wonder if, in this
macabre and unreal situation, I anonymously met one or the other of my later
French colleagues, of whom, indeed, many could have been there.) The political
functionary who had accompanied me was, for his part, positively enthusiastic.
Such mental clarity and reckless abandon, according to him, mirrored with particular effectiveness our consciousness of victory. (Whether he really believed
this or only played along, I could not decide. In any case, he took no offense,
and I even had to give my lecture again in Paris.)

During those years, if one wanted to avoid conflict with the Party, it was necessary to behave unobtrusively. The results of my studies I communicated only

in lectures. There one could function basically in an open and unhindered way. In Leipzig I even held lectures on Husserl undisturbed. Much of what I had worked on and developed during that period saw the light in works by my students, in particular I think of Karlheinz Volkmann-Schluck's excellent dissertation, "Plotinus as Interpreter of Platonic Ontology" (1941).[24]

Since I was professor in Leipzig and, after Theodor Litt's retirement, its only representative of the area of philosophy, I could no longer adjust my teaching to my own research interests and plans. In addition to the Greeks and their latest and greatest follower, Hegel, I had to mediate the whole classical tradition in philosophy from Augustine and Thomas Aquinas to Nietzsche, Husserl, and Heidegger—obviously, as half philologist, I always stayed close to the text. In addition to this, in seminars I dealt also with difficult poetic texts, those of Hölderlin, Goethe, and above all, Rilke. Rilke was, thanks to the highly cultivated mannerism of his style, the true poet of the academic *Résistance*. Whoever talked like Rilke or like Heidegger, or who explained Hölderlin, stood on the margins and attracted those who also stood on the margins.

The last years of the war were naturally lived out in the grip of desperation and were very dangerous for everyone. Still, the intensive bombing which we had to survive and which left the city of Leipzig as well as the university—my means of livelihood—in ruins, also had its good aspects: the Nazi party with its terror was further tied up by the emergency situation then developing. Instruction at the university, switching from one emergency space to another, was continued until shortly before the end of the war. When the Americans occupied Leipzig, I was in the midst of studying the newly published second and third volumes of Werner Jaeger's *Paideia*—which is also an odd fact, it seems to me, that this work of an "emigrant" into the German language should be published by a German publisher in the years of highest war emergency. Total war? The inner schism of our country under a despotic regime made such things thinkable.

After the end of the war, I suddenly had, as Rector of the University of Leipzig, other things to do. Of course, to think of a genuine continuation of philosophical work had for years been unthinkable. Still, my weekends were free, and during them I wrote the majority of the interpretations of poetry that appear in volume two of my *Kleine Schriften*. It occurred to me that never before had I so easily worked and written as in these stringently limited hours, certainly an expression of the fact that during the unproductive, political, and administrative daily work of the rectorship something accumulated which then just poured itself out in this way. Other than this periodic outpouring in the interpretation of poetry, however, writing remained a torment for me. I had the terrible feeling that Heidegger was standing behind me and looking over my shoulder.

In the fall of 1947, after serving two years as rector, I accepted a call to Frankfurt am Main and therewith returned completely and entirely to my teaching and research—as much as working conditions at that time permitted. In the two years I was in Frankfurt, I tried to do my share to deal with the distressed situation of the students at the time not only through intensive hours of teaching but also through the editing of new editions with commentary of Aristotle's *Metaphysics: Book XII* (Greek and German)[25] and also Wilhelm Dilthey's *Outline of the History of Philosophy*,[26] both of which Klostermann Press brought out very quickly. Important at that time, too, was the great conference in Mendoza, Argentina, February 1949, in which we could, on the one hand, get together with old Jewish friends, and on the other, make our first contact with the philosophers of other countries (Italy, France, Spain, South America).

Receiving the call in 1949 to succeed to Karl Jaspers's chair in Heidelberg, for me meant the beginning of a truly "academic" career in an academic "world." Just as I was for twenty years student and *Dozent* in Marburg, I was to be active over forty years in Heidelberg, and in spite of the multiplicity of tasks involved in the years of rebuilding, which claimed time from all of us, it was possible for me to largely disburden myself from politics and university politics and to concentrate on my own plans of work, which in 1960 finally reached a first conclusion in *Truth and Method*.[27]

The fact that along with my passionate engagement as teacher I came to write a large book is due to a natural need I felt to ponder how the various paths of philosophizing which I retraced in my teaching could be made genuinely relevant to today by starting from the current philosophical situation. To arrange them into a historical process that is constructed a priori (Hegel) seemed to me just as unsatisfactory as the relativistic neutrality of historicism. I agree with Leibniz, who once said that he himself approved of nearly all he read. But in contrast with that great thinker, the stimulus of this experience did not lead me to feel I must create one great synthesis. Indeed, I began asking myself whether philosophy could still be placed under the rubric of such a synthetic task at all. Rather, for the continuation of hermeneutical experiences, must not philosophy hold itself radically open, captivated by what remains always evident to it, and use its powers to oppose all redarkening of what it has seen? . . . Philosophy is enlightenment, but precisely also enlightenment against its own dogmatism.

In fact, the rise of my "hermeneutical philosophy" must be traced back to nothing more pretentious than my effort to be theoretically accountable for the style of my studies and my teaching. Practice came first. For as long ago as I can remember, I have been concerned not to say too much and not to lose myself in theoretical constructions which were not fully made good by experience. Since as a teacher I continued to give of myself to the students and in particular to offer intensive contact to my closest students, work on my book had to wait for vacations. This work took almost ten years, and during this time I avoided as much as possible every distraction. When the book finally appeared—and only while it was at the press was the title, *Truth and Method*, chosen—I was really not sure whether it had not come too late and might really be superfluous. For I could already foresee that a new generation was coming on that was in the grip partly of technological expectations and partly the captive of feelings associated with the critique of ideology.

The question of the title of the book was difficult enough. My colleagues in philosophy both in Germany and outside Germany expected it to be labelled philosophical hermeneutics. But when I suggested this as the title, the publisher asked: "What is that?" And in fact it probably was better at the time to banish that still strange word to the subtitle.

In the meantime at Heidelberg my persistently continued university teaching activities were bearing ever more fruit. Also, my old friend Karl Löwith returned from exile and taught along with me, creating a healthy tension. There were several years of highly fruitful interaction with Jürgen Habermas, whom we called to Heidelberg as a young *extraordinarius* after I had learned that Max Horkheimer and Theodor Adorno had gotten into an argument on his account. Well, whoever was able to separate those intellectual brothers-in-arms, Max and Teddy, even just a little bit, must really be something, and in fact the manuscript we requested confirmed the talent of the young researcher, which had been evident to me for some time. —But of course there were also other students who had passionately given themselves up to philosophy. I brought a large group of students with me when I came from Frankfurt, among them Dieter Henrich, who also carried the stamp of his first experiences, which were of the Marburg arch-Kantians, Ebbinghaus and Klaus Reich. In Heidelberg, too, there were also many others who were active in teaching or research, such as Wolfgang Bartuschat, Rüdiger Bubner, Theo Ebert, Heinz Kimmerle, Wolfgang Künne, Ruprecht Pflaumer, J. H. Trede, and Wolfgang Wieland. Others came later from Frankfurt, where Wolfgang Cramer had a strong influence: Konrad Cramer, Friedrich Fulda, and Reiner Wiehl. Also, more and more students from other countries came and blended themselves into the circle of my students. From Italy, I especially remember Valerio Verra and Gianni Vattimo; from Spain, Emilio Lledo; and of course a great number of Americans, many of whom I met again during my many trips to America after 1968, now holding positions of responsibility. A special source of satisfaction has been the fact that from my closest circle of students many emerged who found that what they learned could be carried over into other fields, a good test of the idea of hermeneutics itself.

What I taught above all was hermeneutic praxis. Hermeneutics is above all a practice, the art of understanding and of making something understood to someone else. It is the heart of all education that wants to teach how to philosophize. In it what one has to exercise above all is the ear, the sensitivity for perceiving prior determinations, anticipations, and imprints that reside in concepts. This goes for a good part of my work in history of concepts. With the help of the German Research Foundation I organized a series of colloquia on the history of concepts, and reported on them, and these have triggered a variety of similar endeavors.[28] Conscientiousness and reliability in the employment of concepts requires a concept-history kind of awareness, such that one does not fall into the arbitrariness of constructing definitions, or the illusion that one can standardize philosophical speaking into certain obligatory forms. A consciousness of the history of concepts becomes a duty of critical thinking. I have sought in other ways to accomplish these tasks, for instance by bringing to life, in conjunction with Helmut Kuhn, the *Philosophische Rundschau,* a journal dedicated completely to critique. Helmut Kuhn's critical talent was something I already had learned to admire very early, before 1933, in the last issues of the old *Kantstudien.* Some twenty-three years of issues of the *Philosophische Rundschau* appeared under the strict leadership of my wife, Käte Gadamer-Lekebusch, until it was entrusted to other, younger hands.

But the centerpoint of all my activity in the Heidelberg years, as before, remained my teaching duties. It was only after my formal retirement in 1968 that I had time to present my ideas on hermeneutics in a wider circumference and in other countries, where they met with widespread interest—above all, in America. To that phase of my life I now turn.

II. TRAVELLING SCHOLAR, 1968–

In 1968, when I retired from full-time teaching, I began a whole new life, a life of travel. Throughout the years of my teaching activities, I had always limited my travel for lecturing to the vacations, when I was free of classes. I felt that an excessive number of such events during the periods of time when I was teaching would weaken my presence at the lectern. Indeed, for this reason I had refused a number of earlier invitations to lecture in America. Also, of course, I was conscious of the fact that while I could manage with French quite well in Europe, the English-speaking world had remained basically inaccessible to me because of my limited skill with spoken English. My only contact with English had been through reading it. But on my retirement in 1968, I finally accepted an invitation from Vanderbilt University to visit the university and to present a paper on Schleiermacher at an international Schleiermacher colloquium. On the tour of lectures I gave after the symposium was over I had an opportunity to become acquainted with a considerable number of American universities and in the course of time I developed enough speaking ability in English to manage at least passably in it. As much as possible, I attempted to give my lectures in English and without manuscript, for, in my view, lecturing and especially teaching in the U.S. and Canada would be meaningless if I could not somehow give expression to my own style of thinking in English. In the periods of my presence in America and Canada during the years that followed, I placed our common heritage in Greek philosophy in the foreground of my teaching, and in this way I was able to link my teaching activity during my sojourns in America to my own research studies. I was also able to try out these studies of Greek philosophy in a variety of ways later on in Europe, for example, in Italy, Spain, France, Belgium, Holland, and Scandinavia.

After all the many trips I had made over the years in old Europe, which had necessarily been limited to academic vacations, my venture into the Anglo-Saxon world for longer periods of time certainly represented something new, and it brought with it many memorable experiences. Obviously, the first of these was learning little by little to overcome the language barrier, and here my fondness for lyric poetry was a great help. Through reading T. S. Eliot, William Butler Yeats, and Wallace Stevens, I experienced something of the music of the English language. The philosophical expectations I necessarily had in these journeys into the Anglo-Saxon world also posed new tasks in thinking. It was no surprise to me, of course, that analytic philosophy occupied the greatest share of the philosophical space there and that what was labelled "continental philosophy" was basically eclipsed by it; nor did it surprise me that for this audience the German philosophy of our times was identified with Husserlian phenomenology and Heidegger and hermeneutics were little known. As I learned to speak English a little better, albeit slowly, and got better acquainted with American philosophers, it became quite apparent to me that there were also quite viable bridges from analytic philosophy to hermeneutics. As a matter of fact, already very shortly after I had completed *Truth and Method* in 1960, I had myself begun to read the later Wittgenstein and found there much that had long been familiar to me. By that time, of course, the recognition of Wittgenstein's famous term, "language games," was already widespread in Germany also.

Another connecting link between my own heritage and that of the new continent, was theology. In both Catholicism and Protestantism, the existence of theological faculties signified the presence of Greek, and in the Catholic universities also Latin. Of course, I myself certainly claim no special competence as a theologian. But since Greek metaphysics has had such a profound influence on Christian dogmatics, especially through the adoption of Aristotle in such an encompassing way, the tensions resident in the Roman Catholic metaphysical concept of God as the highest being were long familiar to me. And on the Protestant side, there was in most of the Protestant theological faculties—whose exegetical subtleties I found extremely stimulating—a very good knowledge of the Greek language and of the Greek cultural world. And since the question, "How is it possible to speak about God?" was central to dialectical theology in Protestantism, their interest was philosophically concentrated above all on the nature of the divine instead of on Greek religious cults, and much more on Plato than on Aristotle. The issues and tensions involved here were already familiar to me from my studies of Greek philosophy—especially in terms of the participation of Platonism and Aristotelianism in the history of metaphysics—ever since the dialectical theology of the twenties put theology in a state of suspense with the problem of speaking about God. And, finally, the task of again taking up the Greek problem of being, but now and under modern circumstances, must necessarily confront one with new challenges and tasks.

And just as in Germany, interest in hermeneutic philosophy on the new continent did not limit itself to departments of philosophy. Certainly it is everywhere evident that the great inheritance of Greek and Christian thinking in our age of science is not to be found only in departments of philosophy. And the part of that heritage we may call "the hermeneutical approach" [*die hermeneutische Fragestellung*] has for a long time had its residence rights in several different fields. Thus, in my visits to America I could connect not only with theology but also with departments related to language and literature, especially comparative literature, departments which in the German language we sometimes refer to as the "philological disciplines." And still other disciplines quite different from these also began to acquaint themselves with the problems dealt with in hermeneutical philosophy, disciplines such as law and medicine, as well as the range of fields concerned with the problems of aesthetics. I believe one can say that the *"Geisteswissenschaften,"* as we call them in German, and those disciplines which in English are labelled the "Humanities," and those which in French are broadly called *"Lettres,"* have just as much inherited "Western metaphysics" as philosophy itself has. It makes a huge difference for our *Geisteswissenschaften,* for instance, that in English the word for *Wissenschaft* is "Science"! It makes a difference that earlier the term *Wissenschaft* was not used at all in English in reference to these disciplines and even today is only used out of desperation. Basically, in English, "the sciences" refers to the natural sciences.

This fact, or this contrast, has had powerful consequences in the realm of philosophy itself. Language and words have a completely different place in the tradition of philosophy familiar to us than they do in the Anglo-Saxon tradition of philosophy. Certainly it is true that within Anglo-Saxon philosophy, too, the heritage of the humanistic tradition lives on and is perceivable in their reigning concepts, but these concepts have no different function than they do in the linguistic formulations customary in the empirical sciences. If one wishes to formulate this difference in philosophical terms, I think one needs to go back to the scholastic opposition between nominalism and realism. In this opposition "realism" means of course the realism of concepts in Scholasticism. Here, it becomes immediately clear that the *language* of modern science is totally molded and determined by the nominalism we find described in scholasticism. For in the areas of research in the empirical sciences, word and concept are regarded as instruments, as merely a means of designating what their research is about and what its results are. This nominalistic view of concepts is so dominant in the modern period in general, even in the German tradition of philosophy, for instance—and, not least, even in German Idealism—that the language of their concepts was rarely the object of their philosophical inquiry. In 1918, when I myself began my philosophical studies, the reigning Neo-Kantianism still always spoke the conceptual language of Kant, a language that in turn was derived from the scholastic metaphysics of the eighteenth century which transformed their Latin into German. I think that in the early decades of the twentieth century one was not aware that the project of phenomenology really entailed changing the meaning of "concept" itself. For what was derived from Franz Brentano and continued by Frege, Husserl, Meinong, and others, was really directed towards a new discipline of thinking in which the concept is not merely an instrument and a medium of understanding but becomes the subject matter [*Sache*] of philosophy itself. It is also astonishing to find that, when one goes back to Hegel's *Science of Logic*—the last great attempt at a system in German Idealism—one encounters a logic that leads from "being" to "essence" and then to "concept." This "domain" of the concept, then, is supposed to make up the unity of both being and essence. This unity does not have its right of residence just on one side, the side where our thinking is conducted; rather, it resides precisely in *both* the "true being" of the subject matter [that is, in its concrete immediacy] as well as in its essence [its whatness, its truth].[29] This is still reflected, I believe, in the meaning of the term *"Inbegriff"* [quintessence] in German linguistic usage, where this word refers to the whole essence [*das ganze Wesen*] of the thing being discussed [*die Sache*] and not only to that side of it which is grasped through our conceptual understanding [*das durch unser Begreifen Begriffene*].

In any case, it was a new experience for me when, in my first encounter with Heidegger, I heard the term *"Begrifflichkeit"* [conceptuality], and also when I learned, under the caption of *"Destruktion,"*[30] a critical suspicion over against the concepts resident in philosophical terminology. Slowly I became aware that the language customarily used in German philosophy was not just full of preconceptions and prejudices, but also full of depth and significance. Gradually I came to heed the speaking power of words, a power which still goes on speaking in every linguistic usage and in its antecedents. In sum, the language of philosophy itself began to speak again.

This also involved a slow process of reeducating myself to a viewpoint in marked contrast to that found in the predominant theory of signs, with its instrumentalist view of their function. It was the young Heidegger who, as he recognized the prejudgments behind this reigning conceptuality, called it to account. He took from Kierkegaard the expression "formal indications"—*formale Anzeige*—and with it he brought into play the phenomenological principle of the self-showing of the thing itself [*Sich-Zeigens der Sache selbst*]. It no longer sufficed in philosophy, as it still does in science, to use the term "the given" to link the necessary designation of a thing with what it designates. For in philosophy what is "the designated"? How can a thing, for instance, be so given that we can also introduce a designation for it according to some random convention? And because conventional designation looks like a definition, it sometimes occurs even in philosophy. My own view on this point, however, is very close to that of Wittgenstein, whose thinking I have in mind when I say that in thinking this is clearly not the way that words "work." The words which we use in our speaking are much more familiar to us than this, so that we are *in* the words, so to speak. That is to say, words which are working never become objects. The "use" of words in a language is not a "using" at all. Rather, language is a medium, an element: Language is the element in which we live, as fishes live in water. In linguistic interaction we call it a conversation. We search for words and they come to us; and they either reach the other person or fail him. In the exchange of words, the thing meant becomes more and more present. A language is truly a "natural language" when it binds us together in this way. Of course, in philosophy we constantly use words which do not belong to the natural language, and the same thing also applies to the sciences. There one calls such usages "specialized expressions" or terminology. But the specialized term in the empirical sciences must claim to be a univocal designator in order to make it something confirmable through empirical testing, and fundamentally such a univocal meaning is appropriately fixable only in the symbolic language of mathematics. On the other hand, in philosophy the use of language looks quite different. Each term we use contains a certain saying-power within itself. Our terms are not like signs that point to something but rather themselves tell something of their own origin and from this they form a horizon of meaning which is supposed to lead speaking and thinking beyond themselves to the thing meant. Consequently Heidegger has designated the task of philosophy precisely as a *"Destruktion"* of terms, and in so doing he was heeding the fundamental phenomenological principle that one should avoid all theoretical constructions and get back "to the things themselves." This had been Husserl's famous slogan, a directive which he himself carried out by means of a very finely differentiated use of the German language in those areas that were most his own, namely mathematical problems, logic, and the analysis of basic concepts like time and space. But when Heidegger entered into the teachings of phenomenology with Husserl, and as he learned from Husserl the highly descriptive technique of phenomenological analysis of concepts, the task of "getting back to the things themselves" took on an entirely new dimension: that of a history of the ancestry of terms [*Herkunftsgeschichte*], a history in which the special terminology in philosophy is more or less covered over and in the background, and yet this history still speaks within and along with that term.

Heidegger had already in his early years studied the work of Wilhelm Dilthey intensively, and through this he gained access to the great inheritance that had come to German philosophy from the Romantics, an inheritance otherwise basically unavailable, since it was very little present in the reigning

Neokantianism of that time. The enormous historical-cultural education which Dilthey had acquired as the biographer of Schleiermacher, and which—like Dilthey—the generation of followers had also acquired, stood the young Heidegger in very good stead. Certainly the Neo-Kantian philosophy of that time was not so completely oblivious and inaccessible to the so-called *"Geisteswissenschaften"* as analytic philosophy in the Anglo-Saxon realm has been. Something of the humanistic potential of Neokantianism is, of course, evident in the philosophy of Ernst Cassirer. At that time, Cassirer represented something quite individual and special in Neo-Kantianism. In the end, however, he remained a disciple of the Marburg School, that is to say, of the systematic revival of Kantian thought, a school of thought which through and through placed itself under the factum of the natural sciences just as Kant had done in the *Prolegomena*. Nevertheless, Cassirer was characterized by an enormous flexibility, an astonishing familiarity with literature, and apparently a good bit of natural historical sense, so he was able to make a very fruitful application of transcendental philosophy to the historical world without falling back into scholastic terminology and concepts. But otherwise, the Neo-Kantian school of philosophy was not particulary competent to undertake either a history of concepts or a history of their linguistic presuppositions. Granted, the relationship to the history of philosophy was essential to Neo-Kantianism throughout, but unfortunately Neo-Kantianism, as we noted earlier, understood the history of philosophy as a history of problems, and it held that there were invariant elements in the problems. Thus, one really did not have to bother about their origins at all, which in reality were derived from Hegelian logic; rather, they simply treated them as fixed categories which provided a foundation. Of course, on the other hand, one must also freely admit that in the wake of German idealism the unfolding of historical consciousness in Germany was so intensively cultivated that the Anglo-Saxon visitor before the First World War came to the conclusion that German philosophy was drowning in history. And perhaps with some justification this is precisely what one could say about the scholarly achievements of the majority of the philosophy professors at that time. They had become only an extension and special part of the "Historical School," a school which, in the after-history of German Romanticism, had been the pride of the German universities in the later nineteenth century.

The young Heidegger, however, was not an example of this, for he was certainly no mere historian of philosophy. By education he was a theologian and by temperament truly a thinker. Anyone who was inspired by the appearance of Heidegger on the philosophical scene could no longer make a separation between philosophy and its history. Heidegger was even able to persuade Husserl that Aristotle had been a founder of phenomenology long before its modern founder, namely Husserl himself. Heidegger also had a gift for envisioning the basic experiences which Aristotle had turned over and over in his masterful way. Now, for once, Aristotle was no longer read through the eyes of Thomas Aquinas but rather from the raw materials that were present at the inception of Greek thought itself since Homer.

It was only logical that, in the end, as Heidegger passed through Aristotle, he began to pose the question of the beginnings of philosophy. As is well known, we possess only a few fragments that give testimony about the beginnings of Greek thinking. And even these were preserved primarily thanks to the interest Aristotle had awakened in these beginnings, making it possible for fragments of that beginning to be passed down to us through the centuries of late Greek times in the history of European culture. But this Greek beginning also holds a special significance from a hermeneutical standpoint. Its tradition is, in the strong sense of this word, an almost speechless beginning. Yes, there are citations, but precisely being a citation means that they have themselves been ripped out of the flux of thinking; the context in which these sentences were truly *speaking* is no longer given. All our philological reconstruction can never substitute for what belongs to the very nature of real speaking. So one has to say that the first philosophical texts of the Greeks that we possess are the Platonic dialogues and the so-called "teaching treatises" [*Lehrschriften*] of Aristotle.

Both of these texts, of course, immediately confront us with the fundamental hermeneutical problem of writtenness [*Schriftlichkeit*]. Plato's dialogues are conversations *written down* by a great philosophical and poetic master, and yet we know from Plato himself in his famous "Seventh Letter" that he did not leave behind a written presentation of his true teaching and did not want to. This means he has unequivocally confronted us with the necessity of a mimetic doubling, that is to say, by means of the written conversation to go back to the originally spoken conversation in which the thought found words—a task that can never be fully accomplished. Now certainly one can see quite well through the eyes of Aristotle what had been thought in this conversation. But once again one sees this only in the further mediation of reading a trace of Aristotle's spoken speech in the so-called "texts" of the Aristotelian corpus that have been left behind. It is hardly necessary to add here, too, that the Latinizing of the Aristotelian terminology [in Scholasticism] confronts us in philosophy with yet another task: namely, of thinking in a Greek way on the basis of Latin. One needs to take into account the effort the ancient Romans put into adopting Greek culture for themselves, and, indeed, to take seriously as well the fact that even in ancient Rome in the early Christian era, say, around 200 A.D. or so, philosophy was not pursued in Latin but in Greek. One then begins to sense the significance of the far later step that the schools of Christian humanism took at the threshhold of the modern era, when the language of that cultural heritage was reshaped to fit the measure of the national languages. The word *"Destruktion"* in Heidegger traverses all the layers of this heritage, and it does so not in order to destroy something but to set something free.

The question which I would pose is: What is truly the language of philosophy? What language is the language of philosophy? Is there a "language of philosophy" at all? In the end, as we ask these questions, we recognize that language is the task of philosophy itself, whatever it may be in its own living reality [*Lebendigkeit*] behind all these stages of its historical development; yes, even to recognize in it also the prelinguistic history of humanity in its potential still hidden beneath the ruins of a languageless past. What I am thinking of is not some kind of Indo-Germanic language such as that reconstructed by linguistic research as the basis for most languages in the various European cultures, nor is it anything like a primordial language [*Ursprache*]. Rather, I have in mind the linguisticality, as such, through which and out of which languages are first able to form themselves at all and out of which have been formed the multiplicity of languages, even including those that are not within our own circle of culture.

And one point cannot be left out: that it is the context of problems surrounding *the indissoluble connection between thinking and speaking* which compels hermeneutics to become philosophy. One must always think in a language, even if one does not always have to think in the same language. Hermeneutics cannot evade claiming universality because language as linguisticality—*Sprachlichkeit*—constitutes a human capacity inseparably linked with rationality as such. This only repeats here something Aristotle likewise emphasized: His argument had first to do with the universality of seeing and with the region of differences that were comprehended through seeing. But he also had to distinguish, on the other hand, the sense of hearing, and about it he had to say that he knew no boundaries to hearing at all, because language is among the things one hears, and, as the *logos,* language encompasses simply everything. This is why the project of a hermeneutical philosophy ever and again must go back to Greek philosophy. In the language and the formation of philosophical concepts of the Greeks there still lives the immediacy of experience out of which those concepts were formed. The language of the sciences, indeed specifically this language, has been shaped in such a way that in the end it has led to the development of mathematics. But what holds even more strongly as regards the thinking of the Greek philosophers and the keen pleasure they took in questioning is that they created their thinking from *the language people spoke.* These philosophers profited from and built upon the artful development of the spoken language in Homeric and Hesiodic verse art, and they built upon rhetoric, which had flourished as a highly developed art through which the youth in their claim to education engaged in verbal battles with their peers. It is a language whose influence, through the alliance between rhetoric and dialectic, has continued through many centuries.

This is how the door to Europe was opened—and in the same century that Athens and the Greek culture of the *polis* had victoriously withstood the attack of the Persians.

III. HERMENEUTICS AND PRACTICAL PHILOSOPHY

Hermeneutics and Greek philosophy have remained the two main foci of my work, and *Truth and Method* has been a center of discussion and critique over a period of over thirty-five years since its publication. In the remainder of this essay, then, I should like, first, in this section, to explore the context of factors which has motivated my thinking in hermeneutics, and in particular "practical philosophy," and, in the final section, to make an effort at self-criticism in relation to *Truth and Method*.

First, there was the hermeneutics I developed in *Truth and Method*.

What was this *philosophical* hermeneutics? How did it differ from the hermeneutics that arose in the Romantic tradition with Schleiermacher, who deepened a very old *theological* discipline, and which reached a high point in Dilthey's "*geisteswissenschaftliche*" hermeneutics, a hermeneutics intended to serve as methodological basis for the humanities and social sciences? With what justification could my own endeavor be called a "philosophical" hermeneutics?

Regrettably it is not a superfluous task to go into these questions, because many people have seen and do see in this hermeneutical philosophy a rejection of methodical rationality. Many others, especially after hermeneutics became a stylish slogan, and any and every kind of "interpretation" called itself "hermeneutical," misused the word and the issue because of which I took hold of this term. They reversed its meaning in that they saw it as a new methodology, through which they could justify methodological unclarity or furnish a legitimate cover for their ideology. Others, again, belonging to the camp of the critique of ideology recognize truth in it, but only half the truth. It is fine and good, they say, that preconceptual operativeness of tradition has been recognized, but hermeneutics lacks the decisive thing, a critical and emancipatory reflection that would free it from tradition.

Perhaps it would shed some light on the situation if I presented the motivation for my approach as it actually developed. In this way it may become clear that in reality, the method-fanatics and the ideology-critics are the ones who are not doing enough reflection. For the method-fanatics treat the rationality of trial and error—which is undisputed—as the ultimate measure of human reason; on the other hand, the ideology-critics recognize the ideological prejudice such rationality contains, but they do not sufficiently ponder the ideological implications of their own critique of ideology.

When I sought to develop a philosophical hermeneutics, it was obvious to me from the history of hermeneutics that the disciplines based on "understanding" formed my starting point. But I supplemented these with something that had previously been left out of account, namely the experience of art. Both art and the historical disciplines present us with ways of experiencing in which our own understanding of existence is directly brought into play. Heidegger's

1) Impetus for return to
   Ancients
   → Alienated Method in
     Modernity
   → Heidegger

2) Contribution of
   Plato + Aristotle

3) Hegel + Heidegger

B 3248 .G34 6354 1997

child support obligations, assets, lia
mation.

CIVIL INFORMATION GEN

Worker's Compensation claims a
vant in assessment of ongoing disa
Again, a subject's work and reside
cially if he or she has not been fo
claims may be found through an Ac
the subject's employer. However, jc
quire a subject's authorization, dep
and the accessibility of the personn

Personnel records of a subject wh
yond confirmation of dates of emp
unless attached as part of legal plea
thorize the evaluator immediate an
records. An employer may release
rized investigator in fitness-for-d

unfolding of the existential structure of understanding offered me conceptual help in placing the problematic of "understanding" in its proper breadth. He called this displaying of the existential structure of understanding a "hermeneutic of facticity," that is to say, in its self-interpretation as the human Dasein actually finds itself in "factual" existence. Using Heidegger's analysis, my starting point was a critique of German Idealism and its Romantic traditions. On this basis it was clear to me that the inherited forms of consciousness that we have acquired historically in our education—what we call "aesthetic consciousness" and "historical consciousness"—represent only alienated forms of our true historical being. The unique, originary experiences that are mediated through art and history cannot be grasped within these alienated forms. The tranquil distance from which a consciousness conditioned by the usual middle-class education enjoyed its cultural privileges does not take into account how much of *ourselves* must come into play and is at stake when we encounter works of art and studies of history.

So I sought in my hermeneutics to overcome the primacy of self-consciousness, and especially the prejudices of an idealism rooted in consciousness, by referring to the mode of "game or play" [*Spiel*].[31] For when one plays a *game*, the game itself is never a mere object; rather, it exists in and for those who play it, even if one is only participating as "spectator." In this context, I think, the inappropriateness of the concept of a "subject" and an "object" is evident, a point which Heidegger's exposition in *Being and Time* also has made. That which led Heidegger to his famous "turn" I for my part sought to describe in terms of our self-understanding coming up against its limits, that is, as the "historically affected consciousness" which is "more being than consciousness"—*mehr Sein als Bewußtsein.*[32] What I formulated with this phrase was not so much a task to be accomplished in the practice of art history or historical scholarship—indeed, it did not primarily have to do with the methodical consciousness in these disciplines—rather, it was concerned exclusively, or at least principally, with the philosophical issue of accountability. It was in this connection that I asked: In how far is method a guarantor of truth? It is the role of philosophy to make us aware that scholarship and method have a limited place within the whole of human *Existenz* and its rationality.

My own undertaking was itself conditioned by an "effective history." Obviously it was rooted in a very definite German philosophical and cultural heritage. The so-called "*Geisteswissenschaften*" ["human sciences," or humanities] in Germany had really never before so completely united together in one package their scientific and their world-intuitive functions. Or, to put it more bluntly, they had never so fully and consistently concealed their ideologically conditioned interests behind the epistemological and methodological pretensions of their scientific procedures. The indissoluble unity of all human self-knowledge was expressed much more clearly elsewhere than Germany: in France through the broader concept of "*lettres*," and in English in the newly introduced concept of the "humanities." What I wanted to bring about by insisting on the "historically affected consciousness" was a correction of the self-concept of the historical human sciences, and here I include scholarship about art: that they are not "sciences" in the manner of the natural sciences.

But bringing about the recognition of an "historically affected consciousness" in the human sciences was not my only goal, for the full dimensions of what I have called "the hermeneutical problem" are much broader. In the natural sciences, too, there is something like a hermeneutical problematic. Their path, too, is not simply that of methodical, step-by-step progress. This has been persuasively shown by Thomas Kuhn and was already implied by Heidegger's "The Age of the Worldpicture" as well as in his interpretation of the Aristotelian view of nature (cf. *Physics* B 1). Both make clear that the reigning "paradigm" is decisive both for the questions research raises and for the data it examines, and these are apparently not just the result of methodical research. Galileo had already said, "*Mente concipio*."[33]

Behind all this, however, a much broader dimension opens up, a dimension rooted in the fundamental linguisticality of human beings. In all human knowing of the world and in all orientation within the world the nature of the moment of understanding has to be worked out, and in this way the universality of hermeneutics will become evident. Naturally, the fundamental linguisticality of understanding cannot mean that all experiencing of the world can only take place as and in language, for we know all too well those prelinguistic and metalinguistic inner awarenesses, those moments of dumbfoundedness and speaking silences in which our immediate contact with the world is taking place. And who would deny that there are real factors conditioning human life, such as hunger, love, labor, and domination, which are not themselves language or speaking, but which for their part furnish the space within which our speaking to each other and listening to each other can take place. This fact cannot be disputed; indeed, it is precisely these preconditions of human thinking and speaking which themselves make hermeneutic reflection necessary.

Furthermore, with a hermeneutic oriented to Socratic dialogue like mine one does not have to be reminded that *doxa* is not real knowing, and that the apparent agreement-in-understanding on the basis of which one lives and speaks is not always a real agreement. But even the discovery that something is only apparently the case, which Socratic conversation brings about, takes place within the element of linguisticality. Even the total breakdown of communication, even misunderstanding and the famous admission that one does not know, presuppose that understanding is possible. The commonality that we call human rests on the linguistic constitution of our lifeworld. Indeed, every attempt by means of critical reflection and argumentation to bring suit against distortions in interhuman communication only confirms this commonality.

What I have called the hermeneutic aspect of human life and communication thus cannot remain limited to hermeneutic scholarship, or history, or texts; nor is it enough to broaden it to include the experience of works of art. Rather, as Schleiermacher already knew, the universality of the hermeneutical problem has to do with the whole universe of the rational; that is, with everything about which one can seek to communicate. Where communication seems impossible because one "speaks different languages," hermeneutics is still not at an end. Precisely here the hermeneutical task is posed in its full seriousness, namely finding a common language. Even the common language is never a fixed given. It resides in the play of language between speakers, who must enter into the game of language so that communication can begin, even where various viewpoints stand irreconcilably over against each other. The possibility of communication between rational beings can never be denied. Even the relativism which seems to reside in the multiplicity of human languages is no barrier for reason, whose "word" [or *logos*] all have in common, as already Heraclitus was aware. The learning of a foreign language and likewise even the first learning of language by children do not just involve the acquisition of the means of reaching an understanding. Rather, this learning represents a kind of preschematization of possible experience and its first acquisition. Growing into a language, then, is a path to knowledge of the world. Not only such "learning" but every experience takes place in a constantly developing formation [*Bildung*] of our communicative knowledge of the world. In a much deeper and more universal sense than the great philologist, August Boeckh, meant it when he formulated it in reference to the work of philologists, experience is always an "*Erkenntnis von Erkanntem*"—"a knowledge of something already known." For we live in what has been handed down to us, and this is not just a specific region of our experience of the world, specifically what we call the "cultural tradition" which only consists of texts and monuments and which are able to pass on to us a linguistically constituted and historically documented sense. No, it is *the world itself* which is communicatively experienced and continuously entrusted (*traditur*) to us as an infinitely open task. It is never the world as it was on its first day but as it has come down to us. Always present when we experience something, when unfamiliarity is overcome, where enlightenment, insight, and appropriation succeed, the *hermeneutic process* takes place in bringing something into words and into the common consciousness. Even the monological language of modern science attains social reality *only in this way*. It is because of this that the universality of hermeneutics, which Habermas so resolutely disputed, seems to me to be well grounded. Habermas, in my opinion, never gets past an understanding of the hermeneutical problem one finds in German Idealism and he unjustly restricts my conception of tradition to the "cultural tradition" in the sense that Theodor Litt used this term. The extended discussion between Habermas and myself of this question is documented in the 1971 volume published by Suhrkamp entitled *Hermeneutik und Ideologiekritik.*[34]

In relation to our philosophical tradition, also, I believe we have a similar hermeneutical task. Philosophizing, too, does not just start from point zero but rather has to think further and speak further the language we speak. What this means today, just as it did in the days of the ancient sophists, is that the presently alienated language of philosophy must recover its original saying power and be led back to the uttering of what is meant [*das Sagen des Gemeinten*] and back to the things we have in common, the solidarities that are the bearers of our speaking—*die unser Sprechen tragenden Gemeinsamkeiten.*

Modern science has more or less blinded us to this task, and the generalizing of its perspective into philosophy should be resisted. In Plato's *Phaedo* Socrates puts forward the following demand: he would like to understand the structure of the world and the occurrences in nature in the same way he understands why he sits here in prison and has not taken the offer of flight—namely because he holds it *good* to accept even an unjust sentence against him. To understand nature as Socrates here understands himself, namely in terms of the Good, is a demand that in a certain way is fulfilled through Aristotle's teleological philosophy of nature. But this Socratic demand is no longer accepted and has not been since the science that developed in the seventeenth century, which was the first real "science" of nature, a science that has in some measure made the control of nature possible. But in my view, precisely because of the nonunifiability of philosophy with the modern natural sciences, hermeneutics as philosophy does not have as much to learn from the theory of modern science as it does from the older traditions, which it needs to call back to memory.

One of these is the tradition of rhetoric, a tradition Giambattista Vico, as the last representative of that older tradition, defended with strong methodological awareness against modern science, which he called *critica.*[35] Already in my classical Greek studies during the twenties I had been strongly interested in rhetoric, both as the art of speaking as well as in its theory. Rhetoric for a long time has not been sufficiently recognized. In the older tradition rhetoric was the bearer of aesthetic concepts, as still becomes quite clear in Baumgarten's determination of aesthetics. In any case, this point needs great emphasis today: The rationality of the rhetorical way of arguing, which admittedly seeks to bring emotions into play but works with arguments and with probabilities, is and remains far more a determining factor in society than the excellence of science. For this reason, in *Truth and Method* I have expressly related myself to rhetoric and from many sides found corroboration. For instance, the work of Chaim Perelman, who takes legal practice as his starting point.[36] This does not mean that I underestimate the importance of modern science and its application in the technical civilization of today. On the contrary, there are completely new problems of mediation that are posed by modern civilization. But the situation has not in principle been changed by this. The "hermeneutical" task of integrating the monologicality of science into the communicative consciousness, which entails the exercise of practical, social, and political rationality, has only become more urgent with the rise of technological civilization.

In reality this is an old problem, one that we have been aware of since Plato. The statesmen, the poets, but also the real masters of the individual manual arts, were nevertheless accused by Socrates of not knowing the "good." Aristotle has determined for us the structural difference involved here through his differentiation of *techne* from *phronēsis*. This difference cannot just be talked away. Even if this distinction allows of being misused, and even if the call for "conscience" may itself often conceal unrecognized ideological commitments, it is still a misunderstanding of reason and rationality if one only recognizes them within the anonymity of science as science. So I was persuaded that the Socratic legacy of a "human wisdom," had to be taken up again in my own hermeneutical theory-formation, a legacy which, when measured against the godlike infallibility of science, is, in the sense of *sophia*, a consciousness of not knowing. What Aristotle developed as "practical philosophy" can serve as a model for this fallible and merely human wisdom. This is the second line of the ancient tradition that, in my view, needs to be renewed.

The Aristotelian project of a practical science [*praktische Wissenschaft*] seems to me to offer really the only scientific-theoretical model according to which the scholarly disciplines that are based on "understanding" [*die "verstehenden" Wissenschaften*] can be thought out. Through hermeneutic reflection on the conditions of understanding, it becomes clear that this type of understanding can best be articulated in a reflection that neither starts at a zero point nor ends in infinity. Aristotle has made it clear that practical reason and practical insight do not possess the teachability of science but can be exercised in praxis, and this implies an inner link with the ethos—a point well worth remembering. The model of practical philosophy, then, must be put in place of these "*theoria*," whose ontological legitimation can only be found in an infinite intellect, an intellect about which our experience of human existence, unsupported by revelation, knows nothing. This model must be invoked against all who would bend human ~~The real~~ reason into the methodical thinking that characterizes "anonymous" science. To ~~philosophy~~ present and defend the model of rationality belonging to practical reason over against the perfection of a logical self-understanding specific to the sciences seems to me the true and authentic task of philosophy today, also, and precisely in view of the practical relevance of science to our life and survival.

"Practical philosophy" is much more than a mere methodological model for the "hermeneutical" disciplines. It also offers something like a *sachliche Grundlage*—substantive foundation—for them. The special kind of method that belongs to practical philosophy follows from what Aristotle worked out as "practical reason," a rationality possessing a specific conceptual character.

Indeed, its structure cannot be grasped by means of the modern concept of science at all. Hegel, whose dialectic was successful in rehabilitating many traditional ideas, was also able to renew many of the truths of "practical" philosophy, yet even the dialectical flexibility of Hegel threatens today to become a new, unconscious dogmatism of reflection. For, the concept of reflection that serves as the basis for Habermas's "critique of ideology" implies a highly abstract concept of coercion-free discourse which totally loses sight of the real conditions of human praxis. As has been well documented in *Hermeneutik und Ideologiekritik,* I had to reject Habermas's recourse to psychoanalysis as illegitimately taking the therapeutic situation of psychoanalysis for the program of critique of ideology.[37] In the realm of practical reason there is simply no analogy to the "knowing" analyst who guides the productive reflective processes of the analysand. With regard to the question of reflection, it seems to me that Brentano's differentiation of reflexive self-awareness from objectivizing reflection, a distinction that goes back to Aristotle, is still superior to what we find in the heritage of German Idealism. The same thing applies, in my view, also with regard to the demand for transcendental reflection that Karl-Otto Apel and others have directed at hermeneutics. This demand and my reply to it have also been documented in the volume on hermeneutics and critique of ideology I just mentioned.

So I have to say that the dialogues of Plato, even more than the works of the great thinkers of German Idealism, have left their stamp on my thinking. These dialogues are my constant companions, and what a unique company they are! However much we moderns may have been taught by Nietzsche and Heidegger about how Greek concepts have anticipated everything from Aristotle to Hegel and up to modern logic, so that they constitute a boundary beyond which our own questions remain without answers and our intentions unsatisfied, it is still Plato's dialogical art which serves as an antidote to the illusion of superiority which we think we possess as inheritors of the Judeo-Christian tradition. Admittedly it was also Plato who, with the doctrine of ideas, the mathematization of nature, and the intellectualizing of what we would call "ethics," laid the foundation for the metaphysical conceptuality of our tradition. But at the same time he mimetically limited all his assertions, and just as Socrates knew how to do this with his dialogue partners by using irony, so also Plato through his art of dialogical poetry, robbed his reader of his assumed superiority. To philosophize *with* Plato, not just to criticize Plato, that is the task. To criticize Plato is perhaps just as simple-minded as to reproach Sophocles for not being Shakespeare. This may seem paradoxical, but only to someone who is blind to the philosophical relevance of Plato's poetic imagination.

Of course, one must first learn to read Plato mimetically. In our century some things have happened that make this a little easier, especially through Paul Friedlaender's great study,[38] but also through many other inspired but sometimes not so well-grounded books from the circle of the poet Stefan George (by Heinrich

Friedmann, Kurt Singer, and Kurt Hildebrandt, for instance), as well as the works of Leo Strauss and his friends and students. The task, however, is far from accomplished. It consists of relating the conceptual assertions one encounters in conversations as exactly as possible with the dialogical reality out of which they grow. For one finds there a "Doric harmony" of deed and speaking, of *ergon* and *logos,* which has to do not just with the words. Rather, it is the authentic spirit of the Socratic dialogues. They are in the literal sense, *"hinführende Reden"*—speeches that take you somewhere. Only in these does Socrates open his heart to us and let us know what he really intends, not in his art of refutation that often works sophistically and drives his partners into terrible entanglements.

Yes, if only human wisdom were such that it could pass from one person to another like water over a thread of wool (*Symposium* 175d). But human wisdom is not like this. It is the awareness of not-knowing [*das Wissen des Nichtwissens*], *docta ignorantia.* Through it the other person with whom Socrates is having the conversation, is convicted of his own not-knowing—and this means that something dawns on him about himself and about his living in only pretended knowledge. Or, to put it in the clearer formulation from Plato's *Seventh Letter:* Not just his thesis but his soul is refuted. This applies not only to the young men who believe themselves to be friends and yet do not know what friendship is (in the *Lysis*), as well as to the famous generals (in the *Laches*), who believe they embody in themselves bravery, the virtue of soldiers, or the ambitious statesmen (in the *Charmides*), who think they possess a knowledge superior to that of all others. It applies, likewise, to all those who follow the professional teachers of wisdom, and in the end it even applies to the simplest citizen who must make himself and others believe that he is a just person as salesman, dealer, banker, or craftsman. Apparently, then, a specialized knowledge is not what is involved here but another kind of knowing, a knowing that is beyond all specialized competences and beyond all claims to superiority in knowledge, a knowing beyond all otherwise recognized *technai* and *epistemai.* This other knowledge means a *"Wendung zur Idee"*—"a turning to the idea"—that is, a turning to that which lies behind all the mere positings of supposedly knowledgeable persons.

But this means that in the end Plato does not have a doctrine that one can simply learn from him, namely the "doctrine of ideas." And if he criticizes this doctrine in his *Parmenides,* this also does not mean that at that time he was beginning to have doubts about it. Rather, it means that the acceptance of the "ideas" does not designate the acceptance of a doctrine so much as of a line of questioning that the doctrine has the task of developing and discussing. That is the Platonic dialectic. Dialectic is the art of having a conversation, and that includes the art of having a conversation with oneself and fervently seeking an understanding of oneself. It is the art of thinking. But this means the art of seriously questioning what one really means when one thinks or says this or that. In doing so, one sets out on a journey, or better, is already on the journey. For there is something like a "natural disposition of man towards philosophy." Our thinking is never satisfied with what one means in saying this or that. Thinking constantly points beyond itself. The work that goes on in a Platonic dialogue has its way of expressing this: it points towards the One, toward Being, the "Good," which is present in the order of the soul, in the constitution for the city, and in the structure of the world.

Although Heidegger interprets the acceptance of Plato's doctrine of ideas as the beginning of the forgetfulness of Being, a forgetfulness which reaches its peak in a thinking merely in terms of representation and objectivation, and in a will to power which dominates the era of technology, and although his understanding that even the earliest Greek thinking of Being is a preparation for the forgetfulness of Being that occurs in metaphysics is consistent enough with this, I would argue that the authentic meaning of the Platonic dialectic of ideas is ultimately something quite different from all this. The fundamental step of going beyond all existing things in Plato is a step beyond a "simplistic" ["*einfältige*"] acceptance of the ideas; thus, it ultimately represents a countermovement *against* the "metaphysical" interpretation of Being as merely the being of beings.

Actually, the history of metaphysics could be written as a history of Platonism. Its stages would be, say, Plotinus and Augustine, Meister Eckhart and Nicholas of Cusa, Leibniz, Kant, and Hegel; which means, of course, all those great efforts of Western thought to *go questioningly back behind* the substantial being of the Form and thus behind the whole metaphysical tradition. And in this respect, the first Platonist in the series would be none other than Aristotle himself. To defend this view, and thus to oppose the common interpretation of Aristotle's criticisms of the doctrine of ideas, and to attack also the substance metaphysics of the Western tradition, has been the goal of my writing in this area.[39] By the way, I do not stand all alone in this; Hegel also held such a view.

To make good my point would not be some kind of merely "historical" undertaking. For certainly my intention would not be to supplement the Heideggerian history of the increasing forgetfulness of being with a history of the remembering of being. That would not be meaningful. Indeed, it is certainly appropriate to speak of an increasing forgetfulness. In my view, Heidegger's great achievement was to have shaken us out of too full a forgetfulness by asking in earnest: What is being? I myself recall how in 1924 Heidegger ended a semester seminar on Cajetan's *De nominum analogia* with the question "Was ist das, das Sein?" and how we looked at each other and shook our heads over the absurdity of the question. In the meantime, we have all been reminded, in a certain sense, of the question of being. Even the defenders of the traditional metaphysical tradition, those who wish to be critics of Heidegger, find they are no longer captive to a self-evident understanding of being, an understanding grounded in the metaphysical tradition and accepted without question. Rather they now defend the classical answer *as* an answer, which means that they have again recovered the question as a question.

Everywhere that philosophizing is attempted, one finds in this attempt a recollection of being takes place. In spite of this fact, however, it seems to me there *recollect* is no history of the recollection of being. Recollection has no history. There is not an increasing recollection in the same way that there is an increasing forgetfulness. Recollection is always what comes to one, and comes over one, so that something that is again made present to us offers, for the space of a moment, a halt to all passing away and forgetting. But recollection of being is not a recollection of something previously known and now present once again; rather, it is recollection of something previously asked, the reclaiming of a lost question. And a question which is asked again is no longer recollected; it becomes a question again and is now asked anew. It is no longer a recollection of something that was once asked—it is posed anew. In this way, questioning reconceptualizes [*aufhebt,* to destroy but also to preserve in a higher form] the historicity of our thinking and knowing. In this sense philosophy has no history. The first person who wrote a history of philosophy, that was really such, was also the last to do so—Hegel. And in Hegel, history was cancelled and fulfilled [*aufgehoben*] in the presence of absolute spirit [*des absoluten Geistes*].

But is this *our* present? Is Hegel still present also for us?[40] Certainly one ought not dogmatize and take what Hegel meant in a narrow sense. When he spoke of the end of history which is to be reached through the freedom of everyone, he meant that history is at an end only in the sense that no higher principle can be put forward than the freedom of everyone. The increasing unfreedom of everyone, which has begun to characterize Western civilization—perhaps its inescapable destiny—would constitute for Hegel no valid objection to the principle of freedom. Indeed, he would say, "So much the worse for the facts." At the same time, I would ask, against Hegel: Is the first and last principle in which the philosophical thinking of being culminates really *"Geist"* [spirit, mind]?[41] Cer- *Hegel* tainly, the critique of the young Hegelians was polemically directed against this. *+* But it is my conviction that Heidegger has been the first thinker since Hegel to *Heidegger* present us with a positive alternative possibility, a possibility that gets beyond mere dialectical reversal. This is Heidegger's point: Truth is not the total uncon- cealment whose ideal fulfillment would in the end remain the presence of absolute spirit to itself. Rather, Heidegger taught us to think truth as an uncon- cealing and a concealing at the same time. The great efforts at thinking in the tradition, efforts in which we feel ourselves over and over again to be addressed and expressed, all stand in this tension. What is asserted is not everything. Indeed, it is the unsaid that first makes it, and lets it be, a word that can reach us. This seems to me to be compellingly true. The concepts in which thinking is formulated stand silhouetted like dark shadows on a wall. They work in a one-sided

way, predetermining and prejudging. One thinks, for instance, of Greek intellectualism, or of the metaphysics of will in German Idealism, or the methodologism
of the Neokantians and Neopositivists. In a process of which it is not aware,
each of these formulated its highest principle without realizing its anticipatory
entrapment in its own concepts.

For this reason every dialogue we have with the thinking of a thinker we are
seeking to understand remains an endless conversation. It is a real conversation,
a conversation in which we seek to find "our" language—to grasp what we have
in common. Consciously taking up a historical distance from one's partner and
placing the partner in an historically surveyable course of events must remain
subordinate movements of our effort to achieve understanding. As a matter of
fact, they represent a self-assurance by which one actually closes oneself off
from one's partner. In a conversation, on the other hand, one seeks to open oneself to him or her, which means holding fast to the common subject matter as the
ground on which one stands together with one's partner.

But if this is the case, then the goal of preserving one's own "position" is
in a jam. On the other hand, if one takes such a dialogical endlessness
[*Unendlichkeit*, infinity] to its most radical extreme, does it not entail a complete
relativism? But again, if this were so, would not this position itself be trapped in
the well-known self-contradiction of all relativism? In the end, I think, the way
such a dialogue goes is very much like the way we acquire our experiences in
life: A fullness of experiences, encounters, instructions, and disappointments
does not just conjoin everything in the end to mean that one knows everything;
rather it means that one is initiated and at the same time has learned a bit of
modesty. In a central chapter of my book *Truth and Method* I have defended this
"personal" concept of experience against the deformation the concept of experience has suffered in being institutionalized in the empirical sciences. In this I
feel myself akin to Michael Polanyi.[42] "Hermeneutic" philosophy, as I envision
it, does not understand itself as an "absolute" position but as a path of experiencing. Its modesty consists in the fact that for it there is no higher principle than
this: holding oneself open to the conversation. This means, however, constantly
recognizing in advance the possibility that your partner is right, even recognizing the possible superiority of your partner. Is this too little? This seems to me to
be the only kind of integrity one can demand of a professor of philosophy—but
it is one which one ought also to demand.

It seems to me evident that we cannot get around the original dialogic of
human being in the world and having a world. This holds even if one is demanding some kind of final accountability or "ultimate foundation" [*Letzt-
begründung*]—or for the self-realization of the spirit. The path of Hegel's
thought, above all, should be newly examined. Heidegger has uncovered the
Greek roots of the tradition of metaphysics, and he has at the same time recognized a radical allegiance to the Greeks in Hegel's dialectical dissolution of tra-

ditional concepts as carried out in the *Science of Logic*. But Heidegger's *Destruktion* of metaphysics has not, in my view, robbed metaphysics of its importance today. In particular, Hegel's powerful speculative leap beyond the subjectivity of the subjective Spirit established this possibility and offered a way of shattering the predominance of subjectivism. Was Hegel's intention not the same as that in Heidegger's turn [*Kehre*]: away from the transcendental principle of the self? Was it not Hegel's intention, also, to surpass the orientation to self-consciousness and the subject-object schema of a philosophy of consciousness? Or are there still differences that remain? Do not my orientation to the universality of language and my insistence on the linguisticality of our access to the world, both of which I share with Heidegger, really constitute a step beyond Hegel, or are they a step back behind Hegel?[43]

[handwritten marginal note: Hege l + Heidegger together.]

I could, in fact, say, as a first determination of the site of my own effort at thinking, that I have taken it on myself to restore to a place of honor what Hegel termed "bad infinity" ["*schlechte Unendlichkeit*"]—but with a decisive modification, of course. For in my view the unending [*unendliche*, infinite] dialogue of the soul with itself which thinking is, is not properly characterized as an endlessly refined determination of the objects that we are seeking to know, either in the Neo-Kantian sense of the infinite task or in the Hegelian dialectical sense that thinking is always moving beyond every particular limit. Rather, here I think Heidegger showed me a new path when, as a preparation for posing the question of being in a new way, he turned to a critique of the metaphysical tradition—and in doing so found himself "on the way to language." This way of language is not absorbed in making judgments and examining their claims to objective validity; rather, it is a way of language that constantly holds itself open to the whole of being. Totality, in my view, is not some kind of objectivity that awaits human determination. In this respect, I find Kant's critique of the antinomies of pure reason to be correct and not superseded by Hegel. Totality is never an object but rather a world-horizon which encloses us and within which we live our lives.

I did not need to follow Heidegger, who based himself on Hölderlin against Hegel and who interpreted the work of art as a primordial occurrence of truth, to find in the poetic work a corrective for the ideal of an objective determination of truth, or in order to recognize the hubris that resides in concepts. On the contrary, this was already clear to me in my own first efforts at thinking. From that time on, the poetic work offered my own hermeneutic orientation constant food for thought. Likewise, the hermeneutical effort to think the nature of language in terms of dialogue—inevitable for me as a lifelong student of Plato—ultimately signified that every formulation one might make was in principle surpassable in the process of conversation. The rigid fixing of things in terminology, which is fully appropriate in the realm of modern science and its effort to put knowledge into the hands of its anonymous society of investigators is peculiarly suspect in relation to the realm of motion called philosophical thought. The great Greek thinkers were able to preserve the flexibility of their own language even when it was occasionally carried out in conceptually fixed terms, say, in thematic analysis. On the other hand, there is Scholasticism: ancient, medieval, modern—and the most recent. It follows philosophy like its shadow. That is why the true rank of a thinker or of thinking is almost determinable according to how far the thinker or the thinking is able to break through the fossilization represented by the usages inherited in his or her philosophical language. Fundamentally, Hegel's programmatic effort at this, which in his hands became the dialectical method, had many predecessors. Even a thinker as ceremonially minded as Kant, who constantly had in mind the Latin language of late Scholasticism, established his "own" language, a language which certainly avoided neologisms but in which the traditional concepts gained new applications and new meaning. Likewise, Husserl's higher rank as compared with the contemporary and older Neo-Kantianism consists precisely in the fact that his intellectual powers of intuition welded together the inherited technical expressions and combined them with the descriptive elasticity of his vocabulary into the unity of a personal style. And Heidegger did not hesitate to appeal to the example of Plato and Aristotle to justify the novelty of his use of language, and he is, by the way, far more followed now than the initially provocative effect and public amazement would have allowed one to expect. Philosophy, in contrast to the sciences and also to practical life, finds itself in a peculiar kind of difficulty. The language we speak in everyday use is not created for the purpose of philosophizing. Philosophy continually finds itself in a state of urgent linguistic need [*Sprachnot*]. This is constitutive of philosophy, and this calamity, this distress, becomes all the more felt, the more boldly the philosophizer is breaking new paths. One generally marks oneself as a dilettante in thinking if one arbitrarily introduces terms and zealously "defines one's concepts." Rather, the true philosopher often awakens the intuitive power already resident in language, and every linguistic zeal, or even linguistic violence, can be in place if only this can be accepted into the language of those who would think along with the philosopher, think further with him, and that means if the words are able to push forward, extend, or light up the horizon of communication.

It is unavoidable that philosophy, which never finds its object already at hand but must itself provide it, does not move within systems of propositions whose logical formalization and critical testing for conclusiveness and univocity might somehow deepen its insights. Such a way with language will create from the world no "revolution," not even that proclaimed by the analysts of ordinary language. To illustrate this point with an example, if one analyzes with logical methods the arguments in a Platonic dialogue, shows inconsistencies, fills in gaps, unmasks false deductions, and so on, one can achieve a certain gain in clarity. But does one learn to read Plato by proceeding in this way? Does one make his questions one's own? Does one succeed in learning from Plato instead of just confirming one's own superiority? What applies to Plato in this case applies by extension to all philosophy. Plato has in his *Seventh Letter* rightly described this, once and for all: The means one uses for philosophizing are not the same as philosophizing itself. Simple logical rigor is not everything. Not that logic does not have its evident validity. But the thematization in logic restrains the horizon of questioning in order to allow for verification, and in doing so blocks the kind of opening up of the world which takes place in our own experience of that world. This is a hermeneutical finding which I believe in the end converges with what we find in the later Wittgenstein. In his later writings he revised the nominalistic prejudices of his *Tractatus* in favor of leading all speaking back to the context of life-praxis. Of course, the result of this proposed reduction of philosophy to a praxis-context remained for him a negative one. It consisted in a flat rejection of all the undemonstrable questions of metaphysics rather than in a *winning back* of these undemonstrable questions of metaphysics, however undemonstrable they might be, by detecting in them the linguistic constitution of our being-in-the-world [*In-der-Welt-Sein*]. For this, of course, far more can be learned from the word of the poets than from Wittgenstein.

In the case of poetry, one thing is undisputed: Conceptual explication is never able to exhaust the content of a poetic image. No one contests this. Indeed, this point has been recognized at least since Kant, if not earlier with Baumgarten's discovery of poetic truth as *cognitio sensitiva*. From a hermeneutic perspective this has to be of special interest. In the case of poetry, the mere separation of the aesthetic from the theoretical, and the freeing of poetry from the pressure of rules or concepts is not enough. For poetry still is a form of speech in which concepts enter into a relationship with each other. So the hermeneutical task is to learn how to determine the special place of poetry in the constraining context of language, where a conceptual element is always involved. The question is: In what manner does language become art? I do not pose this question here just because the practice of interpretation always has to do with forms of speaking and forms of text and because in poetry also one has to do with a linguistically created work or composition, that is, with a text. Rather, it is because poetic compositions are text in a new kind of sense: they are text in an "eminent" sense of that word—namely, "eminent text." In this kind of text language emerges in its full autonomy. Here language just stands for itself; it brings itself to stand before us, whereas normally its words are taken over by the intention in the speech and then after being used are just left behind. One could say that, in a sense, the words simply disappear into their function.[44]

Here we have a hermeneutical problem with a difficulty of its own, for through poetry a special kind of communication takes place. In a poem, with *whom* does the communication take place? Is it with the reader? With *which* reader? Here the dialectic of question and answer which is always the basis of the hermeneutical process and which corresponds to the basic structure of dialogue undergoes a special modification. The reception and interpretation of poetry appears to imply a dialogical relationship of its own special kind.

This becomes especially evident when one studies the specific character of the various kinds of speaking. First, the poetic word displays a wide scale of differentiation in the dialogical relationship; for instance, epic, drama, and lyric poetry. But there are also other kinds of speaking in which the basic hermeneutical relationship of question and answer undergoes fundamental modifications. I am thinking, for instance, of the various forms of religious speaking, such as proclaiming, praying, preaching, blessing. One could also mention the mythic saga, the legal text, and even the more or less stammering language of philosophy. All of these involve the hermeneutical structure of application with which I have increasingly occupied myself since the publication of *Truth and Method*. I believe I have been able to get closer to what is involved here by approaching the problem from two sides: first, from my studies of Hegel, in whom I have pursued the role of the linguistic in relation to the logical, and second, from the side of modern hermetic poetry, to which I have dedicated a book, choosing Paul Celan's "Atemkristall" as the object of the commentary.[45] Reflection on them has served to remind me, and can constantly serve to remind us all, that Plato was no Platonist and philosophy is not scholasticism.

IV. *TRUTH AND METHOD* RECONSIDERED

Now that more than three decades have passed since the appearance of *Truth and Method* in 1960, perhaps the time has come to ponder the consistency of a project that brought together several different investigations from several different sides and attempted to weld them into a philosophic statement. So I would like in this final section to make an effort at self-criticism. Do the investigations I undertook in *Truth and Method* constitute the unity of a philosophical whole, or can one perceive glaring gaps in them, inconsistencies in the line of argument as a whole, or structural deficiencies? Has the form of their presentation here and there gotten out of date?

Quite certainly it may seem outdated today to lay the emphasis just on the historical and the philological disciplines within the *Geisteswissenschaften*. In an era of "social sciences" and of structuralism and linguistics, an effort to link up with the Romantic heritage of the historical school can seem no longer sufficient. The limited range of experience with which I began may to some degree account for this. Nevertheless, the intention of all my work has been directed toward the universality of the hermeneutical experience, and if this experience is really a universal, it ought to be reachable from any starting point.[46]

Doubtless the image of the natural sciences that I had in mind when I conceived my hermeneutical ideas for *Truth and Method* was quite one-sided. It is now clear to me in this respect that a whole broad field of hermeneutical problems has been left out, a field which goes far beyond the range of my own knowledge of the processes and procedures of current scientific research. It is really only in the historical-philological disciplines that I have gotten far enough along to participate here and there in the work of genuine research. In cases where I cannot study the original work done, I do not feel that I am justified in wanting to make the researcher aware of what he is doing and what is going on with him. The validity of hermeneutical reflection, after all, depends on the experience that must arise out of concrete hermeneutical praxis.

Nevertheless, the fact that a hermeneutical problematic is present in the natural sciences was already clear to me when I read Moritz Schlick's convincing critique of the dogma of protocol sentences in 1934.[47] When the ideas for my book were developed in the 1930s, which was a time when circumstances entailed an increasing isolation, physicalism and the unity of science were the official image that was pressed upon us. At that time, the "linguistic turn" in Anglo-Saxon philosophical thinking was not yet even on the horizon. Only after I had completed the path of thought that led to *Truth and Method* did I have time to study the work of the later Wittgenstein, for instance, and only much later did I realize that Karl Popper's critique of positivism also contained motifs similar to those in my own orientation.[48]

So I am only too aware of the way in which the points of departure in the formation of my thinking were captive to the times. It is the task of the younger generation to take into account the changed conditions for hermeneutical praxis, and fortunately this has happened. The critiques that have arisen over the years have prompted lively discussion on many sides. So when I came back to *Truth and Method* to prepare it for publication as the first volume in my collected works, I did not attempt to rework it again but to supplement it with a matching volume of essays [*GW* 2].

As I look back today, I see one point in particular where I did not achieve the theoretical consistency I strove for in *Truth and Method*. I did not make it clear enough how the two basic projects that were brought together in the concept of play [*Spiel,* also game] harmonized with each other and how they contrasted with the subjectivism of modern thinking. On the one hand, there is the orientation to the game we play with art and on the other hand the grounding of language in conversation, the game of language. With this, the further and decisive question arises as to whether I succeeded in making it fully clear that the hermeneutic dimension goes beyond the sort of thinking that is based on consciousness, that is, beyond what German philosophy calls "self-consciousness"—"*Selbstbewußtsein.*" This entails showing that the otherness of the Other is not overcome in understanding, but rather preserved. What I needed to do was go back to my concept of game once again and place it within an ontological perspective that had been broadened by the universal element of linguisticality.

In other words, I needed to unite the game of language more closely with the game art plays, which I had designated as the model for hermeneutics. It was certainly obvious that one could think the universality of linguistic world-experience under the model of playing a game. Indeed, already in the foreword to the second edition of *Truth and Method* (1965), as well as in the closing pages of my 1963 essay on "The Phenomenological Movement,"[49] I referred to the convergence of my concept of game with the concept of language-game in the later Wittgenstein.

To say that learning to speak a language is a "learning process" is really only a *façon de parler*—a "manner of speaking." In reality, it is a game of imitation and of exchange. The apprehending child's natural urge to imitate, to form sounds, either in imitation or out of sheer pleasure, is combined in that child's mind with the illuminating flash of meaning. No one can really say how the child's first understanding of meaning comes about. There are always prelinguistic experiences of meaning that have been going on long before that moment, and surely also the exchange of looks and gestures, so all the crossings over from prelinguistic to linguistic understanding flow smoothly. Equally ungraspable is how the result is arrived at. So no one can quite figure out what the term from present-day linguistics, namely "linguistic competence," really means. Apparently whatever it means cannot be objectively described as the possession of an inventory of what is linguistically correct. Rather, what the term "competence" means is that the linguistic capacity has been developed in a person who speaks and cannot be described simply in terms of the application of rules or merely as the rule-governed management of language. One must instead view this competence as the fruit of a within limits unencumbered practice of speaking. A central part of my own endeavor, in contrast to the concept of *Sprachkompetenz,* has been to demonstrate hermeneutically the universality of *Sprachlichkeit* ["linguisticality"]. For I regard learning to speak and the acquiring of an orientation to the world as inseparably woven together in the fabric making up the history of the cultural development of man [*Bildungsgeschichte des Menschen*]. This may be a neverending process, and it is on the basis of *this* that one acquires at the same time something like linguistic "competence."[50] It may be instructive to compare this process to that of learning a foreign language. In general, we can only speak here of *approaching* so-called speaking competence, except in the case of someone who has over a long period of time fully and completely entered an environment in which the foreign language is spoken. Generally, competence is only achievable in one's own mother tongue, or the language one spoke where one lived and grew up as a child. This confirms the fact that one learns to interact with the world through one's mother language, and conversely, the first development of one's own capacity to speak begins to be articulated within one's orientation in the surrounding world.

The question, then, is how the playing of the language-game, which is for each person also the playing of the world-game, goes together with playing the artwork-game. How do both relate to each other? It is clear that in both cases, I think, that linguisticality is incorporated into the hermeneutical dimension. I believe I have rather persuasively shown in *Truth and Method* that the understanding of what is spoken must be thought of in terms of the dialogical situation, and that means ultimately in terms of the dialectic of question and answer. That is always the situation in which one makes oneself understood, and through which one articulates the world both sides hold in common.[51] I have moved a step beyond the logic of question and answer as Collingwood had developed it, in that not only does one's world orientation, as he held, find expression in what develops between the speaking of question and answer; it also happens to us *from the side of the things [Dingen] that are the topic of conversation.* That is to say, the subject-matter [*Sache*] "raises questions" ["*gibt Fragen auf*"]. Likewise, question and answer play back and forth [both ways] between the text and its interpreter. That the text is written does not, as such, change the basic problem-situation at all. It is always the *matter* [*Sache*] which is being spoken about: is it this way or that? A written communication, such as a letter, is merely the continuation of a conversation by other means. Also a book, as it waits for the reader's answer to it, is the opening of such a conversation. Something "comes into words" in it.

But how is it with the artwork, and especially with the linguistic work of art? How can one speak here of a dialogical structure of understanding? The author is not present as an answering partner, nor is there an issue to be discussed as to whether it is this way or that. Rather, the text, the artwork, stands in itself. Here the dialectical exchange of question and answer, insofar as it takes place at all, would seem to move only in one direction, that is, from the one who seeks to understand the artwork, the one who interrogates it and himself/herself and listens to the answer of the work. As this one, which he is, he may, like any thinking person, be both questioner and answerer at the same time, just as in a real conversation between two people. But this dialogue of the understanding reader with himself seems not to be a dialogue with the text, which is already fixed and definitively given. Or is this really the case? Is there any text at all that is definitively given?

The dialectic of question and answer does not here come to a stop. On the contrary, the work of art distinguishes itself in that one never completely understands it. That is to say, when one approaches it questioningly, one never obtains a final answer that one now "knows." Nor does one take from it relevant information, and that takes care of that! One cannot fully harvest the information that resides in an artwork so that it is, so to speak, consumed, as is the case with communications that merely advise us of something. Apprehending a poetic work, whether it comes to us through the real ear or only through a reader listening with an inner ear, presents itself basically as a circular movement in which answers strike back as questions and provoke new answers. This is what moves us to tarry with a work of art, of whatever kind it may be. To be tarrying [*Verweilen*] is clearly the distinguishing mark of the experience of art. An artwork is never exhausted. It never becomes empty. Conversely, we define every piece of non-art that is merely imitation or cheap sensationalism precisely through the fact that we find it "empty." No work of art addresses us always in the same way. The result is that we must answer differently each time we encounter it. Other susceptibilities, other attentivenesses, other opennesses in ourselves permit that one, unique, single, and self-same unity of artistic assertion, to generate an inexhaustible multiplicity of answers. It is a mistake, I think, to try to make this endless multiplicity a denial of the unshakable identity of the work. What this seems to me to be saying, against the reception-aesthetics of Hans-Robert Jauß as well as the deconstructionism of Jacques Derrida (both of which come very close to doing this), is: To hold fast to the identity of sense [*Sinnidentität*] of a text is neither a falling back into the vanquished Platonism of a classicistic aesthetics nor is it an entrapment in metaphysics. The work, the text we read, is not something we dream up.

Likewise, one may ask whether my own endeavor to bring together the *difference* of understanding and the *oneness* of the text or work and in particular whether my holding fast to the concept of a "work" in the realm of art do not themselves presuppose a metaphysical concept of identity: If reflection by a hermeneutic consciousness also leads us to recognize that to understand at all is always to understand differently, is one really doing justice thereby to the resistance and inscrutability [*Unausdeutbarkeit*] that characterize the work of art? Can the example of art really provide a framework within which a universal hermeneutics could be developed?

I answer: This was really the starting point of my whole hermeneutical theory. The artwork is a challenge for our understanding because over and over again it evades all our interpretations and puts up an invincible resistance to being transformed into the identity of the concept. This is a point I think one could already have learned from Kant's *Critique of Judgment*. It is for this reason that the example of art has the function of leading the way, a function which the first part of *Truth and Method* [on aesthetic consciousness] possesses for my whole project of a philosophical hermeneutics. This becomes completely clear if one is to let "art," in all the endless multiplicity and diversity of its "assertions," be accepted as "true."

From the beginning I have regarded myself as a defender of what Hegel called "bad infinity," which keeps me in a kind of nearness, albeit tense, to Hegel. In any case, the chapter in *Truth and Method* that dealt with the limitations of *Reflexionsphilosophie* and then passed over to an analysis of the concept of experience tried to make this point clear.[52] There I go so far as to play off a concept that Hegel used polemically against others, namely *"Reflexionsphiloso-phie,"* against Hegel himself: In his dialectical method I see a dubious compro-mise with the scientific thinking of modernity. When, in his dialectic, he takes the external reflection of ongoing experience up into the self-reflection of thought in the way he does, this remains in the end a reconciliation within thought itself.

On the other hand, one can hardly escape the inner enclosedness of *Bewußt-seinsidealismus*—an idealism based on consciousness—and the whirlpool of its movement of reflection that sucks everything up into immanence. Was Heideg-ger not right when he himself left behind the transcendental analytic of *Dasein* and the approach he called the "hermeneutic of facticity"? Also, in relation to this turn in Heidegger's thought, how have I tried to find a path of my own?

First, I took as a starting point Wilhelm Dilthey and his question about estab-lishing the methodological foundations of the *Geisteswissenschaften* and I criti-cally contrasted my own view with it. Taking this path, I must admit, has made defending the universality of the hermeneutical problem, about which I have been concerned from the beginning, much more difficult.

Indeed, one has the feeling at a number of points in the argument in *Truth and Method,* that my taking the "historical" *Geisteswissenschaften* as a starting point is rather one-sided. In particular, the argument for the significance of tem-poral distance, as persuasive as it is in itself, was a poor preparation for dis-cussing the fundamental significance of the otherness of the other and the funda-mental role played by language as conversation. It would have been more in tune with the subject matter, I think, to speak of distance and its hermeneutic function in a more general way. After all, interpretive distance does not always have to be historical distance; it is also not always the distance in time as such that enables us to overcome false overresonances and distorted applications. Even in simul-taneity, distance can function as an important hermeneutical element; for exam-ple, in the encounter between persons who try to find a common ground in con-versation, and also in the encounter with persons who speak an alien language or live in an alien culture. Every encounter of this kind allows us to become con-scious of our own preconceptions in matters which seemed so self-evident to oneself that one could not even notice one's naive process of assuming that other person's conception was the same as one's own, which generated misunder-standing. Here my insistence on the primary significance of conversation has become important in ethnological research, especially as regards the question-able validity of its questionnaires technique.[53] Nevertheless, where temporal dis-tance does play a role, it remains true that it still offers a special critical help. Certain changes often only then become apparent and certain differences only become accessible to observation with temporal distance. Think, for instance, of the difficulty of evaluating contemporary art, a difficulty which I had in mind especially in my own argument for the importance of temporal distance.

Without question, such considerations as these do extend the significance of distance. Still, they remain within the context of a theory of the humanities and social sciences—the *Geisteswissenschaften.* But the deepest impulse of my hermeneutical philosophy was something other than this. The philosophical context into which I was born was that of subjective idealism and its crisis, which during my youth erupted with the reappropriation of the Kierkegaardian critique of Hegel. This critique gave the meaning of understanding a completely different sense. According to Kierkegaard, it is the other who breaks into my ego-centeredness and gives me something to understand. This Kierkegaardian motif guided me from the beginning, and entered completely into my 1943 lecture, "The Problem of History in Modern German Philosophy."[54] When Heidegger had read that little work in typescript, he nodded approvingly, but immediately countered with the question, "And what about thrownness?"[55] The sense of Heidegger's question was that in the collective meaning of thrownness one finds a sufficient counterinstance to the illusion of a full self-presence and self-consciousness. But what I had in mind was the special autonomy of the other person, and so quite logically I sought to ground the linguisticality of our orientation to the world in conversation. And when I did this I found that a complex of questions opened up to me which had already, long before my first efforts, been addressed by such thinkers as Søren Kierkegaard, Friedrich Gogarten, Theodor Haecker, Friedrich Ebner, Franz Rosenzweig, Martin Buber, and Viktor von Weizsäcker.

This comes to light today when I try to think over my own relationship to Heidegger and my ties to his thought. My critics have viewed this relationship in quite different ways. In general, they focus on my use of the concept of *"wirkungsgeschichtliches Bewußtsein"*—"historically affected consciousness." The fact that I make use of the concept of *consciousness* at all, a term whose ontological bias Heidegger had clearly demonstrated in *Being and Time,* to me only represented an accommodation to what seemed a natural usage of language. Certainly this also gave the appearance that I remained captive to the standpoint of the early Heidegger, which took a *Dasein* concerned with its being and characterized by an understanding of being as its starting point. Of course, the later Heidegger expressly tried to overcome the transcendental-philosophical view of the self found in *Being and Time.* My own intention in introducing the concept of historically affected consciousness, however, was precisely to blaze a trail *to* the later Heidegger. When Heidegger's own thinking pressed beyond the conceptual language of metaphysics, he fell into a *Sprachnot*—lack or need of language—which led him to borrow the language of Hölderlin and to adopt a half-poetic diction. In a recent collection of my shorter works on the later Heidegger which I have titled *Heidegger's Ways,*[56] I have tried to make it clear that the use of language in the later Heidegger does not represent a drifting off into poetry but rather is situated completely in tune with the thinking which led him into a whole new line of questioning.

The end of my apprenticeship to Heidegger coincided with his departure from Marburg and return to Freiburg in 1928, and with the beginning of my own teaching activities in Marburg. Then in 1936 came Heidegger's three Frankfurt Lectures which are today known as *The Origin of the Artwork—Der Ursprung des Kunstwerkes.* I journeyed to Frankfurt to hear them when they were first given. In these lectures, it was the concept of the "earth" with which Heidegger dramatically transgressed the limits of German philosophical vocabulary once again, a vocabulary he had in his lectures long been renewing and filling with vitality after it had so long dwelt outside the linguistic spirit of the German language. These three lectures so closely addressed my own questions and my own experience of the proximity of art and philosophy that they awakened an immediate response in me. My philosophical hermeneutics seeks precisely to adhere to the line of questioning of this essay *and the later Heidegger* and to make it accessible in a new way. In seeking to achieve this goal I reluctantly retained the concept of consciousness, against whose function as an ultimate ground for thought Heidegger had directed his ontological critique. Still, I sought to limit this concept within itself. Heidegger doubtless saw in my use of this term a falling back into dimensions of thought he had gone beyond—even if he certainly also did not overlook the fact that my intention pointed in the direction of his own thinking. In any case, I must leave it to others to decide whether the path I have followed can claim to have kept up, at least to some degree, with Heidegger's own ventures in thinking. But I think one can at least say today that there is an aspect of my own path which makes more identifiable the significance of some of the endeavors of thought in the later Heidegger and which points to something that could not have been done in simply following Heidegger's own lead in thought. Obviously one must read my chapter in *Truth and Method* on historically affected consciousness in the right way. One should not see in it merely a modification of self-consciousness; say, something like an awareness of the way history is working on us; nor even something upon which one could base a new hermeneutical method. Rather, through this term one has to recognize the *limitation* placed on consciousness by history having its effect—that is *Wirkungsgeschichte,* the history within whose effects we all exist. It is something that we can never completely go beyond. The historically affected consciousness is, as I said then, really "more being than consciousness"—"*mehr Sein als Bewußtsein.*"[57]

Therefore I cannot see that it makes sense to regard my continuing to make use of the traditional concepts of philosophy as an inconsistency in my project of thinking, as some of the best among the younger critical participants in hermeneutics have done, such as Thomas Seebohm, Heinrich Anz, or Manfred Frank.[58] This kind of argument, by the way, is similar to the one that Derrida turned against Heidegger.[59] According to Derrida, in Heidegger the overcoming of metaphysics failed; it was really Nietzsche who succeeded in accomplishing this. In such argumentation, the more recent French reception of Nietzsche quite logically ends up in disintegrating the question of being and even the question of meaning as such.

Now I must myself take issue with Heidegger when he says that we have to go beyond "the language of metaphysics." I insist that there simply is no "language of metaphysics." I have already argued for this point in my contribution to the festschrift for Karl Löwith.[60] There are only *concepts* in metaphysics whose content is determined by the usage of these words, just as with all words. The concepts in which our thinking moves are no more governed by some rigid rule of fixed pregivenness than the words used in our everyday language. The language of philosophy, even when it carries such a heavy load of tradition, as is the case in the language used in Aristotelian metaphysics and is translated into Latin, still seeks ever and again the fluidity that belongs to all statements that are offered in language. Even in Latin, old meanings can be transformed into new, as happens in the works of Nicolaus Cusanus, whose genius I have long admired. Such a transformation of meaning need not necessarily take place through some method in the style of Hegelian dialectic or through Heideggerian linguistic force and violence. Even the concepts which I myself have used gain new senses and definitions through being used in the context in which I apply them. And the concepts I have used, by the way, are really not so much those of classical Aristotelian metaphysics as it has been newly unlocked for us through Heidegger's ontotheology. Far more, they belong to the Platonic tradition: for instance, expressions like *mimesis, methexis, participatio, anamnesis, emanatio*—many of which I have often made use of in such modifications as *Repräsentation*[61]—are all terms deriving from Plato. In Aristotle they occur only as expressions he is criticizing, and thus they do not belong to the conceptuality of metaphysics in the form metaphysics later takes in the school founded by Aristotle. Let me refer you here to my treatise on "The Idea of the Good between Plato and Aristotle," which was presented to the Heidelberg Academy of Sciences in 1978,[62] where I tried to make plausible the view that Aristotle himself was far more a Platonist than one would assume, and that the Aristotelian project of an ontotheology (in *Metaphysics,* Lambda) is only one among several problems that Aristotle had treated on the basis of his view of nature [*Physics*] which have now been gathered together in the books of the *Metaphysics* without their forming a true whole.

In this regard, I am finally touching on a point where my deviation from Heidegger's thought is genuine, and it is a point which holds for a considerable part of my work in ancient philosophy, especially my Plato studies.[63] (I have the satisfaction, by the way, of knowing that precisely the essays on Plato which are now in volume 6 and in part in volume 7 of my collected works, meant something to Heidegger in the last years of his life.) In these studies I argue that Plato may *not* be read as the preparation for or the forerunner of ontotheology.

(And, by the way, it is only because Plato was *not* a preparation for ontotheology that Paul Natorp's accentuation—indeed, overaccentuation—of the nearness of Plato to Kant was possible at all.) Even the metaphysics of Aristotle contains other dimensions than those Heidegger unlocked in his work. In this, I believe I was able to refer Heidegger to certain limits in his own interpretations. I am thinking especially of Heidegger's early fondness for referring to "the famous analogy"—*"die berühmte Analogie."* He liked to speak in this vein in the Marburg period. He welcomed the Aristotelian teaching of *analogia entis*—the analogy of being—from early on as a brother-in-arms against the dream of a final grounding, a project which Husserl presided over somewhat in the style of Fichte. Also, Heidegger is carefully distancing himself from Husserl's transcendental self-interpretation when he commonly uses a term like "equiprimordial"—surely an echo of the "analogy of being" slogan and at bottom another element in Heidegger's movement toward a more hermeneutical phenomenological idiom. It was not just Aristotle's criticism, based on his concept of *phronesis,* of Plato's "Form of the Good," then, that put Heidegger onto his own path. He received other impulses from the center of Aristotelian metaphysics itself and indeed directly from the *Physics,* as Heidegger's treatise on the *Physics,*[64] so rich in perspectives, clearly shows. Just from this fact it becomes evident why I have assigned the dialogical structure of language such a central role. What I had to learn from the great dialoguer Plato, or rather from the Socratic dialogue that Plato poetically created, was that the monologue structure of scientific consciousness never permits philosophical thought to achieve what it intends. My interpretation of the excursis in Plato's *Seventh Letter,* it seems to me, stands above all the critical debates about the authenticity of this letter. Only from this letter does it become completely understandable why the language of philosophy developed from that time on in constant conversation with its own history: at first it was through writing commentary, correcting, and varying it; then, with the rise of historical consciousness moving into a new tension between historical reconstruction and speculative transformation. So the language of philosophy remains the dialogue, even when this dialogue is carried on over the distance of centuries and even millennia. The texts of philosophy are for this reason not really texts or works so much as contributions to a conversation going on through the ages.[65]

Perhaps this is the place to say something about identity and difference, or *différance,* if you will—starting with Husserl. Husserl's phenomenology of time-consciousness attempts to describe the temporal foundation for objective validity. This is undoubtedly Husserl's intention, and it has a certain persuasive power. *Identity,* in my view, is not placed in jeopardy when one rejects Husserl's idea of an ultimate transcendental grounding and also his recognition of the transcendental ego and its temporal self-constitution in the *Logical Investigation* as the ultimate instance of grounding.

The identity of the ego, as the identity of a meaning that is constructed between partners in a dialogue, remains untouched by this argument, in my opinion. It is obviously correct that no understanding of one person by the other can ever achieve complete coverage of the thing being understood. Here hermeneutical analysis must clear away a false model of understanding and of agreement-in-understanding. An agreement in understanding never means that difference is totally overcome by identity. When one says that one has come to an understanding with someone about something, this does not mean that one has absolutely the same position. The German phrase meaning "one comes to an agreement"—"*man kommt überein*"—expresses it very well. Or, appealing to the genius of the Greek language, it is a higher form of *synthēkē*, a word that means a putting-together, as in an agreement or treaty. In my view it is just the opposite of a right procedure if one isolates the elements of speaking, of *discours,* and makes them the object of critique. In this case, yes, the same is no longer the same, so one can understand why a person who is fixated on "signs," has to speak of *différence* or *différance*. In the absolute sense of meaning, no sign is identical with itself. Derrida's critique of Platonism in Husserl, which he finds in the *Logical Investigations* and in the concept of intentionality in *Ideas I,* is correct. But this point was clarified long ago by Husserl himself. It seems to me that a clear line leads directly from the concepts of passive synthesis and anonymous intentionality to the hermeneutical experience. And in it, everyone agrees with my dictum—at least everyone who has shaken off the compulsion to method in the transcendental way of thinking—that "if one understands at all, one under-

stands *differently*."[66]

The concept of literature in relation to the complex of questions that makes up hermeneutics has been a preferred theme of my studies throughout the decades since I completed *Truth and Method.* Volumes 8 and 9 of my collected writings contain essays on the theory of literary interpretation as well as interpretations of such writers as Goethe, Hölderlin, Rilke, Kleist, Stefan George, Paul Celan, and others. Also, in volume 2 one finds two essays from the decade of the 1980s that are related to the literary text: "Text and Interpretation" attempts to draw together several of my ideas on the literary text, and "Destruktion und Dekonstruktion" deals with the recent debate about deconstruction, a term which, through Derrida's use of it, has had an important influence on literary theory.[67] As I have already noted, in *Truth and Method* I had not yet defined with enough precision the necessary difference between the game of language and the game of art. As a matter of fact, the relationship between language and art is nowhere so graspable as it is in the case of literature, which is speech—and also writing.

It is significant that since antiquity poetics appears alongside rhetoric; then, with the spread of reading culture—which was taking place already in the age of Hellenism and of course much more fully in the age of the Reformation—the written, the *litterae* [letters], gets combined with the concept of "text." This means that reading moves to the center of hermeneutics and of interpretation [*Interpretation*]. Both hermeneutics and interpretation serve *reading,* for reading is at the same time *understanding.* So when one is dealing with a literary hermeneutics, one is dealing primarily with the *nature of reading.* One may be fully convinced of the primacy of the living word and of the primordiality of language as it lives in speech; nevertheless, one must acknowledge that reading possesses an even wider circumference. This circumference justifies the very broad concept of literature that I have suggested, in a very preliminary way and awaiting future development, at the end of the first part of *Truth and Method.*

Here I think we need to go into the difference between reading and reproduction. I cannot go as far as Emilio Betti does in his theory of interpretation when he totally separates understanding and reproducing.[68] What I must insist on, in this regard, is that it is *reading,* not reproduction, which truly defines the way we experience the artwork itself. I hold that just as the poetic text is "text" in the "eminent" sense of that word, the experience of the artwork shows us what "reading" in the "eminent" sense of the word, is. Reading, I believe, is really the basic form in which all encounter with art takes place. Reading takes place not only in relation to texts, then, but also in relation to pictures, sculpture, and buildings.[69]

Reproduction, however, is something quite different from this, since it has to do with a new realization of something through using the sensory materials of sounds and sound-shadings; and this being so, it has to do with something like a new creation. Certainly a reproduction seeks to bring the work authentically to appearance—the drama on the stage or the musical score through the making of sounds—and this living reproduction rightly carries the name of "interpretation." Precisely because of this, the link in interpretation has to be maintained between reproduction and the cultivation of reading. For to reproduce something is also to understand it, even if it is also more than this. So reproduction is not a matter of free creation; rather it is only an "*Aufführung*" ["performance" or "production"], as the German word so clearly expresses it, a realization by means of which the understanding of a firmly fixed work is led up into the form of a new, real entity. With reading, however, it is a different story, since the sensory reality of the meaning [*Sinnwirklichkeit*] culminates in all its reality in the performance of reading itself, not in something else that happens subsequent to it. So the fulfillment of the event of understanding in the case of reading does not entail—as it does in the case of reproduction[70]—being realized in a new sensory appearance.

Reading aloud demonstrates quite clearly, I think, that reading is a completion-of-meaning which is one's own and is fulfilled within itself in the same act of fulfillment. We can also see from this example that reading is essentially different from a theatrical or musical performance, production, or reproduction.

And this applies all the more to "silent reading," or even when this is articulated out loud as one reads, as was self-evidently the case in classical antiquity. In fact, silent reading is a full completion of meaning, although it is only carried out in a schematizing way by intuition. It remains open to various kinds of imaginative filling out. I once illustrated this point by referring to the work of Roman Ingarden.[71] The same thing also applies to someone reciting a text. The good reciter cannot for an instant forget that he or she is not the real speaker but is serving the process of reading. Although reciting a text is a reproduction and representation for another person, and thus includes a new realization in the sensory world, it still remains enclosed within the intimacy of the reading process.

In connection with these various distinctions, we need to clarify a question I have tried over and over again to think through: What role in the hermeneutic event [or process] does the intention of the author play? In the usages of everyday speaking, where it is not a matter of passing through the fixity of writtenness, I think it is clear: One has to understand the other person's intention; one must understand what the other person is saying as he or she meant it. The other person has not separated himself from himself, so to speak, into a written or whatever other form of fixed speech, and conveyed or delivered it to an unknown person, who perhaps distorts through misunderstanding, willful or involuntary, what is supposed to be understood. Even more, one is not separated physically or temporally from the person one is speaking to and who is listening to what one says.

How well this other person understands what I want to say is even shown by how the person addressed deals with it. The thing that is understood is thus lifted out of the indeterminacy of just moving in a certain direction of meaning and given a new determinacy, which allows it to be understood or misunderstood. That is what happens in a conversation: the thing meant is articulated, and through this articulation it becomes something one has in common. The individual expression is always embedded in a communicative event and may not be understood as a purely individual thing. Discussion of the *mens auctoris* [mind of the author], therefore, really only plays a hermeneutical role where one is not dealing with a living conversation but with fixed expressions, or texts. In this latter case, the question is: Does one understand *only* insofar as one goes back to the author or originator? Does one understand enough if one just goes back to what the author had in mind? And what about when this is simply not possible because one knows nothing about the author?

On this point, it seems to me traditional hermeneutics has still never fully overcome the consequences of psychologism. In all reading and all understanding of writing one is dealing with an event or process through which what has been fixed into the text is elevated into a new assertion and must be concretized anew. Now the nature of true speaking is such that what is meant constantly goes beyond what is said. For this reason it seems to me that to hypostatize the intention of the speaker as the measure of understanding constitutes an ontological misunderstanding that one does not realize. It assumes that one could just somehow reconstruct this intention once again through a kind of identification and reproduction, and *only then* turn to the words as a standard of meaning. But as we have seen, reading is not a process of reproduction that permits a comparison with the original intention. To assume that it can do so is to make an epistemological assumption that has been refuted by phenomenological research—namely, that we have before our consciousness a kind of image of the actual thing that is meant, a so-called *Vorstellung,* that is, a representation. But in my view, all reading goes beyond the hardened trace of the word to the sense of the text itself. It does not reinact the original process of producing the meaning, a process which one would understand as a mental event or event of expression; nor does reading testify to the thing meant otherwise than from the word-trace. This includes, too, that when one understands what another person says, this is not only something meant, it is also something shared, something held in common. When one brings a text to speak through reading, even if such reading be without any audible articulation, one takes up the meaning that resides in the line of meaning that the text has and builds it into the universe of meaning which the reader himself or herself has already opened up. Ultimately this substantiates an insight of the Romantics which I have also taken up: that all understanding is already interpreting [*Auslegen*]. Schleiermacher once put it quite explicitly: "Interpretation [*Auslegen*] is distinguished from understanding [*Verstehen*] only in the way that speaking out loud is distinguished from inner speaking."[72] This does not mean, however, that inner speaking attains the same degree of articulation as the given text, but rather the opposite: that speaking aloud can never fully express one's intended meaning.

The same thing holds for reading. What we call reading means to read with understanding. So *reading itself* is already an interpretation of what is meant. And thus reading is the basic structure that is common to all carrying out, all realization, of meaning [*Vollzuges von Sinn*]. Even if reading is not a reproduction process, every text one reads is only realized in understanding. It therefore also holds that for the text about to be read, the reader who gives the work its full presentness will experience an increase in being. Even when it is not a reproduction on the stage or at the podium, this seems to be the case.

I have in "Text and Interpretation" [1984] analyzed in some detail the various forms of text with which hermeneutics deals.[73] Yet the special case of *Historik*—the historical—I think, requires a further discussion here. In *Truth and Method* I started with the presupposition that historical research is in its final sense interpretation, and thus a performance and a fulfillment of meaning. Even if one starts with this presupposition, however, one has to ask whether the relationship of the historian to the text that is to be researched, namely history itself, is not a different relationship from that of the philologist to the text. The resistance of historians to my arguments in *Truth and Method* (esp. p. 330ff. in *GW*) made me aware that I had assimilated too closely the historian's special type of understanding to the type of understanding of the philologist. As I now see it, this is not just a question of the scale of what I undertook in *Truth and Method*. History [*Historie*] is not just philology writ large, as I suggested there (p. 345). Rather, in the two cases, there is in play a quite different sense of *text,* and therewith also of what understanding the text means.

The whole of the past, which one may take to be the ultimate object of historical understanding, is not *text* in the same sense of the word as the individual textual structure is *a text* for the philologist. Is the totality of history ever given for the historian in the same way as a concrete text is given to the philologist? For the philologist, the text, and especially a poetic text, is there in front of its interpreter like a fixed given that precedes every new interpretation. The historian, on the other hand, has first to reconstruct his basic text, namely history itself. Certainly one cannot draw an absolute line of separation here. The historian, for instance, first must understand the literary or whatever texts that are found, just as the philologist does. And it is equally the case that the philologist often must first reconstruct and review the authentic texts in order to understand them at all, and in understanding these the philologist will let historical knowledge be included in philological work exactly as in his trade he will take into account every possible other knowledge. Also, the view of understanding and of meaning is not the same in both cases. The meaning of a text for a philologist has to do with what the text wants to say. The meaning of an event for a historian, on the other hand, is something that the historian reconstructs on the basis both of texts and other evidence, for a reading which perhaps can even force a transformation of the interpretation one had originally anticipated.

For the sake of clarification, I would like to introduce here a meaning of the term philology that could be the literal translation of the Greek word: Philology is "taking joy [*Freude*] in the meaning which is expressed." In my view, this is just as much the case whether this joy is expressed in the form of a language construct or in some other form. Art, too, as a carrier of meaning, is the object of philology, as well as works of science and philosophy. But even in this broadest sense of philology, as that which understands meaning, philology is still different from history, however much history also seeks to understand meaning. As scholarly disciplines, both history and philology use the methods of their discipline. But insofar as one is dealing with a *text,* even texts of the most varied type and stature, these texts are not only to be understood by taking the path of methodical research. Every text has always already found its reader *before* scholarship [*Wissenschaft*] comes into the picture. The difference between joy in a meaning that is expressing itself and research that is directed toward a meaning that is concealed already articulates the larger realm of meaning in which actually both ways of understanding move. On the one hand, there is the delight in the expressed meaning [the *Sinnanmutung*] as it strikes the "reader"—and, of course, the concept of the reader can easily be extended to the understanding of all kinds of arts. On the other hand, there is also the reader's vague knowledge of her or his own home and origin, that is to say, of the historical depths that belong to one's own present moment. The interpretation even of a text whose meaning is clearly expressed, is always also related back to the interpreter's prior understanding and fulfills itself in the enlargement of that understanding.

Likewise, the sense of the text of history is always already determined, partly through the interpreter's own personal life-history and partly through that which everyone knows by virtue of a knowledge that has been shaped into what it is by culture. Long before historical research begins its methodical work, the historian has formed such a unified image of history, an image that encompasses the whole content of the heritage. Since a certain historicity belongs to all of us as we acquire our knowledge at school, or even before this, the tie in the ribbon of life that links together critical-historical research and the tradition and heritage is never broken. Only a person who imagines him- or herself to be a mere spectator of world history, may seek to blot out his/her own individuality, as the nineteenth century historian, Ranke, sought to do. But such a person still remains, like Ranke, a child of his own time and of his own homeland. Neither the philologist nor the historian can know the conditioning elements at work in his/her own understanding, which in a way lies ahead of them and thereby beyond their methodical self-control. This applies to both of them, but not in the same way in both cases. For the philologist, the simultaneity of meaning that is asserted in the text is constructed through his or her interpretation (when it succeeds). On the other hand, the successful historian undertakes the construction and destruction of meaning-contexts, which amounts to a constant process of correction and emendation, a destruction of legends, a discovery of falsifications, a constant breaking up of former constructions of meaning—for the sake of a meaning they seek that lies behind them. In such a process, he or she is never able to get back to the simultaneity of an evidential meaning.

My studies since *Truth and Method* have also taken me in another quite different direction: into practical philosophy and the problems of the social sciences. The critical interest that Jürgen Habermas showed in my work during the 1960s itself gained critical significance for me and drew my interest into these areas. Habermas's critique and my countercritique first made me aware of the critical dimension into which I entered when I went beyond the realm of text and interpretation and had attempted to move in the direction of the linguisticality of all understanding.[74] This prompted me again and again to go more deeply into rhetoric and the role that rhetoric has had in the history of hermeneutics, a role which relates to a far greater degree to the form of existence of society as such. Testifying to this interest are several studies in volume 2 of my collected works.[75]

Finally, this same kind of problem has compelled me to work out and define more sharply the theory-of-science dimensions that are specific to a hermeneutic philosophy—*die wissenschaftstheoretische Eigenart der hermeneutischen Philosophie*—in which understanding and interpreting as well as the procedures of the interpretive sciences would find their legitimation. In doing this, I once again took up a question which I have been intensively interested in since my earliest beginnings: What is practical philosophy? How can theory and reflection deal with the realm of praxis when praxis does not tolerate distance but rather calls for engagement? This question has deeply touched me from very early on, at first through the existential pathos of Kierkegaard. In addition, I have oriented my thinking to the model of Aristotelian practical philosophy. I sought to avoid the absurd model of a theory and its application which had one-sidedly determined the praxis-concept at the basis of the modern concept of science. Here, Kant has introduced the self-criticism of the moderns. In Kant's *Foundation for a Metaphysics of Morals* I believed I had found, and I still believe this today, what is, within limits, an unshakable truth. Certainly it is only partial insofar as it is reduced to an imperative ethics. It is that the impulses to enlightenment should not lead to a social utilitarianism. Otherwise one cannot defend it against Rousseau's criticism, which Kant confessed was for him decisive.

Behind this whole issue, I think, lies the old metaphysical problem of the concretizing of the general. I had this problem in mind already in my earliest studies of Plato and Aristotle. The first document of my thinking in this regard was written in 1930 although it remained unpublished until 1985, when it found a place in the fifth volume of my collected works under the title "Practical Knowledge."[76] There I have worked out the nature of *phronesis* in close reference to the sixth book of the *Nicomachean Ethics,* taking up initiatives I received from Heidegger. In *Truth and Method* this problem moves to the center. Aristotelian practical philosophy has in the years since that early essay been taken up from many different sides. It seems to me indisputable that it is genuinely relevant today. In my view this has nothing to do with the political omens variously connected today with what is called Neo-Aristotelianism. What practical philosophy is remains a real challenge for the concept of science within the thinking of modernity as a whole, a challenge that one ought not to ignore. What we can learn from Aristotle is that the Greek concept of science, *epistēmē,* means *Vernunfterkenntnis*—rational knowledge, or knowledge through reason. This means that science, for the Greeks, had its model in mathematics and did not encompass the empirical. Modern science, on the contrary, corresponds less to the Greek concept of science, namely *epistēmē,* than to the Greek concept of *techne.* In any case, for Aristotle, practical and political knowing represent a fundamentally different type of knowing than all the teachable forms of knowledge and their "practical" applications. It is this *practical knowledge* which, in reality, assigns and opens the space for each scientifically grounded capacity to do things. This was already the meaning of the Socratic question about the Good, a meaning to which both Plato and Aristotle held firmly. Whoever believes that science, thanks to its indisputable competence, can serve as a substitute for practical reason and political reason, misunderstands the real conditions under which human beings have to organize and design human life. Only practical wisdom is capable of employing science, like all human capacities, in a responsible way.

Now certainly practical philosophy is not itself such a rationality. It is philosophy; which means it is a kind of reflection, or to be more precise, it is a reflection on what a human organization and shape of life is or can be. In the same sense, a philosophical hermeneutics is not itself the art of understanding but only the philosophy of understanding. But both the practical wisdom and philosophical hermeneutics arise out of praxis and are a waste of time without it. That is the special meaning of *Wissen* and *Wissenschaft*—knowing and science—for which hermeneutical philosophy sought to bring a new legitimation. Both in and after *Truth and Method* this has been the goal to which my work has been dedicated.

Postscript 1996

The recognition of my contribution to philosophy which this volume represents is not only a great honor but in many senses constitutes for me the fulfillment of a task. After retirement from full-time teaching in Heidelberg, I learned from teaching in America and Canada to present my ideas in English, and to my satisfaction they have found resonance world-wide. Nevertheless, in the English-speaking world as well as in German phenomenology, what we call the "*Lebenswelt*" has become such a basic orientation in philosophy that now every effort at translation provokes mistrust. Even under these circumstances this volume has still been able to attain the rank of a world-wide conversation, an exchange of ideas that unites a German-speaking author with his many friends and respondents in a common language. I am particularly indebted to the American and Canadian hospitality that has over the years enabled me to have a part in their conversation. And I also want to thank many helpers and friends, like Christopher Smith, John Cleary, and Joel Weinsheimer, for their accomplishments in translating my works into English, and most recently Dennis Schmidt, Matthias Lütkehermölle, and Richard Palmer, who have performed certain important tasks for the editor of this volume, Lewis Hahn. For this, they, along with the editor and the many contributors, have earned my special thanks.

HANS-GEORG GADAMER

NOTES

1. In preparing this account Professor Gadamer has drawn on texts from volumes 2 and 10 of his *Gesammelte Werke*: "Selbstdarstellung," pp. 479–508 in volume 2 as well as the introduction to that volume, pp. 3–23, and in vol. 10, "Mit der Sprache denken," pp. 346–53; but he has freely revised these texts. I want to thank him for reading and occasionally correcting this English translation. I have also benefited from consulting Jean Grondin's eloquent translation of these texts into French under the title "Autoprésentation," which appears along with other significant Gadamer essays in his collection, *La philosophie herméneutique* (Paris: PUF, 1996), pp. 11–62. Also I thank him and Carsten Dutt of Heidelberg University for valuable corrections and suggestions on the final draft of this translation. In the notes of the present translation, Gadamer's citations to the original German are given. I have also supplied the location of Gadamer's writings in *GW,* translations into English, where available, and occasionally an explanatory or bibliographical note. *Trans.*

2. For a review of the earlier years of my life, I refer English-speaking readers to the first chapter of my *Philosophische Lehrjahre* (Frankfurt: Klostermann, 1977), 239 pp., which has been translated into English by Robert R. Sullivan as *Philosophical Apprenticeships* (Cambridge: MIT Press, 1985), 193 pp.

3. Paul Ernst, *Der Zusammenbruch des deutschen Idealismus,* 2 vols. (Munich: Beck, 1920–1922).

4. Oswald Spengler, *Untergang des Abendlandes: Umriss einer Morphologie der Weltgeschichte.* [1919].

5. See Wilhelm Dilthey, *Selected Works,* ed. Rudolf A Makkreel und Frithjof Rodi (Princeton, N.J.: Princeton University Press), vol. 5 (1985) and vol. 1 (1989). *Trans.*

6. See Ernst Troeltsch, *The Social Teaching of the Christian Churches,* 2 vols., trans. Olive Wyon (Chicago: University of Chicago Press, 1981), vol. 1, 446 pp. and vol. 2, 569 pp. *Trans.*

7. The Marburg School is a school of Neo-Kantian philosophy represented by Marburg philosophers Hermann Cohen (1842–1918) and Paul Natorp (1854–1924), Nicolai Hartmann, (1882–1950), and Ernst Cassirer (1874–1945). *Trans.*

8. Hans-Georg Gadamer, "Zur Systemidee in der Philosophie," *Festschrift für Paul Natorp zum 70. Geburtstage* (Berlin: de Gruyter, 1924), pp. 55–75.

9. Hans-Georg Gadamer, "Metaphysik der Erkenntnis: Zu dem gleichnamigen Buch von Nicolai Hartmann," *Logos: Internationale Zeitschrift für Philosophie der Kultur* 12 (1923–1924): 340–59.

10. Hans-Georg Gadamer, "Der aristotelische *Protreptikos* und die entwicklungsgeschichtliche Betrachtung der aristotelischen Ethik," *Hermes: Zeitschrift für klassische Philologie* 63 (1928): 138–64. *GW* 5 (1985): 164–86. [In subsequent notes, the volumes of the collected works, published by J.C.B. Mohr in Tübingen, will be abbreviated *GW* and the year of publication supplied along with the volume, as in this note. *Trans.*]

11. See Julius Stenzel, *Studien zur Entwicklung der platonischen Dialektik von Sokrates zu Aristoteles* (Leipzig, Berlin: Teubner, 1912, 2nd ed. 1931) and *Zahl und Gestalt bei Platon* (Leipzig, Berlin: Teubner, 1924).

12. In this regard see also my essay, "Praktisches Wissen" in *GW* 5 (1985): 230–48.

13. Walter Bröcker later demonstrated this in his *Aristoteles* (Frankfurt: Klostermann, 1935), 231 pp.

14. Deleted sentence [see *GW* 2: 487]: "My uncompleted [early] commentary on Aristotle's *Physics* will perhaps still one day be published." *Trans.*

15. Hans-Georg Gadamer, "Gibt es die Materie?" *GW* 6 (1985): 201–17.

16. Hans-Georg Gadamer, "Antike Atomtheorie," *Zeitschrift für die gesamte Naturwissenschaft* 1 (1935–1936): 81–95. *GW* 5 (1985): 263–79.

17. Hans-Georg Gadamer, *Platos dialektische Ethik: Phänomenologische Interpretationen zum "Philebos"* (Leipzig: Felix Meiner, 1931), 178 pp. *GW* 5 (1985): 3–163. English translation by Robert M. Wallace, *Plato's Dialectical Ethics* (New Haven and London: Yale University Press, 1991), 288 pp.

18. See my essay published in 1974, *Idee und Wirklichkeit in Platos "Timaios"* [Heidelberg: Winter Universitätsverlag, 1974, 36 pp.]. *GW* 6 (1985): 242–70. English translation: "Idea and Reality in Plato's *Timaeus*," in *Dialogue and Dialectic*, trans. and ed. P. Christopher Smith (New Haven: Yale University Press, 1980), pp. 156–193.

19. "Ihr Verhältnis zur historischen Kritik ist schon dann ein positives, wenn diese— in der Meinung, keine Förderung durch sie zu finden—das was sie sagt, für selbstverständlich befindet." Introduction to *Platos dialektische Ethik*, p. 13 (p. 10 in 2nd ed, and p. 13 in the English trans.). The review appeared in *Archiv für Geschichte der Philosophie* 41 (1932): 246. *Trans.*

20. Hans-Georg Gadamer, *Plato und die Dichter* (Frankfurt: Vittorio Klostermann, 1934. 36 pp.) and "Platos Staat der Erziehung" (in *Das neue Bild der Antike,* vol. 1, ed. Helmut Berve [Leibzig: Koehler und Amelang, 1942], pp. 317–33) were reprinted in *Platos dialektische Ethik und andere Studien zur platonischen Philosophie,* 2nd enlarged edition (Hamburg: Felix Meiner, 1968), pp. 179–204 and pp. 205–20, and in *GW* 5 (1985): 187–211 and 249–62. English translations in *Dialogue and Dialectic*, trans. P. Christopher Smith (New Haven: Yale University Press, 1980), pp. 39–72 and pp. 73–92, as well as subsequently in *Plato's Dialectical Ethics* (1991). *Trans.*

21. I have taken up this point recently in "Platos Denken in Utopien," *Gymnasium 90* (1983): 434–55. *GW* 7 (1991): 270–89.

22. For a more detailed discussion of these years and of this promotion, see the chapter titled "Dozentenjahre," in *Philosophische Lehrjahre*, pp. 44–59 and 57–58, cited in note 2, and the corresponding pages in the English translation, pp. 69–81. *Trans.*

23. Robert Musil was a major twentieth-century German author, best known for his three-volume novel, *The Man without Qualities. Trans.*

24. Hans-Georg Gadamer, *Volk und Geschichte im Denken Herders.* (Frankfurt: Klostermann, 1942), 24 pp. *GW* 4 (1987): 318–35.

25. Karlheinz Volkmann-Schluck, *Plotin als Interpret der Ontologie Platos.* (Frankfurt: Klostermann, 1941).

26. Aristoteles, *Metaphysik XII,* Übersetzung und Kommentar von Hans-Georg Gadamer (Frankfurt: Klostermann, 1948), 60 pp.

27. Wilhelm Dilthey, *Grundriß der Geschichte der Philosophie* (Frankfurt: Klostermann, 1949), 268 pp.

28. Hans-Georg Gadamer, *Wahrheit und Methode* (Tübingen: J.C.B. Mohr, 1960), 486 pp. *GW* 1(1986), 494 pp.

29. I have in mind especially the work of the "Poetik und Hermeneutik Arbeitsgruppe," a selection of whose writings from various volumes and years of their meetings have been translated into English in *New Perspective in German Literary Criticism,* ed. Richard E. Amacher and Victor Lange (Princeton, N.J.: Princeton University Press, 1979).

30. ". . . gerade auch in dem wahren Sein und Wesen der Sache." In Hegel, *Sein* [being] refers to the thing in its immediacy, and *Wesen* [essence] is the "truth" of that immediate thing. The *Begriff* [concept] unites these two without losing either side. Thus a "concept" here has a rootedness in being that is not associated with it in merely nominalist uses of this term. *Trans.*

31. *Destruktion* in Heidegger, as Professor Gadamer has emphasized in his essay on *"Destruktion und Dekonstruktion"* (in *GW* 2), does not primarily mean destruction but the polishing of a word or concept to regain its primordial meaning, or as here stated, "a critical relationship to the concepts in [present] philosophical terminology." *Trans.*

32. In German, the same word, *Spiel,* is used to mean both play and game. Our translation will sometimes use one term, sometimes the other, depending on the context, and sometimes also "playing the game," in order to suggest the overtones of motion. *Trans.*

33. As the German word shows, *"sein"* is part of "consciousness" in German, thus Gadamer is suggesting that even when he uses the word "consciousness" the emphasis should be on the *"sein"* that contains historically conditioned structures and not on an empty, flickering awareness. Gadamer has used this slogan elsewhere, generally in explanation of "historically affected consciousness"; for instance, in "Rhetorik, Hermeneutik und Ideologiekritik": "Denn wirkungsgeschichtliches Bewußtsein ist auf eine unaufhebbare Weise mehr Sein als Bewußtsein," *GW* 2: 247. "For historically affected consciousness is in an inescapable way more being than consciousness." The English translation of this essay titled "On the Scope and Function of Hermeneutical Reflection," appeared in *Philosophical Hermeneutics,* ed. and trans. David E. Linge (Berkeley: University of California Press, 1976), p. 38. This collection will be abbreviated *PH* in the remaining notes. *Trans.*

34. ["*I conceive* (experiments) *through the mind."* In other words, it is the mind which first grasps, integrates, and projects. Galileo here is discussing his famous experiment regarding the indefinitely continued motion of bodies projected on a plane in space. He first constructed the experiment in his mind. See *Le Opere di Galileo Galilei,* first complete edition (1842–1856), ed. Eugenio Albèri, vol. 13 (Florence: Società Editice Fiorentina, 1855), *Dialoghi delle nuove scienze (Dialogues on the New Science),* "Giornata Quarta" ("Fourth Day"), pp. 221–22 (first two pages of chapter). I am indebted to Donatella diCesare for this reference. *Trans.*] See my lecture given in 1983 at both Lund, Sweden, and in Boston. In German, the article carried the title "Naturwissenschaft und Hermeneutik," and appeared in in *Philosophie und Kultur,* ed. Arno Werner (Lund: University of Lund Press, 1986), vol. 3: 39–70. *GW* 7 (1991): 418–42. The English translation appeared under the title "Natural Science and Hermeneutics: The Concept of Nature in Ancient Philosophy," trans. Kathleen Wright in *Proceedings of the Boston Area Colloquium in Ancient Philosophy,* vol. 1, ed. J. J. Cleary (Lanham, Mass., 1986), pp. 39–52.

35. Some of my contributions to that volume may be found translated into English in the collection of my essays previously cited as *PH* in note 33, as well as in Josef Bleicher's *Contemporary Hermeneutics* (London: Routledge and Kegan Paul, 1980).

36. Giambattista Vico, *On the Study Methods of Our Time,* trans. Elio Gianturco, and *The Academies and the Relation between Philosophy and Eloquence,* trans. Donald Phillip Verene (Ithaca, N.Y.: University of Notre Dame Press, 1969).

37. See Chaim Perelman and L. Olbrechts-Tyteca, *The New Rhetoric* (Notre Dame, Ind.: University of Notre Dame Press, 1969). *Trans.*

38. *Hermeneutik und Ideologiekritik* (Frankfurt: Suhrkamp, 1971). [See esp. Gadamer's "Hermeneutik, Rhetorik und Ideologiekritik" in that volume. English translation in *PH* 18–43, cited above. *Trans.*]

39. Paul Friedlaender, *Platon,* 2 vols. (Berlin: deGruyter, 1928–1930 [1st ed.], 1954–60 [2nd ed., revised and enlarged]. In English: *Plato,* 3 vols, trans. Hans Meyerhoff (New York: Pantheon Books, 1958–1969).

40. See *G W,* vols. 6 and 7.

41. In a different context, this question parallels Derrida's ironic question at the beginning of *Glas*: "Qu'est-que-ce qui reste de Hegel, aujourd'hui?" *Trans.*

42. For a trenchant critique of the use of this term in Heidegger, see Derrida's *De l'esprit: Heidegger et la question* (Paris: Galilée, 1987); English translation: *Of Spirit: Heidegger and the Question*, trans. Geoffrey Bennington and Rachel Bowlby (Chicago: University of Chicago Press, 1989). *Trans.*

43. See Michael Polanyi, *Personal Knowledge: Towards a Post-Critical Philosophy* (London: Routledge and Kegan Paul, 1958), 428 pp. *Trans.*

44. In the summer semester of 1965 I offered a lecture course titled "Von Hegel bis Heidegger" that raised these questions. Heidegger attended its final session and offered some remarks after my lecture. Basically, in those remarks Heidegger continued to emphasize the fact that Hegel's thought culminates in a form of absolute knowledge.

45. See my discussion of the "eminent text" in "Text und Interpretation," in *Text und Interpretation: Eine deutsch-französische Debatte mit Beiträgen von Jacques Derrida, Philippe Forget, Manfred Frank, Hans-Georg Gadamer, Jean Greisch und François Laruelle*, ed. Philippe Forget (Stuttgart: Fink, 1964), pp. 24–55, esp. pp. 45–46. *GW* 2 (1986): 330–60, esp. 350–52. "Text and Interpretation," trans. Dennis J. Schmidt and Richard E. Palmer in *Dialogue and Deconstruction: The Gadamer-Derrida Encounter*, ed. and trans. Diane P. Michelfelder and Richard E. Palmer (Albany: State University of New York Press, 1989), pp. 21–51, esp. pp. 41–42. The volume will be hereinafter abbreviated *GDE*.

46. Hans-Georg Gadamer, *Wer bin Ich und wer bist Du? Ein Kommentar zu Paul Celans Gedichtfolge "Atemkristall"* (Frankfurt: Suhrkamp, 1973, revised and enlarged, 1986), 156 pp.

47. Further details on this can be found in the essay, "On the Universality of the Hermeneutical Problem" in my *GW* 2 (1985): 219–31. Trans. *PH* 3–17. [Originally published in 1966, this essay provoked lively discussion, some of which is contained in essays contributed by various authors (Karl-Otto Apel, Rüdiger Bubner, Jürgen Habermas, and others) to the collection *Hermeneutik und Ideologiekritik*, Suhrkamp Verlag, Frankfurt am Main, 1971. *Trans.*]

48. Moritz Schlick, "Über das Fundament der Erkenntnis," *Erkenntnis* 4 (1934): 79–99. Also in Schlick's *Gesammelte Aufsätze 1926–36* (Vienna: Gerold, 1938), esp. pp. 290–95 and 300–309.

49. See the instructive introduction of Joel Weinsheimer, *Gadamer's Hermeneutics. A Reading of Truth and Method* (New Haven and London: Yale University Press, 1985), esp. pp. 290–95 and 300–309.

50. Hans-Georg Gadamer, *Philosophische Rundschau* 11 (1963): 1–45. *GW* 3 (1987): 105–46. Trans. *PH* 130–81.

51. In a 1985 conference at the Protestant Academy in Herrenalb on "Linguisticality and its Limits," I made a contribution on this theme, "Grenzen der Sprache," which can be found in *Evolution und Sprache: Herrenalber Texte* 66 (1985): 89–99. *GW* 8 (1993): 350–61.

52. See *GW* 1 (1985): 375ff. *Truth and Method*, rev. trans. by Joel Weinsheimer and Don Marshall (New York: Seabury, 1989), 369ff. All citations will be to this translation.

53. Hans-Georg Gadamer, "Die Grenze der Reflexionsphilosophie"/"The Limitations of Reflective Philosophy," *Warheit und Methode*, Part 2, sec.II, 3a:, *GW* 1 (1985): 346ff., English translation: 341ff.

54. About this, see the recent book by L. C. Watson and M. B. Watson-Franke, *Interpreting Life Histories* (Rutgers, N.J.: Rutgers University Press, 1985).

55. See "Das Problem der Geschichte in der neueren deutschen Philosophie," *GW* 2 (1985): 27–36.

56. "Und was ist es mit der Geworfenheit?"

57. Hans-Georg Gadamer, *Heideggers Wege: Studien zum Spätwerk* (Tübingen: J. C. B. Mohr, 1983), now included in *GW* 3 (1987): 175–332. English translation: *Heidegger's Ways*. Trans. John W. Stanley (Albany: SUNY Press, 1994), 201 pp.

58. See *Wahrheit und Methode* in *GW* 1 (1985): 367, 460 [trans. 361, 456], and also in "Hermeneutik, Rhetorik und Ideologiekritik," *GW* 2 (1985): 247. This essay appeared under the title, "The Scope and Function of Hermeneutics" in *PH*, pp. 18–43, citation p. 38.

59. Thomas Seebohm, *Zur Kritik der hermeneutischen Vernunft* (Bonn: Bouvier, 1976): Heinrich Anz, *Die Bedeutung poetischer Rede: Studien zur hermeneutischen Begründung und Kritik von Poetologie* (Munich: Fink, 1979); and Manfred Frank, *Das Sagbare und das Unsagbare: Studien zur neuesten französischen Hermeneutik und Texttheorie* (Frankfurt: Suhrkamp, 1980), and his *Was ist Neostrukturalismus?* (Frankfurt: Suhrkamp, 1984). English: *What is Neostructuralism?*, trans. Sabine Wilke and Richard Gray (Minneapolis: University of Minnesota Press, 1989).

60. Jacques Derrida, *Marges de la philosophie* (Paris: de Minuit, 1972), p. 77. English translation: *Margins of Philosophy*, trans. Alan Bass (Chicago: University of Chicago Press, 1982), 330 pp.

61. Hans-Georg Gadamer, "Anmerkungen zu dem Thema 'Hegel und Heidegger'," *Natur und Geschichte*, ed. H. Braun (Stuttgart: W. Kohlhammer, 1967), pp. 123–31; "Die Sprache der Metaphysik" in *Heideggers Wege*, pp. 61–69. *GW* 3 (1987): 229–337. *Heidegger's Ways*, pp. 69–79.

62. See *GW* 1 (1985): 74f., 146f., 210f. English trans.: 68f., 132f., 207f.

63. Hans-Georg Gadamer, "Die Idee des Guten zwischen Plato und Aristoteles" (*Sitzungsberichte der Heidelberger Akademie der Wissenschaften*, Philosophisch-historische Klasse, Abhandlung 2), (Heidelberg: Carl Winter Universitätsverlag, 1978), 103 pp. *GW* 7: 128–227. Trans. *The Idea of the Good in Platonic-Aristotelian Philosophy*, trans. P. Christopher Smith (New Haven: Yale U. Press, 1986), 182 pp.

64. In this regard, see volumes 5, 6, and 7 of *GW*.

65. Martin Heidegger, "Vom Wesen und Begriff der *Physis*." Aristoteles, *Physik* B 1. *Gesamtausgabe* I, 9, pp. 239ff.

66. Gadamer here deletes a lengthy discussion of Manfred Frank, Hans-Robert Jauß, and reception aesthetics, found in *GW* 2 (1986): 13–16. *Trans.*

67. *GW* 1 (1985): 302. English trans. 297.

68. *GW* 2 (1986): 330–60, and 361–72. English: *GDE* 21–51, and 102–13. (*GW* 2:23): Discussion between hermeneutics and deconstruction has been lively. See Jürgen Habermas's excellent critique of Derrida in *Der philosophische Diskurs der Moderne* (Frankfurt: Suhrkamp, 1985), pp. 191ff, as well as the discussion of "Text and Interpretation" in English by Fred Dallmayr, "Hermeneutics and Deconstruction: Gadamer and Derrida in Dialogue" ("Dekonstruktion und Hermeneutik," *GW* 10 [1995]: 138–47; English: *GDE* 102–13), my remarks printed on his *Polis und Praxis* (Cambridge, Mass.: MIT Press, 1984), are also supplemented in my essay, "Destruktion und Dekonstruktion," [*GW* 10 (1995): 138–47; English: *GDE* 102–13]. [In the meantime, Gadamer has added another essay to the discussion, "Hermeneutik auf die Spur," *GW* 10 (1995): 148–74. See also Dallmayr's *Language and Politics* (Notre Dame: University of Notre Dame Press, 1984). *Trans.*]

69. See Emilio Betti, *Allgemeine Auslegungslehre* (Tübingen: J. C. B. Mohr, 1967).

70. See my essay, "Das Lesen von Bauten und Bilder," in *Modernität und Tradition: Festschrift für Max Imdahl*, ed. Gottfried Boehm, K. Stierle, and G. Winter (Munich: Fink, 1985), pp. 97–103. *GW* 8 (1993): 331–38.

71. In the case of music, the question of the relationship of reading and reproduction is a special question. One would certainly concede that music is not experienced in the reading of the notes, and this constitutes a difference from the reading of literature. And drama is intended for performance rather than merely reading. Even the epic existed in an external sense before it was given to the bard. Nevertheless, essential differences remain. One has to make the music [*Musik machen*], and the listener must go along with the music [*mitmachen*]. In this question I have learned a lot from Thrasybulos G. Georgiades, whose *Nennen und Erklingen: Die Zeit als Logos* was edited from the posthumous papers by Imgard Bengen. (Göttingen: Vendenhoeck & Ruprecht, 1985), 303 pp. [In English, see Thrasybulos G. Georgiades, *Music and Language,* trans. Marie Louise Gollner (New York: Cambridge University Press, 1982), and *Greek Music, Verse, and Dance* (New York: Da Capo Press, 1973). *Trans.*]

72. See, for instance, Roman Ingarden, *Das literarische Kunstwerk,* 2nd ed., revised and improved. Tübingen: Niemeyer, 1960, 430 pp. English: *The Literary Work of Art,* trans. George G. Grabowicz (Evanston: Northwestern University Press, 1973), 415 pp.

73. See Friedrich Schleiermacher, "Über den Begriff der Hermeneutik mit bezug zu Wolf und Ast," also known as the "Akademie Rede of 1829," published in *Hermeneutik,* ed. Heinz Kimmerle (Heidelberg: Carl Winter Universitätsverlag, 1959), p. 154. English: *Hermeneutics: The Handwritten Manuscripts,* ed. Heinz Kimmerle, trans. James Duke and Jack Forstman (Missoula: Scholars Press, 1977), 225 pp.

74. *GW* 2: 330–60. English: *GDE,* pp. 21–51.

75. See Jürgen Habermas, *Zur Logik der Sozialwissenschaften* (Frankfurt: Suhrkamp, 1970) [English trans. *On the Logic of the Social Sciences,* trans. Shierry Weber Nicholsen and Jerry A. Stark (Cambridge: MIT Press, 1988)] and his essays in *Hermeneutik und Ideologiekritik* (Frankfurt: Suhrkamp, 1971).

76. See, for instance, "Rhetorik, Hermeneutik und Ideologiekritik" (1971), trans. *HP* 18–43; "Rhetorik und Hermeneutik" (1976), trans. Joel Weinsheimer in *In Our Times: Rhetoric and Hermeneutics,* ed. Michael Hyde and Walter Jost (New Haven: Yale University Press, 1997); and "Logik or Rhetorik: Nochmals zur Frühgeschichte der Hermeneutik" (1976), all appearing in *GW* 2 (1985), pp. 232–50, 276–91, and 292–300.

77. Hans-Georg Gadamer, "Praktisches Wissen," *GW* 5 (1985): 230–48.

FOREWORD TO THE ESSAYS
AND REPLIES

Hans-Georg Gadamer

It was an honor for me to be taken up as a subject in the Library of Living Philosophers, and it was the occasion of genuine excitement insofar as I was put to the task of discussion by such an abundance of essays taking positions on my work. However, it was also a great challenge. It is not easy for one of the oldest children of our century—I was born in the year 1900—to go into all of these positions with the appropriate meticulous labor within the limitations of the time and space available to me. Such a task can only be accomplished insofar as I can rely upon the reader's sympathetic patience. The problem of responding to such an international group of philosophers is increased by the fact that the world history of this century only enabled me to break through the isolation of the "German world" after my retirement from teaching duties in 1968. Only then was I able to travel in foreign countries and to learn to think with others in foreign languages.

It is not simply a matter of saying that in my replies to the contributions that follow I was limited by a knowledge of the languages of the European cultural world. Even after many years of teaching activities in countries where the languages were English, French, Italian, and Spanish, I do not feel sufficiently well versed in the standards and levels of research of those lands, since I was able to study more recent publications only in exceptional cases.

So, in the end, there was often nothing more I could do in the replies that follow here, than to give impressions back while the echo of having read a particular contribution remained in my ears. Owing to more or less accidental constellations of reasons I have given more detailed answers to some of the contributions. By that I mean only that I often dealt briefly with those essays which came from those who have been close to my thought for a long time.

Nonetheless, I believe that I was able to risk the conversation across the generations and continents despite the incompetence of encroaching old age that the years will not let one deny. I want to thank the contributors to this volume for the interest that they have demonstrated in my work, and I want to thank even those who really do not know what to make of my work. It is a hermeneutic experience that one feels oneself especially addressed not so much when one believes one has been understood as rather when one believes that one has not been properly understood at all.

Foreword and replies translated from the German by Matthias Lütkehermölle and Dennis J. Schmidt.

PART TWO

DESCRIPTIVE AND CRITICAL ESSAYS WITH REPLIES

1

Karl-Otto Apel

REGULATIVE IDEAS OR TRUTH-HAPPENING?: AN ATTEMPT TO ANSWER THE QUESTION OF THE CONDITIONS OF THE POSSIBILITY OF VALID UNDERSTANDING

I. INTRODUCTION: THE QUASI-KANTIAN RESERVATION ABOUT THE "HERMENEUTICAL ONTOLOGY" OF TRUTH-HAPPENING

Since the author of this "discussion" with Hans-Georg Gadamer is no longer a youngster himself and since he—like the author of *Truth and Method*—has always regarded the solution to the problem mentioned in the above subtitle as the central matter of concern of his philosophy, he may be permitted to introduce the subject matter with the help of an autobiographical retrospective.

Inspired by Heidegger, I arrived at a philosophical position in my 1963 Habilitationsschrift, *Die Idee der Sprache in der Tradition des Humanismus von Dante bis Vico,*[1] which was very similar to the one which I discovered later in Gadamer's *opus magnum.* However, I named it "transcendental hermeneutics" in order to express my intention to hold to Kant's basic question. But I still believed at that time that I could comprehend Heidegger's *hermeneutics of Dasein* as the necessary and sufficient *transformation of the transcendental philosophy* of Kant and Husserl which took into account the linguistic and historical character of our being-in-the-world. I am inclined to think that Gadamer, while he elaborated his "philosophical hermeneutics," had a notion of Heidegger's position very similar to mine.

However, I changed my idea about Heidegger in the years following, mainly, I think I can say today, as the result of reading *Wahrheit und Methode* (henceforth *WuM* or *Truth and Method*).

I now had to recognize with some consternation that Heidegger's assumptions of the hermeneutics of *Dasein*[2] presupposed by Gadamer in *Truth and Method* made something like a normatively controlled *progress in understanding* appear totally inconceivable. The reason for this was not that the

---

Translated from the German by Dr. Ralf Sommermeier

methodologically narrow problem of traditional hermeneutics had been extended in *Truth and Method* with the help of a radically *philosophical (transcendental)* question, as Gadamer kept insisting.[3] The actual reason was that Gadamer did not hesitate to equate the *conditions of the possibility of meaning-understanding* (that is, of the "thrown projection" of a world of manifest meaning, one which goes along with a corresponding hiding of possible meaning) with the *conditions of the possibility of the intersubjective validity of understanding,* in fact of any knowledge.[4] In this respect he followed the line of the transformation of Kant's transcendental question as it had been suggested by Heidegger in *Sein und Zeit* and in the latter's first book on Kant.[5]

I think that the idea which Heidegger supported until 1964, namely the replacing (or deepening) of the traditional binary *correctness* concept of truth with the "more original" concept of *alētheia,*[6] led Heidegger and Gadamer to replace the *counterfactual* and, therefore, *per se intersubjective validity* of truth (this validity had been taken for granted by Kant) with the *facticity* of *meaning* as it becomes *manifest* to us in the particular historical situation. (I must come back to this point later.) In the years following Gadamer could in this way replace the *normatively* oriented, and hence also *epistemologically and methodologically relevant,* conceptions of traditional hermeneutics (for example, Schleiermacher's and Dilthey's) with the *temporal-ontological,* and that is to say, *happening-theoretical* ones. Examples of such conceptions were understanding as "moving into the happening of handing down," "application of understanding as continued forming *(Bildung)* of tradition," "hermeneutic circle" as "bringing into play" and "putting prejudices at risk" in the form of the "fusion of horizons," and finally, in a unique conjunction of a methodologically relevant conception of *reflection* with a conception of *happening,* "effective-historical consciousness."

Remarkably, though, *Gadamer's* notion contrasts with Heidegger's—even after the latter's turn—to the effect that that moment of sense- and truth-happening which must, as it were, replace the normative control of understanding, is located in the *past,* but not in the *future.* In other words, it is not located in the onto-historical "event" of the "opening" qua an "act of mission" of Being. In the history of metaphysics, this opening, according to Heidegger, has underlain not only the epochal uncovering of *beingness,* or of the *essence of beings (ousia),* but also the corresponding withdrawal of Being itself already since Plato; and in fact, it could once again be imminent today after the "destruction," or the "getting over," of this history. Instead, for Gadamer it is located in the *validity authority* of the contents of cultural tradition that needs further continued formation *(Bildung)* by means of applicative interpretation. Evidently, this is connected with the characteristic presumption of the fundamental superiority of the objective validity claims of the *interpretandum* over the interpreter's adoption and assessment. The latter are in fact always already taken to advantage by applying further continued forming (*Bildung*) of tradition (see esp. *WuM*, pp. 261ff.). Of course, this presumption is hard to accept from a post-Enlightenment viewpoint.

This strange primacy of the past (that is, what was thought to be the handing over of contents) is what first provoked my opposition. Or to be precise, it was this primacy together with the following central thesis of Gadamer's, which was directed against Kant, Fichte, and Schleiermacher: "Understanding is in truth not understanding better, neither in the sense of objectively understanding better through clearer concepts, nor in the sense of the fundamental superiority of the conscious over the unconscious moment of production. It suffices to say that one *understands differently if one understands at all.*"[7]

At this place, I do not dispute the thesis that we, as finite and historical creatures, *de facto* understand the *interpretandum differently* in each situational context—which also implies differently than it was meant. I was, and am, quite ready to make this concession to the *temporal ontology* of understanding, that is, the temporal ontology of the accompanying "fusion of horizons" and the effective-historically conditioned context dependence. However, it appears to me that this concession does not indicate anything relevant about the *correctness,* or *depth,* of understanding. In my view, the inevitability of a situation-dependent *understanding differently* owing to the "fusion of horizons" trivially also applies to superficial or even false understanding. It simply applies—today I prefer to put it this way—as *temporal-ontological* determination to preconditions of any human *attempt to understand,* but not yet, however, to the *transcendental conditions of the possibility of valid or nonvalid understanding.* Like the binary concept of truth itself, these conditions relate by their very nature counterfactually and time-independently to all imaginable interpreters' universal capacity for consensus.

Now, if this determination is understood as "regulative idea" in the sense of Kant, Peirce, and Royce,[8] then it may not follow that in a *transcendental hermeneutics,* the *always understanding only differently* could ever be replaced by an *understanding totally correctly.*[9] But it does appear as thinkable, in fact even as a necessary postulate of a normatively oriented hermeneutics, that inasmuch as we understand correctly at all, we understand not *only in a different way*—due to the "fusion of horizons"—but *thereby at the same time in a better, or deeper way.* Put more correctly, hermeneutic understanding is superior not only in comparison with former hermeneutic understanding,[10] but even with the *interpretanda,* or their *authors,* respectively.

This postulate seems to me to take into account the factor of *reflection* (more about this later), which is implied in any creative understanding and thus in any *knowledge.* This integrating factor of all understanding should be more important for the "productivity of the temporal distance" (see *WuM*, pp. 279ff.) than the sheer-temporal-process nature of the effective history of the *interpretandum.* Exactly this seems to me to be the basis of the superiority, emphasized by

Gadamer (see *WuM,* p. 161), of Hegel's theory of the "self-penetration of mind" over Schleiermacher's and Dilthey's theory of the "identical after-understanding." This is true at least in case *understanding* in the humanities and the arts is not comprehended in the sense of "hermeneutic abstraction" from the *judging assessment* (I must come back to this point as well). The history of the sciences and of philosophy, then, seems to suggest that understanding always already *reflectively outstrips understanding* in the respect in which it happens. I should like to cite such examples as the relativization of Euclidean geometry by non-Euclidean geometries and its rehabilitation as "protophysics" by Hugo Dingler, or Paul Lorenzen, respectively; and also the corresponding relativizations and rehabilitations of the validity of Newtonian physics as physics of the "mesocosmos." In philosophy, one could, for example, think of the dehypostatizing reinterpretations of the Platonic doctrine of Ideas; or of the critical and fallibilistic transformations of Kant's unknowable "things-in-themselves" through Peirce's concept of the "knowable" which can never be "known." Finally, I should like to cite Gadamer's own reference to Heidegger's demonstration that the Greek substance-ontology continues in Descartes' concept of consciousness as well as in Hegel's concept of mind, and that this insight "[goes] beyond the self-understanding of modern metaphysics."[11] But how is this assertion of Gadamer's consistent with his fundamental rejection of "better understanding"?

From the things said it does not at all follow, I think, that creative understanding must outstrip the meaning of the *interpretandum* in every aspect; this is virtually impossible in the case of the great works of poetry and philosophy. And in this respect the postulate* *(Resultat)* of *better understanding* does not contradict Gadamer's postulate *(Resultat)* that all understanding must presuppose the "fore-conception of perfection" of the *interpretandum* (*WuM,* pp. 277f); this is also relevant from the point of view of methodology. Hermeneutic understanding should presuppose the heuristic assumption of the superior validity authority of the *interpretandum* as well as—on account of the interpreter's autonomy of reason—the likewise necessary reservation of critical-reflective critique of the understood validity claims. I believe that this double presumption alone is in general accordance with the fundamental *symmetry* of a situation of *dialogical understanding.* This, in fact, also forms a basic premise of Gadamer's philosophical hermeneutics (along or in tension with the paradigm of *meaning- and truth-happening?*). This has been a first lead-in to a possible debate between the "philosophical hermeneutics" as represented by Gadamer, and a "transcendental hermeneutics" which was initially drawn up similarly, but then returned to a more Kantian approach. "Transcendental hermeneutics" is a conception which cannot find the answer to the question of the *validity* of understanding in a *tem-*

---

*Translator's Note: Apel suggests that his word 'Resultat' should be translated in each instance as postulate or hypothesis.

poral ontology of understanding as of a *truth-happening,* but one which looks for *regulative ideas* for a *normative* orientation of understanding.

II. TWO PROBLEMATIC PRESUPPOSITIONS OF GADAMER'S "PHILOSOPHICAL HERMENEUTICS": THE ALĒTHEIA-THEORY OF TRUTH AND THE EQUATION OF THE CLAIM OF THE INTERSUBJECTIVE VALIDITY OF "BETTER UNDERSTANDING" WITH THE OBJECTIVITY IDEAL OF SCIENCE

Nonetheless, serious objections might be raised against the *truth-theoretical* presuppositions of the just-sketched argumentation that favors a regulative idea of *better understanding.* These objections favor Gadamer's concept of the *historical dependence of context and position* of any understanding, in particular, *historical-hermeneutic* understanding. How should it be possible, one could ask, to think a regulative idea of *better understanding* in the sense indicated if it has to be presupposed, along with Heidegger and Gadamer, that all *correctness of knowledge* depends on *truth* qua *alētheia*? (This is to say, if it depends on a linguistically disclosed meaning-world and, hence, on a historically determined *meaning-uncovering,* which implies a simultaneous *hiding* of possible other meanings.) Is not especially the *claim to universality* of Gadamer's "philosophical hermeneutics"[12] well founded on the assumption of the onto-historical *uncovering/hiding-theory of truth*? On the other hand, this claim is also supposed to be founded on the presumptions of *understanding of something* through correct or false arguments, or arguments that prove to be tenable or untenable in discourse, respectively. These presuppositions, I think, cannot be circumvented by philosophers. How is all this to go together?

In my view, the discussion of the questions that were raised at this place requires, first of all, the clarification of two central assumptions in Gadamer's work and in the discussion related to it that have remained unclarified. The first clarification concerns the indicated *concept of truth* which goes back to Heidegger.[13] The second one concerns Gadamer's presupposed relationship of the idea of a "philosophical hermeneutics" (which is held with the claim to universality), first, to the *idea of science qua natural science;* and secondly, to the idea of *hermeneutics* in the sense of the humanities and the arts (*"Geisteswissenschaften"*), as it has been held with the claim to methodological autonomy since Droysen and Dilthey. In the following, I would like to discuss in more detail these two presuppositions of Gadamer's conception of a "philosophical hermeneutics."

II.1 Problematization of the Alētheia-Theory of Truth as Initiated by Heidegger Himself, and Its Consequences

I should first of all like to call into question or at least relativize the scope of Gadamer's concept of truth (which was inspired by Heidegger) with the help of

Heidegger's revocation of the truth-theoretical claim of the theory of *alētheia*. Actually, this revocation has received little attention so far.[14] In his February 1964 lecture, "Heideggers Idee von Wahrheit" (Heidegger's Idea of Truth), Ernst Tugendhat formulated his criticism of Heidegger's adoption and development of Husserl's concept of truth, in the sense of Heidegger's *alētheia*-concept of truth, for the first time.[15] Two months later, Heidegger implicitly confirmed Tugendhat's criticism[16] in his lecture, "Das Ende der Philosophie und die Aufgabe des Denkens" (The End of Philosophy and the Task of Thinking), by noting,

> Insofar as truth is understood in the traditional "natural" sense as the correspondence of knowledge with beings demonstrated in beings, but also insofar as truth is interpreted as the certainty of the knowledge of Being, *alētheia*, unconcealment in the sense of the opening may not be equated with truth. Rather, *alētheia*, unconcealment thought as opening, first grants the possibility of truth. For truth itself, just as Being and thinking, can only be what it is in the element of the opening. Evidence, certainty in every degree, every kind of verification of *veritas* already move with that *veritas* in the realm of the prevalent opening. *Alētheia*, unconcealment thought as the opening of presence, is not yet truth.[17]

At this point, Heidegger does nothing less than revoke that thesis which he had held with growing determination since *Sein und Zeit:* namely, that the more original and the only significant concept of truth is the unconcealment of beings on the ground of the *disclosedness of being-there*, that is, the *opening of Being*. He sees himself forced to revoke his thesis due to his insight that the *unconcealment of meaning*[18] is indeed a *necessary*, but not a *sufficient* condition of *correctness*—that is, it does not operate as the only determining standard. This is the reason why he has to concede that unconcealment is "*not yet* truth" (my emphasis). He is hence explicitly self-critical when he explains,

> To raise the question of *alētheia*, of unconcealment as such, is not the same thing as raising the question of truth. For this reason, it was inadequate and misleading to call *alētheia* in the sense of the opening, truth.[19]

Equally important as this systematically relevant self-correction is Heidegger's revocation of his thesis of the "essential change" of truth in the sense of a Platonic transformation of the *alētheia*-concept of truth into the traditional metaphysical concept of *correctness* or *correspondence*. This thesis lies at the basis of his reconstruction of the history of metaphysics. In factual agreement with Tugendhat's criticism, Heidegger explains,

> The natural concept of truth does not mean unconcealment, not in the philosophy of the Greeks either. It is often and justifiably pointed out that the word *alētheia* is already used by Homer only in the *verba dicendi,* in statement and thus in the sense of correctness and reliability, not in the sense of unconcealment.[20]. . . In the scope of this question, we must acknowledge the fact that *alētheia*, unconcealment in the sense of the opening of presence, was originally only experienced as *orthotēs*, as the correctness of representations and statements. But then, the assertion of a change of the essence of truth, i.e. from unconcealment to correctness, is not tenable, either.[21]

What, now, is the significance of Heidegger's self-criticism for the concept of truth in Gadamer's "philosophical hermeneutics," which is dependent on the concept of *alētheia*?

First of all, it needs to be pointed out that Heidegger's self-correction does not at all mean that he also intended to discredit his discovery of the necessity of a *meaning-disclosedness* of the world as the condition of the possibility of *truth* qua *correctness* (and incorrectness) of statements. This follows from the text quoted and is emphatically confirmed by Heidegger subsequent to the self-correction cited. After Heidegger's self-correction, it certainly needs to be asked with more emphasis what the scope of the discovery of the not-sufficient but yet necessary condition of the meaning-disclosedness (which is always already linguistically articulated) consists in. Could it perhaps consist in having provided the adequate concept of truth of a "philosophical hermeneutics"? This thesis seems to be supported by the fact that a philosophical *hermeneutics* does not at all deal with the correct *knowledge of inner-worldly things* when it reflects upon the *correctness of understanding*. Instead, it only deals either with the *manifestness of meaning,* that is, the manifestness of linguistic meaning as such in the prescientific, life-worldly experience; or with the disclosure of the meaning of works of art or texts on the level of interpretation as made in the humanities and arts. If this interpretation is correct, Gadamer understood with safe instinct the plausibility about Heidegger's theory of *alētheia* and used it to make his conception of a "philosophical hermeneutics" fruitful.

I confess that an argument of this sort was plausible to me not only when originally conceiving a "transcendental hermeneutics," but also afterwards. However, since my conception of a *transcendental pragmatics of language or semiotics,*[22] which was mainly inspired by Peirce, I was unclear about how a *hermeneutics* which was one-sidedly related to comprehensible meaning could at the same time be awarded the status of a *transcendental* hermeneutics that was relevant for the theories of knowledge and science. Briefly put, I was unclear about how it could be awarded the status of a *universal* (and thus methodologically noncircumventable) *philosophy of intersubjective understanding about the world and the knowability of all inner-worldly beings.* As a matter of fact, it appears to me that Gadamer could claim Heidegger's corrected theory of *alētheia* as a sufficient *truth*-theory of his philosophical hermeneutics then, and only then, if he could disregard the *validity claims* of the *interpretanda* which transcend the claim to meaning and which need to be *assessed* or *judged;* in a word, if he were allowed to separate analytically pure *meaning-understanding* from the *evaluative understanding* of the factual problems in the sense of the "hermeneutical abstraction" of traditional, *objectivistic* hermeneutics.

This is precisely what Gadamer does not want. Rather, if I comprehend his conception of hermeneutics aright, it is one of its chief matters of concern to get beyond the value-neutral objectivism of nineteenth-century hermeneutics, which was modeled after the natural sciences. In this way, he stresses the life-worldly unity of *meaning-understanding* and *coming-to-agreement-about-something* (*Truth and Method*, p. 278), in the sense of the dialectical ambiguity of the German expression "Verständigung über etwas."* As I comprehend it, it is this unity on which hermeneutics grounds its philosophical claim to universality and its relevance for theoretical and practical philosophy. And I would like to add at once that, as far as this approach is concerned, *understanding about something* constitutes the common matter of concern of Gadamer's, Habermas's, and of my attempts at an up-to-date "founding" (sorry!) of philosophy in the *a priori of communicative understanding.*

However, if this is so, then the *claim to universality* of "philosophical hermeneutics" seems to me incompatible with the restriction of its *factual reference* to the *meaning-disclosedness* of the world, or even to the linguistically defined meaning of texts. Instead, that *factual reference* which is tied in with the *validity claims* of the *interpretanda* needs to be taken into consideration from the beginning too, both in the epistemologically and ethically relevant senses of *correctness:* and this necessity is already based on the *semantic reference* of language. It needs to be pointed out at this place that the semantic investigations by, in particular, Kripke, Donnellan, and Putnam have recently shown that the thesis which Heidegger put forward as early as in *Sein und Zeit*—that is, the thesis that all *cognition* of inner-worldly beings requires an a priori *understanding* of *something as something*—is not valid without qualification. Heidegger's insight into the "as"-structure of the identification of objects (which is fundamental to the *speech-hermeneutic turn* of phenomenology and has its equivalent in the Fregian/Russellian conception of names as "descriptions"[23]) finds its corrective in the very possibility of using names as *rigid designators* which relate in "as"-free, direct reference to the given that is baptized with the label of deictic or indexical.

In this respect, the given is not yet *known*—hence, not *understood*—"as something" (in the sense of an attributive or predicative modifier). It is, nevertheless, defined by virtue of a direct linguistic reference to its reality which is independent of the *conceptional intensions* of the factually used language. It is defined in a manner which provides evidence criteria, for example, by means of *indexical definitions* of "natural kinds" which are complemented by visual patterns. It is on the basis of these criteria that the *conceptual intensions* of the factually used language can be corrected by the expert in deviating extensions. In this way, Heidegger's thesis of the rigid *ontical-ontological difference* (put differently, of the preliminary opening of scope for *ontical-empirical knowledge* through the *understanding of Being*) is

---

*Translator's Note: This phrase signifies a) communication, b) coming to agreement about something, or more clearly, about theoretical and/or practical validity claims.

corrected in the sense of a *meaning-holism* which is yet conditioned also linguistically.

The epistemological importance of this speech-analytical insight seems to lie in the untenability of the currently influential presumptions of a one-sided predetermination of the scope for scientific discoveries by "epochal openings of the meaning of Being" (according to Heidegger) or by "incommensurable paradigms" (according to Thomas Kuhn) of the preunderstanding of problems and their possible solutions. They have to be corrected at least in the sense that, especially in the sciences, *empirical learning processes* are possible; these, in turn, influence the epochal openings of the meaning of Being, or of the paradigms of "normal science," respectively.

What, now, is the significance of the so-far outlined recent insights for the assessment of Gadamer's conception of *the claim to universality of philosophical hermeneutics*?

So much seems to be clear to me; the recent insights into *meaning-holism* (roughly put, into the possible correction of the *meaning* of language by *reference* of language) elucidate and increase the significance of the insight that a "philosophical hermeneutics" deals not only with *intensional,* speech-immanent *meaning,* but also with the *fact-related validity claims* of human utterances. This insight was implicitly confirmed by Gadamer himself. But if this is so, then Gadamer's previously criticized thesis, according to which our understanding cannot in principle transcend the "always understanding differently" of the *interpretanda* (that is, on account of its dependence on the historically determined situational context of the *manifestation* of meaning in language), appears hardly tenable.

For even if the factual *manifestation of meaning* (*alētheia* in Heidegger's sense) is always context-relative, it has in the meantime become obvious that the *fact-related truth of validity claims* is not yet sufficiently determined by the factual manifestation of meaning. Rather, it requires some additional fact-related insight to assess it, and this insight needs to be *counterfactually valid* at any time, namely, for an infinite community of interpreters. If now this explication of the meaning of truth is to have any pragmatic meaning whatsoever, then it must in principle be possible to presuppose the possibility of progress in knowledge, first of all in the dimension of fact-related correctness. Under the condition of *meaning-holism,* however, such progress cannot in fact be totally relative to a previously determined scope for the factual-historical meaning openings, as Heidegger suggested. It must rather, for its part, be able to influence possible meaning openings (for instance, the intensions of our linguistic terms). But this implies that the consideration of possible progress in knowledge must be constitutive of the speech-mediated understanding of the lifeworld, and beyond that also of understanding in the narrower, methodological sense of the hermeneutics of the humanities and arts. Hence also in this area, *meaning-understanding* must be able to turn into "understanding better and better" on the basis of progress in the research on things. Apparently, this is exactly what is testified by the previously cited examples from the history of philosophy and science (see sec. II above).

All this, I think, is true under Gadamer's assumption—which I share—that *understanding* in the sense of a *philosophical hermeneutics* must have, and maintain, its place in the context of the communicative understanding about things.

However, the consequences we just drew from the problematization of the theory of truth (and meaning) which Gadamer presupposed, still require a more detailed elucidation and substantiation in the context of the previously indicated question of the relationship of "philosophical hermeneutics" to a differentiated theory of knowledge and science. For from Gadamer's perspective, it could immediately be objected that all consequences which have so far been drawn from the theory of truth are still oriented toward the model of the *factual reference* of the *progressive natural sciences*. But it is precisely this model which Gadamer's conception of "philosophical hermeneutics" called into question.

II.2 Problematization of the Equation of the Intersubjective Validity of Progress in Understanding with the Objectivity of Progressive Natural Science

The crucial difference between Gadamer's assessment of the relationship of hermeneutics to the sciences (wherein he follows Heidegger) and the dichotomy between "understanding" and "explaining,"[24] which became popular through Dilthey, it seems to me, can be explicated in our problem context as follows. It is true that Dilthey—like Droysen before him—was interested in working out the epistemological and methodological difference between the factual conditions and the cognitive accessibility of the "objects" of the nomologically explaining natural sciences on the one hand and, on the other hand, the "historical-social reality," which can be relived and comprehended as an expression of life. At any rate, he was intent to do so more radically than the Neo-Kantians, who did not want to let a differentiation occur until the "concept formation," certainly not yet during the constitution of the empirical data. But Dilthey—along with modern, in particular nineteenth-century epistemology—held to the notion that the understanding humanities and arts *(Geisteswissenshaften)* dealt with a *progressively explorable object of knowledge.* He did so in spite of his comprehension of the historical dependence of understanding. Since Dilthey held to the *objectivity ideal of the Geisteswissenschaften* on the one hand but was, on the other hand, willing to reduce philosophy's claim to truth (namely, of the "absolute spirit" as such in Hegel's sense) to that of the "objective spirit" (namely, of a true expression of the diversity of life), he simply had to become hopelessly entangled in the "aporias of historicism" (see *WuM*, pp. 205ff.).

Now, Gadamer believes these aporias can be resolved by giving up as inadequate the *subject-object relation*—which was yet presupposed by Dilthey as well as the entire epistemological tradition—and the accompanying *objectivity ideal of progressive science* for "hermeneutical experience" and the *understanding* of the humanities and arts (see especially *WuM*, p. 437); or by relativizing the two in the sense of treating them as at times useful methodical fictions.[25] According to Gadamer, understanding must be comprehended on the level of reflection of a "philosophical hermeneutics," that is, of a "hermeneutic ontology," as a factor in the onto-historical happening of the mediation of tradition. Put differently, it must be comprehended not so much as an understanding subject's *methodical way of behaving,* but rather as a way of experiencing the world that is conscious of its *effective historical determinedness* and that obtains its possible depth and strength as a response to being addressed by the tradition. For Gadamer, this implies that, all in all, there can be no progressive "better understanding"—since there actually is no progressively explorable object of exploration—but only the context-dependent *self-mediation with tradition,* to wit, a *meaning-* and *truth-happening.*

Accordingly, the above-sketched correction of the *alētheia*-theory of truth apparently can have no consequences for hermeneutics in the sense of a rehabilitation of *understanding's capacity for progress.* For even if the difference between *meaning-manifestation* and *fact-related correctness* is conceded, unlike for natural science, there simply can be no *factual reference* for hermeneutic understanding which allows progress in knowledge. It may be added in special accordance with Gadamer's spirit that this is also true if understanding is comprehended as being embedded in the structural context of *communicative understanding about something* (the *thing!*). For even then, in the end it remains a meaning- and truth-happening which is determined by the "fusion of horizons" between the respective situation-dependent perspectives of the *interpreter* and of the *interpretandum.* What can be said about this?

First of all, I should like to make clear that I indeed do not consider the *objectivity ideal of natural science* (which is based upon the assumption of a homogeneous object of knowledge that is, so to speak, finished and only to be explored progressively) as a possible paradigm for the *factual reference* of hermeneutic understanding. This goes even for the hermeneutic reconstruction of the history of the natural sciences, which is, after all, also based on historical understanding of the matter of the natural sciences. I think that for all historical humanities and arts (which includes "understanding sociology," in the sense it was given by Max Weber), *factual reference* is not determined by an object which is finished and only to be explored progressively, but by history's irreversible happening, which these disciplines themselves constitute by way of "further continued shaping of tradition."

But does it really follow from these "concessions" that one has to agree to Gadamer's notion that, by and large, the possibility of—a normatively regulated!—*progress* in understanding the humanities and arts does not make sense?

This would, in my view, be unavoidable if the concept of *intersubjective validity*—which corresponds with the notion of truth in the humanities and arts—had to be equated with the concept of objectivity in the sense of the objectivity ideal of the value-free natural sciences. As a matter of fact, this widely presupposed equation was suggested by Kant. But could one not also talk of *intersubjective validity of norms*—norms of ethics and norms that guide the evaluational understanding of critical-hermeneutic social sciences, humanities, and arts? It would, however, be imperative to justify philosophically the intersubjective validity of norms which are required in this matter. And this justification would not, for its part, have to return to historically determined contents of tradition, such as the handed-down "*ēthos*" in the sense of Aristotle (see *WuM*, pp. 297ff.), or the authoritative concept of the "classic" (see *WuM*, pp. 269ff.). For what really is at stake here is the provision of normative standards even for the critical assessment of the validity claims of tradition. And it needs to be pointed out that today for the first time, we live in a multicultural world civilization that requires interculturally valid basic norms for the various tradition-dependent life forms to live and responsibly work together.[26]

However, not only Gadamer, but all present philosophers who see themselves as post-Nietzschean, post-Heideggerian, or post-Wittgensteinian seem to be totally confused on the question of the *justification of intersubjectively valid norms,* if the question is recognized as a meaningful one at all. On the whole, the justification is regarded as an impossible task, if one attempts to avoid returning to religious or metaphysical dogmas.

At this point, I should like to go back to the structure of *communicative understanding of something,* which even Gadamer recognizes as the condition of understanding along with the happening of tradition. Put differently, I should like to go back to the structure of *argumentative discourse.* This represents that *form of reflection of communicative understanding* which philosophy—including "philosophical hermeneutics"—takes for granted in the context of the justification of validity. Should this form of reflection, in turn, only be conceivable as an instance of a historically located meaning- and truth-happening? Or should it, as the condition of the possibility and validity of its philosophical function of reflection, imply an intersubjective, and hence historically independent, validity claim per se? And if the latter proves to be the case, what are the consequences for the possibility of a normative justification of understanding in general?

III. The A Priori of the Argumentative Discourse as Historically Noncircumventable Form of Reflection of Understanding on Something, and as Normative Condition of Critical-Hermeneutic Understanding

In the 1971 discussion volume, *Hermeneutik und Ideologiekritik,*[27] J. Habermas and I gave the impression—today I would say, wrongly so—that the "claim to universality" of Gadamer's "philosophical hermeneutics" could be called into question by such social scientific approaches as *psychoanalysis* and *ideology criticism.* More precisely put, we left the impression that it could be called into question by indicating the possibility and necessity of critical-reflective suspension of the hermeneutic "fore-conception of perfection" by means of an objectifying "analysis" of the communicative competence of socialized human beings and, therefore, also of the "authority" of linguistic tradition; and all this, if possible, within the framework of a *philosophy of history* as the comprehensively operating discipline. However, both Habermas and I were at that time developing the approach of a *discourse philosophy,*[28] which proves the above-sketched act of questioning of the claim to universality as impossible. More exactly, it proves it impossible inasmuch as "philosophical hermeneutics" (for example, "transcendental hermeneutics," which after all I had previously supported) may take the place of *discourse philosophy.* What does this mean?

In my opinion, it certainly does not mean that it should not be possible and necessary to analyze the results of—as they are traditionally called—hermeneutic humanities and arts with the help of unmasking social scientific critiques.[29] Not to hold this possible would, I am sure, amount to a hermeneutic idealism of the *Geisteswissenschaften,* which is doubtlessly incompatible with Gadamer's conviction of the superiority of historical Being over any possible kind of reflective consciousness of Being.

It should also be clear, however, that *empirical-self-critical reflection* which both psychoanalysis and all forms of ideology criticism have to take for granted in their human "objects" is not to be confused with *transcendental-hermeneutic, or transcendental-pragmatic,* reflection. The latter refers to the *conditions of the possibility of argumentative discourses* and, consequently, also to those of the critical social sciences. It takes place at the level of *philosophical* discussion and can in no way be replaced, or even in principle be surpassed, by unmasking critique. This is so simply because only this form can reflect on the conditions of the possibility and validity especially of unmasking critiques. As a matter of fact, this constitutes a thesis which currently meets with less popularity than the supposedly more radical, permanently self-contradictory practice of the *total critique of reason*.[30] The disrespect for my thesis is modeled on Nietzsche and is to be found, for example, in Poststructuralism, or Postmodernism, respectively.

I believe that it can now be stated that this noncircumventable *claim to universality* which Gadamer makes of "philosophical hermeneutics" is justified also as far as all critical social sciences are concerned—provided that "philosophical hermeneutics" is so conceived that it can answer the *question of the conditions of the possibility of valid understanding.* But it is exactly this feature which cannot be expected of Gadamer's "hermeneutic ontology" of *meaning- and truth-happening.*

III.1 The Reflective Perspective of Philosophy Indirectly Makes Possible Critical "Better Understanding"

What actually is the perspective of Gadamer's conception of "hermeneutic ontology"? Put differently, what is the relationship between the discourse of understanding, in which Gadamer participates as a philosopher, and the discourses of understanding of the lifeworld and the humanities and arts, the structure of which he analyzes as *meaning- and truth-happening*? The reader of *Truth and Method* receives only an indirect answer to this question, which, I think, is ambiguous. On the one hand, Gadamer himself—just like the later Heidegger—appears not to participate in the discourse of understanding at all, but only to talk about the conditions of understanding as a *temporal-historical happening* in an unreflected, *objectivistic* attitude. (Heidegger had, in the sense of the *ontical-ontological difference,* yet attached importance to distinguishing between the *inner-worldly/inner-temporal happening* in the ordinary sense—that is, empirical happening—and the "bringing about" and "making room" of the world itself in an epochal-eventful meta-happening of the history of Being.[31] As far as I can see, Gadamer abandoned this idea completely. This is why there remains the impression of the *inner-temporal objectivization* of those phenomena which, at least in the classical ontology of the Greeks since Parmenides and Plato, could not have the character of *inner-temporal happening:* that is, *meaning* that can be comprehended in thinking (namely, idea or form and *truth,* or *untruth,* respectively).

Now, it was Hegel who first objectified the spiritual as something *falling into time.* It is true, he did so with the intention of simultaneously making it, as "reflection in itself," nullify time (and history) in its *being-in-and-for-itself,* which required "absolute knowledge." Evidently, Gadamer constantly keeps this quasi-model in mind. But no matter how much he admires it,[32] it is certain from the very beginning that he needs to dissociate himself from it in the name of the *finite nature of human Dasein.* He does so in favor of the objectifying observation of a *happening* purely *within time:* that is, of the *always only understanding differently of the respective* "view of Being."

But is this really a legitimate alternative to Hegel's excessive demands on the reflective powers of the philosophical concept? Can the truth claims of the arts and philosophy (which realizes the relativity of the situation) be thought without contradiction after the model of the inner-temporally appearing "objective spirit"—that is to say, as an "expression of the diversity of life" (Dilthey)—like perhaps the truth claims of art and religion? Gadamer realizes that Dilthey's total reduction of "the absolute" to the "objective spirit" caused Dilthey to become entangled in the "aporias of historicism" (*WuM*, pp. 205ff.). But like Heidegger, Gadamer only seemingly manages an "overcoming" of the *relativism of historicism*. He believes himself to have managed this overcoming by simply giving up Dilthey's *objectivity ideal* and historically-contextually relativizing understanding's validity claim *right from the start*. But is this not making a virtue out of Dilthey's necessity and cutting the Gordian knot of the *relativism of historicism* in two instead of untying it?

Bearing in mind what I said in my introduction, I must at this point qualify my reservations about Gadamer: I am not interested in defending Dilthey's *objectivity ideal* of "critical after-understanding" of uttered meaning. Neither am I interested in renewing Hegel's claim to comprehend the reflectively outstripping "self-penetration of mind"—which is tied with all understanding—in the sense of the possibility of a total mediation of the *form of understanding* (of the "concept") and of the *contents of history*. Instead, I am only interested in being able to think the truth capacity of *reflectively outstripping*—and hence also potentially *critical*—understanding in the sense of the *regulative idea of intersubjective validity per se,* and in this respect of real possible, continuous *progress.* This is of particular interest to me in view of the fact that understanding which is always already reflective cannot, it is true, be raised to "absolute knowledge." However, in *transcendental hermeneutics* it has always already achieved the level of *formal self-reflection with universal validity claim.* This means, the *discourses of understanding* [in the sense of communicative understanding *of* something; R.S.], as a factor of which understanding has to be comprehended (also according to Gadamer), cannot simply be objectified inner-temporally as "happening." For in *philosophical discourse* they have always already achieved a *form of reflection* which can no longer reduce its own truth claim to a historically conditioned perspective among other temporally limited perspectives—as long as one intends to avoid performative self-contradiction.

Of course, this observation is valid only insofar as we are really capable of making universally valid *formal* statements in philosophical discourse on discourses in general, and thereby of relativizing the perspectives of understanding of the individual discourses in the sense of their "belongingness to history" (Gadamer). But this simultaneously opens the possibility of empirically *comparing* between different, context-related perspectives of understanding, both synchronically and diachronically.[33] Nowadays, a number of historical and cultural-anthropological/ethnological sciences take advantage of this. In addition, the radicalization of reflective understanding—which has already been achieved in philosophy—makes possible the "hermeneutics of suspicion" (Ricoeur) which suspends the "fore-conception of perfection," as well as the corresponding methods of the *critical social sciences*.[34]

Should it not, consequently, be possible, even absolutely necessary to comprehend the *formal transcending of the viewpoint dependence of understanding*—which has already been achieved in the philosophical form of reflection of discourse—as a condition of the possibility of synthetically gaining *new, superior perspectives of understanding?* (These are new forms of the *fore-conception of the world* which make possible deeper understanding and which do not simply constitute "further continued development" of traditions, but rather achievements of critical reflection.)

It goes without saying that these new perspectives of understanding (*meaning-openings,* if you will), which are mediated through critical reflection, also will differ *as* perspectives; they open material "views of the world" from out of the formal independence of the viewpoint of philosophical reflective insights; hence they again are historically situated and finite. This, however, does not change anything about the fact that these perspectives of philosophical discourse are subject to the *regulative idea of better and deeper understanding.*

Now Gadamer simply blocks this, so far only indicated, answer of a *reflective, transcendental hermeneutics* to the question of the conditions of the possibility of valid understanding. He does so by polemicizing against "reflective philosophy," and his polemics are certainly indications of "bad prejudices." Although he clearly recognizes how the total historical relativization of all understanding leads to *performative self-contradiction,* he is willing to accept it after the model of Nietzsche, Heidegger, and many of their successors. This reads as follows:

> However clearly one demonstrates the inner contradictions of all relativist views, it is as Heidegger has said: all these victorious arguments have something about them that suggests they are attempting to bowl one over.[35] However cogent they may seem, they still miss the main point. In making use of them one is proved right, and yet they do not express any superior insight of any value. That the thesis of scepticism or relativism refutes itself to the extent that it claims to be true is an irrefutable argument. But what does it achieve? The reflective argument that proves successful here falls back on the arguer, in that it renders the truthfulness of all reflection suspect. It is not the reality of scepticism or truth dissolving relativism, but the claim to truth of all formal argument that is affected.[36]

I must confess that I can only regard this plea for the acceptance of self-contradiction as a fashionable capitulation of reason and as the breaking off of argumentative discourse by means of a word from him. However, it is not this side of Gadamer's "argumentation" which, I think, is interesting, but the question whether this passage does not *express motives* which should be comprehended and taken seriously from a hermeneutic point of view. Should not, for instance, the indication of the "*reality* [my emphasis] of skepticism and of all-truth-dissolving relativism" be taken seriously? Gadamer underscores this indication in the above-quoted passage by remarking that, for example, "Heinrich Rickert, who outright refuted the 'philosophy of life' in 1920 . . . was in no way [able to] match the *influence* of Nietzsche and Dilthey, which began to spread at that time."[37]

My answer is, "Yes and no!" "No" inasmuch as philosophy is not allowed to accept the "actual effect" of arguments as an argument against their validity. "Yes" inasmuch as the great *actual effect* even of defective arguments might contain indication of their possible explication by means of *valid* arguments. Conversely, valid arguments might be practically irrelevant concerning their *significance,* and hence their possible *fruitfulness.* This appears to be Gadamer's motive that needs to be taken seriously. The following passage shows this clearly:

> The consciousness of contingency does not do away with contingency. It is one of the prejudices of reflective philosophy that it understands as a relationship of propositions that which is not at all on the same logical level.[38]

This observation obviously affects the previously indicated circumstance: the *formal-reflective discourse on discourses*—which in fact "does not lie on the same logical level" as those discourses that disclose the contents of the world and about which it makes statements—cannot directly open any new fact-disclosing perspectives *for the time being.* Therefore, it seemingly leaves *everything the way it is* (as Wittgenstein claimed of philosophy in general). However, I have already attempted to show that, and for what reason, this impression of fruitlessness turns out to be erroneous, if you think together the at first only formal-general reflection with its logically possible consequences (namely, the new and superior factual perspectives of understanding that were mediated through reflection).

In the following, I should like to enforce this, in Hegel's sense *dialectical,* aspect in more depth. I shall attempt to show that the (certainly not fruitless) reflection on the presuppositions of the philosophical form of reflection of the discourses of understanding is able to uncover precisely those *intersubjectively valid norms of practical reason and of the critical-hermeneutic reconstruction of history* which hermeneutic reflection, in Gadamer's sense, on the *meaning- and truth-happening* of historically situated understanding cannot discover.

III.2 The Principle of Catching-Up-Itself of the Reconstruction of History As the Normative Basis of Critical Understanding

In contemporary philosophy—for example, hermeneutic phenomenology and Anglo-Saxon philosophy as it is influenced by Collingwood, Wittgenstein, and

American Pragmatism[39]—there is broad agreement on the notion that our *understanding and judging* are dependent on the historical-contingent background preconditions of the "lifeworld" or the socio-cultural "life forms." They are considered to be dependent on preconditions which in principle cannot totally be brought under the objectifying control of consciousness. It goes without saying that this demonstrates a far-reaching and multifold confirmation of the "fore-structure" of the "disclosedness" of "being-in-the-world" as it was worked out by Heidegger and Gadamer—that is to say, of the "a priori perfect of facticity" and of the "thrownness" of our understanding of the world.

The consequences of this epochal insight apply both to theoretical philosophy (including philosophy of science) and practical philosophy. They lie almost without exception in the direction of a *historical-relativistic* approach, even if this is frequently concealed by a strategy which is inspired by Wittgenstein or philosophical pragmatism. This strategy consists in making the problem of *universally valid norms* and *regulative ideas* in theoretical and practical philosophy appear to be an obsolete, wrongly dramatized legacy of traditional metaphysics. In any event, there is general consent that such things as *universally valid norms* or *regulative ideas* could only be generated by a *metaphysical-fundamentalistic* position. Also in my view, however, such an approach does not lie within the sphere of critical philosophical thought. Is there no other way out of this dilemma but to make a virtue out of necessity and see precisely in our insight into the dependence of our thinking on contingent tradition the sufficient solution to all normative problems of ethics and of the hermeneutic humanities and arts? In this respect, Gadamer seems to propose an answer which demonstrates like-mindedness with such thinkers as Rorty and MacIntyre![40]

I have already indicated that I do not regard the above-suggested answer as a plausible one. I do not understand why for the various cultures which today need to live and work together in the *one lifeworld* of humankind (and at many places already do so in the form of multicultural societies) a solution to the normative problem could be achieved if every culture, every socio-cultural life form, merely "continued" its tradition or, in Rortyan diction, showed it off "persuasively" in each particular context. (Particular attention should be paid to the way Rorty uses the words "persuasive" and "persuasion" in their ambiguous meaning between "überzeugen" [to convince] and "überreden" [to talk into]. This ambiguity is characteristic of the entire history of these words in the occidental tradition of rhetoric. Due to his denial of the existence of *universally valid criteria* for *convincing by means of arguments,* Rorty could not even welcome the possibility of dissolving this ambiguity with the help of speech act theory, for instance. I am inclined to think that Gadamer's position is fairly close to Rorty's, certainly closer than to Kant's brusque condemnation of "überreden." Kant regarded this notion as a method of robbing the partners in the discourse of their "autonomy.")

But what is the point of these critical remarks if, in fact, there is no way of justifying universal norms of critically understanding and judging traditions independently of these very traditions? Or should the reflective viewpoint of philosophical discourse on the diversity of traditions open up a solution? In the following, I intend to show exactly this in defiance of all the prejudices against the fruitfulness of the reflective viewpoint. However, I believe it is necessary to make a few preliminary remarks on a *postlinguistic-turn theory of philosophical reflection,* which, in my view, is urgently needed these days.

First of all, it needs to be pointed out that philosophical discourse alone is capable of reflecting on itself and its presuppositions. Herein it is only in accordance with the specific validity claim of philosophical statements, for example, of statements on *discourses in general:* it is universal and hence also self-reflective. I think that through this "self-reflection," philosophical discourse *finishes* the reflective "self-upgrading" of discourses, and hence of language.[41] This self-upgrading process leads from the thematization of the "universality of facts" of natural laws to the empirical-hermeneutic thematization of the "universality of meaning" of language or texts to the self-reflective thematization of the formal, but absolutely universal validity claims of philosophy. In this respect, the "self-reflection" of philosophical discourse also finishes the reflective certainty of the *noncircumventability* of *argumentation* for reflection; this reflective certainty performatively accompanies all acts of argumentation. Any further self-reflection on the part of the participants in the discourse could only have psychological significance, but certainly no validity-theoretical relevance.

This clearly shows that this *reflective self-upgrading of discursive understanding* (which can be carried out in discourse by any participant at any time) has to be distinguished from self-reflection in the sense of traditional *philosophy of consciousness.* As is commonly known, the latter either leads to paradoxes or infinite regress, which corresponds to the regress of the metalanguages (or the metatheories) in metalogic.

The reflection on the *necessary* (that is, under pain of *performative self-contradiction,* nondisputable) *existential* and *rule presuppositions* of philosophical discourse, is, I believe, suitable for bringing to light the *always already* recognized *norms* (in the broadest sense); this reflection has to be carried out in philosophical discourse itself. These norms are definitely different from those which—along with the tradition-dependent "pre-conception of the world" and social "consent"—are *always already* recognized by any finite human being as *contingent a priori of facticity.* They are precisely not part of the "fore-structure" of "everyday being-in-the-world" (the "lifeworld") in the sense of Heidegger and Gadamer (and the later Wittgenstein's "life forms"), but of the "fore-structure" of that reflection on the fore-structure of everyday being-in-the-world which people have tended to pursue since its origin in the "axis age" (Karl Jaspers) of the high cultures of the classical world. (Neither Heidegger nor Wittgenstein ever attempted to analyze the "fore-structure" of *their analyses* of everyday behavior and its accompanying language games. Had they done so, Heidegger would not have been able to put down the *logos* of occidental philosophy together with the "thrownness" of all understanding of the world to an onto-historical "event." And Wittgenstein would have had to answer the question how—that is to say, by virtue of what "healthy" philosophical language game—he would be able "to bring to rest" the disease of the "empty" philosophical language games.[42]

But what, now, are the normative presuppositions of philosophical discourse, and how are they different from those of the contingent preconception of the world? I would like to cite the experience of the *Sixth East-West Philosophers' Conference* in Hawaii (1989) on *Culture and Modernity.*[43] For in this conference, all currently relevant requirements for a *self-reflective discussion* of the problem talked about in this paper were met: an encounter between philosophers and scholars in the humanities and arts from Europe, North America, and the Asian countries; the thematization of the problems of universalism, pluralism, and relativism; and last but not least, the confrontation between the representatives of the various positions I have mentioned (for example, R. Rorty, R. Bernstein, and A. MacIntyre). But most of all I would like to emphasize, as I did in the paper which I gave at this conference,[44] that the conference *as such* offered the opportunity of laying open the—usually not reflected—*normative presuppositions of current philosophical discourse.* For our topic, this would spell out as the presuppositions of an attempted *understanding between members or representatives of the most diverse cultural traditions and philosophical positions.*

I think that I can now honor the following *normative presuppositions* as being of such nature that none of the participants would have been able to contest them without simultaneously committing performative contradiction:[45]

1. Philosophers strive to achieve *consensus* on the *validity* of their own *validity claims* in principle with all (ideally, with all possible) partners in the discourse. They do so with the help of *arguments,* that is to say, by way of *convincing,* but not *persuading,* not to speak of such other *strategic* ways of using language as *bribing* or *threatening.* (They may no doubt expect and accept in the interest of their practical arguments that there will be actual *dissent.* But in spite of Lyotard, they cannot *strive for dissent* by way of arguing.[46] Rather, in the case of dissent, they at least have to strive for a consensus on the reasons for the dissent, provided they continue to argue at all.)
2. When arguing, philosophers necessarily have at least the following *four validity claims* (they always need to presuppose them at the same time, but they can individually emphasize them by the choice of their speech acts):
2.1. Philosophers must have a claim on the *intersubjectively sharable meaning* of their speech acts as a precondition of all further validity claims. (They must

presuppose this claim as sufficiently fulfillable even in case they argue—for example, as linguists or speech psychologists—that, empirically speaking, we can never associate precisely identical meanings with our utterances; or in case they are of the opinion—along with Derrida—that "dissémination" [dissemination] or "différance" [difference] as fundamental happening of any semiotic process makes impossible the present of a sharable "signifié." Derrida, of course, is able to *bear* the ensuing performative self-contradiction.) I believe it is possible to call into question even the claim to meaning of arguments, especially of philosophical questions, in the sense that the *claim to meaning* has to be explicitly defended. (It is true that *comprehensibility* that cannot be problematized any further needs to be presupposed also for the problematizable *claims to meaning* on the levels of linguistic syntax and semantics.)

2.2. In *theoretical discourse,* the *claim to truth* or the claim to the unlimited capacity for consensus of assertions must be at the forefront. (The *claim to truth* includes no *claim to certainty.* It is rather compatible with the explicit support of the *reservation of fallibility,* except in those cases where the presuppositions of the meaning of the thesis of fallibility are concerned. Examples of such presuppositions are those of the binary concept of truth and of the possibility of discourses for the forming of consensus.[47]

2.3. A precondition of any further validity claims—along with the *claim to meaning*—is the *claim to truthfulness,* which refers to subjective *intentions.* If it is called into question, it can of course not be proved by arguments, but only be declared by means of speech acts or be realized *practically.*

2.4. A precondition of the exposition of the *claims to truth* as claims that can be accepted or rejected in a—in principle unlimited—community of communication is an *ethically relevant claim to rightness* in every argument. This fundamental claim to ethical rightness[48] can be explicated in a foundation of ethics which is reflective of its arguments in the following manner: the *solidarity* of an *ideal community of communication,* which follows the tightly interwoven basic norms of *equality* and of *equal responsibility* for the raising and solving of problems in the *mutual recognition of the partners in discourse,* has to be presupposed, and even be *counterfactually anticipated,* as every serious act of argumentation *demonstrates.* (From this, there instantly follows the demand that all moral problems which the participants in the discourse could raise—for example, conflicts of interests in the lifeworld, which otherwise could not be solved without the use of violence—should be solved by means of *practical discourses* by those who are affected.)

What now is the significance of the normative presuppositions of the philosophical discourse of understanding for our debate on Gadamer?[49] More precisely, in what way do we deal with a nonmetaphysical, but transcendental-hermeneutic, or transcendental-pragmatic, basis for the *normative control of all evaluative understanding?* In other words, in what way do we deal with an authority which is independent of the validity claim of tradition (or more exactly, independent of the claims of the various, at least partly, incompatible cultural traditions) inasmuch as it is capable of justifying *universally valid* standards and, hence, also restricting conditions for the recognition of the responsibility of the validity claims of tradition(s)?

In the following, I cannot attempt to unfold the relevance of the *transcendental-reflective* justification of a *discourse ethics* in the current situation of the world by, for instance, discussing a "Neo-Aristotelian" or "communitarian" ethics that only refers to particular traditions (for example, those of a "good polis" or a certain life form).[50] I would only like to stress the following central thesis: the *formal-procedural basic norms of a discourse ethics* relate to the *evaluations of the contents of a substantial morality* in the Hegelian sense, or of an *ethos* in the Aristotelian sense, the same way as the universally valid presuppositions of philosophical discourse relate to the historical-contingent presuppositions of the various life forms. These basic norms of a discourse ethics are not able, and are not supposed, to replace those evaluations or make them superfluous. However, they subject them to the restricting conditions and regulative principles of *practical discourses* in which those norms are to be justified which all people affected (including the next generations) could consent to. Such norms include human rights as well as presently pressing norms of an ecological ethics of global responsibility for the consequences of collective activities in the fields of science, technology, economics, and politics. No doubt, the difficulties involved in this program of a *macroethics of a thousand talks and conferences* are large.[51] But the fact that this program has long been recognized and followed, at least by public pretension, shows that the contemporary world knows no alternative to it.

In the following, I should like to put forward another argument which is able to demonstrate the possibility of justifying the *regulative principles for a critical-reconstructive understanding of all human cultural traditions* (or of the cultural evolution of humankind) on the basis of the universally valid presuppositions of philosophical discourse. In fact, this argument does so more clearly than all so far indicated arguments for the possibility of new, reflection-dependent perspectives of understanding. I am talking about what I named the *principle of catching-up-itself* of all critical-reconstructive social sciences, humanities, and arts.[52]

The point of departure for the following thoughts is reflection on the fact that the *recognition of the noncontingent presuppositions* which form the "fore-structure" of philosophical discourse today also is part of the a priori *of facticity* of our being-in-the-world.[53] In other words, the recognition of the intended presuppositions is not only a noncontestable *a priori of argumentation* for all critical-reconstructive sciences. For them, it also constitutes a *fact of history that needs to be reconstructed*—that is, a fact that needs, in a manner of speaking, to be *caught up* in its capacity and its actuality through understanding the reconstruction of history. Hence, the point of departure for the reconstruction of history, which is presupposed to be transcendental-hermeneutic, functions as the *telos* of this reconstruction. The function of this *telos* as a regulative principle of reconstruction cannot really be contested, provided that one intends to avoid reconstruction to contradict performatively its own validity conditions. I think that this *forestructure of the reconstruction of history* forms the alternative both to *speculative philosophy of history* (which must dogmatically-metaphysically presuppose the *telos* of history) and to Gadamer's *hermeneutics of meaning- and truth-happening,* which is unable to justify a regulative principle of possible progress.

The significance of the *principle of catching-up-itself of the reconstruction of history* can best be demonstrated by confronting it with attempts of a (metaphysical-antimetaphysical) *naturalistic-reductionist explanation* of the history of mind from *external* causal motives. These attempts are characteristic of the modern era in general and, ironically, also of postmodernism's total critique of reason. For instance, it could be confronted with Nietzsche's attempts to call into question absolutely all validity claims of human reason from a *genealogical* point of view; examples would be truth, moral rightness, and in the end, also truthfulness—Nietzsche's "Redlichkeit" or honesty—which he had claimed for himself for so long. In the face of such attempts to *replace understanding* with *explaining* (they are condemned to be performatively contradictory), the *principle of catching-up-itself of the reconstruction* does not at all demand the abandonment of all external explanations. It does, however, demand an—at least validity-theoretical—subordination of the latter to (the act of) understanding in the sense of a rationally evaluating reconstruction.

In my view, Imre Lakatos, in his discussion of Thomas Kuhn's conception of the history of science, provides a model for the relation that I demand at this place.[54] He postulates the general priority of the attempt to reconstruct an *internal history* of progress in natural science (in the sense of the understanding of sound scientific reasons) over any attempt to provide *external* explanations of the history of science by returning to psychological and social causes. On top of that, he demands striving for a maximization of the "internal history" compared with the "external history." (This caused Feyerabend to draw the funny, but problem-annihilating and consequently absurd conclusion that, in that case, it would be best to assume that "anything goes.")

Now, I think that Lakatos's model of the reconstruction of the history of science can be generalized in the sense of a principle of the reconstruction of the history of mind, or of cultural evolution altogether. (For what has to be regarded as an *external* motive from the point of view of the history of science, could certainly be comprehended and appreciated as an *internal* one from the perspective of a hermeneutic reconstruction of the history of mind in general. One example would be Newton's theological, or theosophical, speculations, which motivated him to presuppose the existence of "absolute space.") This way it becomes evident that, basically, Lakatos's postulate constitutes nothing but an analogue of Gadamer's principle of the "fore-conception of perfection," which is applied to history in general. However, this application to history in general also shows, I believe, that this principle in its heuristic-methodological function rather goes with the *principle of catching-up-itself* of *transcendental hermeneutics* (as supported here) than with a *hermeneutics of the always only understanding differently.* For the latter can just not comprehend the "fore-conception of perfection" as a *postulate of progress,* but can only relate it to particular texts, or contexts, respectively.

The same, I think, is true with regard to the "hermeneutic circle," if it is applied to the reconstruction of history. In this case, the principle of *catching-up-itself* again needs to be presupposed in order to "get into it [the circle, R.S.] in the proper way."[55] But this clashes with the later Heidegger's idea that the history of Being has to be comprehended as an—in this respect irrational—succession of "epochal uncoverings/hidings" of the meaning of beings. In the end, an antithetical conflict becomes apparent which I should like to comprehend as one between the *logos of understanding* (which can be caught up through reflection and hence be recognized) and *temporal Being* (that is, the *happening* of the manifestations of meaning). Gadamer's "philosophical hermeneutics" has devoted itself to an *ontology of temporal Being.* In my view, this contradicts its referral to the Socratic-Platonic dialectics of dialogue—that is to say, of argumentative discourse, which is capable of catching up its assumptions maieutically. This is what I attempted to correct.

KARL-OTTO APEL

DEPARTMENT OF PHILOSOPHY
JOHANN WOLFGANG GOETHE UNIVERSITY, GERMANY
AUGUST 1992

NOTES

1. See K.-O. Apel, *Die Idee der Sprache in der Tradition des Humanismus von Dante bis Vico* (Bonn: Bouvier, 1963; 3rd edition 1980).

2. Gadamer called it "philosophical hermeneutics," and he strove to substantiate it in later-Heideggerian terms of a *meaning- and truth-happening* of the "mediation of tradition."

3. See, e.g., the preface to the 2d edition of *Wahrheit und Methode* (Tübingen: Mohr, 1965), pp. xvf., and p. 483. On this point, see K.-O. Apel, *Transformation der Philosophie* (*Towards a Transformation of Philosophy*) (Frankfurt a.M.: Suhrkamp, 1973), pp. 34f.

4. See in particular *WuM*, p. 249; *Truth and Method*, pp. 233–34.

5. See M. Heidegger, *Kant und das Problem der Metaphysik (Kant and the Problem of Metaphysics)* (Frankfurt a.M.: Klostermann, 1951). On this point, see K.-O. Apel, "Sinnkonstitution und Geltungsrechtfertigung: Heidegger und das Problem der Transzendentalphilosophie," in Forum für Philosophie Bad Homburg, ed., *Martin Heidegger: Innen- und Aussenansichten* (Frankfurt a.M.: Suhrkamp, 1989), pp. 131–75. Abridged English translation: "Meaning-Constitution and Justification of Validity: Has Heidegger Overcome Transcendental Philosophy by History of Being?", in E. Agazzi, ed., *Entretiens sur Philosophie et Histoire* (Genova: 1990), pp. 127–46.

6. *Alētheia* is rendered by Heidegger as "disclosure" of the "being-there" or, in his later terminology, "unveiling" or "opening" of Being. In ancient Greek it signifies truth and its personification.

7. *WuM*, p. 280; cf. Apel, *Transformation der Philosophie* (see note 3), p. 46, fn. 70. Emphasis by K.-O. Apel.

8. See K.-O. Apel, "Szientismus oder transzendentale Hermeneutik: Zur Frage nach dem Subjekt der Zeicheninterpretation in der Semiotik des Pragmatismus" ("Scientism or Transcendental Hermeneutics: On the Question of Sign Interpretation in the Semiotic Theory of Pragmatism"), in R. Bubner, K. Cramer, R. Wiehl, eds., *Hermeneutik und Dialektik*, Festschrift for H.-G. Gadamer (Tübingen: Mohr, 1970), vol. 2, pp. 105–44.

9. I am not talking about the *idealistic utopia of complete transparency*, contrary to the suspicion frequently voiced by Gadamer.

10. This was and is even today the methodological precondition of the practicing humanities and arts *(Geisteswissenschaften)*, and of linguistics in particular.

11. This proof is mentioned by Gadamer. See *WuM*, p. 254.

12. This affects in particular its claim to superiority over modern, especially positivist and Kantian, epistemology and philosophy of science.

13. See on this issue J. Grondin, *Hermeneutische Wahrheit? Zum Wahrheitsbegriff Hans-Georg Gadamers (Hermeneutical Truth? On Hans-Georg Gadamer's Conception of Truth)* (Königstein: Forum Academicum, 1982).

14. Compare, however, the thorough revolutionizing of the common Heidegger interpretation by Cristina Lafont-Hurtado's excellent dissertation, *Sprache und Welterschliessung: Zur linguistischen Wende der Hermeneutik Heideggers (Speech or Language and Disclosure of the World: The Linguistic Turn of Heidegger's Hermeneutics)* (Frankfurt a.M., doctoral dissertation, 1992). The dissertation was published under the same title by Suhrkamp in Frankfurt in 1994; an English translation, *Language and World Disclosure*, is forthcoming in 1997 from Sage Publications.

15. Ernst Tugendhat, "Heideggers Idee von Wahrheit," presented in 1964, published in O. Pöggeler, ed., *Heidegger* (Berlin, 1969). See also E. Tugendhat, *Der Wahrheitsbegriff bei Husserl und Heidegger* (Berlin, 1967). See also Tugendhat's *Habilitationsschrift*, in which he elaborated his criticism of 1964.

16. It is not certain but highly probable that Heidegger was familiar with Tugendhat's criticism.

17. M. Heidegger, *Zur Sache des Denkens* (Tübingen, 1988), p. 76. Translation quoted from M. Heidegger, "The End of Philosophy and the Task of Thinking," in M. Heidegger, *On Time and Being*, ed. and trans. Joan Stambaugh (New York: Harper and Row, 1972), p. 69.

18. See M. Heidegger, *Vom Wesen der Wahrheit* (Frankfurt a.M., 1968), p. 97, where that equation which is "decisive" for *Sein und Zeit (Being and Time)* is stressed, that is, the equation of the "question [*SuZ*, 1927] of meaning, for example, of the scope of projection [*SuZ*, p. 97], i.e., of openness, i.e., of the truth of Being."

19. Heidegger, *Zur Sache des Denkens,* p. 77; "The End of Philosophy and the Task of Thinking," p. 70. See n. 17.

20. Heidegger, *Zur Sache des Denkens,* pp. 77f.; "The End of Philosophy and the Task of Thinking," p. 70.

21. Ibid.

22. See K.-O. Apel, *Transformation der Philosophie* (Frankfurt a.M.: Suhrkamp, 1973), vol. 2, part 2. English translation: *Towards a Transformation of Philosophy* (London: Routledge and Kegan Paul, 1980).

23. See C. Lafont-Hurtado, *Sprache und Welterschliessung,* n. 12 and pp. 241ff. See also K.-O. Apel, "Linguistic Meaning and Intentionality," in H. Silverman, D. Welton, eds., *Critical and Dialectical Phenomenology* (Albany: State University of New York Press, 1987), pp. 2–53. (Also in G. Deledalle, ed., *Semiotics and Pragmatics* [Amsterdam/Philadelphia: John Benjamins P.C., 1989], pp. 19–70); and in Apel, *Towards a Transcendental Semiotics* (Atlantic Highlands, N.J.: Humanities Press, 1994), pp. 132–75.

24. Or, between the *"Geisteswissenschaften"* and the "natural sciences," respectively. See K.-O. Apel, *Die Erklären: Verstehen-Kontroverse in transzendental-pragmatischer Sicht* (Frankfurt a.M.: Suhrkamp, 1979). English translation: *Understanding and Explanation: A Transcendental-Pragmatic Perspective* (Cambridge, Mass.: MIT Press, 1984). Also, K.-O. Apel, "Diltheys Unterscheidung von 'Erklären' und 'Verstehen' im Lichte der Ergebnisse der modernen Wissenschaftstheorie," in E.W. Orth, ed., *Dilthey und die Philosophie der Gegenwart* (Freiberg i.B.: Alber, 1985), pp. 285–347. Abridged English translation: "Dilthey's Distinction between 'Explanation' and 'Understanding' and the Possibility of Its 'Mediation'," in *Journal of the History of Philosophy* 25 (1987):131–50.

25. This is how I understand Gadamer's repeated explanations that, due to the point of view of "philosophical hermeneutics," the objectivistic and progressive conditions of methodologically oriented hermeneutics do not become totally invalidated.

26. See K.-O. Apel, *Diskurs und Verantwortung: Das Problem des Übergangs zur postkonventionellen Moral (Discourse and Responsibility: The Problem of the Transition to Postconventional Morality)* (Frankfurt a.M.: Suhrkamp, 1988), in particular index, "Neoaristotelismus" In addition, see Apel's "A Planetary Macroethics for Humankind: The Need, the Apparent Difficulty, and the Eventual Possibility," in E. Deutsch, ed., *Culture and Modernity: East-West Philosophical Perspectives* (Honolulu: University of Hawaii Press), pp. 261–78.

27. See Apel, Bormann, Bubner, Gadamer, Giegel, Habermas, *Hermeneutik und Ideologiekritik (Hermeneutics and Criticism of Ideology)* (Frankfurt a.M.: Suhrkamp, 1971).

28. See J. Habermas, "Vorbereitende Bemerkungen zu einer Theorie der kommunikativen Kompetenz" ("Preliminary Remarks on a Theory of Communicative Competence"), in J. Habermas, N. Luhmann, eds., *Theorie der Gesellschaft oder Sozialtechnologie? (Social Theory or Social Technology?)* (Frankfurt a.M.: Suhrkamp, 1971), pp. 101–41; "Was heisst Universalpragmatik?" ("What Is Universal Pragmatics?"), in K.-O. Apel, ed., *Sprachpragmatik und Philosophie* (Frankfurt a.M.: Suhrkamp, 1976), pp. 174–272; see also K.-O. Apel, "Pragmatics of Language and Transcendental Pragmatics of Language on the Question of Ethical Norms", ("Sprechakttheorie und transzendentale Sprachpragmatik zur Frage ethischer Normen," in K.-O. Apel, ed., *Sprachpragmatik und Philosophie,* pp. 10–173). See also Apel, "Die Logosauszeichnung der menschlichen Sprache," in H.-G. Boflhardt, ed., *Perspektiven auf Sprache* (Berlin: W. de Gruyter, 1986), pp. 45–87.

29. These are meant to include not only those of Freud or Marx, but also of Nietzsche, Foucault, and of Derrida's deconstructionism.

30. See K.-O. Apel, "Die Herausforderung der totalen Vernunftkritik und das Programm einer philosophischen Theorie der Rationalitätsstypen" ("The Challenge of the

Total Critique of Reason and the Program of a Philosophical Theory of the Types of Rationality"), in *Concordia* 11 (1987):2–23. English translation in D. Freundlieb, W. Hudson, eds., *Reason and Its Other* (1993).

31. See K.-O. Apel, "Sinnkonstitution und Geltungsrechtfertigung: Heidegger und das Problem der Transzendentalphilosophie" (see n. 5).

32. Compare the numerous references to Hegel in *WuM*.

33. Gadamer, however, placed very little value on this. Compare *WuM*, pp. 220 and 380.

34. These are methods that employ *external explanations* of motives. Not included, though, are the quasi-nomological behavioral sciences, which stand in the service of social technology. See K.-O. Apel, "Types of Social Science in the Light of Human Cognitive Interests," in *Social Research* 44 (1977):425–70. Reprinted in St. Brown, ed., *Philosophical Disputes in the Social Sciences* (Brighton: Harvester Press, 1979), pp. 3–50.

35. See M. Heidegger, *Sein und Zeit* (Halle: Niemeyer, 1941), p. 229.

36. Hans-Georg Gadamer, *Wahrheit und Methode* (1965), p. 327. English translation from *Truth and Method,* the second edition (New York: Continuum Publishing Corporation, 1975), pp. 308–9.

37. *WuM*, p. 327; *Truth and Method,* p. 308; emphasis by K.-O. Apel.

38. *WuM*, p. 424; *Truth and Method,* pp. 405–6.

39. Examples are Searle's theory of the background and ethical-political "communitarianism."

40. See A. MacIntyre, *After Virtue* (London: Duckworth, 1985); *Whose Justice? Which Rationality?* (London: Duckworth, 1988). Also R. Rorty, *Contingency, Irony, and Solidarity* (Cambridge: Cambridge University Press, 1989); *Objectivity, Relativism, and Truth* (Cambridge: Cambridge University Press, 1991). Also J. Habermas, *Erläuterungen zur Diskursethik* (Frankfurt a.M.: Suhrkamp), 1991, Namenregister. Also K.-O. Apel, *Diskurs und Verantwortung (Explications on Discourse Ethics and Responsibility),* Namenregister; "Das Anliegen des Kommunitarismus in der Sicht der (transzendental-pragmatischen) Diskursethik" ("The Matter of Concern of Communitarianism from the Point of View of [Transcendental-Pragmatic] Discourse Ethics"), in M. Brumlik, H. Brunkhorst, eds., *Gemeinschaft und Gerechtigkeit (Community and Justice)* (Frankfurt a.M.: Fischer, 1992).

41. See Theodor Litt, *Mensch und Welt: Grundlegung einer Philosophie des Geistes (Man and World: Foundations of a Philosophy of Mind)* (München: E. Reinhardt, 1948), pp. 214ff.

42. See K.-O. Apel, "Wittgenstein und Heidegger: Die Frage nach dem Sinn von Sein und der Sinnlosigkeitsverdacht gegen alle Metaphysik" ("Wittgenstein and Heidegger: The Question of the Meaning of Being and the Charge of Meaninglessness against All Metaphysics"), in *Transformation der Philosophie,* vol. 1, pp. 225–75 (see n. 20); in particular see pp. 272ff.; "Wittgenstein und Heidegger: Kritische Wiederholung eines Vergleichs" ("Wittgenstein and Heidegger: Critical Repetition of a Comparison"), in J. Habermas, ed., *Der Löwe spricht . . . und wir können ihn nicht verstehen (The Lion Is Speaking . . . and We Cannot Understand Him)* (Frankfurt a.M.: Suhrkamp, 1991), pp. 27–68, in particular pp. 28f., 53ff., and 65ff. English version in C. Macann, ed., *Martin Heidegger: Critical Assessments of Leading Philosophers* (London; New York: Routledge, 1992), vol. 3, pp. 341–437. Reprint in C. Macann, ed. *Critical Heidegger* (London: Routledge, 1996), pp. 241–44.

43. See E. Deutsch, ed., *Culture and Modernity,* n. 26.

44. Ibid.

45. See the cited works by J. Habermas and Apel at n. 28.

46. J.-F. Lyotard, *La condition postmoderne* (Paris: ed. de Minuit, 1979), p. 66.

47. See K.-O. Apel, *Diskurs und Verantwortung,* n. 24; also *Ethics and the Theory of Rationality* (Atlantic Highlands, N.J.: Humanities Press, 1996).

48. This claim should not be confused with the claims to rightness produced in *practical discourses,* in the form of *demands,* for example.

49. In fact, the presuppositions sketched here are without any pretensions to completeness.

50. See K.-O. Apel, *Diskurs und Verantwortung,* n. 24; also *Community, Language, and Ethics.*

51. See K.-O. Apel, "The Ecological Crisis as a Problem for Discourse Ethics," in A. Ofsti, ed., *Ecology and Ethics* (Trondheim: Nordland Akademi for Kunst og Vitenskap, 1992), pp. 219–60; "Discourse Ethics as a Response to the Novel Challenges of Today's Reality to Co-Responsibility," in *Journal of Religion* 73, no. 4 (1993): 496–513.

52. See K.-O. Apel, "Regulative Ideas or Sense-Events? An Attempt to Determine the Logos of Hermeneutics," in T.J. Stapleton, ed., *The Question of Hermeneutics: Essays in Honor of Joseph J. Kockelmans* (Dordrecht, The Netherlands: Kluwer, 199–), 37–39; "The Hermeneutical Dimension of Social Science and Its Normative Foundation," in *Man and World* 25, 3/4 (1992).

53. This was overlooked by Heidegger.

54. See I. Lakatos, "History of Science and Its Rational Reconstructions," in *Boston Studies in the History of Science* 8 (1971):91–136. German translation in W. Diederich, ed., *Theorien der Wissenschaftsgeschichte* (Frankfurt a.M.: Suhrkamp, 1974), pp. 55–119.

55. See Heidegger, *Sein und Zeit,* p. 153, n. 35.

REPLY TO KARL-OTTO APEL

I am especially grateful to Karl-Otto Apel that he has shown himself to be ready to engage in a fundamental confrontation with my hermeneutic philosophy. Both of us are really no longer young people who are able to adapt themselves to and so learn another style of speaking and thinking.

This is still the case between us although we have been engaged in the process of the give and take of confrontation for a long time. Our confrontation began with Apel's early work *Über die Idee der Sprache von Dante bis Vico* (1964). This book was primarily inspired by Heidegger, and I took it up in those days of my hermeneutic studies after the publication of *Truth and Method*. Now in the contribution to this volume Apel describes what disturbs him in my thought, namely, the "strange [or curious] primacy of the past over the future" (quotation from text).

This, however, must astonish me. The future which we do not know is supposed to take primacy over the past? Is it not the past which has stamped us permanently through its effective history? If we seek to illuminate this history we may be able to make ourselves conscious of and overcome some of the prejudices which have determined us. To Apel the matter seems to look quite different. In this respect I am supposed to ascribe a "legitimizing authority" to the past. He believes himself to be able to read (*herauslesen*) this claim into my sentence with which I take up the well-known proposition that one has to understand an author better than he understood himself. I attempted to mitigate this sentence by saying that one should not understand an author better. One should only understand the author differently if one is to understand the author at all. This decision seems to provoke Apel. In opposition to this decision Apel appeals to the autonomy of the reason of the interpreter and then he is on the lookout for transcendental ideas. To be sure, Apel concedes to me that it can often be the case that one persistently understands the other somewhat differently than the other understands him- or herself. But this, according to Apel, simply is not real understanding.

Here I wonder whether he abandons too quickly the possibility which Heidegger opened up: to think being as time. My proposition really only meant that there are many perspectives of understanding. If someone looked at things in the same way as oneself does, something would simply be repeated. This would not contribute anything new at all. It is true that I indeed do not dare to speak of progress with respect to understanding. In that case, too much regress could result. One perspective darkens the other. A universal perspective comprising everything is a contradiction in itself which at most the metaphysical concept of God could assume. Wanting to understand an author better, even better than he understands himself, would eventually render all communication impossible. Apel then wants to do justice to me and thus he refers to the productive role of the distance between ages in order to understand me correctly. Admittedly, that is a point I make in the first section of *Truth and Method* which does not entirely satisfy me. The systematic treatment of history was too much on my mind there. Later, I indicated that we are not only dealing with the distance between ages but more so with the otherness of the other which makes one reflective. Apel wants to rescue progress in understanding and does so by referring it back to reflection. If by this he only means the use of reason in general, all communication certainly presupposes such a use. This simply lies in the fact that one understands the other. So I went beyond the emphasis on the distance between ages in my works and thus I went further along a path which, it seems to me, comes close to the path Apel went with discourse ethics. Yet a difference remains.

Apel now makes a different distinction. The 'hermeneutics in performance' which I sketched out deals with the understanding of meaning. But, according to Apel, we must be concerned with the correct knowledge of innerworldly things, and for this he appeals to Peirce and his transcendental pragmatics of language. It is difficult for me to see this task assigned to philosophy at all. To be sure, I certainly do not regard the experience of the lifeworld as if all of us in our lifeworld did not need science and its progress. But how can I transfer that to philosophy? What can progress in philosophy mean? Could progress in the human sciences be such a progress? And is progress in terms of the happiness of humanity supposed to result from this? In any case, the concept of progress here seems to me to be fundamentally different from the one which is valid in the natural sciences and their concept of objectivity. No natural scientist would doubt that there is progress in natural research when he takes note of the measurable results of a colleague and is able to establish a new theory based upon them.

Understanding in the human sciences, however, is a quite different matter. In order to understand one another we certainly need the attempt at communication, where communication means reciprocity in understanding the arguments of both interlocutors. But whether communication in the sense of agreement and concurrence will result from this, or whether communication fails, the hermeneutic virtue consists above all in understanding the other without which no possible communication could come about at all. To me this seems to be a necessary distinction, and in this respect I feel that I have been misunderstood by Apel. In the end one certainly also wants to convince the other and in order for this to occur some sort of factual reference (*Sachreferenz*) is required, and it is for the sake of this that we take a philosophical interest in the human sciences at all. One does not want to "understand historically" mere opinions of the other or of the text.

If I am not mistaken, Apel here took the 'ontological difference' too lightly. I regret this all the more since in studying his contribution I discovered many things we have in common, in particular we have both worked to develop the conditions under which it is possible to really understand what an other has meant. We are always dealing with questions of fact (*Sachfragen*) even in the history of philosophy. This must also hold for that which interests philosophy in the other human sciences. Likewise, with respect to the expressive power of art; in other words, the different answers a work of art gives us have nothing to do with relativism. I am not sufficiently familiar with the American philosophy of Peirce and Royce to which Apel appeals. I have sought my philosophical orientation primarily in Greek philosophy and its language. An interest in the progress of science certainly belongs to this, and I have certainly studied Wittgenstein and the *Transformation of Philosophy*. But this did not displace my orientation to Plato and to an Aristotle seen with the eyes of Plato. The doctrine of the inseparability of *ēthos* and *phronēsis* remains fundamental. This holds for Plato's ideal republic as well as for the ethics and politics of Aristotle, and even for a Kant who has been correctly understood.

With this *Testimonium Paupertatis* I have to think through Apel's positive proposal which demands a truly transcendental hermeneutic supposedly superior to all traditions, religious attitudes (*Vorprägungen*), and historical destinies in the life of humanity. This then would be a kind of completed enlightenment. Apparently, this would require a world revolution of pure reason.

But then solidarity would be found only in a world of pure reason, and only through reason would solidarity find its motivation. But then I must ask: would that be the case even for religious life, even without the deeply rooted antipathy to foreigners that one often finds, even for the search for solutions to ecological problems, even for respect of human rights? Should philosophy be able to solve such problems, problems which, in truth, must be borne by the lived solidarity that is alive or should be alive in every culture? It would be just as likely that a stabilization of the world's climate could occur by means of a type of global air conditioning. Could one possibly think such a society of the future? Can one create a solidarity which rests solely upon communal interests? In light of what humanity is and has become, it seems to me to be more sensible for us to take the advice that Aristotle is said to have given Alexander the Great: "To be a Greek to the Greeks, a Persian to the Persians."

H.-G.G.

2

Roderick M. Chisholm

GADAMER AND REALISM: REACHING AN UNDERSTANDING

INTRODUCTION

Philosophy, as Professor Gadamer has emphasized throughout his career, is essentially a dialogue, a mutual attempt to reach an understanding, a *"Verständigung."* Success in such an attempt requires what he calls an adequate setting forth, or *Auslegung,* so that the other can understand one's own position and relate it to his own. In the "Reflections on My Philosophical Journey," which Gadamer prepared for the present volume, he remarks that there are "quite viable bridges between American philosophy and hermeneutics." I write this essay with the hope of contributing toward such a bridge—a bridge not so much between American philosophy and hermeneutics, but between philosophical realism and hermeneutics.

I shall consider, in particular, the realism that is represented in the German-speaking philosophical world by such philosophers as Bolzano, Robert Zimmerman, Brentano, Twardowski, Meinong, and Marty. For here we find a way of continuing the important work that Gadamer has begun.

In early Christian theology, "hermeneutics" was the name for the study of the exegesis and interpretation of texts. Such study involved the formulation of rules of exegesis—rules for the interpretation of biblical texts and rules for filling in "gaps" in the laws. So conceived, hermeneutics was, as Gadamer says, merely an "ancillary" discipline.[1] But, according to Gadamer's own view, hermeneutics is essentially *philosophical* and is also essential *to* philosophy. The hermeneutics that he develops involves two quite different phases. The first is the concern with a type of truth or fact that can be made familiar to us all but which is not known by the natural sciences. The second phase of hermeneutics involves the interpretation of such facts. In addition to their immediate or direct significance, they serve, in a way in which no other type of fact can serve, to extend our knowledge beyond ourselves.

THE FIRST PHASE: THE DATA OF HERMENEUTICS

How are we to describe the facts from which hermeneutics sets out? Gadamer says that "the clearest witness for the claim that there is truth to be found outside of modern science lies in the experience of art."[2] Using a terminology that Gadamer himself might be reluctant to accept, I would set forth this passage in the following theses.

There are two quite different types of truth or fact: those that are propositional and those that are truths of direct *acquaintance.* The truths or facts that constitute the findings of the natural sciences are propositional. Those that constitute the data of the *Geisteswissenschaften,* or humanistic sciences, are not propositional. Of those facts that are nonpropositional, the most significant are the ones that are derived from the direct acquaintance with a work of art; in having such aesthetic experience, we know what the mystery and profundity of the world ("the hermeneutic universe") is really like.

It is tempting to say that such nonpropositional truth is essentially *subjective,* but the word "subjective" can be seriously misleading. In one of its senses, it takes on the role that is played by such modifiers as "ostensible," "supposed," and "so-called," thus depriving the term "truth," or the term "fact," of its ordinary sense and suggesting that the reference is *not* to what can be called truths or facts at all. It is also tempting to contrast such truths or facts with those of "science." What Gadamer wishes to stress, however, is that they fall within the sphere of the humanistic sciences. The subject matter of these sciences is "something quite different from what it is in the investigation of nature."[3] "Truths of inner experience" may be less misleading than its alternatives. For there are certain truths about experiences which can be known only by *having* those experiences. Such truths are *internal* to the experiences themselves. Thomas Nagel has stressed the gulf between what he calls "the objective viewpoint" and that of "the subject of experience." He observes that reality is not just objective reality. "Sometimes, in the philosophy of mind, but also elsewhere, the truth is not to be found by travelling as far away from one's personal perspective as possible."[4]

The point that here concerns Gadamer can also be made by saying that there is more to the world than what is sometimes called "objective reality." Gadamer makes an especially helpful remark in one of his essays on the nature of art. He considers the seventeenth-century view, according to which art should serve to "imitate nature." And he says that "in the complete work of art, . . . nature itself is presented": we have before us *the real thing* and not just an imitation.[5] The starting place of Gadamer's hermeneutics is, in fact, the experience of *certain* works of art—those that present us with what is profound and mysterious about the world. "So the world is like *this,* too!" But a further point should be made. Nonpropositional acquaintance is not at all restricted to what is lofty and profound. And to know what acquaintance itself is, we should also consider experiences of quite a different sort.

William James had described the distinction between nonpropositional and propositional knowledge as being a distinction between "the *what* and the *that,*" and said: "No relation-expressing proposition is possible except on the basis of a preliminary acquaintance with such 'facts,' with such contents, as this. Let [it] be fragrance, let it be toothache, let it be a more complex kind of feeling, like that of the full moon swimming in her blue abyss."[6]

It is important to realize, finally, that by their very nature, indefinitely many nonpropositional truths or facts remain inaccessible to us. Nagel observes, for example, that "we will not know exactly how scrambled eggs taste to the cockroach even if we develop a detailed objective phenomenology of the cockroach's sense of taste."[7] This example—"how scrambled eggs taste to a cockroach"—is quite unlike those to be found in Gadamer's writings; but for that very reason it performs a useful service. The nonobjective truths with which hermeneutics is concerned are not restricted to what may be found in art and in religious experience.

There is another, more positive point to be made about the hermeneutic experience. It is not restricted to what is sensory; it contains *nonsensory* features from which we are able to derive such concepts as those of *beauty* and *fittingness*. This is one of the points that had been investigated in detail by Meinong.

In his important but very difficult work, *On Emotional Presentation* (1917), Meinong observes that, whereas sensation and perception in the ordinary sense of these words may be said to involve *thought-contents,* the apprehension of our own *emotional states* and those of others involves *feeling-contents.* He writes:

> That these are more than mere possibilities is shown by some everyday attributions, as when people talk about a refreshing bath, fresh air, oppressive heat, disturbing noise, beautiful color, stories that are funny or sad, boring or entertaining stories, sublime works of art, valuable people, good resolutions, etc. There is no question as to the close relationship of such attributes to our feelings. And there is no question that these attributes are fully analogous to other properties which are familiarly presented by ideas. When I say "The sky is blue" and then say "The sky is beautiful," a property is attributed to the sky in either case. In the second case a feeling participates in the apprehension of the property, as in the first case, an idea does. And it is natural to let the feeling be the presentative factor in the second case, as an idea is always taken to be in the first case.[8]

This passage should be compared with what Gadamer has to say about the experience of beauty. In the translators' preface to the second edition of *Truth and Method,* Gadamer's view is put this way: "When something is 'beautiful,' its appearance strikes us with immediate self-evidence as valid. It 'appears' or 'shines,' as a 'phenomenon,' and even though it may be a 'mere' appearance, it may also have that special validity that we call the 'beautiful'" (xvii).

THE SECOND PHASE: WHAT THE DATA INDICATE

I have said that "the hermeneutic consciousness," according to Gadamer, has two distinct phases: the one is a concern with those important truths that are unknown to the natural sciences; and the second is the concern with the fact that such truths may put us in contact with *other* individual things.

Gadamer has said that hermeneutics is not concerned with the formulation of *"rules"*; but he was referring to rules for the interpretation of texts and legal systems. He tells us that, when he set to work on *Truth and Method,* his concern was "to work out the *principles* of a philosophical hermeneutics."[9] The formulation of such principles belongs to the second phase of the hermeneutic enterprise. These principles are what indicates the relevance of hermeneutics to philosophical realism.

In his foreword to the second edition of *Truth and Method,* Gadamer writes, "The experience of the Thou manifests the paradox that something standing over and against us asserts its own rights and requires its own recognition, and in that very process is 'understood'" (xxxv).

The experience of *sympathy,* Gadamer goes on to tell us, is a source of insight into the nature of the other; and sympathy may be viewed as a "form of love."[10] Here he refers, appropriately, to Max Scheler's work. Alfred Schuetz formulates Scheler's conclusions in a way that is especially instructive from the point of view of a realistic hermeneutics. Writing on Scheler's "Theory of the Perception of Other Minds" *("Wahrnehmungstheorie des fremden Ich"),* Schuetz says:

> But what else shall we perceive of the other than its body and its gestures? Scheler thinks that we certainly perceive in the other's smile his joy, in his tears his suffering, in his blushing his shame, in his joined hands his praying, in the sounds of his words his thought—all this without empathy and without any inference by analogy. We start reasoning only if we feel induced to distrust our perceptions of the other's experiences—as, e.g., if we feel we have misunderstood him or if we discover that we have to deal with an insane individual. But even those "inferences" are based on perceptions of the other which are rather complicated. In looking at him I not only perceive his eyes, but also that he looks at me, and even that he does so as if he would prevent my knowing that he looks at me.[11]

In 1785, Thomas Reid had seen the epistemological significance of *Verstehen* as providing us with immediate experiences that point to the existence of thinking substances other than ourselves. "Certain features of the countenance, sounds of the voice, and gestures of the body" indicate certain psychological properties of the person whose body it is. This fact confers positive epistemic status upon the proposition that the person in question does have those psychological properties.[12]

What is of first importance to the realist is the fact that, if the immediate experience of *Verstehen* can thus point to the existence of *persons* other than ourselves, then there can be analogous experiences that point to the existence of still other types of substance—for example, to physical things, including physical things beyond our own bodies.

In describing this situation, Meinong said that the objects of perceptual judgments acquire *presumptive* evidence *(Vermutungsevidenz)*. If you judge that you are looking at a garden that is surrounded by trees, then this fact makes it *prima facie* evident that you *are* looking at a garden that is surrounded by trees. The qualification "presumptive" was intended to suggest that the judgment may have such evidence without thereby being true. This suggestion has had considerable impact upon subsequent epistemology.[13] In applying similar considerations to memory, he went on to say that a certain type of ostensible memory, what one might call "mnemic taking," confers positive epistemic status upon the proposition or state of affairs which is the object of that taking.[14]

To see the possibilities of extending, within hermeneutics, the scope of epistemological principles such as those we have been considering, we should consider the full significance of the following passage:

> [An] ancient image of the gods that was displayed in a temple as a work of art in order to give aesthetic, reflective pleasure, and is now shown in a museum, retains, even as it stands before us today, the world of religious experience from which it came; the important consequence is that its world still belongs to ours. What embraces both is the hermeneutic universe.[15]

MUST HERMENEUTICS BE KANTIAN?

Gadamer speaks of "the epoch-making result" of the *Critique of Pure Reason:* it "destroyed metaphysics as a purely rational science of the world." The result, he says, was "the end of metaphysics." But not all philosophers are convinced that Kant *has* shown that metaphysics as a purely rational science is impossible. There are many who still believe that it is premature to speak of the end of metaphysics.

As we have seen, the relation between the self, or subject of experience, and the other is central to all of hermeneutics. Let us try to see what Kant succeeds in proving to us about the *subject* of experience. Much turns on what is said in connection with the so-called "paralogism of substantiality" in the *Critique of Pure Reason.* Kant writes,

> The 'I' is indeed in all thoughts, but there is not in this representation the least trace of intuition, distinguishing the 'I' from other objects of intuition.[16]

Kant appeals to this proposition in order to show that the fact of intentionality does not imply the existence of a subject of experience. His reasoning may be put as follows:

(1) If we have no concept of a thinking subject, then the existence of such a subject cannot be inferred from our consciousness.

(2) We have a concept of a given type of thing only if we have an *empirical* or *sensory* concept of that type of thing.
(3) But we have no empirical or sensory concept of the thinking subject. Therefore
(4) the existence of a thinking subject cannot be inferred from our consciousness.

The crux of the argument is the second premise—what we may call Kant's *empirical* premise. Like many other philosophers of his time, Kant assumed that one is aware of the existence of a thing only if one has an *empirical* or *sensory* concept of that thing. The assumption was shared by those philosophers whom we think of as being "empiricists"—for example, by Hume and Mach, as well as by the members of the Vienna Circle prior to the turn to "physicalism." Noting, then, that we have no empirical or sensory concept of ourselves, Kant concluded that we are not *aware* of ourselves. But to see that Kant's conclusion is problematic, we have only to consider the nature of intentionality.

What Kant says about the experience of the *self*, or the subject, can also be said about the experience of any of our *intentional* properties. There is *no* sensory intuition of judging; there is no sensory intuition of wondering or doubting or hoping or questioning. I now hope, for example, that those who read what I am writing will understand what it is that I am trying to say. And in entertaining this hope now, I do find a certain set of sensory images. But these images need not be the ones that I have entertained at other times when I had such a hope and they need not be the ones that I have next time I have it. For there is no sensory mark of hoping for so-and-so—whatever so-and-so may be. There is *no* sensory content that is either a necessary or a sufficient logical condition for hoping that so-and-so.

And, of course, the other intentional attitudes are analogous. We may say of judging, wondering, loving, hating, and all the other intentional attitudes exactly what Kant had said about the self: "Our awareness of hoping or judging is not accompanied by any *sensory intuition* of hoping or judging." If Kant's reasoning were sound, then we would have to say that there are no intentional attitudes.

We should consider, however, another type of phenomenological datum—one that Gadamer has investigated in detail. I am referring to those experiences that illustrate what has traditionally been called "the unity of consciousness." Kant, himself, suggests the data in question when he sets forth his "second paralogism," the one pertaining to the simplicity of the soul. He writes: "Representations (for example, the single words of a verse), distributed among different beings, never make up a whole thought."[17]

Here is what Gadamer says about the kind of *reflection* that may be involved in listening to a melody:

> If I hear a note, then the primary object of hearing is obviously the note; but I am also aware of a hearing of the note *[ein Hören des Tones ist mir auch bewusst]* and

this hearing is not simply an object of subsequent reflection. It is a reflection that accompanies the hearing and goes on along side of it. *Qua* note that is heard, a note is such that my hearing of it is always there within it *[immer mit darin]*. And this is what one reads in Aristotle.[18]

Robert Zimmerman, one of the associates of Bolzano, suggests a further development of the example, extending it to other senses.[19] We imagine that you are watching a parade and are concerned to find out whether the people who are marching are keeping time with the music. If you find that they *are* in step, then the following intentional properties are exemplified: that of *seeing* the people marching; that of *hearing* the music being played; that of *comparing* the visual and the auditory experience; and that of *judging* that the people whom you see are keeping time with the music. How could this be—*unless* the one who is hearing is identical with the one who is seeing, and, further, unless the one who is making the judgment about the seeing and the hearing is identical with the one who is seeing and with the one who is hearing?

Gadamer, in emphasizing what he calls "the crucial importance of Kant's critique of any substantiality doctrine," refers to "the importance of the transcendental unity of self-consciousness, the synthetic unity of apperception."[20] But if we reject Kant's critique of substantialism, as I believe we should, and if we view the subject of experience realistically, then we will also interpret "the unity of self-consciousness" realistically. Zimmerman, in setting forth the above account, said that he was developing "an ideal view of the world based upon a realistic foundation."

In discussing Husserl's phenomenology, Gadamer sets forth in detail the "opposition between realism and idealism" that Husserl never satisfactorily overcame.[21] And in discussing Dilthey, Gadamer points out in detail the extent to which Dilthey had made use of the insights of Brentano.[22] It should not be difficult to construct a bridge between the two traditions.

CATEGORIAL INTUITION AND THE SUBJECT

Writing about Dilthey, Gadamer refers, approvingly, to the suggestion that philosophy "give up its old claim to be knowledge through concepts."[23] The remark, however, is easily misunderstood. Gadamer means that knowledge through concepts is not *sufficient* to constitute philosophy. Like Heidegger before him, he was impressed by what Husserl had called "categorial intuition."[24] The concept is a Cartesian one. If we view our experience as Descartes had done, we will assume that anyone who is capable of asking epistemological questions is also capable of *understanding* them and is, therefore, a *rational* being. Such a person, Descartes said, is able to "conceive things that are purely intelligible," such *abstracta* as properties or attributes.[25] And in conceiving these things, one is able to distinguish one from another and to see just what it is that they logically require in order to be exemplified. This is the function of a "categorial intuition."

A person, Descartes tells us, is able to grasp or conceive the nature of experience. And in grasping or conceiving this nature, one is able to know, with respect to certain intentional properties, (i) that these properties are exemplified and (ii) that they are necessarily such that they can be exemplified only by individual things or substances.

Does this mean that there is a subject to be found "*in* experience?" The preposition "in" is dangerous here, as the traditional term, "intentional *inexistence,"* may suggest. Our experience cannot be said to *represent* its subject—if we take the term "representation" in its original sense. As Gadamer points out, "to represent" means to be a *representative of.* You represent another person if you are that person's *Stellvertreter,* as the vice president may, on occasion, *take the place* of the president.[26] The point is, the subject is not to be found *in* the experience in the way in which a *copy* or *representative* of a thing may be found *in* an experience. But the experience is *of* the subject.

Gadamer observes, quite correctly, that "givenness in intentional experiences . . . constitutes a new dimension of research."[27] I would put the matter this way. What we find in any experience, in any *Erlebnis,* is a subject *being in* a certain state. There *is* the subject and there *is* the state in which the subject finds himself. But it would not be accurate to say that the *Erlebnis* is directed, in the same way, on each of two different objects, the one object being the *subject* of the experience and the other being a *state* of that subject. We do not find a subject *together with,* or *alongside of,* a state, as we may find one state (say, the state of hearing) together with, or alongside of, another state (the state of seeing). If *this* were the way in which we experience the subject, then one could well say that the subject is a "bloodless abstraction."[28]

What would it be to have an experience wherein the subject does *not* appear as a "bloodless abstraction"? Surely the paradigm case of such an experience is that wherein one experiences oneself *as being* in a certain state. And I believe that Gadamer would not be entirely unreceptive to this conclusion. He tells us, after all, that "Brentano's distinction, traceable to Aristotle, of the objective awareness of objectivating reflection is superior to the heritage of German idealism."[29] I would not presume to suggest that Professor Gadamer give up his Kantian position. I mean only to point out that what he tells us about hermeneutics is not philosophically *dependent* upon that position. One *need* not be a Kantian in order to accept and to appreciate the philosophical significance of Gadamer's hermeneutics. A realist can work together with Gadamer in this philosophical enterprise.[30]

RODERICK M. CHISHOLM

BROWN UNIVERSITY
APRIL 1992

NOTES

1. Hans-Georg Gadamer, *Truth and Method,* second revised edition, trans. Joel Weinsheimer and Donald G. Marshall (New York: Crossroad Publishing Corporation, 1990), p. 505.

2. Hans-Georg Gadamer, "Hermeneutics," in Raymond Klibanski, ed., *Contemporary Philosophy: A Survey* (Florence: La Nuova Italia Editrice, 1969), p. 22.

3. Gadamer, *Truth and Method,* p. 221.

4. Thomas Nagel, "What is It Like to Be a Bat?", in *The View from Nowhere* (Oxford: The University Press, 1986), pp. 25–27.

5. See the essay "Kunst und Nachahmung," in Gadamer's *Kleine Schriften,* vol. 2, *Interpretationen* (Tübingen: J. C. B. Mohr, 1967), p. 18.

6. William James, *The Meaning of Truth* (New York: Longmans Green and Co., 1932), p. 14.

7. Nagel, p. 27.

8. Alexius Meinong, *On Emotional Presentation,* ed. and trans. Marie Schubert-Kalsi (Evanston: Northwestern University Press, 1972), pp. 28–29. The original appears in vol. 3 of the *Alexius Meinong Gesamtausgabe,* ed. Rudolff Haller and Rudolf Kindinger (Graz: Akademische Druck- und Verlagsanstalt, 1972), pp. 316–17.

9. Hans-Georg Gadamer, *Philosophical Apprenticeships* (Cambridge: MIT Press, 1985), p. 146; my italics.

10. Gadamer, *Truth and Method,* p. 233.

11. Alfred Schuetz, "Scheler's Theory of Intersubjectivity and the General Thesis of the Alter Ego," *Philosophy and Phenomenological Research,* 2 (1942): 323–47; the quotation is from p. 334. Schuetz is here setting forth the theory as expounded by Scheler in *Wesen und Formen der Sympathie* (1923).

12. See Reid's *Essays on the Intellectual Powers of Man,* essay 5, chap. 5, in Sir William Hamilton, ed., *The Works of Thomas Reid* (Edinburgh: Machlachlan and Stewart, 1854), esp. pp. 459–60.

13. See Meinong's *Über die Erfahrungsgrundlagen unseres Wissens* (1910), in the Meinong *Gesamt Ausgabe,* vol. 5 (Graz: Akademische Druck- und Verlagsanstalt, 1973), pp. 438, 456–59.

14. See Alexius Meinong, "Toward an Epistemological Assessment of Memory" (1996), in Roderick M. Chisholm and Robert J. Swartz, eds., *Empirical Knowledge: Readings from Contemporary Sources* (Englewood Cliffs, N.J.: Prentice-Hall, Inc., 1973), pp. 253–70. This work appears in volume 10 of the *Gesamt Ausgabe* (1971), pp. 185–218.

15. Gadamer, *Truth and Method,* p. xxxi.

16. Kant, *Critique of Pure Reason,* ed. Norman Kemp Smith (London: Macmillan, 1933), p. 434 (A350). Kemp Smith puts quotes around the word "I," but there are no such quotes in the material being translated. The passage begins: "Denn das Ich ist zwar in allen Gedanken. . . ."

17. Ibid., p. 335 (A352).

18. Hans-Georg Gadamer, "Die philosophischen Grundlagen des zwanzigsten Jahrhunderts" (1965), in *Gesammelte Werke,* vol. 4, part 2 (Tübingen: J. C. B. Mohr: 1987), pp. 5–22; the quotation is from p. 16. Gadamer here refers to *De Anima* 417b19–23, 426b7ff.

19. See Robert Zimmerman, *Anthroposophie im Unriss: Entwurf eines Systems idealer Weltaufsicht auf realistischer Grundlage* (Vienna: Wilhelm Baumüller, 1882). Zimmerman's earlier statement of the unity of consciousness may be found in the first edition of his *Philosophische Propaedeutik für Obergymnasien* (Vienna: Wilhelm Braumüller,

1852), pp. 7–26. Brentano was later to make use of Zimmerman's example. See Franz Brentano, *Psychology from an Empirical Standpoint* (London: Routledge and Kegan Paul, 1973), pp. 155–76; this work was first published in 1874.

20. Gadamer, *Truth and Method*, p. 67.

21. See Gadamer's "Die phänomenologische Bewegung" (1963), in *Gesammelte Werke*, volume 4, part 2, pp. 105–46, esp. pp. 106–12.

22. See Gadamer's "Das Problem Diltheys: Zwischen Romantik und Positivismus" (1984), in *Gesammelte Werke*, volume 4, part 2, pp. 408–28, esp. pp. 412–13. The topic of Gadamer's essay—Dilthey as falling between romanticism and positivism—continues to be of considerable philosophical interest. See the issue of *Topoi* devoted to the topic "Continental Philosophy Revisited," ed. Kevin Mulligan: *Topoi: An International Review of Philosophy*, vol. 10 (1991). Dilthey and Brentano are discussed in the editor's introduction, "On the History of Continental Philosophy," pp. 115–20; see p. 119.

23. Gadamer, *Truth and Method*, p. 229.

24. Gadamer, *Philosophical Apprenticeships*, p. 47.

25. See René Descartes, *The Principles of Philosophy*, part 1, sec. 32.

26. See Gadamer's informative discussion in "The Ontological Valence of the Picture," in *Truth and Method*, pp. 137–44.

27. Gadamer, *Truth and Method*, p. 245.

28. Gadamer uses this expression in discussing Dilthey and Descartes; see *Truth and Method*, p. 506.

29. Gadamer, *Philosophical Apprenticeships*, p. 184.

30. I wish to express my thanks to Johann C. Marek and to Kevin Mulligan.

REPLY TO RODERICK M. CHISHOLM

Maybe I should weigh my points as carefully as I am being led step by step in this contribution by Mr. Chisholm until I reach the point I am really waiting for. When reading this contribution I quickly became aware that the first influences of my youth in Breslau (1918/1919) are being revived here. In those days as a beginner I attended a seminar by Richard Hönigswald, and I heard the names of Brentano and Meinong from him even more often than those of Kant and Husserl. Thus, while studying Meinong, I soon began to gain a critical distance to the then dominant Neo-Kantianism. Then, thanks to Paul Natorp and Nicolai Hartmann, I was able to concentrate on philosophy more generally in Breslau, and then in Marburg. The project I was engaged in I called, quite ignorantly, "phenomenology," and I particularly admired Max Scheler, some of whose lectures I had heard in Marburg. Despite this, I resisted the transcendental framework of Husserl's *Ideas.* This resistance was not so unusual in those days, and Nicolai Hartmann, with whom I aligned myself in particular and from whom I also heard the name of Meinong fairly often, explicitly supported this. In those days Hartmann was already in the process of separating himself from the transcendental idealism in which he had been educated in Marburg. What also gained significance and contributed to the reinforcement of my resistance to Husserl's *Ideas* was that I was quite captivated by Heidegger's early lectures. Thus, when *Sein und Zeit* appeared in 1926, the transcendental framework of that book came as quite a surprise. That did not at all correspond to the expectations cultivated during my years of philosophical apprenticeship with Heidegger and Aristotle. In those days, I tried to avoid all theoretical construction, especially with respect to the ethical and anthropological writings of Aristotle, in order to stay close to phenomena.

To be sure, in moral philosophy I had to play the role of a defender of Kant against Scheler and Hartmann but otherwise, thanks to my philological and literary inclinations, I remained closer to Greek philosophy than to transcendental idealism. Since the publication of the early Freiburg lectures, I see that when I undertook a defense of the sense of performance *(Vollzugs-Sinn)* and especially the truth of art, I was making a connection with the early Heidegger. Much later I came across similar paths when I came to know Alfred Schütz and also Roman Ingarden. In my eyes it is an honor that my works find friendly attention in Mr. Chisholm's contribution, so that a bridge becomes recognizable between the very first inspirations of my youth in Breslau and hermeneutics.

H.-G. G.

3

David C. Hoy

POST-CARTESIAN INTERPRETATION: HANS-GEORG GADAMER AND DONALD DAVIDSON

Interpretation is the central phenomenon analyzed by the German philosophical tradition of hermeneutics. Both Martin Heidegger and Hans-Georg Gadamer have built their philosophies on an argument that human understanding is only ever interpretive, and that philosophy must abandon the Cartesian hope of finding an uninterpreted foundation for all the rest of our beliefs. However, the Continental tradition is not alone in this anti-Cartesian insistence that interpretation goes "all the way down." Donald Davidson has also developed an anti-Cartesian theory that starts from the notion of "radical interpretation." In the present paper I will argue that the hermeneutic account of interpretation can enter into a dialogue with the Davidsonian account, and more specifically, I will draw on some of Davidson's arguments to defend Gadamer's hermeneutic theory against its critics, including not only those who charge it with being relativistic, but also those deconstructionist critics who see hermeneutics as too tradition bound.

In particular, there are two difficulties facing hermeneutic philosophy that I will draw on Davidson's arguments to clarify. The first is the metaphilosophical question whether the hermeneutic assertion of the universality of interpretation is paradoxical. Hermeneutics asserts the universal claim that all human understanding is interpretive. Does hermeneutics thereby exempt this claim itself, since the claim seems to be asserted categorically, or at least as something stronger than an interpretation? This problem emerges specifically for Gadamer, who insists on the universality of his hermeneutic philosophy of language. Philosophical hermeneutics makes universal claims because it investigates language, and understanding requires at least the capacity for language. The universality (or at least the centrality) of language is summed up in Gadamer's famous phrase, "Being that can be understood is language."[1]

Language, furthermore, is always contextualized, as is philosophy itself: "Philosophizing, too, does not start from zero but rather has to think further following the language we speak."[2] This contextualization leads to the second problem, for if in practice understanding is always interpretive, can any given understanding believe in its own cogency at the same time that it believes that other sound interpretations of the same phenomena are also possible? This problem is closely connected to the first, for hermeneutic philosophy itself may seem to be an interpretation that is claiming to be more than an interpretation. Both problems surface frequently in the literature on Gadamer. In the following two sections I will describe how Davidson's approach can help a defender of Gadamer's hermeneutics confront each of these persistent problems.

THE UNIVERSALITY OF HERMENEUTICS

Since there is no historical connection between Gadamer and Davidson, one might think that it is only accidental that they both feature the notion of interpretation so centrally. Davidson's account starts from an analysis of what he calls "radical interpretation." His term goes beyond Quine's notion of radical translation, as I will explain below. First, however, I would like to show how one could derive a similar notion from the German hermeneutic tradition. The way I will get to a hermeneutic notion of radical interpretation will seem completely unrelated to Davidson's. However, I hope that once I have explained how and why such a notion emerges in the German tradition, some useful connections will become apparent despite these differing origins.

To begin to bridge Gadamer's and Davidson's different philosophical styles and backgrounds, I will draw a distinction between two different senses of interpretation. This distinction will reflect Heidegger's own tendency in *Being and Time* to use two different terms for interpretation, *Auslegung* and *Interpretierung*.[3] Typically, *Auslegung* involves ordinary, everyday skills like hammering, typing, driving, and conversing. But Heidegger also suggests that *Being and Time* is itself an interpretation, and in this case he uses the term *Interpretierung*. His philosophy is thus an interpretation of interpretation, or more precisely, an *Interpretierung* (a systematic, reflective interpretation) of *Auslegung* (the everyday activity of ordinary interpretation). These two forms of interpretation are distinguishable, but they are not different in kind. Philosophical *Interpretierung* is itself a form of *Auslegung*, although a more articulated, explicit, reflective, or "theoretical" form. *Interpretierung* is also reflexive in the sense that it can investigate itself to discover conditions that also obtain in *Auslegung*. What leads me to say that *Interpretierung* is more *radical* than *Auslegung* is that *Interpretierung*, at least the thoroughgoing kind evidenced in *Being and Time*, requires one to think about how any particular case of naive or ordinary interpretation could take place. Heidegger's "radical," philosophical *Interpretierung* asks what conditions must obtain when any particular act of interpretation (*Auslegung*) takes place.

There is thus a circle in this hermeneutic philosophy, since what is being interpreted is interpretation itself. Hermeneutic philosophy is itself an instance of this hermeneutic circle since it is interpreting itself, and its self-understanding could also claim to be no more than an interpretation. Or at least Gadamer and Heidegger recognize this circle in their own approach to hermeneutics, in contrast to other theorists of interpretation who do not admit to this circle.

Let me continue to use this distinction between what I am calling ordinary or naive interpretation and radical interpretation to distinguish two different philosophical conceptions of how to do the theory of interpretation. Early hermeneutic theorists (like J. J. Rambach in 1723) drew a sharp distinction between *subtilitas intelligendi* (understanding), *subtilitas explicandi* (interpretation), and *subtilitas applicandi* (application).[4] Contemporary theorists like E. D. Hirsch and Emilio Betti have also maintained that these are separate processes, with the act of understanding the text in its own terms coming before the later moment of interpretation where other terms than the text's are used to explain the significance of that initial understanding. These theorists insist on this distinction so that they can hold that there is really only one right understanding of any text, even if interpretations of its relevance change. They worry that objectivity will be lost without a hard and fast distinction between these moments. In contrast, Gadamer maintains that understanding cannot be broken into pieces like this, and is always conditioned by its context. That is his point in maintaining that understanding is always already interpretation. Furthermore, not only does understanding grow from within a context, it also feeds back into and influences that context. Since an understanding is always responding (even if only implicitly) to the particular problems arising from the context's configuration, Gadamer claims further that understanding is always application as well. On his account it is not possible to isolate the indisputably correct, noninterpretive understanding that could then be distinguished from and serve as the arbitrating foundation for the competing purposes of different interpreters.

I have been emphasizing the distinction between ordinary and radical interpretation to explain why a theory remaining simply on the level of ordinary interpretation might not grant Gadamer's claim that there is interpretation all the way down, but might maintain instead that there must be an antecedent, preinterpretive foundation for understanding. This perspective might be justified from within a particular interpretation, since when one is hammering, for instance, one might not describe oneself as interpreting, but as hitting the nail on the head (or not). Theories of *ordinary* interpretation are therefore likely to be preoccupied with questions of method (for instance, *epistemic* questions about how to distinguish correct interpretations from incorrect ones). Before Heidegger and

Gadamer hermeneutics was thus largely a theory of interpretation in the ordinary sense, debating questions about how the given object could best be represented. There are still theorists who see interpretation in this way. In contrast, Heidegger and Gadamer think of interpretation more radically. They resist the Cartesian picture of the mind as *representing* something that is given prior to or independently of interpretation. Heidegger and Gadamer go beyond earlier hermeneutic concerns with questions about how interpretations could best represent the objects being interpreted. Instead, Heidegger and Gadamer are making the more general claim that all our dealings with the world are contextualized and interpretive.

An interpretation in the ordinary sense is generally thought to be an option, such that we could choose between one interpretive approach to a text and another, or even in the sense that we could choose not to interpret at all and instead go to lunch or take a walk. At the philosophical level Heidegger and Gadamer are asking their readers to assume that interpretation is not optional, but is more generally what we are doing all the time in our interactions with the world. Davidson makes a comparable move, I believe, and the hermeneutic approach is similar to Davidson's in that neither is starting from the methodological questions that preoccupy the Cartesian tradition. Thus, while Gadamer asserts metaphilosophically that his hermeneutics has a universal scope, he denies that he is proposing a universal *method* of interpretation. To think that he is giving us rules or dicta about how to generate better interpretations would be to misunderstand him (and it would make his theory uninteresting *philosophically*). Instead, he is trying to account for the conditions for understanding and interpreting anything. I think that in this respect Gadamer is not far in intent from Davidson, for Davidson also says that "any hope of a universal method of interpretation must be abandoned."[5] That is, neither Davidson nor Gadamer envision a single method that will generate interpretations algorithmically. Instead, they both want to account for the general possibility of understanding.

For that reason I think that they want us to distinguish conceptually between the general conditions of interpretive understanding and the particular interpretations that result. To explain this, I find it helpful to distinguish a sense in which interpretation can be used as a count noun from a sense in which it cannot. When the word interpretation is used as a count noun, that usage often suggests a late and perhaps rare stage where we can say that we have two or more interpretations in front of us, and want to say which one is right. Gadamerian hermeneutics thinks of interpretation in this epistemic sense as "derivative" from a more "primordial" sense where interpretation is not something that can be counted (not even by the number "one"), because when we genuinely understand something (e.g., an utterance), we usually believe that we have understood the utterance itself and not simply a possible interpretation of the utterance. Davidson makes this point in setting up the first general requirement of a theory of radical interpretation. We might be tempted to think of the theory, he says, "as the specification of a function taking utterances as arguments and having interpretations as values." But he says that we should resist this analogy, since then "interpretations would be no better than meanings and just as surely entities of some mysterious kind. So it seems wise to describe what is wanted of the theory without apparent reference to meanings or interpretations: someone who knows the theory can interpret the utterances to which the theory applies."[6]

But then, why speak of such an understanding as a phenomenon of interpretation, or even of "radical" interpretation at all? The point for Davidson, I believe, is that "radical interpretation" is different, at least in degree, from the case of ordinary language where the interpreter already knows the language and tests a theory by seeing whether it yields correct interpretations, that is, results already known to be correct. The case is more basic even than that of Quinean radical translation, where one language is still already known. Davidson's radical interpretation works as if an understanding of particular utterances is not given in advance, and its goal is to explain only how understanding *could* result.

Gadamer's concern has comparable scope, since his intention is the "ontological" one of explaining how understanding even comes into being. When an understanding comes into being, of course, it will contain beliefs about some subject matter (or *Sache*). Whether particular beliefs are true, or whether the understanding represents a correct interpretation of the subject matter is a later and different question, and uses the word "interpretation" in a different sense. Gadamer's point that understanding is always already interpretation is thus an "ontological" and not an "epistemological" one. If these terms are unhelpful, let me rephrase the point, which is that to understand something is not to think that one has produced a countable interpretation. Instead, one has gained the ability to "go on," that is, both to render other utterances intelligibly and to take new data into account coherently. In this more radical sense, "interpretation" is not used in contrast to preinterpretive "evidence" against which interpretive hypotheses are tested. Instead, interpretation is more generally understood as the holistic configuration in which hypothesis and evidence first become contrastable and thus potentially combinable.

So understood, *radical* interpretation does not fall into the paradox of exempting itself from the claim that all understanding is interpretive. Paradox would follow if this claim were asserted absolutely, and thus as an exception to its own rule. Radical interpretation can admit that it is itself interpretation. However, something stronger is meant than that radical interpretation is itself simply one possible interpretation in the ordinary sense (which makes interpretations into countable entities and distinguishes interpretation from some more fundamental, preinterpretive, "rock-bottom" understanding). The claim must be heard as saying that all understanding is interpretive in that it involves the conditions identified by radical interpretation.

Since the task of laying out the conditions for any possible ordinary interpretation is itself a form of (radical) interpretation, someone might worry that paradox could follow from the self-referential character of this interpretation of interpretation. However, self-referentiality is not always paradoxical, for we can perfectly well use English to talk about English (e.g., about what is grammatically correct in English). The hermeneutic interpretation of interpretation is contestable, of course, but insofar as its arguments stand up, it can believe rationally in its own cogency. Hence, we can begin to see why the hermeneutic theory does not have to be relativistic about itself, as if it were simply one possible interpretation among many others. That relativism would follow only if hermeneutics were interpretation in the ordinary and not in the radical sense. In the ordinary sense of interpretation saying that understanding was only ever interpretive might imply that interpretations are largely (or even always) false. Radical interpretation, in contrast, is trying to capture why successful understanding involves minimizing unexplained error and maximizing explanatory cogency. Presumably the success of the philosophical interpretation of interpretation will hang on these same conditions.

For both Gadamer and Davidson a crucial condition identified in and through radical interpretation is that interpretive understanding is necessarily social and requires language. There could be no interpretation that was in principle private. Davidson argues for the social nature of thought by asking us to imagine as a thought experiment what conditions would have to obtain in the most primitive situation of speaking and understanding. For Davidson what is required is not that the speakers be both *speaking* the same natural language but that they both be able to *understand* each other. This mutual understanding requires what Davidson calls "triangulation," with at least two interpreters triangulating on each other as well as on a common object, which forms the third apex. To illustrate this point Davidson asks one to imagine being bolted to the earth in such a way as to be unable to move. Then one would have no way of knowing how close or far from one any visible objects were. By extension, what would be required for linguistic communication would be two conspecific creatures, each interacting with the other while also interacting with (i.e., speaking about) a common object.[7]

Gadamer also argues for the social nature of understanding. He does so by developing his claims about the centrality of the phenomenon of linguisticality (and thus of hermeneutics) from an analysis of a paradigm that resembles Davidson's analysis of triangulation. Gadamer's paradigm is a *dialogue* between two beings, an "I" and a "Thou," which he suggests as the logically primitive case of understanding. Furthermore, Gadamer insists that this dialogue is mediated by the *Sache,* the subject matter that gives the dialogue what I will call its "aboutness." For both Gadamer and Davidson, then, there would be no way to say what a speaker was talking about unless that speaker could be interpreted by a second person as talking about an object or *Sache* that they held in common. For both Davidson and Gadamer this interpretive three-way relation is the minimal structure of understanding and intelligibility. Because at least two conspecifics are required, this relation is necessarily public, and excludes the possibility of a purely private language.

Having suggested this degree of similarity, let me admit that there seems to be a difference between Davidson and Gadamer that may threaten this rapprochement. Davidson is concerned with the interpretation of *utterances,* and Gadamer is concerned primarily with the interpretation of *texts.* I could imagine a Derridean noticing this contrast and taking it as an enormous difference, with Davidson's concern with speech making him guilty of a phonocentric preference for speech over writing inherited from Plato. However, I myself would doubt that this contrast is all that significant. While Davidson takes as his model sentences like "snow is white," his approach is not to take sentences atomistically and in isolation one from another, but to see them holistically. Gadamer would have to approve of Davidson's account of the "inscrutability of reference," which is tied to Davidson's rejection of a "building block" approach that tries to map subsentential units like individual words to individual things. Similarly, Davidson's holism would seem to lead him to approve of Gadamer's claim that sentences (in a text) cannot be understood individually but only through a larger understanding of their inherence in the entire text.

There is another sense in which a difference caused by Davidson's emphasis on speech and Gadamer's (or especially Jacques Derrida's) on texts might suggest divergence. Gadamer's and Derrida's privileging of texts may seem to lead them to exclude extratextual factors such as authorial intentions and causal references. The Heidegger of *Being and Time* may be closest to Davidson's holistic inclusion of such factors in interpretation as beliefs and desires *as well as* sentences. For Heidegger understanding was primordially of the entire Dasein, and both he and Davidson seem to see language as requiring Dasein. In his 1990 Dewey lectures Davidson writes, "But of course sentences are abstract objects, shapes, say, and do not have truth conditions except as embodied in sounds and scribbles by speakers and scribblers. In the end it is the utterances and writings of language users with which a theory of truth must deal; the role of sentences in a theory is merely to make it possible to deal with *types* of utterances and inscriptions, whether or not particular types are realized."[8]

Now this quotation may have identified a basic mistake of Derridean deconstruction, which may depend on taking textual inscriptions as pure types, and ignoring other questions about what particular tokens are realized. For Gadamer, however, I do not see any major obstacles to rapprochement with Davidson on this score. Gadamer's theory tends to exclude consideration of authorial intention because a major rival theory of textual interpretation is intentionalism, which infers from the *causal* claim that the text is produced by an author to the *criterial* claim that the correct meaning of the text can only be what the author intended. Rejecting the intentionalistic theory of Ogden and Richards, Davidson states that "radical interpretation cannot hope to take as evidence for the meaning of a sentence an account of the complex and delicately discriminated intentions with which the sentence is typically uttered."[9] Davidson's point is not simply the practical reminder that we cannot ask the author about those intentions, for even if we could, interpretation would have to proceed holistically: "The reason is not that we cannot ask necessary questions, but that interpreting an agent's intentions, his beliefs and his words are parts of a single project, no part of which can be assumed to be complete before the rest is. If this is right, we cannot make the full panoply of intentions and beliefs the evidential base for a theory of radical interpretation."[10] Gadamer and Davidson both agree, then, that intention cannot confirm or disconfirm interpretation, and is not an independent given that the interpretation must try to "represent" faithfully.

This remark of Davidson that radical interpretation is a "single project, no part of which can be assumed to be complete before the rest is," suggests Schleiermacher's version of the hermeneutic circle. On that version, the parts of the text can be understood only from their inherence in a whole, but the whole can be projected only from the parts. Heidegger reformulated this circle of understanding in terms of a "disclosure" of "meaning" through understanding, with understanding always including a prior grasp of the content (through the triple structure that Heidegger calls the *Vorhabe, Vorgriff,* and *Vorsicht.*)[11] Gadamer claims similarly that understanding is always conditioned by *Vorurteile,* a term that can be translated as "pre-judgments" or even "prejudices." Gadamer thus concludes somewhat contentiously that understanding always involves prejudices. I say that this claim is contentious because it seems to commit Gadamer to a relativistic epistemology that denies the Enlightenment's ideal of overcoming bias and attaining objectivity.

This claim seems to run against not only Gadamer's own preference for hermeneutic awareness of how interpreters' horizons condition their interpretations, but also Gadamer's corresponding thought that interpretation is precisely a way of expanding horizons and transcending provinciality. Gadamer's point about *Vorurteile* should not be overstated, then, and is perhaps better translated using the neutral term "pre-judgments." His claim is that understanding and interpretation always take place in a particular context. While this context can develop and change, contextuality is always a limiting condition on understanding and interpretation. In Heideggerian terms, this contextuality is the disclosedness (*Erschlossenheit*) that makes it possible to discriminate or "discover" (*entdecken*) particular features of the context. Heidegger speaks of these as two different kinds of truth, and claims that disclosedness or *Erschlossenheit* is more primordial than discovery or *Entdecktheit.*

To Davidsonian ears this talk of two kinds of truth will sound strange, particularly when it turns out that the sense of "truth" as discovering through *asser-*

tion, which is the kind that Davidson (and Tarski) usually give as an example, is for Heidegger only derivative from the more primordial disclosedness. Have we therefore reached a point of rupture between Heidegger and Davidson? In the next section I will suggest that Gadamer's theory shows that despite this difference, there is some central common ground between the hermeneutic and Davidsonian theories of interpretation, particularly given some new work on what is called the principle of charity. That principle can illuminate the second problem I raised at the beginning of this paper, namely, whether an interpretation can believe at once in its own soundness and in the possibility of other interpretations.

First, however, let me summarize the answer so far to the first metaphilosophical problem about whether the claim of hermeneutic philosophy that all understanding is interpretive is itself interpretive. I drew the analogy with Davidson to suggest that hermeneutic philosophy is itself a case of radical interpretation. Thus, Gadamer's hermeneutics does not claim to be doing something other than interpretation. However, because what it interprets is interpretation itself, it seeks to identify the conditions required by any interpretation and is thus more radical or thoroughgoing than ordinary interpretation. The conditions thus discovered (such as the impossibility of a private language, or the necessity of understanding being publicly communicable) are not optional, and are thus not features that ordinary interpretations could choose to embody or not. So the conditions are more than "interpretive" in the ordinary sense. But although these conditions may appear to claim universal or transcendental or "philosophical" status, they are not "noninterpretive" in any sense that would be paradoxical for philosophical hermeneutics. There is nothing paradoxical about saying that there could be no actual instances of interpretation taking place unless the conditions obtained. Furthermore, in articulating these conditions philosophical hermeneutics does not purport to be doing something other than (radically) interpreting. But genuine interpretation now means being able to "go on" uttering truths. So the hermeneutic interpretation of interpretation is not aspiring to an understanding that differs in kind, and has different conditions, from the phenomena of understanding that it seeks to describe. If this account makes philosophical hermeneutics seem circular, the circle is not necessarily vicious, as the next section will show.

The Principle of Charity

The hermeneutic circle suggests that interpretation circles holistically between meaning and belief until an equilibrium (which John Rawls calls "reflective equilibrium") is reached. But in practice this equilibrium is never final, and it can be revised when need arises. This model of reaching equilibrium is helpful in pointing up two criticisms of Gadamer: one by Jürgen Habermas, and the other by Hubert Dreyfus. The first can be put by asking the question, does radical interpretation imply an idealized endpoint, a *final* equilibrium? Following Peirce, Habermas (and Karl-Otto Apel) think that an ideal convergence on some final agreement is a necessary assumption. Gadamer demurs from this Peircean idealization, and I will note that even Rawls questions the intelligibility and value of postulating such a final idealization.

The second issue, raised by Dreyfus, depends on a distinction between two kinds of holism, which Dreyfus originally called "theoretical" and "practical" holism.[12] Roughly speaking, theoretical holism takes countable beliefs and desires as all there is, whereas practical holism adds that these grow out of a presupposed background that includes tacit understanding and abilities (like skills) that can never be completely thematized into a final point where all the relevant beliefs and rules are articulated. Gadamer looks like a theoretical holist to Dreyfus, but I think that part of the reason for this is that Gadamer's examples are usually of textual interpretation, and not, for instance, of social interpretation. But Gadamer's model of interpretation should not be applicable exclusively to texts, since he is emphasizing the general form of interpretation.

The contrast between theoretical and practical holism could, I believe, be avoided by using a different model of belief, one more like Davidson's account. The criticism of Gadamer may construe beliefs as denumerable units, perhaps even as isolated, occurrent (or *vorhanden*) entities. But of course, the construction of a theory of the speakers' beliefs must itself be holistic. When an interpreter attributes a particular belief to a speaker, the interpreter does not simply attribute to the speaker that isolated belief, but a "pattern" of interrelated beliefs. "Beliefs are identified and described," says Davidson, "only within a dense pattern of belief."[13] Davidson's principle of charity advises us that this pattern of beliefs must also include beliefs that are mostly true. In "A Coherence Theory of Truth and Knowledge" Davidson suggests that the principle of charity may lead to misconstruing belief as strictly a count noun, and thus as failing to remember the holistic character of attributing beliefs: "there is probably no useful way to count beliefs," Davidson cautions, "and so no clear meaning to the idea that most of a person's beliefs are true." "A somewhat better way to put the point," he adds, "is to say there is a presumption in favor of the truth of a belief that coheres with a significant mass of belief."[14] If belief can function as both a count noun and a mass noun, we get a picture of the identification and attribution of particular beliefs as itself a circular process of abstracting the countable beliefs from the larger, uncountable background mass. But then we have a picture much like Heidegger's view that discrete, *vorhanden* entities are themselves only ever individuated against a background context of significance, including uses and other social practices.

Heidegger repeatedly emphasizes that the circularity of this interpretive process is not a *vicious circle* in the logical sense. I note, however, that Bjørn

Ramberg suggests that the Davidsonian "radical interpretation" is not a circle *at all*. There would be a vicious circle if the field linguist could not construct the Tarskian truth theory without knowing the beliefs and intentions of the speakers of the language in question. But Ramberg argues that there is no circle because all the interpreter needs to assume is *that* the speaker has beliefs and intentions. The radical (as opposed to the ordinary) interpreter does not make any assumptions about the empirical contents of these beliefs and intentions.[15]

One might conclude, then, that Davidson is *not* committed to the hermeneutic circle, since Davidson starts from a primitive concept of truth, and builds, using the tool of Convention T, a radical interpretation that yields meaning as an empirical *result,* and not as an initial starting point. Has Davidson thus "straightened out" Heidegger's claim that understanding is circular in that "any interpretation which is to contribute understanding, must already have understood what is to be interpreted"?[16] One might think that whereas Heidegger starts from the concept of meaning, Davidson shows us that meanings come not at the beginning of the process of interpretation, but, if at all, only at the end.[17] In fact, however, Heidegger shares Davidson's emphasis on extensionality, and he seeks to bypass the idea that what is first understood is an intermediary entity like a "meaning" or a "representation" and not more directly the worldly object: "When entities within-the-world are discovered along with the Being of Dasein—that is, when they have come to be understood—we say that they have *meaning* [*Sinn*]. But that which is understood, taken strictly, is not the meaning but the entity, or alternatively, Being."[18] Heidegger's purpose is to eliminate the idea that meanings are attached by individual assertions to extended entities, and thus are thereby *made true.* Instead, the term "meaning" is used in a broader sense whereby understanding requires the projection or disclosure of a more inclusive context of human interests and purposes. This is how I take Heidegger's claim that "Only Dasein can be meaningful."[19] This assertion suggests to me that Heidegger agrees with Davidson's holism, which for Heidegger results from the fact that something can be intelligible as something only in an interpretation, with the structure of a *Vorhabe, Vorgriff,* and *Vorsicht* (see note 11). But Heidegger is not caught in a *vicious* circle for the same reason that Davidson (on Ramberg's account) is not. Neither asserts that particular empirical beliefs of the interpretee must be known beforehand, since beliefs can be attributed only holistically through their location in a structural pattern (Davidson) or preunderstanding (Heidegger) or interpretation (Gadamer).

The other point of connection of Davidson with Heidegger and Gadamer is their critique of Cartesian subjectivity. From Davidson's standpoint, Heidegger's attempt to show a deeper kind of truth (disclosedness) may be a mistake, and I note that Heidegger himself later avoids using the term "truth" for this level. But a reason for stressing disclosedness is to get away from the idea that the world stands over against "subjects" for whom truths are internal representations of mind-independent reality. Davidson's argument that the subjective is largely a "myth" is compatible with Heidegger's analysis of worldhood, and his insistence that Dasein is being-in-the-world.[20]

A crucial point to add here, however, is that just as Davidson is not a realist, neither is Heidegger, at least not in the sense of the "metaphysical realism" that asserts that reality is so mind-independent that our best-confirmed scientific theories could be entirely false. In the 1990 Dewey lectures Davidson modifies his own earlier use of the term "realist" for his position, and makes clear that he is not a realist in the sense of the epistemological position that denies that "truth is conceptually connected in any way to what we believe."[21] He also abandons the label of "correspondence theory" for his account of truth, for "there is nothing interesting or instructive to which true sentences might correspond."[22] These points, plus his insistence on the "inscrutability of reference," would be shared by Heidegger. One point of the idea of being-in-the-world is that the world is not over against us. We are always caught up in the world, and there is not some further world that could intelligibly be said to be completely alien to our best interpretations. Heidegger and Gadamer thus speak of the "worldhood" of the world. By "worldhood" Heidegger explicitly does not mean either a subjective world, or the totality of *vorhanden* (countable) entities, or the shared conventional world, but the "a priori character" of the phenomenon of being always already in the world.[23] Like Davidson, Heidegger grants that realism is right to think that the ontic, external world is really there. But the Cartesians are wrong to think (ontically) that the world is really "out there" in an independent and occurrent (or in Heidegger's terms, *vorhanden*) manner. So while Heidegger does not deny (ontic) realism, he claims that his view "differs in principle from every kind of realism" and does not think of the problem of external reality as one that is capable of a "proof."[24] Heidegger thinks that Kant's refutation of idealism may be trying to construct such a proof, but I prefer to think that Kant, Heidegger, and Davidson are alike in wanting to show that no proof is even needed.

However, Davidson's version of the argument, I have already suggested, turns on a central principle, the principle of charity, and while the hermeneutic theory of interpretation seems to include some such principle, there has been little direct confrontation of the problems involved with it. So I would like to focus on the question of whether a hermeneutic theory of interpretation should include the principle of charity. Much will depend, of course, on how that principle is itself interpreted. An earlier generation of readers of Davidson, especially Richard Grandy and Ian Hacking, but also Graham MacDonald and Steven Lukes, sometimes tended to see charity as a pragmatic principle of what I am calling ordinary interpretation. They thus argued about whether an interpreter should apply the principle of charity. A later generation of readers of Davidson, especially Bjørn Ramberg and Simon Evnine,[25] now thinks that a mistake is already being made in this debate, since the principle is not an option, one that could (correctly) or could not (mistakenly) be applied. Instead, the principle is one that is required by any act of understanding, and thus by any activity that could even count as interpretation.

Let me first summarize the debate about whether charity is a methodological recommendation or a necessary condition, and suggest my own reasons for preferring the shift in the Davidsonian literature from charity as maximizing agreement to charity as minimizing unexplained error. Hacking reacted to Richard Grandy's formulation of the principle of charity (which Grandy called the principle of humanity) by taking that principle as a recommendation that the interpreter construe any interpretee as sharing most of the beliefs of the interpreter.[26] On an analogy with the Europeans' colonization of the Third World, Hacking saw this principle as leading to the pernicious practice of making the others conform to one's own beliefs and values. Hacking's main worry was probably that in an activity like his own approach to the history of science, the principle would lead to the Whiggish assumption of the superiority of present science over past science, an assumption that can lead to making past science so implausible as to be unintelligible. So instead of making the other more intelligible to us, Grandy's principle of humanity, when used as a pragmatic constraint, would be likely to make some central statements unintelligible. Hacking's critique implies that the principle is potentially ethnocentric and Whiggish.

Where this problem enters the Continental debate is that Michel Foucault appears to be an opponent of the use of charity in the history of science. But this may not be the most charitable reading of what historians of science like Foucault or Thomas Kuhn do. Let's see what Kuhn says and then ask whether it is necessarily "uncharitable" (in an un-Davidsonian way). Kuhn's advice to hermeneutic historians is to take especially seriously those statements by an earlier thinker that seem absurd.[27] Doing so will cause other statements to change their apparent meaning, until finally the whole corpus comes together in a different way than it did on first reading, when we read it with our own expectations. Kuhn suggests that his discovery of hermeneutics is what led him to think of his enterprise in this way, but the point does not seem un-Davidsonian. Or at least I should think that the Davidsonian way of putting the point would be to say that Kuhn is trying to minimize unexplained error, since the historian is faced precisely with many statements from past science that seem not merely false, but absurd and unexplainable. So the historian has to proceed holistically and question other parts, even those that seemed sensible, reworking the various parts until they all seem reasonably understandable.

Gadamer's hermeneutics suggests this solution as well. Two contemporary philosophers, Habermas and Derrida, read him as defending interpretive charity, but they take issue with him in opposite ways. Habermas develops his own theory from what he takes as Gadamer's basic claim that the telos of all language use is reaching understanding and agreement. (Whether Habermas reads

Gadamer correctly here is another question.) So Habermas approves of Gadamer for including charity as a basic assumption of hermeneutics. In contrast, deconstructionists, following Derrida's critique of hermeneutics generally, decry Gadamerian charity. They see hermeneutics as always trying to make the strangeness of the text into something familiar. In contrast to hermeneutics deconstruction appears to be the converse effort of turning the familiar into the strange.

Both these readings are abetted by Gadamer's tendency to characterize the hermeneutic enterprise as follows: "Only the support of familiar and common understanding makes possible the venture into the alien, the lifting up of something out of the alien, and thus the broadening and enrichment of our own experience of the world."[28] Gadamer's technical term that comes closest to charity is the *Vorgriff der Vollkommenheit,* the expectation of the completeness of what is being interpreted. But completeness, which Gadamer insists is only ever anticipated and never achieved, does not entail reducing all that is alien to what is already familiar. While this quotation shows that hermeneutics seems to be committed to *pragmatic,* methodological charity, the notion does not exclude the possibility that the encounter with the alien can make the familiar seem strange. Part of the hermeneutic task of understanding may require the use of deconstructive techniques that bring out the strangeness of what has become too familiar. Hermeneutic understanding may require a confrontation with the alien precisely to keep us from becoming too complacent in our own standpoint. In *Truth and Method* Gadamer echoes the irony in Friedrich Schlegel's critique of complacent historians who rely on the "axiom of familiarity," which states "that things must always have been just as they are for us, for things are naturally like this."[29] So if being charitable is the interpretive strategy of making the strange familiar, and being uncharitable is the strategy of making the familiar strange, Gadamer is not asserting the necessity of either one. These are methods or *strategies,* and each can have its use within the larger project of understanding texts and enlarging our own horizons. Making the familiar strange may even be one pragmatic application of the principle of charity, since challenging one's own assumptions may reveal some hidden and unexplained error in our own standpoint.

Similar considerations have led recent accounts of Davidson to stress that charity as a principle of *radical* interpretation is not an option. Charity is not a hypothesis that we extend tentatively to others' utterances, says Ramberg, so much as a condition for our own linguistic competence. So charity is an abstract condition that applies to what I call "speakerhood," but it does not imply that real speakers will not have widely divergent concrete and particular concerns. Ramberg even argues that the principle of charity is required to recognize these divergences as divergences.

These accounts follow from Davidson's own claim in "The Very Idea of a Conceptual Scheme" that charity is not an option, but a condition.[30] So charity cannot adjudicate conflicts of interpretation, and it is a thinner notion than maximizing prior substantive agreement. Davidson remarks in the introduction to *Inquiries* that we should not confuse agreement with the aim of interpretation, "which is not agreement but understanding" (p. xvii). He says that interpretation should try to bring about the "right sort" of agreement, but grants that no specification of "right sort" is likely. This qualification is important in the current debate between Habermas and Gadamer, since it suggests, contrary to Habermas, that agreement is neither a condition of interpretation, nor the telos of all understanding. If charity is a condition, it does not entail ultimate agreement or final convergence. Charity is instead the condition that makes possible the discrimination of agreement and disagreement, of convergence and divergence.

CONCLUSION

I will conclude by returning to the epistemological questions about ordinary and radical interpretation that are raised by Gadamer's pluralism. Gadamer has been charged with epistemological relativism because of his denial that the ideal goal of any interpretation must be the *single, right* interpretation that everyone should accept. I do not know whether Davidson would accept this denial of the necessity of there being only *one* right interpretation. However, Davidson has subscribed to the "indeterminacy" of interpretation, which follows from the holistic patterning of belief, and would thus seem to allow for some variance in interpretive outcomes, much as Gadamer's theory also envisages.[31] However, pluralism is not the same as relativism, and Davidson has argued strongly against the scheme-content distinction that leads to the latter. At most Davidson would probably allow only for a pluralism such as we find in measuring temperature, where we can use either the Fahrenheit or the Celsius scale without there being a fact of the matter about which scale is right.

The charge of relativism also misses Gadamer's point, which is not to deny that there are some interpretive claims that are right and some that are wrong. Hermeneutics would certainly grant that some "ordinary" interpretations are right on the whole, and that others are wrong about particular principal points. So epistemological questions are not ruled out. Gadamer is not suggesting that interpretation is in general likely to be incorrect, and he is not the skeptic or relativist that some have thought. On the contrary, if he relies on anything like an abstract principle of charity, the point of doing so is to suggest why there need not be skeptical worries about all interpretation being totally off the mark. (Deconstructionists in turn sometimes seem to be advancing such skeptical worries against hermeneutics.) On Gadamer's hermeneutic theory, interpretation involves being able not only to distinguish sound from unsound claims, but also to make a case more generally for the cogency of understanding. Reliance on charity, at least in the thin sense suggested by the Davidsonian model, would not commit hermeneutics to the much stronger ideal of a single final interpretation that would elicit universal consensus. The ideal of the "one right interpretation" is not compelling because it is not clear how that interpretation could be individuated from all other interpretations.

So charity is not pernicious in that it does not rule out some plurality in interpretation. The hermeneutic response to the second problem that I raised at the outset of this paper is thus that any given interpretation can believe in its own cogency at the same time that it holds itself open to the possibility that further interpretation may become required for unforeseeable reasons. But perhaps even to speak of plurality in interpretation makes the mistake of suggesting that interpretations can be counted in some relevant way. Gadamer himself does not assert that an indefinite number of interpretations is possible in every case, and he does not think of interpretive conflict as anything like the intransigence of conflicting conceptual schemes. The point of the enterprise of philosophical hermeneutics is not to provide principles that would explain what makes interpretation correct or incorrect. These principles will be internal to the actual practices of interpretation. The philosophical task of hermeneutics is instead to raise the prior question of how interpretation is possible in the first place. To this extent I believe that Davidson and Gadamer are at least engaged in the same enterprise, however much they may differ in philosophical style and background. Charitable dialogue between their positions is thus possible at least in principle, and I hope that it can begin productively from the shared understanding of interpretation that I have outlined here.

DAVID C. HOY

DEPARTMENT OF PHILOSOPHY
UNIVERSITY OF CALIFORNIA, SANTA CRUZ
MAY 1992

NOTES

1. Hans-Georg Gadamer, *Truth and Method,* second edition, trans. Joel Weinsheimer and Donald G. Marshall (New York: Crossroad, 1989), p. 474.

2. See section 3 of Hans-Georg Gadamer's "Reflections on my Philosophical Journey," published in this volume.

3. For a more detailed discussion of this distinction in Heidegger's *Being and Time,* see my article "Heidegger and the Hermeneutic Turn," in the *Cambridge Companion to Heidegger,* ed. Charles B. Guignon (Cambridge: Cambridge University Press, 1993).

4. See Gadamer, *Truth and Method,* pp. 307ff., and my discussion in chapters 1 and 2 of *The Critical Circle: Literature, History, and Philosophical Hermeneutics* (Berkeley: University of California Press, 1978), especially pp. 51–55.

5. Donald Davidson, "Radical Interpretation," in *Inquiries into Truth and Interpretation* (Oxford: Clarendon Press, 1984), p. 128.

6. Ibid.

7. For the triangulation argument see the last paragraphs of Donald Davidson, "Rational Animals," *Dialectica* 36 (1982): 318–27. Davidson has worked out this argument more extensively in recent unpublished work, which was presented at the 1990 NEH Summer Institute on "Heidegger and Davidson: Critics of Cartesianism" that I co-directed with Hubert L. Dreyfus at the University of California, Santa Cruz. I am grateful to my colleague, Ric Otte, as well as to the participants at that Institute, especially Piers Rawling, for discussion of the issues presented in this paper.

8. Donald Davidson, "The Structure and Content of Truth," *Journal of Philosophy* 88 (June 1990): 309.

9. Donald Davidson, "Radical Interpretation," p. 127.

10. Ibid.

11. For Heidegger "an interpretation is never a presuppositionless apprehending of something presented to us" (*Being and Time,* trans. John Macquarrie and Edward Robinson [New York: Harper and Row, 1962], pp. 191–92; German page 150). Heidegger thus argues that we already relate to what we interpret *in advance* of our explicit articulation of our understanding. There is always already a network of involvements in which what is being interpreted already has some role (the *Vorhabe*). There is also always already a point of view within this network from which we see whatever is being interpreted in advance (the *Vorsicht*). The concepts we will then use to articulate these prior ways of seeing the significance of what is at stake are themselves already prefigured (in the *Vorgriff* or fore-conception).

12. Hubert L. Dreyfus, "Holism and Hermeneutics," *The Review of Metaphysics* 34 (September 1980): 3–23.

13. Donald Davidson, "The Method of Truth in Metaphysics," in *Inquiries into Truth and Interpretation* (Oxford: Clarendon Press, 1984), p. 200.

14. Donald Davidson, "A Coherence Theory of Truth and Knowledge," in *Truth and Interpretation: Perspectives on the Philosophy of Donald Davidson,* ed. Ernest LePore (Oxford: Basil Blackwell, 1986), p. 308.

15. Bjørn T. Ramberg, *Donald Davidson's Philosophy of Language: An Introduction* (Oxford: Basil Blackwell, 1989), pp. 68–69.

16. Heidegger, *Being and Time,* German page 152.

17. See section 5.2 of Simon Evnine's book, *Donald Davidson* (Stanford: Stanford University Press, 1991).

18. Heidegger, *Being and Time,* German page 151.

19. Ibid.

20. See Donald Davidson, "The Myth of the Subjective," in *Relativism: Interpretation and Confrontation,* ed. Michael Krausz (Notre Dame: Notre Dame University Press, 1989).

21. Donald Davidson, "The Structure and Content of Truth," p. 299.

22. Donald Davidson, "The Structure and Content of Truth," p. 303.

23. See Heidegger, *Being and Time,* German pages 64–65.

24. Heidegger, *Being and Time,* German page 207.

25. See sections 6.6 and 8.3 of Simon Evnine's book, *Donald Davidson.*

26. See Ian Hacking, *Why Does Language Matter to Philosophy?* (Cambridge: Cambridge University Press, 1975), and Bjørn Ramberg's critique in *Donald Davidson's Philosophy of Language,* p. 74.

27. Thomas S. Kuhn, *The Essential Tension: Selected Studies in Scientific Tradition*

and Change (Chicago: The University of Chicago Press, 1977), p. xii.

28. Hans-Georg Gadamer, "The Universality of the Hermeneutical Problem," in *Philosophical Hermeneutics,* trans. David E. Linge (Berkeley: University of California Press, 1976), p. 15.

29. Hans-Georg Gadamer, *Truth and Method,* p. 361.

30. See Donald Davidson, *Inquiries into Truth and Interpretation,* p. 197.

31. On indeterminacy see Bjørn T. Ramberg, *Donald Davidson's Philosophy of Language,* pp. 93–95.

REPLY TO DAVID HOY

After reading Davidson's contribution I have studied this contribution with special excitement. In it an expert on my own hermeneutic ideas speaks about what he takes to be the differences and convergences between hermeneutic philosophy and that which the philosophical development of Davidson's position has in mind.

One should not forget that I am here, so to speak, dealing with new information. Thirty-five years ago, when I presented my hermeneutic philosophy in a book which also had its effect in America, I was, in any case, entirely caught up in the further development of the thematic first touched upon in that book. The significance of art for the questions of philosophy today belonged to this work as a primary task, as well as the immanent philosophy of what is called the *humanities* in the English-speaking world. If I may take the information which I owe to the work of Mr. Hoy as a basis, it really seems as if there is a real proximity between Davidson's concept of "radical interpretation" and my own extension of the concept of hermeneutics. I would also say that what has been presented under the concept of the "radical interpretation" corresponds precisely to what I, taking from Plato as the *eumeneia,* the *eumeneia's elenchoi,* indeed regard as a self-evident presupposition for every attempt at understanding. At this point, however, I have certain reservations concerning a further elaboration of the investigation of the relations between Davidson's efforts and my own. There we can entirely disregard the supposed difference between *utterances (Äusserungen)* and text. To be sure, the context of *Truth and Method* primarily speaks of text, but long ago my later works recognized this as only a special case which forced itself upon me through the history of hermeneutics where it had played a special role. The topic of Derrida and deconstruction which, in a different context, I have discussed at length in the meantime in volume 10 of my collected works, under the title "Hermeneutik auf der Spur," releases me from a detailed reply to such matters. The problem lies rather in the fact that it still sounds as if conversation, and the structure of conversation in all areas dealing with understanding, primarily only referred to the attainment of correct knowledge. But what is fundamentally at issue is not primarily science and epistemology but, to speak with Mr. Hoy, the 'ontology' of life communicating itself through language. The form of the proposition, and here I stay close to Hegel, is not suited to express speculative truths. Even the model proposition that Davidson employs—"snow is white"—seems strange to me from this viewpoint. Who uttered this, even if it is true? I am only interested in asking about the precondition of human communication; namely, that one really tries to understand what the other thinks about something. I agree entirely with Mr. Hoy's conclusion that this understanding is not yet agreement. Only a precondition of communication which can be successful is, in this way, satisfied. Yet, this has nothing to do with the anticipation of perfection. Perfect understanding surely never means perfect agreement. Mr. Hoy demonstrates this correctly. So I want to assume that, in this case, we really approach each other. For me, the extension to all sorts of communication is significant for art, for religion, for the concept of law, that is, for jurisprudence, and only in a secondary sense for those sciences we call the *humanities*. These sciences always require a very real hermeneutic ability if something is really going to be said. Of course, there are methods everywhere, in all sciences, even in philology, in history, etc. But apart from the question of method a hermeneutic virtue is needed: one must always be aware that everything, including every text, wants to say something different, for which one should open oneself.

H.-G. G.

4

Joan Stambaugh

GADAMER ON THE BEAUTIFUL

The subject of the beautiful can hardly be said to be the center of much discussion in the contemporary age. Our age could be more aptly characterized as an age of anxiety than one of beauty such as we find in ancient Greece, or even one where beauty plays an important role. Yet Gadamer is not simply reexploring the significance of beauty as dealt with by, for example, Plato, Aristotle, Kant, Hegel, and Schiller. He extends his inquiry to include the questions of contemporary art, the relation of art as a religion of culture with historical consciousness, and art as the self-conscious reflection of the modern artist who deliberately breaks with the past. The expression "religion of culture" obviously needs further explication. At the end of the article we shall examine how Gadamer views the "religious" or spiritual dimension of art.

As Gadamer points out, Kant "recognized for the first time the experience of art and beauty as a philosophical question in its own right" (p. 18).* In his four moments of the beautiful Kant succinctly defined the beautiful as that which pleases universally and necessarily without a concept, does not involve interest, and embodies purposiveness without a purpose. Gadamer probes into the question of the unique nature of aesthetic judgments as distinguished from by far more common and less problematic logical judgments. Logical judgments are based on concepts of objects. Example: this is a dog or this dog is brown. I know what a dog is and subsume this particular animal under the universal concept dog. Aesthetic judgments, on the other hand, are singular. Example: this painting is beautiful. They have universal validity and binding necessity, but they are not based on concepts. I do not possess a universal concept of beauty under which to subsume the painting. On the contrary, I first learn something about beauty from the painting. The painting or the work of art in general has exemplary necessity; it is the "example" of a universal rule that cannot be stated.

Although focused on the beautiful, Gadamer goes further to ask: why does the understanding of what art is today present a task for thinking? He works toward narrowing the gap between traditional art that we enjoy, and contemporary art

---

*All Gadamer quotations are from "The Relevance of the Beautiful," in *The Relevance of the Beautiful and Other Essays* (Cambridge: Cambridge University Press, 1991).

that challenges us to actively try to grasp what is being communicated. This he does by emphasizing the element of participation on the part of the perceiver indispensable to all art, traditional and contemporary.

A major part of Gadamer's essay deals with the anthropological basis of our experience of art. He accomplishes this by inquiring into the three elements of play, symbol, and festival. The source of play, which is a central ingredient in human life, is the basic character of excess and exuberance striving to express itself in the living being. In human beings this involves our reason and outplays the capacity for purposive rationality. No purpose or goal is involved in the free activity of play, but the play itself is intended, not arbitrary or random. I decide to play a game of tennis. A child decides to play with its ball.

Some of the most intriguing insights in this essay are to be found in the section on symbol. Gadamer pursues a different route from such thinkers as Cassirer and Langer. For him the symbol points beyond itself and allows us to glimpse that realm that has always been sought in order to complete and make whole our fragmentary life. In any encounter with art we meet up with the totality of the experienceable world, man's ontological place in it, and above all his finitude before that which transcends him.

Gadamer develops a subtle dialectic, as he has done in other contexts, between showing and concealing, between what is uniquely present in the symbol and what is brought close by that symbol without being literally present. The "symbol," the work of art itself, allows a meaning to present itself. This meaning is present in the artwork in the only way it can be present. In other words, the meaning could not be presented in a literal, nonsymbolic way. Anyone looking at a Cézanne landscape, for example, will be struck by a presence that he, as a nonartist, might not be able to see in the actual, physical landscape. The painter has succeeded in transmitting a landscape experience unavailable to most of us. The experience is actually there, embodied, in the work of art. Thus Gadamer states that the work of art signifies an increase in being. He refers to Rilke's statement that such a thing stood among men. There are also echoes of Heidegger's "not N.N. *fecit,* rather the simple *factum est"* ("The Origin of the Work of Art," p. 65). What is important is not the fact that a particular person made it, but that it was made at all and now stands before us.

And yet that is not all. To return to the example of the Cézanne landscape (not Gadamer's example), we experience the presence of something that was not literally painted. What is present in a way next to impossible to characterize in words is, to resort to what has become somewhat platitudinous, totality and permanence. A dwelling of wholeness comes about in the midst of fleeting transience.

> This activity necessarily reveals the human experience of finitude in a unique way and gives spiritual significance to the immanent transcendence of play as an excess that flows over into the realm of freely chosen possibilities. . . . It seems to me that the advance made now that we have completed our considerations, is that we have seen play's excess to be not only the real ground of our creative production and

reception of art, but also the more profound anthropological dimension that bestows permanence. This is the unique character of human play and the play of art in particular, distinguishing it from all other forms of play in the realm of nature. (pp. 46–47)

Finally, Gadamer makes an interesting distinction between his own interpretation of symbol and the classic understanding of allegory. Whereas allegory traditionally means that what is said differs from what is meant, although what is meant could be said in a direct and immediate way, the symbol or the work of art presents something not literally "contained" in the artwork, and that something could not be presented in any other way.

The last main element that Gadamer discusses is the festival. In this discussion, the influence of ancient Greece is especially apparent. A festival is an experience of community lifted out of the ordinariness of everyday, habitual life. One is reminded of Hölderlin's hymn "As on a Holiday." But Gadamer the philosopher gets into a fascinating analysis of the temporality of the festival. Expressed in Heideggerian terms, the festival lifts us out of inauthentic time into authentic time and thus out of inauthenticity into authenticity in general. This is a "positive" embodiment of authenticity as opposed to Heidegger's more sombre examples of angst and anticipation of death. Gadamer here carries out phenomenologically and hermeneutically what Heidegger only named, but never developed.

> Let us remember that we speak of 'enacting' a celebration. . . . The word 'enacting' removes all idea of a goal to be attained. To enact is not to set out in order subsequently to arrive somewhere. For when we enact a festival, then the festival is always there from the beginning. The temporal character of the festive celebration that we enact lies in the fact that it does not dissolve into a series of separate moments. (p. 41)

Even if the festival gets organized within the framework of ordinary clock time, still its internal temporal structure does not coincide with that of clock time, just as the temporality of, for example, a string quartet does not coincide with the quantity of clock time that it takes to play it.

Giving the example of recurrent festivals, and recurrence is crucial to the celebration of the festival for Gadamer, he states that the ecclesiastical holidays of Christmas and Easter enjoy the primacy of their own time that is not subject to the abstract calculation of quantitative duration.

Quantitative durational time is basically Newtonian in conception. Newton conceived time as a static, empty container waiting to be filled out. This is time *in which* something happens or does not happen. We speak of things being in time in analogy to things being in a drawer or box. Bergson said that we spatialize time. Even Kant was still guilty of this, although he "internalized" the container as a form of sensibility in the mind.

Gadamer discusses the two extremes of the experience of this empty time. They are boredom and frantic busyness. In boredom we experience time as an undifferentiated flow in which nothing at all really takes place. This empty time seems interminable and the interminability constitutes the burdensomeness of boredom. Perhaps the most extreme example of this type of "experience" (or the lack of experience) would be pathological depression. Not only does nothing happen; nothing *can* happen, because no matter what transpires, the person cannot *respond* to it. In frantic busyness we race from one thing to the next and, again, nothing really takes place. Even if it did, we would not have the focus to experience it.

But there is a completely different kind of time available to us in the festival or the work of art that Gadamer calls fulfilled or autonomous time. "It is of the nature of the festival that it should proffer time, arresting it and allowing it to tarry. That is what festive celebration means. The calculating way in which we normally manage and dispose of our time is, as it were, brought to a standstill" (p. 42).

Fulfilled, autonomous time provides us with a different experience of the quality of our lives. No boredom oppresses us from within nor busy bustle from without. Everyone has some experience of this kind of time. The basketball player during practice, the writer who finally gets going on his novel, the violinist practicing his concerto, the person enraptured by love, to name just a few, are all examples of experiences where clock time simply is not there. One forgets that kind of time.

Here Gadamer takes up the distinction between an ideality that he finds in art and the full-blown ideality postulated by the German idealists. Although Hegel, for example, found art infinitely superior to nature because it is the product of human spirituality, ultimately art is superseded by philosophy that achieves the purity of the concept unsullied by any materiality. In contrast, Schelling saw art as the ultimate human achievement, superior to philosophy, precisely because it included nature. Here Gadamer would side with Schelling, maintaining that art provides an ultimacy not available in the concept. Art achieves something that conceptual language cannot.

An essential ingredient of this ultimacy lies in the inclusion of nonconceptual "nature" with its sensuous concreteness and the concomitant transformation of quantitative, measurable clock time into qualitative, autonomous temporality. The creation and the response to the work of art dwell in it to the exclusion of everything else. This is true both of the "static" arts of painting, sculpture, and architecture where the response, what Gadamer calls the "reading," takes time, and even more so in the "transitory" arts of poetry, music, drama, and dance where the "reading" *is* the experience of the artwork. It is this dwelling in the autonomous time of the artwork that constitutes an essential moment of its spiritual dimension, a dimension becoming increasingly difficult to discern in our own disenchanted time. In Gadamer's own words: "The essence of our temporal experience of art is learning how to tarry in this way. And perhaps it is the only way that is granted to us finite beings to relate to what we call eternity" (p. 45).

JOAN STAMBAUGH

DEPARTMENT OF PHILOSOPHY
HUNTER COLLEGE
APRIL 1992

REPLY TO JOAN STAMBAUGH

It was a real pleasure that my little writings on art which have not yet been accessible in English reached my respected colleague, and that she gave them a friendly reception. In my major work, *Truth and Method*, my chief concern was to expand the concept of truth in such a way that we are not only left with the propositional concept of truth which claimed a monopoly over the concept of truth since Aristotle's logic. What was to be learned from Heidegger could be a great help to this end, especially his rejuvenation of Greek philosophy that awoke us to the phenomenological presence of Aristotle. Later, as a professor in Leipzig, I had to extend my course offerings and turned primarily to Kant and the conceptless world of the faculty of aesthetic judgment. When those texts speak of judgments, it is not the logic of propositions that I am referring to but primarily the discovery of beauty itself. Starting with the beauty of nature, the understanding of the sublime and especially the path to art opened up before me. From my youth onwards art had always been with me. That was even the case in my studies on the Greek world: from Pindar to Plato and Plotinus, I found myself again and again placed before the question of what links philosophy and art. For this path of mine, I would refer to volumes 8 and 9 of my collected works (under the titles *Kunst als Aussage* and *Hermeneutik im Vollzug*) from which some essays are now accessible in English. There it is clear that I see the greatest proximity between poetry and philosophy in the art form of lyric poetry which is untranslatable and which remains a mystery almost as great as music.

H.-G.G.

5

Donald Phillip Verene

GADAMER AND VICO ON *SENSUS COMMUNIS* AND THE TRADITION OF HUMANE KNOWLEDGE

Gadamer and Heidegger differ markedly on one thing. Heidegger regards the tradition of humanism as philosophically unimportant. In his *Letter on Humanism* he states, "Humanism does not ask about Being's relationship to man and his essential nature. Humanism even hinders asking this question because, on the basis of its own origins in metaphysics, it neither recognizes nor understands this question."[1] In contrast, Gadamer begins *Truth and Method* with an appreciative discussion of the significance of the humanist tradition in which he introduces his conception of "hermeneutical reflection" through an analysis of the "guiding concepts of humanism" *(humanistische Leitbegriffe).*[2] He calls attention to the great humanist theme of *Bildung,* the Latin equivalent for which, he says, "is *formatio,* with related words in other languages—e.g., in English (in Shaftesbury), 'form' and 'formation'" (16/11). And to memory, another of the great themes of the tradition of humane letters, which he says must be rescued "from being regarded merely as a psychological faculty" (21/16). "Memory must be formed," Gadamer says, "for memory is not memory for anything and everything" (ibid.). Gadamer regards what is known in the German tradition as the human sciences or *Geisteswissenschaften* as part of the general tradition known in other countries as the humanities or "letters"; "in short, everything formerly known as the *humaniora.*"[3]

GADAMER'S UNDERSTANDING OF VICO

Among the guiding concepts within the *humaniora* Gadamer very prominently singles out *sensus communis.* He associates this with Vico and also with Shaftesbury. In his study of the idea of language in the humanist tradition, Karl-Otto Apel sees Vico as the summary figure of the humanist tradition; he says Vico "is truly the Owl of Minerva of Italian Renaissance culture."[4] Gadamer seems generally to hold this view as the background to his specific discussion of Vico's conception of the *sensus communis.* Vico, like Hegel's owl, takes flight at the dusk of the Italian humanist tradition, gathering, in the flight of his works, all the great themes, the wisdom of the Renaissance. To study Vico is to study humanism and to study what humanism is. Vico's works, from his early university orations (1699–1707), to the versions of his *New Science* (1725, 1730, 1744), to his last remarks to the Academy of Oziosi on the relation of philosophy to eloquence (1737) are humanism remembered.[5]

Given the current worldwide renaissance of Vico studies, in which Vico's works are being studied by scholars in all fields of humanistic knowledge,[6] it is easy to forget how unique Gadamer's attention to Vico was in 1960, when *Truth and Method* first appeared.[7] Other than Cassirer, who employs Vico in the *Philosophy of Symbolic Forms* (1923, 1925, 1929) and throughout his works,[8] Gadamer is the only thinker of the first order in twentieth-century German philosophy to involve Vico as part of the basis of his thought.[9] He is preceded in European and British philosophy only by Croce and to an extent by Collingwood.[10] Like Cassirer, Gadamer connects Vico to the philosophy of the human sciences, but unlike Cassirer he emphasizes how Vico's thought is rooted in the humanist tradition of rhetoric. Gadamer approaches Vico as a unique thinker, free of Croce's attempt to understand Vico as the Italian Hegel.[11]

Gadamer's approach to Vico captures a sense of Vico's thought that anticipated a significant part of what has been of interest to many thinkers in the current Vico renaissance: his humanist, rhetorical themes.[12] Gadamer's most concentrated interpretation of Vico is his discussion of *sensus communis* in the first part of *Truth and Method,* but he comes back to Vico in his "Afterword" of 1972,[13] and mentions Vico at several points (226/222, 231/227, 235/230, 281/276, 379/373). Gadamer cites Vico in similar ways in various other writings.[14]

I am concerned in this essay with three questions: (1) How does Gadamer understand Vico's *sensus communis?* (2) What role does *sensus communis* play in Vico's formulation of his philosophy? and (3) What sort of dialogic relation exists between these two "humanist" thinkers? I will take up these questions in turn.

One thing any reader of Gadamer must appreciate is his skill and care in interpreting other texts, whether they be by Plato, Hegel, Dilthey, or Vico. As an advocate of hermeneutics we can apply the adage that he "practices what he preaches." He stands in sharp contrast to what any student of philosophy soon learns, namely, that the least accurate interpreters of major philosophers are other major philosophers. Gadamer's statement of the nature of Vico's *sensus communis* and its connection to Shaftesbury is valuable in itself. Although I wish to suggest a problematic aspect to his interpretation, Gadamer has interpreted, not simply appropriated, Vico.

In the compact section on *sensus communis* (24–25/19–30), Gadamer cites directly only one of Vico's works (ibid., n. 25), *De nostri temporis studiorum ratione (On the Study Methods of Our Time)*. This is Vico's seventh university oration, first published in 1709; it is traditionally considered to be the first statement of Vico's own position, set in opposition to the Cartesianism and modern scientific conception of a single method of knowledge and thinking of his day.[15] Vico's declared aim in this oration is to compare the ancients against the moderns and to assess their relative merits in an effort to strike a balance. Vico is speaking as Royal Professor of Latin Eloquence, or in modern terms Professor of Rhetoric (a position he held throughout his lifetime), and it is in this work that he most directly speaks of the *sensus communis* as a part of the tradition of humane letters. Vico also later directly mentions and employs the notion of *sensus communis (il senso comune)* in his major work, the *New Science*.[16] Gadamer does not cite the *New Science* directly, but from what will be said below it is evident that he does cite it indirectly, and in his discussion of Dilthey he echoes the popular view of Vico's later work, that "Man makes history" (e.g., 226/222).

Gadamer begins his discussion of the *sensus communis* with the assertion that "it is important to remember the humanistic tradition, and to ask what is to be learned from it with respect to the human sciences' mode of knowledge" (24/19). Gadamer makes this point in reference to his claim that nothing can be learned in or of the human sciences by an application of the methodological ideal of the natural sciences to history and the subject matter of the human sciences. In fact, he holds that such an approach would "amount to their self-annihilation" (ibid.). Gadamer says that Vico's conception of human education or cultivation and human knowledge is based on the revival of old truths. These truths involve close ties between philosophy and rhetoric. Gadamer says that Vico "appeals to the *sensus communis,* common sense, and to the humanistic ideal of *eloquentia*—elements already present in the classical concept of wisdom" (25/19).

What Vico wished to revive among the "old truths" that are the subject matter of his conception of *Bildung* or *paideia* in the *Study Methods,* and of the principles of humanity that is the aim of his *New Science,* is the classical and humanist interconnection of *sapientia, eloquentia,* and *prudentia.* Following Cicero, Vico holds that "eloquence is wisdom put into language."[17] Vico claims in his autobiography that in his teaching he always endeavored to be wisdom speaking *(la sapienza che parla).*[18] Gadamer explains that this ideal of "'talking well' *(eu legein)* has always had two meanings; it is not merely a rhetorical ideal. It also means saying the right thing—i.e., the truth—and is not just the art of speaking—of saying something well" (ibid.).

Gadamer says that even with the success of modern science and its mathematical method "we still cannot do without the wisdom of the ancients and their cultivation of *prudentia* and *eloquentia"* (26/20). Vico says, in his remarks to the

Academy of Oziosi, "I hold the opinion that if eloquence does not regain the lus-ter of the Latins and Greeks in our time, when our sciences have made progress equal to and perhaps even greater than theirs, it will be because the sciences are taught completely stripped of every badge of eloquence."[19] Thinking well, speaking well, and acting well are crucial to the life of the civil world. It is this life that contains the roots of the human sciences and of which they are to be a reflection. The possibility of *sapientia, eloquentia,* and *prudentia* presupposes the existence of *sensus communis.* Gadamer says that Vico takes his conception of the *sensus communis* from that found in the Roman classics, and not from the Greeks. It is not a faculty of combining the outer senses and it is not the *koine dunamis* of Aristotle's *De Anima* (28/22). Gadamer says that "The main thing for our purposes is that here *sensus communis* obviously does not mean only that general faculty in all men but the sense that founds community" (26/21).

Sensus communis, then, is not common sense in the ordinary way it is taken in modern thought, but "communal sense." To act well in common life we must be educated into this sensibility, which is governed not by the true or theoretical knowledge but by what is probable—by those *verisimilia* which arise from occa-sions of fortune and from the powers of choice and the will. Gadamer says: "According to Vico, what gives the human will its direction is not the abstract universality of reason but the concrete universality represented by the commu-nity of a group, a people, a nation, or the whole human race" (26/21). This is the most problematic sentence in Gadamer's account of Vico's guiding concept of *sensus communis.* It has been the focal point of extended criticism by John Schaeffer;[20] it has also been singled out in another study by Giuseppe Modica.[21]

Gadamer's sentence above is very close to that of Vico in axiom 12 of his *New Science,* which states: "Common sense is judgment without reflection, shared by an entire class, an entire people, an entire nation, or the entire human race" (142). The problematic term is Gadamer's "concrete universality" (*"die konkrete Allge-meinheit"*), versus Vico's "judgment without reflection" (*"un giudizio senz'alcuna riflessione"*). Gadamer wishes to make a contrast between the "abstract universal-ity of reason" and the "concrete universality" of community. At first this may seem like a harmless slip of the pen, so to speak, and I do not mean that Gadamer has deliberately committed a Fallacy of Accent. But, by dropping Vico's own defini-tion of common sense (*il senso comune*) as "a judgment without reflection" for the Kantian and German romantic notion of "concrete universality," Gadamer has omitted an element that is crucial to Vico's own position.

The important thing for Vico is judgment *without* reflection. Later in the *New Science* Vico identifies reflection with barbarism (*barbarie della riflessione*) (1106). This is the thought of the modern age that wishes to understand reality solely through the form of conceptual language coupled with a language of flat-tery, a kind of pseudolanguage of sensibility, and it has no connection with what Vico calls poetic wisdom or the original poetic speech of mankind. Judgment without reflection, for Vico, takes the form of "imaginative universals" *(universali fantastici)* and such universals are achieved directly through the human power of *fantasia,* understood as an original and primordial power, different in kind from the power of reflection. Judgment accomplished by reflection is tied to "intelligible universals" *(universali intelligibili),* in Vico's terms (e.g., 34 and 934–35). Intelligible universals are antithetical to *sensus communis* in a way parallel to Gadamer's description of judgments that attempt to subsume the individual case under a universal category (27/21).

Kant in the *Third Critique* says: "But under the *sensus communis* we must include the idea of a sense *common to all,* i.e. of a faculty of judgment which, in its reflection, takes account (a priori) of the mode of representation of all other men in thought, in order, as it were, to compare its judgment with the collective reason of humanity."[22] Gadamer's use of "concrete universality" echoes Kant's notion of the aesthetical judgment as bound up with "subjective universality" *(subjektive Allgemeinheit).*[23] This notion of a universality that is subjective is connected in Kant to his conception of reflective judgment *(reflektierende Urteilskraft)*[24] and his distinction between such forms of judgment and a determinant judgment *(bestimmende Urteilskraft)* that subsumes a particular under a rule. "But if only the particular be given for which the universal has to be found, the judgment is merely *reflective.*"[25]

Gadamer connects Vico's conception of *sensus communis* with that of Shaftesbury in order to bring out how it is a "virtue of social intercourse" (30/25) and further, how it is the basis of a doctrine of morality that is developed through Hutcheson and Hume. Shaftesbury connected *sensus communis* with the notions of wit and humor. A sympathetic union—an intellectual and social bond—must exist between persons in a community in order that wit can function and a joke be understood. Shaftesbury says: "A public spirit can come only from a social feeling or sense of partnership with human kind."[26] *Sensus communis* for Gadamer involves not only an aesthetic sense of form that leads to an aesthetic metaphysics, but also a moral perspective, grounded in the social virtue of sympathy.

Gadamer observes,

> It is very characteristic of the human sciences' self-reflection in the nineteenth century that they proceeded not under the influence of the tradition of moral philosophy to which both Vico and Shaftesbury belong and which is represented primarily by France, the classical land of *le bon sens,* but under the influence of the German philosophy of the age of Kant and Goethe. (32/26)

Gadamer is certainly correct in this observation, but is this not equally a description of how Gadamer himself has proceeded in treating Vico and Shaftesbury in *Truth and Method?* It seems to me that he has done just this, as he proceeds to complete his discussion of *Leitbegriffe* moving to the topics of judgment and taste, using Kant as his reference, along the lines discussed above.

The French historian of the eighteenth century, Paul Hazard, has said,

> If only Italy had listened to Giambattista Vico, and if, as at the time of the Renaissance, she had served as a guide to Europe, would not our intellectual destiny have been different? Our eighteenth-century ancestors would not have believed that all that was clear was true; but on the contrary that "clarity is the vice of human reason rather than its virtue," because a clear idea is a finished idea. They would not have believed that reason was our first faculty, but on the contrary that imagination was.[27]

Gadamer has certainly listened to Vico and in him he has heard the whole humanist tradition. As Gadamer makes clear in his autobiographical reflections in this volume, Vico is the key figure for his interest in rhetorical thought.[28] In this Gadamer, as a thinker with the deepest connections to Heidegger, has taken us beyond the provincial attack on humanism found in Heidegger's *Letter on Humanism*.[29] Although Gadamer has listened to Vico, the commentators on Gadamer's hermeneutics have not listened to Gadamer's listening. In such commentators there is no attention given to Gadamer's Vichian-humanist *Leitbegriff* as a beginning point of his whole book.[30] They begin with what is more familiar to them, with Kant and Heidegger, and focus on his criticism of Dilthey or Betti.

VICO'S PROVIDENTIAL METAPHYSICS OF NARRATION

Vico wishes to formulate a philosophy that escapes two alternatives—the deaf necessity *(sorda necessità)* of the Stoics and the blind chance *(cieco caso)* of the Epicureans.[31] To do this, Vico must reinterpret the eighteenth-century conception of providence in accordance with his conception of history as *corsi e ricorsi*. For Vico, God is born headfirst in history. Every nation passes through three ages, that of gods (in which humans first understand their world wholly in terms of gods); that of heroes (in which men apprehend their own virtues and institutions in terms of heroic figures); and that of the purely human (in which humans think wholly in conceptual and reflective terms and have lost the imaginative grasp they once had on the world and their own natures).

For Vico there is not a providential order (as there is for Kant) of events progressing toward a more peaceful and desirable state, a state of affairs closer to the eternal.[32] After the first age, in which religion flourishes, the sense of the divine in human affairs increasingly diminishes as each nation moves through its cycle of three stages, what Vico designates as its ideal eternal history *(storia ideale eterna)* (e.g., 245, 349). The lessons that God might have taught within social life, the connections between things human and divine, are slowly forgotten and unlearned in history. The *ricorso* that any nation will undergo is a successive attempt by the divine once again to assert its truth in an actual history. Because the *ricorso* is built upon a *corso,* there is a memory and in fact a recapitulation of what has gone before, but there is not progress.[33] Vico's position is that there is a divine eternal pattern that is followed by each nation in its rise, maturity, and fall.

This providential order of human life is not the deaf necessity of the Stoics (among whom Vico would include Descartes, who would indeed include himself) because within this eternal pattern of rise, maturity, and fall each nation makes its particular civil world through its own powers of choice *(auctoritas).* To elaborate, within the *sensus communis,* human beings, through their native rhetorical powers, hear each other within any given age, and they make their world together. The providential order is also not the blind chance of the Epicureans (among whom Vico would include Locke)[34] because there is a definite cycle within which history unfolds. This providential order of history, this overall order of the cycle, makes *phronēsis* or *prudentia* possible in human affairs, and all is not governed simply by chance.

What is the connection between this providential order or ideal eternal history in Vico and *sensus communis?* How does this relate to Gadamer's understanding of Vico, and what are its implications for his attempt to include Vico within the general project of hermeneutics?

Vico says that the type of proof that reigns in this science of history's cycles is such that the reader is to meditate *(meditare)* and to narrate *(narrare)* it for himself following the principle that what counts as proof is what had, has, and will have to be *(dovette, deve, dovrà)* (349). In saying this, Vico is citing the ancient power of the Muses, who could sing of what was, is, and is to come.[35] Philosophical proof for Vico is not based upon reflection upon the world of civil things. Nor is it based on any method of scientific reflection. The "method" is rhetorical, that is, the maker of this proof must meditate the material of the civil world in the sense that it must be internalized, taken into the knower's own being. Meditating, in this case, is not equivalent to reflection because there is not the notion of the knower reflecting *on* the object or appearance and learning its nature. Rather, the knower enters into its inner form.

This act of meditation is completed by the act of narration. In order for the material to be known it must be narrated, that is, it must become a speech for the one making the proof. Thus Vico's new science itself is a prime example of wisdom speaking.[36] In it *sapientia* and *eloquentia* are joined. Vico's philosophy is a topical philosophy, one based on the *ars topica,* what is required to make a speech, as opposed to *critica,* which Vico identifies with Descartes. Critical philosophy holds the notion of a single method of truth and thus it rejects as not knowledge anything that cannot be subject to this standard. The method allows us to evaluate any claim to knowledge and dismiss those that fail to measure up. From this can come no possibility of prudence. Prudence requires *copia,* the ability to grasp all sides of a situation, and it requires the interconnection of *eloquentia* and *sapientia* to place the whole of something in mind, and thus to foresee the course that events are taking.[37]

Vico's association of judgment with *sensus communis* and his exclusion at the same time of reflection or reflective judgment from *sensus communis* is crucial to his total philosophical position. Reflection, for Vico, is connected with critical philosophy, not with topical philosophy. Vico's use of *sensus communis* cannot be grasped apart from its connection with two other features of his philosophy—his conception of "sensible topics" *(topica sensibile)* (495) and his conception of the *lingua mentale comune* or common "mental dictionary" *(dizionario mentale)* (145, 161–62, 445). As Galileo understood there to be a book of nature that could be read in mathematical symbols, so Vico understood there to be a book of the civil world that could be read in terms of a common mental dictionary.

The elements of this common mental dictionary are the imaginative universals that are characteristic of the ages of gods and of heroes (34, 204–10, 403, 809, 933–34). In modern terms we might describe such imaginative universals as equivalent to those master images or meanings that lie at the basis of our fundamental understandings of the world and which are first expressed in myths.[38] The words of any language have fabulous beginnings. The common mental dictionary is a notion of what mind itself is, understood as the mind of the human race. The mental dictionary is what all languages share and what all mythologies have in common. In this respect it might be compared to another concept that is crucial to Vico's thought, what he terms *ius gentium naturale*. This is opposed to a notion of natural law that takes it as an ideal conception of right that is common to all law and to positive law or whatever is the law of a given people at a given time. *Ius gentium naturale* is the notion of that part of actual Roman law that is shared by all other systems of laws.[39]

The common mental dictionary is the counterpart in thought of the *sensus communis* as the basis of social virtue and moral life. The mental dictionary is connected with the notion of the sensory topics through which, Vico says, the first humans created their poetic genera or imaginative universals (494ff.). Vico says the first humans were all body—and they thought with their bodies (236, 331). The first thoughts are present in the expressive capacity of the body, in gesture and rituals. Vico says that the first language was mute (401). In such activity the bond of sympathy that Gadamer speaks of as characteristic of *sensus communis* is first manifested. *Topoi* or common places are first realized by common physical actions undertaken to establish places literally, such as the clearing of the great forests of the earth after the flood, in Vico's retelling of the biblical account of the origin of the gentile peoples.

The ability to establish physically a common *place* has its analogue in the notion of a mental commonplace. Vico says that the primary operations of the mind began first "to hew out topics, which is an art of regulating well the primary operation of our mind by noting the commonplaces that must all be run over in order to know all there is in a thing that one desires to know well; that is, completely" (497). To express this in terms of the theory of the syllogism, the mental dictionary is a great repository of the middle terms from which to draw forth the connections between the major and minor terms necessary not only for the invention of a syllogism but also to bring forth a truth in thought. The art of topics is the art of the middle term, which is the art of inventing arguments.[40] Vico says: "Providence gave good guidance to human affairs when it aroused human minds first to topics rather than to criticism, for acquaintance with things must come before judgment of them. Topics have the function of making minds inventive, as criticism has that of making them exact" (498).

For Vico the primordial power of the mind and of all human social life is imagination or *fantasia*. It is through *fantasia* that we originally learn to make the "trues" *(vera)* of our experience, to convert the true and the made *(verum et factum convertuntur)*. The human in its activity of making, in this sense, imitates the divine and thereby enacts that ancient dictum that wisdom is "knowledge of things human and divine."[41] Human making is based on an imitation of divine making that is already present in the world as the providential structure of history. For Vico, imagination is memory *(la memoria é la stessa che la fantasia)* (819). And memory, as Vico says, is memory *(memoria)* when it remembers things, imagination *(fantasia)* when it alters or imitates them, and ingenuity *(ingegno)* when it brings them into new life or proper relationships (ibid.). Vico's topical philosophy sees the civil world as a theater of memory in which every word has a history that takes us back to its fabulous meanings in myths, the *archai* of which are the imaginative universals or commonplaces that make up the common mental dictionary of the human race.

Providence is nothing more in one sense than that there is truly a *sensus communis* of the human race—a fundamental structure of the human being that, when fully understood, shows that there is a divine structure present in the human world. When we meditate and narrate the events of history to ourselves in the pattern of the Muses, we put ourselves in contact with the divine order of things as well as with the fundamental sympathy that makes us human, that is, social animals. The classical notion of prudence requires the study of the actions of great men in history in order that they may serve as guides to our action. Vico has gone beyond this conception of prudence, and founded prudence not in the actions of certain prudent humans but in history itself, in the providential structure of history.[42] Thus practical wisdom or practical philosophy becomes an art based in a knowledge of things human and divine. In this way Vico's new science is a *scienza in divinità* (365). Vico's complaint against both the Stoics and the Epicureans, in relation to moral philosophy, is that they are ethics of solitaries. Vico says: "For they are each a moral philosophy of solitaries: the Epicurean, of idlers inclosed in their own little gardens; the Stoic, of contemplatives who endeavor to feel no emotion."[43]

What I have attempted to note here is the connection between *sensus communis* and providence in Vico's philosophy, something that Gadamer ignores. This may be seen, on first glance, as attributable to the fact that Gadamer relies strongly on Vico's' views in his early work, the *Study Methods*. But Gadamer takes his paraphrase of Vico's definition of *sensus communis* from the *New Science*. Further, I have emphasized that within Vico's definition, *sensus communis* means not just the common sense of a group or a people but of the "whole human race." Although he notes this, Gadamer, I think, through his notion of tradition, focuses only on the more limited sense of the *sensus communis*—the common sense of groups or peoples, as against that of the whole human race.

VICO'S QUESTIONING OF GADAMER

Gadamer says, "The logic of the human sciences is a logic of the question" (375/370). He takes this from the fifth chapter of R. G. Collingwood's *Autobiography*, in which Collingwood projects but never develops a logic of question and answer. Gadamer says that Collingwood, in projecting this logic, "clearly saw what was missing in naive hermeneutics founded on the prevailing philosophical critique" (376/370). Collingwood says, "It must be understood that question and answer, as I conceived them, were strictly correlative."[44] In singling out this important insight of Collingwood, Gadamer has once again gone where other philosophers have not. He has called our attention to something very important that has been overlooked and which, frankly, is overlooked as a means of thinking in most current hermeneutic literature. The art of philosophical question and answer is surely a difficult one, but it is truly the only philosophical art having its roots in the very origin of humane or anthropological philosophy itself—the activity of Socrates.

In the turns philosophy has taken from Socrates to Descartes we lost the sense of the question. What emerged as the basis of modern philosophy has been the argument, the instrument of mathematical and critical philosophy. The question is natural to language as a form of thought that presumes the *sensus communis*—the possibility of dialogue. Cartesian thought endorses logic and the life of logic is the proposition—the clear and finished idea. Vico claims that whoever would attempt to make a speech or live a life by means of the geometric method engages in a kind of rational madness.[45] The question and the speech it engenders, the rhetorical sense of thinking in terms of the particular situation and the ideal of *copia*, of bringing out various viewpoints, is natural to the tradition of humane letters.

Presuming this sense of the question and its honored place in philosophical hermeneutics, I wish to raise three questions, in relation to Gadamer's philosophy, from the standpoint of Vico's new science of the principles of humanity.

1. Why should "reflection" be endorsed as the most desirable or proper form of philosophical thinking? The challenge to reflection in the development of

modern philosophy is Hegel's conception of the "speculative sentence" which Gadamer attempts to integrate into his conception of hermeneutics. He says, following Hegel, "we call what is common to the metaphysical and the hermeneutical dialectic the 'speculative element'" (469/465). He connects Hegel's conception of speculative dialectic with the logic of question and answer (475/471). In this view speculation then becomes the dialectical possibility of reflection. Vico challenges this with his notion of the barbarism of reflection. This barbarism of reflection typifies the third age of the life of any nation. It is in this age that philosophy appears, and had Vico known its name I believe he would have said that hermeneutics appears.

Reflective thinking is barbarous because it is tied to critical philosophy, with its commitment to method. This is a point of view that Gadamer could share with Vico. But Vico considers reflection to be the very form of modern barbarity because it reduces all thought essentially to some form of cognition, whether or not this includes a version of aesthetic form or thought. The medium of reflective thought is the concept. The concept reduces what is known to a single meaning. Reflection cuts us off from the power of fantasia. As Rousseau says, "finally, men chased the gods out in order to live in the temples themselves."46 The temples, from a cognitive point of view, are simply structures; thus they can be occupied as houses. As Vico says, "men first feel necessity, then look for utility, next attend to comfort, still later amuse themselves with pleasure, thence grow dissolute in luxury, and finally go mad and waste their substance" (241). They waste their substance because they can no longer exercise their power to be within the world and thus instead become reflective thinkers and actors. In modern terms, they become technical philosophers.

I suspect that Gadamer's position would allow for the acceptance of most of what has been said above. He, like Heidegger, wishes to get beyond reflective philosophy, but the ghost of "reflection" remains. From Vico's viewpoint what is needed is meditation and narration. Only narration will allow the philosopher to recall something of the original human power of fantasia and to recover philosophy as a process of self-knowledge. It must be remembered here that narration,for Vico, is not just the rendering of the civil world as a story, even an intellectually satisfying story. It is the notion of telling a true story.47 It is, in other words, to put the providential order of things into words. Narration is not merely the recovery of a tradition in language.

2. Why is hermeneutics or hermeneutic reflection unable to offer us a theory of providence? Gadamer's distinction between the natural sciences that aim at explanation and the human sciences that aim at understanding is, from Vico's standpoint, parallel to his own distinction between the Stoic and the Epicurean positions. The natural scientist is essentially a stoic, that is, natural science actually presumes that there is a necessity to things. The search for explanation in natural science is a search for the one cause of anything, and once found, this is

the key to its explanation. This is not to say that accidental occurrence and probability are not part of science. But the metaphysical position of science must still remain that there is a necessary order to the world, no matter how indefinite or complicated, and that this order, if pursued sufficiently and rigorously, can be found, and the nature of nature explained.

The hermeneutic position of Gadamer is one of historicism.48 His endorsement of traditions and of the reality of prejudice, in opposition to the enlightenment prejudice against prejudice is, to my mind, excellent and rare. But any historicist position is committed to chance, that is, to the notion that there is no fundamental structure to human affairs, there is no ideal eternal history, but instead there are just traditions, all to be understood by the human sciences. Given the notion of reflection as the essential notion of hermeneutic thinking, this notion of various traditions to be understood makes sense. But it does not make sense if there is a sensus communis of the whole human race. If there is such a sensus communis then it is possible to tell the story of the human world in accordance with it. Such narration will be not simply the understanding of various nations in their various lives and communalities. It will be a knowledge per causas, to use Vico's term. It will be a relation of the causes both natural and moral and the occasions of fortune of any nation, as seen against the ages of ideal eternal history.

The presentation I have given of Vico's philosophy differs strongly from the way Gadamer presents it when, in discussing Dilthey's conception of history, he says that Dilthey "finds support in Vico" (226/222) in the idea that the historical world is manmade. This may be Dilthey's position, and it is in fact a popular view of Vico, but it is not what Vico actually says. Gadamer is skeptical of this view. Regarding the notion that the true is the made, Gadamer says "Is Vico's oft repeated formula correct?" (235/230). Gadamer is skeptical of the epistemological primacy of this principle, that the notion that man makes history then enables man better to understand history. However, Vico never held that man makes history. The principle that the true is the made is itself not made by man. The providential structure of history is given via the mental dictionary in man's nature. Men make history only within the certain order of corso e ricorso. And in man's attempt to make history is his attempt to envision the divine order that is there but always just outside his comprehension, his understanding. There is no human science of wisdom for Vico that is not also divine science. As Vico closes the New Science, he says that what is required for such science is the connection of wisdom with piety (1112).

3. Is there an alternative to hermeneutic reflection? Is there a way out of the hermeneutic circle? Thomas Seebohm sees the issues present in Vico's philosophy as a necessary part of the history of hermeneutic thought.[49] He as well as

others have wished to include Vico in that hermeneutic circle that is hermeneutics itself (the parts that make up the whole of hermeneutic philosophy). But in expressing this view Seebohm does not consider what providence means for Vico's philosophy. The problem, which is well known, with Gadamer's conception of hermeneutics is that, in the end, he equates hermeneutics with reason itself. The reader of *Truth and Method*, as he goes along, may think how this or that philosophical position would disagree with what Gadamer is saying, only to find, within the next few pages or in the next chapter, that Gadamer brings up that philosopher or that position and weaves it into his tapestry, calling it an essential part of hermeneutic thinking. Hermeneutics so presented is a great intellectual amoeba, from which there seems to be no escape. Any thinker who thinks in terms of understanding the parts of a text in terms of a whole, or the parts of anything in terms of the thing as a whole, is thinking in accordance with the hermeneutic circle. Any thinker who is not Descartes, or who wishes to fulfill the ideal of appending philosophy to the natural sciences by imitating or incorporating their sense of method as the basis of philosophy, is a hermeneuticist.

Is Vico a hermeneuticist? No, Vico is not a hermeneuticist. This must be said, and probably to the dismay of some who have thought he is, but such a conclusion was based on a partial and popular reading of Vico as a historicist. Vico's philosophy is not an example of hermeneutic reflection. Hermeneutic reflection, like all reflection, is cut off from what Vico means by fantasia and from the product of it—the ability to see history as ideal eternal and as a theater of the actions of providence. Thus hermeneutic reflection is barbarism. It is not the barbarism of Descartes, but it is for Vico barbaric because it puts us in history without an origin, without the common mental dictionary.

In the end this makes a difference for the conception of practical wisdom that can be connected to the idea of sensus communis. On the notion that sensus communis is tied to the notion of tradition, that is, to the common sympathy of a group or a people, the standard of such wisdom of human affairs is relative to the people or group in question. On Vico's view the New Science is above all a book of wisdom, in the sense of a prudence or *phronēsis*, but the standard of this practical wisdom is the eternal order of the cycle in history itself, or providence itself is the model for how to acquire the power of foresight and to act in relation to the natural course of events in the civil world.

DONALD PHILLIP VERENE

DEPARTMENT OF PHILOSOPHY
EMORY UNIVERSITY
APRIL 1992

NOTES

1. Martin Heidegger, *Brief über den Humanismus*, 2d ed. (Bern, 1954), pp. 63–64. See Ernesto Grassi's use of this in *Heidegger and the Question of Renaissance Humanism: Four Studies* (Binghamton, N.Y.: Center for Medieval and Early Renaissance Studies, 1983), chap. 2.

2. Hans-Georg Gadamer, *Wahrheit und Methode: Grundzüge einer philosophischen Hermeneutik*, vol. 1 of *Gesammelte Werke* (henceforth *GW*), 7 vols. (Tübingen: Mohr, 1986). English trans.: *Truth and Method* (henceforth *TM*), 2d rev. ed., trans. Joel Weinsheimer and Donald G. Marshall (New York: Crossroad, 1992). Citations are given hereinafter in the text with the page number of the German edition preceding that of the translation.

3. Gadamer, "Foreword to the Second Edition," *TM*, xxix; *GW*, 2: 439. See also "Rhetorik und Hermeneutik," *GW*, 2: 276.

4. Karl-Otto Apel, *Die Idee der Sprache in der Tradition des Humanismus von Dante bis Vico*, 2d ed. (Bonn: Bouvier Verlag Herbert Grundmann, 1975). Apel states, *"Vico ist als Humanist ein Abschluss, wahrhaft die Eule der Minerva der italienischen Renaissancekultur"* (320–21). Grassi takes a similar view, that Vico is the summary of the humanist tradition: see, e.g., *Rhetoric as Philosophy: The Humanist Tradition* (University Park: Pennsylvania State University Press, 1980) and *Vico and Humanism: Essays on Vico, Heidegger, and Rhetoric*, vol. 3 of Emory Vico Studies (New York: Peter Lang, 1990).

5. The view that Vico is an eighteenth-century child of the Renaissance is disputed; see Eugenio Garin, "Vico and the Heritage of Renaissance Thought," in *Vico: Past and Present*, 2 vols. in 1 (Atlantic Highlands, N.J.: Humanities Press, 1981), 1: 99–116. Garin wishes to demonstrate how deeply Vico's conception of a "new science" is connected with the ambitions of his own time. I do not see that the view of Vico's essential humanism shared by Gadamer, Apel, Grassi, and myself is fundamentally at odds with Garin's view, if it is admitted that Vico is struggling to balance the civil wisdom of the ancients and humanists off against the true achievements of the moderns. In his history of Italian philosophy Garin makes clear that the fundamental idea of Vico's *New Science,* the conception of a "poetic wisdom" upon which all later forms of knowledge and culture is founded, is a solution to the problem as started in the Renaissance: "La soluzione del problema rinascimentale della sapienza poetica primitiva conduceva il Vico, attraverso un radicale capovolgimento, alla soluzione del problema della struttura della mente umana" *(Storia della filosofia italiana*, 3 vols. (Turin: Einaudi, 1966), 2: 946).

6. A sense of this worldwide renaissance of Vico studies can be gained through perusal of the issues of *New Vico Studies* (Atlanta and New York, 1983 to present), the *Bollettino del Centro di Studi Vichiani* (Naples, 1971 to present), and the new *Cuadernos sobre Vico* (Sevilla, 1991 to present). The development of current Vico studies is described in Giorgio Tagliacozzo, "Toward a History of Recent Anglo-American Vico Scholarship" (in 5 parts), *New Vico Studies* 1–5 (1983–87) and in "The Study of Vico World-Wide and the Future of Vico Studies," *New Vico Studies* 8 (1990): 20–37. See *A Bibliography of Vico in English 1884–1984* (Bowling Green, Ohio: Philosophy Documentation Center, 1986) and supplements in *New Vico Studies*. Also see Benedetto Croce, *Bibliografia vichiana* (2 vols.), rev. ed. Fausto Nicolini (Naples: Ricciardi, 1947–48), and the following: *Bibliografia vichiana 1948–1970,* ed. M. Donzelli; *1971–1980,* ed. A. Battistini; and *Terzo Contributo alla Bibliografia Vichiana 1981–1985,* ed. R. Mazzola, published as supplements to *Bollettino del Centro di Studi Vichiani.*

7. A picture of this can be quickly gained through the last section of Vittorio Hösle's "Einleitung" to the new German translation of Vico's *Scienza nuova.* See Giovanni Battista Vico, *Prinzipien einer neuen Wissenschaft über die gemeinsame Natur der Völker,*

2 vols., trans. Vittorio Hösle and Christoph Jermann (Hamburg: Meiner, 1990), 1: cclxiv–xxvii. See also Andrea Battistini, "Contemporary Trends in Vichian Studies," in *Vico: Past and Present,* 1: 1–42, esp. 29ff.

8. See my "Vico's Influence on Cassirer," *New Vico Studies* 3 (1985): 105–11.

9. Apel's *Die Idee der Sprache* did not appear in its first edition until 1963. It was, however, a bringing together of views he was developing in the 1950s and it appeared first as his *Habilitationsschrift* in 1957. There are also the essays of Auerbach on Vico and Vichian themes, going back to the 1930s, and the discussion of Vico in Max Horkheimer, *Anfänge der bürgerlichen Geschichtsphilosophie* (Stuttgart: Kohlhammer, 1930). See the English translation by Fred Dallmayr of this part of the work: Max Horkheimer, "Vico and Mythology," *New Vico Studies* 5 (1987): 63–76. There is also the attention to Vico of Emilio Betti; see "The Principles of New Science of G. B. Vico and the Theory of Historical Interpretation," trans. Giorgio A. Pinton and Susan Noakes, *New Vico Studies* 6 (1988): 31–50. This article was originally published in Italian in 1957.

10. Benedetto Croce, *The Philosophy of Giambattista Vico,* trans. R. G. Collingwood (New York: Russell and Russell, 1964; orig. pub. 1913). Collingwood discussed Vico in *The Idea of History* (New York: Oxford Univ. Press, 1956; orig. pub. 1946).

11. This interest went so far as for Croce to write an imaginary conversation wherein Hegel is introduced to Vico's work by an Italian visitor during the last months of his life. Benedetto Croce, "An Unknown Page from the Last Months of Hegel's Life," trans. James W. Hildesheim and Ernesto Caserta, *The Personalist* 45 (1964): 344–45, 351.

12. See, e. g., Michael Mooney, *Vico in the Tradition of Rhetoric* (Princeton: Princeton University Press, 1985); Nancy Struever, "Rhetoric and Philosophy in Vichian Inquiry," *New Vico Studies* 3 (1985): 131–45. Ernesto Grassi, *Rhetoric as Philosophy* and *Vico and Humanism* (n. 4, above); and my *Vico's Science of Imagination* (Ithaca: Cornell University Press, 1971), chap. 6.

13. Gadamer, *TM,* 568, 572; *GW,* 2: 467, 470.

14. Gadamer, *GW,* 2: 111, 192, 273, 280, 311, 342, 498; 4: 133, 368; 5: 358; 7: 222.

15. Giambattista Vico, *On the Study Methods of Our Time,* trans. Elio Gianturco, with *The Academies and the Relation between Philosophy and Eloquence,* trans. Donald Phillip Verene (Ithaca: Cornell University Press, 1990; 1965). Gadamer also cites this work of Vico in "Rhetorik und Hermeneutik," *GW* 2: 280, n. 51. Vico's detailed attack on Descartes' metaphysics was published one year later, in 1710: *De antiquissima Italorum sapientia ex linguae latinae originibus eruenda.* English trans. by L. M. Palmer, *On the Most Ancient Wisdom of the Italians Unearthed from the Origins of the Latin Language* (Ithaca: Cornell University Press, 1989).

16. Giambattista Vico, *La Scienza nuova seconda,* in *Opere di G. B. Vico* (8 vols. in 11), ed. Fausto Nicolini (Bari: Laterza, 1911–1941), vol. 4: pars. 142–45. English translation: *The New Science of Giambattista Vico,* trans. Thomas Goddard Bergin and Max Harold Fisch (Ithaca: Cornell University Press, 1984; orig. pub. 1948). Hereinafter cited in the text by the paragraph enumeration common to the Laterza and Cornell editions.

17. Cicero, *Partitiones oratoriae,* 23. 79.

18. *The Autobiography of Giambattista Vico,* trans. Max Harold Fisch and Thomas Goddard Bergin (Ithaca: Cornell University Press, 1983; 1944), p. 199.

19. Vico, *Study Methods* and *Philosophy and Eloquence,* p. 87.

20. John D. Schaeffer, *Sensus Communis: Vico, Rhetoric, and the Limits of Relativism* (Durham, N.C.: Duke University Press, 1990), chap. 5. Schaeffer's criticisms are important and developed at length and in detail. They are formulated from the perspective of rhetoric and the conception of language that is present in Vico's conception of *sensus communis.* See also Schaeffer's *"Sensus communis* in Vico and Gadamer," *New Vico Studies* 5 (1987): 117–30. My problems that follow, above, focus on the metaphysical dimension.

21. Giuseppe Modica, *La filosofia del "senso comune" in Giambattista Vico* (Caltanisseta-Roma: Salvatore Sciascia Editore, 1983), p. 77, n. 15. Modica does not disagree with Gadamer's emphasis on the importance of the "concrete universal."

22. Immanuel Kant, *Critique of Judgement*, trans. J. H. Bernard (New York: Hafner, 1974), p. 136. *Kritik der Urteilskraft* (Hamburg: Meiner, 1974), p. 144.

23. Kant, *Critique*, p. 46; *Kritik*, p. 49.

24. Kant, *Critique*, p. 28; *Kritik*, p. 29.

25. Kant, *Critique*, p. 15; *Kritik*, p. 15.

26. Shaftesbury, *"Sensus Communis:* An Essay on the Freedom of Wit and Humor," treatise 2 of *Characteristics of Men, Manners, Opinions, Times*, ed. John M. Robertson (Indianapolis: Bobbs-Merrill, 1964), p. 72.

27. Paul Hazard, *La pensée européenne au dix-huitième siècle de Montesquieu à Lessing* (Paris: Librairie Arthine Fayard, 1963), p. 43. My translation.

28. "Reflections on My Philosophical Journey," pt. 3; and in Gadamer's "Selbstdarstellung," *GW*, 2: 498–99.

29. Joel C. Weinsheimer, in *Gadamer's Hermeneutics: A Reading of Truth and Method* (New Haven: Yale University Press, 1985) claims that Gadamer's section on the humanist tradition can be read as a reply to Heidegger's *Letter on Humanism* and that "it affirms Heidegger's critique of humanism as correct in principle but also shows that historical humanism was less 'humanistic' than Heidegger thought" (p. 73). What is meant by the claim: "it affirms Heidegger's critique of humanism as correct in principle"? Gadamer does not specifically say this, and Weinsheimer offers no elaboration. I find Grassi's point correct, in *Heidegger and Renaissance Humanism*, that Heidegger's critique of humanism is based on a misunderstanding of what humanism really is, and so holds against a certain traditional sense of humanism. But this would not make it "correct in principle." I take Weinsheimer's claim more as an act of piety toward Heidegger than a critical observation.

30. Weinsheimer, in his commentary on *Truth and Method*, passes over Gadamer's use of Vico's *sensus communis* as a *Leitbegriff* in a sentence (see p. 74). Georgia Warnke, *Gadamer: Hermeneutics, Tradition, and Reason* (Stanford: Stanford University Press, 1987), a work frequently used as a means for entering Gadamer's thought in English, makes no mention of it; Vico is cited only in connection with Dilthey's conception of history (see p. 39). The contributors to two important collections, *Hermeneutics and Praxis*, ed. Robert Hollinger (South Bend: University of Notre Dame Press, 1985) and *Hermeneutics and Modern Philosophy*, ed. Brice R. Wachterhauser (Albany: State University of New York Press, 1986), pay no attention to the issues discussed above, with the exception of Gadamer's own discussion of rhetoric in the translation of his essay "On the Scope and Function of Hermeneutical Reflection" that appears in the latter volume. The principal commentator who has given important attention to Gadamer's use of humanist rhetorical themes (in addition to Schaeffer; see above, n. 20) is Klaus Dockhorn, in his review of *Wahrheit und Methode* in *Göttingische Gelehrte Anzeigen* 218, nos. 3–4 (1966): 169–206. See the abridged translation in *Philosophy and Rhetoric* 13 (1980): 160–80. Gadamer's response to Dockhorn is in "Rhetorik, Hermeneutik und Ideologiekritik," *GW*, 2: 232–50 and *Continuum* 8 (1970): 77–95.

31. See Vico's letter to Abbé Esperti, "All'abate Esperti in Roma," *Opere di G. B. Vico*, 5: 201–3.

32. Kant says,

> The guarantee of perpetual peace is nothing less than that great artist, nature *(natura daedala rerum)*. In her mechanical course we see that her aim is to produce

a harmony among men, against their will and indeed through their discord. As a necessity working according to laws we do not know, we call it destiny. But, considering its design in world history, we call it 'providence', inasmuch as we discern in it the profound wisdom of a higher cause which predetermines the course of nature and directs it to the objective final end of the human race. *(Perpetual Peace,* ed. Lewis White Beck [Indianapolis: Bobbs Merrill, Library of Liberal Arts, 1957], p. 24)

33. How to understand Vico's conception of cycles is not a matter agreed upon by all commentators of his work. I am simply assuming the position I have worked out in my *Vico's Science of Imagination* and elsewhere.

34. See my translation and commentary, "Giambattista Vico's 'Reprehension of the Metaphysics of René Descartes, Benedict Spinoza, and John Locke': An Addition to the *New Science,*" *New Vico Studies* 8 (1990): 2–18.

35. See my "The New Art of Narration: Vico and the Muses," *New Vico Studies* 1 (1983): 21–38.

36. I have attempted to work out this approach to Vico's philosophy fully in my *The New Art of Autobiography: An Essay on the 'Life of Giambattista Vico Written By Himself'* (Oxford: Clarendon Press, 1991).

37. Gadamer states: "Vico rightly assigns it a special value: *copia,* the abundance of viewpoints. I find it frighteningly unreal when people like Habermas ascribe to rhetoric a compulsory quality that one must reject in favor of unconstrained, rational dialogue" *(TM,* 568; *GW,* 2: 467).

38. On imaginative universals, see *Vico's Science of Imagination,* chap. 3.

39. On the importance of *ius gentium naturale* for Vico's conception of his new science see *The New Art of Autobiography,* pp. 142–45.

40. See Aristotle, *Rhetoric,* 1.1–2 and 2.20–23; *Prior Analytics,* 2: 27; *Topics,* 1: 1.

41. See Cicero, *Tusculanae disputationes* 4.26.57 and *De officiis.* 2.2.5. Seneca, *Letters to Lucilius* 89.5, states that "wisdom is knowledge of things human and divine"; this was taken up later by the Renaissance, and it became a commonplace definition of wisdom.

42. This point is made very well by Alain Pons, "Prudence and Providence: The *Pratica della Scienza nuova* and the Problem of Theory and Practice in Vico," in *Giambattista Vico's Science of Humanity,* ed. Giorgio Tagliacozzo and Donald Phillip Verene (Baltimore: The Johns Hopkins University Press, 1976), pp. 431–48.

43. Vico, *The Autobiography,* p. 122.

44. R. G. Collingwood, *An Autobiography* (Oxford: Clarendon Press, 1939), p. 31.

45. Vico, *Ancient Wisdom,* pp. 98–99.

46. Jean-Jacques Rousseau, *Discours sur les sciences et les arts* et *Discours sur l'origine de l'inégalité* (Paris: Garnier-Flammarion, 1971), p. 52. English translation: *The First and Second Discourses,* trans. R. D. and J. R. Masters (New York: St. Martin's Press, 1964), p. 54.

47. See my exchange with MacIntyre: Donald Phillip Verene, "Imaginative Universals and Narrative Truth," *New Vico Studies* 6 (1988): 1–19; and Alaisdair MacIntyre, "Imaginative Universals and Historical Falsification: A Rejoinder to Professor Verene," *New Vico Studies* 6 (1988): 21–30.

48. Carl Page, "Philosophical Hermeneutics and Its Meaning for Philosophy," *Philosophy Today* (Summer 1991): 127–36.

49. Thomas M. Seebohm, "The Problem of Hermeneutics in Recent Anglo-American Literature: Part II," *Philosophy and Rhetoric* 10 (1977): 274.

REPLY TO DONALD PHILLIP VERENE

This contribution to our volume is especially valuable to me. This study, by a leading expert on Vico's work, of the way in which I have made use of one of the most important early works of Vico for the development of my own thought stands as a real contribution to scholarship. The text at issue was an Italian text. The author is mistaken if he believes that a single citation proves that already thirty-five years ago I was able to really study Italian texts. But when one thinks through an important text, one anticipates, I suppose, some things which become formulated explicitly only later in the life of a thinker. In the face of this limitation, I am extremely happy to have it confirmed by an expert that, on the whole, I rightfully claimed for my own work the testimony of Vico. Verene corrects me when he finds something missing in my rendering of *'senor-reflexion'* without 'reflection', which is an indispensable principle of the Vico of that period. In place of that I say concrete universality. But one might give me credit for my intention to express roughly—as I am learning here gratefully—by means of such a phrase the point that Vico himself makes when he speaks of "topic" *[Topik]* and when he finally even consigns reflection as a form of *critica* even to barbarism. It would have been better if I had avoided the concept of reflection entirely, or if I at least had added that I meant a kind of performance knowledge *[Vollzugswissen]*. I can understand if one is uncomfortable when one finds Kant's theory of the imagination and of the aesthetic faculty of judgment referred to in this context. After all, this is also a theory of the conceptless way of cognition. With regard to the use I make of it I believe that I have been understood rather well by Verene when he says explicitly that reflection is not equivalent to mediation. But for the more detailed presentation I am very much obliged to Mr. Verene. It illuminates, and presents in detail, what I construe in my own thoughts as a philologist and as a philosopher. I am referring to the transition to rhetoric, to the study of eloquence *[Eloquentia]*, to the role of topic, and to the role for the language of the muses. Retranslated into my own language, for my own purposes, I affirm all of that. As a classical philologist I focused especially on rhetoric and that is why I became aware of Vico's critique of Descartes in those days. So I can only gratefully take note of the more precise elaboration of these points in Verene's essay which shows hardly any difference with respect to the matter from my own use of Vico. But more about that later.

This Vico expert also helps me with regard to my skeptical question of why the true and the made, *verum* and *factum,* are exchangeable. It was only against the background of divine providence that this claim became acceptable for me. Moreover, I also see my appeal to Shaftesbury supported in principle, as well as the reference to the bond of sympathy which is apparently an essential ground for the humanity of being human. With regard to the necessary extension of this bond to the entire human race, I believe I have described and justified this extension through the notion of linguisticality. I am also thankful for the clarity with which my reference to Collingwood is emphasized here, and especially for the concluding reference to Socrates. A great part of my research is indeed devoted to him. That the author is apparently troubled by my talk of reflection is due to the fact that he imputes to me the concept of reflection taken in a very narrow, modern, Kantian sense. Thus he apparently is not willing to follow my intention of renewing the concept of the speculative from Hegel's early days explicitly against Hegel's own, later, dialectical self-stylization of that concept.

The speculative is much more a matter of mediation than reflection, and it does not so much belong to the concept but primarily to language, although not so clearly to narration. But after having been able to learn here in what broad sense narration can be understood, I believe that in volume eight of my collected works, *Kunst als Aussage,* I have justified in detail that in art truth is spoken.

And so I can conclude my response with thanks, but also with the question of what a hermeneuticist might be in his eyes. Unfortunately, I do not know this. But I am sure that Vico too would have answered the question as to what he had described in his three world epochs by saying that he himself, in a mysterious way, does not belong to the third epoch of the concept.

H.-G. G.

6

Jean Grondin

GADAMER ON HUMANISM

In this essay, I would like to try to understand Gadamer's step, or leap, beyond Heidegger by concentrating on a theme that might first appear somewhat remote from the major preoccupations of the two thinkers, the problem of humanism. Such generalizations are always hazardous, but one could claim that the issue of humanism was more closely attended to in Latin countries such as France and Italy than in the German philosophical tradition, which seemed more concerned with history and the traditional tenets of Western metaphysics. In that tradition, the "human" perspective takes a second seat to the divine or merely "logical" perspective, which people acquire through the use of reason. Nevertheless, the issue of humanism, far from being incidental, can enable us to understand what is profoundly at stake, and strikingly different, in the philosophies of Heidegger and Gadamer. Many describe Gadamer as a Heideggerian, and he is in many respects. In spite of his evident and often acknowledged debt to authors like Plato, Augustine, or Hegel, the most dominant and persistent imprint on his philosophy and his intellectual development has come from Heidegger, his teacher and mentor. In a sense, any work "on" Gadamer is ultimately a study of his relation to Heidegger. Yet Gadamer distances himself from Heidegger on a wide variety of issues, and these have been dealt with in the extensive literature. Why Gadamer departs from Heidegger can, I submit, be grasped by focusing on the subterranean theme of humanism.

To put the thesis bluntly, Gadamer is a humanist and Heidegger isn't. No moral judgment whatsoever is immediately implied by this (say, Gadamer is "humane," whereas Heidegger isn't), but, more basically, a general philosophical orientation that can make us understand why and at what point a Heideggerian such as Gadamer ceases to be Heideggerian. What is meant shouldn't be understood primarily in a biographical sense either. It is certainly accurate that Heidegger was raised in a provincial form of Catholicism that was hostile to modernism and humanism in general, which was more often than not associated with atheism, and that Gadamer, a Protestant, profited from a more open, classical, and humanistic upbringing. Again, we are referring to a philosophical outlook, that is, to their appreciation of humanism as a leading force in Western culture.

The current literature on the theme of humanism usually singles out three major forms or "high points" of humanism.[1] The first is to be found in the "humanism" of the Renaissance, which resurrected the accomplishments of human artistry and culture in the original works of the Greek and the Latin authors, a focus on "human" achievements, the *studia humanitatis* that was opposed, or added, to a God-centered perspective, the *studia divinitatis,*[2] which was said to be pervasive in the "middle" ages. Since the Renaissance was a "rebirth" of antiquity, one could trace back the seeds of humanism to Greek antiquity itself and more specifically to Socrates and his concentration on "merely" human affairs (exemplified, for instance, in the "know thyself" and in his turning away from the cosmological obsessions of his predecessors). A second form of humanism, of which the Germans are well aware, was found in the Enlightenment and, more specifically, in the works of the German classics of Lessing, Schiller, Goethe, and Winckelmann, all of whom followed the Renaissance in viewing man as a being whose constant task can only consist in perfecting his own self, fulfilling his latent possibilities, again against any heteronomous tutelage of reason. Finally, a "third" form of humanism emerged at the beginning of the twentieth century among classicists like Werner Jaeger who perceived in ancient culture the models of a truly humanistic education. Today, to enjoy a "humanistic" upbringing, in Germany and elsewhere, means that one has studied the Greeks and the Latins.

But in order to put the philosophical debate on humanism in its proper focus, one has to take into account the spiritual situation of Europe after the Second World War. The sheer inhumanity of the Nazi regime and the World War propelled a new discussion on the avenues of humanism. Had humanity exhausted all its possibilities after the death camps and the bloodiest of wars humanity had suffered? Was faith in humanity and its promises of self-formation still possible after Auschwitz? This feeling of disarray was echoed in Jean Beaufret's question to Heidegger in 1946: how can we give a new meaning to the word "humanism"? This question was very typical of the general atmosphere of the times. The dominant philosophy was existential humanism, a philosophy that concentrated exclusively on the human predicament (Sartre,[3] Jaspers, Merleau-Ponty). But the issue, much as existentialism itself, also went far beyond academia. The German constitution, drafted under the shock of the Nazi regime of terror, established as its first and guiding principle the "inviolable dignity of man" *(die Würde des Menschen ist unantastbar).*[4]

But what does it mean to adopt a "humanist" perspective after modernity led up to the barbarism symbolized by Auschwitz? This is the question Jean Beaufret put to one of the leading, if isolated thinkers of the time, Martin Heidegger, whose philosophy of existence was also thought to be one of the roots of the new "humanism." Heidegger was himself very much concerned by the problem, so much so that he immediately took up Beaufret's question—probably the

first and only time he ever responded publicly to a query on his intellectual perspective—in an open letter that became one of the most outspoken testimonies
of his philosophical "turn," the famous *Letter on Humanism*.[5] Heidegger's reflections on humanism weren't sparked by the events that led to the collapse of
national-socialism. As if to document this, Heidegger published his *Letter on
Humanism* conjointly with a seemingly scholarly yet momentous study, *Plato's
Doctrine of Truth*, that dates back to 1942.[6] In this study, Heidegger argues that
humanism is but the latest avatar of metaphysical thinking launched by Plato's
subordination of everything there is to the instance of the *idea*, the *eidos*, which
refers back to an "ideal" perspective, something that can be seen (*eidos* is ety-
mologicaly linked to the verb *oida*, which means "to have seen" and "to know")
or grasped by a looking person, a human eye. For Plato, to understand reality as
it is, is to understand it by way of its "idea," i.e., through the general aspect it
presents to the apprehending eye of the soul. Heidegger sees in Platonism the
most decisive event in the adventure of human culture, which one could translate
as a far-reaching "intellectualization" of all there is or, as Heidegger puts it, as a
forgetfulness of Being. What is forgotten in this strictly human "idealization" of
the world is the sheer gratuity of Being, which simply "is," and into which we
are thrown well before we can undertake to make sense of it with our "ideas."
Platonism erases, as it were, this naked evidence of Being and replaces it by the
ontological precedence of the "idea," of the intellectual and, therefore, human
outlook on what is. This surpassing of being by reaching forth to the "idea" or
"ground" behind it is what distinguishes metaphysics. Thus metaphysics is characterized by the, at first tacit, rise to prominence of the human being that
imposes itself, as it were, as the source from which the whole of Being has to
become accountable, an accountability that culminates in the essence of technology and technological manipulation (carried to its extreme by fascism, Heidegger believed). Metaphysics, humanism, and the essence of technology form an
intertwined whole for Heidegger. This is why Heidegger wants to take some distance regarding the blinding evidence of humanism. In the mind of Heidegger,
humanism is not what is going to save us from the impending catastrophe of
humankind, it could very well be what got us into trouble in the first place. He
thus rejects the implicit premise of Beaufret's question, namely that humanism is
a "good thing" and just needs to be redefined. Clearly swimming against the
tide, his answer begins by stating: "Comment redonner un sens au mot 'humanisme'? The question proceeds from your intention to retain the word 'humanism'. I wonder whether that is necessary. Or is the damage caused by all such
terms still not sufficiently obvious?"[7] Later on, Heidegger will even recommend
"an open resistance to 'humanism'" on the grounds that this would help us to
become dumbfounded by the traditional view of the *"humanitas* of the *homo
humanus"* and its basis.[8] Let's keep in mind this idea of "resistance," since we
will encounter later on a different one in Gadamer's work.

That Heidegger uses Latin titles when he describes humanism is by no means adventitious. For him, humanism arose in the era of the Latins, that is, according to him, at a time when philosophy had ceased to be a creative force and had degenerated into a hollow "technique" of "education." The notion of *"humanitas"* was first entertained, Heidegger claims, in the Roman republic,[9] where the *homo humanus* was single-handedly opposed to the *homo barbarus*. The *homo humanus* proudly adopts the Greek ideal of education *(paideia)* by indulging in the *eruditio et institutio in bonas artes*. This understanding of education is translated in the term of *humanitas*. This perspective was renewed in the Renaissance of the fourteenth and fifteenth centuries as well as in the German humanism of Goethe and Schiller. Everywhere, humanism is to be generally understood as "the care that man can become free for its own humanity and find in this his dignity." Humanism is a perspective that centers on humanity and can see nothing besides it. The anthropocentrism of humanism, concludes Heidegger, prevents one from raising the question of Being or of its relation to humanity. Humanism presupposes an unquestioned understanding of the human being as an *animal rationale,* as a living being endowed with the power of reason that assimilates it to divinity. This understanding, this self-distinguishing of humanity from the rest of being, this claim of humanity to superiority, is what Heidegger wishes to call into question. What enables us to pose ourselves as something beyond animality, as beings that must cultivate their reason, and so forth? For Heidegger, it is urgent to realize that man is not at the center of the universe. He is perhaps a peripheral apparition in the whole of Being, out of which it should gain a new understanding of itself (as a pastoral "shepherd of Being") and its essential finitude, or "thrownness" into Being and by Being. Heidegger thus urges us to go beyond humanism, a transcendence suggested perhaps by the *über* in the title *Letter on (über) Humanism,* i.e., a message thrown into a bottle at sea in the hope of paving the way for what could come after the age of humanism or metaphysics (in German, one would say *Brief über den Humanismus hinaus*).

Heidegger's depiction of the Roman *"humanitas"* is markedly sarcastic in tone and content. The rise of humanism is a typically Roman phenomenon, he underscores time and again,[10] as if to claim for himself a fresh path to the Greeks over and against the "humanist" classicists of his time. He boasts that the Greeks could still think without titles such as humanism and didn't even bother to label their thinking "philosophy."[11] With the later Greeks, who first invented "schools of philosophy," and the Romans, "thinking came to its end," so that its disappearance had to be compensated for by the rise of "philosophy," understood as an "instrument of education and that therefore acquired value as a scholarly enterprise and as a cultural institution," philosophy being reduced to a "technology destined to produce explanations out of the highest causes."[12]

It is now time to confront Heidegger's massive critique of humanism with Gadamer's own philosophy. Even if Gadamer doesn't deal directly with Heidegger's position on humanism, not even, if I read appropriately, in his collection of essays on *Heidegger's Paths* devoted to the later Heidegger,[13] his philosophical perspective can be understood as a defense of humanism and hence as a response to Heidegger's repudiation of the humanistic tradition. This is obvious in at least two ways. First of all, Gadamer's major work, *Truth and Method* (1960), is concerned with a legitimation of the "human" sciences and their importance for philosophy. Human sciences are called *Geisteswissenschaften* in German, but Gadamer is certainly aware that he is dealing with the "humanities" or *humaniora* that formed the cornerstone of the humanist conception of education. Secondly, and perhaps more importantly, the book provokingly opens on a rehabilitation of the forgotten humanistic tradition. In the immediate context of the book, this rehabilitation is directed against the Kantian outbidding of humanism, which stripped the humanities of the title of science. But for a Heideggerian such as Gadamer, it can and should also be read as an answer to Heidegger's own overcoming of humanism.

In a way, Gadamer still follows the lead of Heidegger on this issue. His critique of the overriding dominance of methodical science in contemporary culture is Heideggerian in nature. Where Heidegger denounces the pervasive essence of technology, Gadamer points to the illusions of methodical. Yet the roots of their criticism are very different and perhaps opposed to each other. Heidegger sees technology as the last flagpole of metaphysics or humanism that reduces Being to its functionality for human purposes. Quite on the contrary, Gadamer interprets the dominance of method as the result of the Kantianly motivated abandonment of the humanist tradition, one that his hermeneutics will strive to reconquer.

Kant's importance in this debate cannot be underestimated. Even if his inquiry into the possibility of metaphysics had a positive intent, its result and impact was to establish mathematics and the natural sciences as the sole models of scientificity. What didn't correspond to the methodical criteria of exact science had to be deprived of any cognitive value. Common sense, judgment, and taste, which were cultivated by the humanistic tradition because of their social, political, but also their cognitive importance, were thus relegated to a merely subjective sphere, devoid of scientific import. Everything that isn't "scientific," i.e., verifiable by the norms of methodical science, can only entertain a subjective or aesthetic validity. Gadamer's heroic effort in *Truth and Method* will start off with a repudiation of this aesthetic trivialization of the human sciences. He will call into question the Kantian methodological bias that led thinkers of the nineteenth and twentieth centuries to ground the scientificity of the human sciences on some rigorous "methods" that would be valid independently of the context and the observing subject, very much in the way the natural sciences define their own "method."

Even if Gadamer does not wish to exclude method entirely from the realm of the humanities, it is his conviction that methods alone are not that which make up the scientificity and relevance of the human sciences. More importantly, he argues forcefully, the human sciences have to be understood as "the true advocates or emissaries of humanism," *als die wahren Sachwalter des Humanismus.*[14] This is the first occurrence of the term humanism in *Truth and Method.* It is introduced as a countermovement to the methodical (Heidegger would say technical) model of knowledge represented by the natural sciences. But according to Gadamer, this tradition has been forsaken or forgotten, precisely because of the unquestioned domination, since Kant, of the latter model of exact science. Gadamer will thus have to reacquaint us with this tradition.

It is useful to follow Gadamer closely in his own depiction of the meaning of humanism. The first author Gadamer will evoke in this context will be Herder, who also was in his time an adversary of Kant. Gadamer had devoted to Herder a conference lecture of 1941, which became one of the few articles he published during the Nazi era. Even though some parts of this lecture contain elements on the German idea of *Volk* that one could find objectionable today,[15] it courageously, in a time of inhumanity, portrayed Herder as a defender of humanism. His philosophy of history is indeed grounded on a "faith in the victory of reason,"[16] seeing in history "the spread and promotion of humanity, a humanity however which can only be found in the course of history."[17] What is important to note is that humanity has to *build* itself through history in order to reach its rational potential.

Humanism as a whole, and here independently of Herder's specific views, is not so much defined by the notion that humanity distinguishes itself from animality through reason. Rather, it is defined by the view that humanity constantly has to subdue the animality out of which it stems by developing its rationality, which is actually nothing but the overcoming of animality and its barbaric forms in the history of mankind. Thus the crucial value of culture and tradition for humanism: man never ceases to cultivate himself, never ceases to learn because he is constantly threatened by the darker sides of his animality that can break out anytime.[18] Humanism is thus an attitude of vigilance towards this animal side of human nature, which one can only contain through a process of education or formation and for which there are some models (the "classics" for example), but no scientific rules. Humanism therefore doesn't rest on a fixed notion of what it is to be a human or to have reason. To be human is to have no such algorithmic notion of oneself. Humanism is rather an unending quest for civility in human affairs that can only be achieved or exercised in the process of culture and cultivation of one's own talents.

To be sure, there are theological roots to this conception of humanism that is characteristic of the Renaissance, if not of contemporary humanism. The "lower" side of our nature is to be found in the Biblical notion that man was made out of ashes. What elevates humanity, on the other hand, is that God created man according to his own image. Humanity carries this image within itself, but it has to live up to it, to let its talents flourish and realize what they are destined to accomplish, that is, to elevate mankind to the level of God.[19] The dignity of mankind resides for humanism in this idea that it is made in the image of God, a distinction it can only live up to by cultivating itself and domesticating its "animal" side.

It is therefore no surprise to see Gadamer's rehabilitation of humanism in *Truth and Method* start off precisely with this notion of culture, or *Bildung,* that takes on a historical dimension with Herder, but whose theological origins date back to the Renaissance and the Middle Ages. In the best humanistic tradition, Gadamer characterizes *Bildung* as the "properly human way of developing one's natural talents and capacities."[20] In short, humanity is not something one already has, or some skill one could learn once and for all, it is a sense, a direction one can only try to cultivate. Gadamer will also evoke the theological context out of which this conception arose: "The rise of the word *Bildung* evokes the ancient mystical tradition according to which man carries in his soul the image of God, after whom he is fashioned, and which man must cultivate in himself."[21] What distinguishes mankind from the other animals is exactly this ability to develop itself, to surpass its provincial particularity and lift itself up to the universal. Gadamer won't hesitate to follow Hegel's description of this human elevation above nature: "Man is characterized by the break with the immediate and the natural that the intellectual, rational side of his nature demands of him."[22]

What is striking in all this, is that Gadamer so candidly brings to life again the classical self-definitions of humanism that Heidegger rejected out of hand. In substance, the depictions of humanism they use are the same, but Heidegger evokes them in a distanced and ironic way, whereas Gadamer seems to have no qualms whatsoever with them. This idea that the *homo humanus,* as an "image of God," must devote himself to the *studium humanitatis* and cultivate the *eruditio et institutio in bonas artes* in order to master his *animalitas,* served for Heidegger as a caricature of humanism, as a view of man's "divine" and "cultivated" distinction that he cannot assume anymore. If one takes Gadamer at his word, and I believe one should, it is clear that he fully endorses the conception of humanism from which Heidegger distances himself. As if Heidegger were right in his understanding of humanism, with this small difference that yes, one should indeed keep this tradition of humanism alive.

There is also another latent difference between Heidegger and Gadamer. In order to establish the solidarity of humanism with metaphysics, the *Letter on Humanism* repeatedly states that humanism unmistakably rests on a "fixed" understanding of what man is.[23] One can surmise why Heidegger would want to claim this, but it is far from certain whether it is true or not. If man is a being that is constantly in the process of developing itself through learning, culture, and civilization, then there is no such thing as a human "essence." There is no fixed idea of what man is, only an idea that man has to build himself, his world,

his institutions in order to fight the evil, or "animality," that begets him. Heidegger contrastingly writes on man in his *Letter on Humanism* that he is a "shepherd of Being," that he has to understand himself out of his "essential relation to
Being," that he is "capable of a relation to the Gods and the sacred," that he
"inhabits this world through language or poetry." In this light, Heidegger, not
humanism, is where a clear and definite understanding can be found of what
man's essence really is all about. For humanism, on the contrary, the essence of
mankind is to have no essence and to be able to surpass any fixed essence one
could assign to it.[24]

This is also the lesson that Gadamer draws from the humanistic tradition. If
man never ceases to learn, there is nothing fixed about his essence. Furthermore,
if one has to "build" or "form" oneself through *Bildung,* one will naturally be
open to other points of view, to different perspectives than one's own. The main
characteristic of humanism is thus this thankful openness to the enlightening
perspectives of others and of those who have preceded us and bequeathed to us
the wealth of their experience and wisdom: "That is what, following Hegel, we
emphasized as the general characteristic of Bildung: keeping oneself open to
what is other—to other, more universal points of view. It embraces a sense of
proportion and distance in relation to itself, and hence consists in rising above
itself to universality."[25] What distinguishes our humanity is not any rational
capacity that would catapult us in a divine world of pure ideas, but rather only
the ability to go beyond our particularity, to take into account the heritage that
can help us grow above our limited selves.

When we take into account this heritage of tradition and the wisdom of others, which we always apply differently to ourselves and our situation, we acquire
genuine truths, but truths that cannot be adequately described through the means
of methodical science. These are truths that simply help us become more
"human," more open and also, negatively, more aware of the dangers that surround us. This truly human wisdom corresponds to the form of knowledge that is
pursued in the humanities. Gadamer's rehabilitation of the humanistic tradition
will thus enable him to account for the specific truth claim of the humanities:
"What makes the human sciences into sciences can be understood more easily
from the tradition of the concept of *Bildung* than from the modern idea of scientific method. It is to the *humanistic tradition* [the emphasis is Gadamer's] that
we must turn. In its resistance to the claims of modern science it gains a new significance."[26] While Heidegger advocated a "resistance" *against* humanism,
Gadamer unearths in the forgotten tradition of humanism an instance that can
fuel a resistance against the illegitimate claims of modern science to encompass
all there is to know.

As alluded to at the beginning of this paper, Heidegger's and Gadamer's
stands on humanism point to fundamental differences in their philosophical
bearings. In his break with tradition, be it in his earlier or his later period, something in Heidegger always hoped for a new beginning, for a radical transforma-

tion of the relation between man and Being.[27] For Gadamer, on the contrary, there can be no such thing as an absolute beginning, a zero-point in human affairs where we could start everything anew. We can never jump over our shadows. This is why Gadamer puts so much emphasis on tradition and dialogue. They are the two instances that can help us make things more bearable. Finite beings though we are, we fortunately can learn from our mistakes. And most of our experiences are negative, insists Gadamer in his important chapter on the hermeneutic experience.[28] This has to be stressed against those who accuse Gadamer of nursing a continuous, harmonious, and rosy understanding of tradition. Tradition is not the golden chain that bears witness to the rationality of history; it is, as Hegel's *Phenomenology* taught, the memory of the deceptive experiences stored by our humanity. As a matter of fact, we don't learn anything through positive experiences because they only confirm what we already know. Hermeneutic insight only sinks in when we have been contradicted by events, when we have to change or adjust our perspectives.

Heidegger, to be sure, also spoke of tradition and dialogue, but in ways quite different from Gadamer. The bulk of tradition is there, and it is no less heavy for Heidegger than for Gadamer, but it is something that has to be destroyed if we wish to grasp the things themselves or to make way for a new dwelling on this earth. But how can we destroy that which supports us and allows us to critique the past, retorts Gadamer? There is also talk of a dialogue in Heidegger, and he was the first to call attention to Hölderlin's famous passage on the "dialogue that we are." His seminal lecture of 1936, "Hölderlin and the Essence of Poetry," singled out this passage as one of the leading words of Hölderlin. There Heidegger also wrote that "the being of man is grounded in language and . . . language only happens properly in dialogue."[29] However, Heidegger followed Hölderlin in understanding this "dialogue that we are" as a conversation going on between the mortals and the gods:

> Since we are a dialogue—man has experienced plenty and has named many of the gods. Ever since language takes place properly as dialogue, the gods come to word and a world comes to the fore. But, again, one must see that the presence of the gods and the emergence of the world are not a consequence of the event of language. Rather they happen at the same time as them. And this to such an extent that the true language that we are consists precisely in naming the gods and in the becoming-word of the world.[30]

Yet, as R. Dostal has pointed out, in this alleged dialogue, where real conversation consists in the naming of the gods, "no consideration is given to the conversation among mortals about things mortal."[31]

Gadamer is very much attentive to this earthly dialogue between mortals. He takes Hölderlin at his word when he speaks of the "dialogue that *we* are." The dialogical essence of language[32] does not mean that we are primarily in constant exchange with the gods (who probably don't need conversation anyway), but that we have to rely on what others have to say and what lies there before us if

we want to find some orientation in our earthly existence. What "we are" consists of the traditions that are alive within us. We are what has been bequeathed
to us and, most importantly for a humanist, what we have made out of this
tradition when we constructively applied it to our situation. We are also a dialogue in the sense that we live in a community in which we are exposed to a
plurality of opinions. This plurality of views also lives within us, it constitutes us, it accounts for our all too human stammering and hesitations. To
be in a constant situation of learning means that we cannot entertain the hope
of ultimate foundations in order to decide how the world should be run. All
we have is the experience of those who preceded us, the dialogue with others,
and our good judgment that cannot but be channeled by tradition and the ongoing
conversation.

The focus on the issue of humanism also sheds a new light on Gadamer's account of humanism is not only a defense of the human
sciences, it is also a defense of the utter humanity of our knowledge. What is
meant by this, is that we can never hope to obtain any godlike wisdom, that is a
bird's-eye view that would enable us to transcend our finitude. To be human
means to be deprived of ultimate foundations, to have to educate and cultivate
oneself to our possible humanity. In this, Gadamer takes on the Socratic and, in
his eyes, Platonic heritage of philosophy as an exercise in not knowing: "So I
was persuaded that the Socratic legacy of a 'human wisdom' had to be taken up
again in my own hermeneutical theory-formation, a legacy which, when measured against the godlike infallibility of science, is, in the sense of *sophia,* a consciousness of not knowing."[33]

The focus on the issue of humanism also sheds a new light on Gadamer's
Socratic reading of Plato. As we saw earlier, Heidegger linked the rise of humanism to Plato's metaphysics, to the subordination of all there is to the clarity of
the intellectual idea. To overcome humanism, for Heidegger, is tantamount to
overcoming metaphysics and Platonism. No such motive is to be found in
Gadamer. If he goes back to Plato, it is precisely to retrieve his humanism, as a
humanism of dialogue in the discipline of a merely "human" wisdom:

> From the Greeks one could learn that thinking in philosophy does not, in order to be
> responsible, have to adopt as system-guiding the thought that there must be a final
> grounding for philosophy in a highest principle; on the contrary, it stands always
> under the guiding thought that it must be based on primordial world-experience,
> achieved through the conceptual and intuitive power of the language in which we
> live. The secret of the Platonic dialogues, it seems to me, is that they teach us this.[34]

Gadamer thus heeded Plato's admonition in the *Symposium* (204a): "No god
indulges in philosophy." Philosophy is a truly human and humanistic enterprise,
conducted in the hope of gaining a better understanding of ourselves and the
world through dialogue and by learning from tradition. In the eyes of Gadamer,
Plato can rightly stand as the father of humanism, as Heidegger also believed.
But Heidegger gave this humanism a negative metaphysical interpretation. For

Gadamer instead, humanism is the only resource, or attitude, we have in the absence of a cogent metaphysics.

From Gadamer one can learn that humanism is not necessarily an anthropocentrism. It is not because the only perspective we can entertain is human that man is at the center of Being. As far as one can tell, the individual stands rather at the receiving end of Being, be it of language, of community, or of the cosmic order. An openness to tradition and dialogue in order to contain the animality that threatens us doesn't entail an anthropocentric view of things. In a way, it is very humiliating for mankind to constantly have to learn and to conquer its darker instincts. No triumphalism of reason or of man's centeredness is to be found here. Here Gadamer truly follows the turn of the later Heidegger toward a more modest and peripheral understanding of our humanity. He fully assumes Heidegger's critique of metaphysical subjectivism, but he doesn't forfeit the focus on humanity involved in this process. Perhaps Gadamer's achievement is the protest against the too swift equation of subjectivism and humanism. He rejects, in the footsteps of Heidegger, the subject-centered philosophy of modernity without losing sight of the pervading humanistic trend of Western civilization. Humanism isn't an anthropocentrism, it is the acknowledgment that as finite beings we never cease to learn. Philosophical humanism is nothing but the modest openness to truths that can help us rise above our indigence. Consequently, hermeneutics is a humanism.

JEAN GRONDIN

DEPARTMENT OF PHILOSOPHY
UNIVERSITY OF MONTREAL
MAY 1992

NOTES

1. For a general survey of the problem, see the collective volume *Humanismus,* ed. H. Oppermann (Darmstadt: Wissenschaftliche Buchgesellschaft, 1970; 2nd enlarged edition 1977). Most important in this respect is the work of W. Jaeger, *Paideia: Die Formung des griechischen Menschen* (Berlin: de Gruyler, vol. 1, 1933; vol. 2, 1944; vol. 3, 1947). See also his earlier essay *Antike und Humanismus* (Leipzig, 1925), reprinted in the Oppermann volume. It is to be noted that Werner Jaeger was also a mentor of Gadamer. One of his first publications happened to be a critique of Jaeger's genetic interpretation of Aristotle ("Der aristotelische 'Protreptikos' und die entwicklungsgeschichtliche Betrachtung der aristotelischen Ethik," in *Hermes* 63 [1927]: 138–64, reprint in H.-G. Gadamer, *Gesammelte Werke* [henceforth *GW*], vol. 5 [Tübingen: J. C. B. Mohr (Paul Siebeck), 1985], 164–86.) This essay enjoyed extensive notoriety since it was one of the first to criticize Jaeger's interpretation, whose importance is second to none in the Aristotelian studies of the last century. Gadamer also wrote a separate review of Jaeger's *Aristoteles* in 1928 (see *GW* 5, 286–94). Even if he maintained the trust of his truly ground-breaking

criticism of Jaeger, the later Gadamer could not hide a certain uneasiness at the candor of his early essay in which an immature student attempted to criticize the major work of a renowned scholar. And all indicates this is how Jaeger took Gadamer's criticism. The two scholars remained close in the thirties and forties. Gadamer visited Jaeger often when he traveled through Berlin. Compare also Gadamer's tribute to Jaeger's teacher, Ulrich von Wilamowitz-Moellendorff, in *GW* 6, 271–77.

2. On this distinction see the article *Humaniora,* in the *Historisches Wörterbuch der Philosophie,* vol. 3 (Basel/Stuttgart: Schwabe, 1974), 1215. Unfortunately, the following article in the *HWdP* on "humanism" is far too one-sided, centering almost exclusively on the Marxist interpretations of humanism.

3. See J.-P. Sartre, *L'existentialisme est un humanisme* (Paris: Nagel, 1949).

4. The text of the first article reads: "The dignity of man is inviolable. To respect and protect it shall be the duty of all state authority."

5. On this turning in Heidegger's thought, which became apparent or public in this letter, see my "Prolegomena to an Understanding of Heidegger's Turn," in *Graduate Faculty Philosophy Journal* 14/2, 15/1 (1991): 85–108.

6. M. Heidegger, *Platons Lehre von der Wahrheit. Mit einem Brief über den Humanismus* (Bern: Francke, 1947).

7. See M. Heidegger, *Brief über den Humanismus,* in *Wegmarken,* 2nd edition (Frankfurt am Main: V. Klostermann, 1978), 313; English translation: M. Heidegger, *Basic Writings* (New York: Harper and Row, 1977), 195.

8. Heidegger, *Basic Writings,* 225; *Wegmarken,* 342: "Oder soll das Denken versuchen, durch einen offenen Widerstand gegen den 'Humanismus' einen Anstoß zu wagen, der veranlassen könnte, erst einmal über die Humanitas des homo humanus und ihre Begründung stutzig zu werden?"

9. We are now following *Wegmarken,* 317–18; *Basic Writings,* 200–201.

10. Heidegger, *Wegmarken,* 318; *Basic Writings,* 201: "We encounter the first humanism in Rome: it therefore remains in essence a specifically Roman phenomenon which emerges from the encounter of Roman civilization with the culture of late Greek civilization." On Heidegger's interpretation of "Romanity," compare *Parmenides,* vol. 54 of his Gesamtausgabe (Frankfurt am Main: Vittorio Klostermann, 1984), 57 ff. (from a course of the winter semester of 1942/43, thus contemporary to the lecture on Plato's doctrine of truth and the context out of which the *Letter on Humanism* was written). For a critique of Heidegger's letter on humanism, see the incisive and vehemently antimodern article of G. Krüger, "Martin Heidegger und der Humanismus," in *Studia philosophica* 9 (1949): 93–129, reprinted in *Theologische Rundschau* (1950): 148–78. In some regards, especially in its critique of Heidegger's reading of Plato, Krüger's analysis anticipates, or echoes, the position of Gadamer. But Krüger goes beyond Gadamer when he faults Heidegger for failing to acknowledge a theological grounding of Being and accuses him of "humanizing" Being, an excess against which the Ancients and Plato could immunize us.

11. Heidegger, *Wegmarken,* 313; *Basic Writings,* 195–96.

12. Heidegger, *Wegmarken,* 315; *Basic Writings,* 197.

13. H.-G. Gadamer, *Heidegger's Wege* (Tübingen: J. C. B. Mohr [Paul Siebeck], 1983), repr. in *GW* 3, 1987 (translated by SUNY Press, Albany, 1994).

14. H.-G. Gadamer, *Wahrheit und Methode* (henceforth *WM),* in *Gesammelte Werke,* vol. 1 (1986), 14; trans. *Truth and Method* (henceforth *TM),* revised translation by J. Weinsheimer and D. Marshall (New York: Crossroad Publishing, 1991), 9 ("the true representatives of humanism").

15. See the original version of *Volk und Geschichte im Denken Herders* (Frankfurt am Main: V. Klostermann, 1942). The questionable passages were left aside in the new edi-

tions of the lecture, retitled "Herder and the Historical World," in the *Kleine Schriften* 3 (Tübingen, 1971), 101–17, and the *GW* 4 (318–35). G. Warnke, *Gadamer, Hermeneutics, Tradition, and Reason* (Stanford University Press, 1987), 71, has usefully discussed these critical passages.

16. Gadamer, *Volk und Geschichte im Denken Herders*, 20 (slightly changed in *GW*, 4:332). This passage merits to be quoted in its original version since one can glimpse through it a political indication as to what was needed in 1941: "In der Tat mag der Glaube an den Sieg der Vernunft und der Billigkeit nicht nur dem leidenden Teil der Menschheit wie ein Trost beiwohnen, sondern auch den Helden der Geschichte in ihren Plänen und harten Entschlüssen voranleuchten." In this respect, it is worth remembering that in Leipzig Gadamer was a close friend of the mayor of Leipzig, Gördeler, who was convicted and executed because of his involvement in the assassination attempt against Hitler. We won't credit Gadamer with any heroic implication in this failed assassination attempt, which obviously remained a closely guarded secret amongst the plotters, but can only recall that Gördeler was regularly present in Gadamer's *Gesprächskreis* in Leipzig.

17. Gadamer, *Volk und Geschichte im Denken Herders*, 17 (*GW*, 4:330): "Er sieht in der Geschichte Ausbreitung und Beförderung der Humanität aber eben in der Geschichte."

18. Compare the insightful development of this intuition and its application to the whole of the Western and Roman tradition in the recent essay of R. Brague, *Europe, la voie romaine* (Paris: Criterion, 1992). This book can serve as a useful antidote against the negative view of Romanity espoused by Heidegger and many others.

19. On these theological and forgotten roots of humanism, see H. de Lubac, *Le drame de l'humanisme athée* (Paris, 1944; 7th. ed, Paris: Cerf, 1983), 15ff.

20. "Bildung gehört jetzt aufs engste mit dem Begriff der Kultur zusammen und bezeichnet zunächst die eigentümlich menschliche Weise, seine natürlichen Anlagen und Vermögen auszubilden" *(WM*, 16; *TM*, 10).

21. *WM*, 16 ("Der Aufstieg des Wortes Bildung erweckt vielmehr die alte mystische Tradition, wonach der Mensch das Bild Gottes, nach dem er geschaffen ist, in seiner Seele trägt und in sich aufzubauen hat."); *TM*, 11.

22. *WM*, 17 ("Der Mensch ist durch den Bruch mit dem Unmittelbaren und Natürlichen gekennzeichnet, der durch die geistige, vernünftige Seite seines Weses ihm zugemutet ist."); *TM*, 12.

23. Heidegger, *Wegmarken*, 319; *Basic Writings*, 202: "The first humanism, Roman humanism, and every kind that has emerged from that time to the present, has presupposed the most universal 'essence' of man to be obvious." ("Der erste Humanismus, nämlich der römische, und alle Arten des Humanismus, die seitdem bis in die Gegenwart aufgekommen sind, setzen das allgemeinste "Wesen" des Menschen als selbstverständlich voraus.")

24. On this idea that for humanism, contrary to what Heidegger and Derrida contend, there is no human essence, see L. Ferry and A. Renaut, *Heidegger et les Modernes* (Paris: Grasset, 1988). In this, they are following Jean-Paul Sartre. Compare also H. Arendt, *The Human Condition* (University of Chicago Press, 1958), 10: "It is highly unlikely that we, who can know, determine, and define the natural essences of all things surrounding us, which we are not, should ever be able to do the same for ourselves—this would be like jumping over our own shadows. Moreover, nothing entitles us to assume that man has a nature or essence in the same sense as other things. In other words, if we have a nature or essence, then surely only a god could know and define it."

25. *WM*, 22 ("Eben das hatten wir, Hegel folgend, als das allgemeine Kennzeichen der Bildung hervorgehoben, sich derart für Anderes, für andere, allgemeinere Gesichtspunkte

offenzuhalten. In ihr liegt ein allgemeiner Sinn für Maß in bezug auf sich selbst, und insofern eine Erhebung über sich selbst zur Allgemeinheit."); *TM,* 17.

26. *WM,* 23 ("Was die Geisteswissenschaften zu Wissenschaften macht, läßt sich eher aus der Tradition des Bildungsbegriffs verstehen als aus der Idee der modernen Wissenschaft. Es ist die *humanistische Tradition,* auf die wir zurückverwiesen werden. Sie gewinnt im Widerstand gegen die Ansprüche der modernen Wissenschaft eine neue Bedeutung."); *TM,* 18.

27. For a critique of this utopianism, out of which one can also understand some aspects of Heidegger's entanglement with national-socialism, see my "The Ethical and Young-Hegelian Motives in Heidegger's Hermeneutics of Facticity," in *Reading Heidegger from the Start,* ed. by J. van Buren and T. Kisiel (Albany: SUNY Press, 1994), 345–57.

28. *WM,* 359; *TM,* 353. The hermeneutic primacy of negativity in ethics has recently been stressed by H. Krämer, *Integrative Ethik* (Frankfurt am Main: Suhrkamp, 1992), 234.

29. M. Heidegger, *Erläuterungen zu Hölderlin's Dichtung,* in Gesamtausgabe, vol. 4 (Frankfurt am Main: Vittorio Klostermann, 1981), 38 ("Das Sein des Menschen gründet in der Sprache; aber diese geschieht erst eigentlich im Gespräch.").

30. Ibid., 40 ("Seit ein Gespräch wir sind—hat der Mensch viel erfahren und der Götter viele genannt. Seitdem die Sprache eigentlich als Gespräch geschieht, kommen die Götter zu Wort und erscheint eine Welt. Aber wiederum gilt es zu sehen: die Gegenwart der Götter und das Erscheinen der Welt sind nicht erst eine Folge des Geschehnisses der Sprache, sondern sie sind damit gleichzeitig. Und das so sehr, daß im Nennen der Götter und im Wort-Werden der Welt gerade das eigentliche Gespräche besteht, das wir selbst sind.").

31. R. Dostal, "Friendship and Politics: Heidegger's Failing," in *Political Theory* 20 (1992).

32. In this Gadamer also stands in the footsteps of humanism. On the humanistic conception of language, compare K.-O. Apel, *Die Idee der Sprache in der Tradition des Humanismus von Dante bis Vico* (Bonn: Bouvier, 1963), and E. Grassi, *Einführung in philosophische Probleme des Humanismus* (Darmstadt: Wissenschaftliche Buchgesellschaft, 1986). See also, on the dialogical understanding of language, my *Einführung in die philosophische Hermeneutik* (Darmstadt: Wissenschaftliche Buchgesellschaft, 1991); English: *Introduction to Philosophical Hermeneutics* (New Haven: Yale University Press, 1994).

33. H.-G. Gadamer, "Reflections on My Philosophical Journey," in *The Philosophy of Hans-Georg Gadamer,* ed. L. E. Hahn, The Library of Living Philosophers (LaSalle, Ill.: Open Court, 1996), infra.

34. Ibid. Gadamer's dialogical interpretation of Plato is now extensively documented in volumes 5, 6, and especially in the more recent volume 7 (under the title *Plato im Dialog,* 1991) of his *GW.*

REPLY TO JEAN GRONDIN

It is impressive here how it is shown that the principle of *Truth and Method* turns against the "Letter on Humanism" and the later project of Heidegger in a contrast that is apparently very sharp. In a certain sense, I was surprised to see things worked out in such a confrontational manner. Of course, it is clear that in these questions the declared position and the real historical situations are not always in harmony. Such is the case today with the dispute about the end of metaphysics. Heidegger himself modified the overcoming *(Überwindung)* of metaphysics and replaced it with a coming to terms with *(Verwindung)* metaphysics. Similarly, Derrida, working in Heidegger's wake, did not try to outdo Heidegger as if he could change our entire way of thinking through deconstruction. But, after all, both explicitly thematized, with full consciousness and in their own way, the Heideggerian critique of the full understanding of being. The course of my own studies, too, has been inspired by Heidegger's turn. For me, this turn away from transcendental-philosophical grounding and the transcendental subject proved to be the really liberating advance toward a philosophy of the lifeworld. Although this initially was a Husserlian project, in Husserl's own work this advance into the broad field of anthropology and of history remained essentially restricted.

However, this did not mean that Heidegger's turn away from the transcendental-philosophical format of *Being and Time* did not develop. It moved in a direction which I myself followed in tracing Heidegger's attempt to divert even the question of being from the question of the being of beings. In the end, even the role art plays in my hermeneutic formulation of theories expresses this point that one indeed cannot distinguish determinate beings or even determinate conceptual rules as the proposition of art or of religion. I am very well aware of the problematic nature of this 'or'. In any case, Grondin's essay shows by means of such examples to what extent one's own ways of being conditioned are still effective, even when one does not recognize them oneself. What Grondin's further presentations say about the *animalities* is not entirely clear to me. It is certainly illuminating for us to contemplate the deep insight into the soul of the Greek tragic poets and of Plato or Aristotle. Here, one experiences dramatically the dual nature of human beings: on the one hand, that we are governed by drives *(Triebsteuerung),* and on the other that the governing of one's own actions is never entirely rational. And yet, an unsatisfactory feeling remains when contemplating this view. Should one not rather say that the connection between *ēthos* and *logos*—which in the *Republic* is driven to the point of the utopia of a police state—found its well-considered balance in Aristotle's ethics? It is said there explicitly that *ēthos* and *logos* are as inseparable as the two sides of a coin. Should we not say that this, *mutatis mutandis,* applies to all beings capable of living? One way or the other, all that lives has to endure the struggle of life, and *ēthos* refers to the life forming and life unfolding of all animals and plants. The thinking human being, however, has to pay a price for the leeway found in the freedom of conscious behavior; namely, the price of having to distinguish between what is right and what is not, indeed of having to do this in a world of morals and of a legal order which he gave to himself.

H.-G. G.

7

George R. Lucas, Jr.

PHILOSOPHY, ITS HISTORY, AND HERMENEUTICS

I propose in this essay to examine philosophy's relationship to its own history, a topic which constitutes the single most important aspect of philosophical hermeneutics as taught by Professor Hans-Georg Gadamer. Indeed, it would be appropriate to subtitle this essay, "variations on a theme of Gadamer."

In the history of musical composition, "variations on a theme" signify both a tribute by one composer to another, and also an acknowledgment of profound influence and deep indebtedness. Usually (as in this case) such a tribute and acknowledgment is offered by the lesser to the greater, as well as by the later to the earlier. Especially inasmuch as the fine arts have provided significant inspiration for Professor Gadamer's own thought and work, I trust it will not be deemed inappropriate to make use of this familiar device in paying homage to him.

My own recent work on what is sometimes awkwardly termed "the philosophy of the history of philosophy" developed as a result of my earlier studies on Kant, Hegel, and Whitehead. I have, in addition, been instructed in this emerging interest by a number of contemporary philosophers, including Alasdair MacIntyre, Stanley Rosen, George Kline, Jerome Schneewind, Robert Neville, John Smith, and Richard Rorty—all of whom have played a leading role in recent years in addressing the nature of philosophy's relationship to its past.[1]

The resurgence of interest in the history of philosophy among Anglo-American philosophers during the past decade marks the end of a lengthy hiatus, during which historical studies were relegated to a barely respectable, and decidedly second-class, status within the professional discipline of philosophy as practiced in the United States and Great Britain. Much has been made (and *should* be made) over the recovery by philosophy of its history. I would, in addition, call attention to the concomitant challenge that this recent development poses to the notion of "philosophy" as simply one among many specialized "disciplines" within an academic "culture of disciplines."[2]

All who now contribute to this volume of essays in his honor, however, recognize that the lion's share of the credit for this recovery and restoration of the importance of history to philosophy belongs to Professor Gadamer, and reflects his considerable influence on the practice of philosophy in America as well as in Europe. Indeed, we acknowledge (often with some embarrassment) that what many of us now advocate or embrace as the latest trends in philosophy are little more than "variations on themes" drawn from Gadamer's own work throughout the greater part of this century.[3]

I. ART AND PHILOSOPHY: DEFINING HERMENEUTICS

In the National Gallery of Art at the Smithsonian Institution in Washington, D.C., there hang (in gallery #57) three studies of the Waterloo Bridge in London, painted by the French impressionist, Claude Monet.

The bridge itself, located well above the commercially navigable portion of the Thames, is thoroughly unremarkable: a standard Roman design, in which the road surface is supported by an alternating series of piers and arches. Monet's studies of it, however, are anything but "unremarkable."

We know, of course, that Monet delighted in recording the dramatically different appearances taken on by single architectural objects under a variety of conditions—his much more famous studies of the (north) facade of the cathedral at Rouen, for example, also hang in this gallery. Likewise, the three studies of the Waterloo bridge, undertaken between 1903 and 1904, portray this perfectly conventional structure at different times of day. The first painting in the series, as the gallery visitor encounters it, displays the bridge at sunset, barely visible as a coherent structure within complex patterns of shimmering, rose-hued light. The second study portrays the bridge at twilight. Here the structure and solidity of the bridge are more in evidence, but muted in the softness of evening mists rising from the river below; the veiled edifice seems for all the world to be attended by silent, gaunt-robed priests; votive candles twinkle from some unseen altar, hidden within the dark background of the approaching night.

The third painting in this series, as displayed in the Smithsonian gallery, was actually painted first: it portrays the bridge on a gray, cloudy afternoon. The bridge is stark, solid; it teems with industry. A waterman rows his heavily loaded skiff between the piers; crowds of laborers move in both directions. The robed priests of the twilight are revealed as grimy industrial smokestacks; the votive candles have disappeared; the "altar" which supported them is, in fact, a collection of grim factories. An aura of gloom pervades.

I find these three studies of the Waterloo bridge intriguing for a number of reasons. That a French artist chose to paint, in London, this particular memorial, is worth at least a moment's reflection.

In addition, there is the philosophical question, first raised in book 10 of Plato's *Republic,* regarding the ontological standing of these images or *eikasia* of the Waterloo bridge in relation to the "Brukke-an-sich." The first two studies suggest a beauty and romance that are decidedly lacking in the third; but the third would seem to be the appearance most related to the actuality, the stubborn fact, or the "being" of the structure itself that the majority of nonartists would encounter. The actuality or "being" of the bridge, its ordinariness, might be said to constitute only one aspect of its reality, which would include at least the other two aspects captured by Monet.

Is Monet, in these three paintings, delivering a pictorial intimation of the central Heideggerian notion of the inexhaustibility of being? Like Heidegger's own analysis of the "being" of a Rhine-river dam in "The Question Concerning Technology," for example, the being of this bridge is perhaps also *not* limited to its actuality—to the bricks, stones, mortar, and geographical setting. Being, on Heidegger's well-known account, is not limited to what is disclosed, but also includes what is concealed. Perhaps we should say that the being of a thing consists in its brute facticity together with the infinite ensemble of its possible aspects, appearances, or meanings (*Erscheinungen,* in Heidegger's special sense of that term). The *chronological* order of Monet's paintings seems to move from what we might call the profane to the sacred, from the limited actuality or facticity to the inexhaustible infinity of being.

The Smithsonian curator, however, displays the paintings in reverse-chronological order. Are we to infer that the third painting, on this nonchronological arrangement, is to be taken, in effect, as a reinterpretation, perhaps a kind of deconstruction, of the romantic narrative offered in the other two? Should Monet's rendering of this English memorial to Waterloo be seen as an appropriately complex response by a French artist to England's military triumph over France? Yet the differing manifestations of this memorial (including its underlying grimness and decadence) are at least as complicated and nuanced as are these three very different paintings of the memorial itself.

In this series of paintings we are confronted (to use the language currently in vogue) with a number of "texts"—or (to use Gadamer's words) with a series of paintings which individually and collectively represent *answers* to some set of *questions:*

> One of the more fertile insights of modern hermeneutics is that every statement has to be seen as a response to a question and that the only way to understand a statement is to get hold of the question to which the statement is an answer.[4]

If Monet's paintings in this series are taken (in this instance) as the artist's own "statements," then, in our encounter with them, we are moved to recover and to frame the foregoing questions in coming to terms with the paintings themselves. The questions raised above appear to fall into four categories concerning the following: (1) the bricks and mortar, the being of the bridge itself in its *Sitz im Leben;* (2) the artist's conception or interpretations of this entity; (3) the curator's conceptions or interpretations of the artist's intentions, or the curator's own intentions, in displaying these works; (4) the gallery visitor's reactions to these.

In the end, the *visitor* raises the questions, to which the artistic display is made to yield up an answer or answers as the gallery visitor integrates these works into his or her own self-understanding. The interpreter's or interlocutor's self-understanding may, in turn, range over everything from that visitor's thoughts on war and military history to the relationship between appearance and reality and the manner in which such "philosophical" questions are explored by impressionist artists. But, as Gadamer notes, "just as the artistic statements become integrated with ourselves, in the process of our self-understanding, when they are perceived in their truth, it is no longer art but philosophy at work."[5]

Interpretation is thus interaction and inquiry; it is an immersion within a context in which one gradually becomes aware of the questions to which, in this case, these paintings and the mode of their presentation might represent answers. Such questions emerge from an almost infinite horizon of possible meanings, and prompt a perpetual conversation about those meanings.

This, then, is the meaning that one might plausibly attach to Gadamer's bold claim that "hermeneutics *is* philosophy, and as philosophy it is practical philosophy."[6] Surely what is transpiring here, as Gadamer notes, is no longer art. Indeed, as Arthur Danto (following Hegel) suggests, the emergence of such reflection signifies the "end" of art.[7]

Interpretation, on Gadamer's own account, is a kind of *praxis* characteristic of the human being's immersion in its *Lebenswelt*. While it is thus "practical," it may not be quite correct simply to equate hermeneutics with philosophy. Interpretation, as Gadamer himself has made quite clear, is an activity lying at the heart of numerous preoccupations—art especially, but also poetry, literature, theology, and law (to name the most prominent on Gadamer's own list)—so that hermeneutics necessarily exceeds the confines of philosophy alone. Likewise, in deference to colleagues engaged in logical or linguistic analysis, or immersed in the newly emergent pursuit of cognitive science, we might wish to leave open the question of whether proper philosophical activity might include something other than interpretation.

II. "Being" versus "Meaning": A Problem in Hermeneutics

Philosophical hermeneutics relies heavily on examples and experiences drawn from our encounter with what Gadamer terms "the hundred-eyed argosy that in Hegel's apt words is presented by art,"[8] as well as on analogies (drawn by more recent converts to hermeneutics such as Richard Rorty) with works of literature and poetry. This reliance on illustrations involving works of art, literature, and poetry, however, generates difficulties when such experiences are extrapolated to the domain of philosophy itself. Gadamer notes,

> a philosophic account of things is an unending process . . . realized not only [in] the conversation which each of us conducts with ourselves in thinking but also [in] the conversation in which we are all caught up together and never cease to be caught up.[9]

As critics have noted and disciples of hermeneutics have labored to explain, there is no core to this nested set of questions and interpretations, and hence no ground, no apparent ground-rules, and certainly no clear terminus or resolution for the resultant conversation. It does only moderate good, in the situation described in section 1 above, to address my questions about Monet to the numerous published works of art criticism that might offer informed perspectives on these issues, for the questions and opinions of their authors might stem from an interpretive context wholly alien to, and incommensurable with, my own. These works, while they might stimulate and edify, are not definitive or authoritative. Of the raising of interpretive questions there can be no end—as, once again, Gadamer has claimed. Philosophy, on this account, is the infinite circle of such interpretations.[10]

The comparison of philosophical questioning with the interpretation characteristic of critical inquiry in art, literature, and poetry leads to the cultural relativism that has become the hallmark of contemporary philosophical hermeneutics. In my illustration above, the facticity of the bridge itself plays little role in the narrative that the artist may choose to weave from it. And the artist's intentions, in turn, may be separable from the curator's in providing a telling display of what he or she takes to be the significance of the artworks. Although all of this *informs,* none of this *constrains,* the interpretive freedom of the gallery visitor. Each of us possesses a kind of poetic license to construct the aesthetic world in our own image. If there is what Gadamer, in *Truth and Method,* terms a "fusion of horizons" here, it is largely coincidental. As Stanley Rosen observes, postmodernism's incommensurable plurality of worlds—each world the creation of each one of us, as poet—is the logical culmination of modernism's fatal connection of reason with freedom in the Enlightenment.[11]

I believe, however, that this inference to infinity, and to relativism and incommensurability in hermeneutics, based upon the encounter with aesthetics, is mistaken.

This mistaken inference, I shall argue, stems from the neglect in philosophical hermeneutics of the important conceptual distinction between "being" and "meaning"—a distinction blurred in the bewitching analysis by Heidegger of the "inexhaustibility of being." By drawing its inspiration from areas of experience (such as art) in which this conceptual distinction is relatively unimportant, hermeneutics threatens to collapse this distinction altogether. This collapse or conflation, in turn, would make it impossible to distinguish between history and fiction, or between what George Kline has aptly described as the *being* of the past and the *meaning* (or "interpretation") of the past.[12]

All of the emphasis in hermeneutics is upon interpretation and the interpreter—that is to say, on meaning, as if that is the only sense of being. In *Truth and Method,* for example, Gadamer observes,

> Understanding is never subjective behavior toward a given 'object' but belongs to the effective history of what is understood, to the history of its influence; in other words, *understanding belongs to the being of that which is understood.* . . . The true historical object is not an object at all, but the unity of the one and the other, a relationship in which exist both the reality of history and the reality of historical understanding [my emphases].[13]

In art, where the mundane details of the actual Waterloo bridge are wholly sublated within a web of artistic and critical intentionality, it does indeed seem as if being and meaning are indistinguishable: here, at least, one might plausibly maintain a kind of Heideggerian postmodernist sense of idealism according to which the "being" of an aesthetic entity lies entirely in its ensemble of "meanings," or in which (in Gadamer's own words) the understanding of the artistic object belongs to the being of that object. So it would seem, for example, in the Monet paintings described above.

But this identity of being and meaning does not follow so readily in other areas of human experience. Kline, for example, makes brief but instructive reference to the larger importance of the distinction between being and meaning in psychoanalysis, as this discipline encounters an individual patient's history. Because the technique of psychoanalysis as taught by Freud relied so heavily on the recovery, unweaving, and reweaving of personal narrative, Kline suggests, its practitioners tended uncritically to assume that the being of a patient's past lay entirely in the meaning or interpretation that the patient attached to it. The therapist's emphasis on encouraging a patient to weave a more functional personal narrative in psychotherapy in order to overcome neuroses often led, that is, to an unwarranted *philosophical* assumption among adherents of psychoanalysis that the *past itself* is *never* wholly fixed or unchanging.

But, Kline objects, it is false to assert that, in interpretive acts, the past itself is *remade;* rather, the past is always simply *reinterpreted.* Indeed, the very possibility of the desired therapeutic reinterpretation *presupposes* a conceptual distinction between the raw details, the "brute facts" of the patient's own past, and the dysfunctional interpretation or repression that the patient had attached to these details at the time, or subsequently. If psychoanalysis is effective, it is precisely because there exists a set of forgotten details that can be recollected, and then (perhaps painfully) disassociated from their original dysfunctional narrative context. Once this primordial disassociation is accomplished, the significance of these historical events may then be laboriously recalibrated, permitting these recollected details, in due course, to be rewoven into a more functional narrative interpretation.[14]

Being and meaning are *not* identical, and so may not simply be conflated in this instance. Instead, in confronting the past, we have to do with *one* "being" but *many* "meanings."

III. Theology, Law, and History: Delimiting Hermeneutics

A further source of confusion in philosophical hermeneutics regarding the difference between being and meaning in history stems from a major controversy in Christian theology earlier in this century. Since theology constitutes another of Professor Gadamer's wide-ranging interests and sources of influence, it is instructive to reconsider this controversy briefly.

Rudolph Bultmann generated the controversy by observing that, so far as the historical basis of Christian faith is concerned, *ousia* is largely lost and unrecoverable, obscured behind the veil of *paraousia*. Bultmann's target in this controversial observation was the once-famous "quest for the historical Jesus" by Albert Schweitzer and other immediate predecessors. Bultmann argued that this quest was, in effect, a quest for the unvarnished "being" of past events prior to, and apart from, the variety of meanings that had subsequently been attached to them. Bultmann claimed, however, that the presumed "actual and unvarnished historical events" would be in principle unrecoverable; these "events" were themselves an inference from historical testimony provided by witnesses whose cultural perspective on those alleged events was so thoroughly alien to us as to make their testimony unintelligible and untranslatable in its own terms.

In a historical religion like Christianity, Bultmann argued, there is a paradox or scandal regarding the historical basis of the religion itself. The Kierkegaardian-absurdist paradox is that the only available "historical resources" for authentication consist of a variety of (from our present historical perspective) highly mythologized interpretive accounts in which "meaning" and significance have already long since obscured or utterly displaced what Kline is referring to as the "being" of the past events in question: e.g., the crucifixion and resurrection of Jesus. Simply demythologizing these accounts and peeling away the onion-like layers of subsequent interpretation, on Bultmann's radical view, would *not* (as Schweitzer had hoped) bring us finally face to face with the uninterpreted raw historical data. Rather than confronting us, as expected, with the mundane historical details of a modest carpenter from Galilee at a time when only his mother and a few friends took him seriously, our journey back into history in search of the "being" (apart from the "meaning") of the past, in the Christian case, would be unable to go behind or beyond the *kerygma*—the claim, advanced through the earliest charismatic preaching of the first disciples of the apostolic church, that God had acted decisively in Christ. As this fundamental mythological claim colors the subsequent recollection of historical detail by

Christian disciples, the claim itself, this *belief* of the disciples, is all that history has preserved for us.[15]

Bultmann held that this conclusion regarding the historicity of Jesus left contemporary believers with an existentialist challenge to make a personal faith-commitment, or a Kierkegaardian leap of faith to authentic discipleship. But, in fact, his legacy confronted subsequent Christian theology with other, more immediate dilemmas. The particular vulnerability of a historical religion is that its authenticity rests, or seems (Bultmann notwithstanding) to rest, upon the correspondence of presumed eyewitness accounts with a relatively small number of "actual" historical facts. In other words, there is a very sharp distinction made and understood by adherents of the religion between the "being" and the "meaning" of the past.[16]

Bultmann availed himself of Heidegger's bewitching language concerning the historicity and inexhaustibility of Being and, in effect, tried to preempt the controversy in Christianity over the "scandal of historical particularity" by denying the reality of the distinction between being and meaning. It would not be entirely unfair to characterize subsequent Christian theology as an attempt to recover from the aftereffects of this bold and rather shocking project.

For our purposes, however, it is sufficient to note in summation that Bultmannian existentialist theology is grounded upon this attempt, drawn from Heidegger's thought, to deny and to conflate the distinction between being and meaning. I will leave it to theologians to argue whether this conflation, in the case of theology, will pass muster. I note only that the foundational claim of philosophical hermeneutics, that being and meaning are indistinguishable, is in this case controversial, problematic, and far from obvious. Fortunately philosophy, although it is historical, does not depend upon the verification of a small set of discrete historical details. I shall take up this "scandal of historical particularity," and philosophy's immunity from it, once again in the conclusion of this paper.

The remaining case, apart from philosophy itself, in which the distinction between being and meaning cannot be so easily collapsed is that of legal interpretation. Gadamer himself suggests the point I shall wish to make, although he apparently draws the opposite conclusions. Describing what he takes to be the central role of hermeneutics in juridical practice, he remarks:

> Mediating the universality of the law with the concrete material of the case before the court is an integral moment of all legal art and science. These difficulties become particularly heightened wherever the legal texts are no longer the authentic expression of our experience of the law, rooted in our actual life experience, and represent instead a historical inheritance taken over from a completely different social and historical situation. A legal order that has become obsolete and antiquated is a constant source of legal difficulties, for meaningful interpretation requires adaptation to the actual situation.[17]

This passage describes the possible dissonance between legal precept and changing cultural context. Gadamer has in mind as example the familiar historical conflict generated by the imposition and subsequent maintenance of Roman legal customs (reflecting the needs of a highly organized, culturally sophisticated empire) in later Europe (a loosely organized, culturally unsophisticated frontier-agrarian league). The Justinian code had to be radically reinterpreted in the actual practice of jurisprudence to meet markedly different social needs in postimperial Europe.

The experience of British colonial rule in India, or of the French in Muslim Algeria, would provide a host of additional illustrations. Colonial administrators in both cases were frequently confronted with situations that required dramatic and imaginative reinterpretation of legal statutes to apply to what, in effect, were culturally incommensurable situations. The alternative to adaptation would have been social chaos.

But such instances precisely underscore the *distinction,* rather than the conflation, of being and meaning. Especially in the instances of colonial rule, real persons confront the law as alien, as unintelligible. But the law is the law. The statutes stand as written, even though they are rooted in factual situations that no longer obtain, so that they are forced to confront factual situations to which they are literally not addressed. It is not the *being* of the law, but the *meaning* of the law applied in concrete situations which changes, by means of interpretation and the establishing of legal precedent.

Were this not the case, we would have little need for courts and judges, who, in the ideal situation, are entrusted with the "being" of the law, and charged with continually fixing its "meaning" under changing historical circumstances. This dialectic between being and meaning in legal interpretation is especially evident in American constitutional law, where jurists are constantly faced with the question of the "original intent" of a document and its framers (the "being" of the American Constitution), versus its interpretation (meaning) through subsequent historical precedent established within specific cultural contexts. European jurisprudence, by contrast, in which the role of a fixed constitution is obviated by long historical reliance upon precedent and custom (all of which enfold previous interpretive acts), would understandably tend to blur, rather than to clarify, the distinction between being and meaning in the law itself.

Perhaps the most profound example of the importance of this distinction, however, is to be found in a situation where the law itself, as the very lifeblood and spiritual essence of a people, nevertheless confronts changing historical circumstances—forcing new interpretation to follow upon what are, in effect, alterations in fact. What I have in mind here, consistent with Gadamer's own interest in and emphasis on theology, are the legal traditions of rabbinical Judaism.

The Torah consists of the core Mosaic code—simple, stark precepts well suited to the needs of desert nomads. From Exodus through Deuteronomy, this original code is encased in an elaborate, and culturally incommensurate, blanket of priestly precepts reflecting the adaptation of the original code to the needs of a settled, agrarian population with a centralized, well-organized religious and military authority, empowered to issue edicts in the name of Yahweh. The resulting Torah is literally the speech of God: for the believer, it is not to be changed, nor merely obeyed, but loved: "for his delight is in the Law of the Lord, and on this Law doth he meditate, day and night" (Ps. 1:2).

Well and good. But in the radically altered, postexilic context of the Diaspora, in the absence of priestly authority to petition for augmentation of the Law in the Temple of Yahweh, what had formerly been experienced as the living being of the law threatened to become static, inflexible, and irrelevant. Virtually every cultural situation and need to which this law had been originally addressed was transformed. Yet even in the context of the Diaspora, the Torah is not simply (like colonial or imperial law) some sort of alien Other; rather, it is still, for the member of the covenant people, "myself, my tradition, the narration of my significance as a member of the sacred community." The maintenance of the Law was vital to the cultural integrity and identity of the Jewish exiles in strange lands—yet its precepts no longer governed or spoke to their radically altered historical circumstances.

What, in such an extraordinary circumstance, was required (in lieu, that is, of cultural assimilation and extinction that would normally follow under these circumstances), and what the emergent tradition of rabbinical Judaism provided, was a class of legal scholars who were lovers and sacred custodians of tradition, whose explicit mission was to safeguard and preserve this historical tradition. Torah, the Being of the Law, "is what it is" and must remain unchanged. The Talmud is not itself Torah; it is application of the law to concrete circumstances in the belief that the sacred Law, this "speech of the Lord of the Universe," must be able, by definition, to call upon its own internal resources to address every new circumstance.

And so it is made, laboriously and lovingly, by generations of rabbis, to do. The enormity of the task, and of its *chutzpah,* do not go unnoticed by its practitioners. The Talmud contains a wonderful and touching story of one of Israel's great rabbis, Akiva, that illustrates just how clearly adherents of that tradition are still able to distinguish between the "being" and the radical evolution of "meanings" of the past.

> Rav Judah said in the name of Rav: When Moses ascended on high, he found the Holy One, praised be He, engaged in adding coronets to the letters of the Torah. Moses said, "Lord of the universe! Does the Torah lack anything, that these additions are necessary?" He answered, "after many generations, a man by the name of Akiva ben Joseph will arise, and he will expound heaps and heaps of laws based upon each jot and tittle."

Moses, stunned at this possibility, asks God's leave to see this amazing man who will one day, in effect, reinterpret the Torah itself. His wish is granted, and he is instantly transported into the presence of Akiva and "eight rows of his disciples." Moses listens to Akiva's discourses on the Torah, but becomes "ill at ease, for he was unable to follow their arguments." Finally, one of Akiva's disciples interrupts the Master to ask how he knows that some particularly subtle and difficult point of Akiva's own interpretation of the Law is in fact valid. Akiva responds: "Because it is a law given to Moses at Sinai!"[18]

Moses, in the audience, is amazed! What we who are witnesses to this gradual process of historical reflection observe, however, is a remarkable and wonderful paradox: a cultural tradition, so thoroughly endangered, is preserved intact; and in this preservation, it is nonetheless transformed. It becomes, once again, a living tradition.

IV. PHILOSOPHY'S RELATIONSHIP TO ITS HISTORY

And so we return finally to philosophy itself. Here, I suggest, "interpretation" must likewise be understood in a sense quite different from that appropriate to art, literature, and poetry. The difference is precisely history, and, in particular, the philosophical uses of historical traditions. In the case of philosophy, it is precisely upon history that Gadamer himself has encouraged us to focus.

Interpretation is our conversation with, and serial understanding of, the world in all its manifestations. In that sense, hermeneutics is not philosophy, but is much more than philosophy. Philosophy, I maintain, is our conversation with our own intellectual history, with the record of our own previous thought as a culture. Philosophy is not itself *simply* intellectual history, however; intellectual history is the detailed record of what this or that individual or culture thought to be the case. Philosophy is, as Gadamer rightly surmises, our ongoing interrogation of, and dialogue with that history. Thus, the sort of interpretation that belongs to philosophy is *historical* interpretation, the provision of new meanings to the being of the past.

From Socrates and Plato reflecting on Homeric myths of origin to Heidegger's return to the pre-Socratics, philosophy is a reflective historical dialogue between interpreters and their historical legacy; philosophy is (in other famous words of Gadamer) this historical "conversation that we are." Philosophy is, moreover, a peculiar kind of historical interpretation: as was the case with rabbinical Judaism, philosophy is the act of reflecting on, critiquing, and refining its own activity. Socrates and Plato reflect upon, critique, refine, and transform the previous deliberations of Anaximander, Parmenides, Heraclitus, and Democritus. Aristotle synthesizes and transforms these. Democritus, Plato, and Aristotle are then read, interpreted, refuted, absorbed, synthesized, and transformed by other "philosophical rabbis": by Cicero, Epicurus, Plotinus, and Augustine. They, in their turn, by Ibn Sina and Ibn Rushd, by Moshe ben Maimon and St. Thomas. This historical principle holds, I maintain, even in those instances in which the philosophers in question attempt to deny it. Where would Descartes be without

Aristotle and the Jesuits to refute; or for that matter, where would Carnap and Reichenbach be without the despised Hegel and Bergson?

And yet it is important to note that philosophy is *not* "historical" in the same sense as are "historical religions" such as Christianity, which place almost exclusive emphasis on historical particularity. Accordingly, philosophy does not run afoul of the interpretive-existentialist paradox, the "scandal of historical particularity," that routinely confronts these faiths. A "historical" religion is grounded in the proclamation and continual reinterpretation of some defining historical *sine qua non,* such as the crucifixion of Jesus. And Bultmann *was* at least able to demonstrate the nearly fatal vulnerability of *this* kind of reliance on history: namely, all such "historical" religions are confined and constrained by their own *kerygma,* and cannot "get behind" the initial interpretive act of faith to the historical circumstances that may lie beyond.[19]

But philosophy is *not* "historical" in this sense. There is no single "defining event," no single (or even several) historical *sine qua non.* Philosophy's relationship to history is that of *tradition,* rather than that of *particularity.*

We do not, in philosophy, need to "recover the historical Socrates," for example. Nothing whatever would hinge upon such a quest. There is a natural human interest in the historical details surrounding this venerated figure, but philosophy would not be significantly altered by the discovery that Socrates was somewhat different than we currently suppose, or even by the claim of some future Bultmann-like "demytholigizer" of philosophy, claiming that it is impossible, in principle, to say anything definitive about the "historical Socrates." We require only that there have been, once upon a time, some such figure as Socrates; and that his thoughts and influence were bequeathed to others, including Plato. It is reflection upon and transmission in history of Socratic thought, rather than the peculiar details of the individual, that constitute the essence of philosophy as reflection upon historical tradition.

Gadamer observes that "the art of understanding [a] tradition, whether it deals with sacred books, legal texts, or exemplary masterworks, not only presupposes the recognition of these works but goes on further to shape their productive transmission."[20] Philosophy *does,* in this sense, feed upon itself; its history is not an option for it, but is the raw material for its own continuing activity. Its relationship to its history, however, is not that of the antiquarian, obsessed with minute detail simply for its own sake; nor is philosophy's relationship to its history that of the doxologist venerating tradition for its own sake merely as some sort of Homeric litany of sacred anecdotes and heroic accomplishments. Rather, philosophy's relationship to its history, to its own past, is like the relationship that obtained between the rabbis and Torah: both constitute a peculiar kind of *reflective engagement,* a self-absorption that results in a transformation and reformulation of the narrative tradition that, in this instance, philosophy itself is.

I am suggesting that philosophy is, in effect, the secular counterpart of the rabbinical tradition. Philosophers are not poets, artists, or writers of fiction. They do not simply say or do whatever they please, nor do they simply create or "narrate" the world in their own image. Neither are their deliberations, any more than are legal deliberations, utterly unique or disconnected from their own past. Rather, the love of wisdom requires that philosophers be the lovers, interpreters, and custodians of their cultural tradition, of their predecessors' best and noblest attempts to understand themselves and their world. As in the case of rabbinical Judaism, moreover, the perpetual and ongoing conversation of the custodian with the tradition within the context of his or her own *Lebenswelt* provides, simultaneously and paradoxically, for the preservation as well as transformation of that tradition.

V. Conclusion

I began by considering the claim of hermeneutics to *be* philosophy. Although "understanding" in the particular sense described by Gadamer is indeed central to philosophy, I concluded that hermeneutics is nonetheless both different from, and much broader than, philosophy. Philosophy is, rather, a particular kind of historical self-understanding, one which is most similar to rabbinical and perhaps legal reflection, and least similar to artistic and literary interpretation.

In linking philosophy to history in this "rabbinical" sense of reflective engagement, and in delinking it from art and literature, the quest for philosophic "truth" or wisdom is likewise distinguished in its ongoingness from the endlessness and often relativistic aimlessness that characterize the creativity and interpretive activity in the aesthetic fields. Although interpretation of the law is likewise ongoing and perhaps unending, it does not follow that individuals possess the license to construct whatever legal interpretations they please. In that sense, I have suggested that philosophers are more like jurists and rabbis, and are much less like artists and poets than is currently thought to be the case. The tale of Rabbi Akiva suggests that there is a "Torah-anchor" that grounds all rabbinical reflection and interpretation; I have likewise suggested that there is an anchor of historical tradition that grounds all philosophical reflection.

At the core of contemporary confusion over these points, I have charged that the bewitching and poetic language of Heidegger concerning the inexhaustibility of being has passed over into theological and philosophical hermeneutics, resulting in a fatal and mistaken conflation of the important distinction between being and meaning. That confusion is further exacerbated by the reliance of hermeneutics on illustrations of interpretive understanding in art, literature, and poetry— precisely those areas of human experience in which being may well be reducible to multifold meanings. But this does not justify the conflation; rather, this observation disallows, or at least drastically limits, the comparisons between aesthetic and philosophical hermeneutics. In particular, the rampant relativism in the former does not automatically apply to the latter. Merely from the fact that the last word has not been spoken in the reflective historical engagement that philosophy is, we are not entitled to conclude that any word whatsoever may be taken as edifying, let alone as intelligent, conversation.

Finally, I have distinguished philosophy's reliance on history from that of historical religions like Christianity. The "being" of history from which meanings are to be drawn in philosophy is not the being of discrete historical detail, but the presence within history of a tradition of reflective engagement.

Philosophy is, in this sense, irreducibly historical. The resulting historical dialogue, the "conversation which we are" and which philosophy itself is, is the conversation between ourselves and those who have gone before, concerning what we might, together, become.[21]

GEORGE R. LUCAS, JR.

UNITED STATES NAVAL ACADEMY
MAY 1992

NOTES

1. See my own contribution, as well as that of each of the others in this list (save Smith and Rorty) to a volume entitled *Philosophical Imagination and Cultural Memory: The Philosophical Uses of Historical Traditions,* ed. Patricia Cook (Durham, N.C.: Duke University Press, 1993). Rorty, though not a participant, is much discussed in this volume, as is Professor Gadamer. For Smith, see n. 2 below. My work on the three historical figures mentioned is summarized in *The Rehabilitation of Whitehead: An Analytic and Historical Assessment of Process Philosophy* (Albany, N.Y.: State University of New York Press, 1989).

2. See George R. Lucas, Jr., "Philosophy's Recovery of its History," in *The Recovery of Philosophy in America: Essays in Honor of John E. Smith,* ed. Robert C. Neville and Tom Kasulis (Albany, N.Y.: State University of New York Press, 1996).

3. Richard Rorty's use of the concept of "edifying conversation" in *Philosophy and the Mirror of Nature* provides an excellent example. The notion is taken over straightforwardly from Gadamer.

On the matter of originality: in *The Recovery of the Measure* (Albany, N.Y.: State University of New York Press, 1990), and *The High Road Around Modernism* (Albany, N.Y.: SUNY Press, 1992), Professor Robert Neville of Boston University offers a sustained argument that the European tradition of interpretation, represented by Dilthey and Gadamer, is rivaled by an even older and broader interpretive tradition in American philosophy, represented by the pragmaticism of C. S. Peirce and the instrumentalism of John Dewey. This American tradition of interpretation, Neville argues, includes many of the same features as European hermeneutics, stressing philosophy as active inquiry and the posing of interpretive questions, but has the advantage of including (and indeed, stemming from) the natural sciences, which, in Peirce's own words, consist of "self-correcting communities of like-minded inquirers." One obtains all the insights of European hermeneutics, minus the relativism and bifurcation that result from a disjunction of the

Natur- and the *Geisteswissenschaften,* and from exclusive reliance on the humanities and the fine arts.

4. Hans-Georg Gadamer, *Reason in the Age of Science,* trans. Frederick G. Lawrence (Cambridge, Mass.: MIT Press, 1981), p. 106. In their introduction to Gadamer's work in *After Philosophy: End or Transformation* (Cambridge, Mass.: MIT Press, 1987), editors Kenneth Baynes, James Bohman, and Thomas McCarthy correctly note in passing (p. 321) that Gadamer's "question and answer" dialectical method is similar to that posed by R. G. Collingwood. I am grateful that someone has seen fit to provide such an overdue acknowledgment.

In his *Essay on Metaphysics* (Oxford: Oxford University Press, 1940), part 1, secs. 4–6, Collingwood puts forth the proposition that "every statement that anybody ever makes is made in answer to a question"; that such questions precede their answers both logically and temporally; that the questions, in turn, entail presuppositions (or nested sets of presuppositions); and that metaphysics is an historical science whose aim is to get hold of the absolute presuppositions (which are never answers to questions) that lie at the heart of individual and cultural worldviews (see pp. 23–25, 40–41, 47, 56–57 in the Regnery Gateway edition [Chicago, 1972]). Absolute presuppositions are roughly analogous to Gadamer's "horizons." Like Gadamer, Collingwood views this historical task as open-ended and ongoing: "The historian's work is never finished; every historical subject, like the course of historical events itself, is open at the end, and however hard you work at it the end always remains open" (p. 64). Whereas Gadamer comes to this insight via law and theology combined with his study of Bultmann and Heidegger, Collingwood tells us in his *Autobiography* (1938) that his method was first developed as an attempt to systematize archaeological studies in the 1920s.

5. Gadamer, *Reason in the Age of Science,* p. 19.

6. Ibid., p. 111.

7. Arthur Danto, "The End of Art," in *The Philosophical Disenfranchisement of Art* (New York: Columbia University Press, 1986), pp. 90–115. Danto argues that artistic movements "die" when the artists themselves become consciously preoccupied with the philosophical significance of their work, with its "meaning." What follows, as with Gadamer, ceases to be art and becomes philosophy.

8. Gadamer, *Reason in the Age of Science,* p. 19.

9. Ibid., p. 20.

10. See, e.g., David Hoy, *The Critical Circle: Literature and History in Contemporary Hermeneutics* (Berkeley, Calif.: University of California Press, 1978). As Gadamer himself explains it:

> The very idea of a definitive interpretation seems to be intrinsically contradictory. Interpretation is always on the way. . . . Once we presuppose that there is no such thing as a fully transparent text or a completely exhaustive interest in the explaining and construing of texts, then all perspectives relative to the art and theory of interpretation are shifted. . . . The elaboration of the hermeneutic situation (which means becoming aware of the vague presuppositions and implications involved in a question that comes up), which is the key to methodical interpretation, has a unique element to it. The first guiding insight is to admit of the endlessness of this task. To imagine that one might ever attain full illumination as to his motives or his interests in questions is to imagine something impossible. *(Reason in the Age of Science,* pp. 105, 108)

11. See Stanley Rosen's "Philosophy's Quarrel with Poetry," in *Philosophical Imagination and Cultural Memory: the Philosophical Uses of Historical Traditions,* ed. Patricia

J. Cook; also *Hermeneutics as Politics* (New York: Oxford University Press, 1987); and *The Quarrel Between the Ancients and the Moderns* (New Haven, Conn.: Yale University Press, 1989).

I am not quite content with this way of putting the matter. It would be more correct to focus on the cultural and historical background and horizon of the gallery visitors, in order to account for the "fusing of horizons" within a common cultural context, notwithstanding individual idiosyncracies. The "plurality of worlds" of which Rosen complains, then, would be seen as a plurality of cultures, rather than an infinity of individual interpretations. Poets grow in a common cultural soil; it is not individual numbers and differences, so much as the radical difference and incommensurability between Russian and Japanese poetry, or between English and Yoruba, with which we must contend. But I cannot explore this problem further here.

12. George L. Kline, "Form, Concrescence, and Concretum," in *Explorations in Whitehead's Philosophy,* ed. Lewis S. Ford and George L. Kline (New York: Fordham University Press, 1983); the distinction is introduced in sec. 9 of this paper (pp. 130–32), and discussed subsequently in greater detail in Kline's Presidential Address for the Metaphysical Society of America in 1986, "Present, Past, and Future," *Review of Metaphysics* (March, 1987).

13. Hans-Georg Gadamer, *Truth and Method* (New York: Seabury Press, 1975), p. 268.

14. I have expanded upon Kline's suggestive comments about psychotherapy; he is careful, for example, to distinguish the present *memories* of past events from the past "objects" of those present memories. The *memories of* events, not the events themselves, are reconstructed. In addition, Kline cites numerous other intriguing examples, such as the historical births of subsequently famous figures like Dante and Einstein: the being of such events is fixed; but the meanings took some time to accrue, and are still in process of development.

15. See Rudolf Bultmann, *Jesus and the Word* (New York: 1934), and *Theology of the New Testament,* 2 vols. (New York: 1952, 1955).

16. As one colleague, a university theologian, put the matter to me in contrast to Bultmann: "if there was in fact no resurrection, then it doesn't much matter what 'interpretation' we attach to this nonevent. The entire enterprise is fraudulent!"

17. Gadamer, *Reason in the Age of Science,* p. 95.

18. *Menahot* 29b, in *Judaism,* ed. Arthur Hertzberg (New York: George Braziller, 1962), pp. 200–201. The charming story has, however, a grim ending. The reader is left with the clear indication that Rabbi Akiva's subsequent martyrdom during the Hadrianic persecutions is somehow to be understood as a direct result of this apparent impudence, of his failure, that is, to distinguish adequately between the Being of the Law and his own somewhat convoluted interpretations.

19. Of course it is true that the Exodus plays the role of the "defining historical event" in Judaism. Judaism seems less vulnerable on this score than Christianity, however, in that a multitude of historical particulars, from Exodus to the Davidic epic to Exile, define a historical tradition. As I note, a relationship to history that relies on tradition rather than on a few particulars, while still "historical," is not subject to the "scandal of historical particularity."

20. Gadamer, *Reason and the Age of Science,* p. 97.

21. As Gadamer himself puts the matter:

> Every renewed encounter with an older tradition now is no longer a simple matter of appropriation that un-self-consciously adds what is proper to itself even as it assimi-

lates what is old, but it has to cross the abyss of historical consciousness. . . . [T]he theory of fusion of horizons . . . may provide a justification as to why I maintain that the situation of conversation is a fertile model even where a mute text is brought to speech first by the questions of the interpreter. . . . [W]e cannot change the fact that unacknowledged presuppositions are always at work in our understanding. Probably we should not want to change this at all, even if we could. It always harvests a broadened and deepened self-understanding. (*Reason in the Age of Science,* pp. 98, 111)

REPLY TO GEORGE R. LUCAS, JR.

I read Mr. Lucas' contribution with excitement and, whether he believes it or not, for the most part with agreement. At first I was astonished that one could begin with three paintings by Monet without relating the trinity of the presentations to the question of what this is supposed to tell us. After all, it is revealing when a painter paints his haystack and his cathedral of Rouen again and again. And why do we, of our own accord, look at the repetitions without saying, we know that already? In the face of such an introduction, we cannot entirely dispense with the question which a philosopher instinctively poses to such phenomena. I would like to bracket the application to psychoanalysis. I readily admit that in that regard the interpretation within a therapeutic context requires a deciphering of the unconscious, and that in this sense interpretation certainly cannot be applied arbitrarily.

But after this, the essay continues in a convincing manner. I admit that I was somewhat astonished that Protestant theology in the form of Rudolf Bultmann had to appear on the scene only because he too learned from Heidegger. But he is certainly not alone with respect to the decisive points that are being worked out here, namely 'being' and 'meaning'. The wonderful things which follow about law and its interpretation, and the point that law is primarily applied law, remain as true as the fact that the Torah was the law interpreted through the Talmud and rendered intelligible to us.

But I do not want to take up issues about which Mr. Lucas is certainly more competent. About the history of philosophy as it is discussed, I can only say that one really should begin with Anaximander instead of with Socrates or Aristotle. For how do we know about Anaximander if not through Aristotle. But these are trifling matters which puzzled me in reading this contribution because I always had to assume that sooner or later I would find a point at which the words of reprimand which were directed against the blurring of being *[Sein]* and being-intended *[Gemeintsein]* would concern me. Unfortunately, I cannot find this point. Even such a repetition as the expression 'living tradition' with which I am very familiar and which I find almost touching appears without accusation. When then am I being accused of it? I have not claimed, of course, that only hermeneutics is philosophy, but I did claim that hermeneutics too is philosophy. And maybe it is a philosophy which does not result in confusion when art and poetry are considered as well as when one is in pursuit of philosophical questions? Is that really so striking? Do others not have the same experience that, at least since Hegel, they gain less from what is taking place in philosophy than from *The Brothers Karamazov* or Kafka's *The Trial*? I cannot help it, but in such cases it seems that literature simply says more. Of course, it does not give us an answer. But I suppose all of us are aware of the fact that in truth we are the ones being questioned. I have to confess that what 'being' is supposed to mean in all examples brought forth here is intelligible to me only through 'meaning'. Also, we can hardly disregard entirely the fact that in the eyes of Dostoyevsky the Karamazovs were supposed to be an apology for Christianity, who would have claimed their place next to Pascal, and that Kafka's *The Trial,* too, speaks to us with a power of expression in the face of which we fall silent.

H.-G.G.

8

Herta Nagl-Docekal

TOWARDS A NEW THEORY OF THE HISTORICAL SCIENCES: THE RELEVANCE OF *TRUTH AND METHOD*

Is history a hermeneutic science? In their vehement denial of the possibility, authors such as Walter Benjamin, Theodore Abel, and Michel Foucault, who represent otherwise very divergent positions, agree.[1] They are also alike, however, in that their dissociation from hermeneutics is not based on a thorough discussion of the complex argumentation and the internal development of hermeneutics. Thus, hermeneutics is occasionally accused of what it itself criticizes.[2] For this reason the opening question cannot be considered answered, and to what extent the problems of the constitution of the historical sciences can be clarified by hermeneutic theory must be discussed anew. It is thereby appropriate to proceed by bringing to view the specific thoughts of the individual representatives of the hermeneutic tradition. To this end, in what follows I will focus on Gadamer's *Truth and Method*.

GADAMER'S CRITICISM OF THE SCIENCES

First of all, Gadamer does not aim at questions of the theory of science in a restricted sense. At a time when public opinion increasingly falls under the spell of the sciences, he attempts to uncover the largely unconsidered presuppositions of the sciences in order to clearly punctuate their limits. Thus, for him the question of the method of the human sciences merges with reflection on the way of experiencing on which they are based and which he calls the pre- or extrascientific experience of art and history. This way of experiencing is for him a particularity that must be seen in relation to the "general relationship of man to the world."[3] Gadamer wants primarily to demonstrate that the "objectifying procedure" of the sciences "proved to be an abstraction" and, vis-à-vis this, to draw

Translated by Dr. Murray Woody.

attention to the prescientific, "fundamental relation to the world that is given in the linguistic nature of our experience of it."[4]

At the center of these thoughts of Gadamer's, lies the term hermeneutics. This term, however, is not uniformly defined. Instead, it is given different meanings according to the structure of the argumentation just characterized. More precisely, the word hermeneutics is used with four meanings: (1) the specific method of the humanities; (2) the extrascientific experience of art and history; (3) the general relation of man to the world; and (4) the philosophical reflection on the problematic expressed in 1–3.

If one's goal is to investigate the relevance of Gadamer's philosophy to the theory of humanities, one's course of argumentation should be taken up in the reverse direction. First, one must survey the concept of the fundamental hermeneutic experience and then ask what consequences result for the theory of the human sciences.

Gadamer systematically begins with the situation that man's overall relation to the world is essentially established via language. The thought that language is "not . . . the reflection of something given" is decisive for him. The mediation of 'I' and world in language is not an "activity of the subject" but "something the thing itself does, and which thought 'suffers.'" Speaking appears thus as the "subjective reflex" of this doing, as an execution in which the thing itself brings itself to language. In the further consequence, the things appear as the actual speakers themselves: "Thus we speak not only of a language of art, but also of a language of nature, in short, of any language that things have."[5]

This thought plays an essential role in the further development of Gadamer's theory. It has the effect that the structure of hermeneutics contains, in its most general form, a distinct hierarchy in that the 'I' is determined as merely receptive. As already noted, far-reaching consequences result since, for Gadamer, hermeneutics in this general sense is fundamental hermeneutics (hermeneutics 3)—out of which the special forms of hermeneutic experience (hermeneutics 2) first emerge. These we will investigate below.

If we now turn to Gadamer's discussion of the sciences, one notices that differences between the two major groups of sciences lose, to a great extent, their meaning. Gadamer emphasizes that all sciences agree in two ways: All stem from the one fundamental form of the human relation to the world (the understanding in the most general sense) and they all deny this foundation (thus exposing themselves to the same criticism).

In reference to the natural sciences, Gadamer determines that they have been "abstracted out of the fundamental relation to the world."[6] Their ideal of objectivity betrays, according to Gadamer, an "ontological prejudice," i.e., the picture of the world as a "being-in-itself" that is the object of scientific investigation. The result, he says, is a "false methodologism." On the other hand, Gadamer allows that the natural sciences are "able to serve the growing domination of being."[7] But, one asks, is this compatible with his criticism? If the natural sciences rest on a false ontological estimation, how can their control of nature be explained? Gadamer's statements remain ambivalent, and an analogous ambivalence will be found in relation to the historical sciences.

Based on Gadamer's approach, a criticism along similar lines to that expressed concerning the natural sciences emerges for the human sciences that belong to the historicist tradition. The human sciences, too, create a being-in-itself as the object of their investigations, thereby abstracting themselves out of the original hermeneutic relation. But, as noted above, Gadamer outlines a special formulation of hermeneutics as the fundamental basis of experience from which the humanities have separated themselves. Hence we shall look more closely at this special form of hermeneutic experience (hermeneutics 2). Not until afterwards can the question be asked whether Gadamer's philosophy emits impulses for the constitution of a new type of humanities no longer based on an untenable concept of objectivity.

THE HERMENEUTIC EXPERIENCE OF TRADITION

In order to explain the difference between the humanities' procedure and the original hermeneutic relation, Gadamer chooses the example of art first. He hopes that using art as an illustration will especially facilitate the plausibility that scientific method does not attain that which occurs in the fundamental experience.

> Just as in the experience of art we are concerned with truths that go essentially beyond the range of methodical knowledge, so the same thing is true of the whole of the human sciences, in which our historical tradition in all its forms is certainly made the object of investigation, but at the same time in it truth comes to speech. The experience of historical tradition goes quite beyond that in it which can be investigated. It is true or untrue not only in the sense concerning which historical criticism decides, but always mediates truth, in which one must try to share.[8]

Thus, the special form of hermeneutics which the humanities have "reflected [themselves] out of" involves experience of the truth of the tradition. If one now asks how this experience differs from other forms of experience, it appears that it is the linguistic experience. "But tradition is not simply a tradition . . .; it is language, i.e., it expresses itself like a 'Thou.' A 'Thou' is not an object but stands in relationship with us."[9] For Gadamer, then, the discussion with a 'Thou' as a linguistic experience is the paradigm of hermeneutic experience. In the following, however, it will be seen that this stipulation cannot be held without contradiction.

In a passage significant for the overall train of thought in *Truth and Method,* Gadamer differentiates three ways of treating the 'Thou,' thereby clarifying the difference between the various branches of humanities and also between these and the extrascientific hermeneutic experience. The lowest ranking is the observation of the 'Thou' "that seeks to discover things that are typical in the behavior of one's fellow men and is able to make predictions concerning another person. . . . [In other words,] he is predictable. His behavior is as much a means to our end as any other means."[10] Gadamer summarizes this form of the behavior towards the 'Thou' under the designation *knowledge of human nature.* (Whether it is legitimate to limit the meaning of knowledge of human nature to the manipulative use of other persons cannot be investigated in the current context and is noted solely as a question.)

Elevated to a principle of science, this behavior towards the 'Thou' leads to the "method of the social sciences, following the methodological ideas of the eighteenth century and their programmatic formulation by Hume, ideas that are an imitation of scientific method."[11] The social sciences, too, see that "it is only what is typical and regular that is taken account of in human behavior." For this reason, Gadamer calls them "schematically reduced." "Someone who understands tradition in this way makes it an object, i.e., he confronts it in a free and uninvolved way, and, by methodically excluding all subjective elements in regard to it, he discovers what it contains."[12] What Gadamer calls, on the level of the individual I-Thou relation, knowledge of human nature, finds its counterpart in science in the social-scientific certainty of law-governed relationships. The manipulative use of a seen-through person corresponds to the sciences' already-mentioned authority claim.

The second way of treating the 'Thou' that Gadamer differentiates is "objectively more adequate than the knowledge of human nature, which merely seeks to calculate how the other person will behave."[13] Here the "'Thou' is acknowledged as a person." Gadamer outlines a behavior that is certain that the 'Thou' has a demand to make but that nonetheless does not outreach a "self-relatedness." This failure comes about because the 'I' "claims to express the other's claim and even to understand the other better than the other understands itself. In this way the 'Thou' loses the immediacy with which it makes its claim. It is understood, but this means that it is anticipated and intercepted reflectively from the standpoint of the other person."[14] This behavior exists in a wide range of human relations. Says Gadamer, "Because it is a mutual relationship, it helps to constitute the reality of the 'Thou' relationship itself. The inner historicality of all the relations in the lives of men consists in the fact [that] there is a constant struggle for mutual recognition."[15] The human relationship formed by this behavior is one in which "it is possible for each of the partners in the relationship reflectively to outdo the other."[16]

A further characteristic of this structure is that neither party admits to its existence. "But this dialectic of reciprocity that governs all 'I-Thou' relationships is inevitably hidden from the mind of the individual. . . . In fact, his own self-awareness consists precisely in his withdrawing from the dialectic of this reciprocity, in his reflecting himself out of his relation to the other and so becoming unreachable by him." Gadamer sees an especially conspicuous example of this in charity or welfare work.

By understanding the other, by claiming to know him, one takes from him all justification of his own claims. The dialectic of charitable or welfare work in particular operates in this way, penetrating all relationships between men as a reflective form of the effort to dominate. The claim to understand the other person in advance performs the function of keeping the claim of the other person at a distance. We are familiar with this from the educative relationship, an authoritative form of welfare work.[17]

Elevated to a principle of science, this second form of the behavior towards the 'Thou' leads, according to Gadamer, to the humanities. In reference to history, it leads to that which Gadamer calls "historical consciousness" (as opposed to "effective-historical consciousness").[18] Just as in the reflecting relationship one knows of the 'Thou' as a person, the historical consciousness knows "about the past in its otherness. . . . It seeks in the otherness of the past not the instantiation of a general law, but something historically unique."[19] The historical consciousness, however, also outdoes the demand it faces—traditional hermeneutics aims to understand the authors of the past better than they understood themselves. Gadamer finds, for the element of reciprocity, a pendant in the relationship to history in that the historical consciousness itself depends on history, i.e., it itself is in the midst of a "historical circumstance."[20] And just as the mutuality of the individuals' behavior remains concealed from them, the historical consciousness is likewise unaware of its historical circumstance. Indeed, it is characterized precisely by its failure to consider its own embeddedness. This is expressed by the historian's denial of being "himself influenced by historical circumstances"; he is convinced "that he is free of prejudices" and thereby also of the "objectivity of his procedures."[21] What Gadamer observed in charity and welfare work, he also finds in an analogous way in the historical consciousness, i.e., "it is actually seeking to master, as it were, the past."[22] Thus for him the humanities and the social sciences, despite their differences, agree in that they claim the right to dominate.

The third way of treating the 'Thou', as differentiated by Gadamer, is the model of the fundamental hermeneutic experience. Here he has in mind an acknowledgment of fellow humans that will make a "genuine human relationship" possible. "Belonging together always also means being able to listen to one another. When two people understand each other, this does not mean that one person 'understands' the other, in the sense of surveying him." "Openness" is therefore the central designation of the third way of dealing with the 'Thou'. "Openness" means the "acknowledgment that I must accept some things that are against myself," it means the willingness to "experience the 'Thou' truly as a 'Thou,' i.e., not to overlook his claim and to listen to what he has to say to me."[23] In reference to the coming-to-an-understanding of the past, this method leads to the "effective-historical consciousness."[24] This is essentially different from the historical consciousness in that it considers its own historicality. It admits to its own historical circumstances and thus it can make no claim to authority vis-à-vis tradition. Just as one person listens to another in a personal relationship, the effective-historical consciousness also demonstrates "openness to tradition," i.e., "I must allow the validity of the claim made by tradition, not in the sense of simply acknowledging the past in its otherness, but in such a way that it has something to say to me."[25]

Strikingly, in Gadamer's depiction of this third type, criticism as an element of truth mediation is not discussed. Revealing in this respect is Gadamer's characterization of the "experience of philosophy." He chooses two like-sounding formulations, namely that "a claim to truth" will be acknowledged (in German: *anerkannt*) and that "a truth" will be perceived (in German: *erkannt*), and his usage of these indicates that they are identical for him. But one should bear in mind that they refer to different components of a systematical philosophical discussion of the philosophical tradition. The acceptance of the claim to truth is the starting point that separates the systematic approach to traditional texts from a historical reading in the sense of historicism. As a second step, the truth question itself must be posed. The recognition of the claim to truth means nothing more than the concession to a text that it might mediate truth. Whether it actually does so can be decided only by a thorough critique. Thus it seems significant that Gadamer does not articulate that there are contradictory positions that appear, each with a claim to truth, in the framework of tradition and that each must be weighed and tested against the other, i.e., that therefore even tradition itself requires criticism. For him, tradition is solely a presentation of "truth, in which one must try to share."[26]

FROM A DIALOGUE TO AN AUTHORITY RELATIONSHIP

The omission of criticism as an issue indicates a decisive break in Gadamer's argumentation, making it apparent that Gadamer did not consequently base the hermeneutic experience on the dialogue model. Criticism would not have been incompatible with this model, on the contrary: "being able to listen to one another" in a true dialogue also involves reciprocal criticism. Here Gadamer switches to another model; he chooses the authority relationship as a second paradigm of hermeneutic experience. He sees its compatibility with the dialogue model as established in that he rejects, as a deformation of the concept of authority, an interpretation of authority in which "the prestige of authority takes the place of one's own judgment."[27] But one cannot fail to notice that his own definition of authority does not deviate essentially from this interpretation. "[T]he authority of persons is based ultimately, not on the subjection and abdication of reason, but on recognition and knowledge—knowledge, namely, that the other is superior to oneself in judgment and insight and that for this reason his judgment takes precedence, i.e., it has priority over one's own."[28]

Where the authority relationship becomes the paradigm of hermeneutic experience, a reverse equivalent to the humanities and their fundamental relation to tradition results. If in the humanities it is the researcher who approaches tradition with superiority, then in the hermeneutic experience it is the tradition that is the authority for the current recipient. The scientist's claim of authority, on the one hand, corresponds to the "dominance of history,"[29] on the other. Gadamer interprets the fundamental relationship to history as a direct "stand[ing] always within tradition." "That which has been sanctioned by tradition and custom has an authority that is nameless, and our finite historical being is marked by the fact that always the authority of what has been transmitted—and not only what is clearly grounded—has power over our attitudes and behavior."[30]

Precisely here, where the hermeneutic experience is conceived in the light of the authority model, Gadamer's actual point is made. The focus of his attention is that the possibility of negation is limited because behind its back, in a sense, traditions continue to exist. "Even where life changes violently, as in ages of revolution, far more of the old is preserved in the supposed transformation of everything than anyone knows. . . . That is why both the enlightenment's critique of tradition and its romantic rehabilitation are less than their true historical being."[31] This observation is certainly very plausible, but does it give one the right to view the direct mediation of tradition alone as our fundamental relation to history? Gadamer chooses the "validity of morals" as a paradigm and impressively explains the essence of living tradition. But to interpret this "simplest preservation of tradition"[32] as actual and natural behavior appears, nevertheless, to overstretch a factor. On the one hand, the danger of a historical determinism threatens; on the other, the concept of history itself becomes problematic because the cause of historical change remains open.

At this point I would remind that for Gadamer the hermeneutic experience is a special case of hermeneutics in general, which he calls "something the thing itself does, and which thought 'suffers.'" The consequences of a hierarchical structure already present in the general structure of Gadamer's hermeneutics now become apparent.

THE HISTORICAL CONSCIOUSNESS: A NECESSARY, MERE ILLUSION?

If one now has the fundamental elements of Gadamer's concept of the hermeneutic experience in view, then the question can be addressed, What consequences result for the theory of humanities? Gadamer criticizes, as noted above, the humanities for following the objectivity ideal of the natural sciences and reflecting themselves out of the context of the mediation of truth. One could expect that he is aiming at a new model of humanities, but this expectation will, at first, be disappointed. The reasons for this will now be briefly discussed. Later it will be seen that impulses for a methodological redetermination of the historical sciences do, nonetheless, emanate from Gadamer's thoughts.

If one takes a closer look at what Gadamer means by "reflecting oneself out," it becomes apparent that he differentiates between how the humanities see their nature and how they actually are. He wants to expose "what the human sciences truly are, beyond their methodological self-consciousness, and what connects them with the totality of our experience of world."[33] That means, he emphasizes, that the humanities themselves are a product of living tradition, "that there is an element of tradition active in the human science, despite the methodological nature of its procedures, an element that constitutes its real nature and is its distinguishing mark."[34] In reference to history, this means that the experience of history, because it forms the historian as well as all other individuals, also affects the work of the historian. "Hence historical research is based on the historical movement in which life itself stands."[35]

Historiography belongs thereby in the effective history of the tradition that it treats, apparently detached, as its object. Therefore Gadamer attempts to prove that the "*abstract antithesis between tradition and historical research, between history and knowledge, must be discarded*"[36] and to show "how much there is of *event* in all *understanding*."[37] In historical science the past speaks, in a way, about itself. Thus it comes as no surprise when Gadamer grants historical science the same authority that he otherwise also grants to that which has been "sanctioned by tradition." "Modern historical research itself is not only research, but the transmission of tradition. . . . [I]n it, too, we have, as it were, a new experience of history, whenever a new voice is heard in which the past echoes."[38] Gadamer accordingly summarizes, "The effect of a living tradition and the effect of historical study must constitute a unity."[39]

Examined more closely, these thoughts exhibit some inconsistencies. The observations that Gadamer begins with here are nevertheless plausible. He emphasizes, for example, that "the present and its interests" determine the formulation of the question with which the historian approaches the past and that therefore the "theme and area of research" are constituted by the present.[40] The thought that the historian (as well as all other humans) is always determined more through tradition than he can reflectively overcome is equally apparent. But Gadamer misinterprets both of these observations by deeming them identical. The interests of the present that prescribe the historian's questions are just not the convictions that were uncritically absorbed in the environment of a living tradition. On the contrary, they are the result of those problems which are focused on by public attention and current discussions. Of course the problems of the present are historical givens, and of course tradition keeps norms alive, but the practical discourse implies a discussion in which both an assessment of the present problems and a critical reflection on the, for the time being, directly adopted norms shall take place and which, as noted above, is not itself to be considered a product of history.

When Gadamer claims that we "do well not to regard historical consciousness as something radically new—as it seems at first—but as a new element within that which has always made up the human relation to the past,"[41] he is certainly right, but in a different way than he intends. If he means that the historian, like all other humans, is affected by the past, then contrary to this it must be emphasized that he, like the others, takes part in the discourse of the present, and, based on this, formulates his questions. If the prescientific relation to history is not just receptive but rather reflective and motivated by practical concerns, then historical science also begins here. It has the function of expanding the practical discourse of the present in its confrontation with the past. In other words, history neither "happens" by itself, nor does it speak about itself.

This objection, as noted above, is not intended to deny that the historian is always determined by traditions that he does not see through. But to see in this "the real nature" and the "distinguishing mark" of historical science would be arbitrary. Without referring to the practical encounter of the present with its givens dictated by the past and to the historian himself as participant in this encounter, the essence of historical science cannot be ascertained. This also means that historical research cannot be considered as a direct transmission of truth or as a prereflective mediator of tradition. On the contrary, it makes certain elements of the given tradition visible (certainly without claiming the capability to completely catch up with its own background).

Reflecting on elements of tradition opens a new relation to them: No longer the "simplest preservation" occurs but an argumentative investigation that can just as easily lead to an affirmation as to a break. But Gadamer's concept of the hermeneutic experience precludes his explicating this alternative. Thus Habermas, too, holds against him "the insight that the reflective appropriation of tradition breaks the natural substance of tradition and changes the position of the subject in it." He continues, "Gadamer misjudges the power of reflection. . . . Awareness of the genesis of tradition, out of which reflection originates and to which it refers back, rocks the dogmatism of experience."[42] Despite this problematic, Gadamer undeniably deserves credit for recognizing the constitutive import of the historicity of the researcher for the humanities and for bringing this to light vis-à-vis the historicist interpretation. Thus it is all the more deplorable that the limits of his concept of the hermeneutic experience preclude the possibility of transporting his insights into an alternative model of humanities. His theory of the effective-historical consciousness exposes the illusory character of the historical consciousness but is not itself capable of furthering science.

As the thoughts quoted above show, Gadamer attempts not only to demonstrate that the historical sciences can be traced back to the experience of history but that, above all, they themselves mediate the experience of history. He sees their actual achievement in this. Since he thereby concedes only an indirect feat of the historical sciences—one not part of the explicit research intention—a peculiar situation results in which precisely that which is of importance to Gadamer in the historical sciences is that which is not discussed in them. If he intends to establish the irrelevance of the abstract opposition between tradition and the historical sciences, then he succeeds at the cost of creating a fissure within the historical sciences, namely between research and that which it unreflectively mediates. This crevice could be circumnavigated only if the historical sciences were to acknowledge their historicity and give up their claim to time-lessness. This would mean, however, that a new model of history would have to be developed, and this is exactly what Gadamer excludes. If the historical sciences wish to be sciences, then they must remain obligated to the "methodological means proper to science"[43] that were developed in connection with the natural sciences. The result is that Gadamer's argumentation leads to a paradox. He exposes the false appearance to which the humanities fall victim, but at the same time he blocks the possible escape route out of this appearance.

The convergence of Gadamer's thoughts at this paradox should not obstruct what the current discourse on the theory of the historical sciences can gain from them. This debate should not ignore Gadamer's insight that the researcher's respective historical context is constitutive for the work of the humanities and that the objectivity claim formulated in the historicist train of thought reveals itself as false. And for exactly this reason, it is no longer possible to hold onto the conventional determination of history. On the contrary, a new history that does not deny its historical foundation must be drawn up. A prerequisite, however, is that the historicity of the researcher not be seen only from the viewpoint of the immediacy of living tradition. Otherwise the dissociation from the objectivistic understanding of science would mean the capitulation to the fundamentally unreflective process of tradition, and the transition into a new scientific method would be impossible. This means that the only way to follow Gadamer's insight into the historicity of historical research is to simultaneously negate both sides of the alternative between apparent scientific objectivity on the one hand and extrascientific direct experience on the other.

The historian is, as noted above, a participant in the practical discourse of the present, and as such he approaches the past. Thus, when he considers areas with a liability demand, the abstraction of the truth question will no longer be a desideratum for him. The confrontation of the present with the past is just the point. Here the following becomes apparent: precisely where the paradox should be overcome, one can newly fall back to an aspect of Gadamer's philosophy—it appears as a desideratum to uncover the ever-more-buried model of dialogue. (This applies regardless of how the question is answered concerning whether, in addition to the model of dialogue, still other models must be included for the new definition of history.) The relationship of the historian to the past would then be seen from the angle that Apel chooses when he interprets Gadamer's intent in the sense of a restitution "of the true hermeneutic relationship as a conversation relationship."[44]

HERTA NAGL-DOCEKAL

DEPARTMENT OF PHILOSOPHY
UNIVERSITY OF VIENNA, AUSTRIA
MAY 1992

NOTES

1. See Walter Benjamin, "Über den Begriff Geschichte," in Walter Benjamin, *Illuminationen, Ausgewählte Schriften* (Frankfurt: Suhrkamp, 1977), p. 251; Theodore Abel, "The Operation Called 'Verstehen'," in *Theorie und Realität,* ed. H. Albert, 1st ed. (Tübingen: Mohr, 1964), p. 177 (only in 1st ed.); Michel Foucault, *Archäologie des Wissens* (Frankfurt: Suhrkamp, 1973).

2. In Abel's article it jumps off the page, for example, that differentiations of the hermeneutic tradition are inverted into their opposites. Thus the paradoxical situation occurs that Abel sees the dialogue as decidedly beyond the operation called 'verstehen'. See Herta Nagl-Docekal, *Die Objektivität der Geschichtswissenschaft* (Vienna and Munich: Oldenbourg, 1982), pp. 120ff.

3. Hans-Georg Gadamer, *Truth and Method* (New York: Crossroad, 1982), p. 433.

4. Ibid.

5. Ibid., pp. 431–32.

6. Ibid., p. 433.

7. Ibid.

8. Ibid., p. xiii.

9. Ibid., p. 321.

10. Ibid., pp. 321–32.

11. Ibid., p. 322.

12. Ibid.

13. Ibid., p. 323.

14. Ibid., p. 322.

15. Ibid., pp. 322–33.

16. Ibid., p. 322.

17. Ibid., p. 323.

18. Ibid., pp. 321 and 323.

19. Ibid., p. 323.

20. Ibid., p. 324.

21. Ibid.

22. Ibid., p. 323.

23. Ibid., p. 324.

24. Ibid., pp. 324–35.

25. Ibid., p. 324.

26. Ibid., pp. xii–xiii.

27. Ibid., p. 247.

28. Ibid., p. 248.

29. Ibid., p. 250.

30. Ibid., p. 249.

31. Ibid., p. 250.

32. Ibid., pp. 244–250.

33. Ibid., p. xiii.

34. Ibid., p. 251.

35. Ibid., p. 253.

36. Ibid., p. 251. Gadamer's italics.

37. Ibid., p. xiii. Gadamer's italics.

38. Ibid., p. 253.

39. Ibid., p. 251.

40. Ibid., p. 253.

41. Ibid., p. 251.

42. Jürgen Habermas, "Zu Gadamers *Wahrheit und Methode*," in *Hermeneutik und*

Ideologiekritik, ed. Jürgen Habermas and others (Frankfurt am Main, 1971), p. 47f.

43. Gadamer, *Truth and Method,* p. xii.

44. Karl-Otto Apel, review of *Wahrheit und Methode,* by Hans-Georg Gadamer, *Hegel-Studien* 2 (1963): 316.

REPLY TO HERTA NAGL-DOCEKAL

The contribution by Ms. Nagl-Docekal caused me some difficulties. The text was an English translation. Through the kindness of the author, I then received her book *Die Objektivität der Geschichtswissenschaft* and the nature of the difficulties became clearer to me. Apparently, it is difficult to be open to the philosophical dimension of hermeneutics when one is concerned with the sciences, and in particular the science of history and its methodology.

Thus, already the title of the first section of her text is quite unintelligible to me. It reads "Gadamer's Criticism of the Sciences." What is that supposed to mean? Of course, it did not occur to me to criticize the sciences or their struggle for objectivity—even if for example in historical research, objectivity will always be limited. But I am concerned with philosophy. I ask myself how the spectacular development of modern science with its concept of method and its concept of objectivity is supposed to relate to the lived reality of being-in-the-world which takes place in social praxis, in the family, at work, in politics, and whenever it happens. My critique of Dilthey too, which the author accepts within limits, does not refer to Dilthey as a historian but as a philosopher. I think that in spite of his efforts he did not really free himself from the ideal of the methodology of the natural sciences. *Truth and Method* deals with the experience that art—and not the science of art—is for us. This also comprises history, but not as an object of science, but as the way in which we stand in history and do not know what is happening to us. Due to somebody's acting or suffering, something certainly might eventually result, which will later be seen as part of history. But that is certainly not what one thought or wished by such action or suffering. In contrast to that, my own starting point is the one that really encompasses everything we as linguistic beings share with one another. This is the firm basis on which we try to find our way in philosophy.

By no means then am I speaking of a wrong methodology in the sciences, but of the philosophical attempt to say what they are for us. Of course, this also applies to the natural sciences. One really cannot establish an argument against the finitude of our being human simply because the natural sciences seem to succeed in dominating nature. If such domination succeeds even only to a limited extent, then it does not stand as an objection to the natural sciences. This would only be the case if the application of science leads to the destruction of the basis of our life.

Unfortunately, I thus cannot really understand the comments here that are found under the title "The Hermeneutic Experience of Tradition." There it is said that I appeal to the truth of tradition or even to authority. These are misunderstandings which, after thirty years, really should not occur any longer. However, it is the task of hermeneutic philosophy to remind us of the fact that traditions determine us unconsciously and that learning recognizes authority insofar as it admits superior knowledge on the part of the teacher.

Historians know that especially well, although such a recognition of authority is not a claim to its truth. All of us certainly know that historians are carrying—unknowingly or consciously—a mighty ideological weight when they select their questions and fields of research. One could not understand Ranke and the historical school without knowing the concept and implications of nationality of the nineteenth century. Such is the case with the ideological prejudice *(Voreingenommenheit)* of all people and it constitutes a danger which, especially in the field of the humanities, can only be overcome by critique, and even then only partially. A hundred years from now, much that is now considered secure historical knowledge will definitely appear as ideologically distorted and prejudiced.

I thank the author for her intensive dedication to the problems she takes up. But I would like to add the request that one should first presume that one did not understand the other properly when one believes that one can find contradictions everywhere in the opinion of the other.

H.-G.G.

9

Stanley Rosen

HORIZONTVERSCHMELZUNG

In his seminal work, *Wahrheit und Methode,*[1] Gadamer poses a question to "all of human world-experience and life-praxis" *(Welterfahrung und Lebenspraxis)*: "how is *Verstehen* possible?" (xvii). *Verstehen* designates an understanding that goes beyond the apprehension of facts, rules, inferential patterns, or formal structures. It has more to do with the process by which human beings come to an understanding of each other, and thereby of the significance of human life. In Gadamer's discussion, the term is closely associated with *Erlebnis, Bildung, Wirkungsgeschichte, phronesis,* and *sensus communis.* His investigation is inspired by Heidegger's doctrine of *Verstehen* as *Auslegung* (366), or in other words with the thesis that the mode of existence of human being is that of interpretation. "The human relation to the world is strictly and from the ground up discursive *(sprachlich)* and thereby intelligible. Hermeneutics is, as we have seen, therefore *a universal aspect of philosophy* and not simply the methodological basis of the so-called *Geisteswissenschaften*" (451).

Verstehen takes place in the medium of human historicity. Whereas this notion is in principle "ontological" in the sense of Heidegger's *Sein und Zeit,* Gadamer is clearly concerned with "immanent" history or the medium of the human production of works that both interpret our life-praxis and accordingly require interpretation from other human beings who encounter them in a subsequent time. Perhaps Gadamer would allow the suggestion that he wishes to determine how human beings take a stand within history to their existence understood as historicity. Certainly his book is more fundamentally concerned with works of art and documents in the *Geisteswissenschaften,* as well as with philosophical doctrines about historical interpretation, or more generally with the understanding of life as a process of understanding, than with the logical or ontological structures of existence. In general, Gadamer inquires into the process by which human beings contribute to the formation of sense and significance. This process is the expression of what one may perhaps still call human nature, with the proviso that "nature" is here historical in two senses: it is the immanent expression of local interpretations of the transcendent or ontological historicity of existence. The human being does not simply discover a preordained sense; to be human is also to produce sense. And the production is an actualization of the given or transcending structures, which themselves become manifest to us in our interpretations of them.

Gadamer is therefore concerned, not simply with *Verstehen* as the process of interpreting works of art, law, culture, or more generally, of the human spirit; he is explicitly interested in the "ontological application of hermeneutics" (part 3). It is true that one finds ontological statements in Gadamer's book, in particular the often-cited assertion that *"Being that can be understood is language"* (*Sprache,* 450). But his primary goal is the understanding of textual exhibitions of beings, where "textual" may be understood in the literal sense of "weavings" or productions of the human discursive spirit, including works of art ranging from the explicitly discursive like poetry to the implicitly discursive like music, architecture, and even ornamentation. Stated from another perspective, Gadamer is interested in the historical appropriation of the Western tradition, and thus in the question of how we can understand one another, and in particular the works of the past, precisely as historical beings who derive their multiple senses primarily from their own epochs, but who, as historical beings, are able to dwell within, and hence be understood by residents of, another historical epoch. One concrete manifestation of this question is the fact that we belong to our own historical time and are thus defined in an intrinsic manner by the prejudices of that time. The prejudices of the individual, Gadamer says, much more than his judgments, are "the historical actuality of his Being" (261).

But Gadamer is very far from "historicism" in the sense of the thesis that we cannot understand works from an epoch other than our own. As is evident from his acceptance of Heidegger's existential ontology of historicity, Gadamer believes that we arrive at a transcendence of immanent history precisely by understanding the structure of *Verstehen*. Stated in the terms of immanent history, Gadamer holds that *"Verstehen is itself to be thought as not so much an activity of subjectivity as* [self-] *insertion into an event of tradition [Uberlieferungsgeschehen],* in which past and present continuously mediate one another" (274f.). Gadamer does not mean by this merely that we can grasp the determining moments of the historical process of encounter between a work of the past and an interpreter of the present. To say only this would transform hermeneutics into a pure ontology of historicity, and leave it entirely open whether the concrete interpretation of any particular work of the past has validity. It is perhaps possible to argue on behalf of the later Nietzsche, for example, that Being is interpretation in the sense of the production of perspectives, while also maintaining that each perspective is discontinuous from the others, or in other words, as is frequently held today, that difference is the heart of identity. Gadamer, however, wishes to argue that the very historicity of Being, or in other words, of the discursive essence of human existence, enables us, not to overcome in the sense of disregarding our temporal prejudices or perspectives, but to incorporate them into an interpretation that is true to the nature of that work both in its generality as a work and in its specificity as this work, of such-and-such a nature.

We can see this intention in Gadamer's insistence that to understand a work in its own time—and Gadamer extends this point to a criticism of Leo Strauss' thesis that one must think the thoughts of an author as the author thought them (506ff.)—is to deny its claim to be true for *me*, i.e., for the tradition (287). The *Wirkungsgeschichte* or the history of the effect of the work on its subsequent audiences, is thus a genuine part of the meaning or significance of the work itself (109ff. et passim). It might be objected to Gadamer that this line of argumentation presupposes what is to be proved, namely, that works are not essentially and even largely an intrinsic meaning intended by the author or creator to be understood by the properly equipped interpreter at any historical epoch. In other words, one could object that to understand a work is only partly and secondarily to understand it in its own time; more fundamentally, understanding is the apprehension of the sense or significance of the work as intelligible for all times, as a *ktema eis aei*, in Thucydides' expression. In this case, to understand a work in my terms is to understand it in the author's terms, since these two terms are those of the sense of the work itself.

It seems to me that Gadamer meets this objection at least in part by his doctrine of *Horizontverschmelzung*. Gadamer claims at an early stage of his discussion that the timelessness and the temporality of an artwork must be brought together in the act of interpretation (115). The previously noted insertion into an event of tradition is in fact an entering into the work itself, the existence of which includes the role it has played in the tradition. There is no object in itself of historical knowing; to understand is primarily to come to an understanding with the work, and only secondarily with the thoughts of its producer (269, 278). As a particular example of this thesis, one may note Gadamer's discussion of the performance of an artwork, in particular of a piece of music, and his claim that there is no such thing as *the* objectively correct performance (109–12). Since the being of the artwork includes the moment of performance, it follows that we understand that work, say Beethoven's late string quartets, not simply by studying the score, but by listening to a wide variety of performances from different periods or schools of interpretation.

Arguments from music or dramatic presentation are unfortunately far from conclusive, since it is open to question first whether a piece of music has any discursive sense and more broadly whether the various possible meanings of a work of art have any fundamental relation to philosophical interpretations of art and of the general sense of human existence. Other questions of this sort could be raised, as for example whether the historical rootedness of a drama like *Hamlet* is not simply the medium for the transmission of a universal significance which is intelligible regardless of the manner of performance, provided only that the actors actually deliver the lines written by Shakespeare and follow his settings and occasional indications of action.

As I understand him, however, Gadamer evidently holds that to enter into a work of the spirit from another epoch is to understand it through the act of assimilating it into an interpretation that is in accord with the spirit of the historical horizon of the interpreter. Understanding *is* interpretation; the work is understood, not in its own terms, but as appropriated to my terms. Gadamer's general thesis, it seems to me, stands or falls, not on the changing tastes of connoisseurs, but on the fundamental question of how there can be a "fusion" of the horizon of past and present that preserves the historicity of the sense of human existence as *Verstehen,* and hence as *Auslegung,* without surrendering to historicism, or the thesis that there are no senses but only radically distinct perspectives. In what follows, accordingly, I propose to examine in detail the inner structure of *Horizontverschmelzung,* "fusion of horizons," which Gadamer introduces in the following passage from *Wahrheit und Methode:*

> In truth the horizon of the present is grasped in continuous formation, insofar as we must constantly test all our prejudices. To such a testing there belongs not as the least element the encounter with the past and the understanding of the tradition from which we come. The horizon of the present, therefore, does not form itself without the past. There is as little a present horizon for itself as there are given historical horizons that are to be acquired. *Verstehen is rather always the process of fusion of such ostensibly independently existing horizons.* (289)

At this point in my reflections, I take leave of Gadamer's text in order to carry through the exercise of philosophizing under his guidance. How in fact do we understand a work from the past? What does it mean to speak of a fusion of horizons? It goes without saying that in the compass of a brief essay, we can take only a few steps toward clarifying this crucial question. I begin by noting that the process of understanding a work of art is quite different from that of understanding a work of history, science, or philosophy. I would certainly grant at the outset that works of the types just mentioned do not have a rigid or determinate and circumscribed meaning that is defined explicitly by the author's intention and execution and by nothing else. But there is a fundamental difference between the task of interpreting *Sein und Zeit* on the one hand and the *Mona Lisa* or Beethoven's *Hammerklavier* sonata on the other.

Heidegger claims to present us in *Sein und Zeit* with the first part of a comprehensive interpretation of human being. This interpretation is not local, but valid at least for the current epoch of *Seinsgeschichte.* It therefore speaks not merely to our epoch but to the universal condition of mankind, which is to be understood as epochal. Stated with maximum concision, Heidegger intends his teaching of the relation between Being and Time to be valid for all times. No doubt Beethoven intended the *Hammerklavier* to be accessible to human beings throughout the balance of the tradition in which it was produced. But Heidegger's doctrine is intended to be true even if no one understands it. Again, one could say that the significance of the *Hammerklavier* for human beings of the western European tradition subsequent to the first decades of the nineteenth century does not evaporate even if that tradition should be obliterated. But there is a fundamental difference between a local expression of a universal truth (assuming that universal truth is manifested concretely in works of art) and an expression of the truth about local expressions.

If the universal truth about local expressions cannot be understood *in principle* at any time or in any epoch, and therefore understood in the same way, then philosophy is impossible. Gadamer's own doctrine loses all claim on this hypothesis to anything more than the status of a work of art. Suppose that someone in the twenty-fifth century discovers a copy of *Wahrheit und Methode* in the dusty stacks of a library, where it has been lying unread for hundreds of years. Once the necessary philological preparation has been acquired, can the reader of Gadamer's book understand its universal essence exactly as Gadamer understood it, however various may be the future reader's interpretation of the details or however different may be the works of the human spirit to which he applies that essence?

I want to suggest that there is a difference between understanding and interpretation, although the two are unquestionably related. *In order to interpret something, we must first understand it.* I hold, in other words, that *Verstehen* or the act of coming to a mutual understanding, is not simply the production of a *new* sense through the fusion of two horizons, my own and that of the producer of the work I am inspecting, but that the fusion of horizons is intrinsically the opening of a single horizon thanks to the union of my understanding with that of the producer in the universal sense that the work exhibits. This suggestion, incidentally, is not offered as a criticism of Gadamer but rather as my own "interpretation" of the truth of his doctrine of *Horizontverschmelzung*. I therefore claim to have entered into the universal sense of his doctrine, but not to have thought his thoughts as he himself thought them. Whatever may have been Gadamer's subjective intentions, or the immanent history of his development of the doctrines of *Wahrheit und Methode,* the doctrine of *Horizontverschmelzung* is, I believe, true; and it is true in the same way for Gadamer and me. In other words, if Gadamer should reject my interpretation, he must do so, not by citing his own intentions, or by recording the history of his subjective thoughts as he wrote *Wahrheit und Methode,* but by a philosophical refutation based upon the universal sense of the aforementioned doctrine. And by "universal," I mean nothing more (and nothing less) than that the truth of the doctrine is in principle accessible to every competent thinker.

None of this, of course, is said in a spirit of disputatiousness, but rather I wish to make the point that one cannot deny the difference between understanding and interpretation without repudiating the possibility of philosophy. If we do not first understand, i.e., see the nature of something and hence know the truth about it with sufficient precision to identify and thus to distinguish it from false images or mistaken interpretations, then there is no interpretation but only *creation.* And the word "creation" is here a euphemism, since interpretation, absent a core of common understanding, must always be the substitution of something *different* for the entity to be interpreted. But if each hermeneutical act is the production of a difference, then hermeneutics is impossible; one cannot even interpret a text to oneself without replacing that text by something else. Thus each effort to explain to oneself or to someone else the sense of the new text is itself the production of a difference, and so on *ad infinitum*. If reading is writing, then writing is scribbling.

I am quite confident that Gadamer would repudiate this denial of accessible senses. I am not equally confident that he would accept my distinction between understanding and interpretation; but again, my concern is not so much to establish agreement as to defend the truth of Gadamer's teaching, to the extent that I can discern it. And to repeat, I believe that there is indeed a fusion of horizons that constitutes the heart of an act of interpretation. But the fusion of horizons is itself grounded in a disappearance of horizonal differences, or in the copresence of two intellects within a single horizon. The single horizon is not a fusion or hybrid of two independent horizons, one from the past and the other from the present. It is neither past nor present, nor do we need to worry about the "Platonizing" implications of copresence, since I am not referring to the *parousia* of an *eidos* but to the interplay of presence and absence that constitutes understanding in the sense of openness to the truth, whether with someone else or by oneself.

To restate this pivotal point, I hold that a fusion of horizons is not primarily the coming together or blending of two separate temporal perspectives, but is rather the transcendence or *ekstasis* of time effected through the temporality or historicity of human existence as productive of sense-bearing works. The *ekstasis* is the ground of the subsequent fusion of horizons; and it is here that all of Gadamer's analysis obtains as an explanation of the variations in interpretation from one epoch to another, and indeed, from one connoisseur to another. I believe that this holds true not only of philosophical and scientific texts, but also of works of art.

As the creator of the *Hammerklavier* sonata, Beethoven was obviously a resident within a definite local epoch of the western European tradition. The technical means he employed to compose his sonata were largely given to him by his predecessors; even his original contributions to these means fell within the tradition of European music as it developed in the hands of masters like Bach, Haydn, and Mozart. The radical originality of the *Hammerklavier* does not escape from the horizon of the first half of the nineteenth century; no contemporary listener would mistake it for a piece by Webern or Alfred Schnittke. And one could plausibly argue that the spiritual, emotional, or even intellectual themes of the work are all articulated by the idiom of romanticism or *Sturm und Drang*.

To this it must be added that a listener in the late twentieth century undoubtedly comes to the *Hammerklavier* with an ear that has been indelibly tuned by

Brahms, Scriabin, Ravel, Schoenberg, Shostakovich, and Elliot Carter. The events of the period separating the contemporary listener from Beethoven serve as a continuation of, sometimes as a series of violent changes within, the tradition of Western music. The attempt to return to the historical epoch of Beethoven, whether by a special preparation of one's own psyche or through the artificial device of playing a pianoforte constructed in the nineteenth century, is already a sign of our distance from the historical circumstances of Beethoven's own time. A resident of the twentieth century who dresses in seventeenth-century costumes and lives in a chateau on the Loire remains a man of the twentieth century.

Let this suffice as a sketch of the differences that separate the two temporal horizons at play. What then transpires in a Gadamerian *Horizontverschmelzung?* What transpires in a performance of the *Hammerklavier* in a late twentieth-century salon by a highly literate virtuoso who is thoroughly familiar with the tradition of performance, has studied the circumstances of Beethoven's life and times, and is himself playing on Beethoven's own instrument or one from the same generation of instruments, in the presence of an audience of equally cultivated connoisseurs? We should note, incidentally, that the scene just sketched is very close to ideal, since the usual performance involves no such erudition, sensitivity, or level of competence, whether on the part of the performer or the audience.

As is obvious to anyone who has listened to a wide range of performances of the *Hammerklavier,* the differences in interpretation are marked; each of us will have his own preference, whether it be for Schnabel, Kempff, Arrau, Badura Skoda, Serkin, Pollini, Douglas, or for some other virtuoso. There can be no doubt that the historical horizon in which the sonata was composed is not entirely amenable to fusion with the horizon of the audience. Furthermore, there is not just one horizon of the audience, but the creation of Beethoven must be disseminated through the prism of the multiple perspectives of performer and individual members of the audience. Even if we grant a horizonal unity to Beethoven, it is not the case that each listener is on a par, and constitutes a matching unity that effectuates an isolated fusion, with the horizon of the composer. What I hear will be mediated by the historical accounts I have assimilated of Beethoven's time, the opinions of musicologists, the judgments of critics on the performance styles of the various virtuosos, and so on, not even to consider such transient issues as my mood on the occasion of the individual performance, the acoustics of the hall, and so on.

It follows from these considerations (to which the reader is invited to add others that I may have omitted), that the fusion of the two historical horizons, Beethoven's and (say) my own, can never produce a genuine unity; the result of the fusion is neither the disappearance of my horizon into Beethoven's nor of his horizon into mine. The only possibility is that a *Horizontverschmelzung* results in the production of a third horizon, as defined by my interpretation of the

Hammerklavier. The sense that I attribute to Beethoven's sonata, if it is determined entirely or even essentially by the historically diverse conditions that I have just outlined, is neither simply Beethoven's nor simply my own. In short: if understanding is interpretation, then there is no such entity as Beethoven's *Hammerklavier* sonata, but rather a set of countless interpretations of something called the *Hammerklavier* sonata, which "something" is an indefinable occasion for interpretations.

On the other hand, the sense (or experience) is obviously rooted in the sonata itself. If I am asked to explain my interpretation of the *Hammerklavier,* I will soon be branded as incompetent if I begin with a discussion of the atonal nature of the work as a whole, or of the emotional significance of the key of C-sharp (since the work is written in B-flat). The so-called dissonances of the sonata cannot be correctly explained on the basis of Schoenberg's principles of atonalism, nor does the freedom of interpretation include the right of transposing the piece from one key into another, without altering the composer's original production in a clearly visible manner. Perhaps one might transpose the sonata for a string quartet, just as Bartók's concerto for orchestra has been transcribed for piano. But this example underlines my point: if it is the same piece that we are listening to in the case of the original composition and the transcription, then there must be a universal or universally accessible sense that is constant within alternative interpretations. Let us now assume that the technical manifestation of the sonata is not at issue, and that it can be determined as objectively as can the equations of Newtonian mechanics. What of its spiritual content? What of its significance as an expression of the western European tradition at the beginning of the nineteenth century?

I have purposely chosen a musical composition as my example of the difference between understanding and interpretation because it is especially difficult to decide what we are talking about when we refer to the sense or significance of a nonverbal artwork. It would be easier for a representative of the position I oppose to insist that an artwork is nothing but interpretation than it would be for such a claim to be made about a philosophical, scientific, or even historical text. Nevertheless, it is relatively easy to see that an artwork cannot be mere interpretation. This is self-evident at the physical or technical level; a performance of the *Hammerklavier* is not a performance of Hindemith's *Ludus Tonalis,* as may be confirmed by consulting the scores of the two works.

But what is conveyed by a score if not the creation of the composer? Granted that this creation is prepared and shaped by the historical horizon of the composer's time, does the score of the *Hammerklavier* provide us with nothing but a picture of life in Germany at the beginning of the nineteenth century? If so, it is superfluous to listen to the *Hammerklavier;* we might go to the library and read an encyclopedia article about the cultural scene of the period during which Beethoven lived. On the other hand, if it is held that the *Hammerklavier* provides us with a particular sensual experience that conveys an interpretation of

Beethoven's spiritual response to the tradition, then this response, together with its physical embodiment, provides us with the horizon into which we are assimilated, *exactly as was provided to Beethoven.*

In other words, I am not assimilated into Beethoven's subjective horizon, nor is he assimilated into mine. This is impossible. I agree with Gadamer that it is the work into which we are assimilated. But the work cannot itself be merely the expression of Beethoven's subjective *Erlebnis* of his local perspective onto western European culture. Or rather, if it were, it would be impenetrable to me, except as a kind of sketchily understood occasion to produce within my own psyche some new experience, that of a twentieth-century man listening and responding to a work from an alien historical perspective. This situation would amount to a kind of spiritual Kantianism, in which unknowable works in themselves would somehow register on the transcendental screen of my historical consciousness as the *Empfindungen* from which the transcendental *Geist* constitutes a new work, not in accord with transcendental categories and rules of construction, but rather in accord with transient historical perspectives. The result, in other words, would be that of deconstruction, or the postmodern school of *Écriture.*

The *Hammerklavier* sonata has a physical and technical identity that can be established by any competent person at any historical epoch, regardless of the difference in perspective. Of course, if the difference in perspective is so great that competence no longer applies, or that the principles of composition, the meaning of the notes, and so on, are no longer accessible, this in no way affects the intrinsic meaning of the work. Let us therefore assume that the work can be "decoded" and performed. The performer and the audience are then listening to the same sonic phenomenon as Beethoven heard in his spirit, to the extent that this phenomenon can be registered in the language of musical notation.

The interpretation of the notes, both by performer and listener, will vary from one epoch to another. And if the score were discovered ten thousand years from today by musically competent archaeologists or philologists who nevertheless live in a musical culture removed from that of Beethoven by differences that we can only imagine, it is very likely that the interpretation of the score would differ sharply from those which were established by the nineteenth- and twentieth-century canons of piano performance in general, and of Beethoven performance in particular. To say this in another way, if the historical perspective of the musicians of the 120th century were as different from Beethoven's as was his from, say, King Ikhnaton's, it would still be possible, provided only that the musicians of the future were indeed musicians, and therefore, not simply historical creatures but *human beings,* for them to understand the *Hammerklavier* as the expression of a sensibility of a certain kind. This understanding would not only be independent of differences of interpretation; it would be their indispensable presupposition. For otherwise, interpretations of the *Hammerklavier* would not be interpretations of the *Hammerklavier* but rather creations of their own, related to the original only as are Kantian phenomenal *Gegenstände* to the *Empfindungen* of sensuous experience.

It should at least be mentioned that I have tacitly followed Gadamer in giving precedence to examples of the contemporary attempt to understand a work of the past, or more generally, of attempting to understand future responses to the past. But exactly the same analysis obtains if we try to imagine the transmission of a work backward into the past. King Ikhnaton may not have been equipped, either by personal aptitude or by the conditions of his historical epoch, to respond directly in a positive and comprehending manner to the *Hammerklavier* sonata, but this is not because the sense of the work is inaccessible to him as a human being. Beethoven might well object to Scriabin's Fifth Sonata that it is an expression of decadence, or to Prokofiev's Seventh Sonata that it exhibits a mechanical brutality lacking in all spiritual subtlety, just as Plato would no doubt see in Derrida's *Glas* the ultimate triumph of sophistry. I am not interested in defending these hypothetical judgments, but only in suggesting that they are not implausible. More sharply, they could be defended at some length by appealing to views of the hypothetical judges in each case.

There is nothing intrinsically unintelligible about a backward fusion of horizons. But we ought to resist the temptation to say that the persons of the past would have rejected or even recoiled from the works by masters of the future on grounds of taste or historical perspective alone. Such a claim is equally valid or invalid with respect to the past and the future. The prejudices of the past, precisely on Gadamerian grounds, are as valid as those of the future. But we would hardly rest content with these prejudices as a valid assessment, or a genuinely human appropriation, of the work in question.

It might seem that we of the "future" are in a stronger position than the residents of the past, since we have become accustomed to works from all epochs and so have a wider base of experience upon which to respond to works of art. But what does this mean, if not that we are able to appropriate the *Erlebnis* or to grasp the personal interpretation by the past artist of his or her own historical horizon? And in what does such an appropriation consist if not in the perception of the historically conditioned experience of a fundamental human sense, a sense that we understand exactly as did the resident of the past who transmitted it to us, even though we can never think the transmitter's thoughts or enter completely into his or her historical horizon?

The very notion of a historical horizon presupposes that those who stand within it are thereby enabled to look out upon something, to see or to apprehend something, albeit from a given angle of vision. As a resident of the historical horizon of the twentieth century, I was granted the dubious privilege of experiencing the Vietnamese War as well as the "wise men" whose understanding of human existence that experience conditioned. Hegel in his horizon viewed from his perspective the Battle of Jena, and claims at least to have discerned in

Napoleon "reason on horseback." I cannot truly enter into his horizon nor he in mine. I cannot think his thoughts, feel his feelings, receive his sensations, nor can he take my place in these respects.

On the other hand, the Vietnamese War was no more identical with my perspectival participation in the horizon of the twentieth century than was the Battle of Jena or the significance of Napoleon identical with the nineteenth-century horizon of Hegel. In telling me about the significance of Jena and Napoleon, Hegel is not telling me about himself, nor would I be telling him about myself if I could tell him about the Vietnamese War and its effects on the American psyche. For let me repeat: if the opposite were the case, and such reports were nothing more than the exchange of prejudices, or more sharply stated, the attempted communication of personal perspectives, then there would be no communication and nothing to communicate. Even to the extent that Hegel's report tells us something about himself, or mine about me, it does so on the basis of a shared understanding of what it means to be a human being, on the nature of war, on the wisdom and the stupidity of political life, and so on.

The fusion of two distinct horizons, namely, that of the past as incorporated or represented by the artwork, philosophical doctrine, or scientific theory we are considering, and that of the present as represented by the hermeneutical situation in which I receive or experience the work of the past, does not produce some third historical horizon, blended from features of the first two and located in some other epoch or century. But neither is it a return to the past horizon or a leap forward of the past into the present horizon. Even while granting to Gadamer virtually every one of his descriptive points about the circumstances of our historical condition, and so about the impossibility of becoming identical with the *Verstehen* or act of interpretation of the author of the work we are studying, I argue that all these conditions have the opposite effect to the one that he might seem to assign them. The fusion of horizons leads to the disappearance of historical separation, precisely through the apprehension of the universally accessible sense of the work as mediated by its own historical determinations, determinations which are themselves intelligible as modalities of sense, and so which facilitate our "fusion" into the core of the work rather than hinder it.

If all of this is so, then Heidegger's doctrine of human being as *Verstehen,* and of *Verstehen* as *Auslegung,* cannot be correct, since it teaches us that human existence is the projection of historically determined or perspectively grasped horizons, also known as a world, but a world of such and such a historical epoch. Differently stated, Heidegger's doctrine is not intended by him as an "interpretation" that is marked by the partiality of the viewpoint of a twentieth-century German peasant who became a bourgeois professor and civil servant, an enthusiastic member of the Nazi party, and then retreated into a rhetorical fog of self-justifying obscurantism. All Heideggerians would be outraged by an "interpretation" of their master's teachings that relied upon judgments of the kind I have just indicated. Their outrage would stem from the conviction that Heidegger has not merely interpreted human being from the standpoint of his time and local prejudices, but understood it as it is, not only for himself but for anyone who is capable of thinking his thoughts. And again, to think Heidegger's thoughts has nothing to do with reproducing the exact pattern of his subjective experience. What is to be thought, if I need to say it, is *die Sache selbst.*

It is *die Sache des Denkens* that we interpret; *die Sache* is not itself an interpretation. In my opinion the *Verschmelzung* between theory and interpretation, characteristic of the past two centuries,[2] is the most disastrous development of the modern epoch, one which wherever it is accepted renders impossible all understanding and careful description, hence all genuine communication. It is the ultimate triumph of Nietzsche's doctrine of Being as *Auslegung,* but without Nietzsche's placing of that doctrine within the "Hyperborean" or ahistorical perspective of the prophet of the eternal return. My discussion of Gadamer's doctrine of *Horizontverschmelzung* is intended to preserve it from the deleterious interpretations inspired by an indiscriminate celebration of Nietzschean perspectivism. The interpreter must be a connoisseur of the spirit, not because interpretation is equivalent to the exercise of the local conception of good taste or to the mastery of extensive historical and philological information or aesthetic experience, but because the spirit is what we are, and thus is not a matter of historical perspective, horizon, expertise, or information. On the contrary, all of these are what they are because we are what we are. That we differ widely amongst ourselves in the strength and refinement of spirit is unquestionable. But this is a question of *physis,* not of history.

STANLEY ROSEN

DEPARTMENT OF PHILOSOPHY
PENNSYLVANIA STATE UNIVERSITY
MARCH 1992

NOTES

1. Hans-Georg Gadamer, *Wahrheit und Methode* (Tübingen: J.C.B. Mohr/Paul Siebeck, 1960). Numbers in parentheses in the body of this essay refer to pages in the fourth edition (1975).

2. See my *Hermeneutics as Politics* (New York: Oxford University Press, 1987).

REPLY TO STANLEY ROSEN

I was especially excited to hear what a thinker who has been greatly influenced by Leo Strauss has to say about the "fusion of horizons" *(Horizontverschmelzung)*. I could hardly imagine that one could take to heart the old quarrel of the *anciens et des modernes* in a different way than having to take doubly seriously the truths of the *anciens* in the face of the modernism of modernity. When I published *Plato im Dialog* as the seventh volume of my works, the thought of Leo Strauss and Jakob Klein was especially vivid for me. For I believe that in my recent work I give a new validation to the dominating presence of Socrates within the Greek philosophical tradition. As can be gleaned from our well-known letters, this was also the primary concern of Leo Strauss.

So it was a real surprise to me that Stanley Rosen takes up the concept of the fusion of horizons without charging hermeneutical philosophy with the vulgar reproach that it means historical relativism. However, I continue to believe that Leo Strauss' all too summary thesis—which states that it is all-important to understand an author in exactly the same way as he understands himself—is untenable. That seems to me to be unacceptable in many areas. One only has to think of jurisprudence where one surely is concerned with the *ratio legis* and not the *ratio* of the legislator. Of course, the same holds for the work of art. Otherwise, we would have to be told by the artist what was meant, but was not brought out, in the work of art. But, on the whole, I would agree with Strauss that for all of us in the modern epoch the framework of the ancients must be a common one. I thus welcome Stanley Rosen's effort to really perform this fusion of horizons. I repeatedly expressed how much I made an effort to do this (for example, in *Wahrheit und Methode,* 5th edition, pp. 309ff.) by suggesting that when going back into the history of philosophy, one certainly should not do this as a mere historian. When we are thinking on our own, we always move in a constant dialogue with the history of philosophical thought.

Fortunately, Rosen devotes a precise analysis to a concrete example: the musical performance of a musical piece. Interestingly enough, for such a reproductive artistic exercise we use the term 'interpretation' which has a somewhat different meaning in philosophy. This indicates that the great accomplishments of the reproductive artists, each in his own way, bring to our ears, bring out the composition itself, and that the listener, thanks to the assistance of such artists, 'means' and hears the musical work itself. What this means becomes clear when one refers to the reading of poetical works. When dealing with literary works of art, one does not refer to interpretation as with the musical work of art, but to recitation. This is worth pondering. Apparently, the concept of interpretation is so much at home in the philogical treatment of linguistic texts that interpretation is in truth only an intermediary notion which helps overcome difficulties of understanding and which enlists itself completely for the intelligible performance of texts. In a certain sense, however, a new performance of the text, that is, the recitation, is not an intermediary notion since it does not interrupt the performance. But in being performed, every recitation will, among other things, contribute to the decision about the speaker's understanding. Take the example of the well-known controversy between Staiger and Heidegger about Mörike's poem *"Die Lampe."* One who wants to recite this poem has to decide clearly— there is no possibility of this decision not being heard—in favor of one or the other interpretation of the expression *"wie es scheint."* Spitzer, for example, did this: he had to follow Heidegger although he resolutely rejected his appeal to Hegel.

In any case, we should take seriously the way in which performance marks an answer; such a case deals directly with matters that are 'correct' or 'false'. This means no more and no less than that in such matters even a silent reading of the text has to make a decision. Certainly there are cases in which the question has to remain open for the reader who reenacts that which has been read. In this way, Aristotle indeed reprimands Heraclitus with regard to the first words of his text for the way in which one cannot decide the question of how the word 'always' has to be punctuated, that is, either before or after the word. Obviously, relations of sound gain significance here. That is something which we also know from poetry and which Aristotle does not love in Heraclitus.

One often calls something an interpretation that is really a translation. Thus the special role which the interplay of sound and meaning plays in poetry becomes entirely clear. Translation can always only accomplish a modest, assisting task which is supposed to serve the understanding of the original. However helpful for comprehension such mediation might be, the loss in such cases as lyric poetry, for instance, is enormous. In general, however, the philological meaning of interpretation is that of the intermediary notion which, as a commentary upon a text, interrupts its performance and which, by way of assisting comprehension, is supposed to enable it to be reenacted better.

However, the reader who understands a text is, in the last analysis, in a situation hardly different from that of the musician who presents a convincing interpretation of a musical piece. The listener follows the musical piece even when he knows that the performance of the music could be rendered differently. The same can be said of the reader who feels completely absorbed by a poem. He will nonetheless know that the same poem can say something different another time and that in general something always remains unsaid. Since it always says something new, one likes to read, or better still, to speak, a wholly familiar poem again and again. One who would say, 'But I know that already', would simply be a Philistine. A multiplicity of different statements lies concealed in the text. The inexhaustible statement of a work of art is indeed the 'truth' of the work itself, because one always experiences something new in it. It might even be the case that only another, an interpreter so to speak, reveals this inexhaustible other to, and makes it speak for, a person. But it is equally possible that an interpreter misses the point entirely. There is false understanding, too. That which is false remains false, no matter how often one lets it go unnoticed. There is no last word on that which is unsayable. And yet, that which is beyond sayability is precisely that which makes it say something for a person again and again.

Why these considerations? I want to understand what Rosen means when he says that one must have understood before one can interpret. The reverse seems to me to be convincing too: that the interpretation is precisely supposed to help to finally understand the unintelligible. What then is correct? Both statements? None of them? In the end, the answer must be that understanding is always already interpretation, and that an interpretation is only a 'correct' interpretation if it emerges out of the performance of understanding. Thus, Schleiermacher is finally right in regarding the relation of understanding and interpretation as fluid. On the other hand, Nietzsche is not right in understanding all interpretation from the standpoint of the will to power and in understanding that as an act of positing.

Heidegger did not do that at all, even when he interpreted himself more than the text at hand, which is why he often persisted with a false reading. False remains false and there is no arbitrariness in the sense of historical relativism. Through the notion of the fusion of horizons Rosen's contribution seems to me to confirm precisely that which I had in view in my analysis of understanding. Every interpretation must prove a success in performance, and that means it is taken up into the performance.

Thus I may take up Rosen's last word: "It is the *physis* of humankind that human beings have language—and history."

H.-G.G.

10

Robert Sokolowski

GADAMER'S THEORY OF HERMENEUTICS

I.

Those of us who have had the pleasure of hearing Hans-Georg Gadamer lecture, as well as those who read his writings, know that his philosophical remarks are usually made on the margin of either commentaries on the work of other authors or observations about historical and cultural events. He does not, typically, state or write purely speculative philosophical treatises in the manner of Hegel or Kant or Descartes; instead, he comments, say, on Plato, Aristotle, Nicholas of Cusa, Humboldt, Heidegger, Hölderlin, Rilke, Celan, or *The Magic Flute,* and he discusses, for example, the role of experts in modern society, the development of theology in Marburg, or romanticism and its influence on the understanding of art. While informing us about such diverse matters, Gadamer formulates the components of his own philosophical position.

A style such as this presumes great erudition and extensive experience. It can be practiced only by someone who has mastered many texts and many authors and knows the complex relationships among them, is familiar with the alternative commentaries and interpretations that have been proposed by others, and is thoroughly informed about what is going on in our contemporary social, political, and cultural worlds. The speculative point being made depends on the richness and the accuracy of the information and interpretation that underlie it.

Furthermore, Gadamer's life and character are reflected in his philosophical style. He was born in the first year of this century. His life coincides with the period of time in which historical research has given us a more complete and detailed view of the past than was ever possessed before, a time in which science and technology have taken on worldwide significance, a time in which political, social, and cultural forces have led to a watershed in human affairs. As a student and young teacher, Gadamer lived through one of the greatest periods of philosophical activity, the world of Europe in the first half of this century. He personally knew the leading figures of that era, and he also experienced the political excesses of that same age. He has lived through the diffusion of science and technology throughout the world, a development accelerated by two world wars and the cold war that followed them. The spread of science and technology has been an intellectual and social influence quite different from the expansion of the power, culture, and language of a single nation or people; it is different from, say, the Persian conquest of the Middle East or the Roman conquest of the Mediterranean. Technology and modern science are not the expression of a single people; they do not depend on the grammar of a particular language or the habits of a particular tribe. They are eminently exportable and the way they work their way into new areas of the world and overlay the culture that is in place raises a hermeneutic problem that is different from that which occurs when two cultures blend. Technology and modern science make us think that we can stand free of all traditions and cultures and judge them in a detached way. The quantified way of looking at the world is now, furthermore, being applied to the possession and transfer of information in ways that were never before available in writing and printing; science and technology are developing a language that will either supplement or compete with what are now called "natural" languages. Thus, the development of history, the expansion of science and technology, and the social, political, and cultural changes of our century lead to a moment in which hermeneutics, the active interpretation of what we are and what we are to do, comes to the fore as a philosophical issue.

Gadamer himself is the kind of man who is able to absorb and reflect on all these various currents. He has been engaged in cultural affairs and in academic administration, and thus knows the difference between acting and thinking. With Helmut Kuhn he founded, and for twenty years edited, the *Philosophische Rundschau,* a journal whose name, with its hint of range, detachment, and observation, aptly expresses something of his own attitude toward events. In the last twenty-five years he has taught and lectured in the United States and has traveled extensively. He is informed not only about philosophy but about literature and art. His life, character, and background provide him with a distinctive point of view toward the age in which we live.

Much of what he surveys from that point of view finds expression in his writings, but he is not simply a chronicler or raconteur. On the basis of the rich information and observation that he provides, he builds up a philosophical position, a "universal hermeneutics," a theory about being and the human condition. This theory, as we have observed, is developed on the margins of his commentaries and analyses, and for that reason it is fragmentary. Pieces of it can be found in different places; Gadamer has written no work similar, say, to Michael Oakeshott's *On Human Conduct.*[1] Fragmentariness is not unusual in the philosophical writing of this century. The works of Heidegger and Wittgenstein are fragmentary, and so are those of Husserl, whose manuscripts were written as bits and pieces and whose books are really collections of short philosophical experiments and sketches. And Leo Strauss, like Gadamer, develops his philosophical positions in the margins opened up by commentary. Furthermore, one can also claim that first philosophy itself is essentially fragmentary and marginal because it is a constant approach to the first things, to what Gadamer quotes Plato as calling *ta prôta kai akra*.[2] Since first philosophy does not derive its statements from a single intuition and a primary principle, but strives always to approach that beginning, it is bound to be unsystematic. It does not present a comprehensive doctrine ordered under overarching axioms. But even as fragmentary and marginal, first philosophy can be speculative, so Gadamer's style is compatible not only with the most important figures of recent philosophical thinking, but with the nature of philosophy itself.

II.

Let us attempt to distill some of the elements of Gadamer's universal hermeneutics. He insists on the inevitability of conversation in the pursuit and achievement of truth.[3] The mind is never single but always in conversation with others, whether with one or with many interlocutors. Sometimes the other is bodily present and the conversation takes place in speech, but sometimes the other mind is present in a text or an image, and then the conversation takes place in reading, whether the reading be of something written or of something depicted. In either case, whatever is said cannot be properly understood except as an answer to some sort of question. There are no bald statements coming out of nowhere: whatever is stated is stated because something calls for it, because a question makes a space ready for the statement. The question provides a context. If we do not know the question and the context, we will fail to get the point of the statement, and sometimes will not even understand what the statement means.

Furthermore, the conversation is not merely a matter of propositions being played off against one another; the speakers themselves are engaged in the conversation, which addresses their self-understanding. The speaker has to be willing to understand what the interlocutor proposes and to entertain the questions he raises; for this reason, the speaker is always himself called into question by the conversation. The understanding the speaker has achieved prior to the present exchange must now be ready to be adjusted to the possibilities that the questioner opens up in what he says and what he asks. The speaker has to take the questioner and the question seriously if the conversation is to continue. Indeed, the interlocutors are caught up into the conversation as parts of a larger whole; it is not the case, as we might be tempted to think, that the two speakers are simply independent beings only extrinsically related by their conversational exchange: they are defined as speakers, thinkers, and actors by the exchange and its possibilities. T. S. Eliot's line is appropriate: the interlocutors are "United in the strife which divided them" (*Little Gidding*, III). The conversation has its own substantiality. Gadamer uses the analogy with games to illustrate the force of the conversation. The game too has its own logic and substantiality and the players are established as such by the game that they play; the catcher *is* a catcher and the shortstop a shortstop because of the logic of baseball and the actions permitted by it. The players are not individual agents who are only accidentally related by the activity of the game.[4]

Gadamer's appeal to conversation as the fundamental state of thinking and human existence has an interesting parallel in Michael Oakeshott's concept of "the conversation of mankind" as the fundamental intellectual activity. Oakeshott describes the life of the mind not as a systematic "inquiry about ourselves and the world," nor as an "accumulating body of information," but rather as "a conversation, begun in the primeval forests and extended and made more articulate in the course of centuries."[5] This life is "an unrehearsed intellectual adventure" and there is no way of predicting how it will turn out or what it will turn up. Philosophy, according to Oakeshott, is neither the loudest voice in this conversation nor a way of getting at the truth of things apart from the conversation; it is simply a reflection on the conversation itself, "the impulse to study the quality and style of each voice, and to reflect on the relationship of one voice to another."[6] Gadamer's universal hermeneutics undertakes a similar project.

Experience *(Erfahrung)* is described by Gadamer in a particularly insightful way. He says that both Aristotle, in his notion of *empeiria,* and modern science, with its understanding of experience as experiment, consider experience in relation to the settled conceptual knowledge that can issue from it; they examine experience "in reference to its result."[7] But experience must also be examined on its own terms, as a preparation for yet more experience, as providing ever new empirical perspectives on what it has already established. Gadamer emphasizes the negative aspect of experience: experience corrects the assumptions we originally bring to it, but in doing so it allows the thing we experience to assert itself more truly. The negative contrast with our assumptions thus permits a positive presentation of the thing at issue, a presentation that could not have arisen except as a corrective to what we had taken for granted. (Gadamer's reading of the concept of natural law in Aristotle, incidentally, involves a similar negativity; he says the concept is primarily critical, as nature arises over and against convention when discrepancies in the understanding of what is just have to be resolved.)[8] The sense of consciousness as conversational is thus applied even to our experience of things, where a kind of exchange of question and answer also takes place. Experience, furthermore, modifies the person whose experience it is and makes him into "a man of experience" *(ein Erfahrener).*[9] Experience has an impact on the subject and also on the tradition, which then in turn enables further experience.

Gadamer denies that thinking is the simple contemplation of a scene or the mere contemplation of a series of propositions, in which we give assent to some and dissent to others. In keeping with Heidegger's interpretation of concern as pervading all human activity, Gadamer appeals to Aristotle's notion of prudence and claims that in all that we do, even in the understanding that we achieve of things, we are an issue for ourselves. We never reach sheer detachment and we are never merely lookers on. All thinking reflects our situation and ourselves. At the same time, if we are truly open to who or what is speaking to us, we go beyond ourselves and our situation in the act of interpretation.[10]

Another aspect of prudence that Gadamer appeals to is the fact that prudential decisions require prudential agents; they do not arise from the automatic application of rules and procedures. Just as no serious question can arise except through an intelligent questioner, so no prudential act can be executed except by a prudential agent. Prudence involves the consideration of factors that cannot be brought under preordained categories; it involves the concreteness of a situation the elements of which cannot be specified in advance. It therefore cannot be exercised except by someone whose character and intelligence give him the ability to evaluate what is going on and what ought to be done. Moreover, such prudential judgment, according to Gadamer, is required not only in moral matters but also in the interpretation of texts and the application of science. Gadamer, like Oakeshott, is a critic of the rationalism of the Enlightenment, which believes that thinking can proceed almost automatically by way of expertise and method and that it "strives through its methodology to make itself independent of all subjective applications."[11] He refers to "the great monologue of modern 'method',"[12] and, of course, the title of his *Truth and Method* is ironic: truth requires prudential application and evaluation, not just procedural methodology.

Gadamer's appeal to prudence in the intellectual life finds many echoes in current reflection on thinking. In a recent discussion of the discipline of history, for example, Theodore S. Hamerow writes, in words that could well be used to formulate Gadamer's position, "Historical writing requires the exercise of a form of practical judgment, an ability to assess human beings and their conduct, that cannot be reduced to a science. . . . And therefore we must try to reunite life and learning."[13] In the same discussion, Robert Conquest agrees with the claims that in history "no mechanical criteria for validating or rejecting evidence exist," and that "in the end the crux of the historian's equipment is in all essentials the same as that needed in matters of everyday life, where error and falsehood equally have to be coped with."[14]

Another theme in Gadamer's hermeneutic theory is the interpretation he gives of "prejudice." Obviously, there is a sense in which a prejudice is intellectually debilitating, but drawing on the etymology of the word *Vorurteil*—which is the same as that of the English "prejudice," the sense of a judgment made beforehand and brought to a situation—Gadamer observes that the convictions we bring to an issue allow the truth of the situation to assert itself. We have to begin with convictions and as beneficiaries of a tradition; we cannot stand outside all traditions and evaluate them from no committed point of view; the desire for such an inhuman and detached perspective is another of the misleading hopes of rationalism and the Enlightenment. Prejudgments are harmful only when they are frozen; without prejudgments, we would not be participants in the human conversation and would not be able to react to the insistence of things. Again, a

:tion is expressed by Robert Conquest, who writes, "It is the frank
the historian that he indeed holds specific views that forces him to
,dence as objectively as possible."[15] Another contemporary writer
‹ shows great similarities to that of Gadamer is Alasdair MacIntyre,
w͟ı͟ͅ‿ riticized the rationalism of some modern moral philosophers as the
attempt to stand outside any specific moral tradition and to judge human action
by purely formal criteria.[16]

The theme of linguisticality is another important element in Gadamer's
work. Language, he observes, is not only an instrument but also an embodiment
of thought. A language is not just made up of a vocabulary and a set of grammatical rules, but is also the repository of understandings that have settled into it.
When we learn a language—not just formally, but as something through which
we can live and act—we absorb the opinions or the appearances of things that
have been incorporated into the language. Gadamer uses the cryptic phrase,
"Being that can be understood is language" *(Sein, das verstanden werden kann,
ist Sprache).*[17] The language we live in allows us to approach things with the
prior understandings we inherit and thus allows things to speak to us. Language
is the bearer of a tradition, but it can also be a kind of a participant in the human
conversation and not merely a vehicle for it; if language provides us with understandings, they are understandings waiting to be more fully understood, as we
both reflect on them and let them articulate our initial experience of things.

We have surveyed some of the prominent features of Gadamer's universal
hermeneutics. These and other major themes provide a framework in which he
touches on many minor but significant phenomena: how written correspondence
is a variant on conversation, the distinctive manner in which a telephone call initiates a discussion (the call is essentially an interruption, no matter how much
we may have been waiting for it), the fact that a narrative solicits belief while a
treatise leads to assent through understanding, the way in which jargon differs
from technical language, and so on. Such observations may occur in the inter-
stices of his written argument, or they may be the incidental point we especially
remember from one of his lectures or conversations, but in their variety they
show the depth and range of his philosophical reflection.

III.

Gadamer's hermeneutic theory has often been misinterpreted as a kind of forerunner of deconstruction, a less Nietzschean version of the kind of thinking represented by Jacques Derrida.[18] Because Gadamer stresses the involvement of the
subject in the achievement of truth, his work is sometimes taken as a simple subjectivism or relativism. This interpretation is misleading, as Gadamer's own
remarks in his exchange with Derrida show.[19] I would like to propose some con-

siderations that might reinforce the resistance of hermeneutics to such a deconstructionist reading.

A theme from phenomenology that can be helpful to hermeneutics in this
respect is that of an object's being an identity in manifolds of appearance.[20] The
theme of identity in a manifold is often mentioned by Gadamer in his work on
Plato, but there it is related to the identity of a form in the manifold of individuals in which the form is realized. In Husserl the structure is more widely applied.
To take Husserl's most familiar example, a material object is the identity that can
be seen from this side and that, from near and far, at this moment and that, from
outside and inside; it can be variously seen, felt, heard, smelled, or tasted, and
always it remains one and the same object that is manifested in all its sides,
aspects, and profiles. The identity of the object never shows up as one of its
appearances; the thing is never simply what shows up in this view or aspect or
profile, nor is it equivalent to the sum of its appearances; the identity registered
within the appearances is always distinguished, though never separated, from
them. The identity is of a different order from the appearances through and in
which it is presented.

Various sorts of objects prescribe various manifolds of appearance. A drama,
for instance, is the same identical drama within and across many stagings and
performances; a single text can be realized in many different readings; a single
law in many applications. The identity needs the manifold to be and to appear,
but the identity never becomes simply one member of the manifold of appearances. The drama, for example, needs its stagings and readings to be a drama,
but it is never reduced to any one of its stagings or readings. Each interpretation
intensifies the being of the drama, and some interpretations do so more richly
than others (in some cases the drama is scarcely there at all), but the drama and
the reading never simply coincide, because the drama can be itself once again
even in other readings, just as a perceptual object can be presented as itself in yet
another perspective. The thing itself is what can appear as the same thing again
in a new appearance. Deconstruction and relativism collapse the object into its
appearances and profiles, they reduce it to the way it appears here and now; they
take the drama to be just its interpretation, so that every new staging is like the
composition of a new play; they take the judicial application of a law to be like
the writing of a new law (more accurately, perhaps, they abolish the distinction
between legislation and application).

Deconstruction and relativism are at the opposite extreme from a naive
objectivism, a position that would take the object in isolation from its modes of
appearance. When the problem of appearance and interpretation is formulated in
terms of such extremes, the argument ricochets between either sheer objects
without manifestation or sheer appearance without things. It is like an argument
between a coward and a fool about a matter that can only be settled by courage;
the extreme positions show that the interaction of being and manifestation has

not been grasped with the subtlety that marks its treatment in Gadamer's universal hermeneutics.

Another consideration that can help inoculate hermeneutics against relativism would be a fuller exploration of the range of ways in which a conversation or a reading of a text can fail as well as succeed. It is important to discuss not only the positive side of interpretation but also the negative; the failures are as interesting and as important as the successes, because they define the borders of success. Plato, in his *Seventh Letter*, says that virtue and vice "must be learned together, just as truth and error about any part of being."[21] Acknowledging that a conversation or an interpretation can indeed fail, and spelling out the ways in which it can fail, make it more clear that hermeneutics does not legitimate any and every projection or fantasy as valid. Interpretations have to preserve the integrity of the thing, and not all of them do.

Let us sketch a few elements of such a taxonomy of hermeneutic failures. First, an "interlocutor" may simply be too immature or mentally incompetent to engage in a conversation; if a child starts crying during a discussion, the cries are not necessarily to be taken as a move in the conversation; if a child were to smear food over a portrait, the behavior need not be taken as an interpretation of the painting. Such cases are off the scale of valid interpretation, and even off the scale of valid engagement, but they must be taken into account as parameters when we describe the hermeneutics of interpretation. Second, a speaker may understand the discussion but find the topic disturbing, and may impulsively introduce a different issue. To adapt a passage from Oakeshott, "A girl, in order to escape a conclusion, may utter what appears to be an outrageously irrelevant remark, but what in fact she is doing is turning an argument she finds tiresome into a conversation she is more at home in."[22] Oakeshott uses this example to show the distinction between an argument and a conversation; the conversation is continued but the argument is changed. Third, an interlocutor may try to continue the argument in question but may be quite confused about the issue and his "contributions" may in fact flounder; he may be confused simply because he is uninformed or untrained, or, more radically, he may simply be unable to appropriate the material intellectually. Such an interlocutor may use many of the words associated with the topic in question but he is not able to think with those words. Such confusion is described by Husserl under the theme of vagueness, a topic of immense philosophical importance.[23] Vagueness is different from the immaturity or incompetence we listed above as our first case of failure in conversation. Fourth, the interventions of an interlocutor might be deceptive; they may seem to move the conversation forward but in fact they are part of a strategy to mislead the other participants. Fifth, a person may stay with the conversation but may simply repeat the convictions he has brought to it; nothing that is said in the exchange registers with him, nothing gets through to him. It is not that such a man is intelligently firm in his opinions while listening to his partner; he is, rather, stubborn and soaked—opinionated—in his convictions. Aristotle says that such people "delight in the victory they gain if they are not persuaded to change."[24] Sixth, on the positive side, the interlocutor may be honestly and competently engaged in the discussion. Even in this case, however, he may participate on vastly different levels of success: he may practically run the discussion, he may be an equal partner, he may be only a weak and modest contributor.

More specific categories would need to be elaborated in such a taxonomy of the hermeneutic situation. The contrasts between the various categories can be more fully explored. All the categories are formal and abstract; concrete instances of argument and interpretation will often fall between categories or combine them, and in some cases it may be hard to know which categories apply. But the very description of failure and success in hermeneutics, the description of how a conversation can stall as well as move on, shows that the thing being manifested in a particular instance is not just any thing at all. A conversation is not merely a human interaction, it is also the display of something, and the success or failure of the conversation is a success or failure in the manifestation of the thing in question. The fact that failure can be recognized indicates the possibility of recognizing success and hence of recognizing the identity of the thing being brought to presence by the conversation.

It is true that in some cases what seems to be a failure may turn out to be a success. A particular interpretation may shock the public and we may say that it fails to make its object present, but later we may find that it was an especially original manifestation. But if this can happen sometimes, it does not happen always. There are failures of interpretation; there are performances that deserve to flop because they betray the script or the score, and there are judicial applications that are badly made, that do not present the law they purport to apply. Gadamer acknowledges this, but his emphasis on the negativity of experience—his claim that experience calls our assumptions into question—may make it seem that the new is seen to be genuine precisely because it disturbs the old and because it shakes what has been established. But in some cases—indeed, in most cases—the new confirms the old even as it adds a manifestation to it. To challenge is not necessarily to disconfirm, to adjust is not to repudiate.

IV.

Gadamer provides taxonomies and distinctions in his universal hermeneutics, and when doing so he moves from the style of commentary toward the style of independent philosophical discourse: taxonomies are not gathered from the works of others but presented from one's own point of view. The distinction between commentary and independent writing comes to the fore in regard to another issue in Gadamer's writings, an issue that we have not yet discussed in this paper. It is one of Gadamer's most original philosophical contributions: his interpretation of Plato's unwritten doctrine about the One and the Indeterminate

Dyad, and his critique of Heidegger's claim that Plato's doctrine of ideas was caught in the metaphysics of presence.[25] Gadamer shows that the weaving together of the forms, their combination and sorting out, their "*arithmos*-structure," as he sometimes calls it, is at the heart of Plato's thought; Plato does not think that the forms are contemplated in static isolation and sheer intuition. Gadamer goes on to show that the interwoven character of the Platonic ideas is itself derived from the One and the Indeterminate Dyad, which are reported by Aristotle as the first principles *(archai)* in Plato's thought. The One and the Indeterminate Dyad pervade all discourse and being. They let things be articulated and identified in their articulation, to be shown forth in various ways, to be experienced as many and yet recognized as one. They also permit the vagaries of deception and mistake (although Gadamer thinks that Plato does not sufficiently account for error in his treatment of nonbeing as otherness).[26] The *arithmos*-structure of things, and the role of the One and the Indeterminate Dyad, are the elements of Plato's esoteric teaching, but hints of this teaching are also found in some of the dialogues; Gadamer especially mentions important passages in *Hippias Maior, Sophist, Republic, Parmenides,* and *Philebus.*

These thoughts about the first and ultimate things are developed by Gadamer in his commentaries on Plato, but one would like to know how they can be asserted by a contemporary voice. How is the truth in Plato's esoteric teaching to be stated now? Can we only formulate these things in the terms Plato gave them? It is one thing to state these things as they were stated by Plato, and another to appropriate more explicitly what they are. This is the difficulty that arises inevitably in commentary, quotation, and paraphrase. When we comment and quote and paraphrase, we do indeed speak and articulate something, but we do so by adopting the voice of another; we make a statement as stated by another. To what extent do we *only* quote and comment, and to what extent do we assert? It is often hard to say. The work of Leo Strauss is notoriously difficult in this respect, and deliberately so; according to Strauss's theory of philosophy and interpretation, the writer's voice is concealed when the writer, as commentator, brings the mind of others to light. But if we enter into a more independent philosophical discourse, we cannot hide so easily; we move away from commentary and speak more directly in our own voice, and Gadamer's hermeneutic theory calls on us to do so. The first hermeneutic motion is to be drawn into a text, but the second motion, responding and responsible, is to speak the truth in that text ourselves; we respond by saying, "I say that. . . ."

We can never leave quotation entirely behind in philosophy, since the vocabulary we use will inevitably be drawn from the tradition in which we live, but there are degrees of distancing, and it is instructive to consider what formulation the Platonic first things can be given in our day, in the face of our contemporary science, our history and politics, and our anthropology. Certainly the One and the Indeterminate Dyad cannot simply be equated with historicity, or with linguisticality, or with the endless human conversation; the One and the Indeterminate Dyad are the principles and root of conversation, language, and history. They also stand behind such distinctions as those between facts and propositions, understanding and assent, sense and reference, picture and pictured, present and past, word and thing, numeral and number, element and set. How can the One and the Indeterminate Dyad be stated in our terms, terms that Plato may not have used? To address this problem is not to leave Plato behind, but it does call on us to speak somewhat more in our own voice and from our own perspective. The possibility of speaking in this way, and the injunction to do so, are placed before us by Gadamer's universal hermeneutics.

ROBERT SOKOLOWSKI

SCHOOL OF PHILOSOPHY
THE CATHOLIC UNIVERSITY OF AMERICA
FEBRUARY 1992

NOTES

1. Michael Oakeshott, *On Human Conduct* (Oxford: Clarendon Press, 1975).

2. Hans-Georg Gadamer, "Platons ungeschriebene Dialektik," vol. 6 of *Gesammelte Werke* (Tübingen: J. C. B. Mohr, 1985), 134.

3. On conversation and the dialectic of question and answer, see Hans-Georg Gadamer, *Wahrheit und Methode,* vol. 1 of *Gesammelte Werke* (Tübingen: J. C. B. Mohr, 1986), 368–84.

4. Gadamer, *Wahrheit und Methode,* 107–16.

5. Michael Oakeshott, "The Voice of Poetry in the Conversation of Mankind," in *Rationalism in Politics and Other Essays* (Indianapolis: Liberty Fund, 1991), 490.

6. Ibid., 491.

7. Gadamer, *Wahrheit und Methode,* 358. See pp. 352–64, where Gadamer uses Hegel and Francis Bacon in developing his concept of experience.

8. Ibid., 324–26.

9. Ibid., 359.

10. The fact that we go beyond ourselves and do not play a merely solipsistic game when we engage in interpretation is elegantly brought out in the passage from Rilke that serves as the epigraph to *Wahrheit und Methode.*

11. Gadamer, *Wahrheit und Methode,* 339.

12. Ibid., 375.

13. Theodore S. Hamerow, "Historical Scholarship and Practical Judgment," *Academic Questions* 4 (1991): 30–31.

14. Robert Conquest, "A Letter to a Soviet Historian," *Academic Questions* 4 (1991): 39–40.

15. Ibid., 40.

16. See Alasdair MacIntyre, *After Virtue* (Notre Dame: University of Notre Dame Press, 1981); *Whose Justice? Which Rationality?* (Notre Dame: University of Notre

Dame Press, 1988); *Three Rival Versions of Moral Inquiry* (Notre Dame: University of Notre Dame Press, 1990). MacIntyre insists that human action and moral understanding take place only within the rationality provided by a moral tradition, and he describes several such traditions, such as the Greek heroic culture, the medieval Christian era, and the Scottish commercial Enlightenment. An indication of how close MacIntyre is to Gadamer can be found in the following passage, which occurs during MacIntyre's attempt to define the university as "a place of constrained disagreement": "It is necessary not only to reread the texts which constitute that tradition, but to do so in a way that ensures that the reader is put to the question by the texts as much as the texts by the reader" (*Three Rival Versions,* 233).

17. Gadamer, *Wahrheit und Methode,* 478.

18. A well-known example of interpreting Gadamer in this way can be found in Richard Rorty, *Philosophy and the Mirror of Nature* (Princeton: Princeton University Press, 1979), 357–65.

19. Hans-Georg Gadamer, "Und dennoch: Macht des guten Willens," in *Text und Interpretation,* ed. Philippe Forget (Munich: Wilhelm Fink Verlag, 1984), 59–61.

20. On identity in manifolds in Husserl, see Robert Sokolowski, *Husserlian Meditations: How Words Present Things* (Evanston: Northwestern University Press, 1974), 86–110.

21. Plato, "Seventh Letter," 344b; see *Plato's Epistles,* trans. Glenn R. Morrow (Indianapolis: Bobbs-Merrill, 1962), 241.

22. Oakeshott, "The Voice of Poetry," 489.

23. See Edmund Husserl, *Formal and Transcendental Logic,* trans. Dorion Cairns (The Hague: Nijhoff, 1969), sec. 16.

24. Aristotle, *Nicomachean Ethics,* bk. 7, chap. 9.

25. See the essay in this volume by Thomas Prufer, "A Thought or Two on Gadamer's Plato." Gadamer recognizes the important work done on Plato's unwritten doctrine by Jacob Klein and also by the Tübingen school of Plato-interpretation.

26. Gadamer, "Platons ungeschriebene Dialektik," 151.

REPLY TO ROBERT SOKOLOWSKI

The author of this contribution is well-known to me for some time now, and I remember in particular that he distinguished himself with early works on Husserl's phenomenology. Later I became acquainted with him personally at Catholic University in Washington and since then I have paid close attention to his works. This contribution to the problem of hermeneutics beautifully demonstrates that he is not only capable of presenting good works on phenomenology, but that he also knows how to work phenomenologically. I greatly benefit from this in the present work. For on the basis of this phenomenological talent he succeeds in making clear what one really has to expect from his contribution. My own step toward hermeneutic philosophy consists precisely not only and not primarily in validating hermeneutics as a procedure in the method of the sciences, but as referring to the actual performance of life.

From this viewpoint one should expect that related efforts are under way in the field of Ordinary Language Analysis. I am grateful for seeing this confirmed through a few of Sokolowski's citations. I am also glad that he brings to the fore in his own way the fundamental significance of the chapter on the concept of experience. There is only one point to which I would like to add a remark: one has to view experience in its double direction. To have an experience means to have a new experience. An experience which confirms itself is not experienced as such. This does not mean preferring the negativity of experience, not at all. It rather confirms the immense positive significance of the acquisition and possession of experience. This, however, does not alter the fact that the acquisition of new experiences is based precisely upon negativity, upon the *pathei mathos* of the tragic wisdom of the ancient world.

Without qualifications and in full agreement, I can only confirm what this contribution has to say about *'prudens'*, *'prudentia'*, and related matters. This also holds for the wonderfully clear language in which the one-sidedness of deconstruction, so frequently discussed today, is expressed. It also seems to me that I can find myself really confirmed in Sokolowski's attempt to demonstrate the short-sightedness of seeing a relativism in phenomenologically grounded hermeneutics. I also recognize myself in the way in which my research on Plato is connected to my hermeneutic philosophy. This indeed corresponds to my tendency to seek my own theoretical clarification not only in a dialogue with Kant, Hegel, Husserl, Heidegger, and Wittgenstein, but also with the philosophy toward which the Platonic dialogues point. It is true that I agree with the Tübin-

gen school—which, due to the Aristotle report, relies on the exoteric *Logoi*—
with respect to the significance of the number for the understanding of the theory of the forms. However, I remain skeptical with regard to a point about which
I believe I thoroughly agree with Plato. It seems strange to me when there is discussion of the Aristotelian concept of the one and of the indeterminate duality. Is
it really a coincidence that such a use of the plural of *archai* sounds un-Platonic
to me? I am rather familiar with the formula *ta prôta kai akra,* the first and the
highest, a very indeterminate concept of the highest and most general concepts.
Could it not be the case that Plato aimed at one direction in a variety of forms in
his dialogues and not only for protoseptic reasons. Here it is not only a matter of
the relation of dependence of the geometrical dimensions, which Gaiser demonstrated so beautifully, but also of the doctrine of a philosophy which would be
teachable like Euclidean mathematics. To me it seems to be sufficient to view
these first and highest *(Primatien),* the one and the duality, as directives for
action, as it were, and not as principles in the sense of a syllogistic reasoning
which, I admit, can find their confirmation in the dialogues in limited contexts
too. But that is far from comprising the whole point in a system. I read with
agreement the remarks about both Leo Strauss and Jakob Klein, two researchers
with whom I am very familiar and who are close to me. Yet, they customarily
employ a style in their work that is too much a commentary, so that finally their
own voices are lost. I made an effort to bring out the points in my own language
wherever possible, even though I sometimes use the great models and their clarifying assistance.

H.-G.G.

11

Robert R. Sullivan

GADAMER'S EARLY AND DISTINCTIVELY POLITICAL HERMENEUTICS

I.

The Hans-Georg Gadamer with whom most people are familiar came onto the scene in 1960 with the publication of *Truth and Method,* a book which introduced the reader to a perspective which had hitherto been narrowly associated with theologians and literary researchers in quest of an understanding of a lost past.[1] Hermeneutics had been a 'method', and Gadamer's intent was to turn it into something basic and more creative. He called this a *philosophical* hermeneutics. To put the matter historically, Gadamer argued that before we reduced *truth* to the 'truths' of science, we as a civilization accommodated a different kind of 'truth', one that was more basic and less accessible to the modern penchant for rigidly conscious formulation. This 'truth' is what *Truth and Method* set out to argue.

To put this argument more abstractly, something which Gadamer in fact does in *Truth and Method,* the everyday quest for truth begins in historically determined *prejudices,* not objective ideas or knowledge. Thinking then proceeds to act by means of *conversation* with others, not dialectic in the strict sense of that term. It finally results in agreement, or a *fusion of horizons,* a kind of interlacing of perspectives with the 'Other' being engaged in conversation. Such agreement on 'truth' lasts no longer than the community of thinkers who create it, which means that the agreement reached might endure only a moment or might be sustained by like-minded thinkers for a much longer duration, perhaps centuries, or even eras, as the ancients might put it.

What we call science or take to be objective knowledge apparently takes shape much more narrowly. Conversations turn into rigorous discourses, and they presuppose bodies of established knowledge which function like tools. Words have single meanings, and this limitation is supposed to make misunderstanding impossible. Advances are made, and they take the aggressive form of claims and counterclaims, all more or less hypothetical. They are argued dialectically, with shared standards being met which draw forth the kind of assent needed to proceed. Or alternatively the standards are not met, and the argument collapses. Or colleagues come to the rescue with insights from different perspectives, thus helping a developing argument over an impasse. Finally an agreed-upon formulation is reached, and it provides a model to be tested over against presumed reality, or in the controlled conditions of a laboratory. Throughout there is a shared consciousness of state-of-the-art knowledge, technical terms, standards of evaluation, and even what constitutes an original contribution.

Science is a species of the genus *work,* and as such it articulates the truth-standards of the workshop, which are nothing if not exact. Words are tools and ideally are made for one purpose alone. There is no mystery as to why science privileges coherence and correspondence theories of truth: they work, or rather, they tell us what science must successfully do if it is going to work. It must put together theories which function like well-oiled machines and match these to the actual functioning of reality, recognizing all the while that the theory selects out the reality which supports it. There are no great mysteries here.

The contributions of *Truth and Method* are many, but in my opinion its chief virtue is addressing a problem which has existed for nearly two hundred years in German philosophizing. This has been establishing that there is a 'truth' that is appropriate to the so-called humanities, and it is not of the same order of the 'truth' appropriate to the natural sciences. Kant first attempted this in the *Critique of Judgment.* Schiller articulated the argument in the essay on "Aesthetic Education," and finally Hegel in the *Phenomenology* brought it to the level of systematic philosophy. None of these thinkers wanted to say that beyond the rationality of the natural sciences was only the irrationality of poesy, the vaunted sound-and-fury of history, the brute facticity of the body. They knew that this would be conceding the game. Neither did they want to admit that in dealing with literature they were setting for themselves a lower standard, as is implied in the term 'soft' sciences or 'inexact' sciences. They really wanted to establish that there was a different 'truth', or *logos,* one not easily translatable into the 'truths' of the natural sciences.

Truth and Method redeemed the long-standing claim of the German philosophical tradition, but it would be misleading to leave the impression that it did this with the simple logic of an argument cast in stark terms like *prejudice, conversation, fusion of horizons, and agreement.* Admittedly these were peaks in a mountain chain of argumentation, but they told only part of the story, and the lesser part at that. The greater part of the story was in Gadamer's claims for *language* as such, for here he argued that language contained within itself all that was needed to allow the logic of community to function smoothly. It is precisely because words in their everydayness do *not* have exact meanings that agreements can be reached, meaning that you and I can fuse horizons because I grasp that my perspective is only part of the truth and that I expand my horizon by understanding and fusing with your horizon on the meaning of the thing we are talking about in conversation. We are easily misled into thinking that we give meaning to the words in this hermeneutic process. It is rather the other way round: words give added meaning to the impoverished little things that you and I are at the outset of the conversation. In Gadamer's formulation, "language speaks us before we speak it." Yes, but also: *I speak mere monological language first, and then I succumb to language's metaphorical and allegorical charms to become a larger I, finally a we.* I do not so much fuse my horizon with yours. It is we who fuse our limited horizons into the larger horizon of language.

There is yet more to *Truth and Method* than this. For example, I am not factoring in the dimension of tradition, characterized by Gadamer as *effective history* and its attendant *effective historical consciousness.* I tend to think that this argument about tradition and its effect adds richness to what has already been said in more disembodied terms. It reminds us that words are irreducibly metaphorical because they come loaded with the baggage of history. Put differently, a language is not a compilation of words in a dictionary, all disengaged from their literary traditions. A language is a literary tradition, better, language is tradition, ways of life, spelled out in songs, prayers, epics, and only recently in books, all done for the sake of their power of transmission. This argument should be spelled out, for it greatly enriches the kind of claim Gadamer is making, but that need not be done here. The bare-bones meaning of Gadamer's philosophical hermeneutics should be clear without it, and we can make do with this stripped-down version.

My question in this essay concerns the origins of *Truth and Method,* specifically what Gadamer did in the early years of his career which led up to *Truth and Method.* What I shall argue in the balance of this essay is that there is a compelling logic to the writings Gadamer did in the period between the World Wars. It is not the logic of *Truth and Method,* but it nonetheless establishes a significant position, one which I call *political hermeneutics.*[2] I shall limit myself to one writing, an article Gadamer published in 1934 under the title "Plato and the Poets."[3]

II.

"Plato and the Poets" was conceived, written, presented, and finally published in Nazi Germany. In this light, it takes on an aura which transcends its immediate subject matter: an explanation of Plato's antagonism to the Homeric tradition of transmitting ethical and political verities in the form of poetry. Simultaneously, however, and remarkably openly, "Plato and the Poets" is a reflection on the modern political condition, and one that is directly confrontational to the new conditions of Nazi Germany. Yet because it is arguably one of the best treatments ever written of the problem of Plato's curious hostility to the Greek poetic tradition, it provided its own camouflage. "Plato and the Poets" would have confused whatever oversight Nazi censors might have been giving to academic publications in 1934.

To make sense of this claim, let me step back for a brief moment and sketch in schematically, in terms of a number of steps, the paradigmatic mode of any and all distinctly *modern* political philosophies. The initial move comprises a recognition that there is no *sensus communis,* or common good, meaning that there is no political universal and hence no community. In Nietzschean terms, god is dead, or in more appropriately Hobbesian terms, the dissolution of the idea of the good puts the human condition into crisis, or the state of nature. This basic intuition, itself metaphysical, then leads to step two, which is an empirical observation concerning what is left *after,* as in Alasdair McIntyre's best-known title, or what is *post,* as in the recently fashionable period after modernism, or what happens after the *death of,* as is the mode among Hegelian thinkers. The answer is familiar and simple: There is an atomized condition comprising monads, also known as autonomous egos but more commonly called individuals, each of whom has his or her own idea of the good, meaning that there are now as many ideas of the good as there are individuals. This insight rushes forth through the last three centuries like a wave, beginning with the Calvinists in the seventeenth century and reaching even to contemporary feminists in quest of autonomy from nature.

In such a condition, what is called for is an argument which shows how the semblance of a polity may be constructed out of those individual interests or perspectives not at war with each other. Or alternatively, what is called for is an argument which can either restore the lost community or identify the elements of an entirely new sense of community. To meet this call is the third and final step, and frankly it is decisive, for the first two steps are widely shared, but such clear vision gives no guarantee of creativity. It may of course be argued that the communitarian initiative suggested above is not at all what is called for, that the more pressing task is to make the given condition *just,* to achieve at least a safety net of fairness and equal opportunity while preserving basic, inescapable, and irreversible individualism. There are problems with this argument, not the least of which is that it commits the genetic fallacy of assuming that what *is* will and must be. This argument is endless, and most recently it has taken shape as the 'Liberal-Communitarian' debate in the United States, but that debate no doubt will not put an end to this matter. Both poles of the argument will be provisionally accorded equal legitimacy at this point.

The model is Hobbesian in its original form, but it has proven to be the staple of every distinctly modern political thinker since Hobbes. What we commonly call *liberalism* is made up of a variety of attempts to construct society on the basis of a logic which recognizes that atomized individuals have identical interests in securing life and the conditions of life and hence have *rational* grounds for at least organizing their 'pursuit of happiness' in terms of some ground rules. Locke has faith in such individual rationality, as do Mill and Rawls, but it is fairly clear that they, at least the latter two, are deeply pessimistic about the willingness of contracting individuals to ever really agree on basic principles.

What we call *fascism* is more despairing of the rational capacities of atomized individuals and hence looks for the arrival of a superindividual to impose his idea of the good, hardly a *sensus communis,* but nonetheless order for those who hunger for such a good. By this definition, Hobbes is not at all a fascist, for he introduces the social contract tradition and hence signals his faith in individual rationality. But Nietzsche with his *Ubermensch* is a fascist, at least a protofascist, and so too is Lenin, at least in the collectivized sense of setting up a small, professional, and secret party which will make the revolution and impose truth on a mass of overly 'spontaneous' and hence less than politically rational individuals.

A careful reading of the first chapter of Freud's *Civilization and its Discontents* will show that he adheres precisely to the model sketched above. He first denies the validity of the 'illusion' of religion while agreeing that the vast majority of common men still cling to it. *Mutatis mutandis,* Freud is saying that there is no common good, although it is widely believed that there is. He is thus adding his bit to a series of religious reflections beginning with Baruch Spinoza's *Tractatus theologico-politicus* and continuing through David Hume's *Dialogues Concerning Natural Religion* and Feuerbach's *Essence of Christianity,* up to Weber's essays on the *Protestant Ethic and the Spirit of Capitalism.* Freud's next move is to claim that there are only egos and they are autonomous. At least they seem to be so until Freud announces his discovery of the unconscious. Up to this point, Freud the political philosopher had not said anything original, but with the introduction of the unconscious, he creates a category into which to factor repressed memory, thereby enabling him to argue that *forgetting* is not a matter of destroying the past but is rather a matter of storing it in a way which is not accessible to consciousness in its present form. The past, too, is not simply an individual past. For Freud it is a communal past, and he may be fanciful in his reconstruction of it, but he is still recognizably trying to show what it is like to be a communal being. A distinctly political psychoanalysis will then recover the distant communal past in order to confront it and thereby overcome it or retrieve it.

I am making what is only apparently a *universality* claim. I did not say that every thinker since the seventeenth century has thought in terms of the paradigm I have sketched. I merely said that every distinctly *modern* thinker has thought this way, and so if a thinker does not think this way, I am inclined to question whether he or she has really understood what distinguishes the modern condition. In any case, this is not a problem that need detain us here, for my claim is that Gadamer in "Plato and the Poets" also adheres to this model, although in the very thin guise of discussing the Athenian polity which existed more than two thousand years before Nazi Germany.

III.

Let us begin with the first claim, that there is no longer a *sensus communis*. Gadamer writes early in his essay, "Plato's Socratic insight was that a binding political ethos, which would assure the proper application and interpretation of poetry, no longer existed."[4] The source of this failing, according to Gadamer, is to be found in the theory of justice of the sophists, for they held that justice was merely a convention of the weak to protect their interests against the stronger. Now, we can overlook for the moment the alternative claim that classical Greece entered into political crisis merely because it was modernizing. Gadamer is correct if he means that this new class of educators called the *Sophists* gave the final shove to Homeric Greece's binding political ethos by teaching an alternative and distinctively modern theory of justice.

For the Sophists, "ethical principles are no longer valid in themselves but only as a form of our mutual 'keeping an eye' on one another."[5] What Gadamer is describing is not a surveillance state, but a society that is distinctly Hobbesian in that it rests on individuals. "The 'just'," writes Gadamer, "is that by means of which one person can assert himself against another with help from everyone else and, as such, it [justice] is adhered to only out of mutual distrust and fear."[6] Gadamer goes on to write that it does not matter whether one is speaking of 'left' or 'right' learning Sophists. They are all alike in agreeing on the nature of justice in a society which has lost its *sensus communis*. It is "not the justice intrinsic and internal to me myself," writes Gadamer. It is rather a justice based on the recognition that *"No one does what is right voluntarily."*[7] Individualism rules supreme in this state.

These words, which admittedly are not many, comprise the first two steps of what I have called paradigmatically modern political thinking. They may of course be naively interpreted as merely way stations along the course of carrying out a literary analysis of the essay's stated theme: Plato's problematic relation to the poets. They may, however, also be read as an Aesopian way of introducing the subtext of modern political theory to an essay on a literary topic, which of course is my preferred way of reading this Gadamerian text. There is, as yet, no way to determine which reading is the right one, and frankly, as I have already noted, *both* ways of reading Gadamer continue to work equally well. By this I mean that when and as I schematically present what I take to be the third step in the paradigm of modern political thinking, it will work just as well to sustain the stated theme of explaining why Plato has such a problematic relation to the poets. As noted earlier, I otherwise do not see how Gadamer could have gotten away with this essay in Nazi Germany. But the essay will also work, and much more powerfully, as an antidote to what ails any distinctly modern political society, or more specifically, Germany in 1934.

Gadamer's first step in constructing his own distinctively modern argument is to make a small but highly significant claim. Plato distinguishes himself from all his critical predecessors, Gadamer writes, in that he does not want to reform poetry but rather wants to destroy it. Hence, Plato's problematic relation to the poets turns out to be more simple than might have been thought, given the length of this essay. Gadamer writes that the "very excessiveness of this purification, which exceeds a thousandfold the boldest dreams of power ever attained by any moralist-pedagogue, should teach us the point of a reordering education such as Plato has in mind."[8] What then is that point? Plato's critique, writes Gadamer, *"is not intended to display how poetry would have to look in an actual state. Rather it is intended to disclose and awaken the powers themselves which form the state."*[9] In my words: Plato's critique of poetry is ultimately about politics and not about art, or poetry. The point of education is now decisively political.

Indeed, this sentence, emphasized by Gadamer, virtually disavows the stated poetic theme of the essay and announces a political theme. From this point onwards, I do not think that Gadamer's further arguments can be interpreted as being equally supportive of a literary theme and a political theme. Gadamer's italics convey that he will be concerned primarily with what he takes to be a political theory and only secondarily with what he takes to be Plato's relation with the poets. Everything he says hereafter will bear this out.

Significantly, if one pays attention to Gadamer's *italicized* words wherever they occur, they speak for themselves as a subtext. For instance, soon after shaking Plato loose from the literary theme to concentrate on the political theme, Gadamer goes on to make the point that Plato will be constructing a city-in-speech. This new city will have nothing to do with Homeric tradition, which is to say that it will not be guided by traditional ethical customs. With a keen sense for the efficacy of political theorizing, Gadamer recognizes that the mere construction of an ideal city amounts to little more than moral sermonizing and is therefore not effective. In italics he writes, *"even this state of new habituation must be left behind."*[10] That is to say, the larger signboard of the ideal city is not the definitive statement of Plato's political theory, and therefore it must be left behind. For if the problems are as serious as the modern paradigm makes them out to be, then theorizing must be more radical. The ideal city-in-speech "is intended to lead to a new discovery of justice in one's own soul and thus to *the shaping of the political human being."*[11] With these words, Gadamer reaches the point he wants to arrive at.

To reiterate: Gadamer's *italicized* sentences stick out like sore thumbs, not only because they are italicized but also because they all trumpet the political subtext. Written in 1934, they nearly flaunt the political subtext I have been speaking of, announcing for all to *see* that this piece is not merely about Plato's relation to the poets but is also, and mainly, about a theory of justice in a society in which the idea of the good has died and individuals have become autonomous beings acting in terms of as many ideas of the good as there are individuals. Gadamer's italicized words are tantamount to an announcement that he is pursuing his own idea of the political good in defiance of the neutral theme of his essay. Bearing this in mind, let us follow Gadamer in unfolding this thinly disguised subtext.

The shaping of the political human being will be done by *philosophy,* Gadamer writes. But what is meant by philosophy? Essentially it entails proceeding by means of questioning, and Gadamer means to let us know that this is what he intends to emphasize. In Gadamer's words, "precisely in extending its questioning behind the supposedly valid traditional moral ideas, it [Plato's educational state] is in itself the new experience of justice. Thus this education is not authoritative instruction based on an ideal organization at all; rather it lives from questioning alone."[12] The words are of real significance and deserve to be reiterated and emphasized. First of all, this mode of doing philosophy, which I take to be what we today call 'the Socratic method', is necessitated precisely because there is no binding political ethos. Platonic philosophy, as Gadamer understands it, has nothing to teach, and so it must be creative. Fair enough, but then the claim that the Socratic method is in itself the new experience of justice is at first jarring. How can it be that such a simple device *is* the experience of justice? Here we have one of those points in Gadamer's early career where he is laying down a significant idea but not developing it, instead setting the stage for its later and more mature treatment.[13]

For Gadamer, the question takes priority over the answer and functions to keep thinking closer to the natural movement of discursive inquiry. Hegel understood the natural movement of thinking every bit as well as Plato, but because he was intent upon constructing a closed system, he opted to make the *answer* the basic unit of his dialectical movement, structuring it in such a way that it would generate its opposite, or antithesis. In 1960, Gadamer argued for the superiority of the *question* as the basic unit of dialectical inquiry for the simple reason that it engaged the recipient of the question in dialogue, something that did not happen in the one-sided Hegelian dialectic. The nature of the Hegelian dialectic reveals that its author is intent upon restoring or reconstituting from above the idea of a common good, whereas the nature of the Platonic dialectic indicates that its author is intent upon no such thing. Plato is rather intent on shaping the political human being out of elements which are to be drawn, through questioning, from the existing human being.

Gadamer does not literally dispose of Hegel by demonstrating the superiority of Plato's dialogical method of questioning. That is something he would do twenty-five years later in *Truth and Method.* But he does dispose of another thinker from the classical period of modern German thinking—namely, Schiller—by arguing the specifics of Plato's educational state. Unlike Schiller,

Gadamer's Plato does not presuppose an initially harmonious personality that merely has to be developed. Rather, so argues Gadamer, the human animal is made of conflicting drives. He is at once willful and philosophical, bestial and peaceful, a herd animal and a rapacious wolf, a slave and a tyrant.[14]

The pairings are Gadamer's, and although not developed, they are interesting for two reasons: First, they tell us that the early Gadamer, through Plato, is the kind of *dualist* that the later Freud became. He is not about to construct a theory of human nature on a single principle. Rather, he sees man as made up of conflicting principles, neither one of which can be reduced to the other. Yet unlike Freud, these principles are not so unambivalently good and evil as are the life-instinct and the death-instinct. If we correlate what seem to be the positive terms, we find Gadamer's vision of human nature, ascribed to Plato, as one which is philosophical and peaceful but also slavish and herdlike. If we correlate the seemingly negative terms, we find man to be a wolf, rapacious, and a tyrant, but also simply willful. Consequently, we can reach the conclusion, consistent with Gadamer's forthcoming argumentation, that *the shaping of the political human being* is a complex affair in the sense that both the negative and positive sides have to be integrated to make the desired harmonious whole.

There is nothing unconscious about this construction of Plato, as is evidenced in an extraordinary footnote in which Gadamer nuances the crude dichotomizations mentioned above.[15] At this point I want to note that I am taking Gadamer to be doing an *interpretation* of Plato, and with Gadamer of all people it should not be necessary to explain that interpretation, or *hermeneutics,* involves using the prejudices of the reader, Gadamer in this case, to complete the fragmented picture with which one is dealing. What is necessary to highlight is that Gadamer uses the interpretive occasion to deal with other interpreters of Plato, such as Werner Jaeger or Paul Friedlander or the interpreters of the Stefan George circle. At this point, in dealing with the city of pigs, Gadamer has the opportunity to deal with Germany's master classicist, Ulrich von Wilamowitz-Moellendorf.

According to Gadamer, Plato's rejection of the city of pigs is based on his recognition that the mere provision of life's necessities is characteristic of an *a*historical state, or of no state that has ever been known to exist, and hence the question of justice does not arise. The latter question only arises when states enter into history, where there is flourishing and decay, corruption and recovery. In Gadamer's italicized words: *"The question of justice arises only when injustice has also become possible."*[16] The question of justice arises where there are lords and servants, where there is a desire to invade the sphere of another, and where there is war. "The just state," writes Gadamer, "is the state which has been *brought back* to moderation . . . from a historical excess."[17] As a consequence of thinking along these lines, Gadamer is able to produce a novel conception of the guardian class, and he does so by taking issue with Wilamowitz.

Wilamowitz correctly saw that the failing of the city of pigs was the absence of an *external* threat. This alone made it ahistorical. But because Wilamowitz stopped at this point, his conception of the guardian class is limited. Wilamowitz's guardian class was needed to manage a real external threat, but nothing more. Because Gadamer sees the threat as being *internal* as well, he is able to conceive the guardians as having a twofold purpose. Guarding is not simply a matter of distinguishing between friend and foe. In Gadamer's words, "guarding is both guarding *for* someone and guarding *against* someone."[18] Gadamer's Plato characterizes the ideal guardian as having both the force of the warrior's will and a philosophical nature as well, the purpose of the latter being the development to harmony of the souls of the state's citizens. Such a concept of philosophy is significant. It provides us with reason for looking at it in detail.

But before we do so let me sum up what is rapidly becoming a complex argument. Gadamer very quickly establishes that there is no binding political ethos in Plato's Athens and that everyone acts for himself, thereby perverting justice into a defense mechanism. This is familiar terrain; what is really interesting and creative is what Gadamer goes on to say. He claims that Plato wants to destroy poetry, not reform it, because poetry is incapable of awakening the powers which form the state. Poetry will be replaced by philosophy, and philosophy is conceived as an exercise in questioning precisely because there are no answers to transmit. This concept of philosophy makes it radically creative. Such a philosophy works with the contradictions of human nature, and in making this point Gadamer establishes himself as a complex dualist. More significantly, he is thereby able to establish the guardian class as being itself complex, for it will be charged with developing the political person without the aid of a doctrine.

Notably, Gadamer's Plato proceeds entirely without the famous Platonic doctrine of ideas. Gadamer had already taken this radical approach in his *Habilitation* thesis five years earlier. His claim then was that Plato's ethical ideas are not a prioris, or objective positions being expressed as doctrine. They are rather arrived at dialectically, or through language, and hence they are agreements, or fusions of horizons, worked out from the prejudices of the philosophers. This method comprises *Plato's Dialectical Ethics,* to use Gadamer's title.[19] Gadamer develops this position in "Plato and the Poets."

IV.

With that much said, we can return to the question of just what Platonic philosophy is. In Gadamer's words, "philosophy is what makes man as a political being possible."[20] Now it does this by following two paths, one critical and the other constructive of the new political being which philosophy seeks to achieve. I shall map out each approach in turn.

First of all, and once again in Gadamer's words, "man becomes a political being only *insofar as he resists the temptations of power which arise from flattery.*"[21] Therefore, like the loyal watchdog, political man must learn to distinguish friend from foe, and this is something that cannot be done through poetry because the latter teaches only imitation. First of all, then, philosophy is critical. In Gadamer's words: Philosophy is a *"critique of the moral consequences of 'aesthetic consciousness'."*[22] At this point, Gadamer is introducing a term which later becomes one of the main themes of *Truth and Method,* and it calls for a brief excursus.[23]

In *Truth and Method,* the term 'aesthetic consciousness' refers to the subjectivization of art and is associated with Kant and post-Kantian philosophy, to wit, the German classical tradition of philosophizing. The Kantian argument maintains that the significance of the work of art for the human subject is entirely an inner or subjective experience. In the Neo-Kantian revival of the later nineteenth century, especially in the work of Dilthey, this subjectivization came to be called *Erlebnis,* a term which is often mistranslated as 'experience' but is anything but that. In characteristic Neo-Kantian fashion, Dilthey was dividing the world into the natural sciences and the human sciences and conceding rationality completely to the former. Hence the latter were left with mystifications. *Erlebnis* and even *Verstehen* were the mysterious experience and equally mysterious method of the human sciences.

Unquestionably the most significant post-Kantian in this Gadamerian argument is Schiller, whose *Uber die aesthetische Erziehung des Menschen* haunts Gadamer's early essay for one simple reason: it determines the nineteenth-century German concept of education. Schiller, as I already noted, presupposes a basically (or potentially) harmonious human nature. The encounter with art is the empirical stimulant to the awakening and realization of the pure categories of aestheticism. Art therefore is finally an *inner* experience; it actually creates a certain kind of consciousness. In other words, the effect of the *Erlebnis* of the work of art is to bring into being an 'aesthetic consciousness', and this then shown forth in all its glory in the form of the *gebildete Burger,* or educated citizen. Schiller, more single-handedly than any other German thinker of the classical period, actually creates the German concept of education in the nineteenth century. Hence, Gadamer's frontal attack on *aesthetic consciousness* constitutes nothing less than a frontal challenge to the German educational establishment.

The problem is that this is not at all clear in *Truth and Method.* Indeed, if one judges that book by its reception, then one most easily comes to the conclusion that the whole point of Gadamer's critique concerns art in the modern world. Gadamer seems to be arguing that *the experience of art* is neither subjective nor objective. Rather, it is a dialectical interchange between the objective work of art and the subjective viewer, and what transpires in the metaphorical conversation is a fusion of horizons which changes both the work of art and the viewer.

Hence, there is no such thing as a 'correct' interpretation of the work of art, but neither is there a completely free subjectivity. It is more accurate to say that the subject completes the work of art by his or her interpretation, but it is equally the case that the work of art completes the subject by realizing his or her potential.

Brilliant, but problematic. Gadamer has basked in the fame he has won since the publication of *Truth and Method,* and frankly he has been content to leave things as they are. The problem, however, is that the current fashion in interpreting *Truth and Method* forgets or misses the much briefer original interpretation, which was unquestionably political and which warned in no uncertain terms precisely against the charms of art. To be sure, this was in the context of an argument about Plato's relation to the poets, but it was nonetheless clear that Gadamer, writing in 1934, had to banish art to make room for philosophy. The reason given by Gadamer is emphatic enough—on a single page he uses the term *self* twenty times.[24] It is clear as well: Gadamer argues that precisely the brilliance of art functions to distract the self from its less than brilliant task of constructing a political being. Instead, the self becomes other directed and moves to construct a self in terms of art, a phenomenon which at the level of consciousness results in the construction of *aesthetic consciousness.* This is a kind of false consciousness. Of course Gadamer is presupposing the fallen kind of art Plato treats as poetry, but this is beside the main point that only philosophy has the capacity to create political man. The only kind of poetic art which gains a reprieve from Gadamer's argumentation comprises songs of praise, but these gain their exceptional status because they function like philosophy to bring out the political man. Unless one can argue that art is a functional substitute for philosophy, the move made in *Truth and Method* is highly questionable.

So much for Gadamer's argument about the critical task of philosophy. Its constructive task is actually introduced in Gadamer's comments on songs of praise, for here at last Gadamer returns to the theme which is basic to the concept of a distinctly *modern* political thinking: the absence of a binding ethos, or sense of community. The song of praise is itself praised by Gadamer because it "speaks of that which binds them all to one another and gives them all a common obligation."[25] This is precisely what I earlier meant as the *sensus communis,* or the idea of a common good. "He who praises avows his commitment to praising, for in praising, the standard by which we evaluate and comprehend our existence is made manifest."[26] Now at this point Gadamer needs to note that such a standard only works because it is shared, and he does: "representation of an example in which the standard which we all share becomes evident is certainly more than drama."[27] The song of praise, to the extent that in a society of individuals it is allowed, revives the common standard.

At this point Gadamer introduces what I take to be the decisive idea of his earlier period, the notion that language embodies rather than expresses the binding ethos which indicates the life of the community. As I have already noted,

Gadamer had already argued—once again in the context of a Plato interpretation—the highly unorthodox claim that Plato's ethical dialogues were not based upon Plato's vaunted theory of objective ideas but were rather based on something much more tenuous, namely, the shared language of the participants. Even the title—*Plato's Dialectical Ethics*—of this, Gadamer's first book, was indicative of his claim. The point of the exercise was to show that even in a society of autonomous individuals a binding political ethos could be constructed in the very play of dialogue between partners who intended to reach a common ground. The intention was not a matter of the autonomous will of the actors but was simply implicit in the fact of conversation. Dialogue by its nature intends agreement or, in the words Gadamer would adopt thirty years later, a fusion of horizons.

Gadamer's hermeneutics itself means to indicate that community is not based on the common interest of a collection of individuals, for this would be to confuse community with any number of modern associations. Such phenomena represent collectivizations of autonomous individual wills and individual needs, and they last no longer than the project to realize the needs. Community is rather based on something which is at once more tenuous and more powerful: this is *the play of shared language.* Gadamer says precisely this: "In essence, then, the song of praise in the form of poetic play is shared language, the language of our common concern."[28] And then a few sentences later: The song of praise "does not produce the true ethos; it only represents it poetically. But in the true state, the state of justice, such a representation would be an avowal of commitment to the spirit shared by all, an avowal which in lighthearted play would celebrate that which is taken truly seriously."[29]

But as the last sentence indicates, the song of praise has definite limits, for regardless of what it refers to, it is still a re-presentation of something else and not an embodiment in language itself of the norms of community. Hence, Gadamer can ask, "But what poetic form should praise of true justice take when the communal bond formed in the practices, customs, and patterns of life in the state is no longer felt and when allegiance to it thus can no longer be pledged in a song of praise?"[30] And then Gadamer moves from representation to actual embodiment in another question: "What form must it take so that even as representation it might be authentic praise, a language of what is of concern to everyone?"[31] In the new form, justice remains as an inner certitude of the soul, "no longer clearly identified with any given reality," hence not really representation.[32] In this new form, praise of true justice is "a *philosophical conversation.*"[33] Our final effort in this essay must be aimed at capturing the essence of this philosophical conversation.

It is to be found in the concept of *play.* Once again we find Gadamer introducing a concept which would be deployed more than a quarter century later in *Truth and Method,* and once again, as with the concept of *aesthetic conscious-*

ness, it is desirable to point up the difference.[34] In Gadamer's later book, the concept of *play* is separated out and treated quite literally as a concept, that is to say, as an entity which may be conceived as a tool and used where appropriate. It therefore comes as no surprise to find that it is applied to art, or specifically to the relationship between the viewer and the work of art, or to the literary enterprise, where it describes the work of the hermeneuticist in weaving back and forth between the details and the whole to construct an interpretation of a text. The concept of *play* becomes a tool precisely to the extent that it is disengaged from context, something which occurs almost completely in *Truth and Method.*

This disengagement is not at all the case in "Plato and the Poets." Here the concept is fully and even relentlessly contextualized, and hence I speak of the *concept* of play only metaphorically. It is not a tool which can be applied according to the will and the plan of the individual who comes into possession of it. On the contrary, the vital characteristic of language is what enables language to embody rather than simply construct and express a thing outside language. When language embodies something it gives to it a three-dimensionality which one would normally not expect of a purely expressive, communicative language. Consequently it has an effect, if I may call it that, which destroys the distance we normally presuppose to exist between mind and things. It is only by this means that the atomized individual can transcend the gap which exists between individual and world and achieve a fusion of horizons which completes itself in the vision of *being-in-the-world.* This charged vision is what completes Gadamer's youthful essay.

Play is vital and inseparable from this vision. In Gadamer's words, "the only valid way to represent that [philosophical conversation] becomes Plato's dialogue, that song of praise which affirms what is of concern to everyone and which throughout the 'play' which represents the educational state does not lose sight of the serious issue: the cultivation of the political human being and of justice in him."[35] Gadamer in 1960 himself lost sight of that serious issue, but writing in 1934 he kept it clearly in mind. For example, he finds play to be a vital element of Platonic myths. The content of Plato's myths are not *expressed* by the stories he tells. "Instead it [the content] grows up out of the center of the Socratic truth itself in a play in which the soul recognizes itself and the truth of which the soul is most certain."[36] Further on, Gadamer writes that "one cannot say that the sole function of such myth is to make Socratic truth understandable by expressing it allegorically."[37] On the contrary, "the fact that Socratic knowledge of one's own self is expressed in the form of a play of mythical images tells us something of the kind of certainty which this knowledge has."[38] Even Platonic irony is subsumed in this notion of *play:* "Plato gives his mimesis the levity of a jocular play. Insofar as his dialogues are to portray philosophizing in order to compel us to philosophize, they shroud all of what they say in the ambiguous twilight of irony."[39] And then finally, Plato's "dialogues are nothing more than playful allusions which say something to him who finds meanings beyond what is expressly stated in them and allows those meanings to take effect within him."[40]

The function of play is to give three-dimensional shape to the contradictory elements within us, the willful and the thoughtful, the bestial and the peaceful, the self-seeking and the communal.[41] This is what the building of *political man* amounts to in Gadamer's interpretation of the constructive side of Plato's philosophy, and it is the point at which this essay abruptly halts.

Let me sum up this section as I did the last. The concept of *philosophy* that Gadamer introduces is twofold. Initially it is critical, and this involves it in the destruction of 'aesthetic consciousness', or the other-directedness of beings who no longer have a binding ethos and who look on poetry as a beautiful distraction. The constructive task of philosophy is more ambitious, and it involves substituting Platonic dialogue for poetry because it retains a play which will triumph over the one-dimensionality of other-directedness and enable beings to develop their true selves into a harmonious unity.

V.

A number of questions are left in the wake of this early essay by Gadamer, but I shall forego the obvious temptation and settle for one question which is distinctly hermeneutical and, in my opinion, unanswerable. This is the question why Gadamer decontextualized a set of distinctly political concepts, articulated in writings done from the late 1920s to the early 1940s, when he wrote *Truth and Method*. In some respects, the question is very much like the question which troubled Georg Lukács and caused him to read Marx's *Das Kapital* like a detective trying to unravel a mystery. The problem was not so much that Marx had abandoned the categories of Hegelian philosophy. The problem was rather that Marx had kept them hidden while attempting to write a purportedly materialist political economy. Lukács read between the lines and thought he saw traces of humanist Hegelian categories. With the subsequent publication of the early writings of Marx, Lukács gained the empirical evidence needed to support his position. Lukács was therefore able to reclaim Marx for the Western humanist tradition and establish a powerful defense against the 'scientistic' Marxism of Engels, Lenin, and Stalin.

Similarly with Gadamer, it is possible to read *Truth and Method* as a text in which the parts are often if not always greater than any conceivable whole. This is its genius. It has one brilliant foray after another, and yet there is no whole to make sense of all the parts. The book becomes a brilliant department store in which one can pick and choose, and this is precisely what readers do. Yet when one reads the disengaged sections that deal with the *sensus communis* or *aesthetic consciousness* or *play,* one senses that there might have been a context for these elements, but it is hard to imagine what it is. It is only when one returns to

Gadamer's early writings and discovers their strong political content that one finds precisely what is missing in Gadamer's *opus magnum.*

This is more than a simple omission which can be passed over courteously with comforting statements about authors changing over the course of a lifetime. If one reflects briefly on the problem, it is impossible to avoid coming to the conclusion that *Truth and Method* is not just different but is deficient in a significant way. Precisely by omitting the political context that was so well articulated in the early writings, Gadamer's later book sets the stage for its own successful reception in the kind of civilization his early writings rejected. Gadamer's *Truth and Method* is so written that individual readers with very different ideas of the good, conflicting interests, and autonomous wills—in sum, no binding political ethos—can gain something from their interpretation of the book. To each reader according to his individual interests, in other words. *Truth and Method* enriches precisely the world that the early Gadamer was seeking to trump.

In response one might ask, why not? That is to say, why not write a decontextualized book in which concepts narrowly determined by a notion of the political ethos are freed up and allowed to roam and seek an elective affinity with reader interests whatever they might be? The answer to such an objection is that the early Gadamer's concept of politics is by no means narrow. It is rather a broad vision which brings along with it not only a specific vision of the state as an educational state but also a sociology of existing society and a psychology of the individual person. The *sociology* describes a society in which each individual pursues his or her own interest or idea of the good. The *psychology* denies the simplistic idea of the good of Schiller or Humboldt, and the notion of an educated citizenry, and does so in favor of a much more complex vision of political man. The psychology, in other words, denies the sociology. The *politics* then realizes the psychology, but only by means of education, or a poetic play which draws out and harmonizes the elements of the soul. There is nothing narrow about Gadamer's early concept of politics. On the contrary, what is narrow is the concept of a society in which each individual pursues his or her own interest or idea of the good. What is furthermore narrow is a book, *Truth and Method,* which caters to precisely this fragmented political society.

In response, one might also argue that the above description is indeed that of a *liberal* society and such a society is superior to all other candidates in a world in which god is dead. Any opposing vision which seeks to restore a 'binding political ethos' is suspect and merits heightened scrutiny. This argument is indeed more serious because it presupposes a valid concept of a distinctly *modern* political philosophy. Yet there is also something distinctly deficient about it, for it presupposes that Gadamer's vision of a binding political ethos is fully hostile to this liberalism. But is it? The kind of liberalism with which we are most familiar in the English-speaking world is Anglo-Saxon liberalism, and from Locke through Mill and up to Rawls this liberalism has privileged or at least accepted the pursuit of individual interest as being central to modernity. It has tended to take the individual as he is or, more recently, she is, believing that no one has a right to authoritatively tell anyone else what they may think or do, as long as what they think or do does not harm others. This liberalism has become a kind of civic religion in the United States.

But it does not follow from this that the early Gadamer's program for reconstituting a 'binding political ethos' is illiberal. Ever since Wilhelm von Humboldt was Prussian Minister of Education, there has been a kind of distinctly German liberalism which has focused on the educational development of the individual and devalued the distinctly Anglo-Saxon development of property. Admittedly this German liberalism got badly sidetracked in the nineteenth century, but the memory of it was kept alive by, of all people, Nietzsche, who despised the new *Reich* for its materialism and cultivated a vision of history and education which made sense only in terms of the development of distinct individuality. Gadamer is very much in harmony with this distinctly German liberalism when he conceives his 'binding political ethos' in terms of an educational state which does not impose a predefined ideal of the good citizen but rather uses language to enter into a play with the conflicting elements of the human soul, one that is designed to build a real political man.

Arguably, this kind of liberalism is the only liberalism worth pursuing. Why, after all, privilege the pursuit of property, unless it is for the development of the individual. Property pursued for its own sake is indeed mere materialism, a crude and brutal form of power accumulation. Secondly, why privilege the pursuit of liberty? For the distorted vision of unrestrained liberty leads eventually to the kind of uncivil rights-talk which periodically dominates American public discourse. It is hard to justify liberty or property as *ends* and much more reasonable to justify them as *means* to an end which is close by them, namely, the individual person. This is what Gadamer was doing in his early writings.

It is therefore hard to answer the question in terms of which this conclusion was framed. It is hard to say why Gadamer dropped the political framework of his early concepts. *Truth and Method* is a fine book, but finally it accommodates itself to the modern world by creating the conditions of its own reception. It is autonomous, intriguing, and even cunning in the way it allows itself to be interpreted in multiple ways, thus functioning as a mirror on modern pluralism. It is often profound in its insights and brilliant in its conceptualization. One can concede every point to *Truth and Method* without giving away anything that is vital. But it is only after one has read Gadamer's early writings that one can begin to really understand the whole.

ROBERT R. SULLIVAN

JOHN JAY COLLEGE OF CRIMINAL JUSTICE
THE CITY UNIVERSITY OF NEW YORK
MAY 1992

NOTES

1. Hans-Georg Gadamer, *Wahrheit und Methode,* 4th ed. (Tübingen: J. C. B. Mohr, 1975), first published in 1960, translated as *Truth and Method,* 2nd rev. ed., trans. rev. by J. Weinsheimer and D. G. Marshall (New York: Crossroad, 1989).

2. Robert R. Sullivan, *Political Hermeneutics* (University Park, Pa.: Penn State Univ. Press, 1989).

3. Hans-Georg Gadamer, "Platon und die Dichter," in *Gesammelte Werke,* vol. 5 (Tübingen: J. C. B. Mohr, 1985), translated as "Plato and the Poets," in *Dialogue and Dialectic,* trans. P. Christopher Smith (New Haven: Yale Univ. Press, 1960).

4. Gadamer, "Plato and the Poets," p. 50.

5. Ibid.

6. Ibid.

7. Ibid.

8. Ibid., p. 51.

9. Ibid.

10. Ibid., p. 52.

11. Ibid.

12. Ibid.

13. See Gadamer's "The Hermeneutic Priority of the Question," in *Truth and Method,* pp. 362–79. P. Christopher Smith makes the same point I am making in his footnote no. 3 to "Plato and the Poets."

14. Gadamer, "Plato and the Poets," pp. 55, 56, and 57.

15. Ibid., p. 55, n. 7.

16. Ibid.

17. Ibid.

18. Ibid., p. 56.

19. Hans-Georg Gadamer, *Platos Dialektische Ethik,* in *Gesammelte Werke,* vol. 5 (Tübingen: J. C. B. Mohr, 1985).

20. Gadamer, "Plato and the Poets," p. 57.

21. Ibid., p. 56.

22. Ibid., p. 65.

23. Gadamer, *Truth and Method,* pp. 81–93. Actually, it is one of the main themes of part 1 of the book. P. Christopher Smith makes comments similar to mine in his footnote no. 10, p. 65 of "Plato and the Poets."

24. Gadamer, "Plato and the Poets," p. 65.

25. Ibid., p. 65.

26. Ibid.

27. Ibid.

28. Ibid.

29. Ibid.

30. Ibid.

31. Ibid.

32. Ibid.

33. Ibid., p. 67.

34. Gadamer, *Truth and Method,* pp. 101ff.

35. Gadamer, "Plato and the Poets," p. 67.

36. Ibid.

37. Ibid., p. 69.

38. Ibid.
39. Ibid., p. 70.
40. Ibid., p. 71.
41. Ibid., p. 69, for the reference to three-dimensionality.

REPLY TO ROBERT R. SULLIVAN

This is a very interesting contribution. Here, one of my early works has been chosen as a topic since it lends itself most easily to the interests of political science. It deals with the critique of the poets as presented in Plato's *Republic*. The object of the contribution is a work published in 1934. But it is strange that one always finds the error that one finds here. One assumes that what was published in 1934 had to have been written in 1934. But we are not journalists. Often we write years in advance and what will be published eventually does not at all mirror the historical and political situation of the year of publication. This can lead to misunderstandings: Sullivan did not notice that the topic which motivated me to write "Plato und die Dichter" was ultimately sustained by faith in culture or the cultural hopes of the intellectual class of the Weimar Republic. In those days we believed that eventually we would still learn democracy. But this was of course a premature hope which dissolved into nothingness after the most terrible events and which was reawakened only in the new beginning after World War II. It is equally strange that one is astonished that the publication of a work that did not fit into the party line did not meet with difficulties in 1934. There was not yet control over such trifling matters as philosophy books or articles. Later on, the goal of censorship was achieved more or less indirectly through the necessary granting of paper. But in 1934 the political planning and supervision of censorship was not yet effective in German publishing, although some cautious publishers certainly avoided certain topics. Thus I have to correct this. When the essay was published in 1934, the addition of the motto from Goethe was something of a confession, of course. But a censor—who did not yet exist—could not be interested in that. In those days before the Röhm-Putsch one still hoped for the return to the constitutional state. And even later, the general attitude rather was: Oh these philosophers, that is nothing of importance. When comparing the Third Reich to East Germany, for example, which was dominated by the Communists for decades, one should know what these matters looked like to the minds of these rulers. In the beginning of 1933 there was only an indirect pressure exercised upon intellectual life. The situation changed only after June 30, 1934, that is, after Hitler's pact with the German army. That created an immense increase in the power of the regime and, as a consequence, influenced the population's drive to adjust to the regime. But there never would have been a majority for Hitler in free elections before the start of the war. Precisely that was the terrible situation in which, for example, the soldiers of Hitler's army found themselves after the attack on Russia. The German army was certainly anti-communist. That, however, hardly distinguished the German army from what was the case in other Western countries. But it was difficult even for the army to defend itself against the Nazi party and its barbarism. Such a defense always required a mask, and on top of that it also depended upon the moral and intellectual level of the individual officer.

In any case, when one directs one's interest to the Weimar Republic and the Third Reich before the start of the war, one will have to dispense with the drawing of direct conclusions for philosophy from the political circumstances after 1933. Sullivan knows my works for a long time and I know him too. I was always astonished that he took such a strong political interest in my works on Greek philosophy. For it was always clear to me that they could have validity only as an exercise in liberal democracy and not for the "Thousand Year Reich."

Nonetheless, it is interesting to me to see Sullivan now analyzing my early work with such scrutiny and dedication. This contribution prompted me to reread that work after sixty years. There is one point, however, in which I still cannot follow Sullivan. He thinks that in *Truth and Method* and my later works I have lost my early political interest. Of course, in the beginning, after 1933, one constantly hoped that, after initial confusions, somehow one's own country would stabilize itself within the limits of a cultural or constitutional state. So it was natural that one hoped that the entire thing would be transitory not only for one's own sake but also for all my Jewish friends. That hope seemed legitimate until *"Kristallnacht,"* and when the war started, it was too late for everything.

My critique of aesthetic consciousness, however, which plays a role in the early work on Plato, preserves itself from the beginning until today. My real task became to elevate the philosophical rank of the humanities, not because philosophy is a science and a theory of science but because it comprises the entire experience of life. Political events, and, in like manner, art and poetry, and in general humanity's creating of culture, always cause us to make new experiences. I do share the author's starting point that at least in the intellectual class of the country a demise of the *sensus communis* which has been spreading for centuries, took place. Nietzsche's catchword about the death of god has been confirmed again and again in the twentieth century.

This concern for making new experiences is reflected in my own hermeneutical works primarily in the figure of Socrates and fundamentally in the effort to keep questions open. My chief work precisely begins with the critique of the aesthetic consciousness, and I sought to bring art's claim to truth into a fruitful reciprocal interaction with the experience of philosophical thought. I cannot see this as signifying a real change vis-à-vis my early works. Thus, I remember very well that already in 1934 I marked my beginnings with a lecture on the critique of aesthetic consciousness. Meanwhile, however, the frontlines have shifted. After the second war (and after two years of rectorial politics in Leipzig), in the epoch of rebuilding, a new epoch with entirely different frontlines opened up. It was stamped by the victory of the industrial revolution which resulted in an immense increase in regulations, an increasing bureaucratization, and a constant tendency to conformity. Since that time I saw my task as a teacher in strengthening the courage of the German academic youth to think for themselves and to strengthen their own sense of judgment. This means first of all engaging in the primacy of dialogue in the theory and practice of teaching. In this way we researchers and teachers have to obey the law of the long breath in the field of politics.

H.-G.G.

12

Francis J. Ambrosio

THE FIGURE OF SOCRATES IN GADAMER'S PHILOSOPHICAL HERMENEUTICS

A t the center of Gadamer's philosophical hermeneutics stands the figure of Socrates. This claim, to be explained and argued in the essay that follows, is intended to epitomize a distinctive interpretation of Gadamer's thought as a whole, an interpretation which purports to be:

a) accurate in plotting the trajectory of Gadamer's project in contrast to certain polemical misunderstandings of it;

b) consistent with the primary concerns which inform, structure, and punctuate the development of Gadamer's own hermeneutic practice and theory;

c) comprehensive in scope, avoiding the partialized focus on issues in his thought which, when emphasized in isolation from their full context, tend to distort Gadamer's proper philosophical profile;

d) fruitful in suggesting the significance of both 1) the particular themes and concepts he employs in *Truth and Method* as they emerge when that text is viewed appropriately as a reflective self-explanation against the broader horizon his own hermeneutical practice displayed in his directly interpretive essays, as well as 2) his larger role in the evolution of the philosophical tradition in this century;

e) effective in facilitating both firm commitment to the many important virtues of his philosophical hermeneutics and at the same time, legitimate criticism of his way of thinking, particularly in terms of the necessity to demonstrate the specific limitations which individuate and identify it as his own.

To say that Gadamer's hermeneutics is centered in the figure of Socrates is to say many things at once. First, it says that Gadamer's thought is most properly identified as Platonic in this specific sense: Gadamer shares Plato's commitment to a view of Socrates as embodying the *aretē* (excellence) of the philosophical way of life, dedicated to the "care of the soul," through understanding. This, in turn, says three further things about Gadamer's thought: that it is essentially *ontological, dialogical,* and *metaphorical* in character. In what follows, I wish to consider both what each of these characteristics means in the context of

Gadamer's hermeneutics and also the sense in which each arises from and reflects an element of his interpretation of the Platonic Socrates's way of living and its uniquely privileged excellence. This should not, of course, be taken to imply that such an interpretation of Gadamer, centered on the figure of Socrates, will view as secondary the historical efficacy of Aristotle, Hegel, and Heidegger as interlocutors with Gadamer in his formation of his way of thinking. Rather, the position to be taken here will be precisely that it is in and through his original identification with the Socratic paradigm of philosophy as care of the soul through philosophical conversation that Gadamer is able to listen attentively and respond to all four of these equal partners in conversation, Plato, Aristotle, Hegel, and Heidegger, in a way which is authentically his own. In fact, the conclusion we shall finally reach is that the *integrity* of Socratic existence is what provides Gadamer with the key to holding the center of his thought together in living unity while remaining free for and open to complex interplay with each of these figures regarding the question of truth which is their shared subject matter. The full profile of Gadamer's philosophical hermeneutics emerges when we recognize how the question of truth belongs with, originally and altogether, and is appropriate to, the question of freedom, and how these two questions are integrated in the tension that marks his thought, as they must be in all philosophical existence and discourse.

I.

Gadamer's philosophical hermeneutics is centered in the ontological question of truth. Faithful to the tradition of that question in the West—starting with the Greeks, who first became alert to sophistry as the shadow of philosophy— Gadamer acknowledges the full ontological status of the question. That is to say, he acknowledges that the question of truth can and must be raised only at the same primordial level at which the question of Being itself arises, the question whose power the Greeks experienced and submitted themselves to in the form of the paradox of the One and the Many. At this level, questions of existence, truth, freedom, and beauty come into play and work themselves out; they remain inseparably linked so that in experience and thought we have always to do with them in both their sameness and difference at once. But for Gadamer, following Heidegger, this level of ontological concern is to be engaged in a manner more closely akin to the original Greek experience of it than has been handed over to us in the traditional form of the trinity of metaphysics, epistemology, and ethics. Gadamer's reception of Heidegger's "step-behind" the Western metaphysical tradition culminates in the third part of *Truth and Method* with his sketch of the rudimentary shape of an ontology of language. Here, the human existential concern with the question of Being and its truth expresses itself as an involvement in the question of how, and why, existence occurs as "finite transcendence," that is, as the event of coming-to-be-meaningful as language. In the early Heidegger, this concern takes the form of an analysis of Dasein's temporality. Gadamer follows Heidegger's way of thinking the question of the meaning of Being in its difference from beings through phenomenology and the existential analytic of Dasein until it turns into the question of *das Ereignis.* This vector leads him to *die Mitte der Sprache,* the centering of thought in and on language, or better, to language as the medium of all relation insofar as it is experienced and understood as meaningful. Failure to recognize Gadamer's citing of the question of truth on *die Mitte der Sprache,* and to take the radical consequences of this step of identifying Being as language with full seriousness, has been the source of most of the misunderstanding of the claims that Gadamer makes regarding interpretation in *Truth and Method.* Critics, from Betti and Hirsch through, more recently, Habermas, Warnke, and Bernstein have allowed their focus on Gadamer's approach to the question of truth to be distorted by viewing it through the lenses of the problem of relativism, whether epistemological or ethical. In the case of Betti and Hirsch, this failure arises from a naive assumption of realist metaphysical foundations resulting in a fundamental category mistake. In the cases of Habermas, Warnke, and Bernstein, an excessive preoccupation with the problem of understanding's capacity to arrive at rational agreement in matters of action and the critique of praxis, produces a systematic distortion of emphasis in their reading based on a failure to recognize the metaphysical assumption underlying the conception of rationality which they employ but Gadamer eschews. Whether the charge be that Gadamer's hermeneutics cannot arbitrate rival claims of validity, cannot adequately critique practices, or cannot articulate normative claims, the root of the misunderstanding in all cases is the same: they do not recognize the consequences that result from Gadamer's transposition of the question of the nature of understanding and truth into an ontological context, centered in *die Mitte der Sprache.* This move altogether changes the very way of posing the question from an evidential concern for a transcendental or empirical property of Being, however understood, to a concern for the historical efficacy of truth claims that is, or is not, warranted by the event-structure of meanings as they occur in understanding through interpretation.

Truth and Method approaches the ontological question of Truth from the perspective of an investigation of the way truth comes into play in the experiences of art, history, the human sciences, and finally philosophy. At the outset, in the consideration of whether and how the work of art can make a truth claim on human understanding, Gadamer signals the radical consequences of the ontological shift he is making by focusing discussion on the notion of play. The experience of play, in which the participants are literally "overpowered" and claimed by and for the movement into which they enter, offers us, Gadamer suggests, a more appropriate ontological paradigm for the way truth occurs in understanding than does the metaphysical model of evidential grounding, i.e., foundationalism in all its forms. On this alternative paradigm, the dichotomy between subject and object, knower and known, is taken up into the prior ontological relation of mutual, original co-determination to which Gadamer refers as *Zugehörigkeit*. *Zugehörigkeit* refers to the all-embracing relation at the level of original meaningfulness that is instanced by the movements of harmony in song, rhythm in dance, and plot in drama. The meaning of these movements occurs as the event of the playing. In trying to evaluate, from the perspective of its adequacy to deal with the problem of relativism, the way Gadamer signals the ontological shift concerning the question of truth, the mistake is to misjudge the kind of "seriousness" that appropriately attends that question: as the Greeks recognized, the seriousness of loving the truth is contemplative in nature, not primarily judgmental or practical, although it includes both these elements. Rather, it is a seriousness marked by the liberality of the sacred as opposed to the servility of the profane. It is of the nature of the spectacular to be wondered at and admired, not toiled over, except insofar as toil is necessary to clear and maintain the open and free space of leisure.

The association of play with contemplation as ontological characteristics of the question of truth forms the link that ties Gadamer's consideration of the truth of art with that of the truth of history. In the important passage in *Truth and Method* where he considers the nature of experience, and implicitly the particular human experience of the question of truth, Gadamer emphasizes that all human experience is fundamentally religious, in the sense that Aeschylus's drama and the whole tradition of Greek tragedy makes clear: human experience is always experience of radical finitude, where finitude means being in relation to divine mystery, belonging to and with *(Zugehörigkeit)* the mystery of transcendence. Plato identifies Socrates' enactment of the tragic-comedic paradox of "religion"[1] in the *Apology* by recounting the story of the encounter with the oracle of Delphi under the authority of the injunction to "know thyself." All genuine self-knowledge is religious knowledge, not because it has to do explicitly with issues of the reality, or nonreality, and nature of "god," but more originally, because it is an experience of the mystery of transcendent, divine power by which the human is claimed and which it undergoes and suffers as the passion of need, specifically the ontological "need" to understand itself as being-in-relation to divine mystery *(pathein mathein)*. All necessity, whether existential, logical, ethical, or aesthetic, has its seed in the need for the "divine" mystery of origins and destiny which encircles and circumscribes human existence with its power and which is also the originating truth of history.[2] Gadamer's adherence to the Platonic paradigm of Socratic existence allows him to see, in a way which apparently Heidegger could not, the flesh and blood images of Dasein's "finite transcendence" analyzed as temporality in its philosophically original form in the figure of Socrates. For Plato, to be human is to be in question, because questioning marks the emergence into *Sprachlichkeit*[3] of that passionate need, which is the serious play of truth setting itself to the work of *noesis, poesis,* and *praxis,* the making of science, art, and history, a making which, while originally human, is by no means to be understood in terms of the correlation of subject and object, except, in certain cases, derivatively. For Plato, to be human is to be in question and being in question is the "soul" which Socratic existence cares for as its ontological bond with the mystery of divine power.

The working out of this careful concern for the soul's binding relation to divine mystery, Plato expresses as the question of the Good. This question, as Gadamer points out so lucidly in *The Idea of the Good in Platonic-Aristotelian Philosophy,* Plato shares with Aristotle in a way which is more fundamental than, yet philosophically inseparable from, any and all of the genuine and significant differences that mark each one's way of asking and responding to that question, which of course, is One with the question of truth in all its meaningful manifestations in human experience as *Sprachlichkeit.* Gadamer's identification of language as *die Mitte,* the "center(ing) of relation," upon which experience emerges into the open of freedom and truth as meaning, is a reflection in hermeneutic theory of Plato's identification, in the context of the Greek mythopoetic tradition, of the soul as "halfway in between" the human and divine, the spiritual and the material, the mortal and the immortal.[4] The soul for Plato is the center of all relations, insofar as they can meaningfully come into question and be understood. As such, the soul is the ontologically central locus of the question of the Good, the question which makes us human by always having us in its power. This power which enables us to be human (Latin: *virtus,* virtue; Greek: *aretē*) marks Socratic existence with the question which becomes, through lived conviction, the center of its identity and integrity. Gadamer identifies the aura of this power as it is effective in the linguistic experience of understanding as *die Virtualität des Sprechens,* the "virtuality of living language," by which human language, and particularly the discourse of philosophy, is always held hovering in the tension of the field of force which opens up—through metaphor, as we shall see—halfway in between whatever is said and the "evermore" which, because it is human and born of need as well as resourceful capacity, of necessity remains unsaid, always to be said further. All more specific philosophical questions are virtually present in the question of the Good—the end, goal, and mark toward which questioning itself is destined by divine power. This, of course, accounts for the centrality of *methexis* (participation) as the principal ontological metaphor that dominates Plato's theory of Ideas. It also accounts, however, for the central importance that Gadamer attributes to tradition as the seat of legitimate authority. The "divine" origin of all legitimate authority is a view to which not only the Greeks subscribed, viewing authority as being handed over to humans from its origin source. In this sense Gadamer can say that philosophy is *par excellence* that human endeavor in which there is "no progress but only participation."

On this basis, we are now in a position to state in more precise, if somewhat lapidary, "thetic" form, some propositions regarding the ontological character of Gadamer's philosophical hermeneutics, understood as a theoretical reflection on the original human condition of Socratic existence:

1) Gadamer's most properly philosophical concern is to elaborate an ontology of language.

2) This ontology of language is essentially the view that language is the fundamental and universal "center of relation" upon which human experience emerges as meaningful.

3) In this sense, "language" names the mystery of the emergence of relation out of both power and need as meaning, and understanding names a paradoxical yet appropriately human participation in that mystery.

4) Every relation, insofar as it is properly human, and therefore ontological, is an "internal" relation in the sense that the *"relatio* is prior to the *relata,"* that is, it is meaningless to speak about the elements or individuals apart from their relations to divine mystery, to human existence, and to the world. (*"Sein, das verstehen werdern kann, ist Sprache."*)

5) Gadamer identifies the specifically ontological character of the centering of relation which is language as *"die Virtualität der Sprechens,"* the virtuality of living language. Virtuality is the way living language, as dialogue, holds together the finite determinacy of what is said with the superabundant openness of what always remains unsaid to be said further in a genuine wholeness (integrity) of meaning.

6) The question of truth emerges together with the questions of freedom and beauty in the center(ing) of relation which is language; therefore these questions share an ontological integrity as embodied in human existence and can never finally be meaningfully separated from one another.

7) In these terms, truth, for Gadamer, is the emergence into language of the mystery of human relations to the world as a virtual whole of meaning; that is, truth is integrity of meaning. As such, it bears the marks of its origin, namely, truth is historical, finite, and speculative, in the particular sense in which Gadamer uses this latter term, as we shall see.

8) Virtuality, therefore, names the ontological power of language to create relation through the emergence of meaning in the experience of understanding.

Furthermore, by way of anticipating Gadamer's development of the implications of his ontology of language we can add at this point the following corollaries to these propositions:

9) For Gadamer, the power of language becomes historically effective in dialogue which enacts the dynamics of finite transcendence. The event of truth and experience of understanding occur most originally in dialogue.

10) Metaphor names the way in which human existence experiences and express-
     es the power of language becoming effective in dialogue. The structure of
     metaphor is sameness-amid-difference and as such metaphor is the original
     medium in and through which human beings understand truth.

11) What finally remains unsaid in Gadamer's ontology of language, marking the
     limits of his achievement, is the question of the way truth and beauty belong
     together with freedom.

12) The ontological mystery of human existence most fully expresses itself in the
     integrity of human personal relations of every sort. Therefore, beyond the
     limits of Gadamer's current achievement, his philosophical hermeneutics can
     only be understood as being on the way beyond itself to what can be envi-
     sioned as a metaphorics of the person where person is understood ontologi-
     cally to be a centering in existence of the power to create relation and is in
     no way to be reduced to the metaphysical isolation of an individual subjec-
     tivity for which meaning could be an external, relative, or accidental set of
     relationships into which it enters subsequently at its own initiative.

II.

We have now to consider the next stage of development of Gadamer's ontology
of language, guided by the realization to which the reader of *Truth and Method*
is gradually led: for Gadamer, dialogue, modeled on the practice of Socrates'
philosophical conversation, is the effective essence of language. As the essence
of language, we can presume that from the experience of dialogue, language's
character as historical, finite, and speculative emerges. As historical, dialogue is
always an hermeneutic relation to tradition, and experiences the power of language historically embodied in the authority of tradition, not as a static restriction of thought to what has gone before or is established, but rather as the necessity always to return again to those few fundamental and universal (ontological)
questions that touch upon the meaning of human existence, as such, beyond
every relativity of culture, epoch, and individual psychology, because they are
rooted in the relation to divine mystery which originates all history. History
always repeats itself in that, whatever the novelty of its twisting and turning, the
questions to which human historical words and actions are responses remain
always the same. These fundamental and universal questions are human historicality. Socratic care of the soul is dedicated to them. These questions are always
coming into presence again (essenc-ing) in language, and this historical dedication of human existence to the questions which are its soul/meaning gives tradition its legitimate authority.

But tradition's authority is limited in its legitimacy. The limit of tradition's
claim on experience and understanding, and therefore of its truth claim, is its

ontological relation, which *is* its finitude, to the ever-opening (future) possibilities for meaning which arise from the very nature of ontological questioning itself. Questions of the meaning of the divine, death, embodiment, the Good, freedom, truth, beauty, and their interplay in the human excellence of integrity—these universal and fundamental questions become historically effective only when they lay claim to particular, historically situated, genetically, culturally, socially, and psychologically diverse peoples and persons who, furthermore, differ not merely in their empirical situatedness but in their freedom and imaginative creativity. These questions, for all they remain the same, always occur differently in the concrete historical actuality of their being asked and responded to. This ontological differing, occurring as the historical event of truth in language, is the origin of the free, open space that understanding is, originating not in human subjectivity, but in the ontological relation that centers in language and is human personal existence. Gadamer identifies this ontological freedom and openness of language as its speculative character, its ever-reaching-out into new possibilities of meaning. Dialogue—historical, finite and speculative, same and different—is the way that meaning emerges as living language in the experience of understanding to establish its truth claim on human existence, a claim which demands and measures the truthfulness of every human response. This capacity to respond differently to the ontological claiming of truth is the origin of the human responsibility which Heidegger calls *Sorge,* but which Plato portrays dramatically and ironically as the care of the soul. The identity and integrity of Dasein reveals itself as flesh and blood in the comic tragedy of guilt and conviction enacted by Socrates at his trial. Truth's way of testing and proving itself, the real existential crisis behind the reflection which appears as the problem of relativism, shows itself here: what is required of a human to become and remain, to be historically, true to him- or herself. What does it take to be able to go on questioning in the risk of finitude, the risk which provokes malice and violence, which is stretched out between past and future, between the authority of tradition and the eros of creation, between same and different, between "yes" and "no"? Plato offers his response in the conviction which the *Apology* portrays through its dramatic irony: that Socrates's way of living and dying embodies the human excellence of integrity which allows human existence to hold together through questioning and seeking understanding, its origin in mystery with its destiny in time, in an integrity that carries with it its own truth warrant. Socrates's existence, in its specific temporal structure, i.e., in its way of happening as a humanly meaningful event, is the ironic answer to his own question—what is *aretē?* In terms of the Greek mytho-poetic hero tradition in which Plato sees Socrates as standing, that answer articulates itself in the *Apology* as the need for: 1) the *piety of belief* in the meaningfulness, as opposed to absurd indifference, of human existence in the midst of divine mystery; 2) the *wisdom of admitting one's ignorance* of how that meaning can or will play itself out historically amid the difference of open possibility; 3) *the courage to risk open involvement in the examined life;* and finally 4) the *commitment in justice* to treat all one's fellow citizens as well as one treats oneself by calling them too into the being-in-question which is self-knowledge. This is the rule of life that Socrates follows, the discipline which empowers and regulates his way of living, and which warrants its truth claims. This is the discipline of dialogue, of being in question together through which the virtuality of living language works out its possibilities in the speculative play of history.

Gadamer himself individually reenacts this Socratic discipline of dialogue in the development of his hermeneutic philosophy, and it is precisely this identification with the care of the soul carried out in and as philosophical conversation that gives Gadamer's thought as a whole its own proper character and identity. That is to say, Gadamer's thought is dialogical, in the ironic, double sense that is characteristic of the drama of all authentically human experience: it plays out the tension of something happening—the outcome of which is in question, specifically with regard to its meaning. The dramatic irony of Gadamer's thought is rooted in the experience of his effort to understand what a person of the twentieth century, deeply grounded both in the richness of its tradition and in the crisis of its contemporary need to renew its sense of meaning through both criticism and commitment, can possibly have to say in adequate response to what he hears when he listens attentively through a lifetime to a variety of voices that speak to him of the questions we all share, in ways that are widely diverse and genuinely incommensurable in their range of emphases and styles of philosophical imagination.[5]

In particular, the irony of Gadamer's thought becomes apparent when we recognize in it the drama of a theory of interpretation that presents itself as an ontology of language centered in dialogue, which in fact works itself out precisely by conducting and mediating a four-cornered conversation about the question of the Good with Plato, Aristotle, Hegel, and Heidegger as the primary interlocutors amid a chorus of secondary voices, and resolutely maintains itself at the highest level of tension among them by listening openly and attentively to what each has and does not have to say about one of the ways the mysterious "Good," which always hides itself, shows itself as the question of truth. The central theoretical concepts of Gadamer's ontology can be understood and can make their truth claim only when we become reflectively aware of the hermeneutic logic that governs the speculative unfolding of their meaning through the transformative recovery of Hegelian dialectical method as the interpretive practice of the Socratic discipline of dialogue. Through this discipline, Gadamer takes the shared subject matter *(Sache)* of this four-cornered conversation and applies it to himself by coming to understand and respond to the question of truth differently than each of his interlocutors, yet in a way in which each of them genuinely participates. Concretely, what this means is that Gadamer's hermeneutics can be understood only when we see how in them he is following both Heidegger and Hegel, and is able to do so precisely by employing elements of the analytic, cautious, and conceptually precise formulations with which Aristotle retrieved the Platonic figure of Socrates from its originally existential, dramatic, ironic, and metaphorical context in the Dialogues and reimagined it theoretically as the manifold metaphysical, epistemological, cosmological, and ethical dynamics of *ousia.*

For example, the role of Heidegger's recovery of Aristotelian *phronēsis* in Gadamer cannot be properly understood except by seeing how Gadamer finds an ontologically and theoretically viable way of articulating its structure by rethinking from out of *die Mitte der Sprache* the dynamic interplay of speculation, dialectic, and logic which Hegel presents as the historical process of Spirit's self-appropriation. Yet it is not correct to say that in taking this step Gadamer abdicates his Heideggerian commitment to the historicality, finitude, and epochal play of both truth and understanding and takes refuge with Hegel in a flight from the "scandal of the *Ereignis.*"[6] Rather, as Gadamer himself has said, in working out the dynamics of his ontology of language, he is following the movement of the *Kehre* in Heidegger's thought. Quite precisely, the notion of *die Virtualität des Sprechens* marks the *Wirkungsgeschichte* in Gadamer's thought of Heidegger's thinking of *das Ereignis,* but the articulation of the event-structure of *Virtualität* Gadamer takes from Hegel and transforms it into what he identifies as the "logical priority of the question." Is this mere eclecticism on Gadamer's part, a mendicant's journey through the history of philosophy? Or rather, is there an integrity to Gadamer's Heideggerian retrieval of Aristotelian *phronēsis* in the notion of *Anwendung,* the logic of which is inspired by Hegel, that is large enough to encompass all three of these irascible giants, and the Plato of the theory of Ideas as well? I believe there is, and we recognize in that integrity the figure of Socrates standing behind Gadamer at the center of this four-cornered hermeneutic circle. Gadamer's ontology of language, in the diversity of its philosophical commitments, is centered and held together by the effective power that the discipline of dialogue affords it. In this way, Hegelian Absolute Spirit once again becomes the "soul" that requires Socratic care.

The virtuality of language becomes effective in dialogue through the claim which the universal and fundamental questions of human experience make on understanding. These questions are the subject matter of philosophical dialogue and are effective in two senses: they are the trace-mark in experience of the dynamics of finite transcendence;[7] and, in turn, they lay claim to human experience and require of it a response of understanding. This effective claim establishes in the experience of understanding the logical priority and openness of the ontological question(s) (One and Many) to every human response to it. Consequently, Gadamer can say that there is more truth in the question than in any "answer" to it, because "truth" here signifies the binding power of language to create relation through the question which holds what is said in every "relevant," that is, appropriate response together with what remains appropriate but unsaid in that historical, personal situation, and integrates both elements into a virtual yet historically effective whole of meaning. This "holding-together" is the "coherence" which is one characteristic of truth.

The hermeneutic logic of question and response is experienced as a discipline of dialogical thought which warrants understanding's judgments of truth in response to the prior claims of the question upon it. Adherence to this discipline is the "correspondence" which is another characteristic of truth, here interpreted hermeneutically rather than metaphysically. The logical structure of this discipline of dialogue is the play of language which works itself out as the to-and-fro, yes-and-no dynamics of listening and responding together in conversation to the shared ontological question which initiates truth. On this view, truth is the effective work which occurs in understanding when the power of language plays itself out creating the human relation to the world as a virtual whole of meaning through the discipline of dialogue. Its dynamics of listening and responding are reflected in the tension that characterizes all understanding between openness and commitment, authority and criticism, tradition and revolution, community and individual, mystery and knowledge. It centers itself in the human person and is the center of human integrity. As such, the discipline of dialogue is the universal warrant of the claims of truth upon and among us.

III.

Gadamer's philosophical hermeneutics as a whole is properly understood as metaphorical, because metaphor is the way that language works. That is to say, metaphor is the way language plays out its power to effect meaning by creating relation out of the tension of sameness and difference that characterizes all human experience as being-in-question. This metaphoric quality of Gadamer's thought has two distinct aspects. First, the notion of *die Virtualität des Sprechens,* which identifies the theoretical center of his ontology of language, is the proper name which Gadamer gives to the universal function of metaphor in language, namely, to hold together in creative tension within the dynamics of experience the complementary elements of the known and unknown, the familiar and the mysterious, the sounding and the silent, in such a way as to open up new possibilities of meaning and understanding. Second, Gadamer's ontology of language as a whole is itself a properly philosophical metaphor which, in the dramatic irony of its hermeneutic situation, allows the figure of Socrates to come into presence and maintain itself as the "root," the effective center, of his thought. In other words, Gadamer's ontology of language is a reflective, conceptual metaphor, expressing itself most fully in the concept of the "discipline of dialogue" as the universal warrant of truth, through which we come to understand more fully the meaning of Socratic existence by allowing the question that initiates its movement (what is *aretē?*) to play attentively, imaginatively, and responsively throughout our understanding of the tradition of Western thinking regarding the meaning of truth. An appreciation of the metaphoric character of Gadamer's thought becomes possible when we recognize that these two, hermeneutic theory together with the practice upon which it reflects, on the one hand, and the experiential figure of Socratic existence on the other, are, in fact, one. This is what Gadamer's claim for the universality of hermeneutic understanding finally means: philosophy *is* hermeneutics, because Gadamer's hermeneutics is a metaphor which speaks truthfully about the meaning of philosophy as a human endeavor which is rooted in Socratic existence. A corollary of this claim for hermeneutic universality, which again makes clear the precise sense in which we must understand Gadamer's hermeneutics as "Platonic" in character, is that the figure of Socrates is the root metaphor of every truthful philosophical theory, both in what it shares and in the significant ways in which it genuinely differs with all other truthful theories with which it can always come into dialogue. All that Gadamer has to say in response to Heidegger, Hegel, Aristotle, and Plato on the level of reflection and theory is rooted in the experience of Socratic existence as human being-in-question, which is the one ontological bond which all philosophers share and which warrants the truth of the metaphorically diverse, individual, historical expressions of that experiential bond in which they all necessarily participate differently.

This much, I believe, Gadamer's work makes clear to us, even if he, for a variety of reasons, does not choose to profile himself explicitly in this way.[8] But no attempt to understand the significance of Gadamer's achievement would be even relatively complete until we have asked what remains unsaid, and therefore in need of uprooting, if we are, in some sense, to understand that achievement for ourselves beyond the limits of his own self-expression. We know from him that to understand his hermeneutics, both in theory and in practice, will be to understand it differently. So we now ask, what is the root of this difference? What is rooted in Socratic existence that allows Plato to understand the truth of the same universal and fundamental human questions differently than Socrates and still be true to the living spirit of Socratic existence? Moreover, what allows Aristotle to differ meaningfully and truthfully with Plato, and Hegel with Aristotle, and Heidegger with Hegel, and Gadamer with all four? What is the root of the difference in truth that allows its metaphorical expressions to be many and one together? Is it not what we call "freedom," in response to the question which our experience of the power of language, not as "binding and claiming" but as cutting and judging (*krinein*), provokes in us?

To suggest that Gadamer somehow ignores or underestimates the ontological weight of the question of freedom would, of course, be to fly in the face of his repeated elaboration of thematics directly related to freedom throughout his work and, especially and explicitly, in his later reflections on Hegel. Nevertheless, the question of freedom is not emphasized in Gadamer's thought in the same way that the question of truth is, and this difference of emphasis, itself a trace-mark in historically effected consciousness of the question of freedom, makes a difference. Gadamer characterizes hermeneutics as a movement in dialogue toward agreement, even if this agreement is always primarily regarding the questions that we all must ask, a being-together-in-question. He does not explore the dynamics of difference with the same detailed, lingering attention with which he explores the dynamics of dialogue in pursuit of shared understanding. Similarly, by emphasizing dialogue and living conversation as the paradigm of how language works, he deemphasizes the difference between the interpretive possibilities for understanding that arise when such conversation is carried out through writing and reading, as distinct from the type of conversation that occurs face to face.[9] Granted, both are, or at least can be, genuine instances of "living language" working itself out in the free play of question and answer, but need we not ask about the significant degrees of hermeneutic difference that occur in types of philosophical writing and reading, for example, where the emphasis is explicitly on a deconstructive as opposed to a constructive movement of interpretation, that is, where the emphasis is on the differing rather than on the continuity in the tension-filled relation between what is said and what goes unsaid?

If the discipline of dialogue warrants truth universally, then we shall wish to ask Gadamer how one goes about thinking what in human experience, presumably in the paradigmatic case of Socratic existence, bestows freedom by allowing difference. How shall we speak about freedom? What metaphors are appropriate to freedom's parlance, and how does it set itself to work and play itself out in language? How shall we discuss the way in which Socratic dialogue is related to the silence out of which it arises and to which it returns when enjoined by its *daimōn* not to speak in such and such a way, at such and such a time and place, to such and such a one? What makes the difference? Or better, how does the differing occur? Will an ontology of language, whatever form it takes, allow us adequately to respond to these sorts of questions? I think not, or rather, not until it becomes clearer how language is rooted ontologically in human personal existence.[10] Needless to say, we have to do here, not with another version of grounding a metaphysical foundationalism, but with the question of how to think and speak about the nature of language as metaphoric. By way of conclusion, I offer the following suggestion based on what Gadamer has said, but attempting to go beyond it for myself as well.

The question of freedom is the unsaid in Gadamer's theory of the ontology of language, insofar as it is a reflection of the effective presence at the living center of his thought of the figure of Socrates. I suggest that we think of Socratic existence, the philosophical paradigm of human personal existence in the fullness of its possible integrity, as the root metaphor not only of Gadamer's hermeneutics, but of every possible philosophical theory insofar as it has to make a truth claim upon us. The question for us then becomes how to think and speak philosophically about how the question of truth and the question of freedom

belong together ontologically in the human person as both the origin and the
fulfillment of the universal possibilities for integrity of meaning that are the
virtual reality of human life. The interpretation of Gadamer's thought offered
here would suggest that his philosophical hermeneutics is itself still under way
toward what might be imagined as a way of understanding the meanings that
can and do occur historically in experience as a universally differentiated
metaphorics of human persons, in whom are rooted the questions that give rise
to and structure the finite transcendence of integrity, a wholeness of meaning
amid the interplay of sameness and difference. Whether in science, art, history,
ethical or political praxis, or religion, whenever truth occurs in the experience of
understanding, its occurrence happens as the growth of truthful metaphors in
which our freedom allows us to participate creatively.

FRANCIS J. AMBROSIO

DEPARTMENT OF PHILOSOPHY
GEORGETOWN UNIVERSITY
JUNE 1992

NOTES

1. *"Religio"* has as its etymological source the notion of human existence being
bound back to the power of divine transcendent mystery as the origin of, not merely its
metaphysical existence, but of the meaningfulness of that existence. The fundamental
religious question is, therefore, the question of the meaningfulness or absurdity of human
existence in relation to that which surrounds and transcends it; only secondarily does it
pose the question of the existence or nature of God, and then only insofar as God is experienced fundamentally as mystery. For the simultaneity of the tragic and comedic elements of the soul's religious experience, see *Symposium,* 223d.

2. This is comparable to the point Heidegger makes with regard to Being: *Dasein*
has its need of Being only in relation to Being's need of *Dasein.* It is precisely this relation of mutual, original co-determination which defines the level of ontological questions
and to which Gadamer refers as *Zugehörigkeit.* Needless to say, such a *relationism* as an
ontological position poses a radical challenge to every metaphysical conception of God as
Absolute Being, though interestingly, it is more congruent with the Christian doctrine of
Incarnation and Redemption and with its conception of a divine freedom which allows
itself to genuinely "suffer" its relation to human freedom.

3. *"Sprachlichkeit"* means the original linguisticality of all human experience,
conscious and unconscious (cf. Lacan), precisely in the sense of "living language," which
permeates every level of experience as a continuum oriented toward "coming-to-be-
meaningful."

4. See *Symposium,* 202a–204b.

5. In what follows, I am summarizing in the most schematic sort of way, the substance of several detailed studies of Gadamer's relationship of similarity amid difference
to Heidegger, Hegel, Aristotle, and Plato. The reader is referred to those studies, cited

below, for a presentation of the evidence and arguments that support the conclusions stated here: "Dawn and Dusk: Gadamer and Heidegger on Truth," *Man and World*, 19 (1986): 21–53; "Gadamer: On Making Oneself at Home with Hegel," *Owl of Minerva*, 19 (Fall 1987): 23–40; "Gadamer, Plato, and the Discipline of Dialogue," *International Philosophical Quarterly*, 27 (March 1987): 17–32.

6. This is in fact what John Caputo does say in *Radical Hermeneutics* (1989), marring what is in many other ways an exceptionally valuable work.

7. This is, I believe, the genuine meaning of what Gadamer refers to as *wirkungsgeschichtliche Bewusstein,* which he says should be understood in the sense of *"mehr Seins als Bewusst."*

8. Principal among these reasons, I believe, is the concern which Professor Gadamer once voiced to me in conversation that any attempt to place human existence at the center of philosophical thought as its primary Sache runs the unwarranted risk of slipping back into the kind of metaphysical subjectivism, which Husserl, Heidegger, and Gadamer struggled against for so long. Whether the contemporary historical situation of philosophy has sufficiently absorbed the validity of their critique to make a return to the human person as the center of all mystery and meaning possible is debatable, but obviously that is the venture to which the line of thought presented here is committed.

9. This difference of emphasis is obviously one of the most critical commitments at issue between Gadamer and Derrida. Whether we take it as fundamental will be determined not simply by the way we evaluate Derrida's way of thinking in contrast to Gadamer's, but more basically by the way we understand the relation of both to Heidegger, and all three in regard to the relationship between the questions of truth and freedom.

10. This is not to suggest, of course, that a view of language centered primarily in its deconstructive dynamics would present any less one-sided a profile. Rather, the tension between the deconstructive and constructive dynamics of language in the emergence and concealment of meaning is itself a function of the tension which originally characterizes the question of the meaning of the relation of truth and freedom in human existence.

REPLY TO FRANCIS J. AMBROSIO

Ambrosio's contribution reveals to me in what way he on the whole integrated the philosophical claim of hermeneutical works. By and large I want to regard this as a correct appropriation. It is correct that language has its true reality only in dialogue. This is the guiding viewpoint of all of my studies on hermeneutics. This also holds for my studies on Greek philosophy with which I seek to freshen up and enrich my conceptuality. Thus, I can accept the idea that Mr. Ambrosio has Socrates as a constant point of reference. The approachment between Plato and Aristotle on which I insist also basically refers to their common heritage from Socrates. I sought to make this convincing in volume seven of my works under the title *Plato in Dialogue*. In this context we are not only concerned with the figure of Socrates which we have before our eyes thanks to the masterly hand of Plato, but with the fact that our Greek origin perpetuates itself in all our Western work of thought.

"Philosophy" is the primacy of the question. Ambrosio has stressed this correctly.

But I am missing the name of Kant here whose *Critique of Judgment* plays a decisive role in my work. It is precisely here that I want to contradict Ambrosio when he misses the concept of freedom in my works. I do not want to dispense with Kant and his concept of freedom. However, one cannot say this word in Greek. But if we declare ourselves for the spiritual tradition of Europe, then it is without doubt the fact of reason of freedom which preserves metaphysics since Kant. I see in this Kant's inner connection with Fichte and Hegel, and it is always, among other things, present in my attempt to seek a dialogue with the broad spectrum of the classical authors of philosophy. I want to use this opportunity to add how much I learned from Gerhard Krüger's early book on Kant. Kant's example taught me what the Socratic wisdom basically was: to leave questions open and to keep them open. That is not skepticism but originates from the spiritual need for freedom.

H.-G.G.

13

David Detmer

GADAMER'S CRITIQUE OF THE ENLIGHTENMENT

Hans-Georg Gadamer's critique of the Enlightenment is central to his philoso-phizing, and in particular to his conception of philosophical hermeneutics. For in radical contrast to the Enlightenment, the defining characteristic of which he identifies as a "prejudice against prejudice itself," Gadamer insists that "all understanding inevitably involves some prejudice," and further remarks that this recognition "gives the hermeneutical problem its real thrust."[1]

The importance of Gadamer's critique of the Enlightenment is further revealed in the ever-growing acceptance, since the publication of his influential *Truth and Method* in 1960, of Gadamer's once radical anti-Enlightenment views. Indeed, anti-Enlightenment opinion is currently so pervasive as to embolden one commentator to claim recently that "the failure of the Enlightenment project is by now simply a fact," and to list Gadamer as one of the principal contributors to the "vast arsenal" of fully persuasive anti-Enlightenment arguments that have been "stockpiled" since the early 1960s.[2]

I wish here to examine some of the issues raised by Gadamer's critique of the Enlightenment. I want to determine whether, or to what extent, some of the leading ideas of the Enlightenment can be defended in the face of Gadamer's criticisms. In particular, I will suggest that, since Gadamer's critique takes place almost entirely on the ontological level, it does not seriously undermine the soundness of the Enlightenment's concrete recommendations, on the practical level, for changes in our social, political, intellectual, methodological, and scien-tific conduct.

THE ENLIGHTENMENT

Let us begin with a brief characterization of "the Enlightenment." The term refers to a period in European cultural and intellectual history, and to a cluster of ideas, shared in common by a number of the leading thinkers of the time, that have come to be associated with that period. The period in question is that extending roughly from the early seventeenth to the early nineteenth century, reaching its peak in the eighteenth century, and achieving its greatest prominence in England, France, and Germany.

A clear statement of many of the Enlightenment's central ideas can be found in Kant's 1784 essay, "What is Enlightenment?" There he defines enlightenment as "man's release from his self-incurred tutelage," and declares "Have courage to use your own reason!" to be its motto. Kant further explains that

> laziness and cowardice are the reasons why so great a portion of mankind, after nature has long since discharged them from external direction, nevertheless remains under lifelong tutelage. . . . It is so easy not to be of age. If I have a book which understands for me, a pastor who has a conscience for me, a physician who decides my diet, and so forth, I need not trouble myself. I need not think, if I can only pay— others will readily undertake the irksome work for me.[3]

But the widespread fear that the independent use of one's own reason is "very dangerous" as well as "arduous" is not the only explanation for the prevalence of intellectual conformity, timidity, and servitude. There is also the greed and self-aggrandizement of those opportunists who would take advantage of these groundless fears to "set themselves up as . . . guardians." As Kant rather sarcastically puts it,

> after the guardians have first made their domestic cattle dumb and have made sure that these placid creatures will not dare take a single step without the harness of the cart by which they are confined, the guardians then show them the danger which threatens if they try to go alone. Actually, however, this danger is not so great, for by falling a few times they would finally learn to walk alone. But an example of this failure makes them timid and ordinarily frightens them away from all further trials.[4]

In the light of these remarks of Kant's, and bearing in mind that I am giving special emphasis to those points which are most relevant to Gadamer's critique, I would list the following claims as representing a summary of leading Enlightenment ideas.

(1) Human reason is naturally distributed fairly equally among human beings, and, once it has been adequately educated, is a competent instrument with which to seek an accurate and truthful understanding of all matters of human concern.

(2) The principal cause of intellectual error is not intellectual incompetence or stupidity, but rather the failure to make independent use of one's reason. Such failure is usually manifested in an uncritical overreliance on tradition, authority, and custom.

(3) Even when one does resolve to make independent use of one's reason, genuine understanding can begin only when all prejudices have been cleared away from one's approach to the phenomenon to be understood. What is required is a direct confrontation between one's reason and the object of investigation, unmediated by preconceptions, most of which arise from tra-

dition, authority, and custom. Thus, even when one's reliance on tradition, authority, and custom is not so great as to preclude independent thought, it often gets in the way of *sound* independent thought by placing prejudices and superstitions in the path of one's access to the object of thought.

(4) Since tradition, authority, and custom, and the prejudices which they generate, are the principal obstacles both to the willingness to undertake the effort to think at all and, once this effort has been undertaken, to the ability to think well, it is necessary to devise and make use of methods and principles by which these sources of bias and error can be controlled and overcome. The principles of logic and the methods of the sciences serve as the best examples of means by which such limitations of our particularity can be overcome, and through which an objective, neutral, universal standpoint, or at least a standpoint which is broadly cosmopolitan, and not narrowly parochial, can be achieved.

(5) In addition to making use of the best principles of thought and methods of inquiry known to us, we should develop the habit of regularly subjecting our own beliefs, as well as those of others, to rational criticism, and learn to reject those beliefs which fail to stand up to such criticism, while retaining only those beliefs which can. In this way, the ratio in our thinking of rational, well-grounded beliefs to unfounded prejudices and outright falsehoods should steadily increase.

(6) Such critical methods, principles, and habits of thought should not be confined solely to the logical and scientific spheres, but should be employed in all of our thinking. Indeed, they are perhaps most urgently needed in the social, moral, and political spheres, since it is in these areas that the uncritical reliance on authority and the unchecked dominance of prejudice is most likely to lead to needless misery. Here Kant's explanation of the manner in which the fear of independent thought opens the door for unscrupulous politicians to wield their nefarious influence should be recalled. Moreover, once these politicians are in place, the same intellectual quietude which had initially launched them goes on to stand as an obstacle to their opposition, no matter how nonsensical their ideas or malicious their programs. For the main cause of the acceptance of inhumane political practices is neither a natural human intellectual incompetence nor a natural human cruelty, neither of which exists. Rather, the cause is generally either a refusal to make independent use of one's reason, and thus a refusal to question the authorities, simply because they *are* authorities, from whom the inhumane practices issue, or it is the undue influence of a malicious prejudice which blocks the achieving of an accurate understanding of the nature of these practices. Where these causes are operating efficiently, the fear of reprisals is usually adequate to keep to manageable limits dissent from those few who have achieved sufficient intellectual independence to question these practices.

(7) In short, on the Enlightenment view, the great majority of human beings have
    the natural capacity and predisposition to be rational, decent, and free, and
    will emerge as such given an adequate education and tolerable political con-
    ditions, and provided that the corrupting influences of tradition, authority, and
    custom are kept tolerably at bay. Moreover, even when these conditions are
    quite imperfectly met, and thus when reason is only somewhat independent,
    reason is the emancipating force which is most suited to bringing about a bet-
    ter meeting of these educational, social, political, and intellectual conditions,
    and thus to achieving an expanding scope and competence for itself, which in
    turn increases its ability to bring about better conditions, which in turn brings
    about its own improvement, etc. This is the positive dialectic of the Enlighten-
    ment: reason makes us freer and more decent, and this increased freedom and
    decency in turn makes us more rational. Such is the Enlightenment concep-
    tion of progress.

GADAMER'S CRITIQUE

The discrediting of authority, tradition, and custom, and the attempt to displace
them in favor of pure, ahistorical, unprejudiced reason, is, for Gadamer, not only
the essence of the Enlightenment, but also

> the point at which the attempt to critique historical hermeneutics has to start. The
> overcoming of all prejudices, this global demand of the Enlightenment, will itself
> prove to be a prejudice, and removing it opens the way to an appropriate understand-
> ing of the finitude which dominates not only our humanity but also our historical
> consciousness.
>
> Does being situated within traditions really mean being subject to prejudices
> and limited in one's freedom? Is not, rather, all human existence, even the freest,
> limited and qualified in various ways? If this is true, the idea of an absolute reason is
> not a possibility for historical humanity. Reason exists for us only in concrete, his-
> torical terms—i.e., it is not its own master but remains constantly dependent on the
> given circumstances in which it operates.[5]

Or again, in perhaps his clearest and most comprehensive summary of his
anti-Enlightenment position, Gadamer writes:

> It is not so much our judgments as it is our prejudices that constitute our being. This
> is a provocative formulation, for I am using it to restore to its rightful place a posi-
> tive concept of prejudice that was driven out of our linguistic usage by the French
> and English Enlightenment. It can be shown that the concept of prejudice did not
> originally have the meaning we have attached to it. Prejudices are not necessarily
> unjustified and erroneous, so that they inevitably distort the truth. In fact, the his-
> toricity of our existence entails that prejudices, in the literal sense of the word, con-
> stitute the initial directedness of our whole ability to experience. Prejudices are
> biases of our openness to the world. They are simply conditions whereby we experi-

ence something—whereby what we encounter says something to us. This formulation certainly does not mean that we are enclosed within a wall of prejudices and only let through the narrow portals those things that can produce a pass saying, "Nothing new will be said here." Instead we welcome just that guest who promises something new to our curiosity. But how do we know the guest whom we admit is one who has something *new* to say to us? Is not our expectation and our readiness to hear the new also necessarily determined by the old that has already taken possession of us?[6]

In this brief passage, Gadamer encapsulates many of his specific anti-Enlightenment arguments, which can be conveniently classified, admittedly somewhat arbitrarily, under two main, mutually reinforcing headings.

(1) One of Gadamer's strategies might be described as a presentation of a phenomenology of understanding. That is, Gadamer gives us a richly detailed description of the process of coming to understand something, points out the indispensable role of prejudices in this process, and simply invites his readers to consult their own experiences to test the accuracy of his account. Gadamer has no doubt about the outcome of such a test, remarking, prior to the launching of his discussion, that "the description as such will be obvious to every interpreter who knows what he is about."[7] Gadamer suggests that when we attend carefully to what goes on in the process of undertaking to understand something, we find that we never approach the phenomenon in question with a blank slate. Rather, we always begin with preconceptions or prejudices—preliminary expectations of what the phenomenon in question is likely to mean. While some of these expectations are, perhaps, borne out in our examination of the object before us, others typically are not, and we must consequently revise some of our expectations, or replace them with others. We are then in a position to return to the phenomenon, and the process continues indefinitely, or until we are satisfied that a true understanding has been reached. It is only through this dialectical back-and-forth process of now consulting the phenomenon in the light of our prejudices, and now revising our prejudices in the light of the phenomenon, that genuine understanding can ever emerge.[8]

Thus, to use a phrase which, to my knowledge, Gadamer himself does not use, prejudices are *necessary* conditions of all instances of genuine understanding, without, however, being ever *sufficient* fully to determine the outcome of any instance of real understanding. Because prejudices are necessary to all understanding, the Enlightenment project of achieving unprejudiced understanding is impossible. But because prejudices are not sufficient to determine the outcome of inquiry—they need not preclude genuine understanding of the phenomenon in question, since they are revisable in the light of what is revealed through contact with the phenomenon—the Enlightenment fear that prejudices would block genuine understanding by

merely sustaining and reproducing themselves while obscuring the phenomenon in question is groundless, or, more accurately, overstated.

(2) Gadamer's other main strategy is to advance arguments based upon appeals
to our ontological finitude. For example, in opposition to the Enlightenment's
attempted wholesale repudiation of all prejudices, Gadamer points out that all
criticism of prejudices must proceed from some point of view, which, necessarily, is not itself at the same time subject to critical examination. Thus, it is
impossible to criticize all prejudices at once.[9] Rather, we can question some
prejudices only from the standpoint, at least provisionally, of accepting others. We have no way of jerking ourselves free from all historical and cultural
conditioning, so as to arrive at a perfectly neutral standpoint from which to
subject all of our prejudices to a purely rational critique.

Another way of putting Gadamer's point is to say that it is impossible for
us to overcome our ontological condition of what Heidegger calls "being
thrown."[10] We are always already situated in a world before we can begin to
undertake critical thought. Reason is not something that can ever exist independently of history, and of specific customs and traditions; rather, it is
always conditioned by them, even when it is most critical of them. As
Gadamer puts it,

> In fact history does not belong to us; we belong to it. Long before we understand
> ourselves through the process of self-examination, we understand ourselves in a self-
> evident way in the family, society, and state in which we live. . . . *That is why the
> prejudices of the individual, far more than his judgments, constitute the historical
> reality of his being.*[11]

CRITICAL DISCUSSION

It should be pointed out, first of all, that Gadamer's hermeneutical account of
understanding, despite the anti-Enlightenment rhetoric in which it is formulated,
is in many respects sympathetic to Enlightenment concerns, and decidedly more
hostile towards the many radically anti-Enlightenment forms of relativism which
are currently popular in some quarters. For example, notwithstanding his disagreement with the Enlightenment's attempted wholesale rejection of prejudices,
Gadamer fully agrees with the Enlightenment that prejudices are often a source
of distortion and error, that our understanding of an object should be guided by
our encounter with that object, and that our prejudices are shown to be erroneous
and in need of rejection or revision precisely when they fail to be confirmed
through our encounter with the object. As Gadamer puts it,

> every experience is a confrontation. Because every experience sets something new
> against something old and in every case it remains open in principle whether the new
> will prevail . . . or whether the old, accustomed, predictable will be confirmed in the
> end.[12]

Thus, while Gadamer rejects the objectivism of the Enlightenment, in that he denies that it is possible to approach any object purely as it is, from an unprejudiced, unconditioned, utterly neutral standpoint, it is clear that he opposes those forms of relativism which would draw from this such conclusions as (1) that we might as well simply affirm uncritically as true all of the traditional prejudices of our culture; (2) that we are "trapped" within our own cultural framework, so that we are never in a position to test our culturally conditioned ideas about a thing by seeing whether or not they are borne out by an examination of the thing, or at least that no such examination need ever motivate us to give up or modify our initial ideas; or (3) that such motivation can only be provided by our culture itself, such as by conversation with others within it, on a rhetorical, "consensus and persuasion," model of critical discourse, as opposed to by independently testing our ideas through direct examination of the object of our investigation.[13]

Gadamer's rejection of these forms of relativism, his partial affinity with Enlightenment concerns, and the enhanced subtlety and sophistication of his own views in comparison with both, can all be brought out by considering the following five issues.

(1) The Issue of Perspective. Though Gadamer disagrees with the Enlightenment view that we can (simply) have an unprejudiced, unconditioned, unperspectival approach to an object, this does not entail for him, as it does for some relativists, that we (equally simply) only see our prejudices, conditions, and perspectives, and not the object. To the contrary, we do see the object, albeit from a prejudiced and conditioned standpoint, and from a particular perspective.

(2) The Issue of Openness. Against the Enlightenment view that we can approach the new without prejudice, and thus be completely open to it, Gadamer insists that we are always prejudiced, and thus somewhat predisposed to reject the new. But Gadamer rejects the equally simplified view of those relativists who see our cultural predicament as hermetically sealing us off from an understanding and acceptance of whatever is alien to us. Rather, Gadamer contends that our prejudices are at least somewhat open. They are not totally deterministic, since they always leave open the possibility that our encounter with the thing under investigation will surprise us and motivate us to modify our prejudices. And whenever we do reach out to otherness, our prejudices constitute the standpoint and springboard from which we do so.

(3) The Issue of the Relationship between Reason and Tradition. While Gadamer rejects the Enlightenment conception of tradition as something wholly separable from and other than reason, he is not utterly hostile to the Enlightenment's insistence on the value and importance of reason. Thus, instead of denigrating reason in favor of tradition, Gadamer denies their mutual opposition, underscoring instead their mutual dependence and dialectical unity.

For while Gadamer does contend that reason is always situated in and conditioned by tradition, he also insists, with the Enlightenment, that tradition is always, and should be, subject to modification and revision as a result of its critical examination by reason.

(4) The Issue of Cultural Change and Cultural Stability. Since we cannot challenge all of our prejudices at once, or from an unprejudiced standpoint, as the Enlightenment would have it, it is not possible, on Gadamer's view, for a tradition or a culture to be suddenly scrapped and replaced with another. In this way Gadamer is able to explain the evident fact that cultures change sufficiently gradually as to remain recognizably the same over time. And yet, they do consistently change, and not just, as some relativists would have it, in response to conversations internal to the existing cultural framework, but also as a result of confrontations with that which is alien to that framework.

(5) The Issue of Other Cultures. While the Enlightenment is hostile to the idea of culture as a category, since it favors transcending the particularity inherent in existing cultures through the use of universal, transcultural reason, some forms of relativism go to the opposite extreme in absolutizing the category of culture, and proclaiming genuine cross-cultural communication an impossibility. On such a conception, all such "truths" as we are legitimately able to affirm must be understood as applying only within our own culture, and as not really making contact with, let alone standing in real opposition to, the seemingly contrary "truths" of other cultures.

Once again Gadamer takes a middle path. In opposition to the Enlightenment, he insists that our approach to other cultures cannot help but be launched from the standpoint of the prejudices of our own cultural tradition. And yet, from what has already been said about a culture's openness and capacity for change, it must be obvious that Gadamer also rejects this form of relativism. Indeed, with his concept of the "fusion of horizons," and in his discussion of "transposing ourselves" into another's position, Gadamer's sympathies appear to be very close to those of the Enlightenment:

> Transposing ourselves . . . always involves rising to a higher universality that overcomes not only our own particularity but also that of the other. . . . [O]ne learns to look beyond what is close at hand—not in order to look away from it but to see it better, within a larger whole and in truer proportion. . . . In the process of understanding, a real fusing of horizons occurs.[14]

The idea that Gadamer's project might in many respects be reconcilable with the concerns of the Enlightenment is lent further plausibility by the realization that Gadamer's critique of the Enlightenment takes place almost exclusively at the ontological level, rather than at the level of practical recommendations for changes in our conduct. Thus, even if Gadamer is entirely justified in all of his ontological criticisms of the Enlightenment, it is not clear that this would entail even the slightest criticism of Enlightenment ideas in the practical realm. That is, Gadamer's critique seems not so much to say that we should conduct ourselves in such a way as to violate Enlightenment precepts as to say that, even if we do conduct ourselves in accordance with them, we should *understand it differently*, that is, in hermeneutical terms, rather than in the manner supported by the Enlightenment thinkers.

In making this point it is necessary to distinguish the practical message of the Enlightenment (e.g., "educate yourself; learn the principles of logic and of the scientific method; make use of them in your own thinking; think for yourself; do not trust authorities, customs, and traditions, but subject them instead to a rational critique;" etc.) from its ontological understanding of those aspects of the human condition which allegedly make such conduct possible (e.g., that we have access to a realm of universal, ahistorical, transcultural reason; that through the use of this reason we can wrench ourselves free from the limitations imposed by the particularities of our cultural and historical standpoint and conditioning; that in so disentangling ourselves and using our reason we can come to an understanding of things as they really are, etc.). Now it seems to me that Gadamer reserves all of his critical fire for the latter, ontological, aspect of the Enlightenment project, leaving its practical message virtually untouched. For Gadamer's anti-Enlightenment ontological claims—that all thinking is historically and culturally conditioned; that we can never find a neutral standpoint from which to subject all of our prejudices to critical scrutiny simultaneously; that criticism of any one set of prejudices can only proceed from the standpoint of other prejudices which, for the moment at least, are simply taken for granted; etc.—apply on the practical level equally to the reformer and to the cultural conservative. It simply does not follow from Gadamer's anti-Enlightenment ontological claims that we must all cease to subject our culture and its traditions to criticism, and instead accept them uncritically or become their fervent ideological supporters. What does follow from them is simply that all such criticism, however radical and revolutionary it might be, must be understood as issuing from a standpoint within, or conditioned by, that culture and its history, rather than from an ahistorical, transcultural, utterly neutral and objective standpoint of pure reason. But this seems to leave untouched the question of how we should regard our culture and its traditions—e.g., as the greatest on Earth, as slightly flawed, as seriously defective, as fundamentally rotten, etc. Nor does it dictate whether celebration, passive acceptance, piecemeal criticism and mild activity for change, or radical denunciation and revolutionary agitation are the appropriate attitudes and responses we should undertake in response to our culture. It merely gives an ontological account of the standpoint from which any such attitude must necessarily be assumed, and of the manner in which it should be understood. Thus, while Gadamer's hermeneutical account of understanding might be ontologically conservative in that it denies that it is possible for reason to disentangle itself radically from the cultural and historical context out of which it operates, it does not follow that Gadamer's position entails sociopolitical conservatism—the idea that we cannot or should not engage in vigorous, or even radical, criticism of our culture and its traditions. As Gadamer himself clearly states, "it is a grave mis-understanding to assume that emphasis on the essential factor of tradition which enters into all understanding implies an uncritical acceptance of tradition and sociopolitical conservatism."[15]

Thus, in the light of the distinction, stressed above, between the Enlighten-ment's ontological claims and its practical recommendations, it seems clear that Gadamer's hermeneutical account of understanding, despite the anti-Enlighten-ment language in which it is formulated, lends no real support to what is currently perhaps the most widely used argument against the Enlightenment's normative program. That argument, which might at first appear also to be Gadamer's own, is simply that it is impossible to carry out the Enlightenment's recommended program of independent thinking, of subjecting the prejudices of our culture to reasoned criticism, and of revising and improving our thoughts through direct encounters with their objects, since success in these endeavors is precluded by the inescapable finitude and situatedness of the human condition. Such an argument is serviceable both to sociopolitical conservatives (who stress the radical inescapability of our tradition, and thus call for its acceptance, and for the abandonment of the Enlightenment's call for criticism of it) and to the seemingly anticonservative defenders of "postmodernism" (who welcome cul-tural criticism, but who emphasize both the perspectival nature of all thought and the multiplicity of perspectives, and thus, in opposition to the Enlightenment's quest for "the truth" about things, favor "pluralistic, multivocal and multifaceted critical political discourses.")[16] But the distinction between the Enlightenment's ontological claims and its normative recommendations suggests, as I have argued, that the rejection of the former need not entail the impossibility of carry-ing out the latter. Moreover, as we have seen, Gadamer's hermeneutical account of understanding renders intelligible the idea that these recommendations can indeed be successfully realized even if all thought is inescapably perspectival (as the postmodernists emphasize) and tied to tradition (as the sociopolitical conser-vatives insist).

Thus, Gadamer clears the way for an evaluation of the Enlightenment's practical recommendations on their own (normative rather than ontological) grounds. However, it seems to me that he does not himself address the Enlightenment project directly on normative grounds, operating instead, as I have suggested, entirely on the ontological plane. The one exception I can think of is this. Gadamer sometimes seems to suggest that the Enlighten-ment's great eagerness to criticize tradition and authority betrays, not just a failure to recognize the ontological finitude of human reason, but also an unwarranted prejudice against the past, and an unwillingness to recognize that tradition is not simply a collection of errors, but is rather, at least in part, a great repository of truth and wisdom, of which it would be folly not to take advantage.[17]

My response to this suggestion is that, however accurate it might be as an assessment of the motives of some of the individual Enlightenment thinkers, it cannot count as an objection to the Enlightenment program itself, for the simple reason that criticism of an idea is not the same thing as, and need not entail, rejection of that idea. To say otherwise is to prejudge the outcome of the criticism. Scrupulous, intelligent criticism should make the merits of sound ideas more evident to us, and make us appreciate them more fully, not lead us to reject them. Moreover, it would seem, even on Gadamer's own analysis of understanding, that it is only by such critical probing that a genuine *recovery* of the truth, wisdom, and knowledge embedded in tradition and authority, that is, a meaningful and useful appropriation of them, can be achieved. And even the most ardent cultural conservative surely must admit that traditions tend to include at least *some* foolishness together with their abundant wisdom, and thus that there is also need for "destructive" criticism—the kind leading to rejection. So it is unclear why a belief in the wisdom and truthfulness of (much of) one's own culture and traditions should lead to a repudiation of the Enlightenment's program of vigorous criticism and independent thought.

Finally, since the need for such a program appears even more evident, and increasingly so, the further one moves away from this conservative belief, it is not surprising that most contemporary criticisms of the Enlightenment's practical proposals attempt to demonstrate, not that they are undesirable, on normative grounds, but that they are impossible, on ontological grounds. I have tried to show, however, that it is this kind of criticism of the Enlightenment that Gadamer's hermeneutical account of understanding effectively undermines.

DAVID DETMER

DEPARTMENT OF ENGLISH AND PHILOSOPHY
PURDUE UNIVERSITY—CALUMET
JUNE 1992

NOTES

1. Hans-Georg Gadamer, *Truth and Method,* second revised edition, trans. revised by Joel Weinsheimer and Donald G. Marshall (New York: Crossroad, 1991), p. 270.
2. Tom Bridges, "Modern Political Theory and the Multivocity of Postmodern Critical Discourses." *Inquiry: Critical Thinking Across the Disciplines* 8, no. 1 (September 1991): 3. In addition to Gadamer, Bridges lists Kuhn, Dewey, Wittgenstein, Heidegger, Foucault, Derrida, and Rorty as principal contributors to this arsenal.
3. Immanuel Kant, "What is Enlightenment?", trans. Lewis White Beck, in *Kant Selections,* ed. Lewis White Beck (New York: Macmillan, 1988), p. 462.
4. Ibid.
5. Gadamer, *Truth and Method,* p. 276.

6. Gadamer, "The Universality of the Hermeneutical Problem," in his *Philosophical Hermeneutics*, trans. and ed. David E. Linge (Berkeley: University of California Press, 1976), p. 9.

7. Gadamer, *Truth and Method*, p. 266.

8. See ibid., pp. 266–69.

9. See Gadamer, "Rhetoric, Hermeneutics, and the Critique of Ideology: Metacritical Comments on *Truth and Method*," trans. Jerry Dibble, in Kurt Mueller-Vollmer, ed., *The Hermeneutics Reader* (New York: Continuum, 1985), p. 286.

10. See Joel C. Weinsheimer, *Gadamer's Hermeneutics* (New Haven: Yale University Press, 1985), pp. 10–11.

11. Gadamer, *Truth and Method*, pp. 276–77.

12. Gadamer, "The Problem of Historical Consciousness," in Paul Rabinow and William M. Sullivan, eds., *Interpretive Social Science* (Berkeley: University of California Press, 1979), pp. 108–9.

13. See Richard J. Bernstein's extensive discussion of Gadamer in his *Beyond Objectivism and Relativism* (Philadelphia: University of Pennsylvania Press, 1983). A letter from Gadamer to Bernstein appears as an appendix to this volume.

14. Gadamer, *Truth and Method*, pp. 305, 307.

15. Gadamer, "The Problem of Historical Consciousness," p. 108.

16. Bridges, p. 7.

17. See Gadamer, *Truth and Method*, pp. 279–80.

REPLY TO DAVID DETMER

It is extremely astonishing to me that my project of a philosophical hermeneutics as well as some other such projects are being discussed under the title 'critique of enlightenment' and not with reference to the idealist concept of the 'completed enlightenment' which was coined by Fichte. For what matters to us can only be the question whether a completed enlightenment which would dissolve all human predisposition and societal prejudices is an intelligible claim. The author misses the essence of practical reason through the erroneous assumption that one can appeal to Kant in this matter.

What Kant calls enlightenment in truth corresponds to what hermeneutics has in view. To a large extent, Kant's famous essay to which Detmer refers belongs already to that critique of enlightenment which Rousseau inaugurated and which is directed against the expectation that the progress of the sciences will lead to a moral perfection of humanity. On the other hand, the stubborn clinging to prejudices or even the blind appeal to authority is nothing but the laziness to think. Nobody who thinks for himself will deceive himself about this.

Today, Kant certainly would have to elaborate upon some of the citations which the author quotes: The bureaucratization of societal circumstances, the blind deference to the expert in public life, the general shying away from responsibility so that today, for example, a court assigns the greatest weight and a very significant authority not to the lawyer but to the expert about the matter in dispute. So in general it is true, and here the dialectic of enlightenment is right, that the false development of our scientific-technical civilization is haunted by the blind compliance with rules. Contrary to that, I appeal with Kant to practical reason and the practice of the faculty of judgment. That is what I call hermeneutics as philosophy.

H.-G.G.

14

Robert J. Dostal

GADAMER'S CONTINUOUS CHALLENGE: HEIDEGGER'S PLATO INTERPRETATION

In his writing and in his public lectures Gadamer has often acknowledged his debt to Heidegger.[1] In the preface to *The Idea of the Good in Platonic-Aristotelian Philosophy* we find this debt presented as a "continuous challenge":

> But in the background was the continuous challenge *(beständige Herausforderung)* posed for me by the path Heidegger's own thought took, and especially by his interpretation of Plato as the decisive step toward "metaphysical thought's" obliviousness *(Seinsvergessenheit)* to being *(Sein)*.[2]

He goes on to say that *Truth and Method,* as well as his work on classical philosophy and Hegel, represent his "effort to meet the challenge." In this essay I examine the character of this challenge for Gadamer and the way that Gadamer "meets" it. The question is too large to treat adequately here, but let us look, if only sketchily, at Heidegger's interpretation of Plato in contrast with Gadamer's. We find how Gadamer's reading of Plato follows paths opened, though not followed, by Heidegger. These paths lead us to a Plato quite different from the Platonist of Heidegger's critique.[3]

PART I: THE EARLY HEIDEGGER'S REVIVAL OF ARISTOTLE'S CRITIQUE OF PLATO

We need not here consider the principal tenets of Heidegger's Plato interpretation of which there has been a considerable discussion.[4] Two central aspects of Heidegger's approach to Plato are the following: first, that for Heidegger metaphysics is Platonism; and, secondly, that the task for Heidegger's thought, as it develops, is somehow to be finished with metaphysics. We cannot examine this development here: his early identification with the task of metaphysics, then his call to overcome *(Überwinden)* metaphysics, and then his shift to being-finished or done *(Verwinden)* with it. Throughout the course of his thought there is the recognition that metaphysics is the fate and destiny of Western thought, of the

Abendland. Gadamer's hermeneutics as well as his reading of Plato is deeply indebted to Heidegger, and yet, nonetheless, Gadamer remains, in an important sense, a Platonist. Gadamer resists the deepest historical motive of Heidegger's endeavor, i.e., to move thought beyond what Heidegger considered Plato to have set as the parameters for thinking. Gadamer, rather, gives us a reading of Plato that responds to the Heideggerian critique and shows us how we might recover for ourselves the legacy of Plato.

Gadamer himself directs us to a way to begin to think about this when he writes in his prefatory remarks to the recently published sketch of Heidegger's 1922 Aristotle project: "When I today once again read this first part of the introduction to Heidegger's studies of Aristotle . . . it is as though I have rediscovered the clue *(Leitfaden)* to my own philosophical development *(Werdegang).*"[5] Within the context of Heidegger's early work there is an obvious, if somewhat superficial, answer to our question. Heidegger's project of 1922 was to recover Aristotle phenomenologically. In this attempt Heidegger recapitulates Aristotle's critique of Plato. The direction of Gadamer's effort has been to display the proximity of Aristotle and Plato and thereby to deflate this longstanding criticism. In his essay "Amicus Plato Magis Amica Veritas," Gadamer writes:

> At that time I was strongly influenced by Heidegger's interpretation of Aristotle, the real intention of which was still not completely evident, namely its critique of ontology, and which in essence repeated Aristotle's critique of Plato in the form of an existential, situation-oriented, philosophical critique of the idealist tradition. But does that suffice? It seems to me now that any interpretation which properly adheres to the subject matter under investigation here must start with the assumption that Aristotle's critique of Plato relies on something essential which he has *in common* with Plato.[6]

Though Gadamer did not then fully understand Heidegger's philosophical motives for his appropriation of Aristotle, and although Gadamer's own direction was not then entirely clear to himself, by 1931 when he published his habilitation, *Plato's Dialectical Ethics,* he saw the convergence of Aristotle and Plato, he tells us in *The Idea of the Good in Platonic-Aristotelian Philosophy,* and much of his effort since has been to display this convergence.[7] He had originally intended that his habilitation be a study of the "good" in Plato and Aristotle, but he reduced the scope of his project to Plato's *Philebus,* so that he might finish the work before Heidegger left Marburg in 1928 to return to Freiburg.[8] After almost a lifetime of reading and teaching Plato, Gadamer published an extensive essay on the would-be topic of his habilitation in 1978: *The Idea of the Good in Platonic-Aristotelian Philosophy.* In those fifty years he comes to see more clearly this continuity as well as the limitations of Heidegger's approach to Plato and Aristotle.

The background for Heidegger's own reading of Aristotle is the rejection of Aristotle by Neo-Kantians which left only the Neo-Scholastics of the late nineteenth century to champion Aristotle. The young Heidegger wished to interpret

Aristotle in such a way as to develop the phenomenology of the hermeneutical situation and by virtue of this recovery show the shortcomings of both Neo-Kantianism and Neo-Thomism. In the Aristotle sketch of 1922 Heidegger speaks of his task as, in part, the destruction *(Destruktion)* of Scholasticism.[9] Scholasticism is rooted in Aristotle, yet it is inauthentic. The dismantling or de-construction of the tradition was to allow Heidegger to come to terms with the "radical" and "basic experience" of Aristotle's philosophy from which the tradition is "fallen away" *(Verfallen).*[10] Clearly he is concerned with establishing an appropriate (and Christian) anthropology as a way toward an ontology. This is why Gadamer, with a gesture toward the young Hegel, calls this sketch Heidegger's "theologische Jugendschrift" (theological early work). There is a deep ambivalence in Heidegger as regards his project's relation to Aristotle.[11] He does not mean simply to defend and revive Aristotle.[12] He thinks he has found the fallenness already in Aristotle's ontology, yet there is much to be appreciated in Aristotle's *Rhetoric* and, especially, the *Physics* with its notion of *dunamis (Bewegung* or movement, as Heidegger translates it).

As we shall soon see, Heidegger's retrieval of Aristotle was also a revival of Aristotle's critique of Plato. In response to this effort, Gadamer retrieves from his other great teacher, Paul Natorp, a critique of Aristotle's treatment of Plato. Gadamer develops this in his own way and counters Heidegger's Aristotelian critique of Plato. Yet Gadamer does not claim Plato on behalf of Kant in the way that Natorp does. Nor does he uphold Plato against Aristotle. Rather, Gadamer shows us how Aristotle's Plato (and for that matter, Heidegger's as well) with his version of the doctrine of the forms *(Ideenlehre)* mirrors Natorp's Plato of transcendental subjectivity and the categories. Neither is adequate to Plato's texts themselves.

Yet Heidegger presented Gadamer with the *Leitfaden,* the guide, to his own treatment of Plato—so Gadamer tells us in the prefatory remarks to the recently published early Aristotle essay of Heidegger. This is puzzling in at least two respects. Firstly, in the Aristotle essay Heidegger is more concerned with *sophia* and *theoria,* that is, theory and science, than he is with *phronēsis* or practical wisdom. In his prefatory remarks Gadamer expresses some surprise at this focus.[13] Secondly, Heidegger's lectures on the *Sophist* from 1925 dramatically display a dogmatic critique of Plato, many theses of which Gadamer devotes much of his scholarly effort to reject.

These lectures begin with the stunning pronouncement that Aristotle blocks any approach to Plato.[14] Retrospectively we can see that Aristotle did indeed block Heidegger's approach to Plato, and further, that Gadamer has helped open a way back to Plato. In these lectures, which I will not attempt to summarize here, we find Heidegger adopting many of Aristotle's familiar criticisms of Plato, e.g., criticism of the ideas understood as numbers and of the relation of the ideas to the things of our experience, i.e., the *chōrismos* (separation) and *methexis* (participation) problems. We also find Heidegger, if only briefly, taking up themes that he will develop later, e.g., that for the Greeks Being *(Sein)* is a product (or that-which-has-been-made, *Hergestellt-sein),* that the Greeks did not adequately recognize the ontological difference between Being *(Sein)* and beings *(die Seienden).* Of particular interest for our concern, however, is the way that Heidegger deals with two sets of themes: first, the understanding of rhetoric and dialectic, and, secondly, the concepts of *dunamis* (potentiality) and *genos* (genus) in the last part of the dialogue. What we find here is a dogmatic interpretation of the relation of Plato and Aristotle that retreats from the very insights raised in the reading of the dialogue. Gadamer, as we shall see, recovers some of these insights and, in so doing, makes possible a recovery of Plato.

Heidegger's most comprehensive thesis is that Aristotle provides a more radical treatment of the ontological problems that are raised by the pre-Socratics and Plato. Using a word that is important throughout his work (sometimes in reference to his own work) Heidegger says that Plato, specifically in the *Sophist,* is the *Umschlag* (sudden change or turn) between Parmenides and Aristotle.[15] This change or reversal concerns primarily the development of a concept of motion *(Bewegung).* Attributing to Plato a breakthrough of this sort would seem most significant, but it is as though Plato does not know what he has done and does not develop the notion. According to Heidegger, it is for Aristotle to radically (always "radically") see what is at stake in the concept and to develop it.

With respect to rhetoric and dialectic, Heidegger attacks the view that Aristotle's misunderstanding of Plato's dialectic leads Aristotle to denigrate dialectic. Heidegger claims, rather, that Aristotle grasped dialectic more radically. From our position, looking at Heidegger's other work and his own consistent rejection and disparagement of dialectic, we are tempted to say with Gadamer that Heidegger's own misunderstanding of Platonic dialectic leads him with Aristotle to denigrate dialectic.[16] Heidegger goes on to say that in the *Phaedrus* Plato's treatment of dialectic lays the ground for Aristotle. It is a puzzle *(Rätsel),* he comments, as to why Aristotle did not acknowledge this. Nonetheless, Heidegger goes on to note that Plato does not develop the notion of dialectic and Aristotle does.

Heidegger's claims about rhetoric parallel those about dialectic. Pointing to the *Gorgias* Heidegger asserts that Plato was not successful in coming to a positive understanding of rhetoric, though Aristotle does accomplish this.[17] Heidegger does acknowledge, however, that Plato established the basis for an appropriate and positive understanding of rhetoric but Plato did not develop it. He calls it "remarkable" *(merkwürdig)* that Plato had the possibilities for an appreciation of rhetoric but they never became realized.

If we turn to Gadamer in this regard, the first thing we must note is that Gadamer's habilitation, *Plato's Dialectical Ethics,* written in Marburg (at least in part) with Heidegger is a treatise on dialectic in Plato. The book has only two chapters: the first a general treatment of dialectic in Plato and the second a reading of the *Philebus.* The *Philebus* is chosen because it provides both an excellent example of dialectic as well as an explicit discussion of dialectic. In the context of Heidegger's Marburg lectures, this treatise must be seen as a positive appreciation and defense of both dialectic and Plato. The central thesis of the work concerns the root of dialectic in conversation, the rhetorical dimension of which, especially as shown in the *Phaedrus,* is undeniable. Gadamer's subsequent work both in classical philosophy as well as in hermeneutics maintains and develops the insights of this first book.[18] We can see here not only the continuity of Gadamer's thought concerning dialectic and classical philosophy but that between his work in classical philosophy and hermeneutics, for dialectic and conversation are themes central to his hermeneutics as well as to his reading of the ancients. We shall return to this later.

It is clear from both the early sketch of the Aristotle project and the *Sophist* lectures that for Heidegger the central concept of Aristotle is *dunamis,* which he sometimes translates simply as *Bewegung* (motion) or *Bewegtsein* (being moved).[19] According to the Aristotle essay Aristotle is both the culmination of Greek philosophy as well as the founder of a new approach, which approach is achieved in the *Physics:* "The central phenomenon, whose explication is the theme of the *Physics* becomes the being (or entity, *das Seiende*) in the mode of its being-moved *(Bewegtseins)."*[20] When Heidegger confronts the introduction of the concept of *dunamis* in Plato's *Sophist* where it plays a central function, Heidegger dogmatically attributes this notion to Aristotle. According to Grumach's notes, Heidegger states: "It could also be (something that I do not personally believe) that Plato himself had developed by himself this structural aspect of *dunamis* for the interpretation of Being—it could be, and from this then Aristotle came upon his ontology." Heidegger goes on to say, again dogmatically, that Aristotle views motion positively, that Plato does not, and thus it makes much better sense to say that Aristotle must have given Plato the nudge *(Anstoß)* in this direction.[21] Similarly when the term *genos* ("genus" or "kind") is taken up for discussion, Heidegger comments that the use of the word shows that "Aristotle is at work here."[22] The young Aristotle teaches the elder Plato. In short, in a number of important respects Heidegger in his early work locates significant aspects of the proximity of Plato and Aristotle but dogmatically backs away from this recognition. It is left for Gadamer to reclaim this proximity positively and to overcome Heidegger's dogmatism.

PART II: THE PROXIMITY OF PLATO AND ARISTOTLE

Orienting his reading of Plato primarily around the later dialogues—the *Parmenides, Theaetetus, Sophist,* and *Statesman,* but especially the *Philebus,* Gadamer argues throughout the three volumes of his collected works devoted to classical philosophy for an understanding of the central importance for Plato and Aristotle of *logos* and *eidos* as a shared insight. Though Plato does often orient the discussion of the dialogue to mathematics and the Pythagoreans, while Aristotle orients his discussion to life science, Plato, so argues Gadamer, is not a Pythagorean and neither does he have a doctrine of the ideas which places them in a place beyond the heavens. Gadamer's account of the notion of the good in Plato culminates in his treatment of the mix in the *Philebus:*

> Only when the mixture is no longer thought of as a diminution and clouding of the pure, true, and unmixed, but as a genus of its own, can it be the place where we see how the being of the good and the true is constituted. . . . This doctrine has far-reaching consequences for any appropriate understanding of Plato's dialectic and the problems of *chōrismos* (separation) and *methexis* (participation). If limit and determinacy do not exist apart, for themselves, then neither does the entire noetic realm of the ideas—any more than do the ingredients of this portion of life that is supposed to be mixed.[23]

This notion of the "mix" in the *Philebus* also serves, together with the notion of the "fitting" in the *Statesman,* as the basis for defending Plato against Aristotle's critique concerning the unity of the good in the *Nicomachean Ethics.* The mix requires measure. From this it is a short step to Aristotle's virtuous mean.

If we take a brief look at Heidegger's reading of the *Theaetetus* in 1931/32, we find more examples of abandoned paths of interpretive inquiry that Gadamer has taken up—and taken up in a way to support the proximity of Plato and Aristotle. Heidegger's treatment of this dialogue follows directly on his interpretation of the cave story from the *Republic.*[24] In Heidegger's preliminary discussion *(Vorüberlegungen,* secs. 20–21) of the *Theaetetus* we can find a good summary statement of his criticism of Plato, a criticism that both looks back to his analysis of the cave story and forward to the *Theaetetus.* According to Heidegger here, the question of the dialogue concerns *epistēmē,* and though Plato was not a modern epistemologist, his questions concerned knowledge, *Erkenntnis.* Knowing *(erkennen)* is seeing *(sehen).* Seeing means having something present before one as present *(Gegenwärtig haben von Anwesenden),* or having something at one's disposal in its presentness *(in seiner Anwesenheit zur Verfügung haben),* i.e., in its being present at hand *(Vorhandensein).* Heidegger then puts the question of truth to the text, though he recognizes that the explicit leading question is not truth. He sets up another sequence of rough equivalences that culminate likewise in presentness at hand *(Vorhandenheit): Wahrheit* (truth) = *sich zeigen* (showing itself) = *phantasia* = *Anwesenheit* (presence) = *Vorhandenheit.* According to this interpretation truth for Plato means being present at hand.

The lectures on the *Theaetetus* look closely only at a small section of the dialogue, approximately 184–90, and they conclude by summarizing this central section with the claim that the dialogue exhibits the following four steps:[25]

1. the contrast of re-presenting or bringing to mind *(Vergegenwärtigung)* with making present *(Gegenwärtigung);*
2. the possibility of viewing something as something;
3. the possibility of looking past something, making a mistake, *pseudos;*

4. *pseudos* interpreted as not meeting the attributed predicate, as an incorrect claim.

We cannot here look closely at the interpretation and the derivation of these steps. Heidegger develops the first three steps with some care and positive appreciation of the Socratic argument. In themselves, however, they do not entail the set of equivalences with which he begins his considerations. Nor do the first three steps justify the fourth step. Heidegger jumps rashly to the concluding fourth assertion without textually showing it or logically arguing it. The first three help explain the possibility of the fourth, but the fourth does not exhaust or adequately capture the possibilities of the first three. *Pseudos* is not simply incorrectness, according to Plato. At best, the phenomenon of incorrectness is derived from prior hermeneutic possibilities of *pseudos.* Gadamer corrects Heidegger in much this way.[26]

Two other aspects of Heidegger's reading of the *Theaetetus* are important to note. When Heidegger introduces the term *wissen* (knowing), he suggests two possible ways in which it can be taken: 1) as *sich auskennen* (knowing one's way about in a matter or situation), or as 2) *sehen* (seeing) and *erkennen* (recognizing). And, when Heidegger comes across the discussion of the soul at 184 c–d, Heidegger suggests that the soul has two possible relations to Being: *haben* (having) or *streben* (striving).[27] *Streben* is Heidegger's German for *eros.* He tells us, among other things, that *eros* for Plato is not erotic.[28] "Having" is, for Heidegger, "seeing," which places this in the set of equivalences just mentioned. Further, the gloss on "having" is adumbrated with the notion of perfection *(perfekt)* and completeness *(fertig).* The discussion of Plato with respect to knowing, here as elsewhere, settles on "seeing" and "having." Knowing as *sich auskennen* and the soul understood as *streben* simply drop out of the discussion, even though these are noted as being recognized by Plato. Heidegger is, of course, preparing his critique of the onto-theological character of the metaphysics of Plato and Aristotle. Gadamer draws our attention back to these more human possibilities of knowledge as "knowing one's way about" and of the soul as erotic striving as the genuine Platonic insights into what it means to be human.[29]

Although Gadamer has never provided us with an extended study of the *Theaetetus,* we find him making frequent references to it through his writings. There are, for example, many references to the discussion of the soul at 184c–d. In the essay "Vorgestalten der Reflexion" Gadamer notes Plato's usage of the term *dunamis* with respect to the soul and shows the similarity of Plato in this regard to Aristotle by drawing together discussions of the soul from the *Charmides,* the *Republic,* the *Theaetetus,* and Aristotle's *De Anima.*[30] Similarly, Gadamer returns often to *Theaetetus* 185 for his discussion of the unity of the many in the soul as *logos.* Two basic and much discussed issues with respect to Plato are at stake in this discussion: 1) an understanding of the human soul—of what it means to be human, and 2) the relation of the one and the many.

Both the soul and *logos* exhibit for Gadamer the much discussed relation for Plato of the one and the many. This is the theme and apparent aporia with which the *Theaetetus* concludes. Gadamer argues time and again that this much discussed problem is, in the end, the problem of the "two," the indeterminate dyad.[31] The "two" is not reducible to the one. There are both "two" and "one." Both the soul and *logos* exhibit this structure. Both have a certain sort of unity but both exhibit internal differentiation—twoness. Heidegger, however, finds here only unity, and in the *koinon* (commonality) of the *logos* he finds only the empty and abstract "most general."[32] Gadamer argues further that this logical question of the relation of the "one" and the "dyad" is too often confused with the much discussed problem of participation *(methexis):* how it is that so many things can participate in one idea. This supposed problem is closely connected with the separation *(chōrismos)* problem, i.e., that the ideas dwell somehow in some place beyond the heavens. As we noted above, Heidegger accepts and promotes these Aristotelian criticisms of Plato. Gadamer insists, on the contrary, that there is no problem of participation for Plato since Plato presupposes the participation of the individual thing in the idea.[33] His dialogues show us how we too must presuppose this. Gadamer writes concerning this presumed problem of participation much like Heidegger writing about truth in *Being and Time,* where Heidegger argues that truth is not a problem to be solved but something we must presuppose—an experience to phenomenologically clarify and appreciate.[34] Gadamer would have us appreciate the Platonic insights, especially concerning dialectic, *logos,* and the human soul.

The tension between the "one" and the "two" is closely related, for Gadamer, to the theme of human finitude which is so prominent in his work on Plato as well as to his positive recovery of rhetoric and dialectic. In short, in opposition to Heidegger to whom he is indebted for the very theme of finitude, Gadamer shows us how for Plato knowledge *(wissen)* is not reducible to "having" or "seeing" in the way that Heidegger claims it is. Heidegger reads Aristotelian divinity back into the human soul. For him the human soul in Greek philosophy is a dim shadow of the nonerotic thought which thinks itself in its perfection and completeness—Aristotle's God. Gadamer, on the other hand, returns us to the erotic soul of Plato's *Symposium* and *Phaedrus,* which follows Aristotle's admonition to strive to be divine, yet in a way that recognizes our humanity. We see this, for example, in the positive evaluation of conversation where rhetoric and opinion have their appropriate place.

PART III: GADAMER'S PROXIMITY TO ARISTOTLE AND PLATO

Gadamer's reading of Plato not only shows us how we might see the proximity of Plato and Aristotle, even though Aristotle's sharp critique is an obstacle that has "seduced" so many readers, including Heidegger. Often what Heidegger takes as characteristic of *Dasein* and what he finds lacking in Plato, Gadamer finds already present in Plato. Most important of these characteristics is finitude and the orientation of knowledge within a practical context. If we only note this much, we might conclude simply that Gadamer delivers a Heideggerian reading of Plato and Aristotle that is much more interesting and telling than Heidegger's own. In many ways, this is indeed the case. P. Christopher Smith has persuasively made this case time and again.[35] Gadamer's own numerous professions of his debt to Heidegger support such a view. Yet if we would attend more closely to the themes just discussed as well as to the importance for Gadamer of conversation, the practical context of thought and memory, we would see how in significant ways Gadamer's path is not that of Heidegger. The difference has much to do with Gadamer's own proximity to Aristotle and Plato.

One of the most prominent features of Gadamer's work in general is his attempt to recover Aristotelian *phronēsis,* practical wisdom. This recovery takes place in his writing on classical philosophy as well as in his philosophical hermeneutics. In *Truth and Method* the interpretive act is to be understood as an act of judgment much like the practical judgment of Aristotle's intellectual virtue of *phronēsis.* And in his work on Greek classical philosophy, Gadamer deflates the Aristotelian critique of the Platonic notion of the Good by showing how the notions of measured mixture in the *Philebus* and that of the "fitting" in the *Statesman* anticipate the Aristotelian developments. I would suggest further that Gadamer's work in general manifests this virtue of appropriate measure, finding the right mix, hitting the mark, finding the mean in a way that is not true of Heidegger. Style is substance. Gadamer often characterizes Heidegger's philosophical style and presence as exhibiting "revolutionary force" *(revolutionäre Wucht)*—a description that surely is appropriate but which calls to mind anything but Aristotelian moderation.[36] Nor is Heidegger's call in the *Beiträge* and elsewhere for courage in the face of the abyss *(Mut zum Abgrund)* at all moderate—nor his finding truth in collapse, downfall, and ruin.[37] I need not comment about Heidegger's own political judgments. Gadamer would remind us of Plato's statesman whose character is woven of courage and moderation.

The immediate practical context for theorizing (which is to say, dialectic) for Gadamer is conversation *(das Gespräch).* This theme of dialogue and conversation has had a number of contemporary adumbrations, not the least of which is that by Heidegger.[38] But for Gadamer this theme is rooted in the conversation of the Platonic dialogue as well as in the treatment of friendship in Aristotle's *Nicomachean Ethics* and the treatment of *eros* in Plato. Not only is Socrates a conversationalist but he is an erotic one as well. As just noted, Heidegger also took up this theme, though it is not prominent in his early work. The concept is already at work in Gadamer's habilitation.[39] It is interesting to compare Heidegger on *dialegesthai* in *What is Called Thinking?* with Gadamer on the same concept. Heidegger ignores, for the most part, the *dia* in this term as well as in *dianoia* and cuts directly to their roots in *legein/logos* and *noein/nous.*[40] Though

Heidegger attempted occasionally to write dialogues, and though he often returned to Hölderlin's phrase that "we are a conversation," the form that seems more appropriate to Heidegger is the meditation (not a Cartesian one but a prayerful one).[41] The conversation that most concerns Heidegger is the conversation with the gods, not our conversation with one another. The appropriate role for mortals in such a "conversation" is to listen gratefully. The younger Gadamer seems to have been in agreement with his colleague Karl Löwith's early dialogical critique of *Being and Time*. Löwith developed this critique of Heidegger from the perspective of dialogue in his habilitation which he wrote with Heidegger in Marburg at the same time that Gadamer was working with Heidegger on his own habilitation.[42] In volume 4 of his *Gesammelte Werke* we can find Gadamer's approving 1929 review of Löwith's book.[43] Curiously enough, Gadamer never mentions Heidegger in the review.

Most of Gadamer's efforts in his consideration between Plato and Aristotle have concentrated themselves in practical philosophy. We need only to notice the titles of his two books on classical themes, *Plato's Dialectical Ethics* and *The Idea of the Good in Platonic-Aristotelian Philosophy,* to recognize this. Central to these efforts, as I have suggested, are the recovery of Aristotelian *phronēsis* with its antecedent in Plato and an understanding of dialectic as conversation. Gadamer himself often characterizes hermeneutics as practical philosophy.[44] Yet, just as Gadamer has suggested with respect to Plato and Aristotle, so too is it for Gadamer that practical and theoretical philosophy are closely related. And, though I cannot argue it fully here, I would suggest that theoretically Gadamer differs from Heidegger (or at least the early Heidegger) with respect to the understanding of time and human temporality. Gadamer draws on resources from Plato to find his distance from Heidegger in this regard.

Though Gadamer shares with Heidegger (and with Husserl, for that matter) an understanding of the complex unity of the three dimensions of lived time, Gadamer does not share the thesis of *Being and Time* concerning the priority of the future in this trinity of past, present, and future. Gadamer rather suggests a symmetry of these dimensions wherein memory is essential to the fulfillment of human freedom and the human good. This is not to say, as Habermas once suggested, that there is for Gadamer a priority of the past and tradition.[45] There is rather a reciprocal symmetry of dimensions that mutually implicate one another. If Gadamer returns more often to the theme of memory and tradition than he does to our hopes and expectations of the future, it is perhaps to counter the willful forgetfulness of our age which is thereby lost in the present. Again and again Gadamer returns to the Platonic treatment of *anamnēsis* to explore these themes.

One of the few times that Heidegger takes up Platonic *anamnēsis* is at the conclusion of the 1927 lectures, *Basic Problems,* where he appeals to the Platonic treatment of memory in the *Phaedo* and *Phaedrus* to elucidate what he calls the "mystery of the a priori" *(die Rätsel der Apriorität)*. Immediately thereafter, however, in a gesture that is typical of Heidegger's usage of Plato, Heidegger cites approvingly Kant's disparaging comments about Plato as an enthusiast, *a Schwärmer.*[46]

Clearly a stumbling block for Heidegger with regard to any possible reappropriation of a Platonic notion of recollection or *anamnēsis* is the way that in the Platonic dialogue it often returns us mythically to the timeless eternity of the immortal gods. For radically historical and finite *Dasein,* which is characterized importantly as Being-towards-death, there are no "eternal truths."[47] For Heidegger, Platonic *anamnēsis* becomes Aristotelian *nous* whereby the gods of the myths become thought thinking itself *(noēsis noeseos).* Stories, with beginnings and ends, were appropriate of the gods of the myths, but not for the timeless present of divine *nous.* It is this timelessness and sheer presence as a model for human knowing in Aristotle against which Heidegger objects. Heidegger finds the same understanding of knowing in Plato's ideas, the so-called "doctrine of the forms" *(Ideenlehre).* Gadamer rarely addresses the Aristotelian notion of wisdom or of *nous.* He does attempt, however, to appropriate the Platonic notion of *anamnēsis,* for here we cannot escape our historicity since recollection is a matter of a human memory of the past.

In his early Aristotle sketch Heidegger presents *Verweilen* (tarrying or lingering) as the theoretical mode of the human when we adopt the intellectual virtue of *sophia* (wisdom) and assume, as best we can, the posture of pure thought, that is, of *nous.*[48] *Verweilen* is a temporal concept which expresses our experience of the suspension of time when we are lost in thought. In *Being and Time* Heidegger uses this term to describe the experience of theorizing and science. He does so with clear reference to Aristotle. He writes, for example: "When concern holds back from any kind of producing, manipulating, and the like, it puts itself into what is now the sole remaining mode of Being-in, the mode of just tarrying alongside *(das Nur-noch-verweilen-bei).* . . . This kind of Being towards the world is one which lets us encounter entities within-the-world purely in the *way they look (eidos).*"[49] In a search that has not been exhaustive and thorough, I have found only two discussions of *Verweilen* in Heidegger's later published work. These two are closely related and both concern Anaximander and not Aristotle.[50] It seems as though with the abandonment of the "scientific" *(wissenschaftlich)* and the philosophical project of *Being and Time,* Heidegger loses interest in the possible phenomenological domestication of Aristotelian *nous.* Perhaps Heidegger came to see an unsustainable tension between the experience of knowing in the tranquil and leisurely tarrying of theory and the experience of truth in the authentic moment *(Augenblick)* when suddenly things look differently to us.[51] Heidegger's depiction of the experience of truth is much like religious expressions of the experience of divine revelation. Much of his later work is filled with the notions of a sudden change *(Umschlag),* of a turn or reversal *(Kehre),* of suddenness *(Plötzlichkeit),* of lightning *(Blitz),* and so on.

It is from Heidegger, then, that Gadamer in all likelihood finds his clue *(Leit-faden)* to the temporal concept of *Verweilen,* which he makes central to the understanding of art and aesthetic experience.[52] The objective correlate of tarrying in this context is the permanence of the artwork. This tarrying happens when we get lost in the experience of the artwork and lose track of time. It is tantamount to the suspension of time. Yet, in another respect, time is never suspended, for when our attention returns to the everyday, we find that time has passed and it is later than we think. And just as time is not simply suspended, neither is the artwork simply permanent. Witness the state of the monuments of Europe. Were time to be simply suspended, it would be eternity—the timeless present of thought thinking itself in a life of *nous* perfected by the virtue of wisdom, *sophia.*

Gadamer likes to remind us of Socrates' ignorance and the Platonic defense of his life as a life not of knowledge *(wissen)* and wisdom *(sophia),* i.e., a divine life, but a life of the love of wisdom—*philosophia,* a human life. This is clearly why Gadamer in his work attends more appreciatively to Plato than he does to Aristotle. In his recent preface to the publication of the sketch of Heidegger's Aristotle project Gadamer expresses surprise at Heidegger's focus on *sophia* (wisdom) rather than on *phronēsis:* "In my reading of the rediscovered project sketch I was surprised that in Heidegger's manuscript *phronēsis* is not placed in the foreground but rather the virtue of the theoretical life, *sophia.*"[53] Gadamer seems to have forgotten the young Heidegger's passion for *Wissenschaft,* for philosophy as science. Heidegger, of course, eventually abandons his scientific project and philosophy for something he calls thinking *(Denken).* However much Gadamer finds a guide in Heidegger, he does not abandon philosophy. We have noted how he attempts to positively retrieve in important respects the classical philosophy of Plato and Aristotle. He has shown, for example, both in his reading of Platonic dialogues and his philosophical hermeneutics how the central Platonic themes of *mimēsis* and *anamnēsisis* can be recovered.[54] We must ask if there might be a way to recover the classical distinction between theory and practice and the accompanying distinction between theoretical and practical philosophy. At times in his writing it seems as though there is only the practical for Gadamer inasmuch as we can never escape life's concerns or the human desire for the good. As we have noted, Gadamer characterizes his own hermeneutics (we might want to call it his hermeneutical *theory*) as a practical philosophy, even though it culminates in an ontology. Our question does not ignore the fact that for Aristotle practical philosophy is already theoretical and that theory is essential to the practice of life. Indeed, theory is a certain sort of practice. And we should heed Gadamer's injunction at the conclusion of *The Idea of the Good* in this regard that "we may not absolutize therefore the ranking of the theoretical ideal of life above the practical-political."[55]

Another way to ask this question is to ask simply about philosophy.[56] Throughout his work Gadamer refers again and again to three distinctive and particularly significant modes of discourse—law, religion, and poetry. Each of these brings with it the problem of interpretation. In law and religion the questions of interpretation obviously bear with them questions of practice. Gadamer has insisted on the universality of the hermeneutical situation which he defines in part by this close relation of interpretation and application. As noted above, Aristotelian practical judgment *(phronēsis)* provides a kind of model for interpretive judgment. Clearly, then, for Gadamer the reading of poetry and philosophy similarly displays this close relation of theory and practice. It is remarkable that in Gadamer's extensive writing about these various linguistic domains—of which poetry and art have received particular attention—philosophy as a distinctive mode of discourse has received almost no treatment.[57] What most obviously distinguishes philosophical discourse for Gadamer is its conceptuality *(Begrifflichkeit):* "Philosophy moves exclusively in the medium of the concept."[58] The concept is speculative and its logic is the dialectic of question and answer. Clearly his model of this logic is most informed by Plato and Hegel, yet we should note his comment that Husserl was right to insist that the eidetic reduction "is something that occurs de facto in all true philosophizing. For it is only the a priori essential structures of all reality that have always and without exception formed the realm of the concept of the realm of ideas."[59] If this statement came from the pen of Heidegger, we would read it as a negative criticism—"essential structures of all reality"! Yet Gadamer does not abandon philosophy as Heidegger did, and, as in the title of his self-criticism, Gadamer finds himself between phenomenology and dialectic.

To return to the temporal aspect of these various sorts of discourse, we might ask whether there is a tarrying *(Verweilen)* in thought that is peculiar to philosophy. As we noted above, Gadamer makes tarrying a distinguishing mark of the experience of art. On his own account it cannot be exclusive to art, for he accords this characteristic to religious experience and the festival as well.[60] We are left to wonder if it is not also appropriate to philosophy. We should note that in the essay "In Praise of Theory," which is quite ambiguous about the relation of theory and practice, Gadamer specifies that *theōria* is not a *sehen* but a *Haltung* (comportment or bearing; literally, a way of holding oneself) and a *Dabeisein,* a way of being with what is thought.[61] Here Gadamer implicitly endorses Heidegger's critique of seeing and sight as the most apt metaphor for theory, and yet he refuses to jettison the language of theory and practice. He reinterprets theory in a way that opens the way for an appropriation of the life of the Platonic Socrates. It would make sense to say that this theoretical way of being with what is thought is a kind of tarrying with the matter at hand.

Part IV: Conclusion

This last consideration is a good example of the way that Gadamer accommodates the Heideggerian critique of the classical tradition and its modern legacy but nonetheless sustains the work of Plato and the example of Socrates as a model of the good life. He has shown us how we might, in our contemporary context, recover their work and how we might respect the philosophical accomplishment of Heidegger without accepting his dogmatism with respect to Plato—a dogmatism that has become a pervasive tenet of much of the contemporary discussion.[62] We have seen in the above discussion how some of Gadamer's insights which reject Heidegger's dogmatism seem to have followed leads from Heidegger himself. We have seen how Gadamer finds the clues *(Leitfaden)* to his own philosophical development in Heidegger. In response to Heidegger Gadamer has shown us the proximity of Aristotle and Plato. I have suggested the proximity of Gadamer to Plato and a Platonic Aristotle.

But if we orient ourselves from Heidegger's position, especially in its later development, we might want to say that the proximity of Plato and Aristotle is not particularly of interest since both move in the realm of philosophy and metaphysics which constitutes a fall away from the first beginning. As we know, Heidegger abandons his Aristotle project. The first beginning is earlier in the so-called pre-Socratics. The destruction of late Scholasticism becomes the destruction of metaphysics. Heidegger turns from Aristotle to Kant and then to Hölderlin and Nietzsche. He struggles for another beginning *(einen anderen Anfang).*[63] Gadamer, to the contrary, attends to the insight (an insight that we can find in Plato *and* in Heidegger) that we are already under way *(unterwegs),* that we have already begun, and that we are trying to find our way, in part, by coming to terms with where we have been. We find ourselves in the middle of things and in the effort to move ahead, look back. In short, there is no new beginning for Gadamer. The task of coming to terms with our past is at the same time the task of self-understanding and finding our way. The exemplar of this effort is not the lonely flash of insight but the conversation among friends which we leave and resume, time and again.

ROBERT J. DOSTAL

DEPARTMENT OF PHILOSOPHY
BRYN MAWR COLLEGE
JUNE 1992

NOTES

1. See the autobiographical essay in this volume; see also the collection of his essays on Heidegger originally published under the title *Heidegger's Wege* and reprinted in *Gesammelte Werke,* vol. 3 (Tübingen: J. C. B. Mohr, 1987). We can find similar comments in "Selbstdarstellung Hans-Georg Gadamer (1973)," in *Gesammelte Werke,* vol. 2, pp. 479–94; and "'Platos dialektische Ethik'—beim Wort genommen," in *Gesammelte Werke,* vol. 7, pp. 121–27; in English translation: "Gadamer on Gadamer,"

in *Gadamer and Hermeneutics,* ed. Hugh Silverman (New York: Routledge, 1991), pp. 13–19.

2. Hans-Georg Gadamer, *The Idea of the Good in Platonic-Aristotelian Philosophy,* trans. P. Christopher Smith (New Haven: Yale University Press, 1986), p. 5; in German, *Gesammelte Werke,* vol. 7, p. 130.

3. Gadamer is not the only one, of course, who has provided us with powerfully sympathetic readings of Plato's dialogues and who was significantly touched by Heidegger. Among others we should mention Leo Strauss, Jakob Klein, and Gerhard Krüger—all of whom, together with Gadamer, heard Heidegger lecture on Plato and Aristotle in Marburg in the 1920s. It says much about Heidegger that he, the critic of Platonism, should foster such care for Plato and classical philosophy in his students.

4. For an account of the discussion as well as a criticism of Heidegger's Plato interpretation see my article, "Beyond Being: Heidegger's Plato," *Journal of the History of Philosophy,* 23 (January 1985): 71–98. Recently two publications of particular relevance have appeared: Heidegger's 1931/32 winter semester lectures on the *Theaetetus* and his 1922 sketch of his project to phenomenologically interpet Aristotle. See *Vom Wesen der Wahrheit: Zu Platons Höhlengleichnis und Theätet,* in *Gesamtausgabe,* bd. 34 (Frankfurt am Main: Vittorio Klostermann, 1988) and "Phänomenologische Interpretationen zu Aristotles (Anzeige der hermeneutischen Situation)," in Hans-Ulrich Lessing, ed., *Dilthey-Jahrbuch,* bd. 6 (Göttingen: Vandenhoeck & Ruprecht, 1989), pp. 235–74. Gadamer contributed a preface to the latter under the title, "Heideggers 'theologische' Jugendschrift." (*Ibid.,* pp. 229–34) A third publication by Heidegger, the *Sophist* lectures of 1925, is announced for 1992 but I have not been able to see it before the completion of this paper. I have had a look at Ernst Grumach's unpublished notes from these lectures and will make some use of these notes in this discussion.

5. Gadamer, "Heideggers 'theologische' Jugendschrift," in *Dilthey-Jahrbuch,* bd. 6, p. 229.

6. Gadamer, "Amicus Plato Magis Amica Veritas," in *Dialogue and Dialectic,* trans. P. Christopher Smith (New Haven: Yale University Press, 1980), p. 198. For the German, see *Gesammelte Werke,* vol. 6, p. 74. Gadamer is referring here to his habilitation, which he wrote under Heidegger and which was published in 1931 under the title *Platos dialektische Ethik.* This has undergone several editions; most recently it appears in volume 5 of the collected works. It has just appeared in English translation by Robert M. Wallace, *Plato's Dialectical Ethics* (New Haven: Yale University Press, 1991).

7. Gadamer, *Idea of the Good,* p. 4; *Gesammelte Werke,* vol. 7, p. 129.

8. So Gadamer informs us in "Gadamer on Gadamer"; see n. 1 above. The habilitation was not published until 1931.

9. Heidegger, "Phänomenologisches Interpretationen zu Aristoteles," p. 252.

10. In *Basic Problems of Phenomenology,* winter semester lectures of 1927–28, Heidegger glosses *Destruktion* with *Abbau,* which means to tear down, dismantle, or deconstruct. See *Grundprobleme der Phänomenologie, Gesamtausgabe,* bd. 24 (Frankfurt am Main: Klostermann, 1975), p. 31; in translation by Albert Hofstadter (Bloomington: Indiana University Press, 1982), p. 23.

11. Gadamer notes this ambivalence in his prefatory essay, "Heideggers 'theologische' Jugendschrift," p. 232.

12. In a letter to Jaspers from this same time, June 27, 1922, Heidegger writes that "the old ontology must be built up new again from the ground up" and that this "requires a critique of previous ontology in its roots in Greek philosophy." This does not mean, he explains further, that this amounts to only a renewal of Plato and Aristotle or an enthusiasm for the ancients such that one "preaches that the Greeks already had known every-

thing important." See *Martin Heidegger/Karl Jaspers Briefwechsel,* ed. Walter Biemel and Hans Saner (Frankfurt am Main: Klostermann; München: Piper, 1990), p. 27.

13. Gadamer had had a personal copy of the Aristotle essay but it was lost or destroyed in the war.

14. Heidegger, "Aristotles sperrt gleichsam jeden Zugang zu Plato." This is from the first lecture (January 8, 1925) according to Ernst Grumach's apparently stenographic notes.

15. See especially Heidegger's discussion of the "Idea and Function of a Fundamental Ontology," appendix to section 10 of *The Metaphysic Foundations of Logic,* trans. Michael Heim (Bloomington: Indiana University Press, 1984), pp. 154–59; in German, *Gesamtausgabe,* vol. 26, pp. 196–202. *Umschlag* translates the Greek *metabole* for Heidegger. See also the *Beiträge,* vol. 65 of *Gesamtausgabe,* esp. p. 195. Gadamer glosses *Umschlag* with *Plötzlichkeit,* suddenness—that which comes without transition (*Übergang*). See *Gesammelte Werke,* vol. 7, pp. 48, 76, and 322.

16. Note the comments about dialectic in *Gesamtausgabe,* vol. 29/30, *Die Grundbegriffe der Metaphysik: Welt Endlichkeit, Einsamkeit* (lectures of the winter semester 1929–30), p. 306 but especially p. 276: "All dialectic in philosophy, however, is an expression of *Verlegenheit* (embarrassment or confusion)."

17. Grumach's lecture notes, January 12, 1925: "Es gelang ihm [Plato] nicht, zu einem positiven Verständnis der Rhetorik zu kommen. Dazu kommt erst Aristoteles."

18. In a most recent essay (1990) Gadamer writes how Socratic dialogue culminates in Platonic dialectic. This is a central thesis of his habilitation. See "Dialektik ist nicht Sophistik—Theätet lernt das im *Sophistes,*" *Gesammelte Werke,* vol. 7, p. 346.

19. In the standard English translations *dunamis* is most commonly translated as capacity, ability, or power.

20. Heidegger, "Phänomenologische Interpretationen zu Aristoteles," p. 251.

21. Grumach's notes, lecture February 16, 1925.

22. Grumach's notes, lecture February 19, 1925: "Aristoteles hier mit am Werk ist."

23. Gadamer, *Idea of the Good;* p. 113; in *Gesammelte Werke,* vol. 7, p. 191.

24. Heidegger, *Gesamtausgabe,* vol. 34, *Vom Wesen der Wahrheit: Zu Platons Höhlengleichnis und Theätet* (lectures winter semester 1931/32), ed. Hermann Mörchen. In the afterword Mörchen tells us that these lectures were a development of a 1930 lecture of the same title that had been delivered on a number of occasions and was first published in 1943. A version of this lecture together with "Platos Lehre von der Wahrheit" were collected in *Wegmarken* (Frankfurt am Main: Vittorio Klostermann, 1967). The latter essay goes back to lectures from 1930/31 Heidegger tells us in the afterword to *Wegmarken,* p. 397.

25. Heidegger, *Von Wesen der Wahrheit, Gesamtausgabe,* vol. 34, p. 319.

26. Though Gadamer argues that truth is not correctness and sight for Plato, he does also assert that "in his dialogues Plato fails to deal adequately with the problem of *pseudos.* For *pseudos* does not lie in falsely speaking of one thing as another but only in speaking of it as something which it is not." See "Plato's Unwritten Dialectic," in *Dialogue and Dialectic,* p. 153; *Gesammelte Werke,* vol. 6, p. 151. See also "Plato and Heidegger," in *The Question of Being,* ed. M. Sprung (University Park: Pennsylvania State University Press, 1978), pp. 52–53; in German, *Gesammelte Werke,* vol. 3, pp. 247–48.

27. Heidegger, *Von Wesen der Wahrheit, Gesamtausgabe,* vol. 34, pp. 205.

28. I have attempted to show the critical relevance of Platonic *eros* and Aristotelian *philia* to the ethos of Heidegger's *Dasein* as well as for his political theory. See my "Friendship and Politics: Heidegger's Failing," *Political Theory* 20 (August 1992):

399–423. Similarly I have tried to show the relevance of Platonic *eros* to Heidegger's misinterpretation of Plato in my "Beyond Being: Heidegger's Plato," cited above in n. 3.

29. I find no special usage of "sich auskennen" in Gadamer's writing, but prominent in his habilitation is the phrase "sich auf etwas verstehen" which carries this same sense of a practical orientation in some matter.

30. Gadamer, "Vorgestalten der Reflexion," in *Gesammelte Werke,* vol. 6, pp. 116–28. Gadamer renders *dunamis* as *können,* ability.

31. Gadamer, "Plato's Unwritten Dialectic," in *Dialogue and Dialectic,* p. 132; in *Gesammelte Werke,* vol. 6, p. 135.

32. See, for example, *Beiträge* 206 and 459. In contrast we find Gadamer writing about Being in the *Sophist* what he would also say of the soul and of *logos:* "What Plato is aiming at is rather that the talk of Being implies a differentiation which is not the distinction of various regions of Being but an inner structure of Being itself. To all talk of Being belongs just as much self-sameness and identity as also otherness and variety. And both these aspects are so little exclusive that they reciprocally determine one another." See "Plato," *Gesammelte Werke,* vol. 3, p. 343 (my translation).

33. My thesis is that this is not at all a Platonic problem but rather a Platonic presupposition. Plato had always viewed the participation of the individual in the idea as self-evident and as that which makes the acceptance of ideas at all reasonable. "Dialektik ist nicht Sophistik—Theätet lernt das im *Sophistes,*" *Gesammelte Werke,* vol. 7, p. 343 (my translation).

34. Heidegger, *Being and Time,* trans. John Macquarrie and Edward Robinson (New York: Harper and Row, 1962), sec. 44, pp. 256–73.

35. See Smith's introductions and notes to the two volumes of translations of Gadamer's work concerning Plato: *Dialogue and Dialectic: Eight Hermeneutical Studies on Plato* (New Haven: Yale University Press, 1980) and *The Idea of the Good in Platonic-Aristotelian Philosophy* (New Haven: Yale University Press, 1986). See also his essay, "H.-G. Gadamer's Heideggerian Interpretation of Plato," *Journal of the British Society for Phenomenology* 12 (October 1981): 211–30 in which Smith presents his overarching interpretive thesis: "Gadamer goes on to show that Plato remains an 'early' thinker [i.e., premetaphysical] in part even though the 'metaphysical' as such might finally prevail in him." (211) I am attempting to show important ways in which Gadamer resists Heidegger's critique of Plato as a metaphysician in Heidegger's sense.

36. Gadamer, "Existentialismus und Existenzphilosophie," in *Gesammelte Werke,* vol. 3, p. 182.

37. See Heidegger, *Beiträge,* pp. 28, 241.

38. In Gadamer's formative years, the 1920s, there were a number of thinkers in Germany attempting to develop a dialogical philosophy. These include most prominently Martin Buber and Max Scheler.

39. Conversation is the central theme of the first part (of two) of the first chapter (of two).

40. Heidegger, *What is Called Thinking?,* pp. 197ff.; *Was Heißt Denken?,* pp. 119ff.

41. Two of his dialogues are "Conversation on a Country Path," in *Discourse on Thinking,* trans. John M. Anderson and E. Hans Freund (New York: Harper and Row, 1966), pp. 58–90, originally in *Gelassenheit* (Pfullingen: Neske, 1959); and "A Dialogue on Language," in *On the Way to Language,* trans. Peter Herz (New York: Harper and Row, 1971), pp. 1–54, originally in *Unterwegs zur Sprache* (Pfullingen: Neske, 1959). In "Hölderlin and the Essence of Poetry" Heidegger writes that the real conversation which we are consists in the naming of the gods. See *Existence and Being,* trans. Douglas Scott (Chicago: Henry Regnery, 1949), p. 279; for the German, see *Gesamtausgabe,* vol. 4, p. 40.

42. Karl Löwith, *Das Individuum in der Rolle des Mitmenschen,* in *Sämtliche Schriften,* vol. 1 (Stuttgart: J. B. Metzler, 1981). I wonder if Heidegger's brief remarks about the philosophy of dialogue in *Basic Problems* (lectures of 1927/28) were not elicited by Löwith's criticism. See *Basic Problems,* p. 278; *Grundprobleme,* p. 394.

43. Gadamer, "Ich und Du," in *Gesammelte Werke,* vol. 4, pp. 234–39.

44. See, for example, Gadamer's "Hermeneutik als praktische Philosophie," in *Vernunft im Zeitalter der Wissenschaft* (Frankfurt am Main: Suhrkamp, 1976), pp. 78–109.

45. Jürgen Habermas, "A Review of Gadamer's Truth and Method," in *Understanding and Social Inquiry,* ed. Fred Dallmayr and Thomas McCarthy (Notre Dame: University of Notre Dame Press, 1977), pp. 335–63.

46. Heidegger, *Basic Problems,* pp. 327–30; *Grundprobleme,* pp. 465–69. For Kant's comments see "Von einem neuerdings erhobenen vornehmen Ton in der Philosophie," in *Kant's Gesammelte Schriften* [Prussian Academy edition], vol. 8 (Berlin: DeGruyter, 1923), p. 398.

47. Heidegger, *Being and Time,* trans. John Macquarrie and Edward Robinson (New York: Harper and Row, 1962), pp. 269–70; *Sein und Zeit* (Tübingen: Niemeyer, 1967), p. 227.

48. Heidegger, "Phänomenologische Interpretationen zu Aristoteles," p. 261.

49. Heidegger, *Being and Time,* p. 88; *Sein und Zeit,* p. 61. Here it is Aristotle's *eidos;* at another point (177; German, 138), it is Aristotle's *theoria* which is being appropriated in Heidegger's German with the help of *verweilen.* Curiosity (*Neugier*), the fallen mode of knowing, is explicated in part through "not tarrying" (*unverweilen,* 216; German, 172). In *Being and Time verweilen* is not exclusively an attribute of the theoretical experience. Spending time with the dead at the grave is also discussed in terms of "tarrying" (282; German, 238).

50. Heidegger, *Grundbegriffe* (summer semester lectures 1941), ed. Petra Jaeger, in *Gesamtausgabe,* vol. 51 (Frankfurt am Main: Vittorio Klostermann, 1981), pp. 120–23; "Der Spruch des Anaximander," in *Holzwege* (Frankfurt am Main: Vittorio Klostermann, 1950), pp. 296–343, especially pp. 322 ff. *Verweilen* occurs in both these discussions amidst a play with various forms of the root *Weile* ("while," as in "a while"). Remarkably I have been unable to find *Verweilen* in the extensive discussion of *Langeweile* (boredom) in the *Grundbegriffe* lectures of 1929/30 (*Gesamtausgabe,* vol. 29/20).

51. For Kierkegaard, to whom Heidegger is much indebted in this regard, the "moment" is the intersection of time and eternity. For Kierkegaard we find here a momentary suspension of time.

52. In Gadamer's "Attempt at a Self-Critique" he asserts that "Verweilen ist offenkündig die eigentliche Auszeichnung in der Erfahrung von Kunst (*Verweilen* is evidently the real distinguishing mark of the experience of art)." See "Zwischen Phänomenologie und Dialektik—Versuch einer Selbstkritik," in *Gesammelte Werke,* vol. 2, p. 7. See also *The Relevance of the Beautiful,* trans. Nicholas Walker (Cambridge: Cambridge University Press, 1986), p. 45, where Gadamer writes: "The essence of our temporal experience of art is in learning how to tarry in this way. And perhaps it is the only way that is granted to us finite beings to relate what we call eternity." For the original see *Die Aktualität des Schönen* (Stuttgart: Reclam, 1977), p. 60.

53. Heidegger, "Phänomenologische Interpretationen zu Aristoteles," p. 231.

54. In "Art and Imitation" Gadamer writes: "For when it is correctly understood Aristotle's fundamental concept of mimesis has an elementary validity." See *The Relevance of the Beautiful,* p. 97; for the German, see "Kunst und Nachahmung," in *Kleine Schriften II* (Tübingen: J. C. B. Mohr, 1967), p. 21. In "The Relevance of the Beautiful" he writes: "The essence of what is called spirit lies in the ability to move within the horizon of an

open future and an unrepeatable past. Mnemosyne, the muse of memory and recollective appropriation, rules here as the muse of spiritual freedom." See *The Relevance of the Beautiful*, p. 10; *Die Aktualität des Schönen*, p. 12.

55. Gadamer, *The Idea of the Good*, p. 176; *Gesammelte Werke*, vol. 7, p. 226.

56. I have discussed this question in "Philosophical Discourse and the Ethics of Hermeneutics," in *Festivals of Interpretation*, ed. Kathleen Wright (Albany: State University of New York Press, 1990), pp. 63–88.

57. Two essays which are of some help with this question are "Philosophie und Poesie," in *Kleine Schriften*, vol. 4 (Tübingen: J. C. B. Mohr, 1977), pp. 241–48 (translation by Nicholas Walker in *The Relevance of the Beautiful*); and "Philosophie und Literatur," *Phänomenologische Forschungen* 11 (1981): 18–45. See also the collection of essays in the little volume *Lob der Theorie* (Frankfurt am Main: Suhrkamp, 1983).

58. Gadamer, "Philosophy and Poetry," in *The Relevance of the Beautiful*, p. 137.

59. Gadamer, *The Relevance of the Beautiful*, p. 133.

60. See Gadamer's *The Relevance of the Beautiful*, p. 42; *Die Aktualität des Schönen*, p. 56.

61. Gadamer, *Lob der Theorie*, p. 44. This is obviously quite close to Heidegger's treatment of theory as *verweilen* in *Being and Time*, which we cited above—the "mode of just tarrying alongside." *Haltung* is a translation of Aristotle's *hexis* (habit or state). The theoretical *Haltung* is what Aristotle calls the *hexis* of truth.

62. The work of Jacques Derrida is a good example of the continuation of Heideggerian dogmatism with regard to Plato. See his essay, "Plato's Pharmacy," in *Dissemination*, trans. Barbara Johnson (Chicago: University of Chicago Press, 1981), pp. 61–171, in which he finds aspects of the text that presumably work against the theses of the text. If we adopt a more sympathetic attitude, we see that the text was leading us to the very insights that supposedly undermine or deconstruct the text, namely, an insight into the positive importance of rhetoric and writing.

63. See especially Heidegger's *Beiträge* for which this is a central theme.

REPLY TO ROBERT J. DOSTAL

Like so many contributions from the United States, this work clearly exhibits the immense distance which in this case does not even concern the dominant philosophical and social ideas of value of the new continent. There is rather the amazing certainty and great presence of mind with which a clearly crucial topic which plays a great role in the present volume is being presented. It is true, and I can recognize myself in this, that in spite of the preponderance of Heidegger's ingenious rediscovery of ancient thought, in the end, I did not follow Heidegger's insistence upon the superiority of Aristotle over the Platonic model. This insistence cannot be described briefly and it can be verified at all only through access to Heidegger's early lectures from Freiburg and Marburg that has recently been gained. Heidegger's first attempt to deal with Plato himself was certainly dominated by the basic idea which Aristotelian metaphysics represented for him. It is hard to believe that one could elevate Aristotle to the rank of a model phenomenological thinker and that he did this not only for his teacher Husserl but especially for us, his students. But this Aristotle was lent a voice by Heidegger, so to speak, and it was a voice that reached us in our own lifeworld. It was really only the strange restrictions under which Heidegger finally conducted his appropriation of Plato that brought me on my own path which, in the end, led to a permanent dialogue with Plato. The task thus presented to me was certainly very comprehensive and it could only be carried out to a modest extent: to reveal a great master of language and of the poetic forming of humans such as Plato, a kind of anticipation of Aristotle's later turn to practical philosophy precisely because of Plato's artful and playful style, and to pursue the metaphysical implications of such an insight. But Dostal is correct: the effective unity of Plato and Aristotle, which is increasingly decisive in my later works, more and more finds confirmation in my view. It is on the basis of that view that I can understand our own thinking better, as well as our relation to language and our critique of misplaced logical formalism. I almost imagine that I have learned from Plato what Ordinary Language Analysis tried to accomplish in its own way. One will not believe this, and in a certain sense one is right. I myself cannot accomplish this. Yet in a dialogue with my experiences with Greek philosophers and with the timeless voice of art I can accomplish something which leads "to the things themselves."

H.-G.G.

15

Graeme Nicholson

TRUTH IN METAPHYSICS AND IN HERMENEUTICS

In his short book, *The Idea of the Good in Platonic-Aristotelian Philosophy,*[1] Gadamer shows that, despite Aristotle's criticisms of his teacher over this Idea, the deeper thrust of his thought was to perpetuate Plato's teaching. Both philosophers discerned that the Idea of the Good transcended other Ideas or principles in a special way. The human mind and heart were drawn more deeply to the Good than to anything else, and yet philosophy always found itself embarrassed when seeking to express what the Good was. Like Plato, Aristotle was ready to say that all virtues and sciences and substances had some share in the Good, but like Plato he had to grant that the Good could not be adequately defined in terms of any of them. This is what Plato expressed unforgettably in the *Republic* (509b9) with the statement that the Good lies "beyond being," for Plato means by "being" the form and definition of a given virtue or substance, that whereby our minds could grasp it. Of course, not only Plato and Aristotle inspired the comments of Gadamer, but their common master Socrates. His questionings, his *aporiae,* and his life testified with unique eloquence to the transcendence of the Good. We discover its transcendence clearly in those early Platonic dialogues where Socrates undertakes to question one or two representatives of an important institution or science, a representative of religion or law or the army. The *Laches,* for instance, shows that the generals Laches and Nicias regard themselves as experts on human courage. When Socrates asks them to define it, they do so by reference to the kinds of situation that arise in warfare. But the course of the dialogue shows that their military thought fails them precisely by reducing courage, *andreia,* to military art and science, domesticating something that is a universal human virtue to the habits of one profession. The reason they fail is that no such specialized thinking can express what is *good* about courage, why we regard it as a virtue.

This is a point which Gadamer has also made effectively in commenting on modern society and politics. Nobody should refuse the light that social science and social planning can bring to bear upon decisions that must be made today on behalf of groups and nations. Yet it is a weakness to rely too heavily upon science, administration, and planning. Where a decision must be made, the grounds for it cannot be brought to light through such modes of reasoning. We must learn to understand "the limitations of the expert,"[2] preserve a Socratic awareness of our own ignorance, comprehend that practical decisions stem from the *phronēsis* of the citizen rather than any specialty.

The present paper will argue that not only the Good has this transcendent status—the same thing holds for the principle of *truth*. While many discourses, modes of reasoning, arts, and the like are embodiments of truth and constituted by truth, we are unable to comprehend truth itself and define it through any of them. The Platonic Good could appear in a military context, or an athletic context, or a poetic or erotic or civic context without having an overarching generic definition, and without one such case being reducible to another. In the same way, truth will appear in mathematics, in rhetoric, in perception, in dialectic, and so on, without our being able to formulate a common definition, or reduce one of these domains to another. Actually, this parallel between the Good and the True should not surprise us. In the simile of the *Republic,* book 6, the sun is made into an illustration of the Good, but the rays of light that proceed from the sun and shine upon the intelligible objects and upon the mind are made into the illustration of truth. Truth, like the Good, must enter into the constitution of intelligible things, even while transcending them all.

In the first part of this paper, I shall sketch some passages from Plato and later authors in order to substantiate my claim that metaphysical thinking has always recognized this transcendent status of the principle of truth. By *always* giving us *more than one* concept or definition of truth, metaphysics is conceding the transcendence of truth over each and every one of its realizations. In the second part of the paper, I shall seek to show a parallel in Gadamer's *Truth and Method.* This is a hermeneutical philosophy that focusses attention on art and the experience of art; on history and the knowledge of history; on written works of law, theology, and philosophy and on the interpretation of such works. As *Truth and Method* probes into each of these domains, it pursues the question whether we have grounds for a claim to truth in these cases: is there truth in art? Is there truth in the interpretation of art? in the knowledge of history? in the interpretation of various kinds of text? It will be my case that Gadamer has succeeded in his inquiries—he has shown us grounds for the claim of truth. But I hope to show that his work resembles the metaphysical tradition in that it does not offer a single and unambiguous *definition* or *concept* of truth. It has been a subject of some discussion already whether Gadamer's work offers us a definition or concept of truth,[3] and whether, if it does not, that would be a point to welcome or to condemn. My hope is to show that this very question has a deep metaphysical background, a heritage from the time of Plato at the latest. I also hope to show by way of this background exploration why Gadamer still retains the right to use the word "truth" in the title of his book. There may be no univocal definition of truth, but lack of a definition of the Good or the True does not authorize a philosopher to drop these names or words. The vocation of Socratic-Platonic-Aristotelian thought is to renew our discourse and thought about such subjects ever again, for the subjects that retreat from the grasp of the understanding are the topics of philosophy.

TRUTH IN METAPHYSICS

My concern here will not be with the question whether metaphysics can attain truth in its inquiries—"metaphysical truth"—but rather with the manner in which metaphysics has delineated the nature of truth—"truth *according to* metaphysics." I'll begin with Plato's simile in the *Republic* of the Divided Line. The simile of the Sun proposed a fundamental dichotomy in human experience between intelligence and the intelligible world, on the one hand, and seeing and the visible world, on the other. The Divided Line does not deny the dichotomy, but it modifies it by presenting four kinds of experience and four kinds of object, rather than two, and by sketching ways in which the mind can move back and forth among the four. One consequence of this softening of the dichotomy is that Socrates is quite prepared to speak of truth, *alētheia,* in connection with our ordinary perception of ordinary things like animals and plants—we see this at 510a9–10, and again at the point where he gives this level of experience the name of *pistis,* 511e1–3. That is because, in the Divided Line simile, the four positions are being treated *relatively* to one another: the *alētheia* of one position is spoken of in comparison to another position's lack of *alētheia* or its lesser degree of *alētheia.* (We need not doubt, however, that *eikasia,* the lowest position of all, is utterly lacking in *alētheia,* a feature that is confirmed by the parable of the cave that follows.) *Alētheia* was introduced, in the simile of the Sun, as a bond or yoke that joins an awareness to its characteristic kind of object. This is not changed at all in the Divided Line. Mounting upwards from the bond which links *pistis* to everyday things, through the bond which links *dianoia* to its mathematical objects, to the bond which links *noēsis* to the full world of Forms, we can appreciate a mounting strength of *alētheia* at each step. To express this in modern terms, we would have truth in perception, truth in science, and truth in philosophy. The question is whether there is reason to expect a different *definition* of truth applicable in these domains, a different *essence* of truth, therefore, in perception, in science, and in philosophy. Or must truth itself be one and the same in each domain?

This question is very closely linked to the problem Heidegger addressed in 1947 in "Plato's Doctrine of Truth,"[4] although his focus there was on the parable of the cave, not the Divided Line. Heidegger treats the text of Plato historically, as an event in the emergence and consolidation of metaphysics. Lying at the heart of that history is a transformation that befell the essence of truth: the revision of an original essence of truth qua *alētheia,* unconcealment, to that essence that became normative in Western thought and science, truth qua correctness, *Richtigkeit.* In the early thought of the Greeks, *alētheia* was the unconcealment both of being, *to einai,* and of beings, *ta onta.* Only after a transformation of the essence of truth into correctness would it become possible for Western metaphysics and science to postulate accordance or correspondence, *homoiosis* or *adaequatio,* as the ground of the possibility of truth; correspondence can bring correctness about, but it could never have served as a relevant ground for unconcealedness. Heidegger finds the salient moment in the event of this transformation to be the cave parable of the *Republic.* For at several crucial points in the parable Plato begins to speak about the *orthotes, Richtigkeit,* of the mind's grasp of its objects, appearing to efface the earlier Greek apprehension of *alētheia.* Thus through Plato, metaphysics and science became the orthodox, methodical, self-securing competence over that which is, rather than a response to Being in its unconcealment.

I do not wish to comment here on Heidegger's hypothesis of historical transformation, or on the role of Plato in generating metaphysics and science. Instead, I want to make the point that the textual evidence for Heidegger's hypothesis could be appraised in a different way. Certainly we can discern a twofold discourse in the cave parable: *alētheia* on the one hand and *orthotes* on the other. Heidegger reads this as the transformation or even corruption of the one into the other. But it is possible to interpret the twofold discourse synchronically rather than historically, not as evidence of a macrohistorical transformation, but as a duplicity in the idea of truth that would receive its recognition in the Platonic text. Let me offer a defence of such a synchronous reading.

We first find the comparative adjective *orthoteron* at 515d4, where the released prisoner has turned away from the cave's flickering images, to try to glimpse the figures that were their prototypes within the cave: Socrates calls these figures *more real, mallon onta,* than the shadows, and says that the prisoner would *see them more correctly, orthoteron blepoi,* than he would have seen the shadows. But immediately Socrates adds that the prisoner might not yet be ready for any major insight: he might still think that the things he saw earlier were truer *(ta tote horomena alethestera)* than the things now pointed out to him (515d6–7). This synchrony of the two terms for truth seems to be reinforced later, where the prisoner has made a further advance. Now he has left the cave altogether, yet at first he has great difficulty in seeing *the things which are now said to be true, ton nun legomenon alethon* (516a3), "said," that is, by Socrates, Glaucon, and any philosophers who have completed the journey. Still later, at 517c, Socrates has completed the narrative of the parable and is setting out to interpret it; he says, "in the intelligible world the Form of the Good is the last to be seen, and with difficulty; when seen it must be reckoned to be for all the cause of all that is right and beautiful *(orthon te kai kalon),* to have produced in the visible world both light and the fount of light, while in the intelligible world it is itself that which produces and controls truth and intelligence *(alētheian kai noun*)." Heidegger's comment (*Platons Lehre,* pp. 43f.) seeks to disrupt the apparent parallelism between *orthon* and *alētheian* in these lines; though he might be right on that point, it still seems to me to be exaggerated to speak of the displacement or suppression of the latter by the former. The text will continue to speak of *alētheia* for pages to come, for instance, in describing the philosopher's vision at 520c5.

The best clue to my synchronous reading is perhaps 515d4, mentioned above, in which the prisoner at the beginning of his liberation (still in the cave) is said to see the originals of the images "more correctly," *orthoteron,* than he had seen the images on the wall of the cave. This particular kind of *perception* deserves the credit of correctness, or relative correctness compared to what went before. Earlier I referred to the equivalent passage in the Divided Line, 510a9–10, in which our awareness of living animals and plants was said to have an advantage—in respect of truth and untruth, *alētheia te kai me*—over the awareness of mere images of animals and plants; the proportion of truth to untruth there was the same as the proportional advantage enjoyed by the whole domain of *knowledge, to gnoston* (i.e., the entire upper division of the Line) over the whole domain of opinion, *to doxaston,* (i.e., the entire lower division). Such perception is now referred to in the cave parable as being "more correct" than image-seeing. Thus not only are there different *occasions* or *experiences* of truth—science, perception, etc.—but different *concepts* or *definitions* of it from occasion to occasion. While *alētheia* can be ascribed to science and philosophy, *orthotes* can be ascribed to perception.

This converges with a philosophical point I have tried to make[5] in criticism of Heidegger's own treatment of truth in *Being and Time.* He advances an account of truth as "disclosure," or as "unconcealment," and I do not dissent from that. But in the course of his argument, Heidegger seeks to reject other accounts of truth that focus on "correctness" and "correspondence." My case is that his counteroffensive cannot prevail in the way he thinks; the Heideggerian account of truth is not able to *set aside* or *eliminate* the other, but must find a way to make peace with it. In this way, he finds himself, philosophically, in a position rather like Plato's in the *Republic.*

I have referred to Plato to make a more general point, that any metaphysical thinking will always have more than one concept of truth. To offer a history of the concepts of truth is out of the question here, but I may promote my point by adding a few more examples. It is well known that Aristotle, in *Metaphysics, Epsilon,* chap. 4, claimed that truth was found not in things but in thoughts, and could not occur except through the combination of terms. Yet we find in *Theta,* chap. 10, a view that is most difficult to square with that, where being-true is an element in the very being and substance of things. This duality between a logical and an ontological principle of truth has perplexed scholars for many years,[6] but it may arise from a need similar to that which prompted Plato's twofold meaning: the transcendence of truth itself. Both dualities, Plato's and Aristotle's, could be traced through medieval thinkers, I believe, and would lead us into the varying relations of philosophical truth and revealed truth. But it would be more telling still to call attention to the modern authors who seem to have recognized the multifarious character of truth. Kant's formal-logical account of truth, for example, is explicitly differentiated from a transcendental account of truth at the opening of the *Critique of Pure Reason's* Transcendental Logic. But let me devote some attention here to Spinoza, because Gadamer assigns him a leading role among the Enlightenment philosophers and treats his hermeneutical theory at some length in *Truth and Method.*

For Spinoza, as for Descartes, an *idea* is the subject, or the bearer, of truth and falsity. In an early passage of the *Ethics,* part 1, axiom 6, Spinoza says that "a true idea should agree with its ideal *(ideatum),* i.e., what it conceives," appearing to endorse a correspondence theory of truth. But we see in part 2, definition 4, that a weightier feature of an idea is its *adequacy:* "By adequate idea I understand an idea which, if it is considered in itself without respect to the object, has all the properties or intrinsic marks of a true idea," where "intrinsic" is meant to exclude the agreement between the idea and its ideal. So adequacy is precisely not a case of truth, as truth has been defined. The adequacy of an idea is its presence in the divine intellect, though it can be discovered by ourselves in practice through the capacity of the idea to be generated purely a priori. No mind is an island, complete and entire unto itself, but a portion of the mind of God; and the adequacy of *our* ideas consists in their being thought within us by God (part 2, proposition 11, corollary). Now when that circumstance prevails, our ideas will certainly be true, because in the divine intellect all ideas are true; after all, by one and the same power, intellectual ideas and things are generated by God. On the other hand, images generated in the human mind by sense or imagination are not adequate, but they may be true or they may be false, in the sense that "adequacy" involves a merely adventitious form of truth.

The Spinozist adequacy is the heir of the Cartesian principle of truth, which, after all, was defined in the Fourth Meditation as an outflow of the perfection of God *prior to* any doctrine about the material things of the world, their very existence or nonexistence.

Let me conclude this section with a brief reference to the hermeneutical theory of Spinoza's *Theologico-Political Treatise.* Here, moral goodness and obedience, as exemplified by the prophets, constitute the actual point of religious life and are the guideline for all appropriation of scripture. What is called the "truth" of religious doctrines, on the other hand, is their agreement with history or with nature, and for Spinoza this is an adventitious and secondary question, like the truths of sense and imagination as they were treated in the *Ethics.* It would be a useful inquiry, however, to explore whether some different principle of *truth* does not prove necessary in defining true obedience, true morality, and true religion.

TRUTH IN HERMENEUTICS

I am not concerned here with the attainment of truth in some practice of interpretation or other, but with the question of how the hermeneutical theory of Gadamer has *spoken about* truth.

One point I hope to address is his relation to Heidegger, particularly over the concept or the essence of truth. Gadamer works under the influence of a Heideggerian conception of truth as *alētheia,* though he does not seem to defend it explicitly or in detail in his work. But while *Truth and Method* is indebted to Heidegger, that does not mean that its argument holds only on the condition that truth is understood as *alētheia.* In fact, his hermeneutical argument as such is neutral as to different "theories" or definitions of truth. It would not lose its force for someone who approached it with some other definition of truth, influenced by a Platonic or Spinozist or materialist conception.

Another point is that there is a multifarious meaning assigned to the terms "true" and "truth" here, in just the way I've been reviewing in texts of metaphysics. The main thrust of my comments will be to exhibit three of the contexts which give, case by case, different shadings to the concept of truth.

(A) *Art.* The term "truth" lies at the centre of the introduction to the book, pp. xxv–xxix,[7] which stresses the need to give foundations to the claim to truth that is implicit in our experience of art, art interpretation, historical knowledge, and philosophy. And the lengthy study of art that constitutes part 1 reverts repeatedly to the theme of the *experience* of art. But we learn as we read on that this is also an experience of truth in the work of art. The section called "The Retrieval of the Question of Artistic Truth," pp. 77–96, has a powerful criticism of the idealism or aestheticism that we used to know, views that gave the arts a kind of genteel vocation, a decoration at the margin of real life. This section appeals urgently to the seriousness of art and our encounter with it.

> Is there to be no knowledge in art? Does not the experience of art contain a claim to truth which is certainly different from that of science, but equally certainly is not inferior to it? And is not the task of aesthetics precisely to provide a basis for the fact that artistic experience is a mode of knowledge of a unique kind, certainly different from that sensory knowledge which provides science with the data from which it constructs the knowledge of nature, and certainly different from all moral rational knowledge and indeed from all conceptual knowledge, but still knowledge, i.e., the transmission of truth? (p. 93)

The intention that is expressed in these lines is then fulfilled in the chapter that follows, "The Ontology of the Work of Art and its Hermeneutical Significance." What we encounter in the work of art is truth in the form of play, and truth in the form of structure—something that quite outstrips classical and modern concepts of *mimesis* and *representation.*

> The work of art is conceived as an ontological event and the abstraction to which aesthetic differentiation commits it is dissolved. A picture is an event of presentation. Its relation to the original is so far from being a reduction of the autonomy of its being that, on the contrary, I had to speak, in regard to the picture, of an 'increase of being'. The use of concepts from the sphere of the holy seemed appropriate. (p. 144)

The picture does not point away from itself; it draws us into itself; and its being does not suffer from a deficiency relative to some represented subject; what it gives to us is entirely what it itself *is*. In a later essay,[8] Gadamer expresses this point with a wonderful illustration from poetry in particular.

> The poet Paul Valéry, who must have known, formulated a brilliant metaphor for the difference between words used in spoken communication and the poetic word. The spoken word is like a coin, i.e., it means something that it is not. The gold coin of the past, however, had as well the value which it signified, since the metallic value of the gold coin equaled its value as a coin. So it was itself at the same time what it meant. Clearly, the distinctive value of the poetic word is exactly that it does not refer to something in such a manner that one is directed away from it, in order to arrive somewhere else, as the coin or bill needs its backing. In poetry, when one is directed away from the word, one is also at the same time directed back to it; it is the word itself which guarantees that about which it speaks.[9]

The poem, and generally the work of art, is true in a sense that includes the coincidence between its meaning and its being, its form and its matter. Here truth is experienced, because the truth *of* the artwork is not to be differentiated from the work itself, its being and its meaning. Here we encounter a concept of truth that ties truth directly to being, and it is akin to themes we know from antiquity: the Aristotelian bond of truth with being (*Theta,* 10) and the Platonic discourse about the true things (e.g., *Republic* 515d or 516a). Such an experienced truth is not what we encounter in a scientific or philosophical theory.

(B) *History.* Going from the experience of truth in the work to an interpretation of the work—as in the exposition of a literary work—is a major step, and if truth is to be found in expository interpretation, it may well not be the same as the truth we experience in the work. On pp. 250–90 of the German text, "The Elevation of the Historicality of Understanding to the Status of Hermeneutical Principle," Gadamer is touching on the possibility of truth in textual interpretation, in particular reconciling truth with our being historical, our historicality or historicity.

Gadamer's is a strikingly *modern* hermeneutical theory, very heavily indebted to the Hegelian philosophy, to the nineteenth-century philosophers of history, and to Heidegger. He lays stress on the positioning of every author in the midst of a culture and a tradition, and also upon the equivalent positioning of every interpreter in a culture and a tradition, and he stresses the distance in time and culture that frequently separates the two. He also calls attention to the interior impact of the very flow of time and history upon all human understanding. The event of understanding is never to be separated from the anticipations and interests that drive us in our lives. But what is called *interpretation,* including interpretation of texts, is just one more operation of our understanding. Our own domestic drives and interests, thus, play a central role in our interpretation of Plato or Aristophanes or the Bhagavad Gita.

The quality of this historicism can be made clearest through a contrast with older hermeneutical theories. Let us take a look at Spinoza. The example of Spinoza serves as an ideal counterexample to Gadamer because Gadamer took the trouble in *Truth and Method* to deal with Spinoza, seeing him as the perfect embodiment of the Enlightenment. Gadamer wished to differentiate his own theory of the historical shaping of all understanding and interpretation from the views of seventeenth- and eighteenth-century rationalism, to reject the dichotomies between reason, on the one hand, and tradition or imagination or authority or prejudice, on the other. What is it, then, that Gadamer sets against someone like Spinoza? He sees that Spinoza has an unhistorical, essentialist view of understanding and interpretation, mere implementation of the faculty of reason. But, for Gadamer, as for Heidegger, to understand is to *project.* The section we are scrutinizing is devoted to demonstrating that truth can be obtained in interpretation precisely on Heidegger's premise that understanding and interpretation always have a projective aspect. It follows, according to Gadamer, that our understanding and interpretation will always implement *prejudices.* Indeed, that is one of Gadamer's best-known points. By "prejudice" Gadamer means the finiteness of every understanding we achieve, the circumstance that every understanding and interpretation will be controlled to some degree by preconceptions that are not brought to consciousness and that reflect the viewpoint of the interpreter, and the times of the interpreter, rather than the interpreted text. For that reason, all interpretation is also subject to tradition, and to the pressure of current authority.

> It is the general tendency of the Enlightenment not to accept any authority and to decide everything before the judgment seat of reason. Thus the written tradition of scripture, like any other historical document, cannot claim any absolute validity, but the possible truth of the tradition depends on the credibility that is assigned to it by reason. It is not tradition, but reason that constitutes the ultimate source of all authority. What is written down is not necessarily true. We may have superior knowledge: that is the maxim with which the modern enlightenment approaches tradition and which ultimately leads it to undertake historical research. It makes the tradition as much an object of criticism as do the natural sciences the evidence of the senses. (p. 257)

But the individual and autonomous reason of Cartesian and Enlightenment thought is an obstacle in the way of understanding. Instead of that, the interpreter needs to understand himself or herself as a finite and situated being, subject to social controls that will have a positive sense for the work of understanding. The very agitations of our own being, arising from our own interests and those of our time, have a positive role to play; movement, *Bewegtheit,* is not an obstacle to our encounter with the text but an aid to it. We read the famous sentence: "It is enough to say that we understand in a different way if we understand at all" (p. 280).

When the interpreter understands most drastically his or her situation, finitude, subjection to the needs of the time, and exposure to the nonsubjective power of history, the possibility arises for an interpretation that is subject to *effective* history; here too lies the possibility of that "fusion of horizons" that actually constitutes truth in interpretation. It should be apparent that while this historicality may well be grounds for truth in interpretation, that truth *cannot* be the autonomous identity with being that we discovered in the work of art itself. Truth in interpretation is precisely *not* the same as the truth in the work; Gadamer separates text and interpretation, and has no affinity, either, with modern efforts to assimilate the two of them under a generic concept of *écriture.*

But under what circumstances is truth, fusion of horizons, achieved? We come here to the distinction between true prejudices and false prejudices, pp. 256ff. The principle of true prejudice was defended by German thinkers both of the Enlightenment and romanticism, originally as a true prejudice in favour of Christianity, its myths, its history, and rootedness in nature. Gadamer is not himself defending this content in a neo-romantic fashion, but he recognizes the general category as signifying an orientation of our being that operates in advance of rational reflection. It might be possible for Gadamer to state which true prejudices he himself would authorize in place of the romanticists'. I would suspect they would include prejudices in favour of progress, democracy, freedom, and equality, with the point that purely rational argument could not establish these as modern ideals. In any case, given the historical references with which Gadamer introduced the concept of true prejudice, and in the lack of alternatives to the romantic contents, this is a concept that has always caused me difficulty. At a later page, 282, true prejudices come into the text again: they serve as the condition for a true interpretation. Some readers of Gadamer have suspected a circularity problem here, in that the *truth* of the true prejudices would be *established* by their success in generating true interpretation. This would indeed be a vicious circle, but Gadamer is not guilty of it; the impression arose, I believe, from his hesitation in stating the substance of the true prejudices, such as the prejudice in favour of universal freedom. The concept of truth that is at work here in the prejudice is a priori relative to the truth of an interpretation, and must be defined in some other way. Moreover, the truth of a true prejudice is obviously different from truth encountered in a work of art.

(C) *Language.* As the work moves towards its close, pp. 415ff., Gadamer treats "Language as Horizon of a Hermeneutic Ontology"; the metaphysical dimension implicit in the whole argument is to be broached. Here Gadamer must confront the principle of truth quite directly. He has treated in earlier sections the principle of experience in Hegel and von Humboldt, drawing out from them the way in which a form of life and a form of experience are deposited in a language. But if a language is the record of a given humanity's experience, the question must be asked how it could ever prepare us for the experience of truth. Here Gadamer reveals his debt to Heidegger with a reference to *alētheia;* yet as we shall see he also takes a distance from Heidegger.

> The linguistic nature of the human experience of the world was the guide-line along which Greek metaphysics since Plato's 'flight into the *loqoi'* developed its thinking about being. . . . Greek metaphysics, in considering the being of beings, saw this as a being that fulfilled itself in thought. . . . The articulation of the *logos* expresses the structure of the being, and this expression is, for Greek thought, nothing other than the presence of the being itself, its *alētheia.* It is the infinity of this presence, which human thought regards as its fulfilled potential, its divinity. (pp. 432f.)

Yet I believe that the remark that follows immediately signifies a commitment, Hegelian in tone, to mediation, self-consciousness, and modern responsibility— a tone that separates Gadamer's appropriation of the Greeks from that of Heidegger (and that of Nietzsche):

> We do not follow this way of thinking, in its splendid self-forgetfulness, and so we shall have to consider to what extent we are able to follow its renewal on the basis of the modern idea of subjectivity to be found in Hegel's absolute idealism.

Gadamer does not want to posit a disclosure or *alētheia* that is independent of and prior to our human use of language, and all the contingency and historicity that language brings. Yet the centre of language is nevertheless the event of disclosure—to speak is to reveal the world. And this event should not be separated from the radiance of the beautiful, of which the Platonic dialogues speak, pp. 449ff.

> [Plato] was the first to show that the essential element in the beautiful was *alētheia,* and it is clear what he means by this. The beautiful, the way in which goodness appears, reveals itself in its being, it presents itself. (p. 462)

This radiance brings us an encounter with all the "transcendentals" at once, an experience of being as well as of beauty and truth. Certainly we have returned here to the theme of part 1, the experience of truth in the work of art, but here the theme is made more universal, or, I would say, more metaphysical. The place of the work of art is now secured through a broad philosophical treatment of language. Gadamer is allowing, in this climactic step of his investigation, for the event of truth in philosophical or metaphysical thinking.

GRAEME NICHOLSON

DEPARTMENT OF PHILOSOPHY
TRINITY COLLEGE, UNIVERSITY OF TORONTO
JUNE 1992

NOTES

1. Hans-Georg Gadamer, *The Idea of the Good in Platonic-Aristotelian Philosophy,* trans. P. Christopher Smith (New Haven: Yale University Press, 1986).

2. Gadamer, "Die Grenzen des Experten," in *Das Erbe Europas* (Frankfurt: Suhrkamp, 1989); now translated by Lawrence Schmidt and Monica Reuss in *Hans-Georg Gadamer on Education, Poetry, and History,* ed. D. Misgeld and G. Nicholson (Albany: State University of New York Press, 1992).

3. See the excellent discussions by Robert Bernasconi, "Bridging the Abyss: Heidegger and Gadamer," in *Research in Phenomenology* 16 (1986): 1–24; Jean Grondin, "Hermeneutics and Relativism," in K. Wright, ed., *Festivals of Interpretation* (Albany: State University of New York Press, 1990), pp. 42–62; and Robert J. Dostal, "Philosophical Discourse and the Ethics of Hermeneutics," in Wright, op. cit., pp. 63–88.

4. Martin Heidegger, *Platons Lehre von der Wahrheit; Mit einem Brief ueber den 'Humanismus'* (Bern: Francke Verlag, 1947); trans. J. Barlow in *Philosophy in the Twentieth Century,* vol. 3, ed. W. Barrett and H. D. Aiken (New York: Random House, 1962).

5. Graeme Nicholson, *Illustrations of Being* (New Jersey and London: Humanities Press International, 1992), pp. 74–81.

6. See *Aristotle's Metaphysics,* ed. W. D. Ross (Oxford: Clarendon Press, 1924 and 1966), vol. 2, pp. 274ff.

7. My page citations will be to the 1965 German edition, though where I quote the text in English, I mostly use the phrases of the translators G. Burden and J. Cumming, who first rendered the book into English (London: Sheed and Ward, 1975).

8. Gadamer, "Verstummen die Dichter?", 1970, in *Poetica: Ausgewaehlte Essays* (Frankfurt: Insel Verlag, 1977), pp. 103–18; trans. L. Schmidt and M. Reuss, "Are the Poets Falling Silent?", in *Hans-Georg Gadamer on Education, Poetry, and History,* pp. 73–81.

9. Ibid., trans., p. 73.

REPLY TO GRAEME NICHOLSON

Metaphysics and hermeneutics are confronted here as two fields of philosophical questioning, and both are examined with respect to the way in which truth is the decisive claim. In these fields one moves within the field of the so-called transcendentals, that is, those philosophical concepts that are not generic concepts but that transcend all limitations of the *genus* through their universality. Thus, this essay begins with reminding us of Plato's 'beyond being' which makes the concept of the good an indefinable one, so to speak. It is almost self-evident that the logical conditions of definitions can only be fulfilled within the specification system of genera and kinds. Nonetheless, the Socratic question 'What is that?' is obviously being posed beyond those generic concepts, too. The author then begins first of all with Heidegger's well-known conceptual distinction when he expressly distinguishes truth as unconcealment from *orthotes* as correctness, and when he believes that he, in turn, recognizes in the latter the real fall away from the question of being which, in turn, would be displaced by the concern for correctness and which in a certain sense would mark a concern for certainty instead of truth. The author wants to show now that in truth unconcealment and correctness present themselves as a two-sidedness and ambiguity of the concept of truth itself. After having placed the concept of truth, as it were, into the open in this way against Heidegger, he finds in my own works on hermeneutics, especially those in the field of art, history, and language, a concept of truth such that it could not be related to the opposition of unconcealment and correctness. To speak of definition, however, in cases where we cannot be dealing with the relation between genus and its specifications, is an awkward matter. In logic one usually tries to solve such cases by means of the so-called implied definition. This is quite understandable in the use of the concepts at issue, for example, truth and being-true. But at bottom every implied definition is a determination abstracted from its linguistic usage. If one is being led in this way to the linguistic symbolic power of these highest philosophical concepts, then one finds a commonality wedding them despite the Heideggerian opposition to both concepts. At bottom, *alētheia* of Being refers to what is precisely not a matter of propositional truth. Thus, in his catalogue of concepts, Aristotle did not restrict himself to this meaning of *alētheia*. Only this much might be correct: when dealing with words one always views *alētheia* as a kind of superlative, the absolutely highest, and in *orthotes* as correctness one sees a comparative. Correctness (*Richtigkeit*), as the German word indicates, only refers to a directedness

(Richtung) toward something, it signifies only approximations, just as the correct view, which Plato calls *doxa,* only approximates the view of the thing itself. Of course, you cannot expect unequivocality in the use of words, not even in the use of *doxa* in the Platonic dialogues. This would be entirely opposed to the primacy of the dialogue and of the dialectic. The meaning of a concept is usually determined, among other things, by the word and the use of language. Aristotle demonstrates that in *Metaphysics Delta* with reference to a variety of random examples.

Nicholson now deals with the definition of truth as correspondence or adequation with the help of Spinoza. Then he extends the philosophical concept of truth in metaphysics to the concept of truth in hermeneutical philosophy. The focus of the discussion is the claim that art could speak truth too. One has to admit here, however, that the conceptual imprint of the term "art" has been inherited from metaphysics itself so that this term could enter linguistic usage only after the *Critique of Pure Reason.* In English, for example, one has to say 'fine art' in order to determine more precisely the ambiguity of the concept "art." In German, the term *"die Kunst"* became unequivocal and carries an eminent stream of meaning only after the critical dissolution of Aristotelian metaphysics through Kant and his followers. The author's reference to Valéry makes this evident. One can also certainly use "history" in a very universal field of application as when one speaks of "the history" or the "story." But there is an extension of the concept of truth latent in that use. In this regard the formation of the concept of "historicity" can help us out in certain contexts. The third point discussed by the author concerning the meaning of 'tradition' might be even more convincing. This can refer to the translatability of what is experienced into language, and if that is the case it has unlimited validity. By contrast, when I speak of 'linguisticality' *(Sprachlichkeit),* the meaning of the concept is prior to the event of the building of the tower of Babylon, prior to the multiplicity of languages. At the same time, however, this means that such a concept can hardly be defined unequivocally. Precisely the indefinability of that which is experienced in linguistic wording maintains its own, far-reaching rights over against the artificial tradition of the conceptual language of metaphysics and philosophy—as in pointing toward what is worth knowing.

H.-G.G.

16

Thomas M. Alexander

EROS AND UNDERSTANDING: GADAMER'S AESTHETIC ONTOLOGY OF THE COMMUNITY

Just as recent political events have seen the destruction of walls and barriers which have needlessly separated people, so in the world of philosophy self-imposed barriers between various schools and traditions are beginning to collapse, and new dialogues are emerging. This essay may be a case in point, for I speak here by no means as a specialist of Gadamer's thought. Rather, I come to his work from the tradition of American pragmatism, especially as developed by John Dewey. My purpose, however, will not be to explore in detail all the similarities between Gadamer's philosophy and Dewey's—though they are surprisingly many. I shall try to indicate some common points very briefly. But the primary focus of this essay will be to raise several questions about the side of Gadamer's hermeneutics which points toward what might be called an aesthetic ontology of the human community. I hope to draw out some comments by Professor Gadamer which elucidate further the relationship between Eros, understanding, the other, and the ideal of the community.

In particular, it seems at times as though Gadamer makes both the self and other disappear into the text when there is a genuine fusion of horizons and the claim of the truth of the beautiful shines forth. The dialogic nature of understanding cannot merely be a condition of such communion; instead it is consummated in such a moment. The event of understanding is a moment in the *realization* of community. And though it is true that understanding is objectively focused upon the subject-matter, the event itself manifests the human capacity for genuinely being-with another. We experience the meaning of the world through our dialogical existence, and this existence consequently is governed by a drive or Eros toward such embodied, aesthetically imbued experience. Through our existence as beings-in-community, we come to have a self and to be present to others; moreover, we transcend the individualizing horizons of our mortality in the openness whose configurations are the modes of love. Hermeneutics is above all an ontology of community.

I. Pragmatism and Hermeneutics

If pragmatism has anything to offer Gadamerian hermeneutics, it may be in showing how a robust philosophy of community is possible, where community is understood as a time process in which the human project of living achieves a deep sense of inherent meaning and value. The primary need for human beings, according to Dewey, is to realize as concretely as possible in their actions and experiences a sense of aesthetic fulfillment. When human life is reduced to mindless routine and mechanical boredom, when it is random and chaotic, when it is lived in fear or in isolation, a deep-seated frustration occurs which may be so powerful as to evoke highly destructive and seemingly aimless acts of aggression. It is the major project of the human community to secure those conditions whereby this basic human need can be fulfilled; for Dewey, this is the source of "civilization and its discontents." This basic drive for experiencing meaning and value might be called the "Human Eros," distinguishing it thereby from both Freud's animal eros of sublimated sexuality as well as from Plato's *eros* which seeks to imitate perfect, changeless Being. Gadamer, too, sees human existence as fundamentally a quest for the realization of meaning through the ongoing play of language in which a fusion of horizons allows the intrinsic experience of beauty to become manifest.[1]

Death, however, also structures our world, as Plato, Freud, and Heidegger have each realized, though in very different ways. So, too, for Dewey. Our finite mortality not only shapes our experience of time in terms of generating a sense of our individuality realized through choice and action, but it shapes the social experience of the world. Though individuals die, the culture is passed on. Through the human ability to learn and teach, our mortality is transcended in a very concrete way. Though Dewey often stresses the importance of "reconstructing" our past to shape a better future and Gadamer often speaks of the authority of tradition upon the present, their views are quite complementary. Culture is a process which challenges any philosophy of radical individualization. It is because of culture that helpless human infants are cared for and raised, taught language and behavior, and eventually come to participate for themselves in the symbolic life of a living tradition which they, in turn, may pass on. Our human understanding, then, is shaped by our capacity to be open to the other, both as teacher and student.[2]

Finally, both Dewey and Gadamer see human experience as radically contextual and bound by tragic finitude. As beings-in-the-world, we never find ourselves with the possibility of absolute knowledge of completely determinate Being. We are always in process and on the way. We find ourselves in contexts which are dynamic, in which there is both clarity and ambiguity, determination and indetermination. The sense of meaning of the situation is not strictly cognized intellectually, but is pervaded by a tacit horizon and the dim sense of direction we are taking. The unsaid gives meaning to the spoken, and the spoken, in turn, addresses itself to an as yet unrealized response. In their theories of meaning, both Dewey and Gadamer turn away from objectifications of formal systems, whether of natural languages or artificial ones, to focus on the *experience* of meaning. For Gadamer this is illustrated primarily in the dialogue, for Dewey in the act of communication. But both thinkers see such processes as possibilities for the realization of an inherent aesthetic experience of meaning, which Dewey calls the "consummatory" and Gadamer the "truth" of beauty or *alētheia,* following here Heidegger's interpretation.

Dewey's idea of the consummatory and Gadamer's notion of *alētheia* may seem actually to be a point of strong divergence between their views. Dewey limits the question of truth to what can be successfully predicted on the basis of past experience subjected to methodologies of inquiry: truth is provisional and future-oriented, and so is best called "warranted assertibility." But *alētheia* is the direct presence of the beautiful which authorizes itself and compels us by its own internal closure. In short, Dewey states that meaning is wider than truth and, ultimately, more important.[3] Gadamer states that any methodological sense of truth must be derivative from a more primordial human experience which is the "disclosure" of the thing itself in its meaning. If we recall that the original sense of *alētheia* is really more "not escaping notice" or "unforgetful" (or "mindful"), and the original meaning of "truth" is faithfulness and reliability, *treowth,* "troth," there may be some *rapprochement.*[4] By attending to what shows itself, it is manifest and this establishes the basis of our "faith" with it, depending on its disclosure so that we may again recognize it.

This is a provisional suggestion, which will be expanded later on. The essential point for now is simply that the relationship between pragmatism and hermeneutics cannot be glibly dismissed because of the mistaken notion that the one has a "positivistic" and the other an "intuitionist" view of truth. Both Dewey and Gadamer have sought to develop theories of human experience and have done so by trying to focus on the richest and fullest moments of experience, those in which a work of art speaks to us and addresses us. For Dewey, such consummatory experience is a moment in which human expression realizes itself most completely; it is the highest form of communication. Though Gadamer is not inclined to speak this way, I would like to explore the fundamental role of the other in his theory of language.

II. THE OTHER AS CONDITION FOR UNDERSTANDING

Gadamer's purpose is "to conceive the original phenomenon of language in dialogue."[5] In his "Letter to Dallmayr," Gadamer says, "The word is what one person speaks and another understands."[6] This marks his approach as proceeding phenomenologically from the experience of the event of language rather than from some theoretical construct that assumes language is a fixed totality which speech merely instantiates. It would be hard to find a more profound beginning for any theory of meaning than this, and the variety of philosophical positions in this century deriving from one or the other of these assumptions are testimony to the consequences which can follow from such a seemingly innocuous beginning. Here, I think, we find one of the most significant underlying prejudices of Gadamer's hermeneutics, one which, as I have indicated, he shares with Dewey.

This assumption makes Gadamer think of living speech as the "event of understanding." Though language itself transcends any individual or even group of individuals at a given historical moment, there is implicit in the structure of understanding itself the dimensions of speaker and listener; thus the event itself presents the possibility for the "fusion of horizons," that moment of agreement, toward which the act of speech itself is teleologically directed. For the process of speech is nothing less than the overcoming of alienation for Gadamer. Through it we not only come to develop a range of distinctions and concepts which constitute our self and our world, but we have the genuine ability to become changed or transformed, replacing the limited, provincial world of a former self with the broader and enriched view gained from our ability to open to and appropriate that which at first seemed alien, other, and strange. It is one of Gadamer's strongest objections to the deconstructionists, or to any followers of a "method of suspicion," be it Nietzschean, Freudian, or Marxist, that without the possibility of understanding, there would be no possibility of misunderstanding. In other words, if human beings could not truly come to participate in each other's worlds, and so be genuinely present to each other and agree, they could not even communicate in order to deceive or agree to disagree.

This is in fact the fundamental moral lesson of Gadamer's philosophy. Though he has rejected the possibility of human beings acquiring a universal, absolute, objective science of ourselves or the world, he actively demands that the very dialectic of understanding is to drive us toward a more global point of view, one which has become genuinely educated and humanistically circumspect. The cultivated individual *(Der Gebildete)* is one who has a sensitivity to the histories, nuances, and differences of the range of human experience and who can apply this Goethean breadth with judgment and humanity.[7] *Homo sum: Nihil humanum me alienum puto.* While Gadamer himself sees this virtue exemplified in the ability to understand texts from distant ages or cultures, it is also found in the daily applications of practical wisdom, *phronēsis,* whereby we live with our fellow human beings. The *Geisteswissenschaften* or human studies have the ability to educate our understanding in this fundamental way.[8]

The crucial feature, then, of understanding for Gadamer is its ability to be *open,* and this openness is directly related to the dialogical nature of language. Without the role of the "other" in speech, there would be no process of learning and thus no understanding of self or world. This "other" is no mere dialectical concept; indeed, in *Truth and Method* Gadamer gives it the title of "Thou," or *Du*.[9]

Gadamer's "Thou" deserves some analysis, for it is neither the "Thou" of Martin Buber, though there are clearly similarities and, perhaps, some indebtedness here, nor is it the "Thou" of Emmanuel Levinas. Buber's "Thou" always remains on a fairly equal dialogical footing with the "I." Levinas, on the contrary, has raised his other to the principle of an inscrutable, dominating absolute which demands submission from the I.[10] Gadamer's "Thou," however, can be as radically concrete as the immediate "you" of any conversation; it may be a collective "you" of the community; it may rise to the generality of the speaking voice of a cultural tradition. It may even have almost the grandeur and indefiniteness of Levinas's other, as the eternal other in the structure of the process of meaning itself. In any of these cases, it has the function of revealing the openness as well as the finitude of our understanding. Like the "I," the "Thou" has the capacity to grow. Gadamer has given a reading of the history of hermeneutics, in fact, as an effort to come to grips with the elusive, even paradoxical nature of this "Thou." It is this "Thou" which always surpasses the strategies of any given method and, for Gadamer, makes the question of truth more fundamental and primordial. I will look at three moments of the Thou: as temptation, as communal, and as cultural.

III. THE "THOU" AS TEMPTATION, COMMUNITY, AND TRADITION

The Thou as Temptation: In his essay "Text and Interpretation" (the occasion for his nonexchange with Derrida), Gadamer says, "What we find happening in speaking is not a mere reification of intended meaning, but an endeavor that continually modifies itself, or, better: a continually recurring temptation to engage oneself in something or to become involved with someone. But that means to expose oneself and to risk oneself."[11] This, of course, is the "risk of prejudices" which is also a risk of one's very self. "The mere presence of the other before whom we stand helps us break down our own bias and narrowness," he says, adding that there is in this experience "a potentiality for being other that lies beyond every coming to agreement about what is common."

There is more here, I think, than simply a moment of existential risk followed by the recovered authentic act of choice, which was conceived, whether by Sartre or Heidegger, as a moment of lonely autonomy. It was their principle of individuation, so to speak. Gadamer, instead, speaks of it as a temptation not only to risk oneself and become a "new self," but as a temptation to become exposed to or involved with *another*. One is not merely open to an abstract realm of possibility and freedom, but to another voice which speaks. The other here reveals that our understanding is a power of imagination (a "movement of spirit," as Gadamer might say in one of his Hegelian moments) to go out beyond the self that we are and try to understand our situation and our world through the mediation of another. The other here becomes the incarnation of *our* (not "my") finite freedom. Even where we are involved in a disagreement, we are constantly trying to "read" ourselves from the standpoint of the other, even if only to find words which will convince, silence, or humiliate that other.

This "temptation" to become involved, this "presence" which suddenly illuminates the stasis of our accumulated self, is the first indication, I believe, of the shining of the beautiful. It is an erotic lure which reveals, if nothing else, the possibility for the fusion of horizons which, as I said, drives the human quest for meaning. To be sure, in many instances of our lives this possibility is not realized or is only marginally realized. Nevertheless, this lure was the very one which motivated our development from infancy.

Gadamer does not spend much time discussing the transformation of the prelinguistic infant into the world of language, though much of what he says points to the fact that, like Dewey again, the learning of language is for him more central than such sterile ideals as "linguistic competency." But we begin life full of needs which others must meet if we are not to die. The "other" is a biological necessity for us. The world of these others, the organized family and its sustaining community, exists because of language and communication. If we are eventually to take our place in this world, we too must become communicants. Thus from the beginning, long before we can speak, we are spoken to. It is because we are spoken to, in fact, that we in turn come to speak—very much as Gadamer suggests, by learning to play the language games which constitute so much of infant speech and infant-adult exchanges. As John Dewey and his friend and colleague George Herbert Mead argued, it is by learning to "take the role of the other" that we come to see ourselves as participants and as communicators.[12] It is only after I can imagine how you will interpret a gesture or sound, see how I am a part of your world, that I can then *use* that gesture or sound to communicate. When I have the ability to project myself imaginatively into your point of view, thereby having the ability to understand how you will respond to my action, I can then determine my actions to elicit the response I desire. If you can, in turn, imagine yourself as a feature in my world, then we can indeed communicate and, in participating in each other's worlds through the interplay of gestures guided by a mutual social imagination, be present to each other. Through such interplay, we develop our sense of self along with our sense of the other. The temptation to the other, then, arises from perhaps the most fundamental human needs, the need to be present to another in order to have a self or world at all.

There is one final point to make here, which involves the role of faith and trust in the other. Again, like Dewey, Gadamer has rejected any ideal of knowledge as the quest for certainty possible for an isolated Cartesian spectator-ego. Our objectivity is only a provisional, contextual one. But there is a world of difference between the limited, unreflective context and that which has developed and become reflective through its process of *Bildung*. This has only happened because one has risked the self and so become transformed, a newer and wiser self having grown from the provincial infant. This process, as we have seen, necessarily requires the other and that temptation to the other. In this moment of temptation there is no hope of gaining some absolute; there is not even any guarantee of a successful fusion of horizons which results in a wiser self. Yet the possibility is always there. The moment in which one genuinely becomes open to the other then is very much a "leap of faith." One must have a certain amount of trust in the other for that other, in turn, to have trust in us. Without this mutual faith, the dialogue cannot proceed.

Not only does this explain, I think, the importance of "good will" in communication (a point constantly exemplified in Gadamer's writings as well as noticeably absent in Derrida's comments on this theme), but it is a remarkable instance of William James's "will to believe." James, it will be recalled, located a certain range of events in which the belief had an influence in determining the outcome of the action. James himself used the example of the Alpine climber who had to jump a crevasse and whose faith in his ability to make the jump or not would determine whether he had that last element of strength to do it. James himself applied it to the fundamental issue of whether life had inherent meaning: those who believed it did were likely, he thought, to live meaningful lives while those who despaired would correspondingly find their lives void of value.[13]

We can apply this to Gadamer's view of the risk of the self and the role of the other as well. By a faith in the other which exhibits trust and good will, we not only in fact become open to the other, but *create* the conditions whereby the other can be open to us, and thereby establish the genuine possibility for growth and transformation and that fusion of horizons which we seek. If, however, we approach the other with suspicion and distrust, this too may have the self-fulfilling consequence of creating a situation marked by misunderstanding and intentional deception. Here, I think, we have the final pragmatic distinction between hermeneutics and deconstruction as methodologies. If one approaches another person as someone with whom one might have a conversation, being receptive to that person's claims and experience, the conditions for possible mutual understanding are greatly enhanced. If, on the other hand, one approaches that individual as a mask whose remarks are to be treated with suspicion and as meaning something other than what they seem, the course of the encounter, unless it is in a psychiatrist's office, seems fairly predictable. The same might well be true of how we approach texts: our success in achieving an understanding of them may depend on our "will to believe" in the *possibility* of understanding them. To quote Gadamer, "Without this kind of openness to one another there is no genuine human relationship. Belonging together always also means being able to listen to one another."[14]

Thus, not only is the linguistic event of understanding structured dialogically for Gadamer, but the dialogical other is to be construed as a "Thou" to whom one is willing to risk being genuinely open and who, likewise, can be open to us. Through this mutual openness arises the possibility for the fusion of horizons which is the aesthetic lure in our quest for the experience of meaning. Through this we are "tempted" to the other and in this temptation we either succeed in having faith in the other or not.

The Thou as Communal: For Gadamer, the human community arises more from the ability to listen than the ability to speak. We not only need to hear what the other says, but to hear the questions implicit behind any statement and to sense the direction such questioning might take. Thus the possibility of speech as a joint activity or a process opens up to us in which the other is a partner. Such cooperative partnership is the very nature of a community. The other is "with us" as we proceed. A community is a history of such intertwined projects of cooperative understanding, and its language and traditions are elaborate ways in which the culture as such creates ways in which people can be genuinely present to each other. A community, in other words, resides upon a set of shared prejudices whereby the members can have a common world and engage in the continuous process of listening and speaking. To grow up means to begin to acquire those abilities for listening to the voices in the world of the community, developing that "trained receptivity" in hearing what is truly being said.[15]

The other which arises from our multiple experiences of speaking and listening creates what might be called the "voice of the community." This experience is easily detectable in tribal cultures, though it surely exists as a universal phenomenon. A tribal culture, like those of the American Southwest, will usually refer to itself as "the people" or "the human beings," distinguishing itself from all other tribes by doing so. Involved with this will be a very strong, but not necessarily verbally articulate, sense of what constitutes the "way" of the people, including here often very elaborate customs with their corresponding sense of "rightness" about them. The way one looks at another person, the kind of jewelry worn, the way to fix one's hair or build one's house, even how one tends a corn plant or regards the surrounding hills and mountains (which can be seen, for example, as the sacred, cardinal orientations of the village and the dwellings of the overseeing gods)—all these tacit prejudices flow together in the daily life which constitutes that people. There is, to put it another way, a whole "aesthetic" which organizes and integrates the individual actions, verbal and nonverbal, which succeeds in creating a shared, collective life. An individual living in such a world has a sense not only of what some particular "other" might say, but of what "we" might say.

To some extent this follows Heidegger's description of *Das Man* and the life of the everyday. But Heidegger's phenomenological analysis was far from neutral and had an implicit moral evaluation, and it was so understood: "inauthenticity" was a "fallen" condition. While it may be true that such a life may allow us to forget or hide the fundamental possibilities open before us, to which we can take a creative stance which in turn individualizes us, I think Gadamer can add something positive to Heidegger's negative analysis. Without the sense of the community as a living other, we would not live as *zoa politika,* as creatures-in-community. An essential part of having a self or identity is our capacity to be responsive to a group of others with whom we are a "we."

The Thou as Tradition: Beyond the existing community there is that other which exists as "tradition." Tradition is what can address us from the inherited modes in which a community can engage in self-representation. Here would be included all those facets of culture which help establish the identity of a people through time: religion, rituals, sacred texts, historical narratives, political documents, and so on. Through the encounter with these symbols, the self is addressed as an inheritor of the tradition and as a possible participant in its history. Tradition provides those prejudices which develop understanding and so come to have authority. Tradition is not just what gets taught and passed along from one generation to the next. As Gadamer says, "But tradition is not simply a process that we learn to know and be in command of through experience; it is language, i.e., it expresses itself like a 'Thou'. A 'Thou' is not an object, but stands in relation with us." This "Thou" is not the particular individual "Thou" but is "a meaningful content detached from all bonds of the meaning individual, of an 'I' or a 'Thou'. Still," Gadamer adds, "the relation to the 'Thou' and the meaning of experience in this case must be capable of contributing to the analysis of the hermeneutical experience. For tradition is a genuine partner in communication, with which we have fellowship as does the 'I' with a 'Thou'."[16]

Gadamer is emphasizing here that we can be addressed by something other than the particular individual and whatever might be included under that individual's specifically intended meaning. Gadamer is critical of psychologistic hermeneutic methods which seek to recreate the "author's state of mind" in order to understand the text produced. Though tradition does not rise to the absolute impersonal objectivity which has been the ideal of scientific knowledge, it does transcend particular individuals and even particular communities. Even if at one point in history a community agrees on the given meaning of a text, that text can have indefinitely more meaning which can only be revealed through historical development. A Shakespearian audience, even had it agreed on the meaning of *Hamlet,* would not have been able to produce anything like Olivier's "Freudian" interpretation. But I think Gadamer comes close to over-stating the issue if he means that a "meaningful content" is capable of being detached from any and all "meaning individuals." Meaning will always be historically received through particular communities and particular individuals, and though it may always have "more" than is intended by those cases, it will nevertheless grow from those contexts and from the dynamic interaction historically effected by those contexts. Thus, I would contend, even the highly impersonal "Thou" of tradition must be mediated through concrete contextual understanding. In this sense, though *Hamlet* or the *Agamemnon* are aspects of the Western tradition, I am still addressed in those texts by an "other" who, for lack of any other name, can be called "Shakespeare" or "Aeschylus."

There is, then, an irreducible aspect to meaning which involves the role of the other as "Thou," even if that "Thou" is a community or a cultural tradition. It is this "Thou" which tempts us toward meaning, which makes us present not only to ourselves but to others, and so teaches us our responsiveness and our capacity to be open, whereby we transform our very selves. We achieve the meaning we desire not through acts of ultimate individuation, but through our capacity to stand face to face with the other, and in that mutual openness reveal the possibility for the fusion of horizon in a fundamental act of good will, which is nothing less than the faith in the very possibility of understanding itself, a faith which is instrumental in creating its result.

IV. *EROS, AGAPE,* AND *PHILIA*

At the center of Gadamer's hermeneutic ontology is that feature which he calls "the concept of the Beautiful" *(Der Begriff des schönen).* With Heidegger (and with Dewey once again), poetic speech offers a paradigm of language. In such speech the ontological significance of language is revealed. In the *Symposium,* Plato described the Beautiful-itself as beautiful, a perfect instance of self-representation, whose "radiance" *(ekphanestaton/Hervorscheinen)* constitutes its very being. "The distinguishing mark of the beautiful, namely that it draws directly to itself the desire of the human soul, is founded in its mode of being."[17] There is not only a wholeness in the manifestation of the beautiful, but it draws and compels us by its very nature. Apart from Plato's own ontological conclusions on this matter, which made the Beautiful a supreme substance, Gadamer draws his own results for a hermeneutic ontology: "That being is self-presentation and that all understanding is an event."[18] The metaphysics of the Beautiful, in other words, establishes "the ontological background of the hermeneutic experience of the world." Understanding, like the appearance of the Beautiful, is an *event* and it has the *immediacy of self-presentation,* which Gadamer links with the Heideggerian view of truth as *alētheia.* As he says in *The Relevance of the Beautiful,* "The beautiful fulfills itself in a kind of self-determination and enjoys its own self-representation."[19] It "compels the admission: 'This is true.'" By embodying itself, it not only compels or draws us, but "The ontological function of the beautiful is to bridge the chasm between the ideal and the real."[20]

There are several themes in this aspect of Gadamer's philosophy which can be related to the discussion of the role of the other in understanding. Perhaps nowhere else does Gadamer's admiration of Platonism come out so strongly, but it is important to see how he has radically shifted the ontological commitments away from Plato's transcendentalism. The shining forth of the beautiful is the revelation of the possibility of the embodiment of the ideal in the real by transforming the scattered, fragmentary nature of the everyday world into a moment of harmony, lucidity, and—we should not balk at the word—presence. This is an event, not a flight from time into eternity. In fact it bears, as I have said, a close resemblance to Dewey's description of "an experience" in which the possibilities for aesthetic consummation are so realized as to create a sense of completion, wholeness, and closure. Thus, the "claim" which is put upon us is the very claim that the inherent possibility for understanding has been realized. This "truth" is the capacity for such integrated, fulfilled experience to present itself insistently, and for us, consequently, to recognize it for what it is and recall it in the future, not forgetting it as we do so much of our everyday experiences. This, it might be recalled, is in fact the original sense of *aletheia:* it is that which "does not escape notice" and which is "not-forgotten."

Second, the beautiful is able to have the power for making this claim on us because it fulfills a fundamental drive for the experience of meaning embodied in the world: it is the consummation of Eros in language, the desire for humans to have a reflective awareness of the wholeness and integration of meaning in their lives. I think we can make the claim that, above all else, human beings need to realize in their lives some sense of meaning and value and that if this need is not fulfilled depression, despair, and death can result. This drive toward the direct experience of meaning and value I have termed the "Human Eros."[21] Plato clearly establishes in the *Symposium* that *eros* has an intentional structure: it is directed toward something which fulfills a need, and this Eros is the dynamism whereby human nature can be awakened to seek its ultimate end. It is nothing less than our capacity to be "open" to that which completes.

I think now we can begin to establish the relationship to Gadamer's dialogical view of language, which requires this essential feature of openness. This openness is not merely a moment of understanding, but is a part of the underlying Eros of language itself, which seeks the realization of the beautiful through the mutual openness of speaking and listening. The Eros of language binds individuals together into a community and organizes the life of the community into a history with its traditions. It is that temptation toward the other.

I think it would be helpful here to distinguish three phases of Eros as they were discussed in antiquity by Plato, Aristotle, and St. Paul, namely, as *eros, philia,* and *agape.* Each of these carries with it a different employment of understanding and relates to the other in a unique and, as we shall see, complementary way. And each one motivates language in a distinctive way.

Eros: In the Christian period, when writers wished to contrast *agape* and *eros,* to the detriment of the latter, it was customary to speak of one as selfless and the other as self-centered.[22] But in the classical age, beginning with Hesiod and culminating with Plato, the fundamental feature of *eros* is not that it is focused in any direct way upon the *self;* it is instead primarily oriented toward its *object.* It is in this sense that Hesiod has Eros appear at the beginning of things to act as the (pro)creative dynamism of nature. In the lyric age, Eros is invoked as that which makes the beauty of the beloved stand out and attract the attention of the lover. Plato's discussion in the *Symposium* draws on the implicit meaning of this term in Socrates' refutation of Agathon's speech, which has praised Eros as the most beautiful of the gods. Rather, Plato corrects, Eros is the *desire* for beauty, and a desire implies a need or lack. Eros is thus a highly paradoxical being, full of lack or need (as befits the son of Penia, "Poverty"), but also aware of this lack and full of stratagems to hunt what it needs (which he gets from his father Poros, "Resourcefulness"). This, of course, prefigures the very nature of Socratic *eros* as the ignorance which devises methods (such as dialectic) whereby it can acquire what it lacks, namely wisdom.[23]

The structure of *eros,* then, is to be directed outward toward an object which is sought in order to overcome the need itself. Once the need is met, *eros* wastes away; the everliving gods have no "erotic wisdom" in their eternal contemplation. Also, it should be noted that *eros* carries the strong connotation of the desire for a *kind* of object which then may be fixed upon some particular instance. Hunger desires food, which may take the form of some particular object at hand. This sense too is preserved in Plato's account insofar as *eros* is the desire for the ultimate kinds, the Forms, and even for the "kind of kinds" itself, the Form of the Beautiful.

Eros likewise generates its own language, which might be called a language motivated by desire. In the most literal sense, this will be the language governed by the human projects which seek to satisfy needs, from the necessary to the luxurious. It will also motivate the language which evolves toward the lyrical and romantic. This will not only include the typical form of erotic love poetry (such as we find in the fragments of Sappho) but in the lyrical moment itself which seeks to possess the moment of the beautiful at once and forever. Keats's "Ode on a Grecian Urn" would be a fine example here, since the ode itself *is* the urn in which beauty is forever captured. In another sense, the language of intellectual love, which seeks to attract attention to the need for wisdom and such as we find perhaps best illustrated in the Platonic myths, would be included here, though so would a range of efforts on the part of scientists to write lyrically about their subjects. In this sense, then, *eros* designates the primordial drive toward the aesthetic experience of meaning, the appearing of the Beautiful in which the chasm between the real and the ideal is crossed. It is the teleological dimension of the event of language: it both motivates language as an event and seeks the presence of aesthetic completion. The "Human Eros" is the need to encounter meaning which motivates the project of existence as such.

Agape: This concept reflects another of the erotic dimensions of language, one which comes very close to Gadamer's hermeneutic project.[24] This aspect of Eros, I shall claim, allows us to approach an alien text *as if* it could be understood, and thereby creates the condition for the possibility of understanding it. It also reveals, I think, a fundamental dynamism in any relationship between teacher and student, which, as we have seen, is essential to our existence as social, mortal beings.

To comprehend this, some historical exposition is necessary. In Homeric times, *"agapao"* referred to the affection of close family members, especially of parents for children, and of the appropriate affection conduct. It thus could mean "to greet as kinsman." When Odysseus has slain the suitors, he reveals his identity to Penelope; but Penelope is at first suspicious and so tests Odysseus, telling him he can sleep in his bed, but it must be moved outside the bedchamber. Odysseus explodes with rage, since one leg of the bed was hewn from a living olive tree. This of course proves that he is in fact Odysseus and Penelope rushes to embrace him, apologizing that she didn't "greet" *(agapesa)* him as he deserved. This sense of affectionate family feeling becomes gradually extended through the Greek emphasis on the hospitality due guest-friends, *xenia:* one greets the guest or the stranger in need *as if* he were a kinsman. It has the force, then, of a gracious, friendly reception, even though the ties of blood-relation may be absent and so their corresponding set of moral duties and taboos not in force.

The tribe, or the association of related tribes, was the foundation of the Greek polis, and it was difficult for the Greeks to comprehend how a state could exist without such close bonds of uniting ancestry, shared gods and sacrifices, and commitment in the "family business" of political welfare. Through the democratic compromises of Athens, the rise of the Athenian empire, and then the rise of the empires of Alexander and his successors, such tribal notions gradually broke down. Stoicism provided a range of concepts to interpret this new moral-political phenomenon, but did so by transforming and extending the older tribal concepts. All mankind was a family and the universe itself a divine city, Cosmopolis. The empire-state, Hellenistic or Roman, was still ideologically conceived as a "family enterprise," sanctioned by a "divine ancestry" and often symbolized by the titular head of the family—the ruler—who thus was accorded "divine" status.

With the rise of Christianity, a new set of political as well as theoretical problems presented themselves. First, the early Christian communities were not bound by any tribal notions which lay behind classical political theory. Second, they did not and could not see themselves as part of the political world which involved, among other things, worship of the gods and emperors. Yet the very idea of a community was derived from the concepts surrounding the Greek polis. What was the basis of the community?

The solution lay in the way *agape* had already been extended. With Paul, among others, this word which had meant the "affection" given to anyone as if they were kin, was transformed into the "love" for all those who, though perhaps strangers, wished to be considered as members of the Christian community. It was "unmerited" and freely given, but because of this it succeeded in *creating* the community in which it believed. Thus *agape* became the basis for a nonpolitical community. Of course the source of this ability for two strangers to love each other so that they became friends was seen as deriving from God. With Paul especially, the fundamental relationship of God to humankind was interpreted as *agape*. As such, it was the freely given power whereby a "fallen," self-serving human nature could realize in itself its capacity to live in the spirit of the community.

Aside from its explicit Christian interpretation, I think there are some universal situations in which something like *agape* is illustrated. Of course it can be found in any instance in which an "outsider" of a community is received and treated *as if* he or she were already a member of that community, thereby effecting the deed of *making* that person a member of the community. But I think we can also find this in the relationship of parents to infants and children and, by natural extension, to anyone involved in the role of being a teacher—and almost everyone in his or her life is a teacher at some point.

At birth, each infant is an "outsider" to the culture of the community in the most literal sense: it cannot speak or understand; it doesn't even have a "self" yet; it is a bundle of erotic needs, demanding care, food, attention, and love. The care it receives cannot be realistically given with any thought of immediate response or reward. The parents must give freely, think of the infant's welfare, and seek to imagine *for* the infant. The result of this process, of course, is that over time the infant becomes a child who can in turn love the parent and begin to imagine what others need. The love it needs from birth is a form of agapic love, and this love manages to create the thing it seeks. The child gradually is made a member of the community: a self who has a history, speaks a language, understands traditions, and who can in turn be a giver of agapic love.

One special instance of this is the long process of education. Education might be described as the "art of *agape*," for it is directly concerned with making the student a practicing member of some community, be it the cultural community at large or some special community, such as that of mathematicians or car mechanics. The student is "alien" by the very fact of ignorance. But by the teacher's effort to take the student's interest as his or her own, and responding to that need, the student is gradually given the actual means to become a fully participating member of that community: a fellow citizen, a mathematician, a car mechanic. The process of teaching begins with the ability to "greet and embrace" the alien being *as if* he or she were a member, and by doing so, gradually transforms the outsider, the stranger, into the friend and member. It should perhaps be stressed that as the student proceeds, he or she also must learn to practice the art of *agape*, desiring to care for the subject as the teacher does, trying to imagine the horizon of the teacher in order to transcend his or her own. In short, the teacher must try to imagine the world of the student in order to teach and the student must imagine the world of the teacher in order to learn.

I think it is now rather obvious how Gadamer's approach to texts is a special instance of this. The text is "other"; its horizon is not ours, yet we must make its horizon ours and ours its. We must come to make it a part of our community, and in doing so, it comes to transform our community by making it part of a tradition. To begin the project of understanding we are asked in some very fundamental way to treat it "sympathetically." We may, of course, come to be critical of any text, even to the point of rejecting it. But the first movement of understanding will have to be to "greet" it, so to speak, *as if* it were a member of the community and could speak to us. Only then can we come to understand it. Through the text, we engage our dialogical imagination, trying to recreate its horizon and allowing ours in turn to respond to it. In this manner the text itself can come to teach us, allowing us, as strangers to its world, to become members. If such an attempt succeeds, then there is that fusion of horizons in which a new community is created.

Philia: The greatest classical treatment of friendship, of course, is that given by Aristotle.[25] Here, too, I think we can find a significant aspect which has bearings on the hermeneutics of the community. Friendship is the social and political dimension of *aretē* and *eudaimonia.* Neither virtue nor happiness in the individual would be possible without the proper political and social conditions. If *eros* can be interpreted as the desire for meaning, directed in general toward it, and *agape* is the condition whereby the stranger is transformed into the friend and member of the community, then *philia* is the active exercise or realization, the *energeia,* whereby friends live a shared life, mutually accomplishing the good. It can be found in the active fusion of horizons in which understanding is manifest. But while the object of *eros* is generic, a desire for a *kind* of thing, and the object of *agape* is transformative, changing the unknown stranger into the known friend, *philia* is the action specifically directed toward those who *are* friends. The other is not an incommensurable unknown, but one who bears some proportional likeness to oneself: there is a definite *logos* between the members. We are friends with definite individuals and our friendship is founded upon certain relationships which our two characters create with one another.

Aristotle treats *philia* along with *eudaimonia* as the fundamental object of the art of politics. "Friendship also seems to hold states together, and lawgivers devote more attention to it than to justice," he says in the *Nicomachean Ethics;* in the *Politics,* he says that "the city is not a partnership in a location for the sake of not committing injustice against each other and of transacting business. These things must necessarily be present if there is to be a city, but not when even all of them are present is it yet a city, but [the city is] the partnership in living well both of households and families for the sake of a complete and self-sufficient life." To achieve this there must be all those relationships which constitute "the work of affection; for affection is the intentional choice of living together."[26] This, naturally, is one of the defining marks of friendship.

In the highest kind of friendship, that between good or excellent people, Aristotle finds that there is the presupposition of mutual good will for each other's excellence and happiness which is matched with a corresponding ability in each to realize that end. Such friendships seek to become long-lasting cooperative partnerships in realizing the fullest and deepest aspects of a human life. In this sense, friendship is not so much an "affection or emotion" *(pathos)* but an underlying disposition or characteristic *(hexis),* what Gadamer would call a "prejudice." Each partner wills the good of the other as his or her own, and so the saying, *"touton ton philon koinon":* To friends, all is common.

Such friendships exhibit a kind of *logos,* a ratio or proportionality. Each one is able to "take the measure" of the other with respect to excellence which is also the basis of their speaking to each other and their mutual understanding. The horizon of one is the horizon of the other, so that the good with which they are concerned is truly manifest. And so they seek to spend their days together and finding joy in one another, primarily concerned with giving, rather than receiving, affection. The result is that special association which binds together most strongly: community. "Friendship is present to the extent that men share something in common, for that is also the extent to which they share a view of that which is just. And the proverb 'friends hold in common what they have' is correct, for friendship consists in community."[27] By being able to determine their common share in the realization of happiness, friends create the possibility for each "giving and receiving what is his due." This, it must be recalled, is one of the primary talents of *phronēsis,* the ability to assess situations correctly and respond to them for the sake of the best. But more importantly, the shared life of friends is marked by that freedom of open mutuality in the sharing of happiness, which Gadamer describes as "play."

Gadamer himself has argued that the task of hermeneutics, as he conceives it, extends from Aristotle's account of *phronēsis,* not from his doctrine of science or *epistēmē.* It is *phronēsis,* says Gadamer, which as the *sensus communis* "is the sense that founds the community."[28] "The task of moral knowledge," he adds later on, "is to see in the concrete situation what is asked of it, or, to put it another way, the person acting must see the concrete situation in the light of what is asked of him in general."[29] If fact, Gadamer focuses upon Aristotle's discussion of "understanding" and "insight or fellow feeling" *(sunesis, gnome/suggnome)* as crucial.[30] We can "place ourselves in a concrete situation in which another person has to act." This is to be "united with the other person in this mutual interest"; such a person is not one who "stands apart and is unaffected," but "thinks with the other and undergoes the situation with him."[31] That is, he takes on the role of friend. Insight not only is the ability to interpret the situation well, but leads to forbearance. Gadamer concludes, "we find that Aristotle's analysis is in fact a kind of model of the problems of hermeneutics."

Philia, then, gives us a special way of looking at Gadamer's approach, especially with respect to the issue of the "fusion of horizons." *Eros* may be a generic desire for meaning; *agape* may be a way in which the strange and unfamiliar can be appropriated; *philia* is the consummation, in which the alien horizon and one's own fuse so that a common world of meaning is shared and in truth *"touton ton philon koinon."* The text speaks to us and we hear; our world is enlarged and we are transformed, becoming members not only of a community, but a tradition. This is the active realization of our desire for meaning. The text, in a manner of speaking, becomes a friend with whom we wish to dwell, and our dwelling with the text is an entrance into the play of the text, an enjoyment of its possibilities. The relation is to *specific* texts as well, just as our friends are specific friends. There is something in them which stands in proportion to us and we can "take measure" of each other.

This offers, I believe, a way of interpreting those moments when Gadamer seems to speak of the self and the other dissolving into the text itself. For example, in "Text and Interpretation," he says, "The interpreter has no other function than to disappear completely into the achievement of the full harmony of understanding."[32] The "other" of understanding is still present in this moment—present in the way two friends are mutually present in their common friendship. There is a *mutual* realization which is *consummated* in the event of understanding. The event, activated by *eros,* mediated by *agape,* flowers in *philia.* Language is dialogically configured in each of these erotic moments: lyric, paideutic, playful.

The other of language exists as an erotic horizon of understanding. This is why language really does bind human beings together into friendships, communities, and developing traditions. Plato saw Eros as a fundamental condition for understanding; Aristotle, too, saw friendship as essential to the pursuit of wisdom as well as human excellence. The medievals likewise had a fundamentally erotic view of human understanding in its quest for the divine. One of the radical transitions in Western philosophy which seems to have gone unnoticed, is how the modern era, from Descartes on, "unsexed the mind," that is, removed the relationship of understanding and meaning to Eros. Gadamer, I have contended, has managed to offer a way to restore this aspect which is far more complex and just to the human situation than the post-Freudian approaches. It remains to see how this lays the basis for an ontology of the community in which tradition and progress are intertwined in the project of cultural democracy.

V. THE COMMUNITY OF MEMORY AND THE COMMUNITY OF HOPE

An initial contrast between Dewey and Gadamer might focus upon Dewey's emphasis upon transforming the present toward a more fulfilling future and

Gadamer's stress upon the weight of the tradition in establishing the meaning of
the present. A closer look would reveal that these views are similar, but for the
emphases due to temperament. There could be no significant reconsideration of
the present, for Dewey, without established cultural habits and the cumulative
intelligence of past experience embodied in education. For Gadamer, the horizon
of the future is what perpetually brings tradition to life and moves it beyond the
fixed interpretations of the past. For both thinkers, the fundamental structure of
our human temporality, in which past and future are horizons of the present, is
what dominates. Human nature is radically temporal: we appropriate past and
future, transforming the sequences of events into acts.

In fact, Dewey and Gadamer may be closer here, with respect to the nature
of temporality, than Gadamer and Heidegger. The horizon of the future for Heidegger was revealed only through the lonely moment of individual realization of
my "ownmost possibility," my mortality, marking the finitude of my being. But
as we have already seen, Gadamer's dialogic view of understanding has introduced a moment of transcendence: while I cannot go beyond finitude, I can go
beyond *my* finitude in the moment when I become genuinely open to another.
Indeed, my temporality would remain unreflective if I could not appropriate it
through the other. It is the dialogic event of understanding which opens up the
nature of human temporality, and which thereby balances the individuation of
my own mortality with the possibility of self-transcendence through the other.

In other words, for Gadamer time is not individually appropriated until it has
been dialogically appropriated. The future opens up also as the possibility of the
continuity of meaning through openness to the other. This movement or "temptation" to the other, as I have argued, is in fact an erotic moment. Eros configures
the horizon of temporality as much as Thanatos. Through our capacity to love,
we achieve a finite transcendence. The world as a domain of possible projects, as
a field of human care *(Sorge),* is revealed through the social dialectic of death
and love. This is what motivates the vast project of civilization itself. As Dewey
says, this is what makes us learners and teachers upon the earth rather than self-
contained, timeless Epicurean gods, passively floating in hedonistic bliss in the
tranquil spaces between galactic islands. The future and the past are socially
appropriated. Inherited traditions and organizing social projects are not addenda
to human understanding, but conditions for it. Through these, we are able to be
beings-in-community rather than just cooperative partners temporarily working
for our own benefit.

It will be helpful here to introduce two phrases used by Josiah Royce in his
profound hermeneutic interpretation of the ontology of the community in *The
Problem of Christianity: the community of memory* and *the community of hope.*
Biologically we are isolated individuals, says Royce, except insofar as we interact physically; my actions are mine, and you cannot choose them for me. Yet we
exist as beings who do in some sense live each other's lives. A community is dis-

tinguished from some aggregate of adjacent human beings by this very fact. And this means, says Royce, that "a true community is essentially a product of a time process. A community has a past and will have a future. Its more or less conscious history, real or ideal, is part of its very essence. A community requires for its existence a history and is greatly aided in its consciousness by a memory."[33] A community is possible because of this shared temporality.

Without a memory of the past or some glimmer of a future which is "mine," I might exist biologically, but not as a "self." So too with a community. The present moment, a mere "flash of consciousness," is meaningless unless it *interprets* that moment in terms of some continuous process: "my idea of myself is an interpretation of my past—linked also with an interpretation of my hopes and intentions as to my future."[34] As Augustine says in the *Confessions, memoria* is the power of the soul to gather itself together and recollect itself as a whole rather than to leave it to the dispersion of time.[35]

Moreover, we can each imaginatively appropriate a past which is common, interpreting a set of stories and events as "our history." We can extend the self so that we share a common interpretation of the world. "A community constituted by the fact that each of its members accepts as part of his own individual life and self the same *past* events that each of his fellow-members accepts, may be called a *community of memory,*" says Royce, and "A community constituted by the fact that each of its members accepts, as part of his own individual life and self, the same expected *future* events that each of his fellows accepts, may be called a *community of expectation, or upon occasion, a community of hope.*"[36] A community, then, arises from a shared interpretive time-process in which, ideally, our horizons fuse. But this is also, insists Royce, "a practical conception" because "the community is a being that attempts to accomplish something in time and through the deeds of its members."[37] The meaning of the self we are lies not in the momentary but in the "ideally extended self."[38]

The task of a community does not lie simply in remembering the great deeds or defining events of the past, nor in mere cooperative behavior, but in actually living a shared life. Our lives *make sense together.* Royce uses the example of an orchestra in which the performance of each member is guided by a sense of the composition as a whole. "A community thus constituted is essentially a community of those who are artists in some form of cooperation, and whose art constitutes for each artist, his own ideally extended life. But," adds Royce, "the life of an artist depends upon his love for his art."[39] A community, to accomplish its work, must in some sense embody the love of its members and create a bond of fellowship. "Love, when it exists and triumphs over the complexities which obscure and confuse the common life, thus completes the consciousness of the community," concludes Royce.[40]

Royce was an absolute idealist as well as pragmatist—an "absolute pragmatist," as he said. He believed that in some sense we could identify with the

Absolute and see the finite in the infinite, however concrete. Both Gadamer and Dewey reject this for a doctrine of human finitude. Gadamer traces this back to Aeschylus and the tragic "wisdom won through suffering" which must expect to be "brought up short," to be surprised, to be corrected, to be defeated. "Real experience," Gadamer warns, "is that in which man becomes aware of his own finiteness."[41] This was the domain of what Dewey called the "precarious." This calls for a reconsideration of Royce's views.

We cannot pretend that we are musicians playing a prewritten, rehearsed score whose outcome we know. We cannot simply *will* to see things from the standpoint of the Absolute. Only through our accumulated intelligence, our present ability to cooperate and share good will, combined with a strong sense of our tragic finitude, may we mediate time to preserve the community. This calls for the use of *phronēsis,* the interpretive art which is always under way, provisional, contextual, aspiring. This finitude need not be despairing. If the old men in the chorus of the *Agamemnon* display vain hope, merely wishing that "good will out in the end," we should remember the ending of that trilogy. Orestes brings his case, brought on by the collision of duty and taboo, to the Areopagus of Athens, presided over by Athena herself. Democracy, guided by wisdom, can produce justice, transforming the primitive, destructive drives of human nature into the protective spirits of the state. The task of hermeneutics, which is that of the constant recovery and transformation of the community, can do more than merely hope for future good: it must actively realize it. This process may be called, with Dewey, the "reconstruction of democracy."

Here we can find the relationship between Deweyan "reconstruction" and Gadamerian *Destruktion,* both of which are opposed to "deconstruction." "*'Destruktion,'*" says Gadamer, "never means destruction, but rather dismantling *[Abbau].* Its purpose is to take concepts that have become rigid and lifeless and fill them again with meaning."[42] For Dewey, reconstruction is the creative appropriation of a situation, along with its inherited past, which opens up new possibilities for meaning. These possibilities do not "negate" or obliterate the past, but *grow* from its living possibilities, thereby establishing a process of developmental continuity. As for Gadamer, this involves a thorough awareness of the prejudices of the past, for this is the only way to see beyond their otherwise tacit limitations. Both reconstruction and *Destruktion* are undertaken to critique the present in order to liberate it. For Gadamer, this means to allow the process of dialogic interpretation to continue; for Dewey, it means to keep the members of a society communicating so that they can remain a community dedicated to the realization of meaning and value in human life. To Gadamer, and, one assumes, to Dewey, the idea of playing a perpetual game of dissolving meaning so that only misunderstanding triumphs is perverse. The thought that by such critique one could go back to some primordial moment prior to the dawn of philosophy is merely romantic. As Gadamer says, Western civilization is not the unfolding of Plato's insight into the meaning of Being. It is the exploration of various possibilities historically connected with this view, and if we are to go beyond them, it will be by transforming them further.

The event of understanding can bring about a new way for human beings to share the world of meaning. Beyond a new sense of the vitality of tradition and its many voices there must be the ability to create those ideals which organize our activities toward commonly fulfilling ends and in light of which we interpret each other and our world. This is one reason why Dewey called democracy primarily a cultural problem rather than a political one. No given formal system of government will succeed unless the society embodies the appropriate habits which sustain such a government and give it meaning and legitimacy. Establish the culture of democracy, Dewey said, and the government of democracy will follow. A democratic culture cannot be one in which people do not participate in a shared or common life, each simply pursuing an individualistic course of self-interest. It must be a culture in which people can communicate with each other and work out common goals. We must have the arts of genuinely entering into each other's world and thereby arrive at a common world which gives a sense of fulfillment to us both.

The question of hermeneutics as conceived by Gadamer has great bearing, then, upon the possibility for a democracy. The democratic society is engaged in the project of mutual interpretation; it must creatively grasp its past in order to create a shared future. We must be able to engage each other and participate together in the dialogue that leads the community toward the embodiment of the beautiful. This is not something which can be achieved once and for all or absolutely; it will be partially and contingently realized, and then must be pursued again. Here, then, we may discover the meeting place of hermeneutics and pragmatics, interlocutors in the democratic community with all its traditions and future projects.

THOMAS M. ALEXANDER

DEPARTMENT OF PHILOSOPHY
SOUTHERN ILLINOIS UNIVERSITY AT CARBONDALE
AUGUST 1992

NOTES

1. Dewey's major work, *Experience and Nature,* gives the general argument for this, but *Art as Experience* and *The Public and Its Problems* should also be consulted respectively for their aesthetic and political dimensions of this view.
2. This can be found at the very beginning of Dewey's major work on the theory of education, *Democracy and Education.*

3. This is explicitly stated in Dewey's essay "Philosophy and Civilization," which can be found in his book of the same title.

4. See Liddell and Scott's *Greek-English Lexicon* under *alētheia, lēthē,* and *lanthano.* For example, at *Iliad* 25.355 ff. we read:

> They stood in a line for the start, and Achilleus showed them the turn-post far away on the level plain, and beside it he stationed a judge, Phoinix the godlike the follower of his father, to mark and remember the running and bring back a true story. (Richmond Lattimore translation)

5. Hans-Georg Gadamer, "Text and Interpretation," trans. Dennis J. Schmidt and Richard Palmer, in *Dialogue and Deconstruction,* ed. Diane P. Michelfelder and Richard E. Palmer (SUNY Press, 1989), p. 23.

6. Gadamer, "Letter to Dallmayr," trans. Richard Palmer and Diane P. Michelfelder, in *Dialogue and Deconstruction,* p. 95.

7. See Gadamer's *Truth and Method,* trans. copyright Sheed and Ward (Continuum, 1975), p. 15.

8. See ibid., pp. 277–99.

9. See, for example, the introduction to *Truth and Method,* p. xxiii.

10. See Levinas's comment in "Dialogue with Emmanuel Levinas," in *Face to Face with Levinas,* ed. Richard A. Cohen (SUNY Press, 1986), p. 31: "I must always demand more of myself than of the other; and this is why I disagree with Buber's description of the I-Thou ethical relationship as a symmetrical copresence."

11. Gadamer, "Text and Interpretation," p. 26.

12. See chapter 5 of Dewey's *Experience and Nature* for a synopsis of this theory; George Herbert Mead's classic, *Mind, Self, and Society,* is the fullest exposition. A lucid discussion of Mead's theory can be found in David Miller's *George Herbert Mead.* The recent German study by Hans Joas, *G. H. Mead* (translated by Raymond Meyer, MIT Press) also treats this theme.

13. See William James, "The Will to Believe," in *The Will to Believe and Other Essays.*

14. Gadamer, *Truth and Method,* p. 324.

15. Ibid., p. 17.

16. Ibid., p. 321.

17. Ibid., p. 439.

18. Ibid., p. 441.

19. Hans-Georg Gadamer, "The Relevance of the Beautiful," in *The Relevance of the Beautiful,* ed. Robert Bernasconi (Cambridge, 1986), p. 14.

20. Ibid., p. 15.

21. See my paper, "The Human Eros," in *Philosophy and the Reconstruction of Culture,* ed. John Stuhr (SUNY Press, 1992). When I refer to the specific Greek meaning of Eros, I will designate it by the lower-case italicized form, *eros.*

22. See for example the impressive study by Anders Nygren, *Eros and Agape,* trans. Philip Watson. (Nygren was the Bishop of Lund, Sweden.) See also the impressive historical study by Irving Singer, *The Nature of Love,* 3 vols. The initial meaning of *agape* as special affection for children in particular may have also allowed it to be extended to the love of God as Father for His children. Also, the idea of *agape* as enabling the other to respond in kind can be theologically compared to the way God's *agape* for humankind through *charis* or grace enables human nature to respond with *agape* itself. My point is not that the theological interpretation of *agape must* be taken; rather, it is that the theological interpretation arises from the natural occurrence of agapic love in human life.

23. See *Symposium* 199cff.

24. For a discussion of *agape* in the biblical tradition, see the entry under *agapao* in Stauffer's *Theological Dictionary of New Testament* as well as Liddell and Scott's *Greek Lexicon*.

25. See, of course, *Nicomachean Ethics*, bks. 8 and 9.

26. *Nicomachean Ethics* 1155a23, trans. Martin Ostwald, and *Politics* 1280b29–40, trans. Carnes Lord. See also *NE* 1160a9–30 for friendship as the aim of politics.

27. NE 1159b29–31.

28. Gadamer, *Truth and Method,* p. 21.

29. Ibid., p. 279.

30. NE bk. 6, chaps. 10–11.

31. Gadamer, *Truth and Method,* p. 288.

32. Ibid., p. 41.

33. Josiah Royce, *The Problem of Christianity* (University of Chicago, 1968), p. 243. The original edition appeared in 1918.

34. Ibid., p. 245.

35. See Augustine's *Confessions,* bk. 10.

36. Royce, *The Problem of Christianity,* p. 248.

37. Ibid., p. 254.

38. Ibid., p. 255.

39. Ibid., p. 264.

40. Ibid., p. 267.

41. Gadamer, *Truth and Method,* p. 320.

42. Gadamer, "Letter to Dallmayr," p. 99.

REPLY TO THOMAS M. ALEXANDER

As with some of the other American contributions, reading this one is a remarkable and profound experience for someone like me. After a delay of almost a century it is being made plain to us how powerfully we had been enclosed in isolation since the beginning of World War I despite all efforts to breach such isolation. That there was philosophical pragmatism in America was certainly not unknown to us, but it had no presence for us. One knew about James who had been a friend of my own teacher Paul Natorp, and one knows about Dewey and his enormous influence on American culture. But only now do we begin to understand that American philosophy did have an impact on us and that certain impulses from there became part of German philosophizing. We know today that American pragmatism triggered a real reversal in one of the best younger researchers of Neo-Kantianism, Emil Lask, even before World War I in which he died. Important influences set out from there on several paths. One of those reached George Lukács. The other effect, which cannot be documented in the same way but is also without doubt: the turn toward the 'lifeworld' by the mathematician and phenomenologist Husserl as well as by Max Scheler, Hans Lipps, and Martin Heidegger. This was a crucial step, especially since the fact of science played an important role in Neo-Kantianism, which dominated the times.

One may wonder whether an even stronger retrospective influence set in among us after the second war. Certainly, but such is simply the life of the philosophical spirit: long-dominating traditions are potent. Along with the theory of science we tried to engage in a discussion with analytical philosophy. Thus it should not be surprising that now hermeneutics is being scrutinized as to its proximity to a philosophy that starts with Dewey. For this reason I read Alexander's essay with a certain feeling of homesickness. It is clear that human madness can provoke so much separation and effects which cannot be compensated for entirely even in decades.

Moreover, today we find ourselves in a world situation in which the task of overcoming many other such separations is still waiting for us. East Asia, South Asia, China, Japan, and India are now slowly beginning to become partners in a dialogue, and for the time being we have to be content with a few guests appropriating some basic outlines of German philosophizing in short studies. This holds even more for the reverse, especially since Europeans rarely master East Asian languages so as to be able to think in those languages. The present contribution reveals convergences between hermeneutics and American pragmatism. In doing so, Mr. Alexander demonstrates considerable and extensive knowledge of my writings. However, in this way one cannot learn all those presuppositions, for example, which led my first step from Husserl and Heidegger to my hermeneutical attempts. This took place thirty-five years ago during the decades of our isolated existence.

Thus, I was really surprised that with the 'other' and the situation of the dialogue I am supposed to have had primarily texts on my mind. To be sure, in *Truth and Method* it seems as if I meant Dilthey and his school, and then later Derrida's deconstructivism with which Alexander is apparently very familiar. In truth, however, this is misleading. If there is something I miss in Alexander's careful working through of the topic it is the permanent presence of the Greek philosophy of Plato and Aristotle. The most fruitful impulses for my work came from there. Since then the background for my work was not science but rather art and literature, and, of course, the great thinkers of the Greeks. In this context, the concurrences which Alexander notes are convincing as such. Some American readers of *Truth and Method* will be reminded of *Art as Experience*. In such concurrences, however, the path from Kant to Hegel makes itself felt in a very different way. But precisely this makes Alexander's study so fascinating: how Dewey cherished the optimistic expectation of his time that, with the help of art, the world would turn into a true world democracy. From this perspective even my description of understanding as the fusion of horizons looks like optimism indeed. But that goes too far. After the terrible disappointments on the way to democracy in the world we cannot be too optimistic. But I agree that hope and forgetting characterize the human feeling of life. So I find Alexander's contribution very instructive and I am grateful that starting points of mutual exchange that all of us will need for the future find support here.

H.-G.G.

17

G. B. Madison

HERMENEUTICS' CLAIM TO UNIVERSALITY

Hans-Georg Gadamer's philosophical hermeneutics staunchly maintains a claim to universality, in opposition to a widespread tendency in much of postmodern thought, illustrated perhaps most vividly in the work of Richard Rorty, which denies philosophy's traditional universalist ambitions. Hermeneutics insists that both the general theory of human understanding it embodies as well as the practical implications which follow from this theory (as regards, for instance, ethical and political issues) have universal relevance or applicability. In this way, hermeneutics has likewise resisted the currently fashionable advocacy of cultural and other forms of "incommensurability." While hermeneutics, like other forms of postmodern thought, disavows the essentialism and foundationalism of traditional philosophy, it does not believe that an "overcoming of metaphysics" need necessarily entail the "end of philosophy" proclaimed by many of those who today defend "particularism" or "localism" and reject universalism in any form (often accused by them as being a covert from of "Eurocentrism"). Hermeneutics believes that the traditional claim on the part of philosophical theory to universal validity is not only the defining feature of philosophy itself (as the antiphilosophers correctly perceive, this being the reason for their calls for an end to philosophy), it believes, as well, that this claim is fully defensible and that, moreover, it can be justified in a strictly nonmetaphysical fashion.

Gadamer claims that hermeneutics has universal scope since it is a discipline whose goal is "to discover what is common to all modes of understanding"; it is concerned with "all human experience of the world and human living."[1] Hermeneutics, Gadamer says, is a theoretical, reflective inquiry that is concerned with "our entire understanding of the world and . . . all the various forms in which this understanding manifests itself."[2] What these phrases make amply clear is, as Gadamer would say, "the universality of the hermeneutical problem." Hermeneutic theory is theory in the properly philosophical sense of the term in that it is theory which claims for itself *universal* validity or applicability.

In this paper I would like to focus on one aspect of the claim of hermeneutics to universality, the claim, namely, that it is concerned with "all human experience of the world and human living." More specifically, I would like to defend the claim of hermeneutics to universality against objections leveled against it by various critical theorists (namely, Habermas and others associated with the present-day "Frankfurt School"). Although critical theory joins forces with hermeneutics in upholding the claim to universality on the part of reason, it nevertheless jealously denies universal applicability to the exercise of reason on the part of hermeneutics itself. The position generally taken by critical theorists (the orthodox position, so to speak) is that while a hermeneutic approach to human affairs represents an important stage in their understanding, its usefulness is nonetheless strictly limited. Hermeneutic analysis (it is maintained) goes only so far and must be superseded by critical theory, by what Habermas calls "a critically enlightened hermeneutic."[3] Habermas opposes hermeneutic knowledge (having to do, as he says, with intersubjective communication) to empirical-analytic knowledge (having to do with causal explanations or conditional predictions and technical control) and insists that hermeneutics has to do merely with intersubjective communication (direct person-to-person communication, as well as the understanding of meaning that is embodied in texts and is handed down by tradition). Hermeneutics, Habermas maintains, is incapable of dealing with those instances where communication is "systematically distorted" ("pseudo-communication"). Critical theory, which is guided by a "practical intent," is alone truly "emancipatory."[4]

Moreover, it is objected that to the degree that hermeneutics exceeds the domain to which (according to critical theory) it properly applies and "encroaches" upon areas which critical theory views as its own proper fiefdom (e.g., power relationships [politics] and work [economics]), hermeneutics is overextending itself and is guilty of a kind of disciplinary *hubris,* if not outright intellectual imperialism.[5]

The purpose of this paper is to respond to these objections, which I shall consider in turn.

The debate over these matters has, of course, been going on for some time now.[6] However, Habermas and other critical theorists appear never to have drawn the appropriate lessons from the debate (in which, in the eyes of many, Gadamer clearly came out the winner); generally speaking, they have continued over the years merely to reassert their original position.

At the time of the original debate, Gadamer had responded to Habermas's charge that hermeneutics is limited to dealing with meaning in the narrowly cultural sense of the term as well as the charge that political and economic reality (power, work) fall outside its scope with the following words: "Who says that these concrete, so-called real factors are outside the realm of hermeneutics? . . . [I]t is absolutely absurd to regard the concrete factors of work and politics as outside the scope of hermeneutics."[7] Habermas's opposition to hermeneutics's claim to universality would seem to stem from a fundamental misunderstanding on his part of the actual scope and function of hermeneutic analysis. Habermas and his associates seem to want to fudge the all-important distinction between Gadamer's philosophical or phenomenological hermeneutics and the earlier, romantic hermeneutics that Gadamer set out deliberately to displace.[8]

What I mean is that the Frankfurter crowd appear to believe that Gadamerian hermeneutics is limited merely to explicating the *self-understanding* that authors and agents have of themselves. However, this is most decidedly not the case. For hermeneutics it is not the intention of the author (or agent) but the meaning of the text (or action) that is the proper object of interpretation. As Gadamer himself said in reply to Habermas (to no avail, it would appear): "To limit the understanding of meaning neither to *mens auctoris* nor to *mens actoris* is a point dear to me."[9] More recently, Gadamer has stated that in his opinion Habermas "never gets past an idealistic understanding of the hermeneutical problem."[10]

The Frankfurters' error also serves to immunize critical theory against any objections directed against *it* and to guarantee to it its own uncontested and uncontestable universal validity. If not authors' or actors' intentions, what then is the true object of hermeneutics? Hermeneutics is concerned with all forms of (meaningful) human activity, from the production of texts, in the narrow sense of the term, to the generation and maintenance of cultural forms of life. In all such instances hermeneutics seeks to explicate (lay out, *aus-legen*) not subjective (mental) *intentions* but the *logic* of the order in question (text, culture, etc). Although this logic can be made apparent only by means of the act of interpretation itself, it is not, as the deconstructionists would maintain, created by interpretation but possesses its own kind of "objective" existence. There is a kind of "objective logic" to all products of human action (texts or established modes of praxis). What, for instance, makes a text a *text* is that there is a certain "logic" embodied in it which it is precisely the task of text-interpretation to lay bare (Paul Ricoeur for his part refers to this as "the internal dynamic which governs the structuring of the work"). Likewise, there is a certain objective logic to human events (e.g., the French Revolution) or practices (e.g., those characteristic of democratic societies) which it is precisely the task of a hermeneutic social science to explicate. For instance, the task of a hermeneutic or interpretive economics is that of explicating the logic of market processes. As Eastern European reformers have amply realized subsequent to the demise of socialism, there is a definite logic to a market economy; what exactly this logic consists in is precisely the task of interpretation, i.e., of hermeneutic theory, to determine.[11]

The proper object of hermeneutic understanding is *meaning*. This means, as I have just indicated, that the scope of hermeneutic analysis includes not only texts but all forms of human agency as well, since human action is by definition meaningful (if not always deliberate). The only thing that can set a limit to hermeneutics is the limits of meaning itself, and, as Gadamer says, what lies beyond these limits, "what lies outside the realm of human understanding," is something which is of no concern to hermeneutics.[12]

As a general philosophical discipline, hermeneutics is concerned with everything having to do with linguistically generated and mediated meaning. The critic of hermeneutics might wish to seize upon this disciplinary characterization to underscore what he or she maintains are the limits of hermeneutics. That which falls outside of language (e.g., "power" and "work"), the critic will say, necessarily exceeds the scope of hermeneutics and calls for treatment by a more encompassing discipline (this being, it goes without saying, critical theory). This objection does not hold up, however. For, as hermeneutics insists, there is nothing humanly meaningful that falls outside of language. There is, Gadamer says, "no societal reality, with all its concrete forces, that does not bring itself to representation in a consciousness that is linguistically articulated. Reality does not happen 'behind the back' of language . . . reality happens precisely *within* language."[13] This has to do with what Gadamer calls the *Sprachlichkeit* or essential linguisticality of all human experience of the world, a notion which is meant to emphasize "the fundamental priority of language."[14] Even nonverbal behavior, Gadamer says, "looks to an ever-possible verbalisation, and for which the well tried word 'reason' is, perhaps, not the worst."[15] Gadamer argues for the universality of the hermeneutic problem "precisely because meaning can be experienced even when it is not actually intended,"[16] or expressed in an explicitly linguistic form.

Habermas notwithstanding, this central thesis does not entail any kind of "linguistic idealism," *Sprachidealismus*. When Gadamer proclaims that "Being that can be understood is language,"[17] he is not asserting that language is all there is or that being (reality) is reducible to language (a thesis usually associated with Derrida [*"Il n'y a pas de hors-texte"*]). All he is affirming is that there is nothing in human experience that is meaningful (at however inarticulate or "tacit" a level) which cannot, in principle, be brought to expression (and be interpreted) in and by means of language. "The principle of hermeneutics," Gadamer says, "simply means that we should try to understand everything that can be understood."[18] If the pre- or extralinguistic were not in principle expressible, it would be meaningless to maintain that human existence itself has any meaning (that human existence is intrinsically meaningless is, of course, a conclusion that the structuralists and poststructuralists are in no way hesitant to draw). However, as Gadamer insists,

> Language always forestalls any objection to its jurisdiction. Its universality keeps pace with the universality of reason. Hermeneutical consciousness is only participating in something that constitutes the general relation between language and reason. If all understanding stands in a necessary relation of equivalence to its possible interpretation and if there are basically no bounds set to understanding, then the linguistic form which the interpretation of this understanding finds must contain within it

an infinite dimension that transcends all bounds. Language is the language of reason itself.[19]

More succinctly: "Hermeneutics cannot evade claiming universality because language as linguisticality constitutes a human capacity inseparably linked with reason as such."[20]

Traditionally, hermeneutics was concerned with the right reading of *texts* (biblical, classical, juridical). Following Gadamer's own lead, hermeneuticists have subsequently extended the scope of this discipline to cover the entire range of the human sciences, whose proper object is the meaning of human *action.* The human sciences are concerned with what people do, the meaning of what they do, why and how they do it, and the (often unintended) consequences of their doing what they do. The approach that hermeneutics takes in regard to human action (in an attempt to explicate the meaningful structures embodied in the various orders which are the result of this action) is to view action "on the model of the text," in the words of Paul Ricoeur—as, in other words, a text-analogue.[21] For instance, the interpretive anthropologist Clifford Geertz has likened the work of the anthropologist to that of the literary critic, "sorting out the structures of signification" in those texts we call "cultures." Portraying ethnography as "thick description," he says:

> What the ethnographer is in fact faced with—except when (as, of course, he must do) he is pursuing the more automatized routines of data collection—is a multiplicity of complex conceptual structures, many of them superimposed upon or knotted into one another, which are at once strange, irregular, and inexplicit, and which he must contrive somehow first to grasp and then to render. And this is true at the most down-to-earth, jungle field work levels of his activity: interviewing informants, observing rituals, eliciting kin terms, tracing property lines, censusing households . . . writing his journal. Doing ethnography is like trying to read (in the sense of "construct a reading of") a manuscript—foreign, faded, full of ellipses, incoherencies, suspicious emendations, and tendentious commentaries, but written not in conventionalized graphs of sound but in transient examples of shaped behavior.[22]

If its critics wish to maintain that hermeneutics is limited to the analysis of texts, the hermeneuticist can respond that there is no order of "shaped behavior" or praxis that cannot be read "as" a text. It is in fact only by considering action as a text that we can hope to come to some understanding of it. Text and action are quite simply inseparable. Where Gadamer speaks of "linguisticality," many today prefer to speak of "textuality." As one writer remarks: "Hermeneutics is concerned with the interpretation of any expression of existence which can be preserved in a structure analogous to the structure of the text. . . . Taking it to the limit, the entirety of human existence becomes a text to be interpreted."[23] For his part, Gadamer remarks that "reading is the basic structure that is common in all occurrences of meaning."[24]

Consider the example of economics. Let us suppose that one of our chief concerns in this area is to achieve a conceptual understanding of how it is that a market economy actually functions (revealing thereby the "logic" of this particular order of human affairs).[25] The central problem of market economics is that of accounting for market *coordination:* How is it that out of the multifarious activity on the part of a myriad of independent economic agents, each pursuing his or her own subjective purposes and ignorant for the most part of those of others, an (objective) order (what F. A. Hayek calls a "spontaneous order") emerges that is manifestly the result of human agency but is also clearly not (in contrast to centralized or planned economies) the result of human design? How is it that the workings of the market give rise to such a high degree of social coordination when it is evident that this order is not the conscious product of any number of individual minds?

Hermeneutic economists believe that no significant headway can be made in dealing with this problem so long as the science of economics is itself understood in the objectivistic fashion in which mainline, neoclassical economics traditionally has sought to understand it.[26] Perhaps the chief contribution of hermeneutic theory to economics has to do with methodology.[27] What kind of science is economics? What is its proper object, and what "method" or approach is best suited to that object? Traditionally, ever since the nineteenth century, economists, awed by the Natural Science Ideal (as Lewis White Beck once referred to it), have sought to model their discipline after physics.[28] Precisely this "slavish imitation of the method and language of [physical] science," in the words of Hayek,[29] is being contested today by those economists who have renounced the positivism that still tends to prevail in the discipline and who have turned to hermeneutics. They object to the scientistic attempt to reduce economics to a Newtonian mechanics of human affairs and argue that, to be properly understood, human *action* calls for a different mode of analysis than that which is applicable to merely bodily or physical *motion.* Social reality, they insist, cannot be adequately understood if one does not accord methodological priority to the categories of *meaning* and *purpose* (categories which are obviously inapplicable in the realm of natural reality). As Geertz has said, "man is an animal suspended in webs of significance he himself has spun," and, accordingly, the analysis of human culture (understood as, precisely, an analysis of these "webs") is not "an experimental science in search of [nomological-deductive] law but an interpretive one in search of meaning."[30]

In an attempt to explore these "webs of significance" and to deal with the "coordination problem," hermeneutic economists focus on the role that *prices* play in communicating to economic agents the information that is necessary if they are to interact in an orderly way. The unique feature of a market or self-regulating economy is that monetary prices, as established by the give-and-take of free trade, communicate essential information to economic agents, "telling" them, in effect, how best to allocate their limited resources in order to achieve maximum gain. To speak of the "languages of prices" is more than a mere metaphor. As a means of communicating vital information, prices constitute a semiotic code; they constitute, therefore, a kind of *text*. Those agents perform best who are best able to *read* and appropriately *interpret* the message that prices convey. Economic agents are themselves engaged on a day-to-day basis in a properly hermeneutic task.

Hermeneutic economics thus views the market process as a kind of conversation aiming at "agreement" and conducted in the language of prices.[31] In other words, it maintains, in marked opposition to the position of Habermas, that the market process is best viewed as a mode of *communicative rationality* and not of *instrumental (or technological) rationality*. In opposition to the Frankfurt critics, hermeneutics insists that human agency in the context of a market economy should be treated under the rubric not of *technē* but of *praxis* (i.e., practical reason). Hermeneutic economists believe that to the degree that an economy is a free market economy, to that degree it constitutes (to employ Habermas's own words) "a communication community existing under constraints toward cooperation" and that it is one of those "intersubjective life-contexts" in which communicative reason is embodied.[32] When economic reality is viewed in this way, it is obvious that the domain of "work" does *not* fall outside of the scope of hermeneutics, and thus it is most clearly *not* the case that in extending itself to the realm of economics hermeneutics is *overextending* itself.[33]

I will not consider here in any great detail the related objection that the sphere of "power," i.e., politics, falls outside the legitimate purview of applied hermeneutics. Suffice it to say that Stanley Rosen was much more perceptive in this regard than the Frankfurters when he declared: "Every hermeneutical program is at the same time itself a political manifesto or the corollary of a political manifesto."[34] Of course, Rosen meant this as a criticism, since for him theory should be "pure," uncontaminated by practical concerns. Hermeneutic theory is not at all of this sort, however. Like other forms of postmodern or postmetaphysical thought, hermeneutics subscribes to the "primacy of the practical over the theoretical." It believes that the proper function of *theory* is to enable us to achieve a reflexive awareness of our own *practices* (whether these be understood as everyday, lifeworld practices or the specialized, theoretical, or discursive practices of the various scientific disciplines). It believes that the ultimate justification of theory (as, precisely, a theory *of* practice) is its significance *for* practice.[35] That is, it believes that by enabling us to achieve a reflexive awareness of our practices, theory has a constructive role to play in the shaping or reshaping of these very practices. The role that it plays in this regard is that of "cultivation" (to employ a term of Hayek's). By making us more self-consciously aware of what we actually do (in everyday life as well as in our scientific practices), hermeneutic theory can help us to eliminate from our practices certain inconsistencies or contradictions (what Habermas would call "systematic distortions") which give rise to discrepancies between what we intend or desire and what we actually achieve, as well as misunderstandings with others.[36] With regard to social orders such as a "culture" or an "economy," hermeneutic theory, by enabling us to understand the organizational principles of the order in question, puts us in a position to alter existing practices in such a way as, on the one hand, to eliminate factors which are contrary to the "logic" of the order, and which thus result in malfunctionings of the order (e.g., a particular monetary order), and, on the other hand, to devise new, institutional structures which will allow the order to function in a smoother way and to develop further. In this way, we can contribute to the likelihood that in our lives, both private and social, beneficial results will predominate over disadvantageous ones.

It should therefore be evident that, contrary to the misleading portrayal of it by the Frankfurt critics, the function of hermeneutics is not limited to description or interpretation only; it is of the essence of the discipline itself that it functions also as *critique* (of existing practices). As Gadamer has insisted: "The task of bringing people to a self-understanding of themselves may help us to gain our freedom in relation to everything that has taken us in unquestioningly."[37] In response to accusations by Habermas and others that hermeneutics is essentially "conservative," Gadamer has insisted that it is a "grave misunderstanding" to think that hermeneutics entails "an uncritical acceptance of tradition and sociopolitical conservatism."[38] The notion of communicative rationality defended by Gadamer, the highest form of reason according to him, always holds open, he says, "the possibility of going beyond our conventions" and insures "the possibility of our taking a critical stance with regard to every convention."[39] Hermeneutics is as much a form of "critical theory" as that school of thought which arrogates the name for itself. Unlike Frankfurt critical theory, however, it does not need to ground its critical function on dubious metaphysical notions, such as that of a utopic, ideal speech situation, and social or "species-wide" evolutionism ("historical materialism").[40]

Hermeneutics extends to the realm of politics to the degree that the general theory of human understanding it embodies privileges practical reason, *phronēsis,* dialogue. When Gadamer characterized hermeneutics as *scientia practica sive politica,* he was indeed underscoring its political nature;[41] politics (along with ethics) is the realm *par excellence* of practical reason. There is, moreover, as Richard Bernstein has noted, a radical strain to hermeneutic politics. In attempting to draw out the practical consequences of philosophical hermeneutics, Gadamer appropriates from Hegel, Bernstein observes, the principle of freedom ("a freedom that is realized only when there is authentic mutual 'recognition' among individuals"), and he remarks: "This radical strain is indicated in his emphasis—which has become more and more dominant in recent years—on freedom and solidarity that embrace all of humanity."[42] In many of his writings after *Truth and Method,* Gadamer returns again and again to sociopolitical issues, defending the values of communicative rationality and denouncing the subtle forms of oppression that tend to subvert these values in an age dominated by science and technology and a purely instrumentalist conception of reason. "It is the function of hermeneutical reflection, in this connection [the conservation of freedom]," Gadamer says, "to preserve us from naive surrender to the experts of social technology."[43] Thus, the practical task of hermeneutic theory is precisely, as Bernstein has also remarked, that of fostering "the type of dialogical communities in which *phronēsis* becomes a living reality and where citizens can actually assume what Gadamer tells us is their 'noblest task'—'decision-making according to one's own responsibility—instead of conceding that task to the expert.'"[44] In its application to politics, hermeneutics functions as the legitimating theory of democratic *praxis.*

This, it may be noted, is a theory that is not based on any kind of objectivistic evolutionism or quixotic utopianism but simply on the down-to-earth realization that democracy is the least worst form of government presently known to us. Eschewing appeals to either eschatology or utopia, Gadamer insists: "What man needs is not only a persistent asking of ultimate questions, but the sense of what is feasible, what is possible, what is correct, here and now."[45] The "hermeneutical task," Gadamer says, is that of "integrating the monologicality of science into the communicative consciousness," and this task, he further says, "entails a practical, social, and political responsibility [that] has only become more urgent with the rise of technological civilization."[46]

Not only, therefore, does hermeneutics embody a general theory of human understanding (commonly referred to as "philosophical hermeneutics"), and not only does it contain significant methodological implications for the practice of the human sciences, it also applies, as we have now seen, to "the concrete factors of work and politics." The Frankfurt critics notwithstanding, the scope of the discipline is indeed universal.

While the scope of hermeneutics is universal (applying even to the exercise of theory in the natural sciences),[47] the claim of hermeneutics to universality has nothing "imperialistic" about it, as some critics nevertheless imply. Arguing, as it does, for a *nonessentialist* understanding of universalism,[48] hermeneutics stands in marked contrast to various modernist theories claiming universal validity. In their case, the claim to universality does indeed entail a reduction of difference to homogeneic identity and is therefore "imperialistic." The most notable contrast in this regard is no doubt between hermeneutics and logical positivism and the "Unified Science" movement associated with it. The latter was truly an example, not only of disciplinary *hubris,* but of disciplinary imperialism as well, a fine instance thereof being the work of Carl Hempel who, with his "covering laws" model, sought to impose upon a human science such as history the alien methodology of the natural sciences.[49] This "dogmatic" (to use a Gadamerian term) feature of much of what passes for social science continues in our day to be evidenced in those imperialistic disciplines which go under the names of Sociobiology and Artificial Intelligence (or Cognitive Science). Even as it lays claim to universal applicability, hermeneutics subscribes to methodological *pluralism* (though not, as I shall attempt to indicate, methodological "anarchism").

The position staked out by hermeneutics in this regard could perhaps best be clarified in terms of the classic opposition between *Verstehen* and *Erklärung*—"understanding" and "explanation." In the hermeneutic theory of Wilhelm Dilthey these two concepts were treated as polar opposites: While Dilthey allowed that "explanation" (mechanistic, cause-and-effect analysis) was the method proper to the natural sciences, he insisted that this approach to phenomena was totally inappropriate in the human sciences; their "method" must rather be that of "understanding." By "understanding" he meant *empathetic* understanding, the empathetic *projection* of oneself into an alien form of life. Dilthey equated understanding with a kind of *reliving* of the psychic experience of others. Dilthey's dichotomizing, methodological opposition was revived in the mid-twentieth century by Peter Winch in a famous discussion of methodological issues in the social sciences.[50] In his various references to "hermeneutics," Habermas generally makes little or no attempt to point out how Gadamer's hermeneutics has overcome the Dilthey-Winch opposition between "explanation" and "understanding." Habermas is right, of course, in distinguishing what could be called meaning-analysis from empirical-causal explanation (see above), but he is wrong in thinking that hermeneutics is limited to a narrow kind of meaning-analysis (*Verstehen,* in the classical sense of the term).

What must be noted in this regard is that the distinction between "explanation" and "understanding" is a properly *metaphysical* opposition parallelling that between "man" and "nature." Phenomenology has from the outset rejected this oppositional distinction—and the related distinction between knowledge "from the inside" and knowledge "from the outside"—as untenable and inappropriate. Gadamer's phenomenological hermeneutics, precisely because it *is* phenomenological, carries this rejection of metaphysical dualism even further. Gadamer in fact views Dilthey's dichotomizing distinction as a relic of the Cartesian, metaphysical dualism that has infected all of modern thought.[51] Hermeneutics emphatically rejects any absolute *dualism* in its understanding of human understanding. This is not to say, however, that, like logical positivism, it subscribes to any form of methodological "monism."

Hermeneutics believes that there is a legitimate, albeit limited, place for purely causal or statistical analysis in the human sciences, just as it maintains that causal explanation in the natural sciences must, if it is to be understood properly, be viewed within the wider scope of the interpretive *(verstehende)* frameworks such a mode of apparently purely "objective" or "empirical" analysis actually presupposes.[52] Methodological "objectivists" tend to overlook the fact emphasized by Gadamer, namely, that all knowledge comes only in the form of an answer to a *question*. It is one of the key functions of hermeneutics (of "interpretation") to bring to awareness the often merely presupposed and unthematized question-framework that actually informs and guides all "empirical" research. Take the example of statistics. As Gadamer has remarked,

Statistics provide us with a useful example of how the hermeneutical dimension encompasses the entire procedure of science. It is an extreme example, but it shows us that science always stands under definite conditions of methodological abstraction and that the successes of modern sciences rest on the fact that other possibilities for questioning are concealed by abstraction. This fact comes out clearly in the case of statistics, for the anticipatory character of the questions statistics answer make it particularly suitable for propaganda purposes. . . . Thus what is established by statistics seems to be a language of facts, but which questions these facts answer and which facts would begin to speak if other questions were asked are hermeneutical questions. Only a hermeneutical inquiry would legitimate the meaning of these facts and thus the consequences that follow from them.[53]

As I have mentioned, hermeneutics views "explanation" as a legitimate *moment* (in a quasi-Hegelian sense) in the overall understanding or interpretive process. It is certainly not the case that Gadamerian hermeneutics reduces understanding to mere "empathetic" understanding. On the contrary, it insists that a kind of purely *descriptive* approach (in terms of mental states) is no more appropriate in an analysis of human affairs than a purely "explanatory," cause-and-effect approach; in both cases the object to be understood—meaning embedded in intersubjective practices—would be lost sight of. Human agents are self-interpreting beings, but it is not the task of an interpretive social science simply to "describe" these interpretations. The function of interpretation is not that of *Verstehen* in the classical sense of the term, i.e., that of articulating the self-understanding of human agents in such a way as to achieve an empathetic understanding of them. The self-interpretation of agents *must themselves be interpreted* by the social scientist (this is one of the main reasons why hermeneutic analysis is necessarily *critical*).

Precisely because, as hermeneutics insists, the meaning of things human (texts, action) is not "subjective," there is a legitimate, though limited, place for explanatory techniques of a purely objective nature in the overall interpretive process. For instance, in the case of text-interpretation it may be useful at the outset to approach the text in a purely objective way, in terms of semiological analysis or computer analysis of word distribution. Similarly, a purely statistical analysis may alert social scientists to the existence of patterns of action they might otherwise overlook. In both cases, however, a fully adequate account of human affairs must be one which incorporates these "objective" analyses into a wider, interpretive framework. Ultimately, one wishes to understand the *meaning* of the text (this, of course, is not the author's intended meaning but rather what Gadamer calls *die Sache,* i.e., the "matter of the text," this being in the final analysis the mode of human *being-in-the-world* that the text projects).[54] Likewise, to be made meaningful, social patterns of action must be related back to *individual* human agents and their attempts at achieving meaning or improvement in their own lives (which is not to say, of course, that the results of human action can be adequately understood solely in terms of the [psychological] intentions or motivations of agents; one of the prime focuses of an interpretive *social* science must be the *unintended* consequences of human agency).[55] For instance, the data resulting from macroeconomic analyses is deficient in meaning until it is tied into its microeconomic foundations in the activity of individual economic agents (entrepreneurs, firms, etc.). Economic policies that ignore this methodological requirement are courting social disaster. No "expert of social technology," as Gadamer would say, is capable of managing a market economy on a collective basis and with the aid of macroeconomic indicators; it is possible, though, through democratic processes, to establish a general system of rules and institutional frameworks that will be such as to facilitate and encourage productive activity on the part of individual citizens, the result of this being the enhancement of the good of society as a whole.

Thus, in conclusion, the claim of hermeneutics to universality rests on an approach to human affairs that is *neither* "imperialistic" *nor* "anarchistic" (or "dichotomistic") but rather *pluralistic* and *integrative*. Unlike the approach taken by Winch, hermeneutics recognizes the legitimacy of "explanation," but it also insists that all attempts at "explanation" must ultimately be integrated *(aufheben)* into the wider and all-inclusive attempt at *understanding*. Moreover, the claim of hermeneutics to universality is based on *nothing metaphysical*—neither on an essentialist ("real") human *nature* that all humans are supposed to participate in (in the Platonic-Aristotelian sense of the term) nor on some kind of postulated, transcendental, and universally uniform a priori of human thought processes (*à la* Kant). Hermeneutics does not rest, as Habermas's thought does, on a kind of revamped and quasi-metaphysical a priorism (and on a juxtaposition of this with an uncritical objectivism or empiricism which takes the so-called "objective" social sciences at face value). Like the "ubiquity of rhetoric,"[56] the universality of hermeneutics is based solely on the phenomenological or experiential *fact* that, as the leading Greek rhetorician, Isocrates, pointed out, what makes human beings "human" is their "linguisticality." Humans are distinct from all other animal species in that they possess the *logos;* they are the "speaking animals." "The commonality that we call human," Gadamer says, "rests on the linguistic constitution of our lifeworld."[57] Hermeneutics is nothing other than a systematic attempt to draw all the implications (the normative implications, in particular) that lie in this most primordial of phenomenological facts. This is what makes hermeneutics a truly universal discipline. For wherever "man" is, there also is the *logos*.

G. B. MADISON

DEPARTMENT OF PHILOSOPHY
MCMASTER UNIVERSITY
JULY 1992

NOTES

1. Hans-Georg Gadamer, *Truth and Method* (New York: Seabury Press, 1975), pp. xviii–xix.

2. Gadamer, "On the Scope and Function of Hermeneutical Reflection," in *Philosophical Hermeneutics,* trans. David E. Linge (Berkeley: University of California Press, 1976), p. 18.

3. Jürgen Habermas, "The Hermeneutic Claim to Universality," in *The Hermeneutic Tradition: From Ast to Ricoeur,* ed. Gayle L. Ormiston and Alan D. Schrift (Albany: State University of New York Press, 1990), p. 267. Habermas's self-styled "meta-hermeneutic" is one that "connects the process of understanding to the principle of rational discourse, according to which truth would only be guaranteed by *that* kind of consensus which was achieved under the idealized condition of unlimited communication free from domination and could be maintained over time" (ibid.).

4. See, for instance, Habermas, "Theory and Practice," in *Theory and Practice,* trans. John Viertel (Boston: Beacon Press, 1973).

5. An objection of this sort was made by Richard Bernstein in his commentary on my "Hermeneutical Liberalism," paper presented to the conference on *"Gemeinschaft und Gerechtigkeit"* organized by the *Frankfurter Akademie der Künste und Wissenschaften* (May 1992) and forthcoming in *Gemeinschaft und Gerechtigkeit,* ed. Micha Brumlik and Hauke Brunkhorst (Frankfurt: Fischer Taschenbuch Verlag).

6. Texts of the original debate appeared in Habermas, *Zur Logik der Sozial wissenschaften* (Frankfurt: Suhrkamp, 1970) and Karl-Otto Apel, et al., *Hermeneutik und Ideologiekritik* (Frankfurt: Suhrkamp, 1971). See, in English, Habermas, "A review of Gadamer's *Truth and Method"* and "The Hermeneutic Claim to Universality," in *The Hermeneutic Tradition: From Ast to Ricoeur,* as well as Gadamer, "Reply to My Critics," in ibid. and "On the Scope and Function of Hermeneutical Reflection," in Gadamer, *Philosophical Hermeneutics.*

7. Hans-Georg Gadamer, "On the Scope and Function of Hermeneutical Reflection," p. 31.

8. For a detailed discussion of the basic differences between Gadamer's hermeneutics and romantic hermeneutics, see my "Hermeneutics: Gadamer and Ricoeur," in the *Routledge History of Philosophy* (London: Routledge, 1993), vol. 8.

9. Gadamer, "Reply to My Critics," p. 291.

10. Gadamer, "Reflections on My Philosophical Journey," in this volume.

11. While "logics" such as these are "objective," in the sense that they do not exist merely in the minds of individuals but *in* texts and *in* practices themselves, they are not univocally determined (they are not "essences" in the traditional sense). The products of human activity are always over- (or under-) determined, such that they are amenable to being interpreted in a number of different ways (which is not to say that some interpretations are not better than others and that some are not clearly wrong).

12. Gadamer, "On the Scope and Function of Hermeneutical Reflection," p. 31.

13. Ibid., p. 35.

14. See Gadamer, *Truth and Method,* p. 362.

15. Ibid., p. 496.

16. Gadamer, "On the Scope and Function of Hermeneutical Reflection," p. 30.

17. See Gadamer, *Truth and Method,* p. xxii.

18. Gadamer, "On the Scope and Function of Hermeneutical Reflection," p. 31.

19. Gadamer, *Truth and Method,* p. 363.

20. Gadamer, "Reflections on My Philosophical Journey."

21. See in this regard the highly influential article by Paul Ricoeur, "The Model of the Text: Meaningful Action Considered as a Text," in *Hermeneutics and the Human Sciences,* ed. and trans. John B. Thompson (Cambridge: Cambridge University Press, 1974).

22. Clifford Geertz, *The Interpretation of Cultures* (New York: Basic Books, 1973), pp. 9–10.

23. David Pellauer, "The Significance of the Text in Paul Ricoeur's Hermeneutical Theory" in Charles E. Reagan, ed., *Studies in the Philosophy of Paul Ricoeur* (Athens: Ohio University Press, 1979), pp. 112, 109. Although Pellauer has Ricoeur especially in mind, his remarks apply to phenomenological hermeneutics in general (Ricoeur's work on textuality is a natural outgrowth of his appropriation of Gadamer's own work on the linguisticality of all human experience of the world).

24. Gadamer, "Reflections on My Philosophical Journey."

25. This is a more crucial and pressing task than might readily be supposed; the logic of the market economy is one of the things that, despite its sophistication in the domain of objective measuring techniques, mainline economic theory understands perhaps least of all. As economist Geoffrey M. Hodgson has observed:

> The study of market behaviour is a major theme, if not the major theme, of economic science as we know it. . . . Remarkably, however, definitions of the market in the economic literature are not easy to find, and analytical discussions of the institutional concepts involved are extremely rare. Mathematical models of market phenomena abound, and there is a voluminous literature on the theoretical determinants of market equilibria. Yet if we ask the elementary question, 'What is a market?', we are given shrift. . . . For too long 'the market' has been taken for granted. (*Economics and Institutions: A Manifesto for a Modern Institutional Economics* [Philadelphia: University of Pennsylvania Press, 1988], pp. 172–73)

It should be noted that the kind of *theoretical* understanding of market processes that hermeneutic economics seeks to formulate would have direct *practical* consequences—with regard, in particular, to government economic policy. For without such an understanding, would-be policy makers and interventionists cannot possibly know what it really is that they want to accomplish, as the leading economist, Frank H. Knight, observed a number of decades ago:

> We must always keep in mind the relations between ethical and mechanical aspects of the economic system. In so far as undesirable results are due to obstructions or interference of a frictional character in the workings of the organization machinery, the correct social policy will be to remove these or to supplement the natural tendencies of the system itself. In so far as these natural tendencies are wrong, the effort must be to find and substitute some entirely different machinery for performing the right function in the right way. There is much confusion in the popular mind on this point: critics of enterprise economy who do not have a fair understanding of how the machinery works cannot tell whether to criticize it because it doesn't work according to theory or because it does. (*Freedom and Reform: Essays in Economics and Social Philosophy* [Indianapolis: Liberty Press, 1982], p. 57)

The "confusion on this point" that Knight highlights is to be found in almost all the criticisms that members of the Frankfurt School have directed towards the free-market economy ("capitalism").

26. See my "Getting beyond Objectivism: The Philosophical Hermeneutics of

Gadamer and Ricoeur," as well as other essays included in Don Lavoie, ed., *Economics and Hermeneutics* (London: Routledge, 1990).

27. As one of the leading pioneers of hermeneutic economics, Ludwig Lachmann, remarked,

> The 'market process' is an item high on the agenda of the Austrian [School of economics] research programme. The market, needless to say, offers a particularly fascinating example of an area of intersubjectivity in which vast numbers of men interact with one another in the pursuit of their multifarious needs and interests. It calls for treatment by a method inspired by the hermeneutical style, a method which defies the spirit of orthodox formalism. ("Austrian Economics: A Hermeneutic Approach," in *Economics and Hermeneutics*, p. 145)

28. See in this regard the detailed historical study of Philip Mirowski, *More Heat than Light: Economics as Social Physics, Physics as Nature's Economics* (Cambridge: Cambridge University Press, 1989).

29. Friedrich A. Hayek, *The Counter-Revolution of Science: Studies on the Abuse of Reason*, 2d ed. (Indianapolis: Liberty Press, 1979), p. 29. In this book, the text of which was written in the 1940s, Hayek attacked what he called the "scientism" and the "physicalism" infecting economic theory and methodology and argued for an alternative approach, one which today would be labeled interpretive or hermeneutic. For a discussion of the position defended by Hayek see my "Hayek and the Interpretive Turn," *Critical Review*, 3, no. 2 (Spring 1989).

30. Geertz, *The Interpretation of Cultures*, p. 5.

31. For an excellent treatment of these issues and, in particular, for an attempt to conceptualize the nature and function of *money* along hermeneutic lines, see Steven G. Horwitz, *Monetary Evolution, Free Banking, and Economic Order* (Boulder, Colo.: Westview Press, 1992), as well as his article "Monetary Exchange as an Extra-Linguistic Social Communicative Process," *Review of Social Economy* (1992).

32. See Habermas, *The Philosophical Discourse of Modernity*, trans. Frederick Lawrence (Cambridge, Mass.: MIT Press, 1987), p. 40. An important, as well as apparently irreconcilable, difference between Habermas and the hermeneuticists is that the former seems to accept the purely instrumentalist orientation of neoclassical economic theory (in regard to matters such as equilibrium and rational choice) at face value (thinking, as he does, that the economic realm is a merely technical "subsystem," fully understandable in terms of systems-analysis; see Habermas, *The Theory of Communicative Action*, trans. Thomas McCarthy [Boston: Beacon Press, 1984], vol. 1, pp. 4–5), whereas the latter consider neoclassical theory to be unacceptably positivistic and objectivistic.

Moreover, as Hayek has clearly shown (see his *Law, Legislation, and Liberty* [Chicago: University of Chicago Press, 1976], vol. 2, chap. 10, "The Market Order or Catallaxy"), "the" economy is not a "system" at all (i.e., an order that is goal-directed and uses given means for specific ends). Habermas repeats the error common to Marxists of confusing the economic order of the market with intraeconomy entities such as the firm (which is indeed characterized by technological or instrumental rationality).

It may be noted, in addition, that definite policy implications follow from viewing market processes as a form of *communicative* rationality (as a "conversation," in Gadamer's sense of the term). If the "language of prices" does indeed constitute a kind of "conversation," then it follows, as a policy implication, that the conversation can be a genuine one only if there are no unnecessary extramarket constraints on prices themselves (i.e., only if prices are determined in the very course of unconstrained market transactions) and only if there is no attempt to determine in advance the outcome of the conversation (e.g., governmental attempts to determine the social distribution of wealth ["social justice"]). As Gadamer has remarked, in a genuine conversation—one that "guarantees truth"—"no one knows what will 'come out'" (*Truth and Method*, 447 and 345, respectively). Thus, as economist Don Lavoie observes: "market communication is an extension of the democracy of open verbal communication. . . . Extending to the economy the sorts of values that pertain to democracy-in-the-small points in the direction of a free market system. The free market's discovery process is open-ended in the same sense that a conversation is" (*"Glasnost* and the Knowledge Problem: Rethinking Economic Democracy," paper presented at the Cato Institute conference on "Transition to Freedom: The New Soviet Challenge" [Moscow, September 1990]).

33. The Frankfurters can maintain that "work" falls outside the scope of hermeneutics only because they continue to adhere to the naiveté of "historical materialism" according to which all cultural (linguistic) reality is a mere "superstructure" determined by underlying (and nonlinguistic) "forces of production." (Although Habermas has explicitly called this simplistic distinction into question, his thought continues to be implicitly determined by it—by, in general, a kind of residual and incorrigible Marxism which he maintains as a kind of badge of honor and as proof that he is indeed a "progressive" and "politically correct" thinker.)

34. Stanley Rosen, *Hermeneutics as Politics* (New York: Oxford University Press, 1987), p. 141.

35. For a discussion of the nature and uses of hermeneutic theory, see my "The Practice of Theory, the Theory of Practice," *Critical Review* 5, no. 2 (Spring 1991).

36. To put the matter in a slightly different way, the entire *raison d'être* of hermeneutic theory lies, as Gadamer would say, in its *application*. The hermeneutic elucidation of methodological issues and its critique of objectivism in a science such as economics is one such instance of "application." Hermeneutic self-understanding can be of therapeutic value by enabling us to rid ourselves of various kinds of methodological false consciousness of which we are sometimes victims, as, for instance, when we seek to do sociology in slavish obeisance to positivist prescriptions.

37. Gadamer, *Reason in the Age of Science*, trans. Frederick G. Lawrence (Cambridge, Mass.: MIT Press, 1981), pp. 149–50.

38. Gadamer, "The Problem of Historical Consciousness," in Paul Rabinow and William M. Sullivan, eds., *Interpretive Social Science: A Reader* (Berkeley: University of California Press, 1974), p. 108.

39. Gadamer, *Truth and Method*, pp. 495–96.

40. Far from allowing that critical theory is more encompassing than hermeneutics, Gadamer maintains that the former is actually more limited in scope; he writes: "Ideology criticism represents only a particular form of hermeneutical reflection, one that seeks to dispel a certain class of prejudices through critique. Hermeneutical reflection, however, is universal in its possible application" ("Semantics and Hermeneutics," in *Philosophical Hermeneutics*, p. 93).

41. See Gadamer, "The Power of Reason," *Man and World* 3, no. 1 (1970): 8.

42. Richard J. Bernstein, *Beyond Objectivism and Relativism: Science, Hermeneutics, and Praxis* (Philadelphia: University of Pennsylvania Press, 1983), p. 163. For a discussion of "solidarity" as hermeneutics conceives of it, see my "Hermeneutical Liberalism," cited in note 4 above.

43. Gadamer, "On the Scope and Function of Hermeneutical Reflection," p. 40.

44. Bernstein, *Beyond Objectivism and Relativism*, p. 159.

45. Gadamer, *Truth and Method*, p. xxv.

46. Gadamer, "Reflections on My Philosophical Journey." Gadamer goes on to say:

"the concept of reflection that serves as the basis of Habermas' 'critique of ideology' implies a highly abstract concept of coercion-free discourse which totally loses sight of the real conditions of human praxis." In his "Reply to My Critics" Gadamer states that Habermas' "counterfactual," coercion-free ideal speech situation is "shockingly unrealistic" (p. 292). Habermas' guiding notion of perfect consensus "appears to me," Gadamer says, "to be clearly recognizable as metaphysical in origin" (ibid., 287). Habermas is taking as his model of human understanding, Gadamer says, the intelligence of an angel.

47. Patrick Heelan has dealt extensively with the relation between hermeneutics and the natural sciences; see for instance his "Hermeneutical Phenomenology and the Philosophy of Science," in *Gadamer and Hermeneutics,* Hugh J. Silverman, ed. (New York: Routledge, 1991).

48. See in this regard my "Philosophy Without Foundations," *Reason Papers,* 16 (Fall 1991).

49. See Carl G. Hempel, "The Function of General Laws in History" (1942), reprinted in *Theories of History,* ed. Patrick Gardiner (New York: Free Press of Glencoe, 1959), pp. 344–56.

50. Habermas discusses the views of Winch in *The Theory of Communicative Action,* vol. 1.

51. See Gadamer's discussion of Dilthey in "The Problem of Historical Consciousness."

52. See for instance in this regard Stephen Toulmin, "The Construal of Reality: Criticism in Modern and Postmodern Science," in *The Politics of Interpretation,* ed. W. J. T. Mitchell (Chicago: University of Chicago Press, 1983). The interpretive frameworks that underlie and tacitly guide all empirical research and that inform any community of working scientists were totally ignored by logical positivism and the traditional, analytic philosophy of science. They have, however, become an object of investigation in their own right, by, in particular, the Sociology of Knowledge. Maintaining that what is most primordially given is the activity of interpretation itself, Gadamer remarks: "Even in the domain of the natural sciences, the grounding of scientific knowledge cannot avoid the hermeneutical consequences of the fact that the so-called 'given' cannot be separated from interpretation" ("Text and Interpretation," in Diane P. Michelfelder and Richard E. Palmer, eds., *Dialogue and Deconstruction: The Gadamer-Derrida Encounter* [Albany: State University of New York Press, 1989], 30).

53. Gadamer, "The Universality of the Hermeneutical Problem," in *Philosophical Hermeneutics,* p. 11.

54. See my article originally published under the title "Eine Kritik an Hirschs Begriff der 'Richtigkeit'," in H.-G. Gadamer and G. Boehm, eds., *Seminar: Die Hermeneutik und die Wissenschaften* (Frankfurt: Suhrkamp, 1978); English translation in my *The Hermeneutics of Postmodernity: Figures and Themes* (Bloomington: Indiana University Press, 1988).

55. While some economists refer to this approach as "methodological individualism," when practiced by hermeneuticists it has nothing "individualistic" about it. On the contrary, it represents an attempt to grasp the irreducibly *social* dimension of action on the part of individuals (to understand, that is, the social as having a *logic* irreducible to the *psychology* of individual agents). See in this regard my "How Individualistic is Methodological Individualism?" *Critical Review* 4, nos. 1 and 2 (Winter-Spring 1990).

56. See "On the Scope and Function of Hermeneutical Reflection," p. 24. For a detailed analysis of the relations between hermeneutics and rhetoric, see my "The New Philosophy of Rhetoric," *Texte: Revue de critique et de théorie littéraire* 8/9 (1989).

57. Gadamer, "Reflections on My Philosophical Journey."

REPLY TO G. B. MADISON

As a reliable student of Paul Ricoeur, Madison was well prepared for our later encounter through my works on hermeneutic philosophy. The present contribution to our volume in truth connects with my works, but also with his own. Obviously he wanted to take up anew the dispute that I have had with the Frankfurt School about the universality of hermeneutics. He apparently would like to defend the universal claim of hermeneutics from his own viewpoint. My confrontation with Habermas was primarily concerned with the question whether hermeneutics fails to address the real demand of this time, that is, the emancipation from outlived traditions and conventions, and whether it remains caught in mere understanding and thus fails to deliver what is the most important now, namely critique.

The course of the debate is known well enough. Having been often urged to repeat this public talk after so many years, both Habermas and I rejected this probably because our work moved in other directions over the years. Nevertheless, an opposition that is unbridgeable despite many contacts can be called up in one's memory through discussions of the past. In those days Habermas objected that hermeneutics could have a future only if *phronēsis,* Aristotle's practical knowledge to which I appealed, became science. I responded with the reverse claim: only if science were to be subordinated to *phronēsis* could it fulfill the task of the future.

Madison presents the state of the discussion in a precise and trenchant manner, but he does not merely want to repeat that debate but seeks to extend hermeneutics to cover the entirety of the debate. He agrees with me that in this endeavor one should not only have science in view but primarily human sociality. He then demonstrates this with the example of a science, namely economics. In an interesting manner he presents the development of economics through Hayek. With delight I note that in this hermeneutic extension science itself apparently took the path which I had in view when I criticized the dominance of the concept of method as it determines the natural sciences, and likewise what I had in mind with my own hermeneutic ideas regarding the understanding of the science of the so-called humanities. Madison demonstrates how the development of the economic and social sciences themselves moved further along in this direction about which Habermas claimed that hermeneutics did not have any competence. Of course, in a certain sense he is right here insofar as I myself do not have the slightest competence in economics. Nonetheless, in Madison's presentation it makes sense to me that the market economy presents a convincing analogy to communication in a dialogue. When Madison speaks of the language of prices he could equally well have talked of the balancing-out *(Sich-Ein-spielen)* of prices in the market event, and this corresponds exactly to my own concept of play *(Spiel)* and its model function in the linguistic event as well as in understanding art. I also agree entirely with Schleiermacher that hermeneutics has to grow out of the praxis of understanding and interpretation. Theory should only be developed out of praxis. Thus it seems to me to be justified and understandable that I refer to literature, art, and the history of philosophy for more general theoretical considerations of hermeneutics. In these fields I can rely upon my own research practices, but certainly not in the field of economics. In my eyes, however, it is convincing and important that in the field of the economic sciences one should also speak more of the experience of practice than of the regulative schemata of economic models. This does not mean, of course, that for this reason one should dispense with scientific education. For the unfolding of the free competition of economic practice truly depends upon the right framework conditions. Nonetheless, the model of play finally remains in its proper place here too. The market event is indeed really like a good discussion: one cannot know in advance what will come out of it.

It was quite surprising to me that there was so much evidence which Madison draws from my works that revealed some of the many directions in which hermeneutics can extend itself. It was not a surprise to me that the faculty of judgment accomplishes a decisive contribution in the field of jurisprudence and of the art of medicine. Hermeneutics has been cultivated in those fields since its inception even if it was mostly subordinated to the concept of method. The faculty of judgment, however, renders methods truly applicable in the first place. The natural sciences in general present a similar case in that the hermeneutic dimension plays a certain role. However, Madison seems to me to go a little too far in discussing the opposition of understanding and explaining in Dilthey: he turns Dilthey into a champion of unified science. In this physicalism could hardly remain entirely serious. But with regard to the main points I concur with him. Whenever methods are being employed their correct application is not specified by a method but demands our own judgment. This is a profound commonality of reason itself. It testifies to the depth in which linguisticality is rooted in human life. All methods require judgment and linguistic instruction.

H.-G.G.

18

Carl Page

HISTORICISTIC FINITUDE AND PHILOSOPHICAL HERMENEUTICS

Historicism, like hermeneutics, has an extraordinary philosophical form as well as an ordinary academic one. Just as Gadamer has shown us the meaning of *philosophical* hermeneutics, a hermeneutics separable from all methodologies of interpretation by its focus on the topic of reason's self-knowledge, so too there is a *philosophical* historicism separable from all historicist recommendations for how best to manage the human activities of inquiry and understanding. The latter recommendations are procedural and ontologically uncommitted; the former doctrine is metaphysical, defined by its insistence on the finite historicity of human reason. Gadamer's philosophical hermeneutics is closely linked to philosophical historicism, for both are heirs to the modern philosophical tradition of reason's critique. Gadamer acknowledges the connection in his essay "Hermeneutics and Historicism" which appears as supplement 1 to the English translation of *Wahrheit und Methode.*[1] In that essay, he identifies and endorses a "second-degree" historicism, continuous with his own sense of hermeneutics and marked by its appreciation of "the existence of the knowing subject in his historicity" (TM 533).

Gadamer's second-degree historicism is distinguished from a first-degree historicism he attributes foremost to Droysen, Ranke, and Dilthey as outstanding representatives of a broad historicist tradition rooted in and branching out from nineteenth-century German historiography. In its purest, classical form, historicism rests on convictions about the individual and developmental nature of historical realities (as contrasted with static, universalizing, and naturalistic approaches), rather than on worked-out philosophical views about the nature and circumstances of human understanding. The political historian Friedrich Meinecke and the theologian Ernst Troeltsch have elsewhere and commonly been taken as exemplars of what Gadamer means by first-degree historicism.[2] Individual thinkers do not fall neatly on either side of the distinction—Dilthey and Karl Mannheim, for example, being cases in point—but this does not compromise the meaning of the difference. In classical historicism, the new-found historicity is primarily located in the realities knowable to the human sciences

(Geisteswissenschaften); for philosophical historicism, historicity is a new-found property of reason itself. Hegel, the *éminence grise* of all philosophy's historicist musing, sought to trace the relation entailed by this difference but the style of his resolution is not immediately relevant here: academic philosophy has yet to appropriate his achievement.

Recently amongst English-speaking philosophers, second-degree historicism has become the dominant commonplace of almost all philosophical reflection. Many contemporaries think nothing of presuming the complete and necessary historical contextualization of reason and all its operations: Richard Rorty, Alasdair MacIntyre, Richard Bernstein, and Joseph Margolis may be noted as typical.[3] Gadamer himself was originally more cautious: "in modern life, our historical consciousness is constantly overstimulated" (TM xxiv). Nonetheless he too is inclined to the radical and metaphysically committed thesis of human reason's necessary finitude, an inclination reinforced by the important influence of his teacher, Heidegger.

Despite Gadamer's making the connection himself, there is not a necessary link between philosophical hermeneutics and the sense of historicism now epidemic within philosophy. The central insights of philosophical hermeneutics do not require the thesis of reason's radical finitude, though it still provides a corrective to what may, with some compression and perhaps injustice, be called Enlightenment conceptions of reason. This essay defends the foregoing assertions. Its principal aim is to subvert the pretensions of contemporary philosophical historicism while sponsoring Gadamer's correction of an earlier, and equally mistaken, ahistorical rationalism. [→ between historicism + philosophical rationalism]

I. PHILOSOPHICAL HERMENEUTICS AND THE NATURE OF REASON

The philosophical meaning of Gadamer's philosophical hermeneutics has not been well understood.[4] Part of the reason is that philosophy is never well understood within academic frameworks, i.e., within frameworks that attempt to institutionalize inquiry. Philosophical hermeneutics has constantly been assaulted with demands that it provide, if not a method, at least some sort of procedure or set of guidelines for the activities of interpretation. In direct proportion to this mistaken demand, Gadamer's assertion of hermeneutic universality has also been abused with misplaced criticism. If philosophical hermeneutics were, contrary to fact, a procedure or even a practice, then the claim that there is a universally hermeneutic mode of inquiry and articulation does indeed appear outrageous against the background of the obtrusive differences between, say, mathematics and historiography, logic and ethics, poetry and philosophy. In these cases, the subject matters are so diverse as to make it seem ridiculous that they should all be dealt with in an identical manner. Yet philosophical hermeneutics is not itself procedural or practical, implications for practice notwithstanding.

In the foreword to the second edition of *Truth and Method,* Gadamer writes: "my real concern was and is philosophic: not what we do or what we ought to do, but what happens to us over and above our wanting and doing" (TM xxviii). Later on, he elaborates: "understanding is not just one of the various possible behaviors of the subject but the mode of being of Dasein itself" (TM xxx). The difference between "behaviors of the subject" and Dasein's "mode of being" marks the crucial difference between ordinary and philosophical hermeneutics, locating the latter squarely within the modern tradition of reason's critique. Philosophical hermeneutics "asks (to put it in Kantian terms): how is understanding possible? This is a question which precedes any action of understanding on the part of subjectivity" (TM xxx). Such precedence is the key to the universality of Gadamer's hermeneutics and the ground for its rightly being called philosophical.

The precedence is parallel to Heidegger's distinction of an ontic from an ontological analysis of beings. What is ontic characterizes already constituted beings, their features, their activities, their relationships in space and time, once they are what they are. In contrast, what is ontological concerns the metaphysical constitution of the beings and situations that are the conditions for ontic activity. In Aristotelian terms, the ontic is categorial, while ontological analysis is a matter of aetiology (or archaeology), the tracing of appearances to their primary and universal grounds. All praxis or doing is ontic, because it requires the particularity of resolve or choice (which may be undertaken with varying degrees of self-consciousness). All virtue or excellence is ontological, because it both requires the constancy of disposition and depends on the universality implied by natural capacity.

Human understanding has both an ontic and an ontological face. As an ontic activity, human understanding takes place in a series of acts specifiable through the contents they make known. By "act" here is meant the actualization of the power *(dunamis)* of intelligent self-consciousness. It means that consciousness comes to focus in a content. The specification of that focus may lie anywhere on a continuum from pure self-determination to complete external domination; to be an act of consciousness in this sense is not yet to be marked as either voluntary or involuntary. Nonetheless, underlying the train of individual acts is the single intelligence that is the proper subject for attributions of conscious identity and all forms of intellectual virtue—the identity that constitutes a knower. Intelligence as a power, focused in its manifold acts, is the complex precondition for attributing reasonableness, perspicacity, sense, good judgment, and so on, to a single mind. The power is neither augmented nor diminished by any one act, while its virtues and vices betray its being ill- or well-conditioned.

Correlative to the distinction just drawn, knowers acquire various ontic skills in the manipulation of the contents they apprehend (even as these activities presuppose a cognitive, interpretative machinery behind the scenes of consciousness's actual focus and discursive activity). This gives rise to the procedural interests that mark all forms of ordinary hermeneutics. Their concern is with the typical ways in which one might go about the activities of inquiry and articulation in various domains. It will include metareflections on how to decide about conflicting interpretations and how best to present the results of discriminating cognition. It aims at specifying what counts as rational—nowadays almost always a methodological term, never a metaphysical one—for a given domain of investigation. On the other hand, accounts of understanding's possibility and constitution address themselves to the cognitive and reflective capacities actually being exercised in the procedures of inquiry. They aim at an assessment of the condition and limits of our cognitive and reflective powers, in their own right. Such is the primary task of philosophical hermeneutics. Ordinary canons of interpretation are concerned with how reason should work once it is under way; philosophical hermeneutics with how reason could ever have begun to get going.

Why does Gadamer's critique of reason take the form of a philosophical hermeneutics?

Understanding comes to a focus in judgment. Yet, as Hegel would say, it is not enough to pay attention to the bare result; the result must be comprehended within a whole development. Though the content of completed judgment presents itself as a pure description, as a mirroring without mechanism, the act of judging presupposes a more complex cognitive interaction. Gadamer (encouraged by Collingwood) opens up this prior interaction for analysis by drawing attention to the way in which even the most clearly formulated and adequately defended judgment is not simply a statement but the answer to a question. In other words all human judgment, whether descriptive or evaluative, occurs within the situation of being challenged by experience, an experience that includes both textual and nontextual realities. Thus arises the hermeneutic *Urphänomen:* "no assertion is possible that cannot be understood as an answer to a question."[5] All judgment, and therefore any truth it might contain, must submit to the logic implied by the questionability that is its matrix.

For the critique of reason, such a logic of question and answer implies that the actual situation of inquiry, which aims at judgment, presupposes an already present framework within which what is questioned appears as able to be questioned. This framework does not have to be thematically appreciated and in fact, usually is not. What may strike the experiencing, as yet unreflective mind as immediately given obtrudes into the foreground only on condition of there being a tacit yet precursorily familiar background. In the act of conscious seeing that is stimulated by inquiry, one always knows roughly how to look, what to be looking for. The situation is justly called hermeneutic because an interpretative move has already been made in advance of what is given in encounter, an interpretative move that sets the stage for the latter's possibility and meaningfulness. Nothing is experienced but that it is experienced *as* something. What is met with in encounter has already been referred to horizons that are not written on its countenance. At stake philosophically is the precise ground and origin of this precur-

Hermeneutics "pre-figuring" of the interpretive situation

sory hermeneutic movement, the precise ground and origin of those horizons within which cognitive experience must occur. Significantly different views of those origins may each remain compatible with the basic hermeneutic structure of finding experience questionable *as.*

Human understanding is thus universally hermeneutic for two reasons. First, it is born in questionability. The always inquisitive origin of human judgment reveals that we never immediately understand, and if we do not immediately understand then we are fated to interpret, for interpretation just means the attempt to make sense of things for ourselves. Second, human experience implies a necessary to and fro between the givens of encounter and horizons that have lent and might lend them meaning or intelligibility. This is a to and fro that generates its own experiential, rather than restrictedly textual, hermeneutic circle. If this moment of hermeneutic universality contrasts with anything, it contrasts with the rationalistic naiveté of supposing that understanding is immediate or intuitive in the sense of needing no discursive supplementation within the instant of insight. According to Hegel, exactly this naiveté marks natural, philosophically undisciplined consciousness. It is the gesture of rational self-certainty that drives the whole train of the *Phenomenology of Spirit,* present in every shape of consciousness the latter describes.

Yet the foregoing does not exhaust the meaning of hermeneutic universality for Gadamer: "we are guided by the hermeneutical phenomenon; and its ground, which determines everything else, is the *finitude of our historical experience*" (TM 457). Gadamer's remark is ontological, not ontic. He means that human existence as such is governed by a principle of finite historicity. The appeal to historicity and finitude is inferential, as Gadamer himself indicates by referring to a ground of the hermeneutic phenomenon. But precisely as ground, finite historicity is not necessitated by the phenomena of questionability and precursory horizon. It counts, rather, as an interpretative specification of those generic structures. In like manner, Socrates's hypothesis of the forms *(eidê)* also counts as such an interpretative specification, for the hypothesis is consistent with those deep features of conscious experience. Were it not, Socratic dialectic would be senseless. Finite historicity, therefore, needs more than the logic of question and answer and the necessity of mediation to recommend it as the best interpretation of hermeneutic universality.

II. Finite Historicity

Historicity is, proximately, a piece of Heideggerian metaphysics (although it has an older pedigree). It enters Gadamer's philosophical hermeneutics in the un-Heideggerian form of *wirkungsgeschichtliches Bewußtsein* ("effective-historical consciousness" or "historically effected consciousness"). Two features of Gadamer's conception may be emphasized here.

First, historicity is total. As an ontological principle, it pervades all aspects of human existence: doing, making, thinking. In its barest form, the claim is not objectionable. Few doubt that history, like freedom, is proper to human being. In its details, however, the doctrine must broach more difficult questions. It must account for the exact manner in which history pervades the totality of human existence, it must account for the actual mechanisms of historicity, for how history might determine thought, or anything else. The question is akin to the question of how time may be said to limit and even destroy the things that are in time. The second important feature of historicity responds to this issue: historical process is somehow constitutive of understanding's operation. Central to Gadamer's philosophical hermeneutics is the meaning of this "somehow."

Historicity as constitutive of understanding rules out the cognitive hope of immediately taking up a disinterested, spectatorial stand in relation to what might be known. The historicity of the knowing subject cannot be overlooked, it is part of the actual achievement of understanding. Understanding is not the free reflection of a roaming transcendental eye, at once present within yet somehow unbound by the conditions at work in experience. Gadamer subverts this image of immediate, transcendentally assured objectivity by speaking of understanding as "event" (*Geschehen:* TM xxiii, 164–65, 290; PH 28). Understanding should be thought of "less as a subjective act than as participating in an event of tradition, a process of transmission in which past and present are constantly mediated" (TM 290). Weaving understanding into a web of historicized relations is a rejoinder to picturing it as the pristine act of a transcendental substance, a reified *ego cogitans.*

More important than the foregoing correction is Gadamer's positive point. On the naive, objectivistic view, the historicity proper to the knowing subject is thought of as something to leave behind, while in the picture of understanding as event it becomes an unavoidable and necessary part of a complex interplay in the moment of assimilation *(Anwendung).* The necessity must be understood. Gadamer's central insight is not the vague and popular notion that the subject's historicity cannot be held off from the event of understanding but that this historicity is exactly the condition that makes understanding possible at all. "The historicity of our existence entails that prejudices in the literal sense of the word, constitute the initial directedness of our whole ability to experience. Prejudices are biases of our openness to the world" (PH 9).

The rehabilitation of prejudice *(Vorurteil)* is a hallmark of Gadamerian hermeneutics. Prejudgments are native to human understanding because they structure the questionability primitive in human experience and, structuring questionability, they condition both inquiry and judgment. Yet the historicity implied by effective-historical consciousness means that prejudices in Gadamer's sense cannot be thought of as noetic tools, conceptual wrenches to be employed *ad libitum.* "The prejudices and the fore-meanings that occupy the interpreter's consciousness are not at his free disposal" (TM 295). Exactly how much constraint is implied by Gadamer's view remains to be seen, but his point against a disconnected, separately constituted transcendental onlooker is clear. Prejudgments are modes of understanding's actual operation. According to this picture, one arrives at the moment of questioning encounter already determined *qua* knower by prejudice. It is not enough to possess intellect in order to be a potential knower. To be able to know, the powers of intelligence must always already be partially formed, informed, in order to proceed along the specific paths inquiry naturally takes. Inquiry is experienced as already constituted within an horizon not of its own self-conscious making.

That inquiry finds itself within a historically given horizon does not mean that it is doomed to an historical fate. Gadamer endorses the possibility of critically reappropriating experience, in particular the experience of encountering conflicting claims to epistemic and evaluative validity. There is a crucial difference between "the productive prejudices that enable understanding" and "the prejudices that hinder or lead to misunderstandings" (TM 295). According to Gadamer, the difference may not be told a priori but, properly done in the course of hermeneutic experience, it issues in the well-known "fusion of horizons" whereby different interpretations may be played off one another towards an interim synthesis. It remains "part of the nature of man to be able to break with tradition, to criticize and dissolve it" (TM xxxvii) because it is essential to consciousness "that it can rise above that of which it is conscious. The structure of reflexivity is given with all consciousness" (TM 341). Prejudices are to be purified rather than abandoned. The sort of overcoming to which Gadamer objects is the assumption that noetic validity can be determined from a private, transcendental sphere, in its own nature above and unconditioned by the course of past experience. One must seek not an escape from the historical but a lucid presence within it. In an historicized atavism of Descartes's *lumen naturale,* Gadamer asserts that one must acquire "as much historical self-transparence as possible" (TM xxiv).

Critical appropriation depends on a moment of transparency; Gadamer allows that much in the direction of traditional philosophy. Yet transparency, he adds, cannot be complete. Historicity in its generic sense determines that the knower arrive at the occasion of encounter already conditioned by particular, historically originating prejudices. Specifically, however, historicity for Gadamer entails finitude. Finitude means that even the most disciplined interplay of prejudices cannot ever entirely overcome the parochiality in which it begins: "the illumination of this situation—reflection on effective history—can never be completely achieved. Yet the fact that it cannot be completed is due not to a deficiency in reflection but to the essence of the historical beings we are" (TM 302).

It is important to appreciate that Gadamer is stipulating the meaning of historical here. As a general category, historicity does not mandate specification in terms of finitude. Not only does Hegel's example make this clear, historicity in its generic sense constitutes the doxa from which Socratic elenchus and dialectic begins. (Faithfulness to such necessary beginnings is part of the reason why Plato wrote in the singular, historical medium of dramatic dialogue rather than the universal medium of the treatise.) The necessary structure of prejudice and the universality of the hermeneutic phenomenon have been further interpreted by Gadamer. He means more than that reflection inevitably begins late in the scene of human experience, by which time forces originating beyond individuals have already had a hand in forming who they are and how they think. He means that one cannot in principle self-consciously and wholly undo those effects: "no freely chosen relation towards can get behind the facticity of this being. Everything that makes possible and limits Dasein's projection ineluctably precedes it" (TM 264). In Heideggerian terms, it is impossible to overtake Dasein's thrown-ness.

Finitude names this impossibility, and thus names a metaphysical necessity undemonstrable by historicist resources alone.[6] It is not a property of prejudices, horizons, histories, and traditions themselves but belongs to the activity of negotiating prejudices and horizons. It emerges as a metaproperty of criticism, setting a boundary to how far one can go in the critical appropriation of what has been and what might be. Only when one responds to one's present and prejudiced being in the light of philosophy's natural demands for primacy, universality, and comprehensiveness does one run up against the apparent limitations of this second-degree, and necessary, parochiality. The hermeneutic activity of fusing horizons by itself is not logically committed either way on the questions either of what path the ongoing history of interpretation will take or of where that path will end, if at all. Endless meandering, cyclic repetition, asymptotic progression, arrival at the absolute, are all consistent with the interim achievements of enriched interpretative practice. Therefore, Gadamer's phenomenology of hermeneutic experience cannot have fully described the ground of the finitude he everywhere asserts: "historically effected consciousness is so radically finite that our whole being . . . inevitably transcends its knowledge of itself" (TM xxxiv); "reason exists for us only in concrete, historical terms—i.e., it is not its own master" (TM 276).

The now familiar paraphernalia of prejudices, fore-meanings, traditions, temporal distance, fusion of horizons, and the rest, do not explain why perfect self-transparence is impossible; they set the stage for the task of achieving transparence, determining only that the stage, and not some other transcendental or heavenly locale, is where wisdom may be realized. There is no escape from the historical, to be sure. Reason begins and ends in place—an insight that saves philosophy from absurdity (atopia). Yet the inescapability of our originally historical condition is not immediately equivalent to the impossibility of fully penetrating its apparent darkness with understanding. There always was a fire in the Cave, even as the prisoners mistook what it made visible. They gave even less thought to its light.

III. Temptations toward Finitude

The principle of finitude supervenes on Gadamer's sensitive analysis of the hermeneutic situation, it does not derive from it. This is to say not that the two are incompatible but simply that they do not necessarily go together—as is currently so often assumed. Let me restate the fundamental lacuna: historicity as an essential structure of human reality has not been shown to entail either that understanding is necessarily limited by parochial, contingent horizons or that historical process itself is thoroughly and necessarily contingent, forever lacking an absolute moment. In order to establish such ontological claims one requires a worked-out metaphysics of historicity. To be fair, unlike many contemporary historicists Gadamer is well aware of the need for metaphysically buttressing his phenomenology of hermeneutic experience. For this he points to Heidegger's ontology of Dasein, having rejected Hegel's metaphysics of spirit *(Geist)*. In my view, Heidegger's *Daseinsanalytik* does not furnish the required support, but to establish such an objection is beyond my present brief.[7] Here I confine myself to discussing the manner in which some of Gadamer's own characteristic concerns further encourage the finitistic interpretation of human historicity.[8]

Language looms large on Gadamer's hermeneutic horizon. Sensitized by Heidegger's investigations of truth as unconcealment, as a process of manifestation drawing both thinker and thing into a proximity of illumination, Gadamer seizes on language as the surest sign of the nature of this "between" *(zwischen)*. Principally, closer attention to the phenomenon of language serves to upset the transcendental, reflective image of reason as an isolated, spectating *res cogitans.* Language is native to yet no mere instrument of our subjectivity, it transcends individual consciousness yet remains the enabling medium of all thought. Properly understood, therefore, language does not permit the collapse of self into narcissistic subjectivity while at the same time it furnishes a clue to the necessary mediateness of understanding. There is much of importance in Gadamer's treatment, focused in his insightful dictum—reminiscent of Parmenides—that "being that can be understood is language" (TM 474). Yet while this formula heralds an holistic view of the interrelation between language and being, in Gadamer's case it also serves notice of the hope that language will furnish an independent discipline for reason's universalizing pretensions.

Although he does not neglect the issue of metaphysically accounting for the nature of language, Gadamer's main stated reason for supposing its finitude is the latter's historicity. Within language "the structure of being is not simply reflected; rather, in language the order and structure of our experience itself is originally formed and constantly changed. Language is the record of finitude . . . because every language is constantly being formed and developed the more it expresses its experience of the world" (TM 457). This reproduces the lacuna already noted, without providing an independent principle. Language is no more self-evidently finite (in the required limitative manner) than history. Hence, either we are returned to the unresolved puzzle of proving that nothing absolute could possibly be afoot in history, which has as its linguistic correlate the puzzle of proving the impossibility of ever asserting anything of abiding significance, or we must find nonhistorical reasons for supposing that language really is as finite as Gadamer claims.

That languages are local and have their particular histories might be thought evidence for a strong sense of linguistic determination, but this parochiality would be a sign of reason's necessary finitude only if different ways of speaking forever prevented us from saying the same thing. Indeed it could be argued that the originative function of anything recognizable as full-fledged human language is defined by its being a singular, historical articulation of things common and universal. In other words, that language lives in the between of universal and particular. Moreover, the evolution and alteration of particular linguistic structures itself depends on an horizon not evidently particular in the same way, for the activity of language use is a constant and the conditions for our having been language users has not altered over cultural, historical time. Finally, what sort of a limitation can linguistic practices be supposed to exercise when they alter precisely in virtue of human response to the complex of circumstance? No particular linguistic structure can possibly exhaust the power of human ingenuity on which they all must rest, setting the boundary for all historical manners of speech. Individuals can of course be dominated by the historical accumulation of linguistic innovations but this does not mean that they are in essence overruled by that sediment as if by a foreign, daemonic power; they have in effect been overruled by the memorialized genius of other individuals. It needs to be added that ingenuity as I mean it here does not have to be self-conscious and purposeful in order to be responsible and sovereign; our responses, lucid or not, are always ours and by and large well-founded. The latter point has often been exploited by strongly pragmatic versions of philosophical historicism.

Gadamer's overall treatment comes to emphasize dialogue as a paradigm of linguistic activity. From one point of view this makes very good sense. What better example of how subtle understanding must become and of how little technique avails than the finesse that is needed for truly appreciating the desires, ambitions, and characters of others? But this is not the only lesson Gadamer and other historicists draw from the experience of dialogue. Having ruled out the possibility of ever getting to the bottom of anything, they must replace insight with inquiry as the highest function of the mind. This generates the task of specifying a corresponding set of intellectual virtues (or, in another idiom, canons of justification). Once in this frame of mind, conversational tact commends itself as a paradigm, since the playful, sympathetic to and fro that marks dialogical discussion seems to be both sufficiently serious and satisfying while at the same time apparently unobliged to get anywhere. The conversation continues, upheld by a sense of give and take, of responsibility, of open-mindedness, and by an avoidance of domination, exploitation, closure.

Yet has the phenomenology of conversation been adequately drawn here? In particular, what about those moments of silence between friends who have suddenly, together, come to see what it was they were trying to say? Conversation without such silences is just chatter, the debasement of dialogue. Thus, dialogical skill itself can never be an adequate paradigm for understanding's virtues. All of our serious talk together seeks the closure of judgment, even as we must acknowledge the very real dangers of leaping to conclusions.

Dialogue in philosophy seems to be a manifestation of finitude partly because its judgments are so infrequently come by and partly because there is, as Gadamer maintains, a necessarily dialectical component to reflection and understanding. The problem, however, is that while this dialectical component—equivalent to the mediate articulation of philosophical judgment—is in human context by and large well served by dialogical exchange, actual dialogue is not the mediation itself but its occasion and instrument. Dialogue is a fruitful supplement to the general weakness of philosophical imagination, enabling us to see possibilities hitherto unsuspected. In a sense this is an accidental connection. One of Gadamer's main points, on the other hand, is that only through actual dialogue, either with others or with the manifold bearers of a tradition already on its historical way, can the process of mediation begin; dialogue is not only useful but the necessary origin. Yet neither of these points of departure in themselves specifies how such beginnings must eventually be assimilated. It is clear, neither that the content of history or of conversation contains nothing absolute, regardless of the parochiality of its perhaps necessary occasion, nor that nothing absolute may be done with it.

A rejection of ahistorical rationalism—the assumption that human reason is by nature and immediately adequate to the primary principles of things—is common to all contemporary historicists. Whether the enemy be a priori transcendental subjectivity, Cartesian mathematicism, or naive Platonistic idealism, historicism gains confidence in direct proportion to the excess of claims made on behalf of the self-evident, the eidetically visible, the rationally demonstrable, the timeless, the primary, the universal, the infallible, the absolute.

There is no denying that some of pure reason's champions have been laughable in their extravagance. Moreover, historicists are correct to point out that many of these excesses may be attributed to overlooking what Gadamer has called the historicity of the knowing subject. Thus, the frequent criticism of various rationalistic positions is that they have failed to see the particular historical determinants of their own most cherished, universal principles. The style of such criticisms, however, implies that they can only be entered on a case-by-case basis. It is one thing to maintain that Descartes did not appreciate the contingencies at work in his very articulation of the *cogito,* or that Kant mistakenly assumed the absolute validity of Newtonian mechanics (I endorse neither of these criticisms) but quite another to assert that all thinkers at all times must always remain within limits created by the contingencies of historical circumstances. In order to establish the latter, universal claim, it must be shown first that history itself is wholly contingent, that historical horizons really are parochial and nothing else, and second that reason cannot achieve perfect adequacy to its objects within the horizons of history, whatever they should turn out to be. There is no valid Baconian induction from the errors of individual thinkers to the necessary parochiality of reason, while if we are to make a legitimate interpretative leap from ontic surfaces to ontological depths, more assurance than an observation of what happens for the most part is required. A single example of insight, a single *unzeitgemässige Betrachtung,* ruins philosophical historicism's deflationary program.

What really inspires the historicist leap to a universalized rejection of rationalistic philosophies is, I think, the reasonable conviction that human understanding is never immediate. Being universal in scope, this principle provides a basis for taking on an entire family of philosophical doctrines. It does not, however, provide ammunition against all rationalistic viewpoints. It refutes only those that maintain immediacy, a searchlight view of the intellect, whereby reason has only to fall upon its objects with sufficient concentration for them to reveal their entire logical structure to the inquisitive mind. None of Plato, Aristotle, Descartes, Kant, or Hegel, espoused such a view or were seduced by its imagery. They all suppose a moment of absolute lucidity, which may sound mysterious to some, but in each case the moment of lucidity lies necessarily within a more complex and time-consuming whole from which it cannot be abstracted without violence. Discursivity goes hand in hand with intuition. Furthermore, even if one disagrees with my assessments of the figures mentioned, historicism is still obliged conceptually to show how a lack of immediacy implies inevitable parochiality. The phenomenon of mathematical knowledge—mediate, universal, and intuitive at once—always has been and remains instructive for all attempts to reduce the activity of understanding to its contingent circumstances.

At least two other qualms are often at work in the historicist rejection of ahistorical rationalism. The first is a romantic fear of being philosophically irresponsible toward the contingent and particular. The received theoretical emblem of such fear is Kierkegaard's attack on Hegel, the Terror its practical one. That we should save the contingent by rejecting the absolute is too extreme, a dialectical inversion that has yet to learn of an appropriate synthesis. Yet, quite apart from whether Hegel really did do injustice to the contingent or whether there is not a timeless, rational *politikê technê,* there is no good reason to suppose that appreciation of what is universal and absolute necessarily perverts responsibility in the present. And only if the perversion were necessary, would it make sense to abandon philosophy's natural urge toward understanding things in a cosmic, eternal light. Let it be allowed that there is a danger—attribute it to the austerity of philosophical eros, hankering after the first principles of things—but the possibility of mistaking that austerity is not the same as having to.

The second, obscurer scruple amounts to a failure of philosophic nerve. Specifically, many find so intolerable the conditional inference that if human reason is adequate to what is ultimately real then it must needs be encyclopaedic, that they become prepared to deny the antecedent in order to avoid the consequent. Nonhistoricist philosophies are often abused for the apparent absurdity of supposing that human reason is omnicompetent and comprehensive. That is, if a philosophy claims to know all there is to know or at least to be in a position to know all there is to know, then its underlying conception of reason must be incorrect.

It is difficult to say what grounds the inference, but the following seem to be relevant factors. First, it is simply silly to expect that human beings could ever actually know all there is to know, since there are infinities of knowable facts. Philosophy, however, has never made quite this claim to know all there is to know. Encyclopaedic knowledge is not equivalent to all possible knowledge, it is knowledge of everything worth knowing, everything essential. Everything worth knowing in this sense is the set of primary principles of all that is. It would be a complex debate to establish that such a set is itself within the grasp of human intellect, but a far from silly one. Second, experience clearly reveals the fallibility of all human judgment regarding first principles. Apart from its self-referential instability, this claim is a controversial assessment of at least the history of philosophy and perhaps of other parts of theoretical culture as well; it depends on whose experience one consults. If it were entirely clear that past philosophical judgment were fallible in the way supposed, the history of philosophy could inspire no theoretical desire in the present. The fact that it does not inspire the theoretical desire of all is only to say that philosophy is rare, while the fact that those not suited to it tend to make egregious errors argues only for its difficulty. Third, even if not in principle fallible, all human judgment of first principles should be regarded as fallible. This is a useful heuristic for philosophical inquiry; it is not therefore a standard for philosophical knowing. Finally, philosophy's claim to know is hubristic and inevitably breeds intolerance; the philosopher cuts a despicable figure in placing himself above his fellow citizens. Whether or not the knower of first principles really does aspire to such political superiority, this objection broaches the deep question of philosophy's responsibility to the city. Here, though, it is sufficient to note that the weightiness of this practical issue is no evidence against philosophy's claim to theoretical primacy. In fact, it is precisely the plausibility of such primacy that generates the political problem. If philosophy had no such competence, there would be nothing to fear from its empty arrogance.

In general, the image of philosophy's elitist expertise threatens to obscure an important distinction concerning reason's adequacy to first principles. What I have been calling rationalistic philosophy does not have to maintain *extensive* adequacy; it stands or falls on the axiom of *intensive* adequacy, which may or may not have repercussions for the issue of encyclopaedic knowledge.[10] What Hegel calls the moment of *absolutes Wissen* in the *Phenomenology of Spirit* is not identical with the system of philosophical *Wissenschaft*. One does not need to have a system actually in hand in order to reject philosophical historicism, and one might even have grounds for asserting reason's intensive adequacy while denying that philosophy appropriately realizes that adequacy in a systematic or encyclopaedic way (Plato, for example, seems to have thought this).

The progress of natural science, with its constant revisions, has complicated the question of reason's adequacy. It has led some to suppose that reason, assumed to be paradigmatically at work in that apodictic domain, can never be intensively adequate to a single truth, let alone to all of them. Despite its depressing message, the philosophic inference has not cooled scientific ardor, which suggests that rational curiosity is still being satisfied there and hence that philosophy's skepticism is hasty. Indeed, it is not surprising that natural science should be in essence revisable for it is not itself first philosophy or metaphysics. Only once the hypothetical character of positive science's first principles is discharged within the primacy of a doctrine of being can they achieve stability. Moreover, positive knowledge of the natural domain, or even of the cultural domain, is not the only use of reason relevant to the issue of its adequacy. One still need go no further than the *cogito* to realize that intensive adequacy cannot intelligibly be denied wholesale, regardless of the epistemological naiveté with which the practising scientist rightly presumes its possibility. Thus we are left the task of squaring what makes us adequate for critique with our alleged inadequacy for perfect self-transparence. Even so, this much is evident: the meaningfulness of critique is inconsistent with radical finitude. Consciousness itself "is something that goes beyond limits, and since these limits are its own, it is something that goes beyond itself . . . consciousness suffers this violence at its own hands: it spoils its own limited satisfaction" (introduction to *Phenomenology of Spirit*, sec. 80).

CARL PAGE

DEPARTMENT OF PHILOSOPHY
EMORY UNIVERSITY
JULY 1992

NOTES

1. Hans-Georg Gadamer, *Truth and Method,* second revised edition, translation revised by Joel Weinsheimer and Donald G. Marshall (New York: Crossroad, 1989), pp. 505–41. All references are to this edition, henceforth TM.

2. Cf. Herbert Schnädelbach, *Philosophy in Germany: 1831–1933* (Cambridge: Cambridge University Press, 1984); Gunther Scholz, "Historismus, Historizismus," in the *Historisches Wörterbuch der Philosophie,* ed. J. Ritter (Stuttgart: Schwabe and Co., 1971–84); Rolf Gruner, "Historism: Its Rise and Decline," *Clio* 8 (1978): 25–39; George C. Iggers, "Historicism," in the *Dictionary of the History of Ideas* (New York: Charles Scribner's Sons, 1973); Maurice Mandelbaum, "Historicism," in *The Encyclopedia of Philosophy,* ed. Paul Edwards (New York: Macmillan, 1967); Calvin G. Rand, "Two Meanings of Historicism in the Writings of Dilthey, Troeltsch, and Meinecke," *Journal of the History of Ideas* 25 (1964): 503–18; Carlo Antoni, *L'Historisme,* trans. Alain Dufour (Génève: Librairie Droz, 1963 [1956]); Dwight E. Lee and Robert N. Beck, "The Meaning of 'Historicism'," *American Historical Review* 59 (1953–54): 568–77; Karl Heussi, *Die Krisis des Historismus* (Tübingen: Mohr, 1932).

3. Richard Rorty, *Philosophy and the Mirror of Nature* (Princeton: Princeton University Press, 1979); *Consequences of Pragmatism: Essays 1972–1980* (Minneapolis: University of Minnesota Press, 1982); *Contingency, Irony, and Solidarity* (Cambridge: Cambridge University Press, 1989); *Objectivism, Relativism, and Truth: Philosophical Papers,* vol. 1 (Cambridge: Cambridge University Press, 1991); Alasdair MacIntyre, *After Virtue,* second edition (Notre Dame: University of Notre Dame Press, 1984); *Whose Justice, Which Rationality?* (Notre Dame: University of Notre Dame Press, 1988); Richard Bernstein, *Beyond Objectivism and Relativism* (Philadelphia: University of Pennsylvania Press, 1983); Joseph Margolis, *Pragmatism without Foundations* (New York: Basil Blackwell, 1986); *Texts without Referents* (New York: Basil Blackwell, 1989).

4. For further background see my "Philosophical Hermeneutics and its Meaning for Philosophy," *Philosophy Today* 35 (1991): 127–36.

5. Hans-Georg Gadamer, *Philosophical Hermeneutics,* trans. David E. Linge (Berkeley: University of California Press, 1976), p. 11, henceforth PH. Cf. TM 362 ff.

6. I allude here to the notorious problem of self-refutation. Gadamer is well aware of the issue and has taken it up in dialogue with Leo Strauss whose *Natural Right and History* (Chicago: University of Chicago Press, 1953) elaborates the Platonic objection (cf. TM 532–41). See also, "Correspondence concerning *Wahrheit und Methode:* Leo Strauss and Hans-Georg Gadamer," *Independent Journal of Philosophy* 2 (1978): 5–12; Emil Fackenheim, *Metaphysics and Historicity* (Milwaukee: Marquette University Press, 1961); and "The Historicity and Transcendence of Philosophic Truth," *Proceedings of the Seventh Inter-American Congress of Philosophy* (Quebec: Laval, 1967), pp. 77–92. The force of the self-refutation argument is controversial. I examine it in detail in the third chapter of my *Philosophical Historicism and the Betrayal of First Philosophy.* (University Park; Penn.: Penn State Press, 1995). See also my "On Being False by Self-Refutation," *Metaphilosophy* 23 (1992): 431–34.

7. See chapters 4 and 5 of *Philosophical Historicism and the Betrayal of First Philosophy.*

8. What follows is not intended to be exhaustive. In particular, I have deliberately set aside all treatment of Gadamer's honorable attempt to revive the long tradition of practical philosophy through philosophical hermeneutics (see especially his essays "What is Practice? The Conditions of Social Reason," "Hermeneutics as Practical Philosophy," and "Hermeneutics as Theoretical and Practical Task," in his *Reason in the Age of Science,* trans. Frederick G. Lawrence [Cambridge: MIT Press, 1981]). While I thoroughly endorse the spirit of Gadamer's defending the virtues of *phronēsis* against the incursions of method and technique, I have elsewhere criticized the manner in which both Gadamer and other contemporary pragmatists have pursued this end. See my "Axiomatics,

Hermeneutics, and Practical Rationality," *International Philosophical Quarterly* 57 (1987): 81–100.

9. For Hegel on contingency see Dieter Henrich, "Hegels Theorie über den Zufall," *Kant-Studien* 50 (1958–59): 131–48.

10. For the distinction between intensive and extensive adequacy see Edward Craig, *The Mind of God and the Works of Man* (Oxford: Clarendon Press, 1987).

REPLY TO CARL PAGE

The title of the contribution hits the core of the essential problem in the face of which philosophy became hermeneutics. The essay is quite solid and very interesting. It connects with the old discussions about the problem of historical relativism which come to a head in nineteenth-century German philosophy. In the eyes of the author, the hermeneutics which I developed as well as the works of many other contemporaries necessarily has to result in historical relativism. To me this seems to involve a huge philosophical task that would require going back even beyond Kant's *Critique of Pure Reason*. The language barrier and what is expressed in it is certainly a difficult obstacle, as will be evident in a moment. Therefore I regret that as of yet we cannot get advice from the new publications the author announces. I thus cannot do anything but describe my own obstacles to understanding what is said here.

Among these obstacles is the distinction made early on between a historicism of the first and second degree. The latter is said to be Heidegger's and mine, but also the one advocated by Rorty, McIntyre, Bernstein, and others. The author sees this as a kind of historical epidemic, a historicism of reason itself, so to speak. It is primarily Heidegger, I suppose, whom he has in mind here and he cannot see in the work of the author of *Being and Time* the successful solution to the crises of the century of historical relativism. On the contrary, he sees this as a radical sharpening of radical finitude. This is baffling and cannot be mitigated by placing Heidegger in Kierkegaard's good company. Radical finitude can in truth only mean the limitedness of human beings precisely because we are not just beings of reason. One cannot doubt the emphatic anticipation of death *(Vorlaufen zum Tode)*. The Delphic wisdom "Know Thyself" reminds us that we are not a god but a human being. Should we charge the consequence of historical relativism with this?

For the author, Heidegger's basic thesis and his enterprise of viewing being in the horizon of time via a critique of the Greeks is apparently not worthy of discussion. What then about Kant? Since Kant's *Critique of Pure Reason,* metaphysics can no longer be grounded on science. It has a foundation only in the moral concept of freedom. Hegel's further development of this metaphysics to the concept of the Absolute eventually led to the plays of reflection in historical relativism, up to the point that the radical questioning of *Being and Time* shattered the concept of the Absolute. What then is relativism supposed to mean? In the English text, through the words 'historicist' and 'historicity', one is compelled to think of knowledge and science, and not of the happening of history itself which presents a relativity and diversity of perspectives and views offered by the things.

It is unmistakable that the concept of science which has been dominant since Galileo made possible a certain domination of the powers of nature and with that our entire civilization. Yet one cannot deny that the conduct of life of humans and their organization in family, society, people, and state do not depend upon the mere application of science. Human beings have to live their lives by themselves. Natural instincts do not simply guide us in this. Yet, it is precisely this that lends its science significance. But whether we live our lives one way or the other does not depend upon a science that tells us so. This requires practical reason. In the face of the narrow limitation restricting science through methodical objectification, it really seems better to me to rely upon the true universe of linguistic world orientation, upon "linguisticality." Linguisticality comprises the use and application of science, too, which is the whole of our world orientation; it is on this that the claim to universality in hermeneutics is based. Language, according to its mode of performance, is always conversation with the other. From this structure of conversation all other modifications, speech, text, and every reading, can be derived. But not only dealing with linguistic words is meant. The exchange between human beings consists of silent language, gestures and gesticulation, inflections of the voice, too, and also of eloquent silence. That it creates true comments in the first place holds especially for laughing with one another.

In the end, all of this can find its linguistic expression in the exchange of words although it will always be limited and imperfect. But the attempt to communicate with words is like a step into another world. It is a genuine opening for the other and the entrance into a common world. When I came upon the logic of question and answer in Collingwood's autobiography it became clear to me that in that logic, hermeneutic experience can view itself liberated from the theoretical narrowings found in the scientific orientation to texts. The linguisticality of language frees itself from the restraints of merely following rules in the free search for the right word. That constitutes the real question of hermeneutic experience: that the words we seek and find, be it in our daily dealings, be it in a thoughtful conversation, are never able to convey exactly what we wanted to say. The use of language and the historical origin of the word 'hermeneutic' point toward the truth here even if they do so in measureless exaggeration: words are like oracles. Nonetheless one went to Delphi to ask the oracle. The sounds, uttered by the priestess of Delphi as if in a rapture, required interpretation, and this is the art that we called hermeneutics.

This extreme of nonunderstandability allows the essence of all hermeneutic experience to stand out. Everything happens in the reciprocal interplay of seeking and finding the right words. They are supposed to make the other one think, and his answer is supposed to make us think. This does not imply the claim that reason as such is limited, on the contrary. The discursivity of thinking and the ideal infinity of every conversation means that thinking is without limit. For this reason, I find the recourse to the quote from Hegel at the end of Page's contribution quite surprising. Hegel at least did not want to go back to precritical metaphysics. Already Aristotle demonstrated that *theoria* is the highest praxis, a keeping-to-oneself *(Ansichhalten)* which will thus always remain within the limits of "becoming-immortal." Socrates did not misunderstand the transparency of self-consciousness. Reason, which is supposed to find its purest embodiment in the Aristotelian concept of god, confirms the inseparability of *ēthos* and *logos* for being-human, and this means also that theoretical reason and its exercise presuppose practical reason.

H.-G.G.

Philosophy of HG Gadamer

Ed: Hahn

19

James Risser

THE VOICE OF THE OTHER IN GADAMER'S HERMENEUTICS

The distinguishing feature of Gadamer's hermeneutics in contrast to, let us say, the hermeneutics of Paul Ricoeur, is that it is a hermeneutics of the voice.[1] At one place Gadamer tells us that hermeneutics is precisely letting that which is far and alienated speak again "not only in a new voice but in a clearer voice."[2] Accordingly, it is not enough to say that for philosophical hermeneutics the experience of meaning is linguistic; one must immediately add to this the more specific claim that this experience of meaning takes shape in the language of *speech,* in *living* language, and as such hermeneutics is of the voice. In setting philosophical hermeneutics off in this way one can see, at the same time, how Gadamer separates himself from those thinkers closest to him who come to bear on the project of philosophical hermeneutics. Hegel's dialectic is now reoriented toward the art of living dialogue and Heidegger's project of overcoming metaphysics is continued in the dynamics of a language, not of metaphysics, but "which we speak with others and to others."[3]

If one were to ask for a justification for locating the experience of meaning in the voice one could only assume that it follows from the context of that Socratic-Platonic mode of thinking that comes to bear on the project of philosophical hermeneutics precisely as that corrective to the formalism of Hegelian dialectic and to the Heideggerian preoccupation with the overcoming of metaphysics.[4] This context, which takes human finitude so seriously, insists that one proceeds toward understanding only through dialogical inquiry where one encounters the living word that is of memory *(Mnemosyne).*[5] Here in this space, not just of the voice, but of the voice of an other, logical demonstration yields to the power of communication in language where one must find the right words to convince the other. Here in this space of the voice understanding occurs as a communicative event *(Verständigungsgeschehen).*

Let us consider, then, what is "of the voice," and, more problematical, what is at stake in deferring to the voice. Under this latter consideration the question that arises, already in the Socratic gesture of the turn to the living word, is one of the status of writing. For Gadamer, writing *(Schriftlichkeit)* changes nothing; the text too stands under the voice. The question about the voice thus cannot avoid the question of privileging and of opposition, of the relation between speaking and writing.[6] It would appear, though, that in deferring to the voice the question of the relation between speaking and writing has already been decided in that hermeneutics is committed to a phonocentrism as the condition for the possibility of commensurate understanding. This immediate response to the question is, of course, framed by the project of deconstruction, and to some extent the question has been taken up by Gadamer in his essays that have followed the publication of *Truth and Method*. Here I do not wish to repeat what has already been said there, but rather to take up the question of speaking and writing as it pertains to what is "of the voice." In this regard, I want to explore the question of the voice not just in terms of the Derridian critique of phonocentrism, but also within the project of philosophical hermeneutics itself where a consideration must be given to the element of desire in dialogical inquiry that is rendered by the voice.

Most provisionally, we find both dimensions of the question of the voice taken up by Socrates in the *Phaedrus* where he marks out the difference between writing and speaking in a discussion about the nature of a good *(kalon)* speech— a speech that would not only be in accord with things spoken of, but also written in the soul of the one who hears:

> Soc: It is the same thing with written words; they seem to talk to you as though they were intelligent, but if you ask them anything about what they say, from a desire *(boulomenos)* to be instructed, they go on telling you just the same thing forever. And once a thing is put in writing, the composition, whatever it may be, drifts *(kulindeitai)* all over the place, getting into the hands not only of those who understand it, but equally of those who have no business with it. . . . But now tell me, is there another sort of discourse that is the brother to written speech, but of unquestioned legitimacy? Can we see how it originates, and how much better and more effective it is than the other?

> Phaed: What sort of discourse have you in mind, and what is its origin?

> Soc: The sort that goes together with knowledge, and is written in the soul of the learner, that can defend itself, and knows to whom it should speak and to whom it should say nothing.

> Phaed: You mean no dead discourse, but the living and breathing word *(ton logon zonta kai empsychon)*, the original of which the written discourse may fairly be called a kind of image *(eidolon)*.[7]

Let us consider for a moment what is most decisive in this *locus classicus* for the distinction between speaking and writing. Plato tells us, first of all, that one asks of words what they say from a wish or desire *(boulomenos)* to be instructed. Secondly, he tells us that when these words are written they tend to drift *(kulindeitai)* all over the place. And thirdly, he tells us that the discourse that is the "brother" of written discourse, which appears to be the more proper, is of the living and breathing word *(ton logon zonta kai empsychon)*. Highlighting the text in this way is no guarantee that we have read it properly, for we know that this text has already been subject to radically opposing interpretations. On the one hand, it has been read to say that, despite the seemingly clear indication that spoken discourse has an unquestioned legitimacy, Plato ultimately wants to champion *epistēmē* over *doxa,* which can only come about by the emerging literate revolution.[8] On the other hand, there is a more trenchant reading of it by Derrida who sees Plato promoting the supremacy of spoken discourse over all written discourse insofar as he makes claims for the first order of spoken discourse. Without attending to any one interpretation at the moment, let me reassemble the three highlighted features of the passage into three theses, in no corresponding order, that will enable us to attend to this question of the voice: 1) speaking, which is of the voice, is of the breath; 2) the voice, being of the breath, is situated in the space of desire; 3) communication, occurring through the voice, drifts in the voice.

The Voice Is of the Breath

The living word, according to Plato, is *empsychon,* literally "ensouled," or "of spirit." *Psychē,* following its use in Homer where the word is not yet directly related to the more exclusive "mind" or "intelligence," means primarily the principle that makes one to be alive. But what is of life is of the breath: *Psychē* is related to *psychein,* to breathe, and accordingly could be translated as "breath-soul." According to Snell, Homer does not tell us what he considers to be the function of the *psychē* during life. In dying, though, it is clear that the *psychē,* as the breath of life, is breathed forth, leaving through the mouth or even through a wound.[9] And, what is of breath is capable of flight: in every attempt of Odysseus to grasp the *psychē* of his mother in Hades, the *psychē* flew out of his hands "like a dream." With death, she tells her son, the mighty energy of burning fire overcomes the flesh and bones "and the *psychē* like a dream flies away and flutters."[10]

This etymological determination of *psychē* as breath-soul enables us to grasp the character of the living word as it occurs in the Greek oral tradition. According to Onians, "it was quite natural to say that the speeches of a man who *pepnutai* [has breath] are themselves *pepnumena*. They come forth with the breath that is intelligence in them."[11] The living word is of spirit, and spirit is in flight. A spoken word is said by Homer to be "winged," and an unspoken word "without wings."[12] To speak the word is to breathe it, sending it forth to be heard when the one with ears breathes in.[13] But the word is itself breath, that is to say, being of life, it is of spirit, mind, intelligence.

What then does it mean to say that the voice is of the breath? And how are we to situate philosophical hermeneutics, in particular, in this context? First of all, the voice of which we speak is not identical with *phōnē,* mere sound, for it is possible, following the language of Augustine, for the sound of a word to be an empty voice *(inanem vocem).* The voice that is mere sound must be withdrawn before the voice in which something is given to be understood. A poem is not heard when the mere sound of the words are received by the ear, just as a text is not read when our eyes read the letters that make up the words. What is at stake in the voice, in other words, is the taking place of language as such. The *flatus vocis,* literally, the breathing voice, occurs in the eleventh century as a term for the voice as an intention to signify and as a pure indication that language is taking place.[14] And in language is the most universal field of meaning, namely being. In this context one could perhaps say that the meaning of being is to be found in the experience of the voice.

What is of the voice, then, to use Gadamer's own language, is the inner word *(verbum interius).* In its classical formulation in Aquinas, the inner word is distinguished from the outer word, which is a sound produced by the respiratory tract that has meaning. That the spoken word has meaning allows the word to be distinguished from other sounds produced by the respiratory tract, like coughing. Only the inner word, which is related to the outer word as its efficient cause, is related to understanding; until the inner word emerges we do not understand. What appeals to Gadamer in this notion of the inner word is that this word, which is not expressing the mind but the thing intended, "still has the character of an event," and "remains related to its possible utterance *[Äußerung].*"[15] This is the word that says something beyond its grammatical parts. This is the word *of spirit* that occurs in writing when the word is read. This is the word of breath that is heard by the inner ear.

Now, what appears to be peculiar to the voice of the inner word in dialogical inquiry is that it is always between sound and meaning: in responding to Derrida's charge of logocentrism, Gadamer writes that "conversation defines itself precisely by the fact that the essence of understanding and agreement are not found in the 'vouloir-dire' or intended meaning, through which the word supposedly finds its being, but rather in what aims at being said beyond all words sought after or found."[16] What is of the voice then for Gadamer pertains to the word finding its place. In the rhetorical tradition the distinction is made between *ratio iudicandi* and *ratio inveniendi,* between the art of assuring the truth of a proposition and the more originary art of setting off the very advent of discourse in order for language to reach its place. The place for language was in fact the argument as the illuminating event of language. In the face of such a difficult task though, the ancient topics declined into a technique of "memory places," in which language was conceived as something that has always already taken place and the *ratio iudicandi* was now conceived as making available this already given.[17] But what happens if the word is not already given, as is the case for

Against Logocentrism

philosophical hermeneutics, where the word is enacted in dialogical inquiry? It would appear that in dialogical inquiry, in the "handing over of one's own thinking to another," the voice displaces itself in the intention to signify. This negative dimension of the voice, which is not to be confused with dialectical negation, means precisely that there is no self-identity in the voice, as if the meanings of words possessed a "firmness that could be grasped." But if there is no self-identity in the breath of the voice there is still being, still the meaning of being.

Secondly, that the voice is of breath means precisely that the element of continuity is inescapable in all our speaking. The word that lives and breathes requires a space of continuity. In the oral tradition, this space is the *agora,* the place of assembly for debates and business, but also the place of the gift of speaking. In this space of intimacy and familiarity speaking is granted. And in the granting, by virtue of the continuity, words have no edges; or to propose the lesser claim: the word spoken and heard has only varying edges. For Homer, word *(epos)* means not just a word, that which could possibly have an edge, but includes the meanings "speech," "tale," "song," or "epic poetry as a whole."[18] This means, of course, that in the voice one never finds simply one word. In the *agora* the edge of a word fades into its renewal in another word. When Gadamer says that the word "always already refers to a greater and more multiple unity," a notion one finds in the concept of *verbum interius,* one can readily relate this to the Greek *epos.*[19] For philosophical hermeneutics, there is, by virtue of the voice, never one word. A breathless written word, on the other hand, is encountered as ruptured discourse and accordingly exists in a space of separation. The written word not only separates words from one another, but separates words from reader. Without the reader words do indeed have edges.

But the issue here, especially as it is understood by Gadamer, is not that of a simple opposition between oral and written discourse. Gadamer insists that the same fundamental conditions that hold for oral exchange holds for written conversation. In both writing *and* speaking we are faced with the same problem of understanding what is said. What is at issue in both the printed text and in the repetition of what is expressed in conversation is the return to what was originally announced *(Urkunde).* For written texts this presents the real hermeneutic task, for the original announcement stands under the ideality of the word. The hermeneutic task is accordingly transforming the ideality of the word back into language as speaking—i.e., into the communicative event that is not the "repetition of something past, but the sharing of a present meaning." For writing, the communicative event is accomplished by the reader in reaching beyond the literal inscription of the word in the continuity of words arising in dialogue. This assumes, of course, that reading is in fact analogous to dialogue, that the text stands as an address to an other who fills out and concretizes what is said.

Within the dialogical inquiry, then, the problem is not how to understand writing on the basis of speaking, but, beyond the ideality of the word, of attending to the seduction in the voice that persists in both writing and speaking. In

Truth and Method Gadamer reminds us that "Just as in speech there is an art of appearances and a corresponding art of true thought—sophistic and dialectic—so in writing there are two arts, one serving sophistic, the other dialectic."[20] The voice is continually threatened by what adheres to the voice, namely, a corruption by which it falls away from what is spoken about in the voice. The "binding element" in conversation is, by its very nature, surrounded by idle talk *(Gerede)*, and thus by the mere appearance of speaking. In the art of writing, in particular, then, the writer has an obligation of establishing, in the sense of mooring from the drift, the original announcement such that its sense is understandable.

But to say that the printed text is to be read in terms of what was originally announced implies that the text already stands under the voice. If for Gadamer there is not a simple opposition between writing and speaking, is it because Gadamer wants to understand writing on the basis of speech, because he has privileged the voice? In this context, let us look once more at the relation between writing and speaking. In *On Interpretation,* Aristotle explains the process of signification whereby "that which is in the voice *[phōnē]* contains the symbols of mental experience, and written words *[grammata]* are the symbols of that which is in the voice."[21] According to the ancient commentators, the position of the *grammata* in the passage between these terms was to secure the interpretation of the voice; in a sense it became the ground that sustains the entire circle of signification. As ground, though, the *gramma* has the peculiar status of being not simply a sign but that which is in the voice. As a sign the *gramma* presupposes both the voice and its removal.[22] In this context one can legitimately speak of a voice of a text because there is always already the voice in writing. When Gadamer claims that it is "necessary to separate the concept of the word from its grammatical sense,"[23] he is objecting to the removal of the voice from writing. For Gadamer the communicative situation demands that grammatology not exclude the voice.

Thirdly, and finally, in the claim that the voice is of the breath, there is entailed a further claim—and here we return to the issue of the corruption of the voice—that at the edge of breath is memory. We should not forget that in the *Phaedrus* the issue in terms of which the distinction between speaking and writing is raised is the issue of memory. In the myth told by Socrates, Thamus holds against the invention of writing, against the substitution of the breathless sign for the living voice, because it cannot answer for itself. Consequently, writing, as a recipe for reminding *(hupomnēseos)* rather than memory *(mnēmēs),* will implant forgetfulness in the souls who have learned it. According to Derrida, this myth is meant to instruct us in the danger that Socrates sees in inverting the priority of speaking over writing. In inverting the priority one will have turned from the *origin* for truth and knowledge, and thus the danger is the threat to truth (and morality) that arises in memory as the field of presence.[24] Gadamer, on the other hand, reads the text in a more felicitous manner, which is to say that it is *not* a question for Plato of deciding for speaking over writing, where writing is understood as the fixation of speech. Rather, it is a question of an appeal to a correct use of writing relative to how the soul is to learn.[25] In the writing that would serve dialectics there is an art of writing that comes to the aid of thought, and it is to this that the art of understanding is allied.[26]

There is a particular problem, then, endemic to the voice. What occurs in the breath—that is, in the writing that is to be read and in words that are there only in spoken discourse—is a seduction to the emptying of the word. The problem here is more than the possibility of conversation falling away from itself in the manner of *Gerede*. It is also, by virtue of the element of power intrinsic to discourse, the possibility of truth turning into the lie, of the reading of history turning into propaganda, of the revealed word turning into the secret. To say that at the edge of breath is memory, means, accordingly, that in the breath one faces the constant demand of continual renewal, the gathering-together-anew, of that which is said. Hermeneutic recollection is precisely this rediscovery of the abundance and the attentiveness to what is in the voice. The question before us, then, pertains to what shatters the seduction.[27]

THE VOICE IS SITUATED IN THE SPACE OF DESIRE

In the breathless sign there is no desire. There is, of course, in the chain of signifiers, an interruption, a spacing, but this want and lack, this breech of continuity, is not desire, for desire belongs, if not exclusively to life, then certainly to being.[28] What is in the voice is altogether different than what is in the sign.

Let us recall the distinction in the rhetorical tradition between *ratio iudicandi* and *ratio inveniendi* that was made earlier. The *ratio inveniendi* assumed that the event of language was already completed, and accordingly, the *inventio* of the arguments was related to memory as a reminding. But when we engage in the experience of language precisely as an event, we notice that the notion of memory is otherwise than being reminded. This change in the notion of *inventio* is already present in Augustine. In *The Trinity* Augustine tells us that the etymological origin of *inventio* was *venere in*. It means to *come into* that which is sought; but one can do so only through desire *(amore),* where the word is born if it is united with knowledge.[29] This amorous desire, in which the word arises, is more originary than *inventio* as reminding. Here, then, the event of language pertains to memory rather than reminding; and, most significantly, what is of memory is of desire. At the edge of the breath, then, is not just memory; there is also desire.

But what exactly does this connection between desire and the event of language mean for philosophical hermeneutics and what are the implications for our problematic concerning hermeneutics and deconstruction? Let us first see more precisely what is contained in the notion of desire. In the well-known section from the *Phenomenology of Spirit*,[30] Hegel describes self-consciousness as being in the first place desire, and the end of desire is for self-consciousness to rediscover itself in the heart of life. In this context, desire is both intentional as a desire for the other, and reflexive as a modality in which the subject is discovered. Considered in itself, of course, desire has no real end, for desire generates desire. One could say of desire that it is essentially ontological rupture, the breaking and holding open of being before itself. And yet, desire, as the power of the negative, seeks to transfer this difference into identity. If desire is the pursuit of identity, desire is also what poses for us the question of identity. In effect, desire is an interrogative mode of being.

Wherein might we find the element of desire in philosophical hermeneutics? If dialogue is the condition for communicative understanding, one would have to say that desire is the condition for dialogue. Where does a dialogue begin if not in the space of desire, in the space of the interrogative that allows one to cross over into the word of the other. In *Truth and Method* Gadamer tells us that the first condition of dialogue is "ensuring that the other person is with us,"[31] which requires that one is willing to be addressed by the other. This condition is most evident in therapy that proceeds on the basis of a genuine dialogue model; the exchange cannot move to the question and the modality of discovery without the desire for the question. The interrogative itself appears in the spacing of interrogation that is desire. When Gadamer says in "Text and Interpretation" that in dialogical inquiry "both partners must have the good will to understand one another,"[32] this is saying the same thing, namely, the effort of dialogue is nothing that dialogue itself can accomplish, but is dependent upon being able to turn toward the other and to be open in order to be addressed by the other. If words are winged, so too is desire.

But one would also have to say that desire is *in* the voice in a more direct way not only in that there is the desire *for* the word, in which all speaking is a reaching into language for what it is about to say. In this sense, the relation between desire and language testifies to the space of separation that exists in the voice. What is in the voice is never simply present to the voice. There are no edges in the breath, but there is separation.

Desire is also in the voice in the sense that every speaking is a speaking *to* the other as a desire for the other. There is always in the communicative situation the voice of the other as the desired voice. In this context it is difficult to understand how the event of understanding can be construed as appropriation, as making something one's own, turning the event of understanding into a unity of understanding. In Gadamer's eyes, Derrida, who sees hermeneutics as appropriation, never seemed to grasp the element of otherness that is in play in philosophical hermeneutics. If understanding would be appropriation, which involves the covering up of otherness, then one surely has entered the sphere of logocentrism. But, for Gadamer, it is precisely the voice of the other that breaks open what is one's own, and remains there—a desired voice that cannot be suspended—as the partner in every conversation. The element of sameness in understanding is not an "abiding one," but what takes place in conversation as it goes along. Here the intertwining of desire and breath is most evident: in the language of Merleau-Ponty, the other in the address "draws from me thoughts which I had no idea I possessed."[33] The voice of the other, as desired, draws one beyond oneself, to think with the other, "and to come back to oneself as if to an other."[34] And insofar as the voice is of the text as well, one would want to say that in written discourse, the words—if you will forgive the metaphorical hyperbole—must make love to the reader.

Finally, in this regard, in the claim that all speaking is a speaking to the other, we are able to derive an essential insight concerning the realm of the breath. The *agora,* which is supported by desire,[35] is, first of all, a community of trust rather than suspicion. The fragility of the voice in terms of which propaganda, lies, and secrets are possible, are possibilities because there is trust. If speech is destroyed before it is spoken, there is no speech. What turns the voice out of its element (a seduction that is itself of desire) is, paradoxically, turned back into itself through desire—a desire for the voice of the other that tenuously holds all speaking before its possible truth. Desire is what keeps the space of intimacy intact, and yet the voice is always spaced by the element of desire.

COMMUNICATION DRIFTS IN THE VOICE

Let us return to the passage from the *Phaedrus* that has served to guide our analysis. In the desire of the soul to learn, the soul finds written words to be a dead discourse, infinitely repeating the same thing. In their written form, words are caught up in mere repetition, and drift about. What counters the written word is the spoken word, as it is more effective in defending itself, and thus provides itself with the anchor that can bring a halt to the drift.

In his deconstructive reading of the *Phaedrus,* Derrida insists that this metaphysical opposition between speaking and writing in which writing is viewed as a deficiency of speaking, actually breaks open in the text of Plato. If writing is a danger *(pharmakon)* to good speech, it is also the case that Plato *writes* about good speaking. The reason the opposition breaks open is because writing changes *everything.* The writing Derrida has in mind, though, is not the writing in the soul, where the voice is still present as a kind of psychic *graphē,* where writing is "only a writing of transmission, of education, of demonstration."[36] It is rather a writing where what is signified in the writing is displaced. Derrida demonstrates this in the text of Plato by showing how the word *pharmakon* is itself caught up in the chain of signifiers. Writing changes everything once it is apparent that there is a movement of *différance* in language that institutes the system of language itself. For Derrida, then, a certain kind of writing, which is not opposed to speaking, precedes the voice and disseminates it.[37] This Socratic gesture of holding the determination of meaning open before the reader through a strategy that seeks to disseminate the economy of the text is what ultimately separates Derrida from Gadamer. In Derrida's eyes, there is for Gadamer's hermeneutics no literal writing, that is, no writing that is "external to the spirit, to breath, to speech, and to the logos,"[38] which would disrupt the logos, halt the breath. Gadamer wants to maintain the difference, in other words, between the letter and the spirit of the text, where the concern is always for what is of spirit.

Without attempting to solve the "quarrel" between hermeneutics and deconstruction—for what, in the end, would it mean to decide the matter—let us consider more precisely, by way of conclusion, what it means to say, as Gadamer insists, that writing changes *nothing*. We have already indicated in a general way that for philosophical hermeneutics both writing and speaking are considered as texts that stand under the ideality of the word. Certainly, the ideality of the word is not to be confused with the ideality or absolute identity of meaning—a transcendental signified—that constitutes the logocentrism of Western metaphysics.[39] The ideality of the word is simply the word not spoken; accordingly, for philosophical hermeneutics there is no quest for objectivity as absolute ideality, but only the effort to bring the word to reverberate in the voice so that it can be heard. The question that remains, then, for hermeneutics, concerns the actual proximity of the signified, whether in writing or speaking, in the voice.[40]

That there is a *question* of proximity is a result, not of the dissemination, but of the drift, in the voice. It was said in the *Phaedrus* that words, once written, drift *(kulindeitai)* all over the place. As it occurs in the Greek, *kulindeitai* is often spoken of in relation to speaking; it conveys the sense of being tossed about from mouth to mouth, as a ship is tossed about at sea. The word is also used in the context of rolling around or wallowing as one might wallow in the mud.[41] For hermeneutics, the drift in the voice cannot be avoided because writing changes nothing. Communication, which is accomplished in the sharing of present meaning, will always drift in the voice because the voice is no longer under the control of a controller of words. In this sense, it would seem foolish to want to control the drift, for, if it is the case that our words say more than they say at any one time—that speaking is excessive—it would be fruitful to follow the drift. And yet, the drift in the voice is not entirely aimless precisely because the voice is living. What reverberates in the living voice, in other words, is no mere echo.

A speech that merely repeats what someone else had said is a mere echo. It is a voice for which there is no other—a "voice cast out across a space, only to be returned, almost as if from others."[42] In classical myth, Echo fell in love with Narcissus, who did not return her love. As a result, Echo pined away in grief and in the end what remained of her was only her voice. According to the myth, one could still hear her, for her voice was living. But this voice is actually a voice that is the death of the living voice, for it speaks bygone words in an approximation of a repetition of the same.

[margin notes: Ideality of the word + objectivity]

But not every echo is a mere echo, for, in fact, an echo can pluralize speech and decenter the source of speaking.[43] Such an echo, no longer tied to the classical image-original distinction, does not claim to be a semblance of an original sound.[44] This is what one finds in the living voice, i.e., a plurality of the voice that is granted by the voice of the other. And it is from this voice that the drift of meaning becomes an advent of meaning, an advent of meaning that arises at the edge of breath. To be at the edge of breath, this means either to be at the boundary, the borderline, where one encounters what is on the other side of breath, namely silence. But breath is everywhere. Alternately, then, at the edge of breath means to be at the brink, on the verge, at the interval space at which a different state of affairs arises. The proximity in the voice resides here at the edge of breath where speaking turns into a new speaking—hermeneutics at the edge of the breath.

JAMES RISSER

DEPARTMENT OF PHILOSOPHY
SEATTLE UNIVERSITY
AUGUST 1992

NOTES

1. In an interview with Gadamer from 1986 in which he discusses his teaching and writing, he says, "And so I developed a style of my own by speaking freely (not reading to an audience) and teaching this way. I learned to develop the melody of my own thoughts and although I do not think I am a bad writer there always is the *living voice* behind the writing" (emphasis added). *Hans-Georg Gadamer on Education, Poetry, and History,* ed. Dieter Misgeld and Graeme Nicholson (Albany: SUNY Press, 1992), p. 66.

2. The complete definition is "to let what is alienated by the character of the written word or by the character of being distantiated by cultural or historical distances speak again. This is hermeneutics: to let what seems to be far and alienated speak again. But in all the effort to bring the far near . . . we should never forget that the ultimate justification or end is to bring it near so that it speaks in a new voice. Moreover, it should speak not only in a new voice but in a clearer voice." "Practical Philosophy as a Model of the Human Sciences," *Research in Phenomenology,* vol. 9 (1979): 83.

3. Gadamer, "Letter to Dallmayr," *Dialogue and Deconstruction,* trans. Diane Michelfelder and Richard Palmer (Albany: SUNY Press, 1989), p. 98.

4. Commenting on these influences, Gadamer writes: "Insofar as they are my constant companions, I have been formed more by the Platonic dialogues than by the great thinkers of German Idealism." *Philosophical Apprenticeships,* trans. Robert Sullivan (Cambridge: MIT Press, 1985), p. 184.

5. In *"Destruktion* and Deconstruction" Gadamer indicates that the hermeneutic turn toward conversation seeks to go back to the very presupposition in the Socratic turn to dialogical inquiry, namely "the *anamnēsis* sought for and awakened in *logoi.* The 'recollection' that I have in mind is . . . not only that of the individual soul but always that of

'the spirit that would like to unite us—we who are a conversation.'" *"Destruktion* and Deconstruction," *Dialogue and Deconstruction,* p. 110.

6. In the same interview mentioned above, Gadamer is asked whether one can claim that he has a theory of speech and writing and of their relation. Gadamer responds in the affirmative while noting that "this has not been well considered yet," and goes on to ask rhetorically: "What does it mean, for example, that in all antiquity no silent reading was done, and what does it mean that we no longer hear a real voice when reading? This has implications for writers." When asked further if he is reasserting the primacy of speech, Gadamer says only that "literature and writing must take note of the different conditions under which they occur," and then defines hermeneutics accordingly as "the skill to let things speak which come to us in a fixed petrified form, that of the text" *(Hans-Georg Gadamer on Education, Poetry, and History,* p. 65).

7. Plato, *Phaedrus,* trans. R. Hackforth in *The Collected Dialogues of Plato* (Princeton: Princeton University Press, 1961): 275d–276a.

8. See Eric Havelock, *Preface to Plato* (New York: Grosset & Dunlap, 1967).

9. See Bruno Snell, *The Discovery of the Mind,* trans. T. G. Rosenmeyer (New York: Harper and Row, 1960), p. 9. Note also that the Latin word *"anima"* retains this connection between life, soul, and breath.

10. Homer, *The Odyssey of Homer,* trans. Richard Lattimore (New York: Harper and Row, 1967): Book XI, 222.

11. Richard Onians, *The Origin of European Thought* (New York: Arno Press, 1973), p. 67.

12. See *The Odyssey of Homer,* book 17, 57. A longer study on this topic would require that one pursue this imagery in Plato's dialogues. One immediately thinks here of the winged steeds in the myth in the *Phaedrus.*

13. Onians points out that we literally do not hear so well when yawning, that is, when not breathing in. In the Greek oral tradition the reception of the word—that is, the taking in what pertains to consciousness and intelligence—depended more on the lungs than the ears. See *The Origins of European Thought,* p. 72.

14. See Giorgio Agamben, *Language and Death,* trans. Karen Pinkus with Michael Hardt (Minneapolis: University of Minnesota Press, 1991), p. 34.

15. Gadamer, *Truth and Method,* 2d revised ed., trans. Joel Weinsheimer and Donald Marshall (New York, Crossroad Publishing, 1989), p. 422.

16. Gadamer, "Hermeneutics and Logocentrism," *Dialogue and Deconstruction,* p. 118. Compare this with Gadamer's similar remark in his essay *"Destruktion* and Deconstruction" from the same volume: "[What occurs in dialogue] is the very meaning of the speculative unity that is achieved in the 'virtuality' of the word: that it is not an individual word nor is it a formulated proposition, but rather points beyond all possible assertions" (pp. 111–12).

17. See Agamben, *Language and Death,* p. 67.

18. See Anne Carson, *Eros: The Bittersweet* (Princeton: Princeton University Press, 1986), p. 50.

19. In *"Von der Wahrheit des Wortes,"* a paper presented at and published privately by the Martin Heidegger Gesellschaft in Messkirch, Gadamer writes: "'Das Wort' meint vielmehr immer schon eine größere, vielfältigere Einheit, die in dem Begriff des verbum interius der Tradition seit langsam bekannt ist. Es lebt auch ganz selbstverständlich in userer Altagssprache weiter, wenn einer zum Beispiel sagt: "Ich möchte mit dir ein Wort reden.' Da meint man nicht, daß man ihm nur ein einziges Wort sagen will" *(Denken und Dichten bei Martin Heidegger* [Der Martin Heidegger Gesellschaft in Messkirch], p. 8).

20. Gadamer, *Truth and Method,* p. 393.

21. Aristotle, *De interpretatione,* in *The Works of Aristotle,* trans. E. M. Edghill (Oxford: Oxford University Press, 1971), 16a.

22. See Agamben, *Language and Death,* pp. 38ff.

23. Gadamer, "Hermeneutics and Logocentrism," p. 124.

24. For Derrida the issue here is not to argue for an alternative to self-present speech, but, in carrying out a reading of textual disruption, show that the text fails to achieve what is argued for in the text, namely, the priority of speech over writing. See "Plato's Pharmacy," in *Dissemination,* trans. Barbara Johnson (Chicago: University of Chicago Press, 1981), pp. 61–172.

25. In "Unterwegs zur Schrift?" Gadamer writes, "Ist es aber wirklich eine Verwerfung der Erfindung der Schrift und des Gebrauches der Schrift, die daraus folgt, oder ist es eher ein Appell an den rechten Gebrauch der Schrift, etwas, was man mit einem Ausdruck unserer Tage einen hermeneutischen Appell nennen könnte?" *Gesammelte Werke, 2* (Tübingen: J. C. B. Mohr, 1986), 263. See also *The Idea of the Good in Platonic-Aristotelian Philosophy,* trans. P. Christopher Smith (New Haven: Yale University Press, 1986), p. 119.

26. Gadamer, *Truth and Method,* p. 393.

27. This question can be asked in a number of ways. Rather than seduction one could pose the problem of the speaking in the voice in terms of the shattering of words as such. The problem is captured in the lines from Eliot's "Burnt Norton":

> Words strain,
> Crack and sometimes break, under the burden,
> Under the tension, slip, slide, perish,
> Decay with imprecision, will not stay in place,
> Will not stay still. Shrieking voices
> Scolding, mocking, or merely chattering,
> Always assail them.

T. S. Eliot, *Four Quartets* (New York: Harcourt, Brace and World, Inc., 1943), p. 19.

28. It would be interesting to think the ontological problem of hylomorphism in Aristotle in terms of desire. In the *Physics* Aristotle says literally that "matter desires [*ephiesthai kai oregesthai*] form." *Physics,* 192a22. In a different context this same idea is broached by Merleau-Ponty in his *Phenomenology of Perception:* "If then we want to bring to light the birth of being for us, we must finally look to that area of our experience which clearly has significance and reality for us, and that is our affective life. Let us try to see how a thing or a being begins to exist for us through desire or love and we shall thereby come to understand better how things and being can exist in general." *Phenomenology of Perception,* trans. Colin Smith (London: Routledge and Kegan Paul, 1962), p. 154.

29. Augustine writes: "The word therefore which we now wish to discern and study is knowledge with love." *The Trinity,* trans. Stephen McKenna (Washington, D.C.: Catholic University of America Press, 1963), p. 285.

30. See Hegel, *Phenomenology of Spirit,* trans. A. V. Miller (Oxford: Oxford University Press, 1977), pp. 104ff.

31. Gadamer, *Truth and Method,* p. 367.

32. Gadamer, "Text and Interpretation," *Dialogue and Deconstruction,* p. 33.

33. Merleau-Ponty, *Phenomenology of Perception,* p. 354.

34. Gadamer, *"Destruktion* and Deconstruction," p. 110.

35. Here the question of the *Republic,* which is the question of the community that wants to exclude desire, naturally arises.

36. Derrida, *Dissemination,* p. 154.

37. The kind of writing that Derrida has in mind is described as a "general writing of which the system of speech, consciousness, meaning, presence, truth, etc., would only be an effect, to be analyzed as such. It is this questioned effect that I have elsewhere called *logocentrism." Margins of Philosophy,* trans. Alan Bass (Chicago: University of Chicago Press, 1982), p. 329.

38. Derrida, *Of Grammatology,* trans. Gayatri Spivak (Baltimore: Johns Hopkins University Press, 1976), p. 35.

39. This is the issue in Derrida's reading of Husserl. See *Speech and Phenomenon,* trans. David Allison (Evanston: Northwestern University Press, 1973).

40. The issue of proximity in the voice is the issue of familiarity. In "On the Contribution of Poetry to the Search of Truth," Gadamer speaks of the self-fulfillment of the poetic word in terms of a hold upon nearness as a familiarity with the world. See *The Relevance of the Beautiful and Other Essays,* trans. Nicholas Walker (Cambridge: Cambridge University Press, 1986), pp. 113ff.

41. See *The Iliad of Homer,* trans. Richard Lattimore (Chicago: University of Chicago Press, 1951), book 22, 414.

42. John Sallis, *Echoes: After Heidegger* (Bloomington: Indiana University Press, 1990), p. 1.

43. Sallis pursues the sense of the figure of Echo in turning to the work of Thoreau. There one finds, according to Sallis, an echo of nature in contrast to the Echo of classical culture. This echo is to some extent original sound. Sallis uses this as an occasion to think within the collapse of the image-original distinction. See my remark that follows.

44. A detailed discussion of this issue of the image-original distinction in Gadamer's hermeneutics can be found in my "The Image of Truth in Philosophical Hermeneutics," in *Phenomenology, Interpretation, and Community* (Albany: SUNY Press, 1996), 159–74.

REPLY TO JAMES RISSER

It is certainly a consequence of philosophical hermeneutics that it has significance not only in the field of the sciences but primarily in the shared life of human beings. In today's world where the encounter with the other is submitted to new world standards, this task of philosophizing precisely consists in taking back the overemphasis on the subjectivity of self-consciousness. However, it is less a matter of the voice of the other than the judgment of the other in which the discovery of truth, rather than a methodology, finds its significance. Risser's contribution connects with the debates about the word "phonocentrism" which Derrida introduced. In hermeneutics the orality of conversations allegedly takes precedence over the written form of the text. In truth, there is no real opposition. What is written, has to be read, and so it too "stands under the voice."

Risser wants to reinvestigate the situation of the problem by way of the well-known point in the *Phaidros* where the hermeneutical priority of orality, as well as deconstruction's priority of the written, is based. It is obvious that from the standpoint of hermeneutics too the 'conversation' must not be taken out of the entirety of the life-context. In the *Phaidros* the topic is being dealt with only in a very specific application, that is, the application to rhetoric which had spread in the Greece of those days as a new literary fashion. Derrida consciously connects with the 'literary revelation' which changed the relationship of orality and the written in the Athens of Plato's days as well as in our time. Risser does not want to decide the discussion about the priority of the one over the other. Rather, he wishes to demonstrate that one must not understand the problem without reference to the "place of life." In criticizing the helplessness of the written word and the distance to things of a playful rhetoric as a form of literature, Plato is primarily concerned with the living word. It is obvious that both forms of language, the oral and the written, are exposed to abuse. The possibility fading to a mere empty chatter is an age-old agony of rhetoric. One cannot say, however, that in the age of writing—which, since Gutenberg, defines an enormous field of domination—the emptying of texts and abuse of the means of communication do not occur as much.

Thus, the way in which Risser, following Hegel and, I suppose, also Lacan, draws upon the chapter on desire *(désir)* is interesting. While I appeal to Plato, I can follow this move without any reservations. Of course, every conversation is dependent upon other things beyond that which reveals itself in the voice. A conversation is always a kind of living together and as such it has its incontestable and unreachable priority. This implies at the same time that Derrida falsely sees an appropriation in understanding. The unequivocal mathematical symbol cannot be an ideal for an unequivocal appropriation of the natural and social world, just as one certainly cannot deny that the shared life of human beings could not flourish on such a basis. Maybe today we are really placed in the midst of displacement toward a new orality, but hardly toward an orality of living speech. Such a speech cannot be recognized in the glibness of those who speak through instruments. They all know in advance what they have to say, and that is no speaking at all. Rather, speaking means to seek one's words and to find one's words, whether the relationship between writing and orality displaces itself in one way or another, or not at all. It will always be the case that human beings seek to persuade one another with words and are able to learn from the other's objections—when there is a real, living conversation.

H.-G.G.

20

D. Wyatt Aiken

HERMENEIA: AN ANATOMY OF HISTORY AND *AB-WESENHEIT*

It is my intention here, using the metaphors of heavy and light, *An-wesenheit* and *Ab-wesenheit,* to draft an anatomy of historical re-membering. The inquiry into History and the historical is a process of sifting through the testimony of the past, not only in order to discover what in fact took place, but also to prioritize the spectrum of meanings inseparably woven into the contextual fiber of past-time happenings. The hermeneutical activity is an attempt to reconstitute methodically a cultural milieu now past, now remote and unfamiliar; it is an activity of re-membering the various pieces and bits of past-time into a re-semblance of their original existential cast, a re-semblance that truth-fully and meaning-fully reflects a time in the world's past that has since become *light.*

Among other things, an anatomy of historical reconstitution must attempt to disengage clearly the historical activity of authenticating the witnesses of past happenings, i.e., *text* in the widest sense, from the philosophical process of re-membering past-time happenings into History; for the manner in which historical information is brought together into History is strategically linked to the type of philosophical assumptions holding sway in the historian's mind.

This article is strictly didactic in nature. Structured around an anatomical dissection (Frye 1957, 311) of historical man's *hermeneia,*[1] it seeks to throw light upon the shadowy places of the human animal's impressions of his own historicity, of his own intimate in-the-world mythos. I wish, first, to sketch a profile of the time-constrained animal who cannot seem to just "instantly forget" (Nietzsche 1964, 2:102), emphasizing the delimiting contextual milieu that surrounds and enfolds man-in-process. It is precisely this notion of milieu[2] that has given rise to many of the queries and responses proffered by historical and philosophical hermeneutics.[3] Then I shall give a brief synopsis of History and historicity, and finally, identify what seems to be the principal methodological difficulty confronting the philosophical creation of History.

The hermeneutical inquiry, or the study of how to read the traces-in-time left behind by the historical animal, has become considerably more complex since historical critical scholars originally began investigating the authenticity of biblical documents "qua documents of history, and not simply qua documents of faith" (Aiken 1991, 230). In their pursuit of the historical-in-the-biblical, critical scholars set out first to reconstitute an historically reliable, and credible (Spinoza 1951, 120), biblical Ur-text by identifying the different literary sources and tendencies that initially gave form, and thus potentially substance, to the different narrative traditions reflected in the biblical documents (Aiken 1991, 230–31). Because there are no extant originals of the biblical texts, it was necessary for scholars to re-constitute the supposed form of those missing originals, to create a *Bible* or theoretical Ur-text (Eissfeldt 1934, 2, 693ff.) by clustering together corresponding fragments, references, and manuscripts into a consistent and unified whole.

The authentication and reconstitution of text has always been a stated factor in the goal and method of historical hermeneutics, partly, at least, because historical investigators have always believed that once established, an Ur-text, unlike other types of text, would reveal a previously "concealed or distorted Ur-Sinn" (Gadamer 1986, 2:95; Kisiel 1972, 198), an Ur-truth concerning historical man.[4] Ultimately, then, the inquiry into past-time derives from historical man's search for beginnings. It springs from his drive to dis-cover in the *transient text* of change, and to articulate, his own mythos.

The Lightness of *Ab-wesenheit*

A material heaviness enfolds the human animal actualizing himself in space and in time. Yet his rememberings of past happenings, far from being heavy, are suffused with lightness. In the intimate rememberings of near-at-hand events one reintroduces, in the lightness of the mind's re-collection, the presently in-substantial, the *Ab-wesend,* back into the originating context of its past-time ontological *An-wesenheit,*[5] into the anchoring grasp of "verfließenden Zeit" (Gadamer 1986, 2:135), in order to saturate the *Ab-wesend* once again with in-world substantiality. This is also the case with scholarly attempts to re-member for the present generation the existential heaviness of more remote past-time. Thus, both intimate rememberings of the near-past as well as scholarly re-memberings of the more remote past are processes of re-uniting the in-substantial lightness of *Ab-wesenheit* with the substantial heaviness of *An-wesenheit,*[6] so that clothed in the garments of its own historicity the no-longer-in-the-world can once again cast a shadow of being.

Unlike the eternal Now, the historical moment is a "Pflock des Augenblicks." These furtive flakes of time are the "ghosts" (Nietzsche 1964, 2:101) of the past that the historical animal attempts to assemble into a meaning-full[7] scenario (contextuality) called History. Yet what is man if not himself a nexus[8] drifting toward forgetfulness, if not himself an elusive apparition in the time continuum?[9]

AN-WESENHEIT AS *SUM-PHORE* (NEXUS)

According to Herodotus, when the Lydian king Croesus queried Solon the wise concerning the happiest man he had yet encountered in his travels, Solon responded in what seems a curious fashion. Following a protracted but intriguing calculation concerning days and intercalary months and matching seasons, Solon eventually makes the point that man is a nexus, a junction of converging life currents:

> I set the boundary of a man's life at seventy years, these seventy spaces of yeartime amounting to 25,200 days, not counting the intercalary month. So if one wishes to make every other year longer by one month in order to make the seasons properly agree, then not only are there thirty-five intercalary months beyond the seventy years, but the days of these months total one thousand and fifty, making all together of the seventy years 26,250 days, and each of these days is unlike any other particular day in that which it brings. Thus, then, Croesus, man is nothing more than a junction of happenings *[sum-phore]*. (Herodotus 1990, 1:32)[10]

In response to Croesus's question concerning the happy man, Solon first gives attention to a definition of man, making of him "nothing more than *sum-phore.*" It is only after defining man as nexus that Solon finally addresses the question of the happy man: "If [a man of good fortune] shall also end his life well . . . he is worthy to have been called happy; but if he has not yet died, we must give heed not to call him happy, but only successful *[extuxea]*" (Herodotus 1990, 1:32). Solon's definition of man as *sum-phore* carries with it neither implicit happiness nor unhappiness, neither lightness nor heaviness. Man is an evasive juncture in time linking together an agglomerate of happenings, and the significance of the individual man-nexus at any given moment of his existence is dependent uniquely upon the manner in which an interpreter brings together into *transient text* all the different happenings pertinent to the particular man. Man is a nexus-point in an historical continuum, and whether or not a particular man can be called happy is a judgment rendered only by others, and then only upon the man's death.

Shortly after this passage in which he recounts Solon's conversation with Croesus, however, Herodotus introduces in a much more characteristic Greek existential context the concept of *baru-sumphoros:* heavy-nexus.

Following Solon's departure from the Lydian court, Croesus had a dream that his son would be killed by a spear of iron; and in fact, in spite of all Croesus's precautions the inevitable occurred. Adrastus, an expatriate in Croesus's house, accidentally kills the king's son during a boar hunt. Afterward, when the son's body was placed before the king, Adrastus pleaded for Croesus to slay him as well; but Croesus rendered tragic justice to Adrastus: "I do not hold you to be the cause of this evil, save in so far as you were the unwilling doer of it; rather it is the word of a god, the same who told me long ago what was to be" (Herodotus 1990, 1:45). Adrastus, however, who had unintentionally slain his own brother and thus been exiled from his home, who had been purified by Croesus and received into his house only to kill (once again inadvertently) his protector's son, "slew himself there by the sepulcher, seeing now clearly that he was the most ill-fated *[baru-sumphotatos]* of all men whom he knew" (Herodotus 1990, 1:45).

Man is nothing more than *sum-phore*. Yet whether, like Adrastus, one is weighed down by the happenings that constitute one's own intimate History, being *baru-sumphoros*, or whether one has been generally fortunate enough in life to be thought successful, Solon argues that these are interpretive significations that may randomly apply to a man-nexus during his lifetime, but that it is only after the final card of life, death, has been played that one can be called truly happy.

HEAVINESS AND LIGHTNESS

Solon defines man as a junction of happenings, neither heavy nor light. It is only according to the specific flowing of his days that the individual man becomes either heavy-nexus or prosperous; it is only after a man's death, and because of the conclusive hind-sight afforded surviving spectators of his life, that any particular man can be called happy or unhappy.

This quintessentially Greek tragic sense of heaviness is significantly different from the abstraction of heaviness that later philosophers shall derive from the materiality that constitutes the boundaries of being *(Sein)*. Likewise, the Greek concept of the well-fortuned or successful man, which is clearly endowed with a certain quality of lightness, is yet far removed from the lightness-through-absence metaphor that shall characterize the descriptions of philosophical hermeneutics.

In philosophical hermeneutics, whose method revolves around "a particular 'psychological act', namely understanding" (Connolly and Keutner 1988, 2),[11] the metaphors of heaviness and lightness, *An-wesenheit* and *Ab-wesenheit,* shall instead serve to portray the abstract play between the material weightiness that clothes the potentialities of being-in-the-world, and the lightness inherent to the process of re-membering past-time happenings into an interpretively significant scenario called History.

Hölderlin, among others, clearly recognizes the significance for poetry of the powerful play between *An-wesenheit* (heaviness) and *Ab-wesenheit* (lightness). In his essay "Über Achill (2)" Hölderlin focuses on, and praises, Homer's effectiveness in accentuating in the *Iliad* the immense importance of Achilles to the Greeks. Hölderlin argues that Homer skillfully creates a powerful idealization of Achilles simply by restricting his presense to rare intervals in the action of the poem. The en-lightening or *Idealisierung* of Achilles in the *Iliad* occurs precisely because "the greatest of the Achaians" is virtually *ab-wesend* in the Poet's narration:

> Many have often wondered why Homer, who wanted to sing especially of the anger of Achilles, almost never let him appear [in the *Iliad*]. . . . That which is ideal should not appear all the time [alltäglich]; and [Homer] could not really sing of Achilles any more wonderfully . . . than that he should make him withdraw . . . in order that from that day on every loss of the Greeks . . . reminds one of [Achilles'] superiority over the whole magnificent array of lords and servants, and so that through his Abwesenheit, [Achilles] should be put so much the more in the light in the rare moments when the poet lets him appear before us. (Hölderlin 1977, 495–96)

In another appeal to the metaphor of lightness, the French philosopher Alain includes in his *Système des beaux-arts* a short essay entitled "De l'histoire," in which he emphasizes the dissimilarity between "the type of history that is only the inventory of our knowledge concerning the past" and "the art of painting with words" (Alain 1958, 448). Alain argues that while there are obvious dissimilarities between a history *(une histoire)*, a painting *(un tableau)*, and a novel *(un roman)*, there is yet a very definite resemblance between the historian, the painter, and the novelist, namely, a certain abstraction or lightness in their modes of expression. Because whatever the story being channeled through these different media, viz., "the tragedy, the scenic representation [i.e., le tableau], [and] the analysis of hearts, the whole [descriptive event] is contained in one or two lines" (Alain 1958, 449). The mythos, whether told by *crayon* or *pinceau*, is entirely contained within a few strokes, it is conveyed with brevity through abstraction—*Idealisierung:*

> [O]ne no more sees La Grenadière . . . after one has read Balzac, than one would be capable of drawing or painting Nero and his courtesans according to Tacitus. The reader does not see Grandet at all . . . although Grandet is described from his shoes to his hat; he sees no better the face of Julien Sorel, described here and there with few strokes, who is however as alive and as present as the other. . . . Who then, in reading, sees Gobseck's smile? It is correct to say that he shall find it among men, for a short instant and as an apparition of this character on another face. (Alain 1958, 449)

Karl Jaspers, as well, speculates upon a metaphor of lightness *(Ab-wesenheit)* when, at a Unesco conference celebrating the one hundred and fiftieth anniversary of Kierkegaard's birth, he contends that if Kierkegaard were to return as an *(an-wesend)* contender in today's intellectual arena, he might well say, "If I were your contemporary you would again inflict upon me the treatment I endured in Copenhagen. Now, though, you celebrate me as absent *[passé]*, inoffensive, as a now famous spiritual phenomenon with which you decorate each other, thus making me a spoil of myself" (Unesco 1966, 91).

The play between heavy and light, the existential weight of the present moment and the weightlessness of the past moment, is the quintessential metaphor for the transcendent quality of *Ab-wesenheit,* and thus, for past-time itself—history; for an inevitable consequence of existential ab-*sense* is that by shedding the heavy garments of their in-time nexus natures, happenings and persons and texts[12] are changed into ideal or transcending pre-*senses.* They become strangely lighter and purer, finally *fixed* as en-lightened or transcending re-collections. Gadamer's theory concerning hermeneutic activity revolves precisely around this image of *Idealisierung,* which he likens to the ideal-ization or transcendental re-membering of a loved one over whom death has cast its dis-membering shroud.

> How the *Seinsweise* of this person suddenly changes there, how he has become lasting *[bleibend],* purer *[reiner],* not necessarily better in a moral or loving sense; but in the profile that remains of him *[bleibenden Umriß]* he has become fixed *[geschlossen]* and visible—obviously only because we can no longer expect anything from him, have nothing more to experience from him, and because we may no longer do anything loving for him. (Gadamer 1986, 2:141–42)

HISTORY AND HERMENEUTIC

What precisely is History or historicity? Some have argued that History is restricted to recording actual past-time happenings and events,[13] thus effectively making the historical endeavor a simple inventory of past-time happenings. If this is the case, the historian actually re-constructs the flow of historical past-time following indications educed from the witnesses of that past-time, re-membering from the source material and re-presenting as accurately as possible the *existential unfolding* of that which has become historically *ab-wesend*—light.

Others, such as Merleau-Ponty, argue that History is something more than just a string of discontinuous happenings (Gadamer 1986, 2:138–39), and that "[t]here is no [H]istory if the flow of things is a series of separate episodes," or if History is presented as nothing more than a simple "concord of circumstances" (Merleau-Ponty 1968, 46, 49). If this refinement is accurate, that History is in fact more than an unaffected inventory of past happenings, then Merleau-Ponty's conclusion is defensible; for he argues that the reality of historical events can only be won by a methodical abstraction, that historical truth "is found not in certain existing historical subjects, nor in a theoretical prise de conscience, but in [their] confrontation, in their practice, and in their common life" (Merleau-Ponty 1968, 47; 1964, 55).

In Greek, *history* denotes more than just the process of inquiry into the causes of certain events, but refers, more specifically, to the understanding gained from that inquiry or to the transmission of information gained through historical inquiry. It should come as no surprise, therefore, that Greek historians speak of History as a com-position or com-pilation of deeds and events around a specific thesis,[14] or in order that the knowledge of extraordinary events might not be lost.[15] In the broadest sense every document is historical in nature; but the Greek historians specifically intended so to position events in respect to one another *(sug-grapho)* that the especial emphasis concerning the significance of historical happenings would become evident.

After Spinoza, however, and with the development of philosophical hermeneutics, the horizon of the historian's activity was significantly widened. The historian was no longer seen as the chronicler of happenings that more or less told their own story, but rather, he was re-defined as the interpretive judge and sculptor of History.

Spinoza maintains that Reason, Ratio, is the only acceptable measure for separating the truth of past happenings from their meaning (Spinoza 1951, 99–101). For Spinoza, only Reason, which is anchored in the *current* existential experience of the world, can, ipso facto, determine ultimately and consistently what was existentially possible in the *historical* experience of the world. As the measure of historical experience, however, Ratio obviously allows for only natural and essentially rational explanations of happenings recorded in texts of the past, and specifically in the biblical texts. Gadamer shall stress the importance of this shift in impetus, arguing that it ultimately led to the "conversion into the Historical, which is to say the conversion from the apparent (and incomprehensible) Wonder-histories to the (comprehensible) Wonder-faith" ("Das führt zu der Wendung ins Historische, d.h. zur Wendung von den angeblichen [und unverständlichen] Wundergeschichten zu dem [verständlichen] Wunderglauben") (Gadamer 1986, 2:96–97).[16]

For Spinoza, then, the role of the hermeneut is primarily to transmit understanding[17] concerning historical texts, to translate past-time happenings into a rational framework of relevant understanding in those places "where the truth of a claim is no longer clear or a particular substantive understanding itself needs to be grounded" (Warnke 1987, 10). Spinoza translated past-time through the grid of Ratio, thus transforming the historical inquiry into a systematic and, for all intents and purposes, exclusively philosophical exercise in the meaning-full rationalization of existential experiences of the world.

Following Schleiermacher, who definitively codified the shift from historical hermeneutics to apperceptual or philosophical hermeneutics (Gadamer 1986, 97), philosophers have generally agreed that History is a form of art: the "art de faire re-vivre" (hyphenation mine) (Alain 1958, 450). Philosophical hermeneuts, in fact, argue that History-qua-Art is essentially a form of poetic mimesis, and that it is by means of this artistic re-presentation that the now-silent is once again given voice.[18] Thus, the art of re-membering the past into History parallels the art of re-storing or re-membering statues of antiquity, when, from various pieces of statue that seem to fit together, the sculptor re-sculpts or re-creates an integral and related whole (Statue). This crafting together of happenings into

History is a restitution of sorts,[19] an artistic attempt to render the heaviness of existential *An-wesenheit* to persons or deeds or events made light through *Ab-wesenheit*. Thus, Merleau-Ponty shall argue that the "mental activity" of the historian does not exhaust the "reality of the history that was," but is in fact a process of poetic invention: the making of *histoire-Dichtung* (Merleau-Ponty 1968, 47; 1964, 231). Gadamer, as well, clearly identifies himself with this philosophical tradition when he argues that the hermeneutic re-membering of the past is in fact an artistic reproduction, using as his metaphor of History a quasi-theatrical notion of a modern mise-en-scène whose plot has been supplied by past happenings.[20]

A common denominator of the different thinkers in the philosophical tradition of hermeneutics, then, is that they have "left the domain of historical re-construction, [and] have become engaged in a parallel process of literary creation in which they themselves become the authors of a sort of neo- or pseudo-[H]istory" (Aiken 1991, 233).

THE QUESTION OF AN INTERPRETIVE *AUSGANGSPUNKT*

History is a merging together of re-assembled past-time happenings and the historian's perspective, or *Ausgangspunkt*. It should come as no surprise, therefore, that the historian's *Ausgangspunkt*, which already sanctions prior to any actual *historical* consideration a *philosophical* distinction between acceptable (rational) and unacceptable (ir-rational) experiences of the world, shall also actively influence the process of historical re-membering, and thus History itself as the final product of that process. This interpretive *Ausgangspunkt* is philosophical in nature, and not historical, and it alone shall ultimately determine the spectrum of possible experiences in the modern realm, and of course, the spectrum of possible experiences in the realm of past-time.[21]

The historian's objective in re-membering past-time happenings into History is to obtain historical truth (Aiken 1991, 228). However, the a priori threads of a certain "non-reasoned dogmatic assumption *[Voraussetzung]*" or "pre-condition *[Vorbedlingung]*" (Gadamer 1986, 2:100–101; 2:124; cf. 2:405–6) are also inevitably woven into this re-construction of the past. These philosophical assumptions reflect the attitude of the historian toward certain categories of experience, such as the 'mythical' or the 'fabulous', that are clearly not part of the modern intimate experience of the world. These assumptions, in fact, which are born of critical reason and the progressive enthroning of Ratio as the dominant measure of possible truth in the natural order (Aiken 1991, 228ff.), actually provide the *points de repère* that enable the historian to separate methodically comprehensible types of happenings from the types of happening that the modern world simply cannot comprehend, because it finds them existentially ir-rational.

The principal *Ausgangspunkt* for the modern re-creation of History is the paradigm of world-become-rational, and Ratio remains the conventional a priori interpretive grid through which historical happenings are read and systematically stripped of any ir-rational elements.[22] This rapport between the historian's philosophical perspective and the historical information that he will re-member into History, constitutes the methodological chink in the armor of philosophical hermeneutics; for the general structure through which the historian re-members past happenings into, in this case, Rational History, is already pre-determined by the implicit assumption that happenings in the world are only authentic existentially if they pass the test of Ratio. The actual documents and witnesses of historical happenings, i.e., texts, are only of secondary consideration in the philosophical re-membrance of History.

In general, an *Ausgangspunkt* enables the historian to re-constitute the psycho-apperceptual paradigm through which the chroniclers of man's past perceived and interpreted the events they were narrating. In particular, the rationalist *Ausgangspunkt,* which provides the historian with the point of reference necessary to identify the original paradigms surrounding the descriptions of past happenings, allows the historian to re-define those happenings in terms of a rationally credible picture *(Bild)* of past-time (Aiken 1991, 228). Yet Rational History may not be, in fact, history at all.

The documentary sources and other witnesses of past-time happenings "constitute for the modern historian the unique point of entry into the otherwise inaccessible and obscure world of the past" (Aiken 1991, 228; cf. 243). Thus, the most difficult phase of the historical inquiry is to determine the rapport between mythic, and therefore phenomenally in-comprehensible descriptions and explanations of man's historical being in-the-world, and the modern existential encounter of the world, which is not only immediately accessible but also quintessentially rational. As with any *Ausgangspunkt,* of course, the rationalist *Ausgangspunkt* enables the modern hermeneut to accomplish precisely this: to re-create a harmony or model of the past called History without having to accept as phenomenally possible that which is ir-rational or in-credible, viz., the possibility of an actual existential encounter with the mythic in what is evidently a uniquely natural *Lebenswelt* (Aiken 1991, 229).

The philosophical approach to hermeneutics is not without problems. It is, for example, difficult to defend an interpretive method that sanctions a systematic, rational *dépouillement* of historical experience. For Ratio notwithstanding, there are no indisputable guidelines that allow the historian methodologically to go *behind* a documented experience of the world, an experience recorded in an otherwise authentic historical text, in order to determine what the author of the text could have *in fact* experienced. Philosophical hermeneutics, however, which countenances a rationalist interpretive paradigm of the world, does not profess to re-member historical facts or to re-present actual past-time happenings. Rather, it is engaged in a philosophical process of com-position and textual re-enactment, which is a parallel, and entirely different, activity. "For the philologist, the text . . . is there in front of its interpreter like a fixed given that precedes every new interpretation. The historian . . . has first to reconstruct his basic text, namely [H]istory itself" (Gadamer 1992, 65).[23]

D. WYATT AIKEN

DEPARTMENT OF PHILOSOPHY
UNIVERSITY OF NEVADA
UNIVERSITY OF HULL, ENGLAND
JULY 1992

NOTES

1. "[L]'*hermeneia* est le 'sens' de cet étant que nous sommes, 'hommes', 'interprètes' du *logos*" (Nancy 1982, 10). Cf. Gadamer 1986, 2:93.
2. The notion of milieu is critical to Gadamer's concept of textual *Verstehen*. See Gadamer 1990, 1:305–12, and Gadamer 1986, 2:31–32, 135, 330, 397, 404. In his article "The Science of the Life-World," Gadamer stresses the pervading contextuality contained in the notion of *Lebenswelt*. In defining an acquaintance, for example, Gadamer speaks of all the possible "forms of the world" that may surround and define the acquaintance, concluding: "[O]ne sees that it is the world itself which is concretized by such intersubjective experiences: that, and not an objective world of mathematically describable *a priori,* is the world" (Gadamer 1972, 181). Ranke, likewise, says that "the historian conceives for himself a general picture of the form of the connection of all events. . . . [The ideas he forms] are not being projected into history, but are the essence of history itself. For . . . all occurrences are inseparably linked in space and time" (Ranke 1973, 16; cf. 22 and 26). Husserl argues that any history drawn strictly from facts must remain incomprehensible, and that "[O]nly the disclosure of the essentially general structure lying in our present . . . , only the disclosure of the . . . historical time in which we live, in which our total humanity lives in respect to its total, essentially general structure—only this disclosure can make possible . . . *[Historie]* " (Husserl 1970, 371–72). Heidegger expresses the same idea with the notion of historical inferences: "Die Thematisierung, d. hst. die historische Erschließung von Geschichte ist die Voraussetzung für den möglichen 'Aufbau der geschichtlichen Welt in den Geisteswissenschaften'" (Heidegger 1979 376; cf. Gadamer 1972, 180). French phenomenologist Merleau-Ponty also argues that History is "as a milieu of life," and that the "historical act is invented" (Merleau-Ponty 1968, 45), and French historian George Duby is quoted as saying that "there is no truth of facts [in History], but at very best an ethic. There is not one History, but multiple visions that assemble themselves following the whim of subjectivities" (Simonnet 1992, 47).
3. For a discussion of the progression from historical hermeneutics to philosophical hermeneutics, see Gadamer, "Klassische und philosophische Hermeneutik" (1986), esp. 97ff., and "Hermeneutik und Historismus" (1965).
4. Although the reconstitution of authentic text and the determination of accurate historical facts have been central to the efforts of historical hermeneutics, Gadamer

clearly states that this *historical* process is extraneous to the objective of *philosophical* hermeneutics: "Das eigentliche Urfaktum . . . ist offenbar nicht die Frage. . . . Das eigentliche Problem, das sich hier stellt und als das der Geschichte erkannt wird, findet in dem Begriff der *Geschichtlichkeit* seinen Ausdruck" (Gadamer 1986, 134).

5. For the ontological statement *(Aussage)* contained in historicity *(Geschichtlichkeit)*, see Gadamer 1986, 2:135.

6. The play between lightness and heaviness, absence and presence, is really quite a common metaphor in literature. Nietzsche, for example, grounds his new aesthetic in the shift from Wagnerian weightiness to Mediterranean lightness, because, he says, "[Bizet's] music seems . . . consummate *[vollkommen]*. It comes lightly, spritely, thus with courtesy. It is worthy of love; it does not sweat. 'Goodness is light, everything divine walks on delicate feet': first line of my aesthetic" (Nietzsche 1964, 8:1, 5). Gide describes the marvelous sleights-of-hand of a certain Baldi: "d'un papier chiffonne, déchiré, [il] faisait éclore maints papillons blancs . . . qu'il maintenait suspendus en l'air au-dessus des battements d'un éventail. Ainsi les objets prés de lui perdaient poids et réalité, présence même, ou bien prenaient une signification nouvelle, inattendue, baroque, distante de toute utilité" (Gide 1958, 89). Gide also develops more philosophically upon this metaphor in *Paludes:* "Mais de tout ce que nous faisons, rien ne dure sitôt que nous ne l'entretenons plus. Et pourtant tous nos actes subsistent horriblement et pèsent" (Gide 1968, 123–4). In *The Unbearable Lightness of Being,* Kundera, as well, develops the intermingling play of lightness and darkness, ab-sense and pre-sense: "[Nietzsche's] myth of eternal return states that a life which disappears once and for all . . . is like a shadow, without weight, dead in advance. . . . If the French Revolution were to recur eternally, French historians would be less proud of Robespierre. But because they deal with something that will not return, the bloody years of the Revolution have turned into mere words, theories, and discussions, have become lighter than feathers, frightening no one. . . . [T]hings appear other than as we know them: they appear without the mitigating circumstance of their transitory nature" (Kundera 1984, 2–3). Finally, in *En attendant Godot,* Samuel Beckett might be perhaps suggesting that the most relevant way to speak of the God who is there *(anwesend),* is to speak of the God(ot) who is not *(ab-wesend).*

7. According to Löwith, historical meaning *(Bedeutung)* is distinct from the happenings of past-time; it is the interpretive creation of the historian. "[T]here would be no search for the meaning of history if its meaning were manifest in historical events. It is the very absence of meaning in the events themselves that motivates the quest. . . . Single events as such are not meaningful, nor is a mere succession of events. To venture a statement about the meaning of historical events is possible only when their *telos* becomes apparent" (Löwith 1949, 4–5). Similarly, Gadamer argues that the *Bewußtsein,* in many ways analogous to Kant's notion of *Anschauung,* does not impose a historical structure of *Kontinuität* on the *Erfahrung* of time itself, but rather on the *Erfahrung* of *Geschehens.* For Gadamer, History is not what actually took place in past time, but a meaning-full organization of human *Geschehens,* an imposing of continuity on that which would otherwise remain a dis-continuous cluster of happenings. Past-time does not have an inherent order or structure; it is, rather, an accumulation of days—a *Diskontinuität des Geschehens* (Gadamer 1986, 2:139, 138), and the man-nexus, by the imposition of continuity, creates *(poiein)* his own hermeneia. Thus, Gadamer argues that Nietzsche's concept of interpretation is more radical than Heidegger's, because Nietzsche did not appeal to the "Auffindung eines vorhandenen Sinnes, sondern die Setzung von Sinn im Dienst des 'Willens zur Macht'" (Gadamer 1986, 2:333; cf. 339–40). Finally, Merleau-Ponty argues that the *monde perçu,* which he qualifies as *l'être brut* or *sauvage,* and which he identifies as the object of all apperceptual activity, is more than any painting, parole, or attitude. Of his

two types of interpretive activity, Merleau-Ponty identifies the *logos proforikos* or the logos of perception as fundamentally philosophical in nature. He qualifies this logos of perception by saying that it is an activity that perceives the *être brut*, because when philosophy grasps *être* (Heidegger's *Sein*) in its universality, it "appears to contain everything that shall ever be said, and yet permits us to create it" (Merleau-Ponty 1964, 224).

8. Merleau-Ponty uses the term nexus in this same sense of meeting point or *Urstiftung*. See Merleau-Ponty 1964, 312.

9. Philosophical hermeneutics is an attempt to establish a method of interpreting flux or change—Gadamer's "verfließende Zeit" (Gadamer 1986, 2:135). Cf. Heidegger: "Das Beständige im Vergangenen, dasgenige, worauf die historische Erklärung das Einmalige und Mannigfaltige der Geschichte verrechnet, ist das Immer-schon-einmal-Dagewesene, das Vergleichbare" (Heidegger 1980, 80).

10. All translations from the Greek are mine, based either upon the Greek text of the Loeb edition or the Belles Lettres edition.

11. For the transformation of hermeneutics from the study of objective text to a psychology of *Verstehen* and finally to a psychology of interpretation, see Gadamer's discussions in "Klassische und philosophische Hermeneutik" (1986, 2:98–100, 104), "Zur Problematik des Selbstverständnisses" (1986, 2:123–26, 132), and in "Hermeneutik und Historismus" (1965, 387–88, 393).

12. Texts are the primary informants of past-time, and their idealization is subtle, yet unavoidable. Thus the artistic re-production of a text's milieu, e.g., language, tone, and expression, all elements of what Gadamer calls *Sprachlichkeit* or linguisticity (Gadamer 1990, 1:64f., 73, 112, 143ff., 184ff., 232ff., 387–409, 436, 444, 465, 496f.; Gadamer 1986, 2:143), plays a central role in Gadamer's hermeneutic. Gadamer especially develops the notion of text in the "in-between world of language" in his essay "Text und Interpretation" (1983), (Gadamer 1986, 2:330ff.). Kisiel summarizes Gadamer's concept of text in the following manner: "Detached from its authors as well as its intended reader . . . [the written word] is elevated into the sphere of meaning pure and simple. Finally detached from the contingency of its origin, what is put down in writing is freed for new relations of meaning exceeding that which was intended by the author" (Kisiel 1972, 199).

13. Aristotle, for example, claims that unlike the poet, whose task *(ergon)* is to speak of what *could* come about, the historian's task is to relate things that have *in fact* come about (Aristotle 1979, 1451a36–1451b11).

14. Thucydides com-posed *(syg-grapho)* his *History of the Peloponnesian War* to enable readers "to make a clear assessment both of the events that have happened and of similar such events that, according to the wonts of man, shall again some day come to be; to adjudge these things profitable shall be enough [for me]" (Thucydides 1977, 1:22, 4). For the different uses of *syg-grapho,* see 1:97.2.5, 2:70.5.3, 2:103.2.3, 3:25.2.5, 3:88.4.4, 3:116.3.3, 4:51.8, 4:104.4.7, 4:135.2.3, 5:35.3.8, 5:41.3.4, 6:7.4.7, 6:93.4.7, 7:18.4.9, 8:6.5.8, 8:60.3.8, 8:67.1, 4–5, 8:67.2.5.

15. Herodotus com-poses *(syg-grapho)* his histories "lest the things done by men should be blotted out of memory by time, lest the great and marvelous deeds wrought by both Greeks and foreigners should become without glory, and especially in order to show the cause for which they warred with one another" (Herodotus 1990, 1:1,3). For the uses of *syg-grapho* in Herodotus, see 1:47.8, 1:48.2, 7:142.2, 8:135.8 (transcribing inspired utterances); 3:103.2 (describing or com-posing the form of a camel); 6:14.4 (relating details of a battle).

16. Cf. Heidegger: "Im ständigen Vergleichen von allem mit allem wird das Verständliche herausgerechnet und als der Grundriß der Geschichte bewährt und befestigt" (Heidegger 1980, 80–81).

17. For Gadamer's discussion of historical *Verstehens* and *Überlieferung*, see "Klas-

sische und philosophische Hermeneutik" (Gadamer 1986, 2:96–97), and "Zur Problematik des Selbstverständnisses" (Gadamer 1986 2:122–23).

18. Merleau-Ponty speaks of a second type of interpretive or hermeneutic activity, namely, the *logos endiathetos* or the logos of construction, as an activity of iterating the *Lebenswelt*. Concerning this *logos endiathetos* he says: "We make a philosophy of the Lebenswelt," and "our construction (in the mode of logic) enables us to find again this world of silence" (Merleau-Ponty 1964, 224), concluding that philosophy seeks to guide past-time into new expression—a philosophical construction, through poetic mimesis. Cf. Gadamer 1986, 2:371.

19. Merleau-Ponty uses the term *restitution* to describe the historian's re-creation of the historical life-milieu (Merleau-Ponty 1964, 289, 296–98). Cf. Nancy: *"si l'ekmathesis* consiste à apprendre *ce que dit* le poète à travers son dire, l'*hermeneia* consiste à restituer le poète dans ses vers, à *le faire dire* dans ses propres dires" (Nancy 1982, 57).

20. Among those who have held to this type of History-qua-Art tradition, Humboldt writes that "[a]n historical presentation, like an artistic presentation, is an imitation of nature. . . . We must, therefore, not disdain to apply the more readily recognizable method of the artist to an understanding of the more dubious method employed by the historian" (Humboldt 1973, 10). Ranke also argued for the artistic quality of historical re-production, emphasizing the true character of the historical: "If historical art would . . . succeed in giving life to this subject matter and in reproducing it with that part of poetic power which does not think up new things but mirrors in its true character that which has been grasped and comprehended, it would . . . unite in its own peculiar manner science and art at the same time" (Ranke 1973, 44; cf. 33–34). Finally, Kisiel explains Gadamer's theory of hermeneutical repetition not only as cultural translation, but as an artistic re-presentation of an original piece: "[T]he interpretation is not evoked in place of the text . . . but is in fact the text itself in terms of the meaning it presents in the current situation. . . . The reproduction re-presents the work itself, makes it present again, no matter how far removed in time it originally may have been, and in fact in such a way that the work undergoes an enhancement in Being. And the work depends on the reproduction in order to represent itself, through which it obtains its authentic Being" (Kisiel 1972, 199–200). In a similar summary, the translator of the English edition of *Truth and Method* (New York: The Crossroad Publishing Co., 1989), pp. xiv–xv, states that " [i]n the interrelations of "original" *(Urbild)* and "picture" *(Bild)*, Gadamer wants to stress that we find not mimetic repetition . . . of the real, but a process . . . where the original reality comes to its fullest self-presentation in the picture and where the tie between original and picture is never broken. But as art, this interrelation is fully real only each time it is represented, exhibited, brought into the actuality of our participation in it." Gadamer himself makes very clear statements concerning the nature of History as *Kunst*, which idea of course assumes as a prerequisite the legitimacy of culturally translating past happenings: "die Geschichte [muß] von jeder neuen Gegenwart neu geschrieben werden" (Gadamer 1986, 2:333). Gadamer derives much of his concept of the re-presentative nature of the hermeneutical *Kunst*—the art of making the past *an-wesend* through aesthetic re-production (Gadamer 1986, 2:104, 332–33), from Heidegger's concept of Greek *teknē*: "Die *teknē* ist als griechisch erfahrenes Wissen insofern ein Hervorbringen des Seienden, als es das Anwesende als ein solches *aus* der Verborgenheit *her* eigens *in* die Unverborgenheit seines Aussehens *vor* bringt" (Heidegger 1980, 45; cf. Gadamer 1986, 2:366). In "Die Zeit des Weltbildes" (1980, esp. 101–3, and 106), Heidegger more fully fleshes out the concept of *das Seiende* as an expression of *An-wesenheit.*

21. For a discussion on the rational parameters governing the making of History, see Aiken 1991, 226, 234–36.

22. The *dépouillement* of past-time according to rational criteria is almost impossible to justify methodologically, because the hermeneut is called to go beyond information materially communicated in an historical text in order to determine what *truly* occurred, namely, what the author of the text really must have seen based on what he rationally *could* "in fact" have seen (Aiken 1991, 229).

23. In an argument against "naive history," Nickles would call this a charge of "residual whiggism": "Historians . . . retain the scientists' practice of 'putting the phenomena first.' By explaining . . . the process of research in terms of the products, historians continue to invert history. This practice is unhistorical in smuggling in precognition, in taking as given and unproblematic what had to be historically constructed by human activity, that which now needs historical explanation" (Nickles 1992, section 1:87).

WORKS CITED

Aiken, D. Wyatt. 1991. "History, Truth, and the Rational Mind: Why It Is Impossible to Take Myth out of History." *Theologische Zeitschrift.*

Alain. 1958. *Les Arts et les Dieux.* Paris: Éditions Gallimard, La Pléiade.

Aristotle. 1979. *The Poetics.* Paris: Belles Lettres.

Connolly, John M., and Thomas Keutner, eds. 1988. *Hermeneutics Versus Science? Three German Views.* Essays by H. -G. Gadamer, E.K. Specht, and W. Stegmüller. Indiana: University of Notre Dame Press.

Eissfeldt, Otto. 1934. *Einleitung in das Alte Testament.* Tübingen: J.C.B. Mohr Verlag.

Frye, Northrop. 1957. *Anatomy of Criticism.* New Jersey: Princeton University Press.

Gadamer Hans-Georg. 1972. "The Science of the Life-World." *Analecta Husserliana.* Vol. 2, *The Later Husserl and the Idea of Phenomenology,* edited by Anna-Teresa Tymieniecka. Holland: D. Reidel Publishing Co.

———. 1986. *Gesammelte Werke.* Band 2, *Hermeneutik 2. Wahrheit und Methode: Ergänzungen Register.* Tübingen: J.C.B. Mohr. "Das problem der Geschichte in der neueren deutschen Philosophie." (1943)
"Die Kontinuität der Geschichte und der Augenblick der Existenz." (1965)
"Klassische und philosophische Hermeneutik." (1968)
"Zur Problematik des Selbstverständnisses." (1961)
"Text und Interpretation." (1983)
"Destruktion und Dekonstruktion." (1985)
"Hermeneutik und Historismus." (1965)

———. 1990. *Gesammelte Werke.* Band 1, *Hermeneutik 1. Wahrheit und Methode: Grundzüge einer philosophischen Hermeneutik.* Tübingen: J.C.B. Mohr.

— ———. 1992. "Reflections on my Philosophical Journey." Trans. Richard E. Palmer. Mimeo. (This appears as Gadamer's intellectual autobiography in this volume.)

Gide, André. 1958. *Les caves du vatican.* Paris: Gallimard.

———. 1968. *Paludes.* Paris: Gallimard.

Heidegger, Martin. 1979. *Sein und Zeit.* Tübingen: Max Niemeyer Verlag.

———. 1980. *Holzwege.* Frankfurt am Main: Klostermann.
"Der Ursprung des Kunstwerkes." (1935/36)
"Die Zeit des Weltbildes." (1938)

Herodotus. 1990. *Histories.* Cambridge: Harvard University Press. Loeb Classical Library.

Hölderlin, Friedrich. 1977. *Werke, Briefe, Dokumente.* München: Winkler Verlag.

Humboldt, Wilhelm von. 1973. "On the Historian's Task." (1821) In *The Theory and Practice of History.* New York: The Bobbs-Merrill Company.

Husserl, Edmund. 1970. *The Crisis of European Sciences and Transcendental Phenomenology.* Evanston: Northwestern University Press.

Kisiel, T. 1972. "Repetition in Gadamer's Hermeneutics." *Analecta Husserliana.* Vol. 2, *The Later Husserl and the Idea of Phenomenology.* Edited by Anna-Teresa Tymieniecka. Holland: D. Reidel Publishing Co.

Kundera, Milan. 1984. *The Unbearable Lightness of Being.* New York: Harper and Row.

Löwith, Karl. 1949. *Meaning in History.* Chicago: The University of Chicago Press.

Merleau-Ponty, Maurice. 1964. *Le Visible et l'Invisible.* Paris: Gallimard.

———. 1968. *Résumés de cours* (Collège de France, 1952–1960). Paris: Gallimard.

Nancy, Jean-Luc. 1982. *Le partage des voix.* Paris: Éditions Galilée.

Nickles, Thomas. 1992. "Good Science as Bad History: From Order of Knowing to Order of Being." In *The Social Dimensions of Science,* edited by Ernan McMullin. South Bend: University of Notre Dame Press.

Nietzsche, Friedrich. 1964. "Der Fall Wagner." *Sämtliche Werke,* Band 8. Stuttgart: Alfred Kröner Verlag.

———. 1964. "Vom Nutzen und Nachteil der Historie für das Leben." *Unzeitgemässe Betrachtungen. Sämtliche Werke,* Band 2. Stuttgart: Alfred Kröner Verlag.

Ranke, Leopold von. 1973. *The Theory and Practice of History.* New York: The Bobbs-Merrill Company.

Simonnet, Dominique. 1992. "Quand les femmes rattrapent l'Histoire." *L'Express* (February 14).

Spinoza, Benedict de. 1951. *A Theologico-Political Treatise.* New York: Dover Publications, Inc.

Thucydides. 1977. *History of the Peloponnesian War.* Cambridge: Harvard University Press, Loeb Classical Library.

Unesco. 1966. *Kierkegaard vivant.* Symposium in Paris organized by Unesco in April 1964. Paris: Gallimard.

Warnke, Georgia. 1987. *Gadamer: Hermeneutics, Tradition, and Reason.* California: Stanford University Press.

REPLY TO D. WYATT AIKEN

It is not easy for me to grasp the real point of this contribution. This could be a linguistic problem. Contrary to what is natural to a German, the author does not understand 'absence' *(Abwesenheit)* spatially. He understands it rather temporally and means the past and what has been *(das Gewesene)*. Thus it becomes difficult for us when he understands as the opposite of what is absent *(des Anwesenden)* the present and what cannot be removed, so to speak, and when he contrasts this with what is light, mobile, and stands in bright light, something we know for instance from the peculiar idealization of the deceased. Insofar as the basic structure of historical events is concerned, the author is surely right: it is certainly not simply a sequence of episodes, but presents itself as a firm nexus. The Greek word *Symphora* almost means a heavy fate and, in any case, it cannot be entirely dissolved in *ratio*.

From this the author makes the transition to Schleiermacher and the element of poetic *mimēsis* which he finds there. Obviously, this has its validity for biblical history too. There is certainly a convincing difference between the chronicler who was an eye witness, and who guarantees reality in this way and, on the other hand, the historical tradition which cannot claim the same firmness of reality. What we attribute to myth is certainly not entirely independent of logic, and myth influences our comprehension of the meaning of historical connections. Apparently, this is what the author has in mind. Likewise in the field of the historical he wants to validate something of the rationality of the possible and in this way concede to history a certain proximity to poetic freedom. I think this is implied in the linguisticality of speaking.

H.-G.G.

21

Donald Davidson

GADAMER AND PLATO'S *PHILEBUS*

In 1931 Gadamer published his first book, *Platos dialektische Ethik;* a second edition, with additions, came out in 1968; the first edition was reprinted in 1982; and an English translation *(Plato's Dialectical Ethics)* appeared in 1991.[1] The book was Gadamer's *Habilitationsschrift,* written under the supervision of Martin Heidegger. It would be strange to make this early work, written more than sixty years ago, the launching platform for a discussion of, or reaction to, certain lasting themes in Gadamer's writings if it were not for two things: despite the enormous enlargement in the areas and problems on which Gadamer has worked, the direction in which his ideas were to develop was already quite clear. The second thing is personal: where Gadamer sensed from the start the goal he would pursue, and pursued it with brilliant success, I by chance started in somewhat the same place (but without the clear goal) and have, by what seems to me a largely accidental but *commodius vicus* of recirculation, arrived in Gadamer's intellectual neighborhood.

Plato's Dialectical Ethics is, as its author points out in the preface to the first edition, really two extended essays. The first of these essays is a general discussion of Plato's dialectic, and its basis in dialogue. It is clear that though the ostensible purpose is to allow us to approach the Platonic texts with a fresh eye, Gadamer is also illustrating not only his idea of how the interpretation of any text is to proceed, but the foundation of the possibility of objective thought. Gadamer makes no excuses for the "distance" between the issues he raises and the actual texts of Plato; on the contrary, he advertises this distance: "The closer these interpretations adhere to Plato's text, the more distant they are from their task of clearing the way toward that text. The more distant they are from the world of Plato's language and thought, on the other hand, the closer I believe they come to performing their task."[2]

The second essay is on the text for which the first essay clears the way: Plato's *Philebus.* At first this dialogue seems a curious choice. It is in many ways an awkward piece. The construction lacks the easy grace of many of the early and middle dialogues: highly general and abstract passages are seemingly patched together with the most practical consideration of what makes various pleasures worthwhile; details expand to pages while vital issues are passed over. What role the Forms play, if any, is unclear; yet this is a treatise on the highest good for man. Most unsettling of all is the fact that Socrates practices the elenctic method in ways that are highly reminiscent of the early dialogues, while at the same time promoting doctrines with which he is not explicitly associated in any other dialogue—indeed, doctrines not easy to identify elsewhere in the Platonic corpus. Perhaps it is not surprising that the text is apparently corrupt in some of the most troublesome passages, almost as if copiers could not believe what they were reading, and attempted crude improvements. One has only to glance at Jowett's translation of the *Philebus* to appreciate how strongly he was tempted to warp what is plainly in the text in the effort to make it fit with what Jowett felt was the true Platonic line.

None of this fazes Gadamer. While he is a superb classicist, and discusses textual problems when they seem important, his interest in the *Philebus* is entirely centered on its philosophical content. This makes Gadamer's book unique. There is not, as far as I know, anything like it; not in English, not in German, not in French, is there another book about the *Philebus,* or an edition or translation, which concentrates on the ethical, methodological, and ontological thought in the dialogue. Gadamer's book is, as he plainly intended, not only an eye-opening account of what is to be found in Plato, not only a stunning essay on the origins of objectivity in communal discussion; it is a demonstration of what the interpretation of a text can be.

It was about the year 1938 that I became interested in the *Philebus;* I was an undergraduate at Harvard, studying Greek and philosophy. My concern with the dialogue was more literary than philosophical; to be more accurate, I was interested in the history of ideas. Under the influence of the writings of Cherniss and of my tutors, particularly John Finley, Harry Levin, and Theodore Spencer, I became fascinated with the hints of Pythagoreanism in the *Philebus,* and the suggestion that in this dialogue one finds apparent confirmation of some of Aristotle's reports of Plato's late views. I also proposed that the *Philebus,* if not actually the promised dialogue on the Philosopher which was to follow the *Sophist* and the *Politicus,* could be viewed as a sort of substitute for it. When the time came, a few years later, to write a doctoral dissertation, I naturally turned to the *Philebus.* It was then that I came across Gadamer's book. Being a product of American education, neither my German nor my Greek was very good (they still aren't), and so I unfortunately learned very little from Gadamer; for one thing, the Heideggerian background of his ideas was completely unfamiliar to me. What I did notice, however, was the concentration on the philosophical content for its own sake, and this impressed me.

My progress toward the Ph.D. was interrupted by the war; after the war I took on heavy teaching duties, and it was not until 1949 that I completed my degree. Meanwhile my interests had largely shifted from the history of philosophy to the analytic problems of the period. As a result my dissertation on the *Philebus* was a rather plodding attempt to see Plato as much as possible in the light of the contemporary methods and issues with which I was involved.[3] Plato slowly receded into the background of my thoughts, though from time to time I taught a course or a seminar on the later dialogues until, in 1985, I was invited to give the S. J. Keeling Memorial Lecture in Greek Philosophy at University College, London. This led to a renewed interest in Plato and the *Philebus;* I read some of the more recent literature, and was particularly struck by the treatment of the elenchus by my friend and former colleague from Princeton, Gregory Vlastos. Vlastos was engaged in writing his magisterial book on Socrates.[4] He was mainly concerned to distinguish, even contrast, the views of Socrates and Plato, and so his treatment of the elenchus, which he considered to be characteristically Socratic, was restricted to the early dialogues; already in the *Meno,* he thought, Plato had taken over from his mentor. I was impressed, however, with the extent to which the *Philebus* seemed to mark a return to the earlier methodology, with the extent to which its concern with human virtue looked back to the early dialogues, and with the fact that Socrates again guided the discussion without assuming he knew all the answers in advance. In writing my Keeling Lecture, "Plato's Philosopher," I found it natural to connect my present philosophical interests with what I now found in the *Philebus.*[5] Thus there is a certain parallel between my experience and Gadamer's with one of Plato's oddest dialogues; and a vast difference. The dialogue touched both of us near the beginnings of our professional careers, and it connects with our present interests. The difference is that Gadamer appreciated from the start what was in the dialogue for him, and though his views developed, and his interpretation of Plato underwent some change, he never backed away from the thesis that free discussion is the source of human understanding, nor from his recognition that Plato had revealed and exploited this truth; I, on the other hand, lost my fascination with Plato over a period of decades, and only recently, and by a very different path from Gadamer's, have come to grasp some of what I dimly, if at all, understood the first time around.

The *Philebus* opens with a discussion led by Socrates that is more reminiscent of the early elenctic dialogues in mood and method than anything else in Plato's middle or late dialogues. The question to be decided is what is most excellent and advantageous in a human life; or, as the issue is sharpened, what is the character of the best life. Socrates and Philebus each have a candidate answer: Philebus says the good is pleasure, Socrates that it is wisdom. As in the early dialogues, Socrates does not claim to know the answer; he insists that only a free discussion can hope to illuminate the subject. He is determined that his interlocutor shall say what he really thinks, and not merely strive for a verbal victory. It may well be, as Gadamer suggests, that Protarchus takes over the "defense" of Philebus's position because Philebus seems uninterested in an honest communal attempt to find the truth. Here, as elsewhere, Gadamer shows delicate insight into the human relations that shape the course of the discussion, arguing that only by appreciating all aspects of the context can we hope to understand the philosophical issues. It is a kind of insight for which he gives Plato enormous credit. When Gadamer calls his book *Plato's Dialectical Ethics,* what he mainly has in mind, he tells us, is the moral element in serious philosophical conversation, not the subject matter of the conversation in the *Philebus,* though that too is moral. As recently as 1989, Gadamer remarked, "The formula 'dialectical ethics' indicates an intention that remains throughout all of my later work."[6]

Gadamer is equally interested in how Plato illustrates the creative aspects of discussion, and what he has to say about the dialectical method; this is at least one reason for his fascination with the *Philebus.* Given his (laudable) view that a satisfactory interpretation of a text may be "distant" from it, Gadamer is more than justified in not remarking on several unusual features of the elenctic discussion of the *Philebus.* But there may be a gain in pointing some of these features out. One I have already mentioned: there is no comparable example among the other late dialogues. In fact, there is only one other dialogue now considered late in which Socrates plays a leading part in the discussion, and that is the *Theaetetus.* The reemergence of Socrates thus coincides with the return to the early Socratic method. This is plausibly explained by the return to a typically Socratic subject, the good life; and there may be a further reason, which I shall mention presently.

The method is that of the elenctic, but the pattern is not standard. In the early dialogues, though Socrates claims ignorance of the truth, he is never shown to be wrong; rather, the proposals of the interlocutor are always found wanting. In the *Philebus,* both Socrates's and Philebus's original proposals are rejected in favor of a third position, which is then accepted by the main discussants. This is perhaps the most strikingly original feature of the dialogue's method. That is, the early dialogues end without a clear answer to their various questions, and the middle and other late dialogues put forward answers not in the course of dialogue but as "found" objects; but in the *Philebus* the answer emerges directly from the conversational exchange. While Gadamer titles the first part of *Plato's Dialectical Ethics* "Conversation and the Way We Come to Shared Understanding," he does not emphasize how seldom conversation is seen to result in shared understanding in Plato's writings.

Another, and related, feature of the *Philebus* is the discussion of the "method of collection and division," and the use to which that method is put. The method had been introduced in the *Sophist,* and further employed in the *Politicus* (I assume here that the *Philebus* was composed after those two dialogues). The method could not have been made explicit before the *Sophist,* since it depends on the "blending" of ideas which is shown for the first time in that dialogue to be consistent with the essential unity of the ideas. Collection is the process, for which there is no fixed method, of discovering, intuiting or hunting out, and then defining, the genus to which the subject at hand belongs. Since collection includes definition (or the provision of a "criterion"), the result of collection, and the testing of its adequacy, can include the employment of the elenctic. But collection may differ from the method of the early dialogues in at least two ways: where the early dialogues typically revolve around the search for just one idea, an idea which defines some virtue or ultimate value, collection often arrives at the genus by surveying subordinate universals, and the genus may not define a value or goal, but merely help to place the topic under study. Division is the process of discerning the species and subspecies on down to the infima species which fall under the genus. As in the case of collection, Plato stresses the fact that neither of these aspects of the dialectic can be mechanized; art is required at each stage, both in perceiving the right overarching idea under which to gather the rest, and in "dividing at the joints."

Collection and division are put to quite a different use in the *Philebus* than they were in the *Sophist* and the *Politicus*. The genus which is subdivided in the *Sophist* is art, and the sophist is defined by naming the species to which he belongs, and describing how it differs from other species of art. The statesman is found in a species of science. In theory, the sole function of the method of collection and division in these dialogues is to make clear the essential nature of one of the subdivisions. Contrast this with its role in the *Philebus*. The opening question was: which is the good life, the life of pleasure or the life of the intellect? An elenctic investigation ends with agreement that neither of these lives is as good as a life that combines pleasure with intellectual abilities and activities. The discussion that provides the criteria by which the excellence of a life is to be judged may be thought of as a collection, but this is certainly not a genus that is subsequently divided. Division is rather practiced twice over, once to uncover the differences among the sorts of pleasure, and once to distinguish the various mental aptitudes. These two divisions form much of the bulk of the dialogue, and they serve not only to make clear the "ingredients" that are available for inclusion in the good life, but also to emphasize the aspects of the potential choices that suit them for inclusion or exclusion.

At this point it is obvious that collection and division have done what they can to delineate the good life; it is equally obvious that the good life has not yet been described, for that requires the exercise of judgment in selecting the best blend of pleasures and intellectual elements. Plato's method, at least in the *Philebus,* comprises three parts: collection, division, and combination. Only the third part shows how the purely theoretical exercise that precedes it can be applied to the world, to a life. I am inclined to include the third part in the overall description of the developed Platonic dialectic. This inclusion is not, I confess, directly confirmed by the text: Plato mentions only collection and division in the section on the dialectic (15D–17A). This section is, however, directly followed by two familiar examples of the application of the dialectical method, and reflection on these examples reinforces the idea that combination was part of Plato's method. One example is phonetics, or the "art of letters." What is presented to the senses is undifferentiated sound as it issues from human mouths; this is the subject matter of the art. But collection requires that we discover the "seal of unity" that unites this subject matter. Plato credits an Egyptian, Theuth, with having collected sound into three species, vowels, mutes, and sonants, and these in turn into the generic concept "letter." Collection in this case partly depends on what then becomes the division of the letters into the three sorts; this process is then followed by the division of each of the species into the individual letters. Is this all there is to the art of letters? Of course not: the art must include the ability to assemble letters into words and words into sentences and sentences into narrative or poetry or a lecture. Plato's second example proves the same point. The art of music requires more than that we discover the genus (which may variously be interpreted as note, scale, or interval) and the various subdivisions of the genus; it requires in addition the ability to blend or combine these elements in a pleasing way.

The combining of elements in view here should not be confused with the blending of the ideas of which so much is made in the *Sophist*. That blending traces out the analytic relations among concepts: it tells us such truths as that, while biped and quadruped each blend with animal, they do not blend with each other. These are the truths with which division is concerned, truths of logic in a broad sense. The combining of elements that have been revealed by division is an entirely different matter, and requires a skill of higher order. Plato explains the methodological and ontological considerations that lie behind this skill as involving a fourfold classification of entities: the unlimited, the limit, the mixture, and the cause of the mixture. We can, very roughly, think of these four sorts of entity as follows. An unlimited is any entity viewed merely as determinable; a limit is a defining shape, proportion, or number; a mixture is any definite object—metaphorically, it is a mixture of an unlimited and a limit. Somewhat less metaphorically, it is an entity whose parts or aspects are fixed in relation to one another, as the good life is a mixture of pleasures and intellectual elements. The fourth entity, the cause of the mixture, is the rational agency which creates the mixture.

When this new apparatus is employed to answer the question as to which is the more significant part of the good life, pleasure or mind, the answer is overdetermined. Many varieties of pleasure, but none of mind, are not limited; they depend on alteration, as in the relief of pain. Mind shares with the purer pleasures a part in the final mixture that makes up the good life; but far more important is the fact that mind is the cause of the very mixture of which it is part.

I have reviewed this much of the structure of the *Philebus* for a purpose. I mentioned the fact that this dialogue is in some ways a return to a theme and a method of Plato's earlier works: the theme is a human aspect of the good; the method is elenctic. The return is symbolized by the fact that Socrates here makes a last appearance as the leader of the discussion. Now I want to stress the extent to which the *Philebus* diverges from what might have been expected from the author of the *Phaedrus* or the *Republic* on the same subject.

The essential use of division is justified only by the discussion in the *Sophist* which makes clear the sense in which the ideas can be "divided"; this in turn answers a difficulty raised in the *Parmenides*. The real significance of this discovery is not, however, the discovery of a sense in which the unity of each idea is compatible with its being many. The real significance is the recognition that the ideas cannot serve this necessary analytic or epistemic purpose and at the same time serve as norms, as patterns of positive value. Thus when art is divided in the search for the sophist, a number of the species are of unattractive types: one is the hired hunter of rich young men, another is the maker of false conceits of wisdom. The ideas which represent or constitute these species are not norms that set positive values. Similarly in the *Philebus,* among the classifications are the many impure, or "mixed," types of pleasure; these are all to be rejected in the most desirable life. We also remember Parmenides's teasing question to the young Socrates, whether there are ideas of hair or mud or dirt "or any other trivial and undignified objects." Socrates denies that there are such ideas; Parmenides gently suggests that this is because he is still young; when philosophy has taken hold of him more firmly, he will not despise such objects. Plato took the point to heart: he preserved the epistemological and semantic features of the earlier ideas, but divorced them from their normative role. This also solved another problem: if, by participating in them, particulars came to share some of the value of the ideas, there was the embarrassing question whether this resemblance of particular to idea did not require yet another idea.

Having given up the ideas as the source and explanation of value, Plato needed a new account, and this was provided by the concept of a well-proportioned, rationally generated mixture. Commentators on the *Philebus* have tried to locate the ideas somewhere in the fourfold ontology of unlimited, limit, mixture, and cause, but no consensus has emerged. This is not surprising; the ideas, as employed in the *Philebus,* did their work in implementing collection and division. The remaining task, of combining in the right way the elements revealed by division, was a task for which the ideas could no longer consistently be used. The fourfold ontology has a further purpose, that of providing a framework in which the powers of the mind, of judging, selecting and combining the parts or aspects of a balanced, functioning mixture, can be understood. It is an error to expect to find the ideas in this practice-oriented classification.

In the *Republic* we are led to think of the ideas, particularly the idea of the good, as the source of all that is real. The ideas are therefore generative, a source of existence. In the *Philebus,* the ideas no longer have this power or function: they are neutral classifiers, known, of course, only to the mind, but powerless in themselves to bring anything into existence. Mind has become the sole mover, as well as the source of value. Here, as in the case of the elenctic method, there is a return to the early dialogues: the ideas in dialogues like the *Euthyphro* and *Laches* are what "make" each case of piety a pious act, or an act of courage courageous. But there is no suggestion that this "make" is generative in character. Though for the most part only ideas of virtues are discussed, the ideas themselves are not put forward as a source of value, nor is there a claim that they exist separately from particulars. I think it is no accident that the return, in the *Philebus,* to the early, purely epistemic, use of the ideas, is accompanied by a return to the elenctic method. There is a trajectory in Plato's thinking about how to discover what is good or has value. In the early dialogues, there is little discussion of method; it is simply assumed that the elenchus can lead to truths about what is good and virtuous. Presently Plato appears to have become dissatisfied with this reliance on the elenctic method; the theory of ideas is made explicit, and it is elaborated by adding the doctrine of anamnesis, and the whole metaphysical apparatus of the *Republic.* During this period, as Vlastos emphasizes, the use of the elenchus gives way to an openly didactic style: we are urged to view the realm of ideas as the repository not only of truth but of all value and reality. With the *Parmenides,* various difficulties with the metaphysical doctrine of ideas are aired, but not answered. In the *Theaetetus,* the ideas apparently drop out of sight, and there is a brilliant study of the concept of ordinary empirical knowledge. The *Sophist* and *Politicus,* by stressing the concept of division, reinforce the doubts of the *Parmenides.* I would place the *Philebus* just here, as if, as I suggested in my dissertation, this dialogue were some sort of substitute for the promised dialogue on the Philosopher, following the studies of the Sophist and the Politician. Now deprived of the normative and generative theory of ideas, Plato makes explicit an addition to his methodological tools, an addition which can take their place—the theory of the mixture and its cause.

The renewed and refreshed use of the conversational, interpersonal method of the elenchus makes the *Philebus* particularly relevant to Gadamer's discussion of the dialectic in the first chapter of *Plato's Dialectical Ethics.* This discussion makes little mention of the *Philebus;* its function is to prepare the way for the interpretation of that dialogue (in the second chapter) by drawing its examples from various other dialogues. Thus the organization of the book inadvertently leaves in shadow the extent to which the dialectic of the *Philebus* differs from the dialectic of the earlier dialogues, and, in a quite different way, from the dialectic of the middle dialogues.

Gadamer is, of course, fully aware of the features which make the *Philebus* unique. In the introduction to *Plato's Dialectical Ethics* he writes,

The fact that the *Philebus*'s position in regard to ontology is identical with the general Platonic position that we call the doctrine of the Forms cannot conceal the distinctive concentration of the *Philebus*'s inquiry on the ethical problem—that is, on the good in *human* life. The goal, after all, is to argue from the general ontological idea of the good precisely to the good of actual human existence. In the context of this substantive intention we are given a thorough dialectical analysis of hēdonē (pleasure) and epistēmē (knowledge), an analysis whose positive content and methodological attitude both make the *Philebus* the proper basis for an interpretation of the specifically Aristotelian problem of a science of ethics.[7]

A few pages later, Gadamer speaks of "the derivation and philosophical coherence of the unity of dialogue and dialectic which *only* the *Philebus,* out of all Plato's literary works, presents in this way."[8]

The treatment of pleasure as a necessary ingredient in the good life for a person is particularly emphasized by Gadamer; this shows a human orientation not so clearly marked elsewhere. This corresponds to the quite different role played earlier by the idea of the good:

> One should note that unlike the *Republic,* the *Philebus* does not inquire about the idea of the Good and its function as a paradigm for human life; rather its questioning is the opposite of that. It asks how the concrete life of human beings with all its contingency and impurity, and determined as it is by impulse and pleasure just as much as by knowledge and insight, can nevertheless be good, i.e., can participate in the Good.[9]

In the recent interview mentioned above, Gadamer discusses his view of the *Philebus* as it developed over the years. He sees it as the connecting link between the Socrates of the early dialogues and Aristotle's ethics; in each case there is the concern with "the question of the good for human existence."

The differences between the early dialogues, the middle dialogues, and the *Philebus* are thus not ignored, but at the same time they are muted. These differences, even the differences between Plato and Aristotle, are seen more as a matter of emphasis, of "highlighting," of adjustment of method to subject, than as actual inconsistencies. The picture is not one of stasis, but of a fixed center about which there is movement; for example, "the *Philebus*'s position in regard to ontology is identical with the general Platonic position that we call the doctrine of the Forms." I suppose it is a question how far a "general position" can be stretched before it tears. But it seems to me that it is difficult to bring the Socratic dialogues, which make no mention of a realm of separate ideas which are the only reality, and the source of all value and existence, into line with the middle dialogues which do so treat the ideas. Nor do I see how to reconcile the ideas of the *Philebus* (which are in a clear sense divisible) with either the "ones" which Socrates seeks to define, or the ideas of the *Phaedrus* and *Republic.*

How far to emphasize the continuities among Socrates, the periods of Plato's thought, and the periods of Aristotle's thought on the one hand, and the differences that separate them on the other, is a matter of delicate judgment. If I have been emphasizing the differences, it is not for the sake of airing my particular vision, but because there seems to me some discrepancy between Gadamer's own idea of understanding, and his resistance to finding real development in Plato's attitudes and methods. To put this positively: I think a Platonic dialectic seen as more open to serious revision would cohabit more happily with Gadamer's own conception of dialogue and conversation.

I accept Gadamer's demonstration that the *Philebus,* more than any other of Plato's works, both illustrates and describes "the way we come to shared understanding," "the motives of a concern for the facts of the matter in a shared world." The early elenctic dialogues contained many models of determined and devoted search for the essential nature of one virtue or another, or of virtue itself. There was Socrates's repeated insistence that his interlocutors say only what they really think, his concern that they follow with him every step of the way; and along with the ironic pretense that he could learn the truth from his interlocutors, there was Socrates's genuine modesty in confessing his own ignorance. But it seems to me these dialogues nevertheless fall short of the ideal of a communal search for understanding in at least two ways. First, there is the vast asymmetry, taken for granted by Socrates and his friends, that however ignorant Socrates was of the final truth, he was right in what he did claim; and he made some astonishing claims. Always the interlocutor, never Socrates, turned out to have inconsistent opinions. So even though Socrates sometimes seems genuinely to think he may learn something from the discussion, we are shown no real cases where this happens.

The second way in which these dialogues fail, at least to my mind, to embody the ideal of fruitful communication is that the discussants assume from the start that there is a fixed, definite answer to the deep moral questions asked. There is no suggestion that the goal as well as the search owes something to the human minds at work. Along with this assumption goes the unexpressed conviction that the words that enable the discussion have settled meanings; at the most, the parties to the dialogue may need to determine whether they mean the same thing by the same words; but this is something to find out, not something that may evolve. This attitude makes words the tools of discussion rather than a central aspect of what is to be made intelligible.

In these two matters, the *Philebus* differs from the early dialogues both in spirit and in theory. As I mentioned above, Socrates astonishingly turns out to have held at the start a thesis which must be abandoned. The study of the good life develops from a manifest exchange of originally opposed opinions. The goal is not fixed in advance, for the goal is not represented as a matter of finding the nature of some single idea, but rather as knowing the art of discriminating, judging, selecting, and mixing the appropriate elements of a life in a way that exhibits measure, proportion, and stability. The cause of this mixture is not some abstract, eternal principle, but the mind of the person who lives the life. The goal is in every sense a human goal: an end set by a human being for that human being. This humane conclusion, reached in the course of a collaborative dialogue, seems to me what must, in large part, have attracted Gadamer to the *Philebus* in the first place, and it exudes an attitude we find expressed throughout Gadamer's work.

"Language has its true being only in conversation, in the exercise of understanding between people."[10] This saying of Gadamer's goes far beyond the linguist's insistence on the primacy of spoken over written words, for it implies that only in the context of discussion does language come to have a content, to be language. (This is a view often attributed to Wittgenstein.) But Gadamer has a much more basic claim, that thought itself depends on language: "All understanding is interpretation, and all interpretation takes place in the medium of language which would allow the object to come into words."[11] "Language is not just one of man's possessions in the world, but on it depends the fact that man has a world at all."[12] Putting these themes together, we must conclude that it is only in interpersonal communication that there can be thought, a grasping of the fact of an objective, that is, a shared, world. Not only is it the case that the aim of conversation is "shared understanding"; we must also acknowledge that without sharing there is no understanding.

The reason for this is, in my opinion, that there is no other way to answer Wittgenstein's question, in what consists the difference between thinking one is following a rule, and actually following it. I interpret this as asking how words can have an objective reference, how sentences can have a truth value independent of the individual. Our thoughts and words carry us out into the world; this is why we can have true and false beliefs and say what is false as well as what is true. This connection with the world can be established only by shared reactions to a shared environment. "Speech, in its primordial form, is part of a shared having to do with something," as Gadamer puts it.[13] He goes on:

> Language, in which something comes to be language, is not a possession of one or the other of the interlocutors. Every conversation presupposes a common language, or, it creates a common language. Something is placed in the center, as the Greeks said, which the partners to the dialogue both share, and concerning which they can exchange ideas with one another. Hence agreement concerning the object, which it is the purpose of the conversation to bring about, necessarily means that a common language must first be worked out in the conversation. This is not an external matter of simply adjusting our tools, nor is it even right to say that the partners adapt themselves to one another but, rather, in the successful conversation they both come under the influence of the truth of the object and are thus bound to one another in a new community. To reach an understanding with one's partner in a dialogue is . . . a transformation into a communion, in which we do not remain what we were.[14]

I am in agreement with almost all of this. Where I differ (and this may merely show I have not fully understood Gadamer) is that I would not say a conversation presupposes a common language, nor even that it requires one. Understanding, to my mind, is always a matter not only of interpretation but of translation, since we can never assume we mean the same thing by our words that our partners in discussion mean. What is created in dialogue is not a common language but understanding; each partner comes to understand the other. And it also seems wrong to me to say agreement concerning an object demands that a common language first be worked out. I would say: it is only in the presence of shared objects that understanding can come about. Coming to an agreement about an object and coming to understand each other's speech are not independent moments but part of the same interpersonal process of triangulating the world.

DONALD DAVIDSON

DEPARTMENT OF PHILOSOPHY
UNIVERSITY OF CALIFORNIA AT BERKELEY
JANUARY 1993

NOTES

1. First edition (Leipzig: F. Meiner); German reprinting of the first edition (Hamburg: F. Meiner Verlag GmbH.); English edition (translated and with an introduction by Robert M. Wallace) (New Haven, Conn.: Yale University Press).

2. Gadamer, *Plato's Dialectical Ethics,* p. xxxv.

3. This curious product of my philosophical youth has now been published: *Plato's Philebus* (New York: Garland Publishing, 1990).

4. The book was not published until 1991: *Socrates: Ironist and Moral Philosopher* (Cambridge University Press).

5. "Plato's Philosopher," *The London Review of Books,* vol. 7, no. 14 (1985): 15–17.

6. From an interview published in the *Frankfurter Allgemeine* (October 1989). Translated in *Gadamer and Hermeneutics,* Hugh J. Silverman, ed. (New York: Routledge, 1991).

7. Gadamer, *Plato's Dialectical Ethics,* pp. 1, 2.

8. Ibid., p. 15.

9. *Dialogue and Dialectic; Eight Hermeneutical Studies on Plato* (New Haven, Conn.: Yale University Press, 1980), pp. 190–91.

10. Gadamer, *Truth and Method,* p. 404.

11. Ibid., p. 350.

12. Ibid., p. 401.

13. Gadamer, *Plato's Dialectical Ethics,* p. 29.

14. Gadamer, *Truth and Method,* p. 341.

REPLY TO DONALD DAVIDSON

The style of Donald Davidson's study is especially exciting and suspenseful. What characterizes both of our scholarly paths is no more nor less than a mutual overtaking of each other. I devoted my beginner's work, *"Platos dialektische Ethik,"* to the Platonic dialogue *Philebus,* and Davidson too devoted his first work, his dissertation with Werner Jaeger at Harvard, to this dialogue. In the interim, we have both let that theme fall away. Several times I made retractions with regard to my first work, and Davidson too returned to my later works again and again. One might be led to think that such a conversation during many decades should have led to a real proximity between us, and if a mutual appreciation is assumed as well, then one is certainly right to expect that proximity. It is thus all the more astonishing how great the distance and the differences with respect to the treatment of the same topic are on both sides. To a certain extent, Davidson is aware of this, and it is indeed the topic of his contribution to this volume. It is really astonishing for me to see how difficult it is to reenact the train of thought and the basic position of the other. It is hardly possible to discuss step by step this new work. But to make a beginning I will simply content myself with a few marginal comments: we are certainly not dealing with a competition between a classical philologist, which Donald Davidson was when he wrote his first work, and a philosopher, who was educated by Heidegger. That is not the point. Rather, the point is that more and more what both of us mean by philosophy is what we find in Plato. Through the provocations of Davidson's essay I cannot help but reply with a few new thoughts of my own about this point.

The primary theme of the *Philebus* is whether pleasure or contemplation is the highest in human life. It is not as it may sound, namely that two contradicting positions regarding the evaluation of human life are opposed to each other. In truth, right from the beginning the dialogue is concerned with two inseparable universal perspectives. Pleasures (in the broad sense of *hedoni*) are, so to speak, a true flourishing in the enactment of life, and so the title hero of the dialogue is not introduced as an interlocutor, he is rather a reluctant listener to the entire duel of the thought carried out in the dialogue. Right from the beginning one has to see—and this does not really surface in Davidson's treatment—that two theses about the meaning of life are not being confronted with each other. Rather, two basic conceptions of the enactment of life, which are in truth inseparable in all things alive, are being opposed to each other. This is so evident that even

Socrates, who is leading the discussion here in a late form, is hardly being endowed by Plato, the great describer of humans. It is more like an objective weighing of both theses where it is obvious right from the beginning that we cannot be dealing with a simple either-or. Pleasure or joy, this elevated feeling of existence, is certainly impossible without the consciousness of it. Similarly, the opposite thesis of consciousness and its wakeful presence is filled with the plenitude of existence that is bestowed on a human being as both uplifting and fulfilling. We are thus faced with an opposition that is no opposition, and the issue is how to measure out both ways to live a life defined by their cooperation.

Thus, it does not seem right to thematize, with Davidson, the role of Socrates in the entirety of the Platonic dialogues. However, he is correct in the sense that the leading role of Socrates in this dialogue signifies an astonishing return. But one can hardly imagine seeing Socrates—who regarded knowledge as *aretē,* and that as exhibiting the elevated feeling of life that is meant by *hedoni*—represented by somebody else. This is less obvious—and this is what I miss somewhat in general here—when one thinks about the role Socrates plays in the *Republic.* Whereas he usually appeared as the critic of the others' knowledge, he can hardly be recognized as playing the same role in that dialogue. Apparently, the ancients felt this role to be so strong that they, as a preparation, placed the *Clitophon* as a kind of introductory conversation at the beginning of the utopian republic. In any case, it is not only in the *Philebus* that Socrates appears in a different role. The transformation leading from the *Phaedo* to the *Republic* appears to me to be at least as great as the transformation which occurs later with the *dihairesis,* the dialectical division, and which eventually even displaces the figure of Socrates. All in all the differences might be described in such a way that we must not view the Platonic dialogues as the source of Platonic philosophy in the same way as we are accustomed to viewing the *Corpus Aristotelium* as the source of the Aristotelian doctrines. They are incomparable inheritances. In Plato an immense playful joy triumphs in the transformative acts of the figure of Socrates. The writings of Aristotle we know are not published writings at all but they were only intended for teaching. I cannot see that the development of the image of Socrates in the early dialogues through the middle period up to the later one has a different meaning than merely a dramatological one. The great number of scenes in which Socrates presents himself in the magical hand of the writer Plato is certainly overwhelming. But it is still the one Socrates. Thus I cannot really admit that I deprive myself of an interlocutor when I try to understand the Platonic dialogues as a unity. One is constantly being implicated in the conversation with Socrates because in the style of the Socratic conduct of the conversation the other participant in that conversation has hardly anything to say. Of course, here too one can learn much from Davidson's observations, but why does he not take seriously the chief testimony which he does not mention at all, namely the *Seventh Epistle*? It clearly says there that only in conversation is one able to convey thoughts to another so that the spark of an idea passes over to the other. From this vantage point, I think we can understand why the *Philebus* does not at all speak of the Forms any longer, but in truth speaks always of the relationship of the Forms to each other. That is the real topic of Platonic thinking, and it does not at all become conspicuous only with the *dihairesis* and its methodological elaboration. The proof of immortality in the *Phaedo* is only such a proof if one recognizes that the real topic is the relation of the Forms to one another. On this point I never really could follow Stenzel who does not want to admit the uniformity of the dialectical topic in Plato's dialogues. There is a single topic: how are the great accomplishments of reason, the numbers, mathematics, and logical stringency present in Plato's work? If we can say 'mixture' as well as 'participation', then this is already and truly a clear rejection of pseudo-Platonism which is indeed expressly being rejected in the dialogue *Parmenides* along with the two-world doctrine. Apparently, Plato is not interested in determining with greater precision the concept of *methexis*, of 'participation'. What should be retained rather is the fact which Aristotle emphasizes explicitly, namely that *mimēsis* is no longer being discussed, but *methexis*. Thus, the real point is the inseparability of *eidos* from its visible appearance—and Aristotle assumes that *methexis* is only another word for *mimēsis*.

H.-G.G.

22

Diane P. Michelfelder

GADAMER ON HEIDEGGER ON ART

On the occasion of Martin Heidegger's eighty-fifth birthday in 1974, Hans-Georg Gadamer published in a German newspaper some reflections on the life of his former teacher.[1] In the course of his reflections, Gadamer described the experience of encountering Heidegger's thinking for the very first time. Despite its indirect and removed character—Paul Natorp had turned over to Gadamer a manuscript by Heidegger on Aristotle to read—this encounter produced a tremendous effect. The unusual way Heidegger had of putting things hit him, Gadamer recalled, like *das Getroffenwerden von einem elektrischen Schlage,* the impact of an electric shock. Heidegger simply made Aristotle come alive. Later on, when Gadamer came to Freiburg and started hearing Heidegger lecture in person, he realized that this effect was not limited to the case of Aristotle. Heidegger had the remarkable gift of making whatever things he was talking about come to life in front of his students. These things would appear so vividly, reports Gadamer, it was as though they had taken on physical form.

Gadamer's youthful impressions of Heidegger as a highly engaging, stimulating lecturer, who had no interest in the academic game of playing around with ideas whose terminological precision exceeded their range of truthfulness, were to form the basis of a lifelong engagement with the creative, winding path of Heidegger's thinking. As Gadamer developed his own approach to questions of what role understanding has to play in interpretation, an approach that would get the name of philosophical hermeneutics, Heidegger would turn out to be never very far behind. Gadamer's description of Heidegger's initial effect on him makes one recall Heraclitus's "lightning bolt that steers all things," and to entertain the image of Heidegger as Gadamer's lightning bolt. In general, when Gadamer addresses himself to the matter of the relationship between his own thinking and Heidegger's, he tends to confirm this image. For instance, he writes of his interest in "developing the implications for hermeneutics of the Heideggerian insight into the central significance of finitude" or in understanding the essence of language as dialogue "in full accord with Heidegger's critique of the concept of subject."[2]

Interests such as these, though, are not the only signs through which one can catch a glimpse of this image. It is also possible to take Gadamer as attempting to do for Heidegger what Heidegger did for him. As we have just mentioned, against an academic style of doing philosophy that prided itself on preciseness of expression, Heidegger made the philosophical tradition come alive in Gadamer's presence. Likewise, against the charge that the lack of immediate clarity in Heidegger's language was certain evidence of poetic vagueness, Gadamer responded by clarifying or "translating" Heidegger's thinking in such a way that it came alive as philosophy. Because doing this involved situating Heidegger's questions within the stream of sources out of which these questions arose, Gadamer also heightened the liveliness of the Western philosophical tradition.[3] In this way, he continued with Heidegger's task of maintaining "within an increasingly technical age and its antihistorical ideal the great heritage of Western thought"; a heritage that, Gadamer felt, Heidegger had indeed "appropriated with a new passion."[4]

Even in the face of the rush to discredit Heidegger's work following discoveries of the extent of his avowal of National Socialism, Gadamer has stood firm in his commitment to his youthful perception of Heidegger's greatness as a thinker.[5] Considerations such as these take us into the territory of some familiar questions. Just how closely affined is Gadamer's philosophical project with Heidegger's? How critical is Gadamer's engagement with this project? When addressing himself to Heidegger's questions, what sorts of questions about Heidegger does he in turn raise for us?

One place to which we might turn in order to look for some answers to these questions is the area of Gadamer's appropriation of Heidegger's thinking about the meaning of the work of art; and, in particular, to Gadamer's introduction to the 1960 Reclam edition of Heidegger's essay *Der Ursprung des Kunstwerkes*.[6] Written at Heidegger's request, this introduction gives us a special opportunity for exploring the relation between Gadamer and Heidegger, given its status as one of the few texts by Gadamer to speak in an extended way *to* something written by Heidegger rather than *about* it.[7]

The activity of textual interpretation, as Gadamer is fond of saying, is much like the activity of carrying on a conversation with a live partner, for the purpose of understanding what the other has to say. Keeping this in mind, we shall consider the following questions in looking at Gadamer's reading of this essay: What does Gadamer understand Heidegger to be saying in it? What aspects of this essay does he emphasize, and what elements does he downplay or simply ignore? How is Gadamer's reading of this essay connected to his own later discussions of the meaning of art? What can other, more recent readings of Heidegger's essay contribute to our understanding of how Gadamer has appropriated Heidegger's thinking about this matter?

So our line of questioning in the following will be twofold. Through exploring the questions mentioned immediately above, the hope is to be able to respond to the challenge of those mentioned before that, and thereby become clearer about Gadamer's relation to what Heidegger thought, thought in such a way as to have come across with the fervent intensity of an electric shock.

I

Given the fact that the introduction to *Der Ursprung des Kunstwerkes* was aimed at a general audience, it is not surprising that Gadamer starts out by situating Heidegger's essay within the context of its own time. This essay, first published in *Holzwege* in 1950, originated as a single lecture a number of years before, in 1935, and had expanded to a group of three lectures by the following year.[8] These dates, coupled with the recognition that these lectures had received widespread attention before their initial publication, leads Gadamer, from the outset of his introduction, not only to place this essay within the unsettling time period between the two world wars, but to make a connection between the general explosiveness of new trends and movements of thought during this time and the startling intensity of Heidegger's inquiry into the nature of art. He takes this inquiry to be part of an overall wave of intellectual excitement in Germany, a wave which Heidegger himself had earlier on helped to swell by his "passionate protest," found in *Sein und Zeit,* against the pseudo-vitality of the sociocultural world and its new forms of organization inspired by the rise of modern technology (*WK* 82/HLP 214). The lectures of 1936 produced a similar effect. In Gadamer's assessment, there was no doubt about it: they caused nothing short of a "philosophical sensation" (*WK* 84/HLP 217).

It might seem surprising for Gadamer, in this context, to have so readily drawn a picture of Heidegger as an emphatically passionate thinker. It is an approach that runs the risk of fueling exactly what Gadamer takes to be the most serious challenge to Heidegger's thinking about art. In 1934–1935—that is, during the time period immediately preceding the lectures on art—Heidegger lectured on two of Hölderlin's hymns: *Germania* and *The Rhine.* These lectures developed from a study of Hölderlin's work whose "passionate intensity" *(leidenschaftlicher Intensität)* also stood out in Gadamer's mind while writing this introduction (*WK* 84/HLP 217). Gadamer's emphasis points out Heidegger's vulnerability to the charge leveled against his lectures on art: that the "philosophical sensation" they produced was more a result of poetic influences than philosophical insight. To come to this conclusion, one need presumably only point to how Heidegger here interpreted the "happening of truth" in art as essentially poetical: *"Die Kunst geschieht als Dichtung,"* he wrote (*UK* 64/OWA 77);

or that when Heidegger spoke of how this "happening" occurs, his language seemed to trail off into a mythic-poetical luminosity. Consider, regarding this point, his talk of the truth of the work of art being held in the figure *(Gestalt)*, which in turn is the place of the rift *(Riss)*, which keeps the strife *(Streit)* and holds it in the earth (*UK* 52/OWA 64).

All of this was indeed a far cry from what was then the conventional style (as found, for example, in work of Hermann Cohen) of looking to a methodology to insure the universality and necessity of one's thinking. The main task Gadamer thus assumes in his introduction is to defend these lectures—with all their unusual stylistic and linguistic turns—as philosophy. He takes it upon himself to make the philosophical concept hiding behind the poetic word more visible and to justify the appropriateness of its usage. Heidegger had brought both the words "earth" and "world" into his account of the being of a work of art: he claimed it both sets up a world and also sets forth the earth while it retreats into it (*UK* 33–36/OWA 44–47). Given that Heidegger's general goal in coming up with this account was to show that the work of art is accessible to hermeneutic interpretation, his reliance on speaking about a "world" appeared legitimate, since the hermeneutic meaning of world as found in *Being and Time,* the world as the "wherein" of our acts of self-understanding, was carried over into these lectures.[9] But the same could not be said about his use of "earth" *(das Erde).* This is the concept whose justification provides a challenge for Gadamer here. Although the earth resists attempts to disclose it, and thus bears some similarity to the *existentiale* of "mood" in *Being and Time*—the feature of Dasein that shows its facticity in revealing how deeply it is thrown into and bound up with its world—Gadamer readily admits that no pathway from this form of self-disclosure to the notion of the earth can be found.

So Gadamer is continually moved, throughout his introduction, to pay closer attention to the admittedly "startling" concept of earth than to the concept of world because of the greater need the former concept has for justification. Such is his eagerness to concentrate on this one aspect of the "philosophical sensation" caused by these lectures that he sets aside other of Heidegger's radical ideas, including (and we will have more to say about this as we go on) the idea that art is the "act that founds whole historical worlds" (*WK* 84/HLP 217). In dealing with this question of the legitimation of the concept of the earth, even though Gadamer is unable to draw a straight line from *Being and Time* to the lectures on art, he does adopt an approach that in its general form is suggestive of what Heidegger did in that earlier work. Just as Heidegger demonstrated that a grasp of the being of Dasein would lead to a recognition of Dasein's limits to its ability to project itself—and, as a consequence, of the limits to the truthfulness of German idealism—so Gadamer attempts to reveal how using Heidegger's new conceptuality to grasp what the work of art is in its being will produce an understanding of art that will surpass that made possible through idealist aesthetics in various historical forms: Kantian aesthetics, Hegelian speculative aesthetics, and Neo-Kantian aesthetics.

The difficulties with these forms of aesthetics, from Gadamer's viewpoint, can be briefly outlined as follows. The shortcoming of Kantian aesthetics is connected to its attempt to legitimate the universal character of aesthetic judgment. This universality had its roots in the subjectivity of the experiencing subject, which in turn was able to locate itself as part of the created order of nature. With the fading of the general belief in such a divinely inspired order, the possibility of rooting aesthetic judgments in anything outside of a purely subjective context was severely threatened. Secondly, although Hegel took both art and nature to be objectifications of absolute spirit—a move which had the virtue of providing a comprehensive ontological picture within which art could receive a place—it was at the expense of the truth of art being treated as an inferior expression of philosophical truth. Finally, within Neo-Kantianism, a different ontological view presented itself, but one with the same effect of diminishing the status of art. For the Neo-Kantians, anything with real being was objective, thinglike, and thus accessible to scientific understanding. This implied that art needed to be viewed from the perspective of a thing in order for its truth to be identified; and thus any "aesthetic" qualities it had would need to be considered as subjective ones (*WK* 85–87/HLP 217–19).

Gadamer's point in going over the history of idealist aesthetics more deeply than Heidegger does in these lectures is to intentionally place what Heidegger is saying within a conversation with the history of philosophy. Statements such as these from the epilogue to the lectures—"Truth is the truth of Being. Beauty does not occur alongside and apart from this truth."—show Heidegger deliberately trying to reorient the problem of the nature of the work of art away from the perspective of such aesthetics. To make this reorientation work, he has to show how it is possible for the being of the work of art to be related to the whole of being in such a way that its truth can still stand on its own. Gadamer's most productive insight in his introduction is to show that if Heidegger's task can be clarified up to this point; that is, if Heidegger can be shown to be responding to a problem arising out of previous philosophical talk about art, then his use of terms such as the "earth" will no longer seem predominantly poetically determined.

To spell out this insight further, it seems appropriate to start with the clue that was most significant for Gadamer: Heidegger's claim that truth *(alētheia)* emerges from the work-being of the work of art. This claim simply means that nothing strikes us *more* about a work of art than the fact that it is. The truth of the work of art comes directly from the work itself. This means it is accurate to say that it is the being of the work that we experience when we encounter a work of art, but its being does not depend on our experiencing it. This is Heidegger's answer to the difficulty posed by Kantian aesthetics. Likewise, because Heidegger claims that what the artwork opens up is not simply its own being but also the being of a new world, he is able to show that it does not appear as a thing within the world. In fact, by contrasting the being of a work with the being of a thing, a contrast that makes sense when we consider how nothing strikes us *less* about a thing than the fact that it is, he shows that its being is not thinglike at all. These claims respond to the problem posed by the Neo-Kantian view. Lastly, Gadamer indicates, the truth belonging to the work of art is not an imperfect truth, in need of the philosophical concept to attain real being. Instead, the truth *of* the work of art is the truth that *is* the work of art itself. So Gadamer sees Heidegger as being able, in addition to everything else, to "upgrade" the truth of art and thus side-step the view proposed by Hegelian aesthetics.

But what of the alleged troublesome concept of the "earth"? As Gadamer develops a dialogue between Heidegger and the representatives of idealist aesthetics, he emphasizes how the "earth" is not a darkly suggestive poetic image but rather names the part of the ontological structure of the work of art into which the work settles, stays, and hides itself. To take an example, the captivating blues, reds, and yellows in Mondrian's paintings disappear as colors as soon as we try to penetrate them cognitively. "Earth" refers to the part of the artwork that escapes objectification and conceptual understanding. By means of this concept, Heidegger reveals the limitations of idealist aesthetics; and thus, Gadamer argues, despite its apparent "mythical" and "gnostic" overtones (*WK* 84/HLP 217), talk about the "earth" does have a legitimate place within philosophical language.

At the same time, Gadamer wants it to be kept in mind that this concept is connected to a more general point Heidegger wants to make about truth. If the being of the work of art is the event of its truth, its coming-into-presence, and if hiddenness belongs equally to this being, then its truth can no longer be conceived from within the framework of presence alone, but must be thought of from within the interplay of presence and hiddenness. This teaches us something that holds true for every being, Gadamer stresses, not just the one of the work of art. No special complications present themselves here when we try to figure out whether this could be true. It can be "confirmed by everyone" that there is a richness and depth subsiding in all things that is simply more vivid in the case of the work of art, whose truth, in Gadamer's words, is not "its simple manifestation of meaning, but rather the unfathomableness and depth of its meaning" (*WK* 92/HLP 226). Although Gadamer does not explicitly say so at this point, herein lies the significance of the concept of the earth for hermeneutic interpretation. It is suggestive of what Gadamer would come to speak of later on as the "fundamental relation of hermeneutics": *"Vieles ist zu sagen";* "There is much to say."[10]

By the end of his introduction, Gadamer's efforts to free Heidegger's concept of the earth from poetic language have involved him in demonstrating its force in Heidegger's challenge to aesthetics and his efforts to open up the sphere of hermeneutics to include the work of art, as well as in its larger role in validating Heidegger's idea that truth as *alētheia* is the truth of beings in general. What Gadamer does not discuss is the question of just upon whom the work of art—in the deep, rich, inexhaustibility of its meaning—has an impact to make.

II

If the phrase "there is much to say" captures the basic hermeneutic relation, then Heidegger's lectures on art are a clear-cut illustration of this relation. In the thirty-odd years since their publication with Gadamer's introduction attached, the historical horizon from within which they originally appeared to be meaningful has undergone a substantial shift. Newer texts have appeared that make it much less possible to read these lectures without giving increased attention to the question mentioned just above. These "introduce" us to other passions than those that struck Gadamer as significant. In the contentious atmosphere surrounding the arguments over Heidegger's work triggered by the publication of Victor Farías's book in 1987, the concepts of the "earth" and "world" once again appear troublesome, but for different reasons: for their ties to the concept of a "historical people" *(das Volk)* whose "vocation," Heidegger claimed, is opened up by the work of art.[11] Even if one takes Farías to be exaggerating when he claims that this new conceptuality does not dominate these lectures as much as the concept of the formation of the German people, one is still left with the blunt fact that it now seems disturbing more for political than for academic reasons. One is also left with the consideration that Heidegger did not just put this conceptuality in these lectures to the use of trying to develop a philosophical investigation, but also to the task of the formation of a people, a task of which the line that "history is the transporting *(Entrückung)* of a people into its appointed task as entrance *(Eintrükung)* into that people's endowment" is indicative *(UK 64/OWA 77)*.

Rereading Gadamer's introduction today in the light of these developments, one's attention is drawn in two directions at once, both towards what he did say and towards what he did not. The simple matter, for example, of the way Gadamer put a date to Heidegger's lectures now appears to have a degree of disingenuousness about it, as though its neutral tone (from the "time between the two world wars") overlooks a certain ominousness. Likewise, the way Gadamer situated these lectures in the immediate light of *Being and Time,* a move which went along with his emphasis on Heidegger's distrust of academic philosophy, now seems oversimplified; and any line now drawn between these two works seems to need to pass through such texts as Heidegger's 1933 *Rektoratsrede,* other public speeches from the same year, and his 1934–1935

Hölderlin lectures. All of these are places where Heidegger spoke to the importance of the people, the connection between the work of art and the work of the
state, the need to assume one's historical destiny, the role of decision making
and resoluteness in this assumption, and the challenge to view the moment at
hand as a historical moment in the most fundamental sense, that is, of being
the origin of history itself: topics which are all present in varying degrees in the
lectures on art.

One could even argue that nowadays Gadamer's introduction to Heidegger's
lectures has more to teach us about hermeneutic interpretation in general, about
what goes on in holding a conversation with a text, than about the hermeneutic
character of the artwork or other subjects Heidegger addressed. One of the most
striking things about Gadamer's reading is its almost total lack of references to
the historical character of the world opened up by the work of art, and to Heidegger's project of showing how art lets history happen. One might be surprised
by this absence for a couple of reasons. First of all, as we have already pointed
out, Gadamer develops his reading with an eye to showing that Heidegger's
thinking cannot be accommodated within the history of idealist aesthetics, and
thus represents something new within the larger history of philosophical reflections upon art. This view, which clearly takes Heidegger's reflections to be an
improvement on such aesthetics without constituting its perfection, matches up
well with the de-Hegelianized approach to history Heidegger presented as
involving a succession of world views none of which is to be judged as more
rational than any other.

A second, more significant reason is related to the general task of hermeneutics itself. This task, from Gadamer's perspective, is to consider how we form an
understanding and interpretation of ourselves from within the context of our own
historicity. The activity of understanding, so defined, involves all temporal
dimensions: past, present, and future. It implies that we project our own possibilities from within a present situation that has been handed over to us, rather than
perform an act of consciousness to represent ourselves to ourselves as who we
are.[12] Heidegger's statement to the effect that the event of the work of art "brings
out what is as yet undecided and measureless, and thus discloses the hidden
necessity of measure and decisiveness" would seem to reflect such a definition
of hermeneutic understanding (*UK* 51/OWA 63). In fact, statements of this type
could lead us to see how the event of the work of art is an example of what
Gadamer describes as an "existential moment": a point in time where the "basic
historical condition of human existence is experienced."[13] In other words,
although all understanding is hermeneutic, there are some occasions when this
fact appears to us more vividly and stunningly than on others; and one of these
times is when we enter the world that the work of art opens up.

If anything might prevent one from being surprised, it would be seeing how
Gadamer's reading of Heidegger is a good example of the hermeneutic principle

that one needs to continually test one's prejudices in interpreting a text. Gadamer's eagerness to respond to concerns relating to the unheard-of use of "earth" in philosophical discourse results in his not spending long enough time with the concept of "world" in order to let the controversial issues stirring within it come to the surface. Gadamer is able to show how Heidegger moved beyond the false prejudices of idealist aesthetics, but this demonstration is at the expense of depending on what appears to a contemporary reader to be a false prejudice itself. As Gadamer underlined in *Truth and Method,* "We are always affected, in hope and fear, by what is nearest to us, and hence we approach the testimony of the past under its influence."[14] What was nearest to him were certain passions and not others. This, in turn, caused him to let Heidegger's concern with history, destiny, and the political side in general of both the poetic and mythic element of these lectures slip silently into the background.

That Gadamer was affected by what was nearest to him in a way that *then* overly restricted the scope of the horizon he depended on to approach Heidegger makes us wonder about Gadamer's relation to these topics *since* the publication of his introduction. How has Gadamer dealt with them? In what way has he added to the discussion of the political-philosophical issues that now appear so central to what Heidegger was thinking about the work of art? Just how open— or how reticent—has Gadamer been in addressing these matters?

A quick look at other of Gadamer's writings bearing on Heidegger's writings on art could easily create the impression that he has simply continued to endorse those ideas of Heidegger's towards which he was initially favorable, and avoided any in-depth contact with the politically related questions arising in connection with these writings. As Gadamer developed his own reflections on art in these essays, he has never wavered in his beliefs of what the genuine insights were that the lectures contained, nor have his criticisms of their political content been outspoken. Consider, for example, the following passage, taken from "The Universality of the Hermeneutical Problem" (1966):

> Despite its misuse by the National Socialists, we cannot deny that the idea of art being bound to a people involves a real insight. A genuine artistic creation stands within a given community, and such a community is always distinguishable from the cultured society that is informed and terrorized by art criticism.[15]

Gadamer does not comment on whether this idea as it is found in Heidegger tends more towards being a "misuse" or "genuine insight." Likewise, when Gadamer had occasion to take up Heidegger's lectures again, in the course of the memorial address he delivered for Heidegger in 1976, he did not deviate from his earlier observations about what was truly perceptive about this piece:

> that "earth" now became the theme of philosophy—this elevation of a poetically charged word to the position of a central conceptual metaphor—signified a true breakthrough.[16]

Likewise, whereas he did not exactly sidestep the question of how Heidegger's political views played a role in his interpretation of art, he certainly did not entertain it in this context to any extent, and rather seemed to dismiss this as a nonquestion simply by mentioning that by 1936 Heidegger had "recognized his political error."[17]

Now particularly in the light of claims such as that made by Philippe Lacoue-Labarthe that Heidegger brought out the essence of Nazism in the lectures on art, it looks as though one could justifiably say that such an easy dismissal is unwarranted.[18] Still, just as it would be a mistake to suppose Gadamer's entire reading of Heidegger on art consisted of reaffirmations of what he had initially found to be truthful, it would likewise be a mistake to think that Gadamer does not deal with the politically significant elements in what Heidegger has to say about the philosophical significance of art: elements such as the idea that the work of art calls together a people, and that it also has the power to open a new epoch in human history. The signs of a more critical engagement with Heidegger are there. They are almost never direct, but they are clearly decisive. Gadamer tends not to meet questions about art and politics in Heidegger with political answers. But we know from Heidegger that silence speaks; and, with respect to the matter here, Gadamer's silence often speaks against Heidegger.

Over the course of his numerous essays on art, Gadamer has shown how *extending* and *expanding* one's understanding of the hermeneutic character of art—in other words, pursuing the philosophical implications of Heidegger's discovery of the hermeneutic dimensions of art—can reveal basic weaknesses to Heidegger's ideas about the political side of art. At the same time as he takes Heidegger's original insight into the hermeneutic truth of art further, Gadamer makes us more conscious of how it had become waylaid, and thus limited from the outset, by political untruth.

In order to defend this last point, I want to briefly look at two of Gadamer's other works that deal with the experience of art. The first of these, "Aesthetics and Hermeneutics," followed Gadamer's introduction to Heidegger's essay by four years (1964); the second, "The Relevance of the Beautiful," comes from the following decade (1977).[19]

III

In "Aesthetics and Hermeneutics," Gadamer raises once again Heidegger's question of whether it is legitimate to try to make sense of the experience of art from within the hermeneutic standpoint. Taking the idea that hermeneutics "operates wherever what is said is not immediately intelligible" as a starting point, he moves to justify this legitimacy by defending the claims that there is indeed a language to art (art can "speak"), and that no matter what the direct strength of an artwork's impact is, it still occupies a position at a distance from us, a distance brought on by the very abundance of its meaningfulness. The hand of Heidegger is clearly visible in Gadamer's reliance on what he took to be the most lasting insight from the lectures on art: the truth of art as *alētheia*. Even as the artwork presents itself to an observer, it holds something back in reserve, so that the entire effect created, Gadamer indicates, can best be named with the word *surprise*. An artwork—one could say—is not very careful with the person who notices it. The very fact of its existence, its "that it is," can shock, astound, amaze—or, alternatively, captivate, entice, or excite. In either case the consequence is one of surprise, brought about by suddenly having to face a situation that one did not anticipate.

Although Gadamer speaks here simply of surprise, it is important to note that he takes this emotion to arise not just as a result of what is unexpected in general, but of what is unexpected as that which presents a contest and a challenge, and makes a demand upon us. This demand, as Gadamer perceives it, is an ethical one. The "increase in being" that the artwork represents disturbs the feeling of compatibility that one generally has with life itself. Without warning, one becomes destabilized within a world that one was previously able to count on, and exposed to questions such as the following: *What is there in life that is truly valuable? Where am I headed? What is it that I ought to be doing?* Such questions, if sincerely addressed, could likewise lead to the experience of an increase in one's own being.

No doubt we have all been under the pressure of being asked difficult, unexpected questions that reach into the depths of our being. Forced to deal with such questions, we feel singled out. It is a similar situation with a work of art. The more it surprises us, the more deeply, Gadamer suggests, does it present a problem of self-interpretation. "It says something to each person as if it were said especially to him" (*AH* 100). The voice belonging to such a work, in its strangeness and otherness, makes us look at our own strangeness, which we begin to grasp when we ask the question "Who am I?" This is, for Gadamer, the activity involved in recognizing the meaning of an artwork, an activity fundamentally different from replacing a muddle in one's mind with a clear picture of what was originally intended by another's consciousness.

Precisely this self-isolating element of the experience of the artwork is what Gadamer emphasizes in this essay, just as much as Heidegger ignored it earlier. Recall Heidegger's claims:

Poetry is the saying . . . in which a people's world historically arises for it. (*UK* 61/OWA 74)

The origin of the work of art . . . which is to say of a people's historical existence, is art. (*UK* 65/OWA 78)

Heidegger understood the artwork to appeal to oneself insofar as one *simultaneously* was able to identify with a group that, in turn, was tied to the earth. He took the artwork, so to say, to be casting its appeal in an uncanny albeit public voice. But because of the nature of Gadamer's approach to the question of the legitimacy of putting hermeneutics and aesthetics together, he is led to pay very close attention to the question of just what it means to say that an artwork speaks, and is thus able to find a dialogical, ethical side involving the apprehension of otherness to this speaking that Heidegger passes over. For Gadamer, the artwork no more addresses a people than would any other situation that demands an ethical decision. Both demand a response from an individual self.

Hence Gadamer's willing endorsement of Heidegger's idea that the truth *(alētheia)* of an artwork is also an "overflow" *(Überfluss)*—so that when we experience it the sheer existence of other things shows itself to us as well—is not a corresponding endorsement of the belief that there is a similar "overflow" on the part of those towards whom the artwork extends itself, so that they are effortlessly grouped into a people. Gadamer's insistence that the artwork makes "others" of us can reasonably be interpreted as indicating that there is no warrant for the idea that it immediately binds us into a political group that would be "other" to similar groups. As he says in this essay, art certainly can speak from the past, and does so whenever it appears as a part of culture or a historical monument. In these cases, it does present itself as intimately connected to a people: we see a Greek temple, a Tudor ceiling, or the like. But just because we are able to identify a work of art as belonging to a people, and often do make such an identification, does not mean that it addresses itself directly *to* a people. The essential element in the language of art, as Gadamer uncovers it in this essay, is the way it speaks out at a personal level. It is likely that, as he would say, we can recognize something like this in our experience, and unlikely that we can recognize being addressed by an artwork as part of a people—as unlikely as that we would experience, to take an analogous example, the reality of being an American to be an intrinsic part of that particularly demanding "upsurge of being" that we call "falling in love."

Now certainly the underspoken critique of Heidegger on art that can be drawn from the pages of this essay is given from a philosophical rather than a political viewpoint. Indeed, as has already been mentioned, Gadamer has publicly barely touched upon the political aspect of this lecture of Heidegger's, and even then only to call attention to the dangers of overestimating its importance. His approach suggests an arguably more valuable way of judging the connection between Heidegger's philosophy and Heidegger's politics than many currently in favor. Rather than claiming that Heidegger's philosophy should be dismissed because of the sheer presence of indefensible political ideas, or taking the opposite view that somehow good philosophy can be recovered after all from these ideas, Gadamer, so it seems, would have us raise the following question: How is Heidegger's philosophical insight frustrated by his political interests? He challenges us to see how Heidegger's attempt to link the question of the experience of art with the questions of philosophy—that is, of hermeneutic interpretation—clashes with the attempt to bring both questions under the umbrella of politics. Certainly Heidegger took a step forward in understanding the connection between hermeneutics and aesthetics by revealing the hermeneutic *dimension* of the artwork in its saying, the excess of meaning that is the happening of its truth. What he overlooked, by taking the work to be making a direct appeal to a people, was the hermeneutic *task* that Gadamer expresses straightforwardly as "the task of integrating [the experience of art] into the whole of one's own orientation to a world and one's own self-understanding" (*AH* 102).

This task of integration can only take place in one's own language. It is with respect to this basic feature of experience that Gadamer's earlier-mentioned remark affirming the essential truthfulness of the idea that art is bound to a people can be understood. Because one's own language must be at the same time the language of a people, carrying out the hermeneutic task of integration necessarily involves understanding how one's own individual life is bound up with others. Such understanding is not that of a means towards an end lying outside of it; one does not struggle with the task of hermeneutics only to emerge a more solitary human being. But neither does one emerge having forgotten one's otherness by being caught up in the singularly dramatic moment of a world-historical task.[20]

Gadamer's lack of a direct, sweeping critique of Heidegger's treatment of the relation between aesthetics and politics does not thereby imply an absence of critical perspective. In Gadamer's development of Heidegger's insight into the hermeneutic character of art—a development which negotiates a course between idealist aesthetics and Heidegger's aestheticized politics—his criticism of this treatment can be seen. Although in "Aesthetics and Hermeneutics" Gadamer does not once mention the name of Heidegger, this essay can nonetheless be seen as an attempt to disassociate the hermeneutic character of the artwork from Heidegger's emphasis on the character of a people. Gadamer's exploration of the hermeneutic task involved with the experience of art shows how what goes on in responding to the saying of art involves a struggle of a more modest and personal dimension than Heidegger assumed. In later essays dealing with this same experience, Gadamer has revealed further aspects of this struggle; and it is in order to see another of them—again in its modesty and difference from Heidegger—that we now turn.

IV

A connection other than the one between aesthetics and hermeneutics is at stake in "The Relevance of the Beautiful." In this essay, Gadamer confronts the problem of how art can be justified by dealing with the question of whether there can be a common history to traditional art—art that depends on perspective and a representational subject matter—and the nonobjective art of our own time, which rejects the standards of traditional art to such an extent that it often appears as anti-art.[21] His response to this question will be anchored in Heidegger's idea of the truth of art as *alētheia*. At the same time, though, he will skillfully let this concept emerge from the temporal framework with which it was surrounded in Heidegger's discussion: the promise of a new beginning, on a monumental scale.

In doing this, and in showing that the experience of art is indeed connected to a *different* experience of time, but one involving more modest temporal dimensions than Heidegger had envisioned, Gadamer is able to demonstrate that these two vastly different styles of art are not entirely alienated from each other, but can be brought together into a single whole. Again, although he is not overtly critical of Heidegger in this essay, Gadamer's insight into how art allows us to make a break with ordinary time can be understood as having such a critical dimension to it, particularly when we keep in mind that his approach yields a positive response to the question at stake here, a response which Heidegger was apparently unable to entertain.[22]

At the start of this essay, Gadamer proposes three starting points or clues as potentially helpful in coming to grips with the question of the existence of a connection between traditional and contemporary art. Each clue—the word "art" itself, the concept of the beautiful, and the discipline of aesthetics—looks immediately promising. For instance, regarding the concept of the beautiful, Gadamer indicates that we can still hear traces of the original meaning of *kalon* (beauty in both an aesthetic and a moral sense) in contemporary expressions about beauty such as *die schöne Sittlichkeit*. He takes Plato's discussion of the love of the beautiful in the *Phaedrus* to be communicating an idea that is still relevant today—namely, that the beautiful is not simply to be identified with the ideal but rather is that which links together "the chasm between the ideal and the real" (RB 15). And yet, with only these pointers at hand, Gadamer's attempt to tell a coherent story about art falters. One runs up against the problem that the word "art," for example, cannot easily be stretched to accommodate what is produced, say, by a John Baldassari, a Barnett Newman, an Anselm Kiefer, and so on. Neither, as Gadamer readily points out, do the conceptual resources of aesthetics shed light on what Marcel Duchamp was up to. The clues Gadamer initially suggests turn out to be inadequate when it comes to giving us an understanding of the artworks of our own time.

So it is that Gadamer turns once again to Heidegger's notion of *alētheia*. Unlike anything else, and particularly technological objects, he reminds us, the work of art—any work of art, from no matter what historical period—signifies "an increase in being" (RB 35). More specifically, with regard to its irreplaceability, "the work of art is no mere bearer of meaning, as though the meaning could be transferred to another bearer" (RB 33).

With regard to its meaning, Gadamer assures us it is better to say that "art is the containment of sense, so that it does not run away or escape from us, but is secured and sheltered in the ordered composure of the creation" (RB 34).

To be aware of this sheltering and withdrawing of the artwork is to recognize its "thereness." Without reference to his concept of "earth," Gadamer brings forward his debt to Heidegger concerning this point:

> He enabled us to perceive the ontological plenitude or the truth that addresses us in art through the twofold movement of revealing, unconcealing, and manifesting, on the one hand, and concealing and sheltering, on the other. (RB 34)

Heidegger's notion of *alētheia* is helpful, but not enough to solve the problem Gadamer faces in this essay. It offers a preliminary insight that needs to be supplemented. Gadamer finds what he needs to supplement it in the idea of the "hermeneutic identity" of the work of art. This is nothing other than the "thereness" of this work presenting itself as an "invitation" or, in stronger terms, a "challenge" for interpretation (RB 26–27). We know already from "Aesthetics and Hermeneutics" that this challenge is made at the personal level, and is specifically a challenge that we integrate the artwork into the whole of our orientation to the world. What Gadamer now clarifies is the temporality involved with this integration. Integration does not entail fitting an already completed work into a conceptual schema. The demand the work makes to be interpreted is likewise a demand that it be constructed. The act of interpretation does not follow the work. Rather, the work's withdrawal makes for a kind of limited open space within which one needs to make an active contribution. As Gadamer puts it, "The participant belongs to the play" (RB 26).

Gadamer brings up Cubist paintings as an obvious example where a contribution is required on the part of an observer in order to bring the work together into a whole, but he is quick to emphasize that there is nothing special in this regard about Cubism. Even the most unrelenting representational artworks—portraits, for example—need to be "filled out" by the onlooker. Thus, by drawing out what is involved in the *experience* of the work of art, Gadamer finds a way of unifying the art of our times and the art of the past. In this way Gadamer is also able to offer a critique of Heidegger's view, developed in his lectures on art, that such an experience could provoke a new historical beginning. By showing that the hermeneutic identity of the artwork is bound to the idea of truth as *alētheia*, Gadamer demonstrates that part of what it is to experience art is to experience a sense of discontinuity with the flow of ordinary time, a discontinuity whose dimensions, compared to those found in Heidegger, are far more modest in scale.

This works as follows. If an artwork required no effort from us to constitute it, then the immediate response of "I get it!" when faced with a problematic work for the first time would be an appropriate one. With this response, we would have moved the work into our world, and life could go on as usual. But the hermeneutic identity of a work means that whatever public meaning it has needs to be filled out by a private contribution. This means that one needs to move into the world of the artwork, rather than the other way around. This takes time, and the time it takes is time out from ordinary time. The withdrawing of a work of art creates a break with the continuity of ordinary time, at the same time as it draws one into another "whole" of time that forms as a result of one's inter-action with the work.

Part of the work of art, then, is a particular temporal structure, which emerges in experience as an interim, a temporary yet seamless "whole," which can best be designated as a "while."

Like a festival, which sets up its own time, and like periods of life such as childhood and middle age, any work of art, Gadamer contends, has its own self-contained time. In this sense art presents itself as an "overcoming" of time (RB 46). All of this is quite a long way from the dramatic unfolding of the likewise self-contained epochs of Being that one finds in Heidegger. Gadamer down-scales Heidegger's concern with world historicality to an emphasis on more localized temporalities. Reading *alētheia* in this way, Gadamer is able to dis-tance it from the metanarrative impact it has in Heidegger. This does, though, lead to a productive insight into the history of art, an insight to which Heideg-ger's own path was blocked by his politicization of *alētheia*.

Perhaps nowhere else in "The Relevance of the Beautiful" does Gadamer's difference from Heidegger appear so clearly than in the following passage on the autonomous temporality of architecture:

> when we actually stand before one of the great architectural monuments of human culture for the first time, we are apt to experience a certain disappointment. They do not look as "painterly" as they seem from the photographic reproductions that are so familiar to us. . . . This feeling . . . shows that we still have to go beyond the purely artistic quality of the building considered as an image and actually approach it as an architectural art in its own right. To do that, we have to go up to the building and wander around it, both inside and out. Only in this way can we acquire a sense of what the work holds in store for us. (RB 45)[23]

This "great architectural monument of human culture" could be a Greek temple, towering above the earth as we find it in Heidegger (*UK* 30–32/OWA 41–42). And yet there is nothing here to suggest that, were it to be a Greek tem-ple, its "Greekness" would be in any regard important. To what culture, to what people, the work belongs is irrelevant. The important thing is for one to make one's own way around such a work and to spend time with it. If this experience should lead to a greater sense of community with others, as Gadamer suggests here that it can (RB 38–39), there is no reason to suspect that this community must adhere to a national identity. Thus Gadamer's response to the hermeneutic challenge of art leads him, as it led Heidegger, to consider how a new history can be written. At the same time he clearly shows that for this history—the unified story of art—to be written with *alētheia* as a guiding concept, this concept must be depoliticized and dedramatized: in other words, heard in another voice from that resonating in Heidegger's lectures on art.

V

One thing that Gadamer does not mention, either in his enthusiastic introduction to Heidegger's lectures on art or in his quietly stated critical engagement with the political side of these lectures that was to follow, is the way in which Heidegger, despite his use of the concept of *alētheia* to undermine idealist aesthetics, remains close to Hegel. One of Heidegger's aims in demonstrating the limitations of these aesthetics was to put the decisiveness of Hegel's famous judgment that "art is a thing of the past" into question. Hegel believed art to be irrelevant to his own times because its truth was better represented by the conceptual truth philosophy could provide. He enfolded the already monumental history of art into the larger, even more monumental history of philosophy. The effect of Heidegger's argument against idealist aesthetics was to display the fragility of Hegel's claim. If art could indeed set up a new beginning for history, then it could not at all, at the same time, be a thing of the past. It is with regard to this point that the similarity between Hegel and Heidegger is to be found. When Heidegger disputes Hegel's claim, it is still within a framework of monumentality and a drama of huge proportions. In his perception, art has the power to overhaul the past and open up an entire new way, a way that affects an entire people, for beings to be understood. *Seinsgeschichte, Volksgeschichte, Kunstgeschichte*—Heidegger puts all of these together and thus responds to Hegel's contention about art on a scale worthy of Hegel himself.

Gadamer fashions things in a different manner. As he draws the connection between aesthetics and hermeneutics more firmly, undermining the particular tie Heidegger believed existed between aesthetics and politics, *alētheia* turns, in his hands, into a concept with more modest, less publicly dramatic implications. For example, the modest space of time—the "while"—that art opens up gives us an opportunity, perhaps the only one "granted to us finite beings," to experience "what we call eternity" (RB 45). In *"Ende der Kunst?"* (1989), Gadamer does not oppose Hegel's idea of a monumental end to art with a monumental beginning to history, but rather suggests that "every purported end of art will be the beginning of a new art." *("Jedes vermeintliche Ende der Kunst wird Anfang neuer Kunst sein.")*[24] This concern with modesty and humbleness that comes out in Gadamer's writings on art is illustrative of the emphasis it gets when Gadamer reflects in a more general fashion on what it means to speak philosophically.

Those who devote themselves to a life and career of philosophical thinking, according to Gadamer, have to continually remind themselves that when it comes to finding solutions for problems associated with everyday life, nothing gives them an edge over other responsible, reflective human beings.

In making this remark in "The Political Incompetence of Philosophy," Gadamer had Heidegger specifically in mind. It could however be applied to anyone whose "extravagance"—the word Gadamer chose to describe Heidegger's thought that history was on the verge of a new beginning in the 1930s—prevents them from realizing they have no special advantage in dealing with practical matters.[25] It is not that philosophers have no alternative but to be incompetent when making political claims, but rather that any competence they might have does not stem from the fact of their being philosophers. Once again here Gadamer speaks of passion:

> Human beings everywhere pose philosophical questions that no one is in a position to answer—concerning the future, death, the meaning of life, happiness and so on. There is evidently a passion for philosophical questioning that exists in all human beings, not just the professional philosopher.[26]

Philosophers, as Gadamer sees it, have to let their own passions for confronting difficult questions about life help others better understand and better pursue their own passions for philosophical questioning. They need to remember, as Heidegger on critical occasions did not, how their own finitude means that they have always to be rethinking as they think, and beginning again and again in less than spectacular ways. Sometimes a philosopher can provide the right word, but there is never room for a final word. Often the right word turns out to be one that is quite modest. This is one of the lessons of Gadamer's philosophical hermeneutics.

DIANE P. MICHELFELDER

DEPARTMENT OF PHILOSOPHY
CALIFORNIA POLYTECHNIC STATE UNIVERSITY
AUGUST 1992

NOTES

1. Hans-Georg Gadamer's article, which appeared in the *Frankfurter Allgemeine Zeitung* on September 28, 1974, was reprinted under the title "Martin Heidegger—85 Jahre" in *Heideggers Wege* (Tübingen: J. C. B. Mohr [Paul Siebeck], 1983), pp. 94–102. An English translation appears in *Philosophical Apprenticeships* (Cambridge, Mass.: MIT Press, 1985) as the chapter on Martin Heidegger.

2. Gadamer, "Text and Interpretation," trans. Dennis Schmidt and Richard Palmer, in *Dialogue and Deconstruction,* ed. Diane Michelfelder and Richard Palmer (Albany: SUNY Press, 1989), pp. 23–24.

3. See, for example, Gadamer's "The Phenomenological Movement," in *Philosophical Hermeneutics,* trans. and ed. David E. Linge (Berkeley: University of California Press, 1976), p. 141.

4. Ibid.

5. Gadamer, "The Political Incompetence of Philosophy," in *The Heidegger Case: On Philosophy and Politics,* ed. Tom Rockmore and Joseph Margolis (Philadelphia: Temple University Press, 1992), pp. 364–69.

6. This introduction appears under the title *"Zur Einführung"* on pages 102–25 of the Reclam edition. It is reprinted under the title *"Die Wahrheit des Kunstwerks"* in Gadamer's *Neuere Philosophie* 1 (Tübingen: J. C. B. Mohr [Paul Siebeck], 1987), and in *Heideggers Wege,* pp. 81–93. The English translation of this essay, "Heidegger's Later Philosophy," appears in *Philosophical Hermeneutics,* pp. 213–28. Future references will be in the text to the German edition (*WK,* with page numbers from *Heideggers Wege)* and to the English translation (HLP).

7. Gadamer has also written a very brief essay, *"'Was ist Metaphysik?'"* (1978, first published in German in *Heideggers Wege,* pp. 41–44) dealing with Heidegger's lecture by the same name and, in particular, with the new introduction Heidegger wrote for the fifth printing.

8. "Der Ursprung des Kunstwerkes," in *Holzwege* (Frankfurt: Vittorio Klostermann, 1972), pp. 7–68; translated as "The Origin of the Work of Art," in *Poetry, Language, Thought,* trans. and ed. Albert Hofstadter (New York: Harper and Row, 1971), pp. 15–87. Future references will be in the text to *UK* and OWA.

9. See particularly section 19.

10. Gadamer, *"Die Marburger Theologie,"* in *Heideggers Wege,* p. 40. (English translation: "Heidegger and Marburg Theology," in *Philosophical Hermeneutics,* p. 211.)

11. Victor Farías, *Heidegger and Nazism,* trans. Paul Burrell (Philadelphia: Temple University Press, 1989). The section on "The Origin of the Work of Art" is to be found on pp. 239–41. Other recent publications treating the relation between Heidegger's politics and his writings about art include *Heidegger, Art, and Politics* by Philippe Lacoue-Labarthe, trans. Chris Turner (Oxford: Basil Blackwell, 1990); Michael Zimmerman's *Heidegger's Confrontation with Modernity: Technology, Politics, and Art* (Bloomington: Indiana University Press, 1990), particularly chapters seven and eight; Jean-Francois Lyotard's *Heidegger et "les juifs"* (Paris: Editions Galilée, 1988); *The Heidegger Case: On Philosophy and Politics,* ed. Tom Rockmore and Joseph Margolis (Philadelphia: Temple University Press, 1992); and, to a lesser extent, Tom Rockmore's *On Heidegger's Nazism and Philosophy* (Berkeley: University of California Press, 1992) and Richard Wolin's *The Politics of Being: The Political Thought of Martin Heidegger* (New York: Columbia University Press, 1990). Also of interest on this topic is the issue of *Diacritics* on "Heidegger: Art and Politics" (vol. 19, nos. 3–4, Fall-Winter 1989).

12. See Joel Weinsheimer, *Gadamer's Hermeneutics: A Reading of Truth and Method* (New Haven: Yale University Press, 1985), especially section 2, "The Critique of Historicism," pp. 133–212.

13. Gadamer, "The Continuity of History and the Existential Moment," trans. Thomas Wren, *Philosophy Today,* vol. 16 (1972): 232.

14. Gadamer, *Truth and Method,* revised translation by Joel Weinsheimer and Donald G. Marshall (London: Sheed and Ward, 1989), p. 305.

15. Gadamer, "The Universality of the Hermeneutical Problem," in *Philosophical Hermeneutics,* p. 5.

16. Gadamer, "Being, Spirit, God," trans. Steven W. Davis, in *Heidegger Memorial Lectures,* ed. Werner Marx (Pittsburgh: Duquesne University Press, 1982), p. 67. The

German text *("Sein Geist Gott")* appears in *Neuere Philosophie* 1, and is the final essay in *Heideggers Wege.*

17. Ibid.

18. Philippe Lacoue-Labarthe, *Heidegger, Art, and Politics,* trans. Chris Turner (London: Basil Blackwell, 1990), especially chapter six.

19. "Aesthetics and Hermeneutics" appears in *Philosophical Hermeneutics,* pp. 95–104. (Hereafter abbreviated in the text as AH.) The German text, *"Aesthetik und Hermeneutik,"* appears in *Kleine Schriften* 2 (Tübingen: J. C. B. Mohr [Paul Siebeck], 1979). "The Relevance of the Beautiful" (trans. Nicholas Walker) is from *The Relevance of the Beautiful and Other Essays,* ed. Robert Bernasconi (Cambridge: Cambridge University Press, 1986), pp. 3–53. (Hereafter abbreviated in the text as RB.) The German text, *Die Aktualität des Schönen,* was published by Philipp Reclam (Stuttgart, 1977).

20. It is worthwhile noting in connection with this point that, at least with respect to *Truth and Method,* Gadamer has thought it necessary to remind readers of the place his discussion of aesthetics occupies in that work. He has written that his analysis of aesthetic experience has there merely an introductory function, leading up to a discussion of the more fundamental matter of dialogue. In other words, understanding the "other" of the artwork is important in order to better understand the "other" who is part of humanity *("Ethos und Ethik,"* in *Neuere Philosophie* 1, p. 357).

21. For another look at this question, see Gadamer's *"Ende der Kunst? Von Hegels Lehre vom Vergangenheitscharakter der Kunst bis zur Antikunst von heute"* in *Das Erbe Europas* (Frankfurt: Suhrkamp Verlag, 1989), pp. 63–86.

22. In a lecture given in Athens in 1967, Heidegger appears to privilege Greek art over modern art *("Die Herkunft der Kunst und die Bestimmung des Denkens,"* in *Distanz und Nähe,* ed. P. Jaeger and R. Lüthe (Würzburg: Königshausen and Neumann, 1983), pp. 11–22. Two years later, in a short work concerning sculpture *("Die Kunst und der Raum,"* in *Gesamtausgabe* 13 [Frankfurt: Klostermann, 1983], pp. 203–10) Heidegger strikingly gives no examples of particular works of art, but does ask one to pay attention to the original meanings of some words. Both texts point to Heidegger's difficulty in seeing modern art to be of the same order as the art of the past.

23. Of interest here is Gadamer's description of his own experience of an architectural work, the cathedral of St. Gallen, in *"Hermeneutik und bildende Kunst,"* Neue Zürcher Zeitung, September 22/23 1979, pp. 65–66.

24. *"Ende der Kunst?"* p. 86.

25. "The Political Incompetence of Philosophy," p. 368.

26. Ibid., p. 365.

REPLY TO DIANE P. MICHELFELDER

It is not surprising that my text which is taken as a starting point here is not taken up for the sake of aesthetics or the philosophy of art but rather for the sake of the question how Heidegger's involvement in National Socialism is reflected in my eyes. To be bridged here are huge distances between which lies not only the ocean but half a century. For a contemporary American the interest that dominates runs directly counter to my own interest. It is indeed clear that for someone like me—who from the beginning observed Heidegger's entire political adventure, if only from a distance, from Marburg, entirely without preparation and surely not without terror—the task presents itself under very different presuppositions than for the contemporary reader. For us in 1960 the task was to see how we could keep alive the philosophical impetus that issued and that, despite everything, continued to issue from Heidegger. That was the task presented to all of us.

For these purposes, a more infelicitous starting point than my (1960) afterword to Heidegger's Reclam edition of "The Origin of the Work of Art" could hardly be found. In those days, after the nightmare was gone, I accepted Heidegger's invitation and, as a philosophical reader, I saw it as my task to work out the uniform line in Heidegger's thinking which leads from the thing to the word. This was supposed to facilitate a comprehension of the late Heidegger. For this reason the selection of my text seems to me to be at the same time infelicitous and understandable. What was already possible to "think away" *("wegzu-denken")* and to forget when listening to the text in 1936 becomes the real topic here. Since the dictatorship, and behind it the *Wehrmacht,* dominated the field, we in Germany could only continue to disregard all of that and to push aside the contemporary resonances so that the ingenious insights of the thinker Heidegger could further our own thought. With appreciation I noticed that Ms. Michelfelder, despite the abyss between our interests, recognized all the same a philosophical insight of Heidegger in the example of "earth" in my essay, and that she probably also felt the experience Heidegger made and worked through at the columns of Pastum. I remember clearly how we, in 1936, passed over the fantastic dead-end reverie of the 'people' with the most embarrassed discretion. Heidegger's successor in Marburg—Erich Frank who lived with us in Marburg before he took that position—certainly complemented the problematic and, like us, understood 'community' instead of 'people' to be that which every significant work of art creates *(stiftet)* around a great artist.

To be sure, in 1936 Heidegger had already fallen into political disgrace with the "Party." However, in the Frankfurt lectures which we listened to together, one still felt very strongly his political identification with what was called the National-Socialist "awakening" *("Aufbruch")*. I was interested in how Heidegger, from his philosophical perspective, thought about the work of art and its statement *(Aussage),* and to see how this could be found not only in a translation of Hölderlin's later poetic works into the conceptual language of philosophy. My first attempts in the field of aesthetics began as early as the 1930s. It should be noted that Cohen's voice could be heard less then; his aesthetics in general met with little consideration. Instead, Paul Natorp appropriated Beethoven and Dostoyevsky from the viewpoint of German mysticism and handed it down impressively. But for me there were further important impetuses. They came primarily through Richard Hamann who, having completed his doctorate under Dilthey, led me to Georg Simmel, Jonas Cohn, and the young Lukács. Apart from these, the productive effects of the George circle could be seen in those days in Marburg, for example, in Friedrich Wolters and, last but not least, in Ernst Robert Curtius. Heidegger's interest in modern art, as well as his turn to Hölderlin, grew less out of his erroneous political paths than out of his tireless search for God, a goal which he could never attain. Even the point of my own strongest deviation from Heidegger's philosophical thoughts belongs to this context. Heidegger always viewed Plato through the lens of Aristotle, and by so doing he missed something that could have assisted his later thinking much better than his complete absorption in Hölderlin.

I do not want to avoid the guiding interest of Ms. Michelfelder's contribution, but I cannot really share it. In the meantime I have taken my own path which I sketched in *Truth and Method.* By no means do I believe that it points toward a completely new direction leading away from the late Heidegger, but, to the contrary, I believe that it pursues a better, and that means a more explicable, path. It was supposed to be a hermeneutic grounded in 'conversation'. Heidegger's later works and his slowly emerging agreement with my Plato works confirmed my enterprise, and when he called my commentary on Paul Celan the second volume to *Truth and Method* I did not feel misunderstood at all. In any case, the impetus for thought which Heidegger meant for me continued to influence my later works as can be seen in volume eight of my collected works *(Kunst als Aussage).* Today I wish more than ever that one does what I attempted to do: to seek to utilize for one's own paths even Heidegger's later thought efforts.

H.-G.G.

23

Bjørn T. Ramberg

THE SOURCE OF THE SUBJECTIVE

What follows is a schematic calibration of Hans-Georg Gadamer's hermeneutic ontology of interpretation and an externalist analysis of intentionality. This is no arbitrary juxtaposition; they both work, along different axes, to provide a conception of the subject which breaks free of Cartesian metaphors. In a nutshell: the former points to a conception of the mental as essentially temporal, while the latter helps us shed the myth of inner space. The two, I claim, are made for each other.

I shall begin by pursuing the hermeneutic critique of an aspect of subjectivism—specifically, the idea that we interpret objectifications of mind ultimately in terms of intentional states of the originating subject. The point of this critique is that subjectivism assumes, if not the actual atemporality of interpreting subjects, then at least a conception of subjectivity which fails to recognize historicity as an essential determinant of all understanding. The burden of this first section is to suggest how our abandoning the Cartesian subject leads us to give up the determination of the originating subject's mental states as the ideal target of interpretations of meaningful phenomena.

Nevertheless, I do actually believe that interpretation is intrinsically and irreducibly of subjectivities, that an account of one is *eo ipso* an account of the other. Accordingly, the point of the second part is to modify the overzealous conclusion drawn from the hermeneutic diagnosis of the first part. In the end, I suggest, a non-Cartesian picture of content-bearing mental states will retain both the hermeneutic account of the historicity of meaning as well as a tight connection between interpretation and subjectivity.

Along the way I shall make assumptions, both exegetical and philosophical (if readers still find this distinction a useful one), to which various objections may be raised. If there is a decisive justification for these bare claims, it will be found in the virtues of a larger view the articulation of which Gadamer has made possible. In that context, the present ambition is modest; the announced superimposition is really a matter of a regional pixel adjustment, a local enhancement for the viewing of a fragment of that larger vista.

1. GOODBYE TO THE *MENS AUCTORIS*

In denying that we understand intentional phenomena by recovering the intentions that bring them about, Gadamer distinguishes himself fundamentally from the methodological hermeneuticists. Certainly, the historicism of Dilthey, in particular, brings to the fore the temporality of all human efforts to understand, and so is a valuable corrective to the Enlightenment conception of Reason. However, Gadamer takes Dilthey's response to historicity to be conditioned by the very prejudices he attempts to overcome, in so far as his hermeneutics was developed as a methodological response to the truth of the subjectivist thesis that Gadamer rejects. From Gadamer's perspective, Dilthey fails to fully realize his own insight that their historicity is not a contingent fact about persons but an essential determinant. This failure finds expression in Dilthey's wish to do for the *Geisteswissenschaften* what Kant did for the natural sciences, and so to produce a general method designed to free the interpreter, the humanist scientist, from the distortions of particular prejudices of time and place.

For Gadamer, such a method, were it conceivable, would produce not clarity but emptiness of mind. The understanding does not receive, it reaches out. Though it does not do so in a way that might be formalized through Kantian transcendental analysis; Kant's understanding is from Gadamer's point of view as receiving as that of Hume, although the formatting procedures are somewhat more extensive. The reaching out to the phenomena that Gadamer has in mind is achieved precisely through the vast, unarticulated mass of beliefs, interests, and perceptions which forms the involvement with the world of an individual, her historical situatedness, and which Kant's transcendental philosophy leaves behind as contingent matter for the pure and immutable form of the understanding.

Gadamerian hermeneutics emphasizes the understanding as perspectival interrogator of the world, a poser of substantive questions from a point of view. What is understood, is understood as an answer to a question, and a question is a question only in a particular context. The prejudicial structure of the understanding provides that context; any particular question we have in mind has, as its roots, an indefinite number of beliefs. In interrogating the phenomena that hold our reflective attention, we indirectly give expression to these unreflective beliefs as biases and prejudices. These, however, are not encumberings from which methodology will deliver us: "Prejudices are biases of our openness to the world. They are simply conditions whereby we experience something—whereby what we encounter says something to us" (Gadamer 1966, 9).

The point is not only the trite one that at any given time we believe more than we are aware of believing and are guided by unarticulated interests. The point is that this fact is what enables us to entertain any given belief or question, or to pursue any clearly grasped interest. For Gadamer, the situated, prejudicial structure of cognition is the *condition of the possibility* of any understanding whatsoever. Before the reflective understanding can consciously inquire about a particular object, that object is constituted as object of inquiry by the subject's involvement with her world. This involvement manifests itself cognitively as prejudices which direct the understanding, and can therefore never be fully objectified by the reflective consciousness.

As Gadamer conceives of them, there is, to understate the matter, nothing inherently pernicious about prejudices. They are simply attitudes we think and act on (quite literally; they are the basis on which acting and thinking can happen), attitudes that we might not at the moment be attributing to ourselves. Some of these are pernicious, of course, some are deceptive, some obscure, and some plain foolish, but, as a body, they constitute our orientation to the world; as our preunderstanding they are the required context of our questioning of the phenomena we encounter.

It should be obvious that our preunderstanding is not a fixed block of desires and beliefs; like our physical body, the body of our prejudices is unstable and in constant, though not homogeneous, metamorphosis. This is a process over which we can, and ought to, exert some influence: We might become aware of prejudices as such, for example, when we find ourselves in situations where they suddenly appear unjustifiable, or at least to be in need of justification. And so we may come to understand ourselves better, more deeply, when we expose ourselves to that which is different, unfamiliar, distant, even threatening. In this way, we bring aspects of our preunderstanding to reflective consciousness. As Gadamer says, "Reflecting on a given pre-understanding brings before me something that otherwise happens *'behind my back'"* (Gadamer 1967, 38).

The understanding subject, then, is a being for whom the world is already constituted by preconceived expectations, which in portions of varying sizes may become explicit, or change, or both, in the very process of our coming to understand the world. This is true whether or not we are dealing with intentional phenomena; our cognitive grip is always secured by virtue of the directedness of our preunderstanding. Every judgment we might make is based on the prejudices which guide our eye to particular features of the world. Intentional phenomena are not a special case; understanding the meaning of a text, as well as identifying an object as a can opener, is a matter of construing it as providing answers to certain questions. The notion of prejudice, expressing the involvement with the world which allows this questioning to take place, is intended to suggest something that precedes any cognitive act of the self-conscious subject. For Gadamer, therefore, understanding is at its most fundamental an event—it is something that happens to us, that makes us the subjects we are. As an explication of understanding, consequently, Gadamer's hermeneutics is not reducible to methodology. Its claims are ontological.

However, the specific implications for the domain of classical hermeneutics, the interpretation of texts, become apparent in Gadamer's appropriation of the

Husserlian concept of *horizon:* "With this concept . . . Husserl is obviously seeking
to capture the way all limited intentionality of meaning merges into the fundamental continuity of the whole. A horizon is not a rigid boundary but something that
moves with one and invites one to advance further" (Gadamer 1975, 245).[1]
Embodying the suggestion of a limited perspective which fluidly moves beyond
itself, mediating limited particularity and cohesive totality, the metaphor of the
horizon lends itself to an account of understanding which emphasizes the temporality of interpreting subjects.[2] On the one hand, the horizon of understanding is,
for Gadamer, the total present orientation of the historically situated individual.
As "the range of vision that includes everything that can be seen from a particular vantage point" (302), the horizon is the "initial directedness of our whole
ability to experience" (Gadamer 1966, 9). Yet on the other hand, just as our
prejudices are not fixed, so Gadamer's horizon is essentially impermanent.
While everything is understood from a point of view, this point is changing and
enabling, rather than fixed and restricting. Gadamer underlines this point with a
specific modulation of Husserl's metaphor. The temporal, dynamic nature of
understanding is not to be envisaged as a sequence of horizons, each superseded
by the next, but as an ongoing process of fusion:

> In fact the horizon of the present is continually in the process of being formed
> because we are continually having to test all our prejudices. An important part of this
> testing occurs in encountering the past and in understanding of the tradition from
> which we come. Hence the horizon of the present cannot be formed without the past.
> There is no more an isolated horizon of the present in itself than there are historical
> horizons which have to be acquired. *Rather, understanding is always the fusion of
> these horizons supposedly existing by themselves.* (306)

We must take the last, emphasized phrase quite literally, for it in fact encapsulates Gadamer's critique of the subjectivist conception of understanding. The
notion of a continual fusion of horizons, which Gadamer elaborates in the context of historical understanding, captures our appropriation of all intentional phenomena, all embodiments of consciousness. It has as a direct consequence that
to grasp the content of such objectifications is not—cannot be—a matter of
reproducing the horizon of the producer, since, Gadamer says, we only imagine
such a discrete, isolable entity to exist. It is, instead, a matter of drawing the
product itself, as a manifestation of the mind of another, into active question-
and-answer dialogue with one's own understanding. Interpreting the content of
an object or event is to bring out possible questions to which it might be an
answer. This process is as much a matter of self-understanding as it is a matter
of understanding something other, since the questions one is able to raise bring
to light, or to view, aspects of one's horizon. This process becomes reflective
when the phenomena to be interpreted are perceived as in some sense alien or
puzzling, when the hermeneutic issue is explicitly raised. The experience of,

e.g., cultural distance, which in such cases might prevent immediate understanding, is the effect of being confronted with what we can only understand as the productions of people whose actions and thoughts are informed by relevantly different preunderstandings or collections of prejudices. Overcoming this distance always involves changes in the body of prejudices of the interpreter. At the same time, our interpretations must, Gadamer holds, transcend the understanding of the producer. The questions the interpreter is able to call forth will bring to bear on the interpreted object a position in the world and time which is always to some extent different from that of the producer.

> The real meaning of the text [Gadamer claims], as it speaks to the interpreter, does not depend on the contingencies of the author and his [or her] original public. It certainly is not identical with them, for it is always co-determined also by the historical situation of the interpreter and hence by the totality of the objective course of history. . . . Not just occasionally but always, the meaning of a text goes beyond its author. (296)

Nevertheless, might there not be some component of meaning that is internal, as it were, to the object, determined as that which valid interpretations succeed in correctly applying to their unique contexts? If this were so, we might have it both ways: it would be true, as Gadamer says, that "[e]very age has to understand a transmitted text in its own way" (296), yet at the same time we could preserve the idea that there is *something* about the relation between author and text that grounds validity in interpretation. Perhaps one might even admit that there is no way to say what this something might be other than by appealing to the notion of valid interpretation, and so be willing to grant that the idea of the *mens auctoris* therefore serves no epistemic or methodological purpose. One could still maintain, in a spirit of metaphysical realism, that it remains the (ineffable) core of any correct interpretation.[3] One might, in short, accept Gadamer's account as a phenomenology of interpretation, an account of how interpretation does and must proceed, while remaining committed to a Cartesian ontology of meaning.

The question here is whether it even makes sense to think of an object such as a text as having a kind of content, however partial, however ideal, which it possesses independently of any particular interpretative encounter, and which does metaphysical duty as truth-maker of valid interpretations. For Gadamer, the answer is clear: in the making of sense the relation between the subject and object is primary with respect to its relata; they are constituted as subject and object of understanding in the interpretative encounter. This is the burden of Gadamer's discussion of the classic hermeneutic distinction between understanding, interpretation, and application (see 307ff.). While Gadamer's romantic predecessors "recognized the inner unity of *intelligere* and *explicare*" (307), Gadamer insists that the moment of application, too, must be seen as an integral part of any understanding.

Here he is making a point of ontology: there is no meaning separable, even in principle, from application in a context. This is the thrust of his critique of psychological hermeneutics, which aims precisely to capture contents across contexts.

Gadamer makes this very same antisubjectivist point when he claims that we only imagine horizons to exist apart from their fusion; the fusion, the encounter, is not what expresses or transmits meaning, it is not a synthesis of separable components of meaning, it is literally what constitutes it. Gadamer shows us that the failure to isolate a canonical notion of "internal" meaning or preinterpretational content—something which, as the object's contribution to the encounter, might serve as a foundation for invidious comparisons of alternative interpretations—is not the persistent failure of a human practice to perfectly instantiate its regulative ideal, it is a failure springing from a misconceived ideal.

A text, then, has no definite meaning to be recovered, but is to be construed, in the words of the Gadamer scholar David Linge, as "an inexhaustible source of possibilities of meaning" (Linge 1976, xix). On this view there can be no canonical interpretation of anything. Determining the content of an object or event is, it appears, a matter of specifying questions to which it may be an answer, and this, it would appear, is not to determine originating states of mind of a producing subject.

To sum up: Gadamer's conception of interpretation takes as fundamental rather than accidental the fact of the concrete historical situation in which all understanding takes place, and this surely represents a great advance in our conception of what it is to be a subject. Our historicity is what permits understanding, it is not something to be abstracted away through Kantian suspension of content or to be overcome by the self-transformational methodological constraints of romanticist hermeneuts. To put the Gadamerian point with un-Gadamerian bluntness: the idea of interpretation as recovering the intentions of a producing subject is ultimately linked to a normative conception of a universe of ahistorical, free-floating receptivities, bumping into objects with essences that are determinately what they are independently of any particular description or point of view. While not *denying* that any actual view is a view from a particular point, this conception neglects this fact as purely contingent; as a consequence of our finitude rather than an essential characteristic of subjectivity, it is allowed no bearing on the *ideal* of understanding, and so our historicity becomes nothing more than a methodological challenge in the actual practice of interpretation. This failure to see that our historicity is no limitation, which *happens* to make the God's-eye point of view an unrealizable ideal, but on the contrary an essential determinant of subjectivity which implies that there *is* no God's-eye point of view (it is precisely not a *point* of view at all) is in the end what undermines the notion that we interpret an intentional object by determining the originating states of mind.

2. SUBJECTIVITY EXTERNALIZED

The view that the meaning of a text is cut loose from the author seems to be a common assumption of much current theory. Understandably, too; fashion aside, the assumption arises, on the current picture, from considerations about understanding which seem to leave no viable alternative open for the historically self-conscious theorist. Nevertheless I suggest that this position is both counterintuitive and conceptually unresolved. It is conceptually unresolved, because it fails to break free of the picture of mind it attempts to replace; the move that severs meaning from states of author's mind seems compelling, I will argue, only to someone who thinks of states of mind in an essentially Cartesian way. As for the claim that it is counterintuitive, this can best be supported by turning our attention from texts to actions. The claim then becomes: to understand an action as an action is not a matter of correctly ascribing intentional states. If intuition balks at this, while reason remains generally sympathetic toward the hermeneutic critique of subjectivism, we have a problem. What is the principled distinction between acts and texts, qua objectifications of mind, that warrants this fundamental difference in the determination of their intentional content?

Unless we can come up with one, and I know I can't, it would appear that the meaning of an action transcends the intentions of the agent in the same way that the content of a text purportedly goes beyond the intent behind it. Textualism entails actionalism; agents drop out of the picture along with authors. However, unless we are eliminativists (or, in a different mood, metaphysical realists) with respect to the subjective, we should be reluctant to bite this bullet; for doing so is to insert a conceptual chasm between interpretation and subjectivity. This is tantamount to giving up the idea that interpretation is a matter of understanding subjects qua subjects, that is, as being unique precisely (and only) in having—being—a point of view, an orientation to the world. And to preserve subjectivity as the defining purview of interpretation, to preserve the idea of interpretation as distinctively and literally a meeting of minds, is a fundamental concern of the hermeneutic historicist critique of Cartesianism in the first place, one that Gadamer shares with Schleiermacher and Dilthey.

This tension may be relaxed if we, instead of assimilating actions to texts, assimilate objectifications of mind in general to what I will treat as central intuitions about actions. Now, Gadamerian considerations might appear to preclude this, in so far as they are taken to imply that the interpretationally mediated relation between objectifications of mind and producing subjects entails that interpretations of the former cannot amount to a determination of mental states of the latter, but must necessarily go beyond these. In fact, however, we still have the choice of viewing texts, like actions, as manifestations of paradigmatically subjective states like intentions. This would restore a direct and immediate connection between the content of both texts and actions and the mental states of subjects. Gadamerian hermeneutics would appear to rule out what we may as well frankly call neosubjectivism only when it is co-opted by an implicit view of the content-bearing mental states of agents and authors as internal states with natures or identities independent of interpretation. But this, surely, would be to saddle Gadamer with a prejudice he does not share; it would, as I suggested above, be to methodologize what is intended as ontology. What is needed to spell out in analytic terms the full implications of Gadamer's historicizing of understanding, is a noninternalist picture of what it is for a subject to have something in mind.

What is at issue here, as particularly John McDowell (1985, 1986) and McGinn have made clear, is the idea of mind as substance (that is, at least, the idea of mental properties as intrinsic and autonomous [see McGinn, 24–25]). Making the mind a nonspatial substance is an attempt to capture both the idea of the subjectivity of the mental and the idea of the objectivity of any legitimate domain of understanding. Subjectivity, understood in terms of privacy and, primarily, in terms of self-transparency, is preserved by making the mind nonspatial: nonspatiality ensures the phenomenal nature of what is before the mind, rendering the mind's access to its objects immediate and complete. The substantiality of the mental ensures that it is an objective realm of reality, thinglike, i.e., not metaphysically dependent for its existence on other substances. This picture gives us mental properties that are intrinsic, properties of the sort of ontological entity that is capable of entering into and sustaining relationships with other autonomous substances.

The difficulties of this picture are well known, and usually expressed in epistemological terms: what are the evidential relationships between the phenomenal entities immediately available in and to the mind, on the one hand, and, on the other, the properties of the substances beyond the mental which the mind somehow represents to itself?

Responding to the difficulties of the Cartesian mind simply by making the mind physical is to throw the baby out while retaining the bath water (see McDowell 1986, 152–55). It is to keep the bath water, because the move retains the debilitating view of mental properties as intrinsic and autonomous, leaving methodologically solipsistic psychology intact. And the hermeneutic baby is thrown out, for the motivation behind the nonspatial bit of the Cartesian determination of the mental was to preserve the intuition that to talk of subjectivity is to talk of something *sui generis*. Rendering the mind inner, but physical, makes the challenge of accounting for the semantic, representational aspects of mind an impossible one; internalist physicalism leads to eliminativism. This is to say that if we think *dualism* is what is fundamentally wrong with Cartesianism we end up with substance and no subjectivity—and mind is simply no longer anywhere in sight.

If, on the other hand, we follow for example McDowell's lead and regard the implausibility of dualism as an expression of the impossibility of thinking of subjectivity in terms of substance—as a distinct ontological realm with objectively characterizable features—our response is likely to be different. The mind is not, on this view, something which enters into relation with other things—it exists *as* a system of relations. Mental properties, then, are not autonomous, not intrinsic features of some entity; they are essentially relational. They are individuated, and constituted, (in part) by objects beyond the subject or person. A person's mental properties are a system of relationships between the person and her environment.

That the mind should involve, or be constituted by, what is more or less distant from the person is still intuitively strange. This felt strangeness, though, resulting in notions like narrow content, is a symptom of the obstinacy of the conception of mind as substance. So obstinate is this conception that even an explicitly anti-Cartesian, relational account of understanding such as Gadamer's, which insists that all understanding draws on what is spatially or temporally beyond the object of interpretation, is often taken to imply that any understanding of objectifications of mind always leaves the states of mind of the producer behind. But this leaves us without any account of what such states might be, without an account of the subjective. Fortunately, it follows only if we assume the autonomy and ontological exclusivity of the mind, which is exactly what the externalist view of the mental explicitly denies.

While externalism entails that a mind is not a substance which stands in causal or representational relations to the world, but is essentially world involving, this is not to suggest that we capture the mental *merely* by giving a constitutive role to causal chains that run between a person and her environment. Shifting from a substantialist to a relationalist account is not by itself sufficient to bring the distinctive nature of the mental into view. This happens only once we give full play to the idea that the difference between the mental and the physical lies not at the level of ontological categories but in the purposes and kinds of description and explanation. The trick is not done by substituting at best only partly known external objects for the perfectly known but merely phenomenal intentional objects of the Cartesian mind. The distinctiveness of the mental simply cannot be captured in terms of the nature of purported objects of thought at all (see Davidson 1987).

What distinguishes content-bearing mental states from physical states defined in terms of relational properties is their being described in a vocabulary the terms of which embody a constitutive commitment to a particular normative ideal. To interpret something as content bearing is to explain that something not as an instance of how things tend to happen, but as an instance of how they ought to happen. Explanations that invoke mental states are instances of (to borrow a term from Philip Pettit) normalizing explanations (see Pettit 1986). Citing beliefs and value attitudes as causes for action is certainly to affirm the presence of causal connections, but, in so far as we are talking about actions and reasons, the intelligibility of such accounts derives from the *rationality* they confer upon the action, not from the acknowledged causal connections. We *understand* the action as action only in so far as it is brought under norms of rationality by the cited attitudes. As with Gadamer's account, the point here is ontological, not merely epistemic.

If the attribution of beliefs, desires, fears, hopes, and so on, is essentially a rationalizing or normalizing process, then to attribute one attitude is to attribute many. Beliefs are not rational intrinsically, taken atomically. Normalizing explanations attribute mind-clusters—sets of attitudes—which approximate, more or less imperfectly, some guiding ideal of rationality. Attitudes are attitudes only in such clusters. Mental content *comes to be* in a holistic attribution of states which rationalizes the relationships between persons and their environment. The greater the distance between the normative ideal and the states attributed, the less intelligible becomes the claim that we are dealing with mental states, with something that is an orientation to the world.

The hermeneutic critique of Cartesianism emphasizes the social and historical situatedness of subjects as an essential determinant in all understanding. The externalist conception of mental content allows us to think of this explicitly as a claim about what intentional states are; empirical objectifications of subjectivity are understood when we articulate the perspective, the point of view, which comes to expression in them, but this understanding does not transcend the point of view of the producer, it is part of its constitution. We can take Gadamer's evocative metaphor of understanding as a fusion of horizons, which emphasizes the primacy of the relation over the *relata,* as expressing the fact that meaning arises in the encounter between subject and subject, embedded in a shared world, in a question-answer-question dialectic which constitutes both interpreting and interpreted subject as such. This picture of intelligibility as an emerging relation corresponds neatly to the constitutive role assigned rationalizing explanation on the externalist view I have sketched. For what is at issue in this process are not just the actions and productions of the interpreted subject, but equally the necessarily imperfect grasp of the rationality ideal that guides the interpreter. Our efforts to find something or someone intelligible may involve a change in our very conception of what is intelligible.

At this very point, though, an Anglo-American considering the interpretative account of content might decide to opt out. For the account seems to force a choice between cognitive relativism on the one hand, and, on the other, some form of skepticism-inducing metaphysical realism about rationality. Regarded from the point of view of someone who has taken to heart Gadamer's historicized conception of meaning, however, this dilemma itself appears to be founded on subjectivist preconceptions. It is an instance of the idea that we can speak meaningfully and comparatively of separate semantic horizons, existing independently of constitutive moments of fusion. To put it differently: the grim choice presupposes that the question of the source of the validity of norms of rationality can be generalized in such a way that it can be raised without substantive reference to particular contexts of interpretation. And this, if I read Gadamer correctly, is one version of the subjectivist illusion. For hesitant externalists, then, it is not the least virtue of Gadamer's thoroughgoing antisubjectivism that it reveals the contingency of this particular dilemma, providing a basis for an alternative account of the dialectical, mutually transforming relationship between interpretative practice and the ideals that guide it.

The hermeneutic-externalist joint account rejects not just contemporary vestiges of the idea of mind as inner space, but also the view of mental attitudes as instant. To see interpretation both as essentially historical and as constitutive of content, is to grant that there is no definite, particular point at which the contents of the intentions, actions, or productions of a subject crystallize.[4] To be an intentional being is to engage and be engaged in a certain kind of process, rather than to be the bearer of individual, atomically specifiable states. In this very process, in the interpretation of certain objects and events as expressions of the intentional totalities of others, we hermeneutically constitute ourselves and each other as subjects with thoughts and intentions. Dropping the prejudice that what is temporally distant cannot enter into the mental content of a subject, allows us to free our account of subjectivity from any remaining Cartesian moorings. By consistently reading Gadamer as an externalist, as giving an account of how mental content emerges, we can close the rift between sense and mental content with which the first part of this paper concluded.

What we lose on this conception of meaning is the possibility of employing notions like original intention to anchor canonical criteria of correctness that would allow us to judge the validity of competing interpretations. From Gadamer's perspective, of course, this is no loss at all. What is gained is, I think, significant. Firstly, as I have stressed, we retain the intrinsic—indeed, constitutive—connection between interpretation and subjectivity understood not in terms of privacy or self-transparency but as a locus of coherence, as an orientation to and in the world, or, still more metaphorically, as a field of intention stretched out in the world and through time by interpretation. Secondly, we can strengthen the case for the externalist-interpretative picture of content by drawing on Gadamer's account of the relation between the practice of interpretation and the norms that guide it. Thirdly, and conversely, we are able to conceive of content in a manner which gives full weight to the historicity of subjects without falling prey to relativism or idealism. The essentially world-involving nature of the mental, depicted in externalist accounts of content, alleviates the threat of linguistic idealism that allegedly stems from Gadamer's Heideggerian claims about the linguistic nature of being; for while it is true that things are what they are only under descriptions, it is clear, too, to the externalist, that descriptions are descriptions only in a world of things. This view of content ensures the public nature of the world in and through which subjectivity appears as normatively constituted points of view.[5]

BJØRN T. RAMBERG
DEPARTMENT OF PHILOSOPHY
SIMON FRASER UNIVERSITY
JULY 1992

NOTES

1. Further citations from *Truth and Method* will be by page number only.

2. See p. 304: "Everything contained in historical consciousness is in fact embraced by a single historical horizon. Our own past and that other past toward which our historical consciousness is directed help to shape this moving horizon out of which human life always lives and which determines itself as heritage and tradition."

3. A model for this sort of response might be Jerry Fodor's defense of narrow content in the face of Twin Earth difficulties (see Fodor 1987, chapter 2). Fodor's realism expresses itself here in his efforts to insulate the ontology of meaning from the epistemology of interpretation.

4. As Karsten Stueber has pointed out to me, this certainly places in question the nature of mental causation. Still, I don't think viewing the notion of temporally localized contents as a reification forces one to give up the view that beliefs and desires can be described as causes of actions. The issue turns on what conceptual requirements we might think supervenience relations impose, and I cannot usefully pursue that question here.

5. In developing this paper I have drawn on the generosity and expertise of colleagues and friends, none of whom are going to be entirely happy with the final result. I hope, nevertheless, they will forgive me for acknowledging their contributions, which have greatly improved the final result: John Tietz's extensive comments on the earliest recognizable incarnation of the paper pointed me in the right direction. Later versions owe much to discussions with faculty and graduate students at Emory University and the Universities of Connecticut and of South Carolina, and also with fellow participants at the 1990 summer seminar on Heidegger and Davidson at the University of California at Santa Cruz. In particular, talks with Jerald Wallulis affected the focus of my exposition of Gadamer. More recently, both Karsten Stueber's insightful and constructive remarks and John Russon's illuminating and generous commentary on the penultimate version (CPA Conference, May 1992) have helped me see more clearly the implications of my argument. Thanks to them all.

REFERENCES

Burge, T. 1986. "Cartesian Error and the Objectivity of Perception." In J. McDowell and P. Pettit, eds., *Subject, Thought, and Context*. Oxford University Press.

Davidson, D. 1982. "Mental Events." In *Essays on Action and Events*. Oxford University Press.

———. 1987. "Knowing One's Own Mind." APA (Pacific Division) Presidential Address.

Fodor, J. 1987. *Psychosemantics.* MIT Press.

Gadamer, H.-G. 1966. "The Universality of the Hermeneutical Problem." In D. Linge, 1976, *Philosophical Hermeneutics.* University of California Press.

———. 1967. "On the Scope and Function of Hermeneutical Reflection." In D. Linge, 1976, *Philosophical Hermeneutics.* University of California Press.

———. 1975. *Truth and Method.* Seabury Press.

Linge, D., ed. 1976. *Philosophical Hermeneutics.* University of California Press.

McDowell, J. 1985. "Functionalism and Anomalous Monism." In E. LePore and B. McLaughlin, eds., *Actions and Events.* Blackwell.

———. 1986. "Singular Thought and the Extent of Inner Space." In J. McDowell and P. Pettit, eds., *Subject, Thought, and Context.* Oxford University Press.

McGinn, C. 1989. *Mental Content.* Blackwell.

Pettit, P. 1986. "Broadminded Explanation and Psychology." In J. McDowell and P. Pettit, eds., *Subject, Thought, and Context.* Oxford University Press.

REPLY TO BJØRN T. RAMBERG

It is extraordinarily difficult for me to situate myself with regard to the language of this contribution. Already the first sentence contains problems for me: "Externalist Analysis of Intentionality." Is this being opposed to hermeneutic philosophy? Or perhaps both are being placed in close proximity to each other? I can understand what might be an opposition, namely, I apparently meet with a certain agreement here on the form of reflection of the *'cogito me cogitare'*, and thus also with the critique of the singular power of the ideal of methodology and certainty. This is the anti-Cartesian element which I believe received its standard from the basic modes of behavior of the modern mathematical natural sciences. Apparently, the author sees my critical distancing from Dilthey in the same way, and he is right in this. However, I miss something here: Kant is not only found in the *Critique of Pure Reason*. His real persisting presence lies in practical philosophy, that is in the concept of freedom which cannot be understood as fact of cognition but only as fact of reason—with all its far-reaching metaphysical consequences. If one were to understand Kant in this broader sense, then Hegel and the whole of romanticism, in truth even the basic impulses of the entire modern world, would be grasped along with it. That the mere transparency of subjectivity as the self-confirmation of the methodological domination of the world cannot be advanced as the final truth most definitely has to be kept in mind. It is difficult for me to understand, however, why Heidegger is being mentioned in this context as an idealist of language. Thus, I fear that I will lose again all of my credit when I also hold the opinion that only the universality of our reason conveying itself linguistically gives the real framework within which we articulate world as world, world as our lifeworld. That the transformative force of the methodologically constructive natural sciences and of technology integrates itself into this great framework certainly does not mean that all the rest is abandoned to the mere arbitrariness of possible interpretations.

To be sure, in the face of our own limitations and our deficient competence we always have to view the difference between correct and false interpretations as a relative, that is, revisable, interpretation. But there are certainly also simply false interpretations. I would say that here we have a trait in common with research into nature which has to relativize its final pieces of knowledge from the viewpoint of the progress of research. I think that this applies to hermeneutics in the same sense, although not on the basis of scientific progress. Our understanding always expects that our understanding of the world changes. That does not at all mean that it makes progress in the same sense as research into nature does. But it does mean that our present understanding of the world will be changed by new points of view. That is the essence of hermeneutics. In this sense the appeal to the *mens auctoris* is inappropriate for the hermeneutic way of thinking. The truth value of an interpretation always depends on us, too, and the process in which we all participate. That does not have to mean that historical experiences have to determine us. There can also be lasting results that give weight to our knowledge of the world. So in principle I would agree that the relation takes precedence and not the single member of the relation. The concept of play plays a decisive role not only in the field of language, as Wittgenstein emphasized, but also in many other areas of cultural life. Thus, I cannot entirely agree with efforts to trace the extension of the hermeneutic formation of horizons back to actions, as if they were the sole issue. That sounds as if it depended upon our will. In general, experience is not always the confirmation of what we want, wish, or plan.

I fear that my marginal notes did not illuminate the sense in which serious philosophical research of younger researchers can utilize my ideas on hermeneutics. But I think it is good that we try a conversation and that we learn from ourselves.

H.-G.G.

24

John Sallis

REREADING THE *TIMAEUS:* THE
MEMORIAL POWER OF DISCOURSE

In his essay "Idea and Reality in Plato's *Timaeus,*"* Gadamer focuses on the very exceptional position and character of this dialogue. Attentive to the hermeneutic preconceptions that have come to govern the reading of the Platonic text, Gadamer notes that the *Timaeus* "occupies a singular position on the periphery of the works of Plato" (158). Behind this marginalizing of the dialogue lies the attitude stemming from Aristotle's *Physics,* which would replace the story of the demiurge with an account more rigorously scientific. Even the reliance on the *Timaeus* of both medieval theology and, in a very different respect, the seventeenth-century founders of modern science, has not sufficed to recall the *Timaeus* from the periphery and to prompt an integration of its discourse with that of the other dialogues, most notably those regarded as presenting—in contrast to the mythical narrative—Plato's dialectic. Although Gadamer does not stress the fact, this marginalization of the *Timaeus,* especially since the era of German idealism, is nonetheless paradoxical, since of all the dialogues it is the one that has been most continuously read and that has most consistently and thoroughly governed the very sense of Platonism. To say nothing of the fact that one of the legacies that had its inception in the era of German idealism was a renewed attentiveness to the literary character of the dialogues, an openness to forms of discourse and aspects of discourse not governed by a single model derived from allegedly scientific canons. So then, a paradoxical marginalization, to be sure, and yet one that no doubt was still largely in force when Gadamer composed his essay in the early 1970s. More recently there are signs of renewed interest in the *Timaeus* and of a reading that would resituate the dialogue at the center of Plato's work. No doubt Gadamer's essay has been instrumental in spurring this new interest and in prompting a challenge to the older interpretations of the dialogue.

While fully acknowledging the need to investigate the literary character of the dialogue, in the way inaugurated especially by Schleiermacher, the need to establish the philosophical significance of the scene, the setting, of the dialogue and to interrogate the relationship of each speaker to what is said, Gadamer notes that even in this respect the *Timaeus* presents a special problem, since the scene and even the other speakers recede so thoroughly into the background, giving way to the long narrative by Timaeus that occupies most of the dialogue, continuing to its end without a single response or interruption from the other speakers, not even from Socrates. And yet, even if the other typical dialogical elements fall away, Timaeus's long monologue is nonetheless quite distinctive in its literary character. Indeed, Gadamer calls special attention to the character of the discourse, noting that it is "a kind of story which, in fairy tale fashion, is peculiarly loose, incoherent, and allusive." He continues: "The incoherence is especially obvious in the way the natural sequence in which a narrative would usually unfold is interrupted by regressions, corrections, repetitions, and abrupt new beginnings" (160). In particular, he calls attention to the abrupt new beginning that is made when Timaeus, absorbed in the particulars of human perception, suddenly interrupts himself and, insisting that things ought to be considered in relation to ἀνάγκη, makes a new, second beginning in his narrative on the cosmos. Or rather, he launches, as Gadamer says, a "search for another, more fundamental beginning," which "cannot be inserted straightaway and unobtrusively into the story being told" and which opens a discourse that *"has a completely new look to it"* (170).

In the spirit of Gadamer's essay and following the clues it provides, I would like to focus on the peculiar character of the discourse in the *Timaeus* and especially to draw out the way in which that discourse is characterized within the discourse itself. I shall want also, moving in the orbit of Gadamer's broader work in hermeneutics as such, to consider the memorial power of discourse, its power to bring things back in their presence to one's vision. I shall be concerned also with the limits of that power, that is, with those points at which a gap opens in memory, at which discourse proves incapable of bringing things back in their full presence, those points at which certain kinds of things prove to resist and to escape the memorial gathering of speech. These are also the points at which discourse addressed to others ceases to call so imperatively for direct response, for an affirmation, negation, qualification, or interrogation based on a restoration of presence in the would-be interlocutor by the discourse. At these limits conversation would be exposed to silence and communication disrupted insofar as it involves the requirement that something come to be shared, held in common before an essentially common vision. At these limits necessity may prescribe that dialogue become monologue. As in the *Timaeus,* in which the opening, conversational remembrance of the πόλις gives way to a series of monologues, some presented, some only promised. The most extensive of those presented is of course Timaeus's monologue on the cosmos, itself broken into three distinct discourses by the abrupt new beginnings ventured by Timaeus.

Gadamer has noted how from the outset of the first of these discourses a twofold distinction—he calls it the distinction between being and becoming—

comes into play in the form of the schema of paradigm and image, a schema directly linked to making or production (ποίησις). This distinction, thus construed, thoroughly governs the development of the first of Timaeus's discourses: here it is a matter of telling how the artisan god, the δημιουργός, made the cosmos by looking to the paradigm and producing the cosmos in and as its image.

The most decisive interruption is the one by which Timaeus breaks off this first discourse and launches then on another, very different one, the one that Gadamer insists cannot be "inserted straightaway and unobtrusively into the story" as told up to that point, the one that *"has a completely new look to it."* What prompts the interruption is the fact that the first discourse, moving from vision of the paradigm to the fabrication of its image, proves to have passed over entirely—that is, to have taken for granted—the four so-called elements from which the god is said to have made the body of the cosmos. Timaeus's second discourse turns back, then, to this beginning that precedes the beginning of the god's fabrication of the cosmos. This turn culminates in the addition of a third kind, the receptacle, the χώρα, which comes thus to supplement the twofold that governed the first discourse, that is, to complete or ground the discourse of the twofold while, at the same time, undermining it, exposing it to an abyss. Timaeus's second discourse, especially its culmination in the discourse on the χώρα, the chorology, is the most perplexing in the entire dialogue. It is also the discourse in which the most extreme limits come into play.

In speaking of the cosmos and then of the precosmic beginning, Timaeus broaches three kinds of discourse, that is, three ways in which the memorial power of discourse can come into play, also, correspondingly, three ways in which the limits of discourse come to operate. Not only does Timaeus broach these kinds of discourse but also, remarkably, he distinguishes the kinds and indeed in the course of the dialogue refers back repeatedly to the most explicitly drawn of the distinctions.

Before beginning the first of his discourses, Timaeus speaks of discourse as such (*Tim.* 29b–c). Construing it within the framework of the twofold, he declares that discourse about an image or about its paradigm will be akin to that which it is about, will be of the same kind (συγγενής) as that of which it is spoken. Those discourses that tell of what is permanent and stable, of the selfsame paradigms, are themselves permanent and unchanging; insofar as it befits discourse to be irrefutable and invincible, these discourses will be such as are not to be pushed and swept aside by others. On the other hand, discourses about images of the paradigms will share in the image-character, will be of the same kind as the images told of in the discourses: whenever the λόγος is about an εἰκών, it will be an εἰκώς λόγος. One can say: *likely discourse*—though it is imperative to bear in mind that such discourse is likely, not in the sense of probability, but in that it is a discourse about a likeness, an image. It is an imaginal discourse and as such no less distant from the truth than the images of which it speaks are from the original, the paradigm. Furthermore, such discourse will be just as impermanent, as changing, as the images of which it speaks: such discourse will be multiple, one discourse changing into another or coming to sweep another aside, one discourse developing into another or coming to interrupt it.

But what do such discourse and its typology have to do with remembrance? In what way are these kinds of discourse memorial? How in general does discourse function memorially? What is the character of the remembrance achieved through it? What is remembrance as such?

To remember is to bring something back to mind, to bring back before one's inner vision something remote, something past. It is to bring back into presence something that nonetheless, in its pastness, is, and remains, absent. In a more radical sense, to remember is to bring and to hold before one's vision things that in and of themselves pass away, things that are always already past as soon as they come to presence, things that are not just singularly past but rather characterized by passingness. Such remembrance is precisely what is thought in the Platonic texts (for instance, in the central books of the *Republic*) as the ascensional movement from the things that come to be and pass away *to* the εἶδος that shines through and gathers such things. In coming to have before one's vision the εἶδος, the unchanging "look" of the things that come and go, one brings those things back in their full presence, indeed in a presence of which they themselves, stamped as they are by passingness, are incapable. Thus it is that learning, that is, coming to know something, is nothing other than a kind of remembrance.

Thus it is also that discourse is memorial. For it is in speech that the gathering εἴδη are themselves already gathered and borne. It is through discourse, in speaking, that the εἴδη are first set forth in such a way that they can then be beheld in remembrance of those passing things gathered by them, gathered to the common look.

Such is, then, the irrefutable and invincible discourse that tells of what is permanent and stable, the discourse of the paradigm. It is itself, in a sense, paradigmatic in its orientation to the restoration, the vision, of full presence.

What, then, of that other kind of discourse, the εἰκὼς λόγος in which Timaeus tells of how the god, looking to the paradigm, made the cosmos in its image, as its image? Such discourse recoils from the εἶδος. In it the directionality is reversed: it is a descensional discourse, proceeding from the paradigm back to the image, taking distance thus from full presence. As imaginal discourse it sets forth the image in which the cosmos is gathered into presence—or rather, it sets forth a developing, multiple, manifold image, that is, it unfolds as a narrative, indeed as a narrative that Timaeus comes eventually to interrupt precisely because it has failed to *present* the *full* development of the cosmos, passing in silence over the fire, air, earth, and water that the god is assumed to have had at his disposal when he came to fabricate the cosmos. Not only is the εἰκὼς λόγος a moving, developing, narrative discourse but also—and not only in this respect—it is limited: before its beginning there is another beginning that will have escaped it.

Not that the eikonic character simply vanishes once Timaeus turns to his second discourse, once he turns toward the so-called elements and ultimately toward what he calls χώρα. If anything, the eikonic character of the discourse becomes more obtrusive, as it drifts from one image to another, from receptacle to nurse, to a mass of gold modeled into different figures, to a block of wax on which designs are stamped, to the mother, to a base for fragrant ointments. Yet, through this drift, through what this discourse manages to say of what finally comes to be called the χώρα, the necessity of another kind of discourse is exposed, one that would no longer remain within the ascensional-descensional compass of the twofold.

What determines the character of the choric discourse, of the chorology that finally comes both to consummate and to interrupt—though only briefly—the discursive drift of images? What is, finally, at stake when one comes to say that third kind that Timaeus calls "most difficult to catch" (*Tim.* 51 a–b), so difficult indeed that it slips away from every one of those images that he poses of it. The difficulty is precisely that it is a third kind, that it is a kind of kind beyond kind, that it is neither an intelligible εἶδος nor one of those things that, from a distance, share the look and the name of such an εἶδος. The difficulty is that speech is eidetic, whereas the χώρα is neither identical with, nor determinable by, nor an image of an εἶδος. It will not be possible to reach the χώρα by uttering a legitimate discourse. For the χώρα refuses every attempt to say it by way of an εἶδος. It withdraws from the remembrance that would bring it to presence because—and here the language cannot but begin to coil up and recoil—it is not something present. Any remembrance of the χώρα, any discourse that would stand a chance of touching it, would have to be, as Timaeus says, a bastard. It would have to say it in such a way as also somehow to grant in the very saying its withdrawal from saying as such.

In the *Timaeus* this third kind of discourse, this discourse on the third kind, unfolds in a way that is hardly less elusive than the third kind that it would bring to speech. The relevant passage is one of the most complex and most disputed in the entire dialogue, and here I can give only the briefest indication. The passage begins by taking up those very things that escaped Timaeus's first discourse, those nonthings called fire, air, water, and earth. These, it turns out, are still more fleeting than what is called χώρα. Indeed, says Timaeus, they cannot be properly called by those common names, for they never remain the same but are always passing into one another. They are so lacking in self-sameness and determinacy that they cannot be caught and held by discourse. Whenever it attempts to touch them, they take flight in a way unthinkable within the twofold of paradigm and product made to look like the paradigm. It is this flight of fire and the others, their flight from discourse, their flight beyond the twofold, that serves to point to the third kind, which would harbor them outside, receiving them in their self-extinguishing withdrawal.

Yet, Timaeus contrasts the fugitive, properly unspeakable four (fire, air, earth, and water, as they are—improperly—called) with that into which they flee, by which they would be received. Most notably, what is called χώρα proves less resistant to discourse than the elemental fugitives, for, as Timaeus says, it can be called *this* (τοῦτο) and *that* (τόδε), whereas fire can only be called *such-like* (τοιοῦτον). But if the χώρα can be called *this* and *that,* it can at least be held sufficiently stable to be pointed to, even if the indicators themselves, fire and the others, are extinguished through the very flight by which they indicate it. Indeed, Timaeus says of them that "they have only a trace (ἴχνος) of them-selves" (*Tim.* 53b). They are no more than traces drawn in the direction of the χώρα. Choric discourse would be one that, setting forth the χώρα as *this* and *that,* would delineate the self-extinguishing traces drawn toward it.

So, then, a discourse of traces. Or, extending the figure in a way to which the text alludes, it would be a matter of a discourse that would follow the traces, thereby tracking the χώρα so as perhaps finally to catch it, to snare it. Or, more precisely, a discourse that would, as its very condition, appeal to the peculiar appearing of the χώρα in and through the flight of the self-extinguishing traces of the so-called elements.

Such discourse will be no less memorial than that in which Timaeus recalls the fabrication of the cosmos. But it will be a different kind of remembrance. For one of the things that Timaeus describes as being made along with the cosmos is time: time and the cosmos were made at once, at the same time, the word ἅμα marking a simultaneity that cannot itself be simply of the order of time. Thus, when Timaeus turns to his discourse on that which preceded the god's fabrica-tion of the cosmos, the discourse that he then presents on what are called fire, air, water, and earth and on what is called χώρα will be a remembrance of a pre-cosmic time, of a time before time and before the beginning of the cosmos. What had been taken as the beginning is thus referred back to a prior beginning—a fig-ure often repeated in the *Timaeus.* The discourses are thus archaic and, as such, memorial, though in precisely such a way as to put in question the ἀρχή at which the remembrance would arrive. In the *Timaeus* nothing is more vigorously interrogated than the question of the beginning.

JOHN SALLIS

DEPARTMENT OF PHILOSOPHY
THE PENNSYLVANIA STATE UNIVERSITY
AUGUST 1992

NOTE

* "Idea and Reality in Plato's *Timaeus*," in Hans-Georg Gadamer, *Dialogue and Dialectic: Eight Hermeneutical Studies on Plato,* trans. P. Christopher Smith (New Haven, Conn.: Yale University Press, 1980), 156–93. References to this essay will be given in the text by page numbers alone.

A portion of the present text was presented, along with additional material, at a conference on Gadamer's work held at the University of Heidelberg under the direction of James Risser and Lawrence Schmidt. The conference, "Das Gespräch in der Hermeneutik: Das Wort, der Dialog, und die Mitteilung," took place on July 3–5, 1992. Professor Gadamer participated in the conference.

REPLY TO JOHN SALLIS

Sallis's study directly connects with my analysis of the composition of the report about the genesis of the world given in the *Timaeus*. To be sure, Sallis follows my description, but he is looking for a different background for that report and that is very interesting. For him, the narrative form mirrors the form of recollection and its limitedness. It is not entirely clear whether this refers to Plato's description that lets the limits be felt, or whether Plato's description itself encounters its limits. In any case, Sallis attempts to get at the things more concretely and deals with the important question of how far a pretemporal event *(vorzeitliches Geschehen)* forces itself into cosmology. It really cannot be overlooked that the jumble of the elements which reorder themselves into different fixed constructions points to a kind of prehistorical background, and that it exhibits a profile that lacks a narrative order. But in my eyes it is precisely at this point that the most interesting part begins; namely, how the step from mathematics into corporeality is suggested as a kind of layering of triangles one over the other to form a package, as it were. That is certainly one of the most naive and truly challenging ways to view the dimension of corporeality: to see it was mere quantitative increase of expansion on a plane. Nevertheless, during my studies, and even later, I recognized in this point the important problem of why modern physics sees itself anticipated in the mathematical construction of the world. According to the analysis of Eva Sachs I treated that as a mathematical digression and interpreted it in an aside (which, however, did not meet with agreement by Ms. Alt in Berlin).

Willingly I take up Sallis's suggestion that we see the workings of memory and the arrival of recollections at work in the narrative confusion of the *Timaeus*. Given that, the mathematical exercises do not fit into the framework, which is what I believe that I have demonstrated.

H.-G.G.

25

Dennis J. Schmidt

PUTTING ONESELF IN WORDS . . .

I ask that you pardon the script, since I have not acclimated myself to forming these letters.

—Martin Heidegger to Elisabeth Blochmann

Hermeneutic theory remains committed to the remark that Gadamer makes in part 3 of *Truth and Method:* "being that can be understood is language."[1] Consequently it need find itself in accord with Cratylus's claim that "language is perhaps the greatest topic of all"[2] as well as with Levinas's claim that language is the medium of our most intimate "contact" and so an essential element of ethical life. Among the most distinctive trademarks of the hermeneutic approach to language is the effort to attend to the double force—both finitizing and fusing—of language in every human affair and to do so in a manner that resists any abstraction which results in the construction of an artificial rational language. Attentive to the self-effacement of language, its capacity to throw itself ever anew into a darkness beyond the reach of its own reflexivity, hermeneutics has been first and foremost a theory alert to the finitude of all understanding and the compressions placed upon every human affair. Guided by such convictions and commitments, hermeneutic theory has paid special attention to the conflicts and complexities of the struggle, ultimately—and I believe that this is important in the final analysis—an ethical struggle, to put oneself in words. This struggle to find words goes beyond the strategic problem of merely communicating information. Rather, it is a struggle that finally concerns the relation of language and being, and so it is among the most profound struggles in which one can engage. In a very real sense, the question of language always inevitably becomes a question of who one is—and is not. Hermeneutics pays homage to this relation of language and being insofar as it recognizes that when we understand something about the need for words, about how it is that we make contact with one another insofar as we put ourselves in words, we understand something important about ourselves.

In a letter to Gadamer dated 29 February 1972, Heidegger makes a point and raises a question about this struggle in and with language to which hermeneutics addresses itself. Heidegger writes, "the more precise determination of hermeneutics presses forward to the question whether and in what manner the special universal claim of information, as an extreme case of the deficient mode of 'communication', can be recovered in hermeneutics.—Taking this task up [means suffering through and acknowledging] the *language-neediness of think-ing. . . .* [It also means asking why] *thinking necessarily stays in the language-neediness of finding words?"*[3] Now, after Gadamer cites this remark from Heidegger, he comments in return that "Of course Heidegger is right when he sees in information the extreme case that poses the most strenuous task for hermeneutics. But I must also ask myself here what the language-neediness of thinking really means."[4] The question about language, about putting oneself in words, that I want to take up today ultimately concerns this question which Gadamer puts to Heidegger; that is, how are we to understand this notion of "language-neediness," this "need of language" with which one struggles in try-ing to put oneself in words? How does one "acknowledge" and "suffer through" the neediness of language? What might language "need"? Can we meaningfully speak about the need *of* words within our need *for* words?

Later in the same letter to Gadamer, Heidegger specifies his own understand-ing of this topic when he asks if there is a name for this need, a name for nam-ing, a word for the need of the words into which one struggles to put oneself. As a sort of challenge, he asks Gadamer if there can be a "hermeneutic of such names," if, in other words, hermeneutics can acknowledge the finitude proper to the neediness of language itself. It is a perplexing question, one reminiscent of Heidegger's concern with arriving at an experience of language that is suffi-ciently radical to give a "word for word." But while this question which Heideg-ger asks is, as Gadamer suggests, puzzling, the direction in which Heidegger takes it is clear: this radicalization of the experience of language drives Heideg-ger to address the topic of language in the poem and to enlist Hölderlin's claim that such naming, which is the province of poetry, is so unique that it must be called holy. Likewise, this problematic of the neediness of language leads Heidegger to speak of the "translation-neediness" *(Übersetzungsbedürftigkeit)* of language,[5] and to take up the issue of the relation of language and translation. A relation that in turn becomes of such fundamental importance that Heidegger is willing to say "Tell me what you think about translation and I will tell you who you are."[6] Despite his hesitations regarding Heidegger's notion of the neediness of language Gadamer's work moves in a direction congenial to Heidegger's on these themes and so is aware that language pays tribute to its own needs and lim-its in poetry and translation, both of which stand as reminders that the guiding sentence of hermeneutics, "being that can be understood is language," means that "that which is can never be completely understood."[7]

One should not forget that poetry, which "fulfills itself in the ideal of untranslatability,"[8] and translation are decisive for every effort to think language *as* language and to do this outside of the orbit of metaphysical presumptions; that is, to think it independently of the empire of representation. When language is sharpened, when it is experienced "like the point of a spear,"[9] that is, when the finitude proper to it is experienced, then both poetry and translation come forward as questions, bringing language to the question of the idiom—the question at which the communicative character of language reaches its crisis.

I do not intend to take up the themes of either translation or poetry here, but I do want to note their proximity and final import for the special topic of my concern today.[10] Rather, my approach to this enigmatic question about the limits and "need of language" in the struggle to put oneself in words will pursue another, admittedly peculiar, angle. Nonetheless, I believe that it is a crucial question for those of us committed to the effort to solicit an understanding of language at its extremities. It is a question that Gadamer himself raises in his 1983 text entitled "Unterwegs zur Schrift" when he asks "Does not the use of words always already contain something like an urge to being fixed [in writing]?"[11] This is not simply the question of the difference between orality and literacy. Nor is this question one that finds its stakes in determining some sort of hierarchy between speech and writing. In the end, I believe that Gadamer is quite right when he says that "there is no sharp division between orality and literacy."[12] The inner connection between speech and writing is a powerful one, so powerful that it seems a senseless practice to try to pull them apart in any fundamental way. But there is a question to be asked about what we must think about language if we pay heed to the idea that language not only lets itself be written, but—as Gadamer suggests—might even need to be written. Of course, this is the same question that Plato projects upon every other question raised in the dialogues. One might even argue that Platonic texts can only be read if one understands that they have been written out of the logic of a worry about this urge to fix language in writing. Plato's concern is well known and put concisely when Socrates speaks to Phaedrus, who has fallen in love with a written text on love. Socrates speaks to Phaedrus about the peculiarly static character of the written word by saying that

> Writing, Phaedrus, has this strange power, quite like painting in fact; for the creatures in paintings stand there like living beings, yet if you ask them anything they maintain a solemn silence. It is the same with written words. You might imagine they speak as if they were actually thinking about something but if you want to find out about what they are saying and question them, they keep on giving the one and same message eternally. (275d–e)

As Heidegger will remind us later, there is a curious Parmenidean problem to be faced in the problematic of writing. Socrates suggests that a written text is like the corpse of thinking; mute and unresponsive, it captures nothing of the living eternity which the mind is capable of knowing, delivering instead only a 'now'

immobilized for all time. It is not an accident that the subject of the text that provokes Socrates's remark is *eros* nor is it insignificant that the text arrives in the
dialogue smuggled by Phaedrus under the cover of his cloak. Both desire and the
secret belong to the full question of writing as Plato understands it. But I want to
prescind from the full issue for now and simply make some remarks about what
it means when a written text arrives.

Without diminishing the riddle of human and nonhuman productions that do
not happen as written language, it is possible to argue against Plato that with the
arrival of the written word, what Schelling referred to as "a second empire of
experience" opens up before us. Gadamer puts this point eloquently when he
writes that

> there is nothing so strange and so demanding as the written word. Not even the
> encounter with speakers of a foreign tongue can be compared with this strangeness,
> since the language of gesture and of sound always contains an element of immediate
> understanding. Writing and what partakes of it—literature—is the intelligibility of
> mind transferred to the most alien medium. Nothing is so purely the trace of mind as
> writing. . . . The remnants of the life of the past, what is left of buildings, tools, the
> contents of graves, are weatherbeaten by the storms of time, whereas a written tradi-
> tion . . . is to such an extent pure mind that it speaks to us as if in the present.[13]

For the most part, hermeneutics has been focused upon reading and the event of
the realization of meaning in sound and voice; that is, it has pressed upon the
experience of language *as* language by means of attention to the reenactment
and revitalization of "the living voice behind the writing."[14] That is why
Gadamer can say that "I would define hermeneutics as the skill to let things
speak which come to us in a fixed, petrified form, that of the text."[15] Or: "Writing, in all its spirituality, is only there when it is read. So words are what they are
only as spoken discourse."[16] In other words, for the most part, hermeneutics has
been directed to the recuperation of the already written word, to the recovery of
voice in script, to the reanimation of already petrified language rather than the
process whereby language becomes "petrified"—if indeed "petrified" is the
appropriate word for what happens in writing.

But this seeming privilege of reading and the voice in hermeneutic reflections on language does not exclude the "other end" of language in the text,
namely, the question of the transformation of word into writing. I should also
note that this question about word become script does not deny that in the act of
writing one might necessarily hear a sort of voice speaking. That language seeks
voice and "asserts its creaturely rights in sound"[17] is clear, but there remains
nonetheless a question of how this voice lets itself be recorded in writing. A
question not of the semiological, but the iconographic, potential of language.
Gadamer alludes to this in *Truth and Method* when he notes that "The legitimate
question whether the word is nothing but a 'pure sign' or has something about it

of the 'image' is thoroughly discredited by the *Cratylus.* . . . ever since in all discussion on language the concept of the image *(eikon)* has been replaced by that
of the sign *(semeion* or *semainon).* This is not just a terminological change, but
it expresses an epoch-making decision about thought concerning language."[18]
Against this Gadamer argues that "The word is not just a sign. In a sense that is
hard to grasp it is also something almost like an image. The word has an enigmatic bond with what it represents, a quality of belonging to its being."[19] It is, I
believe, worth asking whether or not this sense in which the word is "almost like
an image," this "bond with what it represents," is to be thought in trying to
understand what it means that language lets itself be written. Can we imagine a
language that *could not* be written?[20] What would have to happen in language
for it to *refuse* the relation between speech and writing, voice and script? Certainly there are languages that can only be written in ways alien to our alpha-
betic writing, and, in the end, I believe that the unique aspects of the alphabet
might be decisive for the issues I am trying to raise. It is worth noting that Plato,
who confronted the alphabet as a relatively recent innovation, seems to find it
worth remarking upon on several occasions.[21] In particular he asks about the difference between noise and breath, between consonants and vowels as for
instance in the following passage in the *Philebus* which draws that dialogue
close to the story about the discovery of writing told in the *Phaedrus.* In the
Philebus Socrates speaks about the elements of writing and says,

> The unlimited variety of sound was discerned by some . . . godlike man . . . in Egypt
> called Theuth. He was the one who originally discerned the existence . . . of
> the vowels—not vowel in the singular but vowels in the plural—and then of other
> things which, though they could not be called articulate sounds, yet were noises of a
> kind. . . . in the end he found a number of such things and affixed to . . . each single
> member the name 'letter.' It was because he realized that none of us could ever get to
> know one of the collection by itself, in isolation from all the rest, that he conceived
> of 'letter' as a kind of bond of unity, uniting as it were all these sounds into one.
> (18b–d)

But of course Gadamer is pointing to the *Cratylus* as a dialogue in which
Socrates, who did not write, asks most directly about the relation of word and
image. There, shortly after Hermogenes asks "what sort of imitation *(mimēsis)* is
a name *(onoma)?"* (423c), the often comic discussion moves through the question of the imitations found in sound (music) and image (painting) to the point at
which Socrates introduces the topic of script: "That objects should be imitated in
letters *(grammasi)* and syllables *(syllabais),* and so find expression, may appear
ridiculous, Hermogenes, but it cannot be avoided" (425d). What follows this is a
discussion of the relation between image *(eikon)* and word *(onoma).* It is a
strange and difficult discussion about the shape of letters and the sounds of words.
A discussion that, as Gadamer notes, takes the topic to the point of absurdity and

ridicule. It finally leads Socrates to say, "Do you not perceive that images are very far from having qualities which are the exact counterpart of the realities which they represent?" (432d). The ironic reason for this is that if an icon were perfect, its perfection would destroy the image-original relationship. An icon, says Socrates, "dares not reproduce every particular if it is to be an icon" (432b). He then suggests that it is important to stay alert to the necessary difference between icon and word—a suggestion that Walter Benjamin will make as well in his "Trauerspielbuch," only Benjamin, who is quite fascinated by the idea of hand-writing, will say that in being alert to this difference one is permitted a "gaze into the depths of language."

Plato's conclusion in the *Cratylus* notwithstanding, the topic of the relation of word and icon, and the possibility that such a relation is to be thought in the idea of script, is one that appears in several Platonic texts.[22] Nonetheless, it seems clear that the conclusion expressed in the *Cratylus* won the day and now what is most surprising is that we are no longer surprised by the conclusion that supersedes this one. Namely, that number bears a deeper relation to the truth of words than icons. Leibniz becomes the true inheritor of that conclusion. Today, the prospect that the question of script, the iconography of language, might belong to the topic of language does strike one as somewhat ludicrous—and I must confess to my own trepidations about taking such a topic seriously even though I am convinced that it is a topic needing to be addressed. It is also a topic that I have come, much to my surprise, to take seriously and to find a quite active concern in a number of texts with which I once believed myself to be familiar. An autobiographical note might help me explain this.

When I broke the wrist of the hand with which I write I found myself curiously tongue-tied, unable to put myself in words in all of the ways to which I was accustomed. Now, for an academic, being cut off from writing poses special dilemmas in one's daily life. But my sense was that the experience of being unable to write, ultimately of being compelled to learn the rudiments of writing, frustratingly slowly, with my other, untrained, hand, was not problematizing my relation to language so profoundly simply because of my special academic circumstances. If you want your empirical confirmation of this simply try to write for some days with your untrained, your other, hand. Rather, I came to realize that this was an experience that went beyond the endurance of a mere inconvenience to something very much at the center of an experience of language that is bound up with the phenomena of alphabetization and the strange mimesis of script. It was an experience that gave new weight to claims such as the one that Hegel makes in the *Phenomenology* where he writes that "the hand does not seem to be an external factor to fate; it seems rather to be related to it as something inner. . . . It is the living artificer of his fortune. . . . Thus the simple lines of the hand, the timbre and compass of the voice as the individual characteristic of speech—this too again as expressed in writing, where the hand gives it a more durable existence than the voice does, especially in the particular style of hand-writing."[23] It also seemed to provide testimony that was a sort of photographic negative of Heidegger's celebrated claim that "Only a being who can speak, that is think, can have a hand."[24] I discovered that I needed a hand to speak. But, in the end, what was surprising to me was that this broken arm turned out to be not so much an experience "about" my hand as an experience "with" language. Heidegger again: "the hand has the essence of man within, because the word as the essential realm *(Wesensbereich)* of the hand is the essential realm of man."[25] Of course, this reciprocity between word and hand not only problematizes language, but should make us realize that the hand here is not simply to be understood according to an anatomical body that itself is profoundly shaped by a metaphysics that every hermeneutic sensitivity to language renders suspect.

Simply put: my problems with handwriting, my frustrations, have driven me, with a strange ineluctibility, to take seriously the quite strange claim that Heidegger makes in his 1942–1943 lecture course on Parmenides that "Being, word, reading, script name an original and essential matrix in which the signing-writing hand belongs. The relation of being to man, namely the word, is, in handwriting, inscribed in a being."[26] It is a baffling remark, one that I nonetheless found oddly compelling in light of my own experience, but it is neither as strange nor compelling as the remark that follows in which Heidegger writes that "When then writing is taken away from its essential origin, i.e. the hand, . . . a transformation in the relation to being takes place."[27] Now Heidegger is interested in asking about "the 'invasion' of the typewriter into the realm of the word,"[28] and though he speaks of the "destruction" and "degradation" of the typed word, he never quite explains his reasons for this judgment. He does however make two comments that lead one to suspect that the point to be made concerns the iconographic potential of language. First, he claims that the written word is language that is exposed to the eyes *("dem Blick sich zeigende");*[29] second, he claims that the essential belonging together of hand and word finds its summit in the image which is formed out of the sign *("die . . . Zeichen zu Gebilden bildet")*[30] That is why I have come to take the questions one finds in Plato about the icon and writing with a newly found seriousness. I do not want to overstate the issue. It should be clear that the role of the question of writing has other concerns than this: different types of writing, the relation of writing and the formation of traditions and disciplines, the relation of writing and desire, as well—and this is not far removed from the topic at hand—as the relation between writing and the body (a theme that even belongs to the subject of voice and breath as yet another manner in which the body extends itself into the world),[31] all these questions surround the question that I have taken up from Gadamer: what does it mean that there seems to be something like an "urge" in words to be fixed in writing. But it also seems clear that this question about the inner connection between word and script, the transformation of thought into its own hieroglyph, is one that cannot be dismissed as easily as Socrates seems to do in the *Cratylus*.

The point, as Gadamer notes in *Truth and Method,* is to ask how far we can think language independently of the sign and the representational conception of language that has governed metaphysics. When he develops this project in *Truth and Method* he does so by noting how it moves beyond the Greek understanding of language. In the move from the section on "Language and *logos*" to the section on "Language and *verbum*" Gadamer notes that "There is an idea that is not Greek and that does more justice to the nature of language and prevented the forgetfulness of language in Western thought from being complete. It is the Christian thought of *incarnation*."[32] I want to note this move, and acknowledge—as Hegel and Benjamin also argue—that, in the end, it might be a move that cannot be avoided. But, for my present purposes, I want to try to pursue the question still in a Greek context because I believe that a crucial issue—the temporality of the iconographic potential of language—is found at the center of Plato's concerns and that it is precisely this issue which is erased in the Christianization of the matter. To that end, Gadamer makes a remark in "Unterwegs zur Schrift" that is especially helpful. There, citing the *Philebus* (39b), he notes that "It is *'mneme'* which 'writes' *logoi* in our souls."[33] According to Gadamer, this reference to memory marks "the entry of temporality and departure in time, which gives the finite being of man its stamp."[34]

In the *Phaedrus* Socrates contends that writing is a ruse that *must fail* since it is designated as *the illusory effort to outwit time by arresting it.* It is, he argues, only the semblance of eternity. At best it is the memento, the *aide memoire,* of a knowing that has already seen the idea and so in truth dispenses with writing in recollection; at worst it becomes the mechanism of the mortification of the dialectic. Two passages from the *Phaedrus* make this point. In the first, Socrates says that while "any discourse ought to be constructed like a living creature" Lysias's text, like every written text, is more like the "writing on a tomb" (264c–d). Interestingly he refers specifically to the tomb of Midas, one who immobilized all that his desire touched. In the second passage I have in mind, Socrates notes that the "inventor" of writing, the Egyptian King Theuth, who thought that his discovery "provided a recipe for memory" (274d), eventually learned that "it implants forgetfulness in the soul [and] . . . is not a recipe for memory *[mneme],* but merely for reminder *[hypomnema]"* (275a) which is the semblance of memory, the illusion of time outwitted by the materiality of language as the icon.

The question is how far this temporal liability of language is to be understood as the trap of the icon. Here the issues broaden and are driven to take up a complex of problems that include the relation between language, painting, and music.[35] Heidegger has taught us the insights that come with thinking works of art as modes of communication with time and history, and if we take that move seriously—especially with regard to the new directions in which that thought leads with respect to our understanding of the relation between painting and image—then it is necessary that we rethink the temporal meaning of the iconographic potential of language that lets itself become script. It means remembering as well Gadamer's insight that writing is only in reading; that the temporal arrest of writing finds its truth in the temporal recovery of the act of reading. But Heidegger takes this temporal movement and need of writing even further when he says: "Writing, in its essential origin is hand-writing. We have named the disclosive taking up and taking notice of the written word 'reading,' i.e. gathering, in Greek *legein, logos;* but this word in originary thinking is the name for being itself."[36]

Let me conclude by returning this discussion to my opening remarks about the "neediness of language" to which Heidegger refers. I have limited my remarks to the way in which this "neediness" is to be thought in the relation of word and image in the iconographic character of language. I am aware that such a limitation is severe and poses serious problems, especially since even the special questions of writing can only be taken up by addressing the character of the transition between language that is spoken, written, and read. In that transition, in the moves between the ideality of meaning and the materiality of the word, language both completes and argues with itself at its limits.

But however it is that language becomes the bearer of ideality and the imaginary, it is important that we understand how language bears its truth as temporal possibilities: how, that is, writing—even if it is not able to outwit time and touch eternity—is the act of taking up a *temporal distance,* a distance that is found in the difference between word and icon. A distance that, as Gadamer has shown, is felt in the strangeness and authority of the text.

I conclude with a speculative question that I believe is important to ask, even if my remarks up to this point have not fully prepared for it. I said at the outset that—as both Hegel and Levinas explicitly argue (and I would argue that Gadamer might say as well)—the questions of language are, at heart, ethical questions. If that is true—and I believe that it is—then it is worth asking *just what sort of ethical act the taking up of this temporal distance in writing is.* Of course, that means asking as well about *the ethical meaning of the effort to cross that distance in reading.* Any understanding of Plato's contributions to these questions must then ask: *what sort of ethical act is Socrates's refusal to write?*

Let me end by giving Plato's Socrates the last word. In the *Cratylus* he gives a remarkable etymology of *"onoma,"* he gives a word for word which establishes *word as the refusal of any final word.* He says simply that "word" is the word "for that reality for which we are still seeking" (421a).

What is the life of man? An image of the divine.
Just as they wander beneath the heaven, those who are
earthly, look to it.
As if reading, as if in a script, men imitate infinity
and the treasures.
Is the simple heaven a treasure?
How the silver clouds blossom. Yet from them
dew and mist rain down. But when the
blue is effaced, the simple, mat as marble, shines
like ore,
pointing to treasures.

—Hölderlin, "Was ist der Menschen Leben . . ."

DENNIS J. SCHMIDT

DEPARTMENT OF PHILOSOPHY
VILLANOVA UNIVERSITY
JUNE 1993

NOTES

1. Hans-Georg Gadamer, *Wahrheit und Methode* (Tübingen: J. C. B. Mohr, 1960), 450: "Sein, das verstanden werden kann, ist Sprache."

2. Plato, *Cratylus,* trans. Jowett, in *Collected Dialogues,* ed. Hamilton and Cairns (Princeton: Princeton University Press, 1961), 427d.

3. Hans-Georg Gadamer, *Das Erbe Hegels* (Frankfurt: Suhrkamp Verlag, 1979), 90–91:

> Die nähere Bestimmung der Hermeneutik drängt jedoch zugleich in die Frage, ob und auf welche Weise der eigentümlich universale Anspruch der Informatik als ein im äußersten Maße defincierter Modus der "Verständigung" in Hermeneutik zurück-geholt werden kann.—Die Übernahme beider Aufgaben muß für deren Austrag die *Sprachnot des Denkens* nicht nur durchleiden und anerkennen. . . . *Weshalb bleibt das Denken notwendig in der Sprach-Not der Wortfindung?"* (emphasis added)

4. Ibid., p. 91: "Heidegger hat sicher recht, wenn er in der Informatik den Extremfall sieht, der der Hermeneutik die äußerste Aufgabe stellt. Doch frage ich mich auch hier, was die Sprachnot des Denkens eigentlich bedeutet."

5. Martin Heidegger, *Gesamtausgabe,* 53: 79ff.

6. Ibid., 76: "Sage mir, was du vom Übersetzen hälst, und ich sage dir, wer du bist."

7. Hans-Georg Gadamer, "Text und Interpretation," in *Gesammelte Werke* (Tübingen: J. C. B. Mohr, 1991), 2:334.

8. "Kultur und das Wort," in *Lob der Theorie* (Frankfurt: Suhrkamp, 1983), 23.

9. Martin Heidegger, *Unterwegs zur Sprache* (Pfullingen: Neske Verlag, 1975), 37.

10. See my "Fission and Fusion: Gadamer on the Edges of Language," in *ellipsis . . .,* vol. 2, no. 2 (1992): 1–24.

11. Hans-Georg Gadamer, "Unterwegs zur Schrift," in *Gesammelte Werke* (Tübingen: J. C. B. Mohr, 1991), 7: 258: "Ist nicht in dem Gebrauch von Worten immer schon so etwas wie ein Drang zur Fixierung enthalten?"

12. Ibid., 261–62.

13. Hans-Georg Gadamer, *Wahrheit und Methode* (Tübingen, J. C. B. Mohr, 1960), 156:

> Es gibt nichts so Fremdes und zugleich Verständnisforderndes wie Schrift. Nicht einmal die Begegnung mit Menschen fremden Zunge kann mit dieser Fremdheit und Befremdung verglichen werden, da die Sprache der Gebärde und des Tones immer schon ein Moment von unmittelbarer Verständlichkeit enthält. Schrift und was an ihr teil hat, die Literatur, ist die ins Fremdeste entäußerte Verständlichkeit des Geistes. Nichts ist so sehr reine Geistespur wie Schrift. . . . Keine sonstige Überlieferung, die aus der Vergangenheit auf uns kommt, ist dem gleich. Die Überreste vergangenen Lebens, Reste von Baute, Werkzeuge, der Inhalt der Gräber sind verwittert durch die Stürme der Zeit, die über sie hingebraust sind—schriftliche Überlieferung dagegen . . . ist so sehr reiner Geist, daß sie wie gegenwärtig zu uns spricht.

14. Hans-Georg Gadamer, "Writing and the Living Voice," in *Applied Hermeneutics,* ed. Misgeld and Nicholson (Albany: SUNY Press, 1992), 66.

15. Ibid., 65.

16. Hans-Georg Gadamer, "Hermeneutics and Logocentrism," trans. Palmer and Michelfelder, in *Dialogue and Deconstruction* (Albany: SUNY Press, 1989), 124.

17. Walter Benjamin, "Ursprung des deutschen Trauerspiels," in *Gesammelte Schriften,* bd. 1, 1, p. 384: "Die Sprache, die einerseits in der Klangfülle kreatürlich ihr Recht sich zu nehmen sucht."

18. Gadamer, *Wahrheit und Methode,* 391:

> Die berechtigte Frage, ob das Wort nichts anderes als ein 'reines Zeichen' ist oder doch etwas vom 'Bild' an sich hat, wird durch den 'Kratylos' grundsätzlich diskreditiert. . . . so daß seiendem in der gesamten Reflexion über die Sprache der Begriff des Bildes *(eikon)* durch den des Zeichen *(semeion,* or *semainon)* ersetzt wird. Das ist nicht nur eine terminologische Wandlung, sondern in dieser drückt sich eine Entscheidung über das Denken dessen, was Sprache ist, aus, die Epoche gemacht hat.

19. Ibid., 393–94: "Das Wort is nicht nur Zeichen. In irgendeinem schwer zu erfassenden Sinne es es doch auch fast so etwas wie ein Abild. . . . Dem Wort kommt auf eine rätselhafte Weise Gebundenheit an das 'Abgebiltete', Zugehörigkeit zum Sein des Abgebilteten zu."

20. So far as I have been able to discover, among the 5,053 languages which are said to be in existence today, all possess the possibility of being written.

21. See especially *Theaetetus,* 203a–204a where the question of the whole and parts is illustrated by means of a discussion of the relation between letters forming a syllable. There Theaetetus points out that consonants are "not articulate sound" and "inexplicable," while vowels are "a sound" but no account can be given of them either (203b). One curious point of note is how frequently Plato links the discussion of writing with Egypt. That is the case in the *Phaedrus, Timaeus,* and *Philebus.*

22. See, for instance, *Phaedrus,* 274d, 276c; *Charmides,* 159c, 160a; *Protagoras,* 326c; *Laws,* 7.809e; *Philebus,* 18b; *Theaetetus,* 203b. Reference to the letters of the alphabet even play a role in a decisive move in the *Republic* when Socrates suggests that "I think we should employ the method of search that we should use if we, with not very

keen vision, were bidden to read small letters from a distance, and then someone had observed that these same letters exist elsewhere larger and on a larger surface" (368d–e). Platonic dialogues also frequently employ an analogy between the general process of education, but especially education with regard to laws, and the specific process of learning to form the letters of an alphabet. (Foucault makes a similar point when discussing the pervasive nature of discipline when he discusses the process whereby handwriting is taught in the schools. See Michel Foucault, *Discipline and Punish,* trans. Sheridan [New York: Random House, 1979], 152.) The general point is simply to note that Plato is indeed fascinated by the Greek alphabet. It was, as scholars have noted, a remarkable invention, since "The Greek sign, and this for the first time in the history of writing, stands for an abstraction, the isolated consonant" (K. Robb, "Poetic Sources of the Greek Alphabet," in *Communication Arts in the Ancient World,* ed. Havelock and Hershbell [1978], 31).

23. G. W. F. Hegel, *Phänomenologie des Geistes* (Hamburg: Meiner Verlag, 1952), pars. 315/316:

> Die Hand freilich scheint nicht so sehr etwas Äußers für das Schicksal zu sein, son-
> dern vielmehr als Inneres zu ihm sich zu verhalten. . . . Sie ist der beseelte Werk-
> meister seines Glückes. . . . Die *einfachen Züge der Hand* also, ebenso *Klang* und
> *Umfang* der *Stimme* als die individuelle Bestimmtheit der *Sprache,*—auch dieselbe
> wieder, wie sie durch die Hand eine festere Existenz also durch die Stimme
> bekommt, die *Schrift,* und zwar in ihere Besonderheit als *Handschrift.*

24. Martin Heidegger, *Was Heisst Denken?* (Tübingen: Niemeyer Verlag, 1971), 51: "Nur ein Wesen, das Spricht, d.h. denkt, kann die Hand haben."

25. Heidegger, *Gesamtausgabe,* 54:119.

26. Martin Heidegger, *Gesamtausgabe* (Frankfurt: Klostermann, 1982), 54: 125: "Sein, Wort, Lese, Schrift nennen einen ursprünglichen Wesenszusammenhang, in den die zeigende-schreibende Hand gehört. In der Handschrift ist nun der Bezug des Seins zum Menschen, nämlich das Wort, in das Seiende selbst eingezeichnet."

27. *Ibid.:* "Wenn also die Schrift ihrem Wesensursprung, d.h. der Hand, entzogen wird . . . , dann hat sich im Bezug des Seins zum Menschen ein Wandel ereignet." I should note that the passage that I omitted from the citation refers to the substitution of the type-writer for the pen ("und wenn das Schreiben der Maschine übertragen ist"). Much of Heidegger's concern in his remarks about script is guided by the effort to exhibit the "'meta-physical' essence of technicity" (127) via a discussion of the way in which the typewriter "conceals the essence of writing and script" (126) thereby "accelerating the destruction of words" (129). The question of the technics of writing is not insignificant here. A fuller treatment of that question would need to pay attention to the fact the pen was a radical innovation of Greek writers introduced for use on papyrus. While Egyptians wrote with the stem of a rush cut on a slant to form a brush which painted words, the Greeks devised a pen out of the stiff hollow reed called *kalamos* which was sharpened to a point that produced a fine line. See E. G. Turner, *Athenian Books in the Fifth and Fourth Centuries B. C.* (London, 1952), 11; also A. Carson, *Eros: The Bittersweet* (Princeton, 1986), 58–60.

28. Heidegger, *Gesamtausgabe,* 54:124.

29. Ibid., 119.

30. Ibid., 125.

31. As does the way language spoken shapes the face in exercising its muscles.

32. Gadamer, *Wahrheit und Methode,* 395: "Es gibt aber einen Gedanken, der kein griechischer Gedanke ist und der dem Sein der Sprache besser gerecht wird, so daß die

Sprachvergessenheit des abendländischen Denkens keine vollständige werden konnte. Es ist der christliche Gedanke der *Inkarnation*."

33. Gadamer, "Unterwegs zur Schrift," 261: "Es ist die 'Mneme', die in unseren Seelen Logoi 'schreibt.'"

34. Ibid., 264.

35. Here one might also consider Merleau-Ponty's text "L'oeil et l'esprit," as well as Nietzsche's *Geburt der Tragödie*. See also my "Acoustics: Heidegger and Nietzsche on Words and Music," in *Dialectic and Narrative*, ed. Flynn and Judowitz (Albany: SUNY Press, 1992).

36. Heidegger, *Gesamtausgabe*, 54:125.

REPLY TO DENNIS J. SCHMIDT

This contribution explicitly takes up some points which I myself pursued in my connection with Heidegger. Dennis Schmidt thematizes what I once formulated as a question in a correspondence with Heidegger: Why does thinking press forward into the word? There is a rich convergence of many questions here, particularly with respect to the concept of language-neediness. For a long time I have sought to bring this concept to bear upon the later Heidegger and his resolute, but violent, treatment of language, and it also seems to me to be central to the poetic language of Hölderlin. Indirectly, the problem of translation seems to be posed here too, indeed lyric poetry radiates with a special significance in this regard because of its untranslatability. Schmidt's reflections refer primarily to Plato's critique of script which we know from the *Phaedrus, Epistle Seven,* as well as other texts. In *Truth and Method,* I tried to retrieve the question found in the difficult Platonic dialogue *Cratylus.* It is obvious that the word, in a certain sense, is a conventional sign, but is it not also more than that, something almost like an image *(Abbild)*?

In a peculiar way, the relation of word and image *(Bild)* now intertwines itself with the question of script and image. Schmidt pursues this problem, but the figurative problems at hand are then peculiarly complicated in connection with Heidegger's suggestions. Schmidt is concerned with a double issue: on the one hand handwriting, that is, the image of script *(Schriftbild)* which occurs in handwriting, and on the other hand the quite different problem of language's power of imagery, and through this power one is faced with the question posed by the suggestivity of the imagination as it is achieved in the discovery of the proper choice of words and word constructions. In his essay, both problems are being dealt with, as far as I can see, in the formula of the ichnographic potential of both language and script. He is less concerned with finding an answer to this inner interweaving of abstract letters and living events which is evoked through script; rather, it seems to me that he follows my own contrasting of *logos* and *verbum* to a certain extent as well as the development that can be traced from Greek *logos* to the Augustinian *verbum.* In this lies the real problem which really came to my full attention only through Heidegger and which found expression in the Scholastic distinction of *actus signatus* and *actus exercitus.* It concerns the fact that not everything which one knows and can know in the performance is sayable in a thematic assertion. Some things we know, and can know, without this being possible. When, at the end of Schmidt's essay, we are confronted with the question of what this distinction between performance and thematic assertion really means and whether it does not comprise the world of memory *(Erinnerung)* in so far as word and image turn up in memory *(Gedächnis)*, then one might wonder with Schmidt why the refusal of script by the Platonic Socrates is necessary. Apparently, the answer to that question must be: Where there is no other, the critical response must be brought forth by the writer him/herself. However, no one is as alert in one's self-critique as one is when one is critiqued by another.

H.-G.G.

26

Robin May Schott

GENDER, NAZISM, AND HERMENEUTICS

*Catch only what you've thrown yourself, all is
mere skill and little gain;
but when you're suddenly the catcher of a ball
thrown by an eternal partner
with accurate and measured swing
towards you, to your centre, in an arch
from the great bridgebuilding of God;
why catching then becomes a power—
not yours, a world's.*

Rainer Maria Rilke, quoted at the beginning of *Truth and Method*

*De nobis ipsis silemus.
(About the self it is better to keep silence.)*

Paul Natorp, quoted at the beginning of *Philosophical Apprenticeships*

Gadamer's announced intention is to turn away from a philosophy of the subject. He argues that a philosophy of the subject such as is present in romantic hermeneutics, emphasizes the author's creativity while overlooking the situatedness of understanding. Hence, a subjective starting point in philosophy underestimates human embeddedness in language and tradition. Gadamer follows his own advice, and in his intellectual autobiographical pieces—*Philosophical Apprenticeships* and the introductory essay to this volume—Gadamer gives us little clue about himself as an individual, a political agent, as opposed to Gadamer the philosopher. But if one believes, as I do, that the scholar is not separated from his/her existence as a sexual and political being, the few clues about his concrete life become troubling (both in their limited number and in their content). I intend to take these "autobiographical" works as my text in order to raise questions and criticisms often raised by "ideology critics" (and I would not be uncomfortable in being included in this category). Does Gadamer's philosophy adequately deal with social and material life? Can he account for the different positions of individuals in language, a position which entitles some to legitimacy in participating in intellectual and academic conversations and relegates others to silence? If the answer to these questions is "no," is Gadamer's hermeneutics "conservative," not merely in that it refers back to an inherited tradition? Rather, is it a fundamentally conservative perspective that separates out concrete personal identity from philosophical expression, and thus explicitly refuses to raise questions that could possibly challenge existing social relations? In my brief contribution to this anthology honoring Gadamer's work, I will raise some questions which may be developed in greater length in the future.

Because philosophy cannot be all things to all people, and Gadamer is acknowledgedly *not* a social and political philosopher, my criticisms may seem irrelevant. But it is my contention that when one is the "catcher of a ball," one cannot always choose the decisions that must be confronted as part of one's historical destiny. Gadamer's life has spanned the twentieth century, a period in which fundamental challenges have been raised by women concerning their historical subordination and their exclusion from higher education and politics. Moreover, it is a period marked forever by the barbarism of Nazi Germany. Using these axes as reference points, I will try to elucidate Gadamer's personal and intellectual choices, in order to return to the philosophical questions concerning the relation between philosophy and material life—which includes the domains of history, politics, and personal identity.

In the translator's introduction to *Philosophical Apprenticeships,* Robert Sullivan claims, "The entire German twentieth century is here channeled to us through the life of one man."[1] In this context Sullivan refers to the political contours of twentieth-century German history that are present in some manner in Gadamer's tale—from World War I to Nazism to the Soviet control of portions of East Germany. It is my conviction, after reading Gadamer's autobiographical writings, that much of the history of twentieth-century Germany left this philosopher untouched. He continued to carry on a dialogue with classical texts, once claiming to a colleague, "I basically only read books that are at least two thousand years old."[2] His apparent oblivion to the issues posed by twentieth-century politics indicates a vision of philosophy that is divorced from the surrounding lifeworld, a vision that violates Gadamer's own conception of hermeneutic consciousness with "the constant operativeness of history in his (sic!) own consciousness."[3] History does not operate in consciousness merely through abstract formulations, nor can its effect on consciousness be understood merely abstractly. Rather, to acknowledge and accept the "operativeness of history in consciousness" requires also a concrete engagement in making history. Gadamer's flight from concrete existence through a life lived in the "Ivory Tower" provides little inspiration for those seeking to take the relation between consciousness and history seriously.[4]

At the beginning of *Philosophical Apprenticeships,* Gadamer raises the question of how to write a memoir, how to return to those earliest times in his life. What aspect of those times should be remembered? "Certainly not simply the things that flare up in memory from earliest childhood: the red roundness of an

Edam cheese, a spinning fan in the window on Afföller Street in Marburg, the fire engine pulled by heavy stallions thundering along the Shoe Bridge in Breslau. Such early remembrances are ridiculously intimate and irrelevant because of their very communicativeness."[5] Gadamer evinces an obvious discomfort with the mundane details of daily life, devoting a mere 5¼ pages to the period of his life before his university education began. These details are apparently too "communicative" about the self, so Gadamer quickly leaves them and this style of writing for that which "people today are more interested in," for example, the progress of technical civilization. In this brief opening chapter, then, Gadamer tells us of the Zeppelin, the Titanic, and the fact that his father was a pharmaceutical chemist, a significant researcher, and an authoritarian. About his mother (presumably she was alive for he later speaks of his liberation from his parents),[6] his dreams, and desires aside from his love for philosophy, he is silent. (He does indicate that he was interested in "strategy" and that people said he had an officer's career in front of him, until he was pulled away by the dreams of the "inner man, poetry, and theater." One cannot help but speculate about the course of his life had he chosen a military career.)

Not only is Gadamer's mother completely absent in his memoirs, but so are other women who are apparently more significant to his adult life. We know that he was married, because on page 14 he mentions that during his Heidelberg years he asked his wife to read his dissertation, so he could better evaluate the dissertations he was receiving from his students. But when he married, the name of his wife, whether she had read his dissertation earlier—all these observations belong apparently to the too intimate, too communicative details of life. Since *Philosophical Apprenticeships* is devoted to the great men who have influenced him,[7] other references to the existence of the female sex are brief. On page 17 one hears that a "very tender, soft, almost girlish voice brought up a few clever things about Nietzsche" only to discover that this is the voice of Jacob Klein. On page 29 we learn that Scheler was, among other things, a "lover of beautiful women." On page 35 Gadamer describes himself in 1923 as "an immature doctor of philosophy and all-too-young-husband," though he misses yet another opportunity to name his wife and provide any information about her. The existence of women does reappear on page 70 when he refers to Heidegger's penchant to give a lengthy talk "much to the despair of his wife as we were sitting in front of full dishes." (Though one might expect a scholar of the Greeks to have a sense of the "chairetic" moment for talking and for eating.)[8] On page 96, Gadamer's cowhide briefcase-turned-schoolbag becomes the means to introduce that he had a daughter by his first marriage and a daughter by his second marriage. But when his daughters were born, and whether his first marriage ended in death or divorce, remain outside the province of this story.

The only reference to women's presence in the academy (since Hannah Arendt doesn't make it onto his list of important persons), is to the "temporary predominance of female students during the war."[9]

In "Reflections on my Philosophical Journey," the introductory piece to this anthology, much the same pattern of description is repeated. He paints a life of work, in which weekdays are devoted to his teaching and his administrative work (serving as rector of the University of Leipzig at the end of the war) and weekends are devoted to his own work (without a hint about his family life). He paints a picture of himself as a man amongst men, and he introduces the whole medley of contemporary male German professors who were once students of Gadamer's. Finally, on page 18, a woman is named. "Some twenty-three years of issues of *Philosophische Rundschau* appeared under the strict leadership of my wife, Käte Gadamer-Lekebusch, until it was entrusted to other, younger hands." Although he "brought to life" the journal, she led it. (Was she also a philosopher? Did she have an intellectual relationship with her husband?)

But to what avail are these questions? How do they have philosophical as opposed to merely "intimate" import? Is my admittedly angry recounting of Gadamer's virtual silence about women in his personal and professional life merely the ranting of a latter-day American feminist, tasteless and out of place in these austere circles, and reflective of an American empiricist penchant to count up women? Even if my motives are "impure," I would venture that they do have philosophical bearing. In the past, Gadamer has defended himself against the criticism that he has detached language from sociohistorical processes and action. He argues that concrete factors such as work and politics (and one might add sexual identity) are not outside the scope of hermeneutics. Instead, language reflects everything that is. Gadamer notes that language is a game of interpretation that we are all engaged in every day: "everybody is at the center, is 'it' in this game. Thus it is always his (sic!) turn to be interpreting."[10] Although Gadamer effectively argues that one can never be outside an interpretive framework, his assumption that "everybody is at the center" presupposes that all interpreters are equally legitimated in being "it" in this game.[11] As his own chronicles announce, however, only very select persons (exclusively male) are dialogic partners for Gadamer. When one's conversational partners are drawn from such an exclusive club of like-minded men, it is easier to display the hermeneutic generosity of spirit that assumes the openness to one's opponents' position and the probability that they are right.[12] Whether this conversational experience can be normative for understanding in general, and whether it proves that hermeneutics is "universal," remains highly questionable. (If I were to carry on a conversation with the leaders of Operation Rescue, should I assume that they are probably right?) From this point of view,

Gadamer's depiction of hermeneutic understanding seems to echo the "bloodless academic philosophizing"[13] which he thought he had abandoned when he turned to Heidegger as his mentor.

Gadamer's references to national and academic politics under Nazism is somewhat more explicit than his acknowledgment of women, though less than a satisfying "Auseinandersetzung" with Nazism. He writes in *Philosophical Apprenticeships* of Hitler's ascent to power in 1933: "It was a terrible awakening, and we could not absolve ourselves of having failed to perform adequately as citizens. We had underrated Hitler and his kind, and admittedly we made the same mistake as the liberal press in doing this. . . . It was a widespread conviction in intellectual circles that Hitler in coming to power would deconstruct the nonsense he had used to drum up the movement, and we counted the anti-Semitism as part of this nonsense."[14] He goes on to talk about the grotesqueness in Marburg, where soon a refusal of the Hitler salute would become an immediate ground of dismissal. By the stylization of the greeting, students could recognize the convictions of the teacher. Gadamer continues, "Certainly it remained difficult to keep the right balance, not to compromise oneself so far that one would be dismissed and yet still to remain recognizable to colleagues and students. That we somehow found the right balance was confirmed for us one day when it was said of us that we had only 'loose sympathy' with the new awakening."[15]

Gadamer's use of the Hitler salute, certainly not zealous but convincing enough to enable him to carry on a successful academic career in Nazi Germany, epitomizes his strategy of survival. Although unlike his teacher Heidegger (Heidegger's Nazi moment is treated only obliquely in Gadamer's memoirs), Gadamer evinces no sympathy with National Socialism, nonetheless he was intent on accommodation in order to further his academic career. Gadamer speaks of his Jewish friends who "had to leave us or to live quietly," without ever discussing the government's representation of its policy toward the Jews. In giving a piece on Plato that has been printed under the motto "he who philosophizes is not at one with the premises of his times"— a quote from Goethe—Gadamer claims for himself some small act of resistance. But in the 1930s, Gadamer's "little ship had run aground," and he sought ways to save his academic existence in Nazi Germany. Although refusing to enter any party organization, he voluntarily registered for a "rehabilitation camp"—a political course for Dozenten that was required for habilitation. By means of this camp Gadamer won an influential friend, and in 1937 he finally got the professorial title. Soon he was called to Leipzig, where he also served as rector after the war. Of the Russians in charge of Leipzig after the war he writes that although he might disagree with them, they could "be certain that I would carry through their directives exactly, even against my own convictions."[16]

Gadamer's picture of his survival under Nazism is of a man who "does not want to make a martyr of oneself or voluntarily leave the country," but who seeks to find small ways of affirming his identity in the midst of enforced conformity.[17] "Indeed, from that time on (1933) the fact that one strenuously avoided politically relevant themes (and publication in journals outside one's special field altogether) was in accord with the same law of self-preservation."[18] Clearly, Gadamer is a strong individual, intent on survival, intent on his career, and willing to make accommodations for the sake of his life and work. What is rather more surprising than his accommodation during Hitler's regime is that in the post–World War II period, when many German intellectuals have been trying to come to grips with the phenomenon of Nazism, Gadamer has become no more explicit on the political and cultural implications of this period. It is as if Gadamer's penchant for reading very old books made it easy for him to turn away from any politically relevant themes, and he has continued that practice when the political conditions themselves no longer demand that silence.

In this historical context, the claims of a hermeneutic philosophy to be "radically open,"[19] to not "lose (oneself) in theoretical constructions which were not fully made good by experience,"[20] seem dramatically unrealized. Moreover, amidst these historical events, it seems hardly adequate to develop a philosophy of language that presents the following vision: "Language is the element in which we live, as fishes live in water. In linguistic interaction we call it a conversation. We search for words and they come to us; and they either reach the other person or fail him."[21] This very abstract notion of language as "the element in which we live" does not deal with the particular features or failures of linguistic interactions. Why, as far as these memoirs are concerned, did Gadamer never have a conversation with female students, colleagues, friends, or spouses? Is it because these women's words have "failed him"? What is responsible for that failure? His own prejudices? The entrenched male chauvinism of the German academy (where even today there are only very few female philosophers)? Is an ontological approach to language rich enough, and concrete enough, to provide the resources to answer these questions? Similarly, where did the conversation go wrong between German Jews and their anti-Semitic persecutors? In order to understand this failure, aren't we obliged to delve into the history of anti-Semitism, its economic justifications, the psychological and existential factors which support it?[22] Can Gadamer's ontological approach to language, and his goal of developing a universal hermeneutics, help us to come to terms with these most pressing historical demands? And if not, if contemporary politics is defined as outside the scope of hermeneutic reflection, can hermeneutics really be said to explore the relation of consciousness with its historicity, to understand the ways in which historical context is reflected and appropriated in intellectual thought?

It is important to remember that Gadamer's philosophical choices are existential ones as well. There are philosophers and artists, whose work spans some of the period of Gadamer's long life, who have chosen more explicitly to address personal and political currents omitted both from Gadamer's hermeneutic writings as well as from his autobiographical ones. As one contrast, I will mention briefly Audrey Flack, feminist painter and sculptor. The curator of the current retrospective exhibit on Flack's work describes it in the following terms: "It is personal and self-revelatory. Historically conscious and emotionally charged, it is passionate, involved and unashamedly sentimental. Flack's art is about people and objects she cares for and which she often sees as extensions of herself. Both her portraits and still lives have a positive physical and moral presence and a sense of respect for living beings."[23] Flack's work ranges from self-portraits ("Self-Portrait Holding Charcoal Stick," "Self-Portrait in Underpants," "Triple Self-Portrait"), to photorealist images of public figures (Kennedy, Hitler), to scenes of Mexican workers and market women, to paintings of religious and sexual icons, to bronze goddess figurines which celebrate the female figure, strength, and energy. Here we have a radically different vision of the relation between high culture and the social world than is present in Gadamer's work. Flack purposely breaks the rules of high culture in order to create art "for the people."

I am not interested in comparing these two figures, Gadamer and Flack, with such different life histories and cultural contexts. Nor am I interested in setting up a female artist who paints herself in her underpants as normative about the relation between personal identity and creative production. Rather, my references to Flack are meant to serve as a sort of shock therapy and reality test. Her art reminds us that the parameters in which one creates, whether art or philosophy, are at least partly self-chosen ones. Although Gadamer chose to keep silent about the self, this very silence is self-revelatory. It indicates a desire to maintain a safe distance from troublesome issues on both a personal and political scale. The huge gaps in his intellectual auto-biographies about his own historicity give us ample grounds to question his view that about the self it is better to keep silent.

What then does this critical reading of Gadamer suggest about the relation between philosophy and material life, the question posed at the beginning of this essay? For me, it suggests at the very least that the question is unavoidable, however much a philosopher might seek to turn away from it explicitly. But limitations of time and space preclude a fuller examination of this question here. I will instead briefly indicate the kinds of strategies that might be useful in pursuing it. One strategy might be to develop comparisons between hermeneutics and other leading currents of twentieth-century intellectual life—for example, German critical theory, French post-structuralist theory. And indeed, there have been many projects devoted to this debate (for example, the debate between Gadamer and Habermas, the attempt to set up a debate between Gadamer and Derrida). However, such a debate continues to function on a high level of abstraction.

I find it more fruitful to look at theorists engaged in philosophical reflection on world-historical events (while acknowledging that these theorists have a theoretical perspective that may itself be debated). Hannah Arendt, for example, sought to grapple with issues of Jewish identity, anti-Semitism, violence, and authoritarianism in her works *Rahel Varnhagen, The Origins of Totalitarianism, Eichmann in Jerusalem.* More recent philosophers, like Berel Lang, have written on the Holocaust and on genocide. Were philosophers to turn their attention to the urgent political tasks of our time, there would be attempts to grapple with the motivation for massacres and rapes such as are taking place in the civil war in the former Yugoslavia, with the resurgence of anti-Semitism and violence against "Gastarbeiter" in newly reunified Germany, with questions of individual and collective responsibility for racism and inequality, with the existence of institutionalized homophobia in the United States. I would argue that contrary to the insular model of Gadamerian hermeneutics, philosophers might become engaged in their historicity and situatedness, might abdicate the struggle for abstract justifications of universality, might challenge the practices of the university system that perpetuate the mythology of this institution as an Ivory Tower. To develop a fruitful understanding of the relation between intellectual understanding and concrete existence, one has to acknowledge that the philosopher is also a historical, contingent, embodied being, to acknowledge how one is implicated in one's personal/historical identity, and to develop theories as a means of resistance and not merely as tools that are innocuous and complicitous with existing inequalities and injustices.

ROBIN MAY SCHOTT

DEPARTMENT OF PHILOSOPHY
UNIVERSITY OF COPENHAGEN
APRIL 1993

NOTES

1. Hans-Georg Gadamer, *Philosophical Apprenticeships*, translated by Robert R. Sullivan (Cambridge: MIT Press, 1985), p. viii.

2. Quoted in Sheldon S. Wolin's review of *Philosophical Apprenticeships*, "Under Siege in the German Ivory Tower," *New York Times Sunday Book Review*, July 28, 1985.

3. Gadamer, "On the Scope and Function of Hermeneutical Reflection," in *Philosophical Hermeneutics*, translated and edited by David E. Linge (Berkeley: University of California Press, 1976), p. 28.

4. See my discussion of this flight from concrete existence in an earlier article, "Whose Home is it Anyway? A Feminist Response to Gadamer's Hermeneutics," in *Gadamer and Hermeneutics*, ed. Hugh Silverman (New York: Routledge, 1991). In that article, I connect Gadamer's notion of re-appropriation, of making a second home away from home, with a flight from the temporality and materiality of existence that has characterized much of the masculine tradition in Western philosophy.

5. Gadamer, *Philosophical Apprenticeships*, p. 1.

6. Ibid., p. 4.

7. Chapter headings are entitled "Paul Natorp," "Max Scheler," "Martin Heidegger," and so forth.

8. "Chairetic" comes from the Greek "chairos," referring to the most opportune moment in the body's healing process for a physician's intervention. Metaphorically it refers to the importance of timing in life.

9. Quoted in Wolin, p. 11.

10. Gadamer, "On the Scope and Function of Hermeneutical Reflection," p. 32.

11. See my earlier discussion, "Whose Home is it Anyway?" pp. 208–9. In that piece, I argue that Gadamer's philosophy is oblivious to issues of legitimacy and illegitimacy faced by oppressed groups. The problem of oppression is not only external, but also internal, as de Beauvoir and Baldwin amongst others have so eloquently argued. If one has learned to be inferior, one will not feel entitled to be "it" in the game of interpretation, and individual feelings and thoughts become suppressed.

12. See Gadamer's "On the Scope and Function of Hermeneutical Reflection," p. 42 (typescript).

13. Ibid., p. 8 (typescript).

14. Gadamer, *Philosophical Apprenticeships*, p. 75.

15. Ibid., p.76.

16. Ibid., p.107.

17. Gadamer, "On the Scope and Function of Hermeneutical Reflection," p. 14 (typescript).

18. Ibid.

19. Ibid., p. 18 (typescript).

20. Ibid., p. 19.

21. Ibid., p. 25 (typescript).

22. Sartre seeks to explore these factors in *Anti-Semite and Jew*. Though his analysis has often been criticized for equating anti-Semitism with other forms of prejudice, and thereby ignoring its specificity, he at least faces as historically inevitable the task of understanding anti-Semitism.

23. Thalia Gouma-Peterson, curator of "Breaking the Rules: Audrey Flack; A Retrospective 1950–1990," exhibited at the Speed Museum, University of Louisville, January 12–February 28, 1993.

REPLY TO ROBIN MAY SCHOTT

I can only be sorry for Ms. Robin May Schott who wasted her time by using my little autobiography *Philosophical Apprenticeships* as a basis for her criticisms instead of the autobiographical texts presented to her for this volume. That small text was written in response to the urgings of my former and current students. On top of that Ms. Schott became the victim of a very misleading translation of the motto of the autobiography. The motto does not mean: 'it is better to be silent about myself' but rather 'I want to be silent about myself'. One may doubt whether I heeded this good intention with sufficient care. But it is completely impossible, in defiance of the clear intention of the author, to try to learn something about the person and the life of the author from these little notes. For that purpose I must be allowed to refer to the statements in the *Living Philosophers.*

Robert Sullivan, the translator of my *Philosophical Apprenticeships,* did not follow my warnings, but out of a political-scientific interest insisted on the translation. I could not see how my little book could have any utility from this viewpoint. By contrast, his new contribution to this volume has a solid foundation in my interpretation of Plato's *Republic.* In my reply to Sullivan's essay, I expressed clearly enough that the *Philosophical Apprenticeships* are no basis at all for the interests of Ms. Schott.

The sole philosophical content I added to the little sketch of life of *Philosophical Apprenticeships* consists in a few essays which Ms. Schott does not mention at all. In the essay "Über die politische Inkompetenz der Philosophie," I illustrated with Plato and Heidegger what I myself think about the relation between philosophy and politics. With modesty, I lay claim to the same incompetence.

H.-G.G.

27

P. Christopher Smith

THE I-THOU ENCOUNTER (*BEGEGNUNG*) IN GADAMER'S RECEPTION OF HEIDEGGER

> *He [Werner Marx] sees the danger here in a counterpower* (Gegenmacht) *building up in the human being against* (gegen) *the power that is presenting itself to us in the countryside* (Gegend). *I [Gadamer] would have expected the opposite difficulty, which was always a problem for me, namely whether Heidegger does not go too far when the human being is so totally eased into waiting for the countryside to open itself that no 'counterresponse'* (entgegnen) *at all 'toward'* (gegen) *can be found any more in the human being.*
>
> Gadamer, "Gibt es auf Erden ein Mass (W. Marx)"

In the fall of 1961 I came to Heidelberg with a grant from the German Academic Exchange Service for what I thought was to be a year of study under Karl Löwith. Löwith was on leave, however, and Gadamer, largely unknown outside of Germany at that time, graciously offered to take me under his wing in Löwith's absence. I soon realized what a stroke of good fortune this was, for once in Gadamer's hands I experienced his unique Socratic ability to find and elicit intellectual strengths in beginners in philosophy of which they themselves had had hitherto not an inkling—combined, of course, with his equally Socratic talent for first disabusing students of the intellectual phantoms filling their heads. At the end of my year, and in the hopes of staying on, I submitted to Gadamer a dissertation proposal on Martin Buber and Martin Heidegger. He was kind yet firm in rejecting it, as well he should have been. Indeed, it was so unfocused that I no longer have the slightest remembrance of its content save that, after two years of logical analysis at Columbia, I was determined to do something "existentially relevant" and that I had found Buber's I-Thou philosophy a good deal more "existentially relevant" than Heidegger's "thinking about Being" had turned out to be after a year of trying in vain to decipher it.

For I had been drawn initially to the traces in *Being and Time* of the Heidegger of 1921 who could cite Kierkegaard's *Training in Christianity* as a motto:

> Modern philosophy in its entirety is based, both in regard to what is ethical and to what is Christian, on a mere bit of frivolousness. Instead of jolting human beings and calling them to order by talking of the radical doubt of despair and by getting

angry with them, philosophy has quietly beckoned to them and invited them to indulge the fantasy that they are doubting and have doubted. The rest of philosophy floats, abstract, in the indeterminacy of the metaphysical.[1]

And like Socrates with Anaxagoras in the *Phaedo,* I fancied that I too had soared high with Heidegger only to have my hopes dashed when I found him too "floating" in the very abstractions he first seemed to have sworn off.

But it was Gadamer's way to purify the element of what was good in a student's ideas from the dross in which it was hidden. Thus while telling me that I would have to start from scratch, he told me too, reassuringly, that I was on to something. Although Heidegger always spoke of a "Zurückschlagen des Denkens in die Existenz," of thought's returning to have an impact on our existence, there was indeed, he said, a "Gnostic" turn to Heidegger's thought, a tendency to withdraw introspectively from the world "between" *(zwischen)* human beings. And Buber, the philosopher of the I-Thou encounter, to be sure, but primarily the preacher of the word who calls us back into it, had seen this tendency and rejected it.[2] Since my dissertation ought, of course, to be philosophical, not homiletical, it would draw upon the *thinker,* Heidegger, in elaborating the experience of the Thou as one more of the instantiations of otherness and being that cannot be founded in acts of subjectivity—alongside Heidegger's being-there *(Dasein),* being of the thing, being of the artwork, and being of the word. (Indeed, Gadamer himself had already explored the "experience" *(Erfahrung)* of the written artwork, the text, as analogous to the the the I-Thou encounter (WM 340ff.). And thus the dissertation would be titled, "Das Sein des Du: die Philosophie Martin Bubers im Lichte des Heidegger'schen Denkens an das Sein."[3] But it would also explore, critically and in starting from Buber, the deficiencies in Heidegger's treatment of our being together with others and pursue the reasons for the neglect of this being in Heidegger later on. To be sure, Gadamer always contended that given the task with which Heidegger saw himself confronted, namely to resist modernity's obsession with calculating and making, a certain single-mindedness was inevitable and indispensable. And this single-mindedness would, of necessity, preclude the pursuit of a number of avenues of thought that his thinking had in fact opened, not closed, among these, exposition of the I-Thou encounter. Still I sensed then what I was to confirm as I went ahead in my studies with Gadamer: namely that Gadamer's own reception of Heidegger, however dedicated and loyal it was to the man to whom he owed so much, was not at all uncritical in the uses it made of his thought.

Accordingly, in what follows here I wish, first, to outline those things in Heidegger from which Gadamer derives his own hermeneutic philosophy and without which it would be unthinkable. But I will do this in order, second, that we might see where Gadamer at the same time has always diverged from Heidegger, in particular, from his latent "Gnosticism," and has thereby succeeded in recovering important realms of our experience lost sight of in Heidegger, in particular, our being together with others in the I-Thou encounter. Finally, I will probe how in starting from Gadamer one might go on even to recover the Biblical dimensions of the I-Thou encounter as an encounter with God and neighbor *(der Nächste)*, dimensions that were pervasive and fundamental not only in Buber but in Kierkegaard, from whom perhaps more than anyone Heidegger received his initial, "theological" impetus, yet who nonetheless fades from view with Heidegger's "Gnostic" turn to heeding Being's call to the solitary thinker.

(1) GADAMER'S APPROPRIATION OF HEIDEGGERIAN THEMES

At the center of *Truth and Method* we find, as a kind of hinge to the whole work, a section entitled "Heidegger's outline of a hermeneutical phenomenology." Here (WM 240ff.) Gadamer begins to apply Heidegger's "hermeneutics of facticity" in rectifying the deficiencies Gadamer had been exposing up to this point in previous hermeneutic philosophies (Dilthey *et alii*). The "hermeneutics of facticity," as this is elaborated in Heidegger's *Being and Time,* might be taken as a further contribution to Husserl's project of transcendental founding in the acts and performances of subjectivity, with the qualification, of course, that in Heidegger these acts of subjectivity had become being-there's *(Dasein's)* projections of itself. A deeper reading of *Being and Time,* however, and in particular a reading in retrospect from Heidegger's later work, reveals that in Heidegger's hands the idea of founding had undergone a radical change. For even in *Being and Time* the active center or foundation was already being displaced from the self-projection of being-there to what is other than being-there, other than consciousness. Even in *Being and Time,* that is to say, the emphasis was already shifting from being-there's *Sich-Entwerfen* to its *Geworfenheit,* from its thrusting itself forward in its existence, to its always finding itself already having been thrust into a situation that it itself did not define and that is thrust upon it. Activity of the "self that relates itself to itself" thus gives way to receptivity insofar as in its own projection of itself it must take upon itself what is *not* of its own making. Hence if one looks for a ground or *principium* here, if one looks for that from which one may start and for which, in being given in itself, no further grounds need or can be given, if one looks for a "fact" and foundation behind which one need not and cannot go, this is not to be located in being-there itself but rather in the given "fact" of its always already having been determined by something other than itself.[4]

We are, for example, not in control of the mood or passion *(Stimmung)* we happen to find ourselves in, say anxiety or boredom, to take two of Heidegger's examples, a mood or passion that nevertheless is fundamentally constitutive of how our world is construed. Similarly, in regard to temporality, Heidegger faults Husserl's transcendental philosophy for trying to account for time in starting from what is retained in consciousness of the past and projected in consciousness of the future. In both cases presence in consciousness was supposed to be the ground and foundation. But Heidegger shows us time is better understood in starting precisely from what is *not* retained in consciousness but forgotten and no longer present and precisely from what is *not* foreseen and projected but, like the Biblical "thief in the night" (1 Thes. 5:4), comes upon us from the future, wholly unexpected. Indeed, Heidegger's question, which was about Being and precisely not about consciousness, displays that anything that is temporally in this way, is *to* us and *toward (gegen)* us starting from what is other than we (compare GW 3: 274–75). Hence, in the temporal event of being we are shown to be not so much the active subjects of transitive sentences as the indirect, dative objects "to whom" something is given. And with this insight the project of transcendental "founding" collapses altogether.

But not only this. All detached knowing of objects by subjects, all "Wissen auf Abstand," all knowing at a distance, as Kierkegaard would say, is shown up as derivative and abstract. At its basis knowing, *scire,* science, proves to be acquaintanceship with something, knowing one's way around *in* it and from *within* it. At its basis *Wissen,* knowledge, is *Verstehen,* understanding.

In "The Language of Metaphysics" (GW 3: 233ff.), Gadamer lists four exemplifications and concretions that show us what Heidegger has in mind and that provide tangible evidence, as it were, of the validity of his thesis that what is precisely *not* consciousness or subjectivity, is the origin and "ground" of Being: first, there is the tool, of which, in its being ready at hand and in its smooth functioning, we are precisely *not* aware and whose being is, accordingly, not to be accounted for in starting from consciousness. There is, second, the thing, that *of itself,* and not as a result of any action on our part, singles itself out in its irreplaceability. There is, third, the artwork, which, like the thing, is characterized not so much by what it does display to us of itself as what it does not, by what it withholds from us in "keeping to itself." And there is, fourth, the word spoken whose meaning comes forth toward us only from within the silences of what remains unsaid.

Gadamer, who sees a task for *Truth and Method* precisely in providing such verifiable instantiations of Heidegger's thinking about being, appropriates in particular the last two of these in focusing, to begin with, more narrowly on the artwork and in proceeding then to the wider concern of speech and language. Following Heidegger he elaborates our "dativity," if I may call it that, in the interpretation of art, namely our being the ones "to whom" the work is both given and withheld in its temporal being "toward" *(gegen)* us and being away from us. Then, in the final part of *Truth and Method,* and again following Heidegger, he elaborates speech and language with regard to the "virtuality" of the word, its infinite potential to always mean more than what we can expressly say on any given occasion. Thus here too, we are not so much active as receptive. We learn from an utterance's very withholding of its meaning from us that it itself is the active center, not we, the ones who say it. More than our doing things with words, then, we undergo what words do with us.[5]

Now precisely this displacement of centrality from consciousness to what is other than consciousness, Gadamer finds, puts the difficulties of previous hermeneutics in a completely new light: "Heidegger," he finds, "achieved a new position vis-à-vis the perplexities besetting historicism" (WM 245). Hence in Gadamer's new hermeneutics, where Heidegger's understanding *(Verstehen)* becomes understanding of texts, Heidegger's *Geworfenheit,* our always having already been thrust into a situation and having had things thrust upon us, becomes our always already belonging to a tradition of interpretation of these texts. For Gadamer, Heidegger's "facticity" becomes our inability to get out of, and to get behind the past tradition that is constitutive of us, to get around its authority and prejudgments.

To illustrate and document this phenomenon of our "always already" (Heidegger: *immer schon)* finding ourselves under way within a historical tradition that "effects" us even as we are in the process of further "effecting" it, Gadamer turns, naturally enough, to legal theory, to jurisprudence *(dikast⁻e phronēsis),* with its presumption and dependence on precedent (WM 301ff., 307ff.) and to prudence *(phronēsis)* itself, of which jurisprudence is but a special form (WM 297ff.). Gadamer shows that *phronēsis,* as Aristotle explicates it, is precisely a kind of knowing that is not "at a distance" but involved in, and itself effected by the decisions *(proaireseis, kriseis)* it makes in taking over decisions already made. *Phronēsis* is thus not methodical science, *epistēmē,* nor even the art, *technē,* of making something, but the more basic understanding or *Verstehen* that Heidegger uncovered beneath these.

In his "Marburg Theology" (GW 3: 197ff.) Gadamer describes the Heideggerian background for his own appropriation of *phronēsis* as a paradigm for hermeneutic understanding, i.e., for understanding and interpreting texts. Here he introduces Heidegger's own account of *phronēsis* in conjunction with Heidegger's recourse to the scholastic distinction between an *actus exercitus* and an *actus signatus,* which correspond, for example, to directly asking a question as opposed to reflectively focusing on and objectifying what it is to ask questions (200ff.). *Phronēsis,* the knowing that guides our deliberations about ethical choices, Heidegger shows, is the kind of prereflective knowing-in-execution where what is known is not yet singled out as such and signified and, consequently, is not yet an object put before us and at our disposal. And as knowers we, consequently, are not yet removed from the direct encounter *(Begegnung)* with what is known, not yet detached and "at a distance" from it but affected, and historically effected, by it in each of our decisions about it. Nor is our knowing of it ever yet complete and adequate. For in this infinite process, not of an *adequatio intellectus et rei* but of a *mensuratio intellectus ad rem,*[6] the *res* or thing, in "keeping to itself," is always more than what we could know of it at any given time. And, Gadamer goes on to argue in *Truth and Method,* it is this way with *dikastē phronēsis*'s, jurisprudence's, interpretation of a law, within which judges who render their decisions still find themselves under way, and it is this way, correspondingly, with our "judicious" *(phronimos)* interpretation of all texts and artworks.

(2) THE I-THOU ENCOUNTER AND GADAMER'S IMPLICIT CRITIQUE OF HEIDEGGER

Still, the exposition of Aristotle's *phronēsis* in Gadamer proceeds quite differently from its exposition in Heidegger, as we learn from Gadamer's own account in his "Marburg Theology." Gadamer tells us that on one occasion Heidegger, in a seeming *non sequitur* typical of him, broke into his students' struggle over the difference in Aristotle between the knowledge of art or *technē* that can be forgotten and the knowledge of prudence or *phronēsis* that cannot: "That's conscience!" he interjected, putting an abrupt halt to the class (GW 3: 200). And, Gadamer adds, "With this violent way of dragging Aristotle's text into his own questioning one is reminded of how in *Being and Time* the call of conscience is what first of all makes the being-there in the human being visible in its structure of temporal occurrence" (ibid.).

Of course Gadamer, despite the apparently sharp tone of this comment, is not concerned to criticize Heidegger. Heidegger's "violence," he would always remind us, was a part of his genius, and Heidegger, precisely in linking *phronēsis* to the call of conscience, Gadamer would show, has uncovered *phronēsis*'s own structure of being something, not that we do as subjects, but that happens to us. Nevertheless, it is also clear that Gadamer does see a violation, however creative, of Aristotle here—and of *phronēsis* itself. For in Gadamer, far from being the call of consciousness to the solitary individual, the call that calls him back from the "world" to which he had "fallen" and lost himself (SZ 272ff.), *phronēsis* remains the *social* phenomenon that it is in Aristotle. And now we begin to perceive what Gadamer might have meant when he spoke to me of a "Gnostic" tendency in Heidegger.

For in Gadamer Aristotle's *phronēsis* is not torn out of its context in *boulē, bouleusthai,* and *euboulia* (advice and counsel, taking counsel, well-advisedness) nor out of its context in *synesis, syngnōmē,* and *epieikeia* (understanding for someone, consideration, clemency). In brief, in Gadamer *phronēsis* remains tied to social relationships. And consequently, in Gadamer, the *Verstehen* or understanding for which *phronēsis* could be paradigmatic becomes, in the third and final part of *Truth and Method, Sich-Verständigen,* our coming to an understanding with each other.

To be sure, Heidegger does not by any means omit this social dimension of our being-there from his considerations. For him the Thou, like the thing, artwork, and word, was always an instantiation of being that could not be reduced to an act of subjectivity and that therefore resisted Husserl's attempts to account for it in terms of "intersubjectivity." And for Heidegger, as Gadamer himself often points out (see GW 3: 184, 234, 275–76), to begin with *(zunächst)* one "always already" finds oneself together with others from whom one has "always already" taken over a construed world. But this notwithstanding, the experience of the Thou undergoes a remarkable diminishment in Heidegger's thinking quite in contrast to the amplification it receives in Gadamer's.

To see why, we should note, first, the very location in *Being and Time* of Heidegger's exposition of our being-together-others, our *Mitsein* (SZ 118ff.): it immediately precedes the exposition of *das Man,* the "everybody," of the "world" and, in fact, introduces this exposition. As is signaled by the qualification "zumeist," or "for the most part," characteristically predicated of it and indicating its decadent *(verfallen)* "everydayness," our being together with others thus occurs in Heidegger primarily as a deficient, inauthentic, fallen mode of a being-there that has not yet been disconnected from others in anxiety and called back from the world by conscience and called into its absolutely singularized, very ownmost being toward death.

To be sure, even in this context Heidegger makes a crucial distinction in the caring for others or *Fürsorge*—our worrying about them—in which our being together with others manifests itself. There is the usual everyday sort of care for others in which I "jump in" and take over another's existence for him or her thus depriving him or her of free decision. But there is also, says Heidegger, in what amounts to a kind of excursus here, the special authentic sort of caring for others in which I leap ahead, opening the way, and thus give back to the other his or her possibility of free, authentic decision and resolve precisely by helping him or her become free for this. And here Heidegger is certainly not reducing care for others to an aspect of our decadent everyday existence.

Clearly, however, the reference here is to a kind of being-together-with which paradoxically could exist only between essentially solitary individuals, both of whom are no longer "numbed by" and "taken up with" *(benommen)* a social world that they are jointly taking care of: for here, says Heidegger, "The shared commitment for the same subject matter is defined by each having in each case seized, on his own *(eigens),* his being-there. Only one's own, authentic *(eigentliche)* connectedness makes possible the right matter of factness that lets the other go free in his freedom" (SZ 122). The subject matter here that each, in leaping forward, gives back to the other, would be, we must presume, his or her ownmost *(eigenstes),* authentic *(eigentliches),* intrinsically unsharable being-towards-death. And of necessity this is ultimately a (subject) matter for the solitudinous individual in "flight alone to the alone," as Plotinus would put it, and no longer lost in the world of what "everybody" does.[7]

The point is that even in this passing reference to an authentic caring for others Heidegger gives us no way of thinking positively of social being, of our being together with others as participants in a public subject matter, a tradition, a world, that we can and do share. In Heidegger the human animal who has speech, the *zōion logon echon,* hears the call of conscience by himself. He is no longer, as he must still be in Aristotle, the *zōon politikon,* the social animal who takes counsel with himself only on the basis of always already having taking counsel with others, *philoi,* friends, in the community. In Gadamer, however, this is not at all the case.

That it is not can readily be shown if we turn to Gadamer's own exposition of the I-Thou encounter in *Truth and Method* (WM 340ff.). Indeed, from the start we note a crucial difference, one that should not surprise us given the quotation with which we began (GW 3: 342): in Gadamer the I-Thou encounter, our being together with others, is characterized by mutuality. As we have just seen, in the Heidegger of *Being and Time* the one self, thinking it knows better, might look out for others, or, being in advance of them in its own authentic existing toward death, might even give their existence back to them, but there is nothing said of a reciprocal interchange here. And Heidegger, after the "turning" from acts of a self that relates itself to itself to actions of Being on our being-there, only reverses this one-sidedness, as Gadamer has pointed out (ibid.). But in Gadamer, in contrast to Heidegger, what I do unto others they also do unto me and vice versa, except that to begin with, at least, the model is not so much the New Testament as it is Hegel's dialectic of civic recognition:

> Thus, simply speaking, the process here is a doubled one of both self-consciousnesses: each sees the other doing the same thing it does. Each does itself what it demands from the other and does what it does only insofar as the other does the same. One-sided action would be useless because what is supposed to occur [acknowledgement, recognition] can only come about through both.[8]

Gadamer sees something like the greeting in this, say a tip of the hat or wave, which falls humiliatingly flat if the other does not acknowledge it by responding in kind. Thus in Gadamer, as opposed to Heidegger, in my being with others I give as much as I receive. Action is interaction, reciprocal relation. It is meeting, encounter, *Begegnung,* and not Heidegger's "Begegnis" or the one-sided "towardsing" of the other in our direction *(gegen uns)* (again, compare GW 3: 342).

There are, of course, distortions of the I-Thou encounter that are not reciprocal, and precisely in order to highlight the reciprocity of the true I-Thou encounter Gadamer begins with two of these. First, I can deal with you on the basis of my knowledge of "what people are like." I can deal with you, that is to say, by having "figured you out" and having "got your number," in which case I have only objectified you and put you at my disposal while maintaining my own dispassionate detachment (WM 341). (If anything exemplifies "knowing at a distance," it is surely this!) Furthermore, in a variation of Heidegger's inauthentic caring for someone, I can even recognize you as a person *(persona),* but in a kind of psychoanalytical one-upmanship I claim to know better than you, and in advance, what you really mean to say or what you really want. To be sure, in this case you are no longer just a thing *(res)* that I would fit into my scheme of things. Hence there is a measure of reciprocity here—you will, after all, be playing the same "mind games" with me—but recognition of the *persona* of each of us is still being fought out in a kind of jousting where each party still seeks to get recognition from the other while not having to extend it him- or herself. Each party, in other words, seeks, as a kind of spoilsport and killjoy, to preserve self-referentiality and to avoid yielding to the interplay that exists between the two of them.

But in the true I-Thou encounter, Gadamer goes on to show, I must allow that both I and you belong not so much to ourselves as to the world and its language in which we both participate and communicate, the world and language between us and constitutive of who each of us is in the first place. Here I am willing to listen to what you have to say, to let it stand, and to join with you in coming to deeper insight into the significance of it. This demands more than mere acknowledgement of you and recognition of the individual "person" with rights that you are, and consequently only here is the self-referentiality really overcome that mere civic acknowledgement and recognition tacitly perpetuate. For here we both do yield to the "game" to which we belong, a game we are no longer trying to win but simply to enjoy. And, hence, where there was isolation, estrangement, and conflict, here there is now community, kinship, connection.

As Gadamer puts it early on in *Truth and Method,*

> All single individuals who are raising themselves from their physical nature find in the language, customs and institutions of their people a pre-given substance, which, as in learning language, it is their task to make their own. Thus single individuals are always already under way in shaping themselves and becoming cultured, always already in the process of canceling their physical aspect insofar as the world into which they are growing is a human world shaped by language and custom. (WM 11)[9]

Quite in contrast to Heidegger, the education, *Bildung, paideia* that Gadamer stresses here, is not at all learning to hear the innermost call of conscience that calls the single existing individual back from the world's "talk" and back to his or her ownmost self. And neither is it learning, as in the later Heidegger, to listen, in pastoral solitude, to the call of Being that calls thinking back from its obliviousness and self-dissolution in the "metaphysical" languages of Western culture. Rather it is precisely the reverse, namely learning to rise above our initially individuated and private existences and to participate in the communities of language and culture to which we have always already belonged from time out of mind.[10]

There is little in Heidegger that could prepare us for this insight. For central to it is that we win our true selves, not by getting ourselves back from the language we find ourselves speaking and by idiosyncratically forcing it into new forms of expression, but by coming to participate ever more fully in its expressive power.[11] We win our true selves, this is to say, not by recovering ourselves from the social world constituted by this language, as if it were some sort of alien fate that has come over us and estranged us from our original, solitary being, but precisely by coming ever more fully into our being together with others in this very social, cultural world.

To be sure, we cannot overlook the fact that we do *not* find Gadamer's exposition of the I-Thou encounter in part 3 of *Truth and Method,* the last part, which is specifically concerned with these wider questions of our participation in language and speech and with our reaching an understanding with each other in language and speech. Rather this exposition comes in the specifically hermeneutic part 2 of this work, which is more narrowly concerned with *an* interpreter's understanding of texts. And indeed, the I-Thou encounter is presented there *only as an analogy* for the interpreter-text relation, the two wrong forms of the I-Thou illustrating the two wrong forms of hermeneutic understanding, and the right form pointing the way out of mistaken conceptions of interpretation. Thus the "experience" with the otherness of the Thou serves there, *as it did in Heidegger,* to point us beyond any theory of understanding that would found itself on performances of subjectivity. And the same is true of Gadamer's splendid exposition of the dialectic of question and answer (WM 344ff.): as beautifully as this might have served as a phenomenological description of what happens in the I-thou exchange, it is not Gadamer's intention here that it should. Rather, once again we are to see in this dialectic an analogy for the interpreter's experience with the text—the single interpreter's, or so, at least, it might seem at first glance. The "Thou," then, would really be a semi-anthropomorphized "it," namely the "text," and the later Heidegger's solitudinous "devotional contemplation of Being" *(Andenken an das Sein)* might seem to be the model after all.

However, the shift in part 3 of *Truth and Method* from *an* interpreter's understanding of texts to the dialogical process of *our* reaching an understanding about something in speech and language, makes unequivocally clear that for Gadamer understanding was never monological. For instance, on p. 422 we find, at first quite in unison with Heidegger,

> What is thus thought of as existing and being, is not really the *object* of things we say, rather it 'comes to be spoken of' in things we say. That is how it attains its truth and comes to be plain in human thinking. Hence Greek ontology is founded on speech or language being tied to what it is about, for it thinks the essence of speech and language in starting from the things we say.

But then Gadamer adds,

> *Of course it is to be emphasized in opposition to this that speech and language first get to be what they are in discussion, which is to say, in the exercise of getting each other to understand (Verständigung).* (emphasis added)

In retrospect, from this passage we can see that Gadamer always intended that understanding be construed dialogically and triadically, that is, as a discursive occurrence between two or more who together with each other are in the process of reaching an understanding about some thing and subject matter they share between them. Thus in the end the key here is not so much *phronēsis,* or my understanding *(Verstehen)* of some thing, as *synesis,* or my understanding *(Verständnis)* for someone. And this *synesis,* Gadamer tells us, is based on our both wanting what is right and based in the fact that the other one and I are bound together in this communality (WM 306). Thus when I show understanding for someone, I do not presume to set myself apart from the other and, detached from him and unaffected by his lot, to judge him impartially. Rather, as a friend *(philos)* and in specifically belonging with him to a community of language and obligation, in sharing with him its principles and ways, and in being touched by the other's predicament, I "think together with the other" (ibid.).

Thus it becomes clear that in Gadamer, in contrast to Heidegger, *synesis,* the understanding shown to each other by friends and kin who are dear *(philoi)* to each other, is even more than the mere adjunct of *phronēsis* that it seems to be in Aristotle. In Gadamer it is its basis. For *phronēsis* is the guide of our taking counsel with ourselves *(bouleuesthai)* in regard to our ethical decisions or choices *(prohaireseis;* see Aristotle's *Nicomachean Ethics* [EN], 1111b4ff.). But in Gadamer's hands taking counsel with ourselves *(Mitsichzurategehen;* WM 304) is at its root precisely not something that one does with oneself alone, but that we do with each other together. And we can take counsel only together with other friends and kin who show us understanding or *synesis* (WM 306). Precisely in this Gadamer breaks with Heidegger's "Gnostic" introspection.

Put in theological terms, which are certainly not Gadamer's, the kingdom of God is not "within you," rather it is "among you" and "in your midst" (Luther: "mitten unter euch"; Luke 17:21). Gadamer, of course, is not thinking of the kingdom of God, but of the civic community, the *polis.* Still one might ask if his appropriation of the word "Mitte" or "midst" in such coinings as "die Mitte der Sprache" or "the 'midst' of speech" (WM 405, 432ff.) does not derive after all from Luther rather than from the more immediate source, the "deiner Mitte" or "to your center," in Rilke's poem on the frontispiece for *Truth and Method.* For obviously the "midst" of speech is among you people *(euch)* and is not yours *(dein)* individually. Is not Gadamer, then, implicitly extending a theme of Luther's and Luke's anti-Gnostic theology?

(3) RECOVERY OF THE BIBLICAL DIMENSION

In any event, Gadamer's extrospective return to our social experience, to what occurs among participants in a community of speech and language, occurs in their "midst," has a theological consequence perhaps unintended but of great significance nonetheless. It reopens the way back to the initial Biblical underpinnings of Heideggerian thinking, underpinnings in dialectical theology that were increasingly obscured as Heidegger came to focus ever more exclusively on his question about Being.

For as Heidegger, in an effort to recapture an "inceptive thinking" *(anfängliches Denken)* before philosophy's deviation into "metaphysics," turned more and more to Greek beginnings, the once predominant Biblical strands in his thought, our fallenness from grace, our debt *(Schuld),* our anxiety, our despair, Biblical strands appropriated from Augustine, Luther, Dostoyevski, and Kierkegaard, lapse into near imperceptibility. Indeed, from early on the place of all of these in our relationships to others and to God, their place in I-Thou relationships, is obscured. Most notably in this regard, *Verborgenheit* and *unverborgen,* "hiddenness" and "unhidden," words whose origins are surely to be traced to Luther's "Verbirg dein Antlitz nicht vor mir, verstosse nicht im Zorn deinen Knecht (Hide not your face from me; do not in wrath push your servant away)" (Ps. 27:9), become in Heidegger the Greek philosophical, impersonal concepts of *lēthē* or "concealment" and *a-lēthes* or "true" in the sense of "disconcealed." And with that the interpersonal dimension, the original locus of *Verborgenheit* and *unverborgen* in what happens in the "midst" of the I and Thou, between them in their mutual encounter, vanishes. For once "true" has become in his hands *a-lēthes* or disconcealed, it no longer characterizes you in your relationship to me and me in my relation to you, but rather some*thing,* a pitcher, a pair of shoes, an artwork, a word, in what it discloses of itself to being-there. And how different that is from some*one* who had withdrawn from me in anger, drawing near again in forgiveness, where "true" would continue to mean "faithful" despite all my "unfaithfulness."

Again, we could certainly ask whether precisely this interpersonal *Ereignis* or occurrence is not the actual but obscured background for the "being" that the later Heidegger would characterize as concomitant *Abwesen* and *Anwesen,* drawing away and drawing near. Are these not best understood as God's being far away and coming near, His wrath and *parousia*? (See GW 3: 314.) But in Heidegger the dimension of wrath and grace so central to some*one*'s hiding his or her face and then showing it to me is lost. In Heidegger's ultimate Hellenization of Christianity, the Hebrew *sathar* behind Luther's "verbergen" has become the purely Greek *lanthanein* from which comes the *lēthē* or hiddenness in Heidegger's *a-lētheia* and *Unverborgenheit* or "unhiddenness." And with that, the Thou-art being of God, *who* in response to our violations of faith seems to have turned away from us, to have become angry, remote, who even seems not to be there at all when we call upon Him, has become the it-is being of the divine *which* has receded into "forgottenness," i.e., *Vergessenheit,* Heidegger's other rendering of *lēthē.*

But Gadamer, by returning *phronēsis,* prudence, to its communal setting in *synesis,* and even *syngnōmē* and *epieikeia,* which represent understanding for someone as well as considerateness and clemency (WM 306), reopens the way back to the Biblical context of what occurs between persons in the I-Thou encounter. And with that the way is reopened to a God *who* could respond to the psalmist's bidding and petition in drawing near again and forgiving. Put another way, Gadamer, even if his aims are quite different, reopens the way from Heidegger back to Bultmann. Heidegger, driven by his single question about

Being, must move ever further from the initial coincidences of his work with Bultmann's existential theology, and in his *Letter on Humanism* seems even to sever definitively any remaining connection,[12] while Gadamer, in relying on *synesis, syngnōmē,* and *epieikeia,* makes possible once again a return to Bultmann's very Kierkegaardian, very Lutheran, very Biblical account of mercy and forgiveness: "We can get clear about what takes place in [God's] forgiveness," writes Bultmann,

> in reference to what forgiveness means in the I and Thou between human beings who love each other. When one human being has transgressed against another—not to say sinned [against him or her]—then nothing can bring the first back into the former relationship except the forgiveness of the other. . . . Only one thing can help: if something new occurs, if the Thou finds the strength to forgive the I and thereby to make him into a new I. If something new occurs—this is to say that the forgiveness that can come to pass is not something that can be derived from the essence of the Thou, not something on which the I can count. (Then he would not be worthy of it.) Rather it is just this, an occurrence *(Ereignis),* one originating in the gratuitous kindness of the Thou and entirely a gift.[13]

Now I grant that it is counterintuitive to suggest that Gadamer, the consummate Greek scholar, would be the one to have preserved the Biblical I-Thou where it threatens to disappear in Heidegger—and also paradoxical, for of the two Heidegger was the avowed theologian and seeker after God, and the one in whom the religious motif is most obviously pervasive (see GW 3: 309ff., "The Religious Dimension"). Moreover, precisely Heidegger's "violent" transformation of *phronēsis* into *Gewissen,* of prudence into conscience, with which we began our delineation of the differences between Gadamer and Heidegger, is plainly a superimposition on Plato and Aristotle of the New Testament (and intertestamentary [Wis. 17:10]) idea of *syneidesis,* that internal and intensified knowing, con-science and *Ge-wissen,* which warns me of the ways of the "world." Yet Heidegger's turning exclusively to just this "Gnostic" theme in Christianity—is not "Welt" in Heidegger the Johannine "kosmos"?—blocks his recovery of its Hebraic dimension and, hence, of the I-Thou encounter. In contrast, Gadamer's relocation of *phronēsis* to its setting in *synesis, syngnōmē,* and *epieikeia* keeps this Hebraic dimension alive.

For in Gadamer, as we have seen, the reciprocal transaction which occurs *between* participants, which exists in the "midst" of them and from which they derive their being, is never displaced by a turn inward and away from the social world. And though Gadamer thinks of this communal exchange entirely civically and not in the least ecclesiastically, thinks of it, that is, as a local occurrence among citizens and not at all as a religious occurrence in the church of those "called out" by God to the catholic communion of all with all, clearly in Gadamer the way from *phronēsis* through *synesis, syngnōmē,* and *epieikeia* to the Biblical *charis,* pardon, and *katallagē,* reconciliation, is still open even if it is not explicitly traversed.

There should be nothing astonishing about this, for there is, after all, a tacit Lutheran German semantic field within which Gadamer's recurrence to Aristotle's *synesis, syngnōmē,* and *epieikeia*—and to the vocabulary of the I-Thou encounter in the first place—takes place. And precisely this Lutheran German semantic field provides the hermeneutic horizons for his exposition of these. Granted, in Gadamer the initial context for the explication of these words is, as it is in Aristotle, juridical. *Epieikeia,* for instance, is taken primarily to be a legal matter and rendered accordingly as *Billigkeit* or equity. The reference here is to the discretion required in the nuanced application of a law to circumstances unforeseen by its legislators (WM 301ff.). But in recurring to the word's components—*eikein* (drawing) and *epi* (off)—Gadamer also renders the word with *Nachlassen* meaning to "ease off" or "let up" from the letter of the law (WM 301), and in this accentuation he comes close to Luther's rendering of St. Paul's use of it as "Lindigkeit" or clemency (2 Cor. 10:1; Phil. 4:5) and, with that, to the whole Biblical tradition of mercy *(chesed, eleos, Barmherzigkeit).* Compare, for instance, Luther, "Ich habe Wohlgefallen an Barmherzikeit und nicht am Opfer" (I delight in mercy and not offerings) (Hos. 6:6; Matt. 9:13). Similarly, in Gadamer's appropriation of *syngnōmē* as *Nachsicht* (WM 306) something more than mere consideration is meant. For surely Luther's *Geduld* or patience is in the background here, as is his *Verzeihung* or forgiveness, which Gadamer specifically invokes (WM 306).[14]

But most striking in this regard is Gadamer's rendering of Aristotle's *synesis* as *Verständnis* or the understanding we show for someone else. For though justified in the end, this reading of the text (EN 1143a35ff.), which directs us past it to the subsequent discussion of *syngnōmē,* is far from self-evident. (Translators, for instance F. Dirlmeier, generally stay with the more usual rendering of *synesis* as *Verständigkeit* or a grasp of things.) But Gadamer, accentuating Aristotle in a quite particular way, writes that *synesis,* as *Verständnis* or understanding *for someone,*

> is present when the concern is not with myself, but with the other. Hence, it is a kind of ethical judging. Plainly, one speaks of understanding [for someone] when, in passing judgment in this fashion, one puts oneself in the situation in which the other must act in all its concreteness. Here too it is not a matter of knowing in general, but of concretion in the instant. (WM 306)

Here we have language that goes back through Bultmann and Kierkegaard to Luther and St. Paul: compare "Freuet euch mit den Frohlichen und weinet mit den Weinenden" (Rejoice with the joyful and cry with those who cry) (Rom. 12:15). And how very Lutheran-Pauline is Gadamer's idea of the *Zugehörigkeit* on which our understanding for someone else is founded, our belonging with him or her to a community transcending us as individuals (WM 306; see also

434ff.); compare, "alles is euer, ihr aber seid Christi, Christus aber ist Gottes" (All things are yours, but you are Christ's and Christ is God's) (1 Cor. 3:22–23). Indeed, it is precisely because of continuing overtones of Luther's German in Gadamer that *die Begegnung* itself, the reciprocal encounter, say of David with the prophet Nathan (2 Sam. 12), need not be reduced, as it is in Heidegger, to the one-sided *Begegnis* or "towardsing" of the countryside to the awaiting solitary thinker.

To be sure, I must conclude here with an important qualification: it is patent that *synesis, syngnōmē,* and *epieikeia* will, in fact, have to be understood very differently if they are seen as universal, ecclesiastical virtues than if they are seen, as they are in Gadamer, as political virtues, virtues of a particular *polis.* As we have seen, if political *synesis, syngnōmē,* and *epieikeia* all presuppose a local *philia* or kinship (compare WM 306), they come into play among those close friends and relatives who already hold each other dear *(philos),* and consequently they have no bearing on how we stand in relation to outsiders and enemies. If, however, these virtues are to be made universal, they presuppose not *philia* but *agapē,* namely that "malice toward none" and "charity for all" which extends precisely to outsiders and, above all, to enemies. And on the basis of this *agapē, synesis* becomes *eleos* or mercy, *syngnōmē* becomes *aphesis* or forgiveness, and *epieikeia* becomes *makrothymia* or forbearance, all of which extend precisely to those who are not akin to us at all. It follows that in these modified senses these virtues come into play not in a scene of domestic peace but in a scene of interethnic war and that they guide a process that does not begin, but that ends with the *katallagē* or reconciliation of differences between those who had been estranged, alien, other—a reconciliation where at long last "There is neither Jew nor Greek, there is neither slave nor freeman, there is neither male nor female" (Gal. 3:28).

Hence, if this deeper, Biblical dimension of the I-Thou encounter is to be recovered, we must indeed move decisively beyond Gadamer's starting point. But is this not inevitable? In a time of resurgent ethnic rivalry I have come to believe that our starting point can no longer be the political, ethnic, national entities to which we may have happened to belong. The uncircumventable "facticity" of our life now, with which we must begin and from which we must recover, is strife. Gadamer himself does not go so far as to say this, but in following out his way back from Heidegger to the I-Thou encounter, we most surely can.

P. CHRISTOPHER SMITH

DEPARTMENT OF PHILOSOPHY
UNIVERSITY OF MASSACHUSETTS AT LOWELL
AUGUST 1992

NOTES

1. Quoted by Gadamer, *Gesammelte Werke,* band 3 (henceforth "GW 3") (Tübingen, 1987), 449. (This volume contains the majority of Gadamer's invaluable Heidegger studies.) Gadamer's *Wahrheit und Methode (Truth and Method)* (Tübingen, 1965) will be referred to here as "WM" and Martin Heidegger's *Sein und Zeit (Being and Time),* as "SZ." Translations from these and other German and Greek works are my own.

2. See in particular "Die Lehre Heideggers," in *Das Problem des Menschen,* in Martin Buber, *Werke* (Heidelberg, 1962), 1:360–80.

3. *The Being of the Thou: Buber's Philosophy in the Light of Heidegger's Thinking about Being,* Dissertationsdruck (Heidelberg, 1966).

4. In his "Der eine Weg Martin Heideggers" Gadamer points out that even the term "facticity" originates in theology, which speaks of the resurrection as precisely such an uncircumventable, given fact (GW 3: 431–32).

5. For an exposition of Gadamer on Plato's *pathos tōn logōn (Philebus* 15b), the "Wiederfährnis der Reden" or experience of what words do to us (WM 433, 441), see my *Hermeneutics and Human Finitude* (Fordham, 1991), 148ff.

6. Not an "adequation of the intellect and the thing"—to each other—but a "measuring of the intellect against the thing."

7. Ἀπαλλαγὴ τῶν ἄλλων τῶν τῇδε, βίος ἀνήδονος τῶν τῇδε, φυγὴ μόνου πρὸς μόνου" ("escape from the others here, life taking no pleasure in things here, flight of the alone to the alone"), *Ennead* 6.9.11.50–51.

8. G. W. F. Hegel, *Die Phänomenologie des Geistes* (Hamburg, 1952), 142. See Gadamer's interpretation of this passage in his *Hegel's Dialectic* (New Haven, 1972), 64 ff. Significantly Gadamer, like Hegel, moves beyond this level in drawing on *Biblical* concepts: "The common sphere that obtains between the single individuals, the Spirit that binds them to each other, is love: I that is thou, thou that is I, I and thou that are we" (GW 3: 323).

9. See my *Hermeneutics and Human Finitude,* 179ff.

10. In this Gadamer comes very close to the urbane "Socrates" of Plato's *Phaedrus,* who would rather be in the city conducting discussions *(Gespräche, logoi)* with others than in the countryside: "For I am a lover of learning, but the countryside and the trees are not wont to teach me anything, whereas the people in the city are" (230d). And in just this urbanity of Gadamer's, I think, we have the deeper reason why Gadamer turns to Plato even as Heidegger turns away from him. For Gadamer, like Plato, whose dialogues are his paradigm, thinking is carried out within the city and *polis,* carried out, that is, in the "midst" *(Mitte)* of the community of those who share a culture and language. (But compare GW 3: 229–30, 238ff., 302–3.)

11. To be sure, Gadamer would not fault Heidegger either for his "violence" in wrenching language to force new meanings from it. Heidegger, he argues, had no way left apart from this always objectionable, often futile, but sometimes brilliantly illuminating "etymological" strategy. For his task was to break the hold on us of a flattened and technocratic vocabulary that had deadened our perception for any other kind of being except that which we could put at our disposal. Hence, radical revolutionary that he was, he could not go on in the pervasive language of our day, but needed to jolt both us and himself loose from it (see Gadamer GW 3: 226ff., 307, 383ff.).

12. Martin Heidegger, *Über den Humanismus* (Frankfurt am Main, 1960 [Bern, 1947]).

13. Rudolf Bultmann, *Jesus* (Hamburg, 1964 [Tübingen, 1926]), 137–38.

14. Heidegger too mentions *Nachsicht* (SZ 123) but precisely by establishing the

correlation of this aspect of our *Fürsorgen,* or taking care of others, with *Umsicht* or circumspection as an aspect of *Besorgen* or taking care of things. With that he has already removed the word from its natural semantic neighbors, *Geduld* or patience and *Verzeihung* or forgiveness. In Heidegger *Nachsicht* has become *Nachsehen* (ibid.) or looking after someone.

REPLY TO P. CHRISTOPHER SMITH

B asically, Christopher Smith deals with his own educational history in his contribution. I myself play a certain role in it insofar as he found himself confronted with the explosive power of Heideggerian thinking through me. But at the same time, his own earlier influences would not let him overcome a resistance to Heidegger, and this is especially evident with regard to the later turn in Heidegger. Thus, he takes up the occasional comment of mine that Heidegger represents the gnosis, so to speak. This can be said of Heidegger in today's circumstances and after the way in which our early Christian influences developed in the age of the European Enlightenment. After all, Ferdinand Christian Bauer in his day dealt even with Hegel, along with Plotinus, in a book that is still a classic, bearing the title *Gnosis.* Admittedly, Smith's questions make my own contribution to hermeneutics very clear even to me. Smith is not at all mistaken that, as a child of modern Enlightenment, I have been led to my path via the great humanistic heritage. I owe my early formative impulses to it insofar as I could never entirely follow Heidegger in his search for God with full devotion.

Christopher Smith describes his own educational history. Consequently, in the first essential point of his contribution he takes up Heideggerian philosophy with respect to his own forms of thinking-further through Heidegger. The decisive role Kierkegaard played for the young Christopher Smith becomes clear in this, a role even more crucial for him than for the early Heidegger or for me. But at the same time the way in which the scene fundamentally changed for Smith since Heidegger helped us to the reawakening of Greek thinking is unmistakable. When I myself dared to take the first steps of thinking, still under the domination of Neo-Kantianism, the image of Greek ethics was stamped by the concept of intellectualism. To get beyond that and to attain our own thinking required a powerful breakthrough which we owe to Heidegger. The decisive point was to acknowledge the independence of practical knowledge, of *phronēsis.* From this vantage point, Smith takes over with great care the concurrences as well as the connections of my own thinking with Heidegger's, but he also does not miss the modifications I made. In any case, *phronēsis* played the important role. The way in which Heidegger reformulated the Greek concept of *phronēsis* and its role in Aristotelian ethics toward the Christian concept of conscience, *syneidesis,* was indeed almost a violent act.

Aristotle's practical philosophy attained a powerful presence through this. One really was shocked that the intimately known concept of knowledge, that is of conscience, is not intellectualistic at all and, despite Nietzsche, meets with a full echo and the strongest resonance in our own linguistic life. Nevertheless, Smith succeeds in reappropriating for a more humanistic sensibility the violent twist in which Heidegger's revolutionary temperament of thought expressed itself. The number of dianoetic virtues which according to Aristotle follow the distinction between ethical and technical knowledge confirms this: there are some concepts that accompany *phronēsis: synesis* as understanding, *syngnōmē* as forgiving lenience, and finally *epieikeia,* the mitigating application of the laws in the search for the just sentence. These concepts are not borrowed from Christian ethics and its language. This holds especially for the role of friendship *(philia)* and all that goes along with it in Aristotle. There is no resonance here with the Christian commandment to love one's neighbor.

If we follow Smith's essay, which never loses sight of nuances, we nevertheless can hardly deny that the tradition of European thinking, at least within the process of its modern secularization, contains elements that can be found outside of the Christian world in other European cultures. The radical Enlightenment that began on European soil certainly is the fruit of a long humanistic and Christian history of the soul. There is no objection to this. Thus, I understand that from the viewpoint of Kierkegaard, Heidegger, as well as my own further elaboration of the impulses received from him, gained a special significance for Christopher Smith. What he could not accept in Heidegger is not being demanded of him by the moderate form in which I pursued Heidegger's suggestion. Finally, the work here moves fundamentally beyond the thematic circle of Heidegger as well as my own reformulation of Heidegger. The author demonstrates how the voice of Luther, and thus the soulful voice of Christian biblical language, resounds on the semantic level, that is, in the vocabulary and the conceptual world within which my own thinking moved. This is made obvious without any false proximity assumed, and yet precisely because of it. How could someone who experienced his own formation to a large extent with German poetry not expect to have heard, among other things, the voice of Luther?

H.-G.G.

28

Richard E. Palmer

RITUAL, RIGHTNESS, AND TRUTH IN TWO LATE WORKS OF HANS-GEORG GADAMER

In 1991–1992 Hans-Georg Gadamer produced two new essays that sum up and significantly augment statements in his previous writings on the nature of language and the nature of art. They were titled "Zur Phänomenologie von Ritual und Sprache" and "Wort und Bild—'so wahr, so seiend'" ("On the Phenomenology of Ritual and Language" and "Word and Picture—'so true, so existant'"). As the final two essays in volume 8 of his *Gesammelte Werke: Kunst als Aussage (Art as Assertion),* they hold a special place in his writings on art and language. Yet without fanfare or prior announcement, each essay appeared in print there for the first time. Unfortunately, they could easily be neglected because they were not published separately. The present essay will call attention to these two significant essays and discuss several of their more important contributions.

It should be noted that each of the two essays is over double the average length of all other writings in volume 8 except "Die Aktualität des Schönen" (1977), which was immediately published as an inexpensive paperback book and later appeared in English as the title piece of *The Relevance of the Beautiful and Other Essays* (1986), edited by Robert Bernasconi. Taken together these three very substantial essays in volume 8 constitute important statements of Gadamer's post–*Truth and Method* thinking on language, art, and truth. While they bring together many things that Gadamer has said earlier, they also each contain new arguments and enrich the meaning of key terms in his thought. In the two more recent essays we have singled out three central terms whose meaning Gadamer deepens in the essays. They will serve as foci for discussing what is interesting and new in these two significant writings from 1992. The terms are: ritual, rightness, and truth.

I. "ON THE PHENOMENOLOGY OF RITUAL AND LANGUAGE": ON RITUAL, RIGHTNESS, AND LANGUAGE

Although "Zur Phänomenologie von Ritual und Sprache" ("On the Phenomenology of Ritual and Language") represents the first time that the term "ritual" appears in the title of a work by Gadamer, it is not the first time he has shown an interest in the anthropological basis for linguistic practices and usages. For instance, in "The Relevance of the Beautiful," Gadamer's reflections on the *"Aktualität"* (contemporaneity, present meaningfulness, topicality) of *to kalon* (Greek for "the fine, the good, the beautiful") took what might be called an "anthropological turn," as he explored *"mimēsis"* and "festival" as basic participatory experiences in Greek cultural life. Instead of appealing to Heidegger, or Hegel, or Plato, or even to "the experience we all have," Gadamer reminds his reader of how the Greeks experienced religious festivals, including tragic dramas, and of the terms in which Greeks thought of their art, religion, and being-in-the-world. His purpose was in part to deconstruct the static conceptualities, the scholasticism and scientific objectifying, in our present ways of thinking and to go behind the received interpretations of Plato and Aristotle. In this *Destruktion* Gadamer is following the lead of Heidegger, as he does when he "polishes" ("putzt") words to make their earlier meaning come through.[1] Also, he is consciously taking a phenomenological approach in "letting things appear from themselves" rather than pursuing the methodical questioning typical of other approaches, when he proposes to go back before the distinction between pointing *(Zeigen)* and naming *(Nennen)* to look for "their inner commonality," and especially when he says that in this connection "we want throughout to proceed descriptively and not with ungraspable concepts like consciousness, soul, spirit, reason, and community meaning *(Gemeinschaftssinn),* as the well known great ones have done" (411). The reference to phenomenology in the title of the article, then, is not accidental.

As the title, "Zur Phänomenologie von Ritual und Sprache," also implies, there may be a previously unexplored relationship *between* ritual and language. Does ritual require language? Gadamer answers no. A burial, for instance, can take place in complete silence. In terms of human behavior, rituals occupy a place in the life of human beings prior to language. Rituals are *actions* in which the whole community participates. Like games/play, which Gadamer makes reference to in *Truth and Method,* in discussing the being of language, they pull the individual participant up into themselves, dictate the rules and procedures to follow, and heavily penalize violations of the protocol. Even if language is part of the ritual, Gadamer notes, it becomes an action, it functions as the performance of an action. We might say, following J. L. Austin's *How to Do Things with Words,* it becomes a "performative utterance."

Like festivals (which Gadamer took up in *The Relevance of the Beautiful,* 1977), rituals do not have as their purpose conversation *(Gespräch)* or reaching a new agreement in understanding *(Verständigung)* with another person; rather, they carry out a preset activity of a whole group, like a celebration of something past or the establishment of something new. The title of the section in which the discussion of ritual occurs is significant: "Language—Conversation and Ritual."

Gadamer's goal is to "locate" language by exploring the margin between two forms of human activity. Conversation, Gadamer notes, does not belong to ritual and in fact would be out of place in it. He asks what this means for our understanding of language in a way that goes decisively beyond the pragmatist project of describing language as a tool to be used pragmatically by human beings in specifiable performative ways, such as to perform marriages, make promises, announce verdicts, or pass sentences.

In order to probe at a deeper level the borderline between ritual, as an action of a whole community, and conversation, as an interaction between two persons seeking an agreement in understanding, Gadamer introduces a distinction he says is prior to language. In doing so, however, Gadamer is not satisfied, as he was in the case of festival, merely to go back to anthropological roots. In order to "determine the place of language" as a medium in the "lifeworld of humankind," Gadamer decides to "broaden the whole horizon of questioning" (409) to include scientific research on the "lifeworld" of animals. In other words, he goes back this time to biology rather than anthropology, to the behaviors one finds in animal life, to the behaviors of establishing relationship and the modes of togetherness in animals, of courting gestures in animal communication. Research into the behaviors of animal species, he finds, shows "a frightening and even touching nearness" to the behaviors of human beings. Here he approaches but draws back from the *"angebliche Biologismus"* (alleged biologism) of Nietzsche.[2] With Nietzsche and Freud, Gadamer recognizes the instinctual basis of human life. Humans, too, have the instincts of animals for self- and species-preservation, Gadamer allows, but unlike animals humans are not enslaved to their instincts. "The power of nature flows through all life, humans' too" (410), he notes, but human beings are able, through rituals, signs, and naming within the interwovenness *(Ineinander)* of a human community, to move up into a lifeworld that can develop moral codes and laws that offer at least a limited freedom from the ironclad governance by instinct (410).

Gadamer puts forward two terms that are new in his writings to articulate the distinction he has in mind: *"Mitsamt"* and *"Ineinander."* *"Mitsamt,"* in ordinary German usage, is a preposition that takes the dative case and is generally translated as "together with" or "as well as" or "inclusive of": for instance, the phrase *"seinen Freund mitsamt dem Stuhl"* is translated "his friend, *together with* the chair." For Gadamer, *"Mitsamt"* designates basically the animal forms of togetherness, being-with, and communicating with each other. The word *"Gesamt,"* to which it is related, means "the whole"; *Mitsamt* points to the fact that as members of a whole, a species, animals are rigidly governed by species-wide instinctive behaviors. On the other hand, *"Ineinander"* in German means "interwoven," literally "to relate to one another," or "to enter into [relationship with] one another." In German, *Ineinander* combines with words like *arbeiten* (to work) to form *ineinanderarbeiten,* meaning "to work cooperatively," or with *greifen* to form *ineinandergreifen,* "to mesh (like gears), to work together." Gadamer designates with *Ineinander* primarily the way human beings relate to each other. He remarks that seemingly "nature has not bestowed on animals any real *Ineinander;* rather their behaviors are locked into an enslavement to a species-specific *Mitsamt* that causes all behavior of animals to appear specific to their species" (409).

Within the *Ineinander* of the human lifeworld, language arises and with it the function of giving understanding. The miracle of language, Gadamer asserts, is that it can "turn on a light," as it were, and, lightning-like, cause understanding to occur. Still, "all understanding is rooted in *Miteinanderleben*—our life with, our interwovenness with, each other" (412). Instead of Heidegger's impersonal *Bewandtnisganzheit* (relational totality), whose key example is the relationship to a tool, to a hammer one lifts and finds "too heavy" for the purpose, Gadamer focuses on language as it arises in the context of human interactive life. He is not recanting what he previously worked out so carefully (building on Heidegger) about historicality, tradition, and preunderstanding; but he is adding back into consideration a dialogical relationship Heidegger seemed to leave out of his concept of *Mitsein* (being with)—*life* and conversation in living language. But living language still operates always in a situation of interrelationships within a "lifeworld"; for, as Gadamer points out, it is never an isolated individual who uses language, and words are only mere vocabulary items when one is learning a foreign language in a classroom. To understand living language deeply, then, one must return to it in the lifeworld of human beings.

In ritual, as we have stated, Gadamer has noted that real "conversation" is out of place, even when language is used. Ritual *uses* language but does not require it, and when it uses it, language becomes subordinate to the action of the ritual, indeed becomes an action. Still, in this context language takes on a special power to speak, although not the power of conversation. What Gadamer calls "real speaking," then, *can* occur in conversation but does not require it; what it does require is the context of our ongoing interwovenness in a lifeworld of relationships and customary actions with other human beings. Real speaking *can* occur in rites, however. When we examine real speaking, Gadamer asserts, "we find that the rites of life also have a share" (413). It would seem, then, that "real speaking" *(wirkliches Sprechen)* is a category more encompassing than "conversation," as important as this term may be in Gadamer, and it can occur powerfully not just in conversation or in poetry, but more inclusively, more universally, in the rituals of our communal life. In ritual, the abstractness of a concept like tradition *(Überlieferung,* what is handed down), so important to Gadamer, becomes more concrete, personal, and participatory.

Rites also seem to unite two functions usually held separate: showing *(Zeigen)* and naming *(Nennen),* again suggesting the primordial site of ritual in the lifeworld and its importance to understanding more deeply the nature of language. Exploring what showing and naming have in common, Gadamer finds this to be a "directedness toward sense or meaning"—*Richtung auf Sinn.* We may observe that this extends Gadamer's remarks in "Text and Interpretation" and elsewhere that *"Sinn ist Richtungssinn,"* i.e., that to mean something is to point in a direction *(Richtung);* meaning is directional. Here the emphasis is on the lifeworld in which the pointing *(Zeigen)* or the naming stands. A sign *(Zeigen)* can point in a direction; naming requires a word, but both stand within the lifeworld of human meanings and translations. While individual words have meanings, Gadamer acknowledges, it is in the transactions within a world of living interactions with others that words take on their special power to name, a power that builds up the shared human world: "In linguistic exchange the world grows for us, and *naming* brings it about that in the use of language the power of the word to name is enriched; and through the continued use of the same language the world we hold in common *(die Gemeinsamkeit der Welt,* the commonality of the world) is formed" (412).

Rightness, too, belongs to rites, since it is offensive to err in a sacred or other rite. Rightness *(Richtigkeit)* in this case is not just a matter of following a rule one has learned, or of somehow reaching the prescribed goal of the action; it belongs to one's sense of the proper, a sense that one does not have to defend against doubt because it is something one maintains *(behauptet)* without requiring proofs. And significantly, Gadamer adds that "it is the same way with speaking"—*"ebenso ist es beim Sprechen."* The situation and the speech community customs of daily life prescribe what is appropriate. In a way parallel to the enslavement of animals to species-wide instinctual behavior, humans are bound by linguistic usage and custom. Gadamer notes: "There is no freedom in the use of words, no real choice of words. . . . In the use of words the hidden order of behavior is expressed. But this is a quite different understanding from that which one seeks when one wishes 'to tell someone something'" (414). At a level deeper than conversation, deeper than language in the conventional sense, Gadamer finds in the patterns of human being-together constraints that maintain one's relationships with others in the lifeworld.

The case of ritual, then, reaching as it does into the depths of actions and ceremonies that support human solidarity, shows us a preconscious level of human belonging to each other. "It belongs to a rite that it is supported by the whole of those gathered together or of their representatives, who insist on keeping the usage" (415). A rite does not establish something, Gadamer notes; rather, it celebrates and preserves. Like a festival, it belongs in the category of *Mitsamt* (being gathered into one) rather than *Ineinander* (entering into each other): "How little is there of being-with-each other *(Miteinander),"* Gadamer exclaims, "how little is there of conversation *(Gespräch),* and how much is everything a whole *(ein Gesamt)!* This everyone can feel in the celebration of a festival. The distinguishing mark of a festival is not pleasant talk but that everyone participates, for example, through music or festive speeches" (415–16). Whether the occasion be joyous or sorrowful, whether it be a festival or a ritual, everyone participates. And a strong protocol arising out of the requirements of the action dictates the right forms and formulas of the day. The "rightness" for the situation is known and powerful.

In contrast to this, the "true life of language," Gadamer asserts, "is formed in the interaction between human beings [das Miteinander] and above all in conversation" (416)—not in a monologue where only one person speaks but in the give-and-take of question and answer. Human life in community relies on ritual and festival to undergird solidarity, and in this it reaches down into the prelinguistic realm, yet Gadamer reaffirms that the "true life of language" comes forward not in Mitsamt but in Miteinander—"above all in conversation." Even when words speak powerfully in rite and ritual—and also, one might add, in poetry and sacred text—this is not the "true life of language," which occurs in the give-and-take, the question and answer, the Ineinander—the interwovenness—of human cooperative work and the interplay of communication.

One does well to distinguish participation in a ritual action from interpretive interaction with a text. In interpretive interaction with poetic, legal, and sacred texts, unlike ritual actions that use language performatively, the interpreter's search for an understanding is the lively one of question and answer, of letting the text speak as a dialogical partner; the text poses questions and offers answers to questions. Gadamer's basic position has not changed. It has only taken a step back phenomenologically in order to situate the problem of language not in linguisticality as such but "in the lifeworld where action as well as speaking are found" (414). There Gadamer sheds light on the phenomenology of ritual and marks the borderline and the contrasts between language used in ritual and language used in conversation.

For Gadamer, however, the significance of ritual to language is not exhausted in its contrasts with conversation. In the remaining two substantial sections of this essay, he turns to language as it occurs in poetry and in philosophy. What he is really after is "what language is as language and what in it comes to language when it is there as language; for this we must range further into the language of poetry and the language of concepts" (421). In doing so, however, Gadamer now turns to poetry and philosophy of Greek antiquity, now under the sign of ritual and lifeworld, in an effort to reinsert himself phenomenologically more fully into the lifeworld of antiquity.

In the section of the essay that discusses the poetic dimension, "From Legend to Literature," he attempts to describe legend and mythos as they were prior to the existence of written forms, and thereafter he takes up the significance and impact of writtenness. For instance, he asks, "What does it mean that the free rule of the reciter's fantasy is placed under limited circulation [through writing] and how did this happen? Here we must above all take a look at the cult forms and rituals that lie before all poetic forming of language and all writing, as the true life-basis [Lebensboden, the soil of life] of literature" (421). In the primordial oral forms, the legends are uttered by the living voice; they are uttered and uttered again, prior to and "beyond all distinguishing between bodiliness *(Leiblichkeit)* and spirituality *(Geistigkeit)"* (421). Again, ritual plays a role, for the earliest forms of the legend, Gadamer asserts, "were probably embedded in ritual action" (421). In all those singing reciters of the great legends, Gadamer asserts, there reigned a kind of freedom which basically resisted any written fixity in language, and it was out of this prewriting narrative freedom that the great form of the epic arose. This freedom, this "joy in narration" (422) prior to all writtenness, is what Gadamer's quest for the lifeworld of earliest poetry uncovers and probes. In spite of the constraints of the ritual action in which the legends may have originally been embedded, then, Gadamer still finds a freedom belonging to the language-game of narration that overcomes the constraints. Indeed, language in narrative song resists the constraints of writing, surviving writtenness to speak powerfully to us today. For the great narratives of the Greek epics are not just stories; they powerfully evoke a "world," offering us access to a lifeworld otherwise closed to us.

In his effort to understand more deeply "what language is as language and what in it comes to language" Gadamer in the concluding section of the essay turns to philosophical language, i.e., the language of concepts. Again, he finds a special freedom in the prewritten stages of philosophy. Socrates, philosopher *par excellence,* never wrote anything down. The figure of Socrates comes down to us transmuted into the literary form of the Platonic dialogues, with their occasional negative references to writtenness (as in the *Phaedrus*) and even the suggestion in the *Seventh Letter* that the true doctrine was not the written one. Likewise, although Aristotle was famous in antiquity as a writer, none of the writings on which his fame rested has survived; Aristotle's writings as we have them were mostly notes for lectures given orally. In a certain way, Gadamer's reemphasis on the richness of living language and the constraining effects of writtenness, contrast with the adulation of writing found in Derrida. In both Plato and Aristotle, Gadamer finds a struggle against the fixity of writing, against the alienation one feels from what stands forever frozen into the fixity of the text.

In a parallel way, Gadamer argues, the history of Western philosophy has been a struggle against the hardening of living ideas and questions into metaphysical concepts. Latin antiquity embalmed/translated the philosophizing of the Greek philosophers that took place in the living language of the day into Latin terms that translated them literally and robbed the terms of their tentativeness and their original connotations in Greek usage. Medieval Scholastic thinkers recovered Aristotle, but again out of context. It is this tradition of Scholastic formulations of problems and Latinized Greek thinking that Hegel sought to overcome through the dialectic, Heidegger through *Destruktion* of the "language of metaphysics" and wanderings on the forest paths of poetizing and thinking, and Gadamer through a return to language in dialogue, the "hermeneutical problem," and now in this essay more primordially through reestablishing what language was in the lifeworld of antiquity, which did not even have a name for "language," as poetry and philosophy made the transition from oral forms to writtenness.

II. "WORD AND PICTURE—'SO TRUE, SO EXISTING'": THE BEAUTIFUL, RIGHTNESS, AND TRUTH

"Wort und Bild—'so wahr, so seiend'" is quite possibly the most exciting and impressive of Gadamer's essays on art, surpassing even *The Relevance of the Beautiful* in its scope, originality, density of thought, and significance. Completed only in the spring of 1992 and appearing for the first time in *Gesammelte Werke* 8:373–96, this essay renews and carries further the question Heidegger had posed at the beginning of his seminal essay, "The Origin of the Work of Art" (1935): What is the nature of art—what makes an artwork *art?* As we know, Heidegger's essay played a key role in Gadamer's undertaking to defend the truth-claims of art in *Truth and Method* (1960) and it is not accidental that Gadamer edited and published an inexpensive paperback edition of *Der Ursprung des Kunstwerkes* in 1960, adding to it a twenty-four-page introduction of his own.[3] While the 1992 essay on the phenomenology of ritual and language was focused on the nature of *language* and returned to ritual as a way to place the problem of language "in the lifeworld, where action as well as speaking are found" (414), "Word and Picture" focuses on the question "What is *art?*" with its larger purpose being to redefine the place of art in modernity. To accomplish this it posed to itself the challenge of finding the deeper grounds of commonality between works of visual art and works of art in words—or theater, music, or dance. Like the essay on language and ritual, it also returns to Greek antiquity; now, however, his effort is not primarily to get back to the primordial lifeworld in which language becomes truly language, but through revisiting certain texts of Plato and Aristotle *"to work out, with older concepts, what is common to all art"* (385, emphasis added). His goal is, as he puts it, "to grasp conceptually what we today call 'art' and what artists create in such a way that the claim of art to truth becomes understandable" (385). In the essay, he succeeds in finding more than a dozen comprehensive concepts that apply to all art; we will limit ourselves here to those links to the themes of the beautiful, rightness, and truth.

"Word and Picture" takes up again many themes found in *Truth and Method* (1960), and also the goal of a philosophical justification of the truth of art. Indeed, in the essay Gadamer explicitly links his discussion (*GW* 8:374) to that of the beautiful and truth found in the final section of *Truth and Method,* also mentioning this section in "Text and Interpretation" (1984; *GW* 2:330–60). Since "Word and Picture" self-consciously resumes discussion of issues important in these two key texts as well as *The Relevance of the Beautiful,* it must represent for us an important statement. Indeed, one may see it as something of a "swan song," undertaking one last time, as the project of gathering the essays to be included in the collected works drew to a close, to restate and carry forward certain guiding themes in his thought.

One may note some contrasts between *The Relevance of the Beautiful* and "Word and Picture": Both have recourse to Greek culture as a source of concepts that could lead to a renewal of the claims of art. In both, Gadamer seeks comprehensive concepts, but in this case, he does not turn to game, symbol, or festival as sources of insight into the experience of the artwork; rather, he returns to Plato and Aristotle and also to his own experiences of artworks in various forms. In the course of the essay, he refers with regret to the shift in aesthetics from "the beautiful" to "art" in and after Hegel, and he again takes up the theme of the beautiful as it was experienced in Greek culture in an effort to step back behind modern conceptualities we have taken for granted since Kant and Hegel. In *The Relevance of the Beautiful* the major gap Gadamer had confronted in modern art as a problem was that between the representational forms of art and literature, on the one hand, and the less accessible nonrepresentational forms of art, including a good deal of modern poetry, such as the "dark lyric" found in French symbolists like Mallarmé and many twentieth-century poets, including Paul Celan, to whose dark lyrics Gadamer dedicated a book, *Wer bin ich, Wer bist du? Ein Kommentar zu Paul Celans Gedichtfolge "Atemkristall"* (1973).[4] In "Word und Picture," however, the gap is deeper; it is between works of art in language and all the forms of art that make use of shaped images or pictures *(Bilder)* rather than language to make their statements. *Bildende Kunst* in German even includes architecture, which Gadamer will still seek to defend as "true" insofar as it becomes "art" for its perceiver. A final part of his essay is devoted to the challenge of architecture and the decorative arts to his argument. In fact, "Word and Picture" is misleading as a title in that Gadamer also attempts to include music, dance, theater, and architecture in his essay. What he is in fact seeking is a concept of art that can account for the widest range of the arts: those that present themselves in words and those that present themselves in forms other than words, especially pictures but also music, dance, theater, sculpture, and even architecture. A major term he deals with in the quest is "the beautiful," but this is anticipated by a substantive discussion of "the beautiful" in *Truth and Method*, to which we must turn before examining the discussion of this topic in "Word and Picture."

1. Prolegomenon: The Beautiful and Truth in Truth and Method

Gadamer's major discussion of the beautiful and its connection to truth occurs in the culminating section of *Truth and Method* (1960), which is titled "The Universal Aspect of Hermeneutics" (*GW* 1: 478–95). After alluding to major points established by his arguments in the book—that language is the point where "I" and "world" come together, that the speculative structure of being in language is finite rather than a dialectical mediation of concepts, and that "the coming into language of meaning points to a universal ontological structure" and thus, "Being that can be understood is language" (478)[5]—Gadamer reaffirms that his purpose has been to overcome the abstraction at the heart of natural scientific investigation that ignores "the fundamental relation to the world that is given in the linguistic nature of our experience" in favor of a relation to nature that seeks to dominate it (479–80). In the face of this, he says, "in view of the experience we have of art and history, we were led to a universal hermeneutics focused on the relationship of human beings to their world" (480). The speculative ontological turn of this hermeneutics, which gave it "the same universal compass as reason and language" (480), led him "into the neighborhood of a metaphysical idea whose significance we must make fruitful by tracing it back to its source: *the concept of the beautiful*" (481). Thus Gadamer, at the culmination of his quest for a universal hermeneutics that takes the ontology of the language-event of understanding as its guide, turns to a seminal concept in aesthetics: the beautiful. The abruptness of this turn may be justified by the fact that all along Gadamer has appealed to "the experience of art" (as well as history) in order to show the limits of objectivizing scientific methods. His "ontological hermeneutics" in *Truth and Method* is primarily focused on understanding in its historical and linguistic dimensions rather than on texts per se (although methodology of text interpretation had been a traditional focus of hermeneutics); but in this closing section the emphasis is on works of art (including textual works), and more broadly on the category of the beautiful. As important as historicality and linguisticality were in Gadamer's description of the process of understanding, he chooses to focus on an encounter—the experience of the beautiful—that to some degree overcomes time and history. We may observe that with this shift to the concept of the beautiful, Gadamer has already in *Truth and Method* gone beyond the distinctions among types of art to a more comprehensive concept.

Gadamer in this final section is quite explicit about *why* he turns to "the beautiful" here. He notes with regret that while the concept of the beautiful held a central place in eighteenth-century aesthetics, it was virtually omitted in the nineteenth century in favor of a focus on the "work of art." Yet as a metaphysical concept, a concept having to do with the universal consideration of being, the beautiful was "by no means limited to the aesthetic in the narrower sense" (481). This older idea of the beautiful, Gadamer argues, "can be of service to a comprehensive hermeneutics" (481). The context in which Gadamer takes up the concept of the beautiful in *Truth and Method* is his quest for a universal and ontological hermeneutics, then, a hermeneutics that encompasses and at the same time shows the limits of methodical understanding in the sciences, social sciences, and humanities.

The Greek word for beautiful, he notes, is *kalon*, an equivalent to *schön* in German (481). The *schönen Künste* in German, he explains, are the "fine arts," as contrasted with the technical or useful arts; *schöne Literatur* is basically *belles lettres* (literature as art); and *schöne Sittlichkeit* may be translated the "superior morality." And for Plato, beautiful things are "in closest relation to the Good *(agathon),*" Gadamer notes, because like the Good, they are *chosen for their own sake* and "are not regarded as a means to something else" (482). This corroborates the Platonic linking of the Idea of the Beautiful with the Idea of the Good in the *Symposium*. There, the path or ladder up to the Idea of the Good is the path or ladder through levels of beauty: beautiful bodies, beautiful institutions, customs, and laws, the beautiful relations of numbers in mathematics, to the "wide ocean of beautiful utterances" and beyond. Still, Gadamer notes that "Plato apparently means that the teleological order of being is also an order of beauty, and that beauty comes to appearance in the intelligible realm more purely and clearly than in the sensible" (282). Thus, Gadamer follows what Plato says about the beautiful rather than what he says about art and artists, which is rather disappointing. In the Middle Ages, too, Gadamer notes, the link of *kalon* with the Good was so close that "in a classical text of Aristotle, it was translated simply with *bonum*—good" (282). Thus, the link between the beautiful and the ethically good, the beautiful and the very order of being, was seeming self-evident in antiquity and the Middle Ages.

Gadamer points to a further basis for these connections in the Platonic-Pythagorean concept of measure. For, "Plato defines the beautiful in terms of measure, appropriateness, and right proportions, Aristotle names the moments of the beautiful 'order' *(taxis),* right proportions *(symmetria),* and decisiveness *(Bestimmtheit, horismenon)*" (482–83). This close connection with mathematical proportion links beauty with the order of the heavens and thus with the order of things, the order of being. The cosmos is the pattern of all right and beautiful order and thus "the highest example of beauty in the realm of the visible" (483). Nature has a beauty and a goodness superior to any human work of art or goodness. What this means is that beauty is closely tied to what is right, fit, proportional, and thus to what Gadamer will later call "rightness" *(Richtigkeit)*. In apprehending the beautiful one is at the same time apprehending what is fitting, what is morally right, what is in harmony with the cosmos, and therefore also ultimately what is "true."

But Gadamer's analysis here in *Truth and Method* goes one step further to distinguish the beautiful from the good—and to assert the superiority of the beautiful: "The beautiful is distinguished from the absolutely intangible good, in that it can be laid hold of. It is part of its own nature to be something that is visibly manifest. . . . That which manifests itself in perfect form draws one towards it in the longing of love" (484–85). Furthermore, for Plato, the morally good in the human realm involves appearances and decisions that are imperfect. "But it is different with the beautiful. 'Beauty alone . . . has its own radiance . . . it is most radiant *(ekphanēstaton)* and lovable'" (485, quoting *Phaedrus* 250d7). Gadamer finds in this "anagogical" (drawing on upward) function "an ontological structural element of the beautiful and with it a universal structure of being" (485). More importantly, Gadamer observes that "it is obviously the distinguishing mark of the beautiful over against the good that *it presents itself from itself, that it makes itself immediately perceptible in its being*" (485, emphasis added). What this means is that because the beautiful comes forward in sensible appearances, it is able to show its being from itself. The phenomenological and hermeneutic ideal situation of something that shows itself *in its being* and *from itself* is found here. Plato speaks of this in terms of "participation" *(methexis)*, and Gadamer also, but what Gadamer has in mind by "participation" is not so much a metaphysical explanation as it is an opening of oneself to the event of encounter and standing in it in such a way that the being of the work of art shows itself, steps forth, *appears.*

The disclosure of being that takes place in this "shining forth into appearance" *(Hervorscheinen,* to shine or come forth into appearance), which is translated as "radiance" in *Truth and Method,* "is not just one of the qualities of what is beautiful," says Gadamer, "but constitutes its actual being" (486). And this radiance draws the soul to it in desire. "The harmoniousness of being is such that it does not let the soul be just what it is but also causes it to *emerge* as a harmonious whole that is proportioned within itself. This emerging is the disclosure *(alētheia)* which Plato speaks of in the *Philebus* and which is part of the nature of the beautiful" (486). Here the radiance of the beautiful becomes the disclosure of truth—*alētheia* (disclosure of what *is).* The several streams of Gadamer's analysis in *Truth and Method* come together here at the end. Art, like language, happens in time, and therefore can emerge from undisclosedness to disclosedness—a process which the Greeks, Heidegger, and Gadamer call *alētheia* (unconcealment, truth). The disclosure of being, i.e., of the way things are, is therefore the happening of truth. The category of the beautiful, then, brings together not only the beautiful and the good but also the true. The deeply hermeneutic significance of this point, as Gadamer observes, is that "both the appearance of the beautiful and the mode of being of understanding have the character of an event; the hermeneutical experience as the experience of transmitted meaning, has a share in the immediacy which has always distinguished the experience of the beautiful, as it has the experience of all evidence of truth" (488). The references to truth in art, here, are set in the context of an ontological definition of truth as *alētheia,* a truth whose appearing in art is sensibly present.

We shall conclude our brief review of the concluding section of *Truth and Method* with a phenomenological observation on truth. Truth, here, is what shows itself from itself in a process of phenomenological disclosure. Gadamer credits Plato with being "the first to show that the essential element of the beautiful was *alētheia"*—that is, truth as unconcealment. Phenomenology and ontology combine, then, when Gadamer notes that Plato intended to say that "the beautiful, the way in which goodness appears, reveals itself in its being, it presents itself. What presents itself in this way is not different from itself in presenting itself. . . . We have attempted to show in the analysis of the work of art that self-presentation is to be regarded as the true being of the work of art. To this end we invoked the concept of play" (491). Because what presents itself presents itself from itself as it is, this is the truth of the being of the work. In sum, we see that a full-fledged hermeneutic, ontological, and phenomenological view of art is already contained in this culminating section of *Truth and Method*. It is this discussion that Gadamer explicitly links with and supplements in "Bild und Wort."

2. The Beautiful, Rightness, and the True in "Word and Picture—'so wahr, so seiend'" (1992)

While it continues the discussion of the beautiful and truth found in *Truth and Method*, "Word and Picture" stands in the context of a different project and a different era from that of *Truth and Method* (1960). The project of *Truth and Method* was to put forward a universal hermeneutics based on the nature of language, and in this context the experience of art and its claim to truth served to demonstrate the limits of objectivizing modes of understanding. The basic project of "Word and Picture," on the other hand, is to find out what makes art art by looking for commonalities shared by works of art in words and works of art in nonverbal images. It proposes through philosophical and philological analysis to restore art to a more respected place than it has recently occupied in modern culture, an aim it shares with *Truth and Method*.

Its guiding question, "What makes art art?" makes its project more parallel to that Heidegger set for himself with a similar question in *The Origin of the Work of Art* (1935). Indeed, there are a number of interesting parallels to this work of Heidegger which had such a liberating effect on Gadamer as he worked on *Truth and Method*. Both *The Origin of the Work of Art* and "Word and Picture" accord the artwork an autonomy that lifts it above all ordinary communication to something like disclosure of being. In both essays, works of art "open up a world"; one tarries before artworks almost in a suspension of ordinary time; and in both writings, artworks are seen as powerful enough in their impact to strike one like a blow. It is certainly clear that Gadamer in "Word and Picture" builds on the insights in Heidegger, including his seminal work on art, and now offers his own exploration of "the origin of the work of art." In it he situates that origin in "the beautiful" and embellishes his discussion with further characteristics that testify to the power and priority of art.

In "Word and Picture" the concept of the beautiful as reflected in the Greek word *kalon* provides the comprehensive term Gadamer is seeking that will apply to all that is art: to poetry, sculpture, to architecture, to painting, or to music. As in *Truth and Method* he notes the close connection in Greek thinking between the beautiful and the good, mentioning here the term *aretē*—which means excellence in all things, the perfection of being human on the physical, moral, and mental levels (it is often inadequately translated as "virtue")—and also *kalokagathia* (adding *agathon,* the good), another word meaning "human excellence." As in

Truth and Method, Gadamer notes that *kalon* is associated with unchanging things like numbers and geometry, and by extension with *taxis, symmetria,* and the determinate. Thus, "the beautiful remains near the realm of knowing and coming to know *[Wissen* and *Erkennen]"* (380). As in the earlier work, Gadamer notes that "the concept of *kalon* brings us into contact not only with the concept of the good but also the concept of the true—and thereby with the standpoint of metaphysics as such" (381), which is to say, the standpoint of Being and the way of being of nature. Gadamer notes that for Plato the heavens in their mathematical beauty are also embodiment of the truth of the cosmos, and thus beauty is linked not just with goodness but truth. In its richness of associations, then, the ancient concept of *to kalon* not only bridges the gap between arts of the word and other arts, including music, but between works of art and works of nature. In the Greek word for the beautiful, Gadamer has truly found a term of inexhaustible richness.

One of the distinguishing characteristics of *kalon,* and also of the German word *schön* often used to translate *kalon,* which Gadamer mentions at the end of *Truth and Method* and also in "Word and Picture," is that art as art is a good in itself rather than useful for something else. This, too, connects it with truth: "In the concept of the 'free' arts one already discerns the closeness that exists between the *theoretical* and the *aesthetic,* and therewith the closeness between contemplating the beautiful and knowing the true—*Schauen des Schönen, Wissen des Wahren"* (380). For Aristotle, too, Gadamer notes, there is a "closeness which exists between the semantic field of *poiesis,* art, and work, and the semantic field of the beautiful and the true. The beautiful, for the Greeks, remains close to the realms of knowing and recognizing *[Wissen und Erkennen]"* (380). The encounter with a work of art is an experience of coming to know something, not just a disinterested aesthetic pleasure in form. Indeed, in the most powerful of these experiences it is not unusual to say, *"Es ist so!"*—"It is so!" This brings us to another term important in this essay: Rightness *(Richtigkeit).*

In "rightness" Gadamer finds another term that encompasses all the arts. It links with his discussion in *Truth and Method* of what is appropriate and fitting and therefore "right," an association discussed at still greater length in this essay. Here, Gadamer chooses texts from the *Philebus* and the *Statesman* to establish the connection of the beautiful with measure, fitness, appropriateness, rightness. Gadamer acknowledges that Plato's negative comments on the art and artists of his time (in *The Republic* and *Ion,* for instance) are not useful for his project, but he finds Plato's inquiry into the beautiful and its connection with the good and the true are helpful: "We find in the profound late dialogues of Plato that the concept of the beautiful, along with the concept of *alētheia* [truth] and the concept of the Good step into the foreground. In these dialogues, what Plato seeks in the 'good life' is not a pure exactness of a mathematical type but the measured proportionality *[maßvolle Gemessenheit]* of a well-mixed drink of life *[Lebenstrankes]"* (381). It is here, in the finite world of measure, in the sensible world

of the visible, of choices and of art, that the Good is to be sought. And in a further step it is remarked, at 65a of the *Philebus,* that "the Good which they had
been seeking as the right mixture of being *'has taken refuge in the beautiful'"*
(381). The Good, then, "only permits of being grasped in the threefold of beauty,
symmetry, and truth" (381); rightness and truth are inseparable from the beautiful and the good. Measure is not just moderation in the "well-mixed drink of
life" but at one with rightness and with truth.

The expression "It is so!" also leads Gadamer to other important connections.
He remarks that his early studies in the areas of literature, art history, and classical
philology led him "again and again into the circle of problems in pictorial art and
poetry," and already at that time, he notes importantly, "I wanted to prove the
claim of art to truth" (375). In his studies of early culture and practices prior to
written culture he uncovered profound experiences of understanding and communication. When he encountered the prehistoric cave paintings that had been discovered and the earliness of legends *(Sagenfrühe)* from "the mythic world that stands
behind our literary heritage," he found that they evoked in him "the same affirmation, 'It is so!', as when we recognize that a work of art is 'right' *('richtig')"* (375).

Later in the essay, he connects this exclamation with another assertion one
makes as one experiences the artwork: one finds that "'it' comes forth *['es' her-
auskommt]."* Says Gadamer, "We recognize in this [the expression, "'it' comes
forth"] the basic experience we have in encountering a work of art, the experience we have when we say, *'So ist es'—so ist es 'richtig'!"* ['It is so'—it is
'right' so!] (386). Thus, Gadamer connects this exclamation not only with the
experienced sense of "rightness" that is essentially a measured, finite truth to
being, but with the "radiance" of *"es herauskommt."*

Gadamer also links the experience of beauty (and his explanation of
alētheia) with the concept of *energeia* (a term Aristotle coined) and remarks,
"With the new conceptual expression *'energeia'* a problem-horizon is opened up
which might permit new light to fall on the way of being of the artwork" (386).
Energeia in Aristotle designates not something completed, like a work, but
something which has its being in being-in-motion, in the performance *(Vollzug,*
the carrying out), a *Vollzug* that "has its fulfilled being *in itself"* (387). Gadamer
suggests, "Now I think that Aristotle described *energeia* with the word *hama* in
order to designate the immanent simultaneity of duration: not a one-after-
another but an at-the-same-timeness *(ein Zugleich)* belonging to that which possesses the time-structure of tarrying *(die Zeitstruktur des Verweilens)"* (387).
This is the duration of tarrying—*des Verweilens*—in which one is "totally
absorbed" into the thing contemplated and at the same time one is fully alive—
am Leben ist: "It is not a being directed toward this and that, first this and then
that, rather it is a whole that is present in the seeing, the thinking something
over, or the gazing at something, in which one is immersed" (387). Gadamer
says that this *"Verweilendes Sein"*—being that is tarrying in time—"is like a

richly varied conversation that does not come to an end but rather lasts until it is ended." And during this tarrying in time, "you are 'totally *there' (ganz dabei)"* (387). This is the state of being in which one experiences the work of art. When one reads a poem, Gadamer asserts, one is "there with it" *(dabei)*—and "in the end our impression grows ever deeper: 'It is so'" (388). Thus, the experience is ontological—i.e., of the way things are—but now is rendered sensibly present by the artwork in an event of appearing, a happening of truth. Gadamer is not just repeating Heidegger here but clarifying, embellishing, and offering Platonic variations on what Heidegger had offered the world in *Der Ursprung des Kunstwerkes* and elsewhere, albeit without the "fourfold" and other Heideggerian metaphorical constructions.

Continuing his discussion of *energeia,* Gadamer describes the experience of the presence of an artwork as "like a growing fascination which holds on and even outshines temporary disturbances because the harmonious consistency of the whole—*die Stimmigkeit des Ganzen*—is growing and demands our consent, our attunement—*Zustimmung"* (388). And when this all takes place, one knows that "'it' has come forth"—*"'es' herausgekommen ist"* (388). To experience an artwork, then, is not a doing something but a being absorbed in something. The work of art, for Gadamer, is an "assertion" *(Aussage)* but one that is not made up of affirmative propositions, "yet it is by far the most telling of statements" (388). It is "like a myth, [or] like a legend" that both offers and withholds and that "will always speak again" (388). What the work says is persuasive without being a scientific demonstration. Its truth is the truth of rightness, of "it is so"—and of *energeia:*

> Bringing in the concept of *'energeia'* here has a special value because in using it we are no longer moving in the realm of propositional truth. By means of this conceptual word Aristotle was able to think of a form of motion, a being-moved, that was without path or goal: something like aliveness itself, like being awake, like seeing, or 'thinking'. All of this he called 'pure *energeia'—and this allows us to think more adequately about art.* (389, emphasis added)

Gadamer's consideration of *energeia* also deepens our understanding of such Greek words as *"theōria,"* which, Gadamer says, does not mean just to look at something but rather "to participate and be fully there in a festive activity. . . . It means to be totally there *[ganz dabei],* which is to say it is a highest form of activity and a highest reality—*höchste Tätigkeit und Wirklichkeit"* (389). It is interesting that Gadamer turns at this point back to cultic activity (which suggests a connection with the essay on ritual), as he notes that "whoever takes part in a cultic event in this way lets the divine come forth in such a way that it is there, as if the divine were appearing in bodily form," and then he adds, significantly: *"Das gilt bestens für das Kunstwerk*—This holds best of all for the work of art." For Gadamer, then, to experience a work of art is like being in a festival activity in which one is fully there and in which the divine—what truly is—comes forth. What truly is, is truth, whether it stands before us in philosophical propositions or in the presentness of the artwork. Ritual participation, rightness, and the experience of truth all are parts of the beautiful, and therefore, in Gadamer's philological, anthropological, phenomenological, ontological, and hermeneutic philosophy of art, they are parts of parts of what makes an artwork art.

3. The Absoluteness and Contemporaneity of Art

There are still other encompassing concepts that Gadamer advances and explains in this crowning essay which are also related to the rightness and truth of art. One is the "absoluteness" of the artwork, a concept Gadamer notes originated in Plotinus but became a "key word" in the period of German idealism. The word in classical Latin is the counterconcept of the relative. It means, says Gadamer, *das Abgelöste*—the detached, removed, independent. In Hegel, absolute *Geist* (spirit, mind) is "a constant, full presence to itself that is fulfilled in absolute knowledge" (375). According to Hegelian phenomenology, art, religion, and philosophy were the three forms of absolute spirit, and "in all three cases this had to do with an absolute certainty of being" (375). Spirit disclosed itself in sensuous form, or in symbol and ritual, or in the invisibility of the concept. Art, for its part, stands in a special relationship to time: it "attains a timeless presentness *[zeitlose Gegenwärtigkeit]* to the degree that it, like religion and philosophy, is detached from and independent of historical-social conditions. Art claims absoluteness because it transcends all historical differences between times" (375). While Gadamer's hermeneutic commitment to the finitude of all interpretation and its inescapable situatedness in time and place prevents him from accepting the metaphysical assumptions of Hegel or Plato, he finds in the concept of the Absolute in Hegel and of the beautiful in Plato conceptual pointers for describing the special status one experiences the artwork to have.

The "timeless presentness" of art has a parallel, Gadamer notes, in Kierkegaard's concept of *Gleichzeitigkeit*—contemporaneity, one's sense of belonging to the same time as the original Christian message. Gadamer asserts that this same concept also applies in philosophy, which is in constant dialogue with all the great adventurers in thinking "who belong to our Western tradition as if they were contemporary partners with us" (375). The same point applies for art, so again religion, philosophy, and art all assume a certain "simultaneity" with the work or text to be understood. The peculiar temporal character of this simultaneity is pointed to, Gadamer says, in the German word for the present: *Gegenwart*. Since *warten* in German means "to wait," he says, the future is always in play in the present moment. Our expectations, however, are also based on our past experiences, and so past and future are both contained in the present. But philosophy and art have a special presentness: They "take their start *from their own present—"so sehr stellt sich Kunst und Philosophie als eigene*

Gegenwart ein" (376). This means that in art and philosophy "one does not have
to know at all from what past, from what distance, from what foreignness, what
one encounters comes. It has its own presence . . . and draws one into its path"
(376). The fact that art has the power to overcome even the greatest distance and
foreignness of time and place and still speak "demonstrates its absolute presentness to all times and places *[Allgegenwart]"* (376). Even in the literary arts "one
can speak of a certain presentness and contemporaneity *[Gegenwärtigkeit und
Gleichzeitigkeit],"* and in the pictorial arts (*die bildende Künste,* including sculpture) this is even more the case because the language barrier does not need to be
overcome (377). The absoluteness of art here is seen in that it possesses its own
presentness and is able to overcome foreignness in space and time and still
"draw one into its path" (376). This absoluteness also testifies to the power of art
to disclose, and thus to render present a truth of being. What Gadamer has in
mind, however, is not exactly a metaphysical absoluteness but rather a description of one's experience of the power and independence of art.

In closing, one may mention, although space does not permit their adequate
exposition here, three other related encompassing concepts Gadamer puts forward which belong to art as art and support the concepts of rightness, beauty,
and truth we have discussed here: the priority of art, its normative power, and its
Heiligkeit. The artwork always has a certain priority over the viewer, listener, or
reader. It makes a claim and demands to be heard in its own terms, just as a
sculpture requires that the viewer find an appropriate distance in order to appreciate it properly. The "normative power" (*normative Gewalt,* normative force) is
perhaps a consequence of the priority of art. Gadamer links them explicitly:
"What I have been describing is the sovereignty of the image *[Bildhoheit]* in the
visual arts *[bildende Künste]* and the dictatorial force *[Diktatur]* of the text in
'literature'. In both cases we have to do with a powerful normative force." Of
course, this force would not be so powerful if its appeal did not seem to contain
a certain truth and rightness. Finally, there is the fact that artworks possess a certain "sanctity"—*Heiligkeit* (cognate: holiness). This word in German is also
associated with what is hale, that is, healthy, as well as healing, not just the
sacred or holy per se.

In explaining *Heiligkeit* Gadamer alludes to Walter Benjamin's concept of an
"aura" about the work of art. Art is unique and irreplaceable, and one feels a sac-
rilege has been committed if a great work of art is marred or destroyed. Thus, in
the nineteenth and twentieth centuries, even with the loss of prescientific cosmo-
logues, when the heavens and the earth seemed to lose their sacredness, art
gained a new significance.[6] Gadamer notes that actually art attained "its highest
rank" in the nineteenth century, when "the experience of order as such—as
mediated by the visual arts, poetry, and above all music—took its place at the
center of middle-class cultural life, and the miracle of art was celebrated as the
last pledge [*Unterpfand,* guarantee] of an untarnished world—*eine heile Welt"*
(384). The experience of art remained and remains an access to "an untarnished

world." The absoluteness of art, its contemporaneity, priority, rightness, and normative power, along with its uniqueness and irreplaceability, give it overtones of transcendence, a transcendence that in a desacralized world make art "a last pledge" of a realm of wholeness and incorruptibility—*"die heile Welt."*

Gadamer's lifelong goal of defending the "truth" of art philosophically here attains its final realization in a defense of the beauty, absoluteness, rightness, normative power, truth, and incorruptibility of art. In seeking what is common to both verbal and nonverbal arts, he develops a powerful philosophical account of the nature of art. Structurally, his argument has analogies with the fugue in music, where themes are brought in one by one until four, five, and six are going at once and all in harmony. The issue of art leads to the word *kalon,* which leads to issues of goodness, rightness, exactness, and truth. Some of these are themes that have occupied Gadamer for a lifetime. A surprising number of them come into play here in what is like a complex final movement of a symphony or string quartet, or what Plato called "the measured proportionality of a well-mixed drink of life" (381).

RICHARD E. PALMER

DEPARTMENT OF PHILOSOPHY
MACMURRAY COLLEGE
JUNE 1995

NOTES

1. Gadamer affirms the connection to Heidegger quite explicitly in this essay: "In truth, I am a follower of Heidegger in that, starting from linguisticality, my own efforts also seek a way to leave Greek metaphysics behind" (419).

2. Cf. Martin Heidegger's heading in *Nietzsche,* vol. 1 (Pfullingen: Neske, 1961), 517ff., in part 3: "The Will to Power as Knowledge." In English translation see vol. 3, *The Will to Power as Knowledge and as Metaphysics,* ed. David F. Krell (San Francisco: Harper and Row, 1987), 39ff.

3. See Martin Heidegger, *Der Ursprung des Kunstwerkes* (Stuttgart: Reclam, 1960), with an introduction ("Zur Einführung") by Hans-Georg Gadamer, pp. 102–25 (reprinted in *GW* 3: 249–61). A translation of Gadamer's essay, under the title "The Truth of the Work of Art," can be found in Gadamer's *Heidegger's Ways,* a book translated by John Stanley (Albany: SUNY Press, 1994), 95–109, as well as in the collection *Philosophical Hermeneutics,* ed. David E. Linge (Berkeley: University of California, 1976), 213–28, under the title "Heidegger's Later Philosophy."

4. *Who am I, Who are You? A Commentary on Paul Celan's series of poems "Breathcrystals."* Untranslated.

5. This citation is found on page 574 of the English translation of *Truth and Method* (2nd rev. ed.; 1989). To locate subsequent citations in the English translation, simply subtract four pages. For example, (478) becomes (474).

6. See "Geschichte des Universums und Geschichtlichkeit des Menschen" (1988), *GW* 10 (1995): 206–22.

REPLY TO RICHARD E. PALMER

Like his contributions from earlier years, Richard Palmer's precise structuring of my work *"Wort und Bild—'so wahr, so seiend'"* (from volume eight of the Collected Works) here shows how closely he follows my thought. So this is the place to thank him for his early efforts on behalf of my hermeneutic philosophy and for his untiring readiness to assist the present volume.

H.-G.G.

29

Thomas Prufer

A THOUGHT OR TWO ON GADAMER'S PLATO

Gadamer's reading of the first nonfragmentary and nonquoted philosophical texts available to us, the Platonic dialogues,[1] especially of *Sophist* and *Philebus,* calls into question Heidegger's reading of Greek philosophy[2] as a falling off from a beginning caught up in the interplay *(Gegenwendigkeit)* of hiddenness and display *(alētheia),* a falling off through Plato toward Aristotle's apotheosis, in *Metaphysics* 9.10 and 12.7 and 9, of presence without absence: for Aristotle the primary sense of *ousia* is *nous* without the otherness *(krinein)* and the motion *(kinein)* of *logos.* For Gadamer the root of the Platonic dialogue form is the Indeterminate Two of Plato's unwritten teaching. The dialogue form displays *(in actu exercito)* the protectedness *(Bergung)* of the open-ended and intrinsically never-ending interplay of speakers and of speeches, a protectedness Plato is said to have called the Indeterminate Two, the wedge of doubleness inexorably splitting and delaying presence and display. Protecting absence and hiddenness from being swallowed up in presence and display, the Indeterminate Two protects the *lēthē* in *alētheia* and thus prevents philosophy from degenerating into doctrine and pursuit of the honoring of doctrine. Gadamer reads Plato by using Heidegger's *Bergung* against Heidegger's reading of Plato. He lets us see Heidegger's *Bergung* in the context of (Gadamer's) Plato and of Aristotle, Aristotle's apotheosis of presence and display without absence and hiddenness: *ousia* as *nous* without the otherness and the motion of *logos,* mind without the form of dialogue.

The One and the Indeterminate Two of (Gadamer's) Plato let (or lets) come about a *not (not$_1$)* different from the *not (not$_2$)* of *eidē* to one another; *not$_2$* is the *not* of otherness of *eidē* to one another: *eidos$_a$* is merely other than *eidos$_b$*; *eidos$_x$* and *eidos$_y$* exclude each other. *not$_2$* lets a being display itself or be viewed as another what *(eidos),* as *another* what which it nevertheless *is,* or as a what *(eidos) other* than any what which it *is* (or which it could be), as a what which it is *not.* a/b: a human being (Theaetetus) sits [said while Theaetetus sits]; x/y: a human being (Theaetetus) stands [said while Theaetetus sits] or a human being (Theaetetus) flies.

*not*₁ lets a different doubleness of *Sein/Schein* come about, a doubleness which is simpler and more widespread than those othernesses which *not*₂ lets come about: the othernesses $eidos_a/eidos_b$ and $eidos_x/eidos_y$. This different doubleness of *Sein/Schein* is to be *(Sein)* "is/is not" display *(Schein);* display is out of hiddenness: display is not hiddenness but not without hiddenness: one (hiddenness) and another one (display) both together are one two: to be:

to be

hiddenness/display.

To be is one two: to be is the hendiadys *alētheia:* hiddenness/display.³

From the doubleness of *Sein/Schein* as *esse/lucere (sich darstellen)* comes about the doubleness of *Sein/Schein* as *esse/videri (sich verstellen).* Here is the place of both the sophist and the politician *(dēmologikos),* the two together, in difference to the philosopher. The sophist and the politician both prefer honor to inquiry *(plus videri quam esse):* they speak in order to be honored.⁴

In book 12, chapters 7 and 9 of Aristotle's *Metaphysics* (see also book 9, chapter 10) the primary sense of *ousia, noēsis noēseōs,* is display without doubleness: *alētheia* without *lēthē;* presence without the double difference: without absence and without that-which-is-present/absent;⁵ *nous* without *kinēsis* and without *logos, nous* without *psychē; energeia* without *dynamis; eidos* without other *eidē* (being without being with others, without honor and friendship) and without *genos* (being without having a common background, a background shared with others).⁶

For Heidegger this *ousia-nous* is the apotheosis of what he calls "metaphysics." Heidegger takes a step back behind what he calls "metaphysics," a step toward *Bergung;* this step back is both a step back behind Heidegger's "Plato," a "Plato" without *Bergung,* a Plato stylized by Heidegger into the forerunner of Aristotle's *ousia-nous,* and a step around (Gadamer's) Plato, the Plato of the One and the Indeterminate Two: *Bergung.*⁷

THOMAS PRUFER

SCHOOL OF PHILOSOPHY
CATHOLIC UNIVERSITY OF AMERICA
NOVEMBER 1991

NOTES

1. Hans-Georg Gadamer, *Gesammelte Werke* (Tübingen: Mohr), 3:16–22, 245–48; 6:129–53.

2. *Gesammelte Werke,* 2:12; 3:302–3, 410–13; 4:481; 7:82, 280, 367.

3. *Reductio ad absurdum:* "To be is display; to be is hiddenness; display is not

hiddenness; hiddenness is not display: therefore to be is not to be; if display is and if display is not hiddenness, then hiddenness is not; if hiddenness is and if hiddenness is not display, then display is not."

Conclusion of the *reductio ad absurdum:* to be is *both* hiddenness *and* display; to be is the hendiadys *alētheia.* Heidegger is a (Gadamerian) Platonist, but not a Heideggerian "Platonist." Q.E.D.

4. There is a twisting *(ver-stellen;* "twist": *Zwist, zwei),* twisting$_1$, other than the twisting, twisting$_2$, in which error fails truth. In twisting$_1$ something true *discovered* through inquiry, something evidenced, is spoken by a speaker who wants to be *honored* for making public the discovered truth—and a philosopher can err (twisting$_2$) even though he lives in inquiry for its own sake and not in order to be honored.

> Because that-which-is is both hidden and manifest, there can be false *doxa* (view: both the show itself and how we take the show, what we take the show *as* being). False *doxa* comes about when that-which-is both shows itself ("is manifest") and, because it is also being beyond the show ("is hidden"), is taken *as* being other than it *is.* The difference between show and *as* is formulated when we say something *of* something. When there is one show (snub-nose) and two *as* (both Theaetetus and Socrates), then error is possible: we take the shown snub-nosed one we see *as* being Socrates, but is Theaetetus. We say falsely "The snub-nosed one is Socrates." When there is one show and two *as,* two (both Theaetetus and Socrates) having the same show (snub-nose) in common, we can take the common show *as* being the show of the other (Socrates) rather than of the one (Theaetetus): we twist and falsely say something *of* something. Hidden/manifest is thus reduced to saying incorrectly and, set against and contrasted with this incorrectness, to saying correctly: true assertion is assertion not twisted but in line with that-which-is: true assertion corresponds to that-which-is.

Thomas Prufer, "Glosses on Heidegger's Architectonic Word-Play: *Lichtung* and *Ereignis, Bergung* and *Wahrnis," Review of Metaphysics* 44 (March 1991): 611.

5. Ein "da," das nicht das "da" von etwas ist; ein "da" ohne etwas, das da ist. See *Gesammelte Werke* 5:293.

6. Why does Gadamer insist on infecting the *nous (noēsis noēseōs)* of Metaphysics 17.7 and 9, with *kinēsis* and with *logos,* with *psychē* (Aristotle understands soul in terms of movement, *kinein,* and discrimination, *krinein)*? Of course "first for us" *energeia* is embedded in *dynamis,* "first for us" *alētheia* is embedded in *ti kata tinos,* "first for us" *zōē* is embedded in *psychē,* but Aristotle intends to free *nous* as *energeia, alētheia, zōē* from these embeddednesses. That Aristotle does not succeed in doing what he intends to do is owed, for the Platonist Gadamer, to the power of the Indeterminate Two. See *Gesammelte Werke* 3:11, 295, 403–4; 6:170.

7.

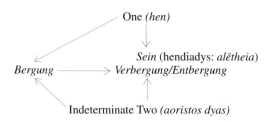

Just as *Bergung* is not *Verbergung/Entbergung (alētheia),* so the One/the Indeterminate Two "are" (or "is") not the one number two (hendiadys): the "eidetic number" two: *Sein.*

REPLY TO THOMAS PRUFER

This is the shortest of all contributions: three pages. These three pages were mailed by Thomas Prufer years ago as the outcome of a conversation that lasted for years. He died soon afterwards and thus his present contribution is the continuation of the conversation. It is almost impossible, of course, to integrate into the series the conversational relationship—which had been led over many years despite a long interruption and which now meets its end—in such a way that the end turns into a continuation of that conversation for readers of this volume. This last contribution which has the cryptic brevity of all of his works demonstrates anew how much Thomas Prufer was engaged in a confrontation with my Greek studies. Apparently he was permanently accompanied by my way of going along with Heidegger and of the way I tried to go further through the distance that I managed to gain from Heidegger.

This contribution shows this. Here, on the basis of my Greek studies, Prufer sees the short-cut that Heidegger undertook in viewing Plato as merely a preparation for metaphysics, toward the overcoming of which he directed all of his thinking. To Prufer it seems that Heidegger read Plato with Aristotelian eyes, so to speak, whereas I myself conversely attempted to read Aristotle with Platonic eyes. Precisely Heidegger's last word is represented by what is meant by the mysterious formula *to en kai ē aoristys duas* ('the One and the indeterminate duality'), and this confirms that Heidegger's real concern takes place in the duplicity of concealment and recovery. Whatever the indeterminate duality might signify, without doubt a certain conceptual formulation can be found in Aristotle: what is without limit is being maintained there as a *dynamei,* that is, as what is only possibly without limit, and not as an *energeia,* that which is without limit in reality. For all of us that is inevitably to be taken for granted insofar as the number and the series of numbers include the unlimited possibility of the continuation of counting. This is the reception of the Pythagorean *apeiron.* For us this could be represented in the concept of space, too, which Aristotle, however, thinks only as *topos,* as the abode of beings. What now is the testimonial value of this formula? We know very little about this, and if we take the *Seventh Epistle* seriously, then it is the point of this formula itself that resists. One might see a concrete answer in the *Seventh Epistle* in which Plato communicated his thought. Dialogical poetry testifies, as it were, to the fact that what seems final, for instance what has been written down, sublates its own finality and lets the

Socratic background be seen as that which is really permanent: the *docta igno-rantia*. This *docta ignorantia* is the self-sublation of all dogmatism. Wherever Aristotelian dogmatism in its critique of Plato might lead, what Aristotle demands of himself looks in any case like a fall from Socratic ignorance. I sup-pose it is at this point that I separate myself from Prufer, or rather, here I would like to continue the conversation with him. Does he not do Aristotle an injustice by seeing in him a violation of the inscrutability of being? Despite his mastery of logical argumentation did Aristotle not remain aware of the limits of logic? The books of *Metaphysics,* especially the chapters 6–9 of Zeta and his circum-stantial transition to the concept of *energeria* in the following book, seem to be attempts of thinking rather than results.

True, in the *Physics* Aristotle again and again surpassed the aporetical prepa-ration of his propositions to a large extent, but probably we forget too often that the Aristotelian written corpus consists of documents written for teaching pur-poses. This means, however, that all that is reflected in Aristotle as firm results of conceptual investigation must be capable of being understood as a proposal and not as established dogma such as one finds in a textbook. If we keep this per-spective in mind we will have to view with an open critical eye, too, the concept of *nous* which, in *Metaphysics Lambda,* is raised to a kind of metaphysical cos-mology. I wonder whether the full self-transparency which is supposed to perfect itself in the *energeia* of *theorein,* the divine presence of knowledge, was what the Aristotelian concept really meant? Why then is that called *energeies?* Why is the verb *'energeia'* which corresponds to this *energeies?* Did the young Heideg-ger look for and read into the *Physics* precisely that which he intends as the overcoming of metaphysics and of being and as a new preparation of the ques-tion of being? Thus he does not reduce being to the measurability of what is available which marks the limits of science and of the knowledge of domination. If I might dare to read Aristotle with Platonic eyes, which is what I have attempted to do, then the last hour of the great effective unity of Plato and Aris-totle is surely still not over. In any case, the unusual weakness in book Lambda—which sounds like an encyclopedia—can lead one to such thoughts: suddenly and without any preparation, the analogical movements of thought that had been developed in chapter 4 turn into the doctrine of the first mover—god. As far as I can see, this seems to be the move with which Aristotle stepped beyond the limit of Socratic ignorance. Did he perhaps take this step back? Maybe the *Physics* and *Metaphysics* were not his final words.

That, however, might be as it may. Prufer is correct in any case that, in the appendix to his work on Nietzsche and other places, Heidegger saw in Plato nothing but a preparation of the understanding of being as time. In the beginning Heidegger had apparently still hoped to rediscover being as the true concept of time in Aristotle, Anaximander, and Parmenides. This would have meant that

Aristotle believed that he was able to deal with the aporias of logic, and that he had dared to think being as recovery *(Entbergung)* and as recovering conceal-ment *(bergende Verbergung)*. Might this finally be implied in the Aristotelian *'energeia'* and in the description of *theoria* as the highest praxis?

H.-G.G.

PART THREE

BIBLIOGRAPHY OF HANS-GEORG GADAMER: A SELECTED BIBLIOGRAPHY

Compiled by
RICHARD E. PALMER

BIBLIOGRAPHY OF HANS-GEORG GADAMER

RECOGNITIONS OF MERIT, AWARDS, AND HONORARY DEGREES

A. ELECTED MEMBER OF ACADEMIES OF ARTS AND SCIENCES

Leipzig — Sächsische Academy of Arts and Sciences
Heidelberg — Heidelberg Academy of Sciences
Darmstadt — Darmstadt Academy for Language and Poetry
Athens — Academy of Sciences in Athens, Greece
Rome — Accadèmia Nazionale dei Lincei, Italy
Budapest — Budapest Academy of Sciences, Hungary
Brussels — Académie Royale de Belgique
Torino — Academy of Turin, Italy
London — British Royal Academy, United Kingdom
Boston — Member American Academy of Arts and Sciences

B. ELECTION TO MERITORIOUS ORDERS AND A SELECTION AMONG MANY PRIZES AND AWARDS

1971 — Reuchlin-Prize of the City of Pfortzheim
1971 — Elected Knight of the "Order of Merit" ("Pour le Mérite") for Arts and Sciences — highest academic honor given in Germany
1972 — Grand Federal Cross of Merit with Star
1975 — Honorary Member American Academy of Arts and Sciences, Boston
1979 — Hegel Prize of the City of Stuttgart
1979 — Sigmund Freud Prize of the German Academy for Language and Poetry
1986 — Jaspers Prize from the University of Heidelberg
1987 — Martin Schleyer Prize
1990 — Bundesverdienstkreutz mit Schulterband (Service Cross with Shoulderband)
1990 — Named Honorary Citizen of Naples
1993 — Großkreutz Bundesverdienst (Grand Cross of Service to the Republic)
1995 — Internationale "Antonio Feltrinelli" Prize of the Accadèmia Nationale dei Lincei (18 Nov. 1995)

C. Doctorates 'Honoris Causa'

Leipzig University, Leipzig, Germany
Bamberg University, Bamberg, Germany
University of Tübingen, Tübingen, Germany (in theology)
Catholic University of America, Washington, D.C., U.S.A.
McMaster University, Hamilton, Ontario, Canada
University of Ottawa, Ontario, Canada
Wroclaw University, Poland (formerly Breslau University)

HANS-GEORG GADAMER:
PHILOSOPHICAL WRITINGS 1922–1996:
A SELECTED BIBLIOGRAPHY[1]

This bibliography is divided into five sections:

A. Books and Monographs in German, with their English Translations
B. Books in English That Are Collections of Gadamer's Articles (listing their contents)
C. Published Articles and Their English Translations (in order of first publication)
D. Interviews and Videos: Published Interviews and Archival Tapes
E. Secondary Sources: Bibliographical Resources, Book-Length Studies, Collections of Essays

LIST OF ABBREVIATIONS USED IN BIBLIOGRAPHY

DD	*Dialogue and Dialectic* (1980)
EE	*Das Erbe Europas* (1989)
EH	*The Enigma of Health* (1996)
EPH	*Gadamer on Education, Poetry, and History* (1992)
FAZ	*Frankfurter Allgemeine Zeitung*
GDE	*Dialogue and Deconstruction: The Gadamer-Derrida Encounter* (1989)
GG	*Gedicht und Gespräch (1990)*
GW	*Gesammelte Werke* (10 vols., 1985–1995); e.g., *GW* 5:22 = vol. 5, p. 22
HD	*Hegels Dialektik* (1971)
HDt	*Hegel's Dialectic* (1976), trans. of *HD* (1971)
HW	*Heideggers Wege* (1983)
HWt	*Heidegger's Ways* (1994), trans. of *HW* (1983)
KS	*Kleine Schriften* (4 vols., 1967–1977)
LPD	*Literature and Philosophy in Dialogue: Essays in German Literary Theory* (1994)
LT	*Lob der Theorie* (1983)
MGV	*Die and Moderne und die Grenze der Vergegenständlichung (*1996)
PA	*Philosophical Apprenticeships* (1985), trans. of *PL* (1977)
PC	*Poetica* (1977)
PDE	*Platos dialektische Ethik* (1931)
PDEt	*Plato's Dialectical Ethics* (1991), trans. of *PDE* (1931)
PH	*Philosophical Hermeneutics* (1976)
PL	*Philosophische Lehrjahre* (1977)
PR	*Philosophisches Rundschau*

1. This bibliography is heavily indebted to Etsuro Makita's *Gadamer-Bibliographie: 1922–1994* (Frankfurt/Berlin/Bern/New York: Peter Lang, 1994). I wish to thank him for his support and for permission to select from his bibliography, without which I could not have undertaken this project. It is a reliable and indispensable research tool for every serious student of Gadamer's thought. I also want to thank my student assistant, John P. Werry, who patiently entered the items in this bibliography into the computer, and MacMurray College for its generous support of my work. Finally, for expert suggestions on the final draft I thank Jean Grondin of the University of Montreal.

RAS   *Reason in the Age of Science* (1981), trans. of *VZW*
RB   *The Relevance of the Beautiful and Other Essays* (1986)
TM   *Truth and Method* (1975, rev. trans. 1989)
VG   *Über die Verborgenheit der Gesundheit: Aufsätze und Vorträge* (1993)
VZW   *Vernunft im Zeitalter der Wissenschaft: Aufsätze* (1976)
WM   *Wahrheit und Methode* (1960)
WW   *Wer bin ich, wer bist Du* (1973, 1986)

A. BOOKS AND MONOGRAPHS 1922–1996

1922   *Das Wesen der Lust nach den platonischen Dialogen.* Dissertation, University of Marburg. 117pp.

1931   *Platos dialektische Ethik. Phänomenologische Interpretationen zum «Philebos».* Leipzig: Meiner, 1931; 2d ed. 1968, 3d ed. 1983. *GW* 5: 3–163. Trans.: *Plato's Dialectical Ethics: Phenomenological Interpretations Relating to the "Philebus,"* by R. M. Wallace. New Haven, Conn.: Yale University Press, 1991.

1934   *Plato und die Dichter.* Frankfurt: Klostermann. 36pp. *GW* 5: 187–211. Trans.: "Plato and the Poets." In *DD* (1980): 39–72.

1942   *Volk und Geschichte im Denken Herders.* Frankfurt: Klostermann. 24pp. *GW* 4: 318–335.

1946   *Bach und Weimar.* Weimar: H. Böhlaus Nachfolger. 15pp. In *GW* 9: 142–49. Trans.: "Bach and Weimar." In *LPD* (1994): 109–17.

1947   *Goethe und die Philosophie.* Leipzig: Volk und Buch. 34pp. *GW* 9: 56–71. Trans.: "Goethe and Philosophy." In *LPD* (1994): 1–19.

1947   *Über die Ursprünglichkeit der Wissenschaft.* Leipzig: Barth. 16pp. *GW* 10: 287–94. Trans.: "On the Primordiality of Science: A Rectoral Address." In *EPH* (1992): 15–22.

1948   *Über die Ursprünglichkeit der Philosophie: Zwei Vorträge.* Berlin: Chronos. 30pp. Reprinted in *KS* 1 (1967): 11–38. Not in *GW*.

1949   *Vom geistigen Lauf des Menschen: Studien zu unvollendeten Dichtungen Goethes.* Godesberg: Küpper. 56pp. *GW* 9: 80–111. Trans.: "On the Course of Human Spiritual Development: Studies of Goethe's Unfinished Writings." In *LPD* (1994): 31–66.

1952   *Gedächtnisrede auf Oskar Schürer* (Eulogy to Oskar Schürer). Darmstadt: Neue Darmstädter Verlagsanstalt. 23pp.

1960   *Wahrheit und Methode: Grundzüge einer philosophischen Hermeneutik.* Tübingen: Mohr. 503pp. 2d ed., 1965; 3d ed., 1972; 4th ed., 1975; 5th and 6th ed., 1986 and 1990, same as *GW* 1. Trans.: *Truth and Method,* by G. Barden and J. Cumming. New York: Seabury Press, 1975. 2d rev. ed. (from German 5th ed.) is translated by J. Weinsheimer and D. G. Marshall, 1989. Other translations: Italian (1972), French (1996), Spanish (1977), Serbo-Croatian (1978), Japanese, part 1 only (1986), Hungarian (1984), Russian (1988), Chinese, part 1 only (1987). Shorter excerpts have been published in Czech and Danish.

1963   *Le problème de la conscience historique.* Louvain/Paris: Béatrice-Nauwelaets. 90pp. Trans.: "The Problem of Historical Consciousness." *Graduate Faculty Philosophy Journal* (New School for Social Research) 5 (1975): 1–52. Also in *Interpretive Social Science: A Reader,* edited by P. Rabinow and W. M. Sullivan, 103–60. Berkeley: California University Press, 1979; 2d ed. 1987.

1964   *Dialektik und Sophistik im siebenten platonischen Brief.* Heidelberg: Winter. 34pp. *GW* 6: 90–115. Trans.: "Dialectic and Sophism in Plato's *Seventh Letter.*" In *DD* (1980): 93–123.

1967   *Kleine Schriften 1. Philosophie, Hermeneutik.* Tübingen: Mohr. 234pp. Translations of some essays from this volume appear in *PH* (1976) and *RB* (1986). Abbrev.: *KS* 1.

1967   *Kleine Schriften 2. Interpretationen.* Tübingen: Mohr. 2d. ed., 1979. 324pp.

1968   *Platos dialektische Ethik und andere Studien zur platonischen Philosophie.* Hamburg: Meiner. Title essay was published as a monograph 1931. The 1968 collection was translated by P. Christopher Smith as *Dialogue and Dialectic* (1980). See *DD* in sec. B below for contents.

1968   *Werner Scholz.* Recklinghausen: Bongers. 158pp. A book of the artist's paintings with commentary by Gadamer.

1971   *Die Begriffsgeschichte und die Sprache der Philosophie.* Opladen: Westdeutscher Verlag. 24pp. *GW* 4: 78–94 (appendix 91–94). Trans.: "The History of Concepts and the Language of Philosophy." *International Studies of Philosophy* 18, no. 3 (1986): 1–16 (appendix 12–15).

1971   *Hegels Dialektik: Fünf hermeneutische Studien.* Tübingen: Mohr. 96pp. 2d ed. enlarged to six studies, 1980. Trans.: *Hegel's Dialectic: Five Hermeneutical Studies* by P. C. Smith. New Haven, Conn.: Yale University Press, 1976. The translated volume substitutes "Hegels Dialektik des Selbstbewußtseins" (1973) for "Hegel und die Heidelberger Romantik" (1961).

1971   *Über die Naturanlage des Menschen zur Philosophie.* Pforzheim: Stadt Pforzheim. 18pp. *VW* (1976): 110–24. Trans.: "On Man's Natural Inclination Towards Philosophy." *Universitas,* 15, no. 1 (1975): 31–40. Also translated as "On the Natural Inclination of Human Beings Toward Philosophy." In *RAS* (1981): 139–50.

1972   *Kleine Schriften 3. Idee und Sprache: Platon, Husserl, Heidegger.* Tübingen: Mohr. 271pp. Some essays are translated in *PH.* See sec. B below.

1973 *Wer bin Ich und wer bist Du?: Ein Kommentar zu Paul Celans Gedichtfolge Atemkristall.* Frankfurt: Suhrkamp. *GW* 9: 383–451.

1974 *Idee und Wirklichkeit in Platos Timaios.* Heidelberg: Carl Winter Universitätsverlag. 36pp. *GW* 6: 242–70. Trans.: "Idea and Reality in Plato's *Timaeus.*" In *DD* (1980): 156–93.

1976 *Rhetorik und Hermeneutik.* Göttingen: Vandenhoeck und Ruprecht. 19pp. *GW* 2: 276–91.

1976 *Vernunft im Zeitalter der Wissenschaft: Aufsätze.* Frankfurt: Suhrkamp. Trans.: *Reason in the Age of Science,* by F. G. Lawrence. Cambridge: MIT Press, 1981. Abbrev.: *VZW.* Translation abbrev.: *RAS* (1981).

1977 *Die Aktualität des Schönen: Kunst als Spiel, Symbol, und Fest.* Stuttgart: Reclam. 77pp. *GW* 8: 94–142. Trans.: "The Relevance of the Beautiful: Art as Play, Symbol, and Festival." The title essay in *RB* (1986): 3–53.

1977 *Kleine Schriften 4. Variationen.* Tübingen: Mohr. 261pp. Some essays in this volume are translated in *RB* (1986).

1977 *Philosophische Lehrjahre: Eine Rückschau.* Frankfurt: Klostermann. Abbrev.: *PL.* Translation abbrev.: *PA* (1985). A list of figures discussed in this volume is given below in sec. B under *Philosophical Apprenticeships.* Gadamer selected a number of these essays for inclusion in the final section of his collected works. See *GW* 10: 375–403.

1977 *Poetica: Ausgewählte Essays.* Frankfurt: Insel Verlag. *GG* (1990) is an expanded version of this collection. Most essays from this volume appear in *GW* 8 or 9.

1978 *Die Idee des Guten zwischen Plato und Aristoteles.* Heidelberg: Winter Universitätsverlag. *GW* 7: 128–227. Trans.: *The Idea of the Good in Platonic-Aristotelian Philosophy,* by P. Christopher Smith. New Haven, Conn.: Yale University Press, 1986.

1982 *Lectures on Philosophical Hermeneutics.* Pretoria: University of Pretoria. 34pp.

1983 *Heideggers Wege: Studien zum Spätwerk.* Tübingen: Mohr. GW 3: 175–332. Trans.: *Heidegger's Ways,* by John W. Stanley. See *HWt* (1994) in sec. B for contents.

1983 *Lob der Theorie: Reden und Aufsätze.* Frankfurt: Suhrkamp Verlag. 176pp. Abbrev.: *LT.*

1985 *Die Vielfalt Europas: Erbe und Zukunft.* Stuttgart: R. B. Stiftung. 36pp. Trans.: "The Diversity of Europe: Inheritance and Future." In *EPH* (1992): 221–36.

1985 *GW 5. Griechische Philosophie I.* Tübingen: Mohr. 394pp.

1986   *GW* 1. *Hermeneutik I: Wahrheit und Methode.* Tübingen: Mohr. 516pp. 5th ed. of *WM* (1960).

1986   *GW* 2. *Hermeneutik II: Wahrheit und Methode Ergängungen, Register.* Essays supplementary to *WM*, plus index. Tübingen: Mohr. 540pp.

1986   *GW* 6. *Griechische Philosophie II.* Tübingen: Mohr. 347pp.

1986   *Die Universität Heidelberg und die Geburt der modernen Wissenschaft.* Berlin: Springer-Verlag. 16pp. Originally published as a newspaper article in 1986. See Articles. GW 10: 336–45. Translated in *EPH* (1992): 37–46.

1987   *GW* 3. *Neuere Philosophie I: Hegel/Husserl/Heidegger.* Tübingen: Mohr. 455pp.

1987   *GW* 4. *Neuere Philosophie II: Probleme/Gestalten.* Tübingen: Mohr. 508pp.

1988   *Platon als Porträtist.* Munich: Verein der Freunde und Förderer der Glyptothek und der Antikensammlungen München. 37pp. "Plato als Porträtist" is expanded in *GW* 7: 228–57.

1989   *Das Erbe Europas: Beiträge.* Frankfurt: Suhrkamp, 1989. 175pp. 2d ed. 1990. Abbrev.: *EE*.

1990   *Gedicht und Gespräch.* Frankfurt: Insel, 1990. 186pp. A revised and expanded edition of *Poetica* (1977). Abbrev.: *GG*.

1991   *GW* 7. *Griechische Philosophie III: Plato im Dialog.* Tübingen: Mohr. 480pp.

1993   *GW* 8. *Ästhetik und Poetik I: Kunst als Aussage.* Tübingen: Mohr. 440pp.

1993   *GW* 9. *Ästhetik und Poetik II: Hermeneutik im Vollzug.* Tübingen: Mohr. 481pp.

1993   *Hermeneutik, Ästhetik, Praktische Philosophie: Hans-Georg Gadamer im Gespräch.* Ed. Carsten Dutt. Heidelberg: Universitätsverlag C. Winter. 80pp. Interviews with Gadamer.

1993   *Über die Verborgenheit der Gesundheit: Aufsätze und Vorträge.* Frankfurt: Suhrkamp Verlag. 215pp. Abbrev.: *VG*. Trans.: *EH* (1996). See *EH* for a list of its fourteen essays.

1995   *GW* 10. *Hermeneutik im Rückblick.* Tübingen: Mohr, 1995. 488pp. IMPORTANT NOTE! Volume 10 includes *the tables of contents for each of the ten volumes,* and it indexes titles and translations into English, French, and Italian for all the essays found in *GW* 1–10! This eliminates any need to list the contents of each of the ten volumes here.

0000   *Die Moderne und die Grenze der Vergegenständlichung.* Ed. Bernd Klüser, with two essays by Gadamer and contributions by Hans Belting, Gottfried Boehm, and W. Ch. Zimmerli. Munich: Bernd Klüser, 1996. 125pp. One of the two essays, "Vom Wort zum Begriff" (1995) does not appear in *GW*.

(Forthcoming) *Der Anfang der Philosophie.* Stuttgart: Reclam, 1997. ca. 150pp. Authorized trans. by Joachim Schulte from the Italian, *L'Inizio della filosofia occi-
dentale: Lezioni raccolte da Vittorio De Cesare.* Milan: Guerini e Associati,
1993. 150pp. Ten lectures on early Greek philosophy given at the Instituto per
gli Studi Filosofici in Naples, between January 11 and 22, 1988, transcribed
and edited from the tape recording by Vittorio De Cesare.

B. BOOKS IN ENGLISH THAT ARE COLLECTIONS OF GADAMER'S WRITINGS

1976   *Hegel's Dialectic: Five Hermeneutical Studies.* Translated by P. Christopher
        Smith. New Haven, Conn.: Yale University Press, 1976. (Substitutes "Hegels
        Dialektik des Selbstbewußtseins" (1973) for "Hegel und die Heidelberger
        Romantik.") Abbrev.: *HDt.*
        Included Essays: "Hegel and the Dialectic of the Ancient Philosophers"
        (1961), "Hegel's 'Inverted World'" (1966), "Hegel's Dialectic of Self-
        Consciousness" (1973), "The Idea of Hegel's Logic" (1970), and "Hegel and
        Heidegger" (1971).

1976   *Philosophical Hermeneutics.* Edited and translated by David E. Linge. Berkeley:
        University of California Press. 301pp. Abbrev.: *PH.*
        Included Essays: Editor's introduction (xi–lvii). Part 1, The Scope of
        Hermeneutical Reflection (1–104): "The Universality of the Hermeneutical
        Problem" (1966), "On the Scope and Function of Hermeneutical Reflection"
        (1967), "On the Problem of Self-Understanding" (1961), "Man and Language"
        (1965), "The Nature of Things and the Language of Things" (1962), "Seman-
        tics and Hermeneutics" (1971), "Aesthetics and Hermeneutics" (1964). Part 2,
        Phenomenology, Existential Philosophy, and Philosophical Hermeneutics
        (105–240): "The Philosophical Foundations of the Twentieth Century" (1965),
        "The Phenomenological Movement" (1963), "The Science of the Life-World"
        (1972), "Martin Heidegger and Marburg Theology" (1964), "Heidegger's Later
        Philosophy" (1960), and "Heidegger and the Language of Metaphysics"
        (1967).

1980   *Dialogue and Dialectic: Eight Hermeneutical Studies on Plato.* Translated and
        edited by P. Christopher Smith. New Haven, Conn.: Yale University Press.
        221pp. Abbrev.: *DD.*
        Included Essays: "*Logos* and *Ergon* in Plato's Lysis" (1972), "The Proofs of
        Immortality in Plato's *Phaedo*" (1973), *Plato and the Poets* (1934), "Plato's
        Educational State" (1942), "Dialectic and Sophism in Plato's *Seventh Letter*"
        (1964), "Plato's Unwritten Dialectic" (1968), "Idea and Reality in Plato's
        Timaeus" (1974), and "Amicus Plato, Magis amica Veritas" (1968).

1981   *Reason in the Age of Science.* Translated by Frederick G. Lawrence. Cambridge:
        MIT Press, 1981. Abbrev.: *RAS.*
        Included Essays: Translator's introduction (ix–xxxiii), "On the Philosophic
        Element in the Sciences and the Scientific Character of Philosophy" (1976),
        "Hegel's Philosophy and Its Aftereffects until Today" (1972), "The Heritage of

Hegel" (1979, but not found in *VW*), "What is Practice?: The Conditions of Social Reason" (1974), "Hermeneutics as Practical Philosophy" (1972), "Hermeneutics as a Theoretical and Practical Task" (1978), "On the Natural Inclination of Human Beings Toward Philosophy" (1971), "Philosophy or Theory of Science?" (1974).

1985   *Philosophical Apprenticeships.* Translated by Robert R. Sullivan. Cambridge: MIT Press, 1985. Gadamer's autobiography, recalling many contemporaries. Abbrev.: *PA*.
Included Chapters: "Breslau," "Marburg," "Paul Natorp," "Max Scheler," "No-one's Years," "Martin Heidegger," "Rudolf Bultmann," "Gerhard Krüger," "Teaching Years," "Richard Kroner," "Hans Lipps," "Leipzig Fears," "Leipzig Illusions," "Frankfurt Intermezzo," "Trip to Argentina," "Karl Reinhard," "Heidelberg," "Richard Benz," "Geshom Scholem," "Jan van der Meulen," "Karl Jaspers," "Karl Löwith," and "On the Origins of Philosophical Hermeneutics."

1986   *The Relevance of the Beautiful and Other Essays.* Edited and introduced by Robert Bernasconi. Translated by Nicholas Walker. Cambridge: Cambridge University Press. 191pp. Abbrev.: *RB*.
Included Essays: Editor's introduction (xi–xxi). Part 1 (pp. 1–53): "The Relevance of the Beautiful: Art as Play, Symbol, and Festival" (1975). Part 2 (pp. 55–153): "The Festive Character of Theater" (1954), "Composition and Interpretation" (1961), "Image and Gesture" (1967), "The Speechless Image" (1965), "Art and Imitation" (1967), "On the Contribution of Poetry to the Search for Truth" (1971), "Poetry and Mimesis" (1972), "The Play of Art" (1977), "Philosophy and Poetry" (1977), "Aesthetic and Religious Experience" (1978). Appendix essay (pp. 155–70): "Intuition and Vividness" (1980).

1989   *Dialogue and Deconstruction: The Gadamer-Derrida Encounter.* Edited and translated by Diane P. Michelfelder and Richard E. Palmer. Albany, N.Y.: SUNY Press. Abbrev.: *GDE*.
Although this volume contains essays by other hands, it contains five translated essays by Gadamer: (1) "Text and Interpretation" (1984), (2) "Und dennoch: Macht de guten Willens" (1984), (3) "Letter to Dallmayr," a trans. of "Dekonstruktion und Hermeneutik" (1988), (4) "*Destruktion* and Deconstruction" (1985), and (5) "Hermeneutics and Logocentrism," a trans. of "Frühromantik, Hermeneutik, Dekonstruktivismus" (1987).

1992   *Hans-Georg Gadamer on Education, Poetry, and History: Applied Hermeneutics.* Edited by Dieter Misgeld and Graeme Nicholson. Translated by Lawrence Schmidt and Monica Reuss. Albany, N. Y.: SUNY Press. 238pp. Abbrev.: *EPH*.
Included Essays: Editors' introduction (vii–xxiii). Part 1: *The Philosopher in the University* (pp. 1–59), "Interview: The German University and German Politics. The Case of Heidegger" (1992), "On the Primordiality of Science: A Rectoral Address" (1947), "The University of Leipzig, 1409–1959: A Former Rector Commemorates the 550th Anniversary of Its Founding" (1960), "The

University of Heidelberg and the Birth of Modern Science" (1986), "The Idea of the University—Yesterday, Today, Tomorrow" (1988). Part 2: *Hermeneutics, Poetry, and Modern Culture* (pp. 61–131): "Interview: Writing and the Living Voice" (1992), "Are the Poets Falling Silent?" (1970), "The Verse and the Whole" (1979), "Hölderlin and George" (1968), "Under the Shadow of Nihilism" (1987), "Interview: Historicism and Romanticism" (1992). Part 3: *Europe and the Humanities* (pp. 133–236): "Interview: The 1920s, 1930s, and the Present: National Socialism, German History, and German Culture" (1992), "The Philosophy and the Religion of Judaism" (1961), "Notes on Planning for the Future" (1966), "The Limitations of the Expert" (1989), "The Future of the European Humanities" (1983), "Citizens of Two Worlds" (1985), and "The Diversity of Europe: Inheritance and Future" (1985).

1994   *Heidegger's Ways.* Translated by John W. Stanley. Introduction by Dennis J. Schmidt. Albany, N.Y.: SUNY Press. A translation of *HW* (1983). 212pp. Abbrev.: *HWt*.

      Included Essays: Translator's preface and introduction by Schmidt (pp. ix–xxiii), "Existentialism and the Philosophy of Existence" (1981), "Martin Heidegger—75 Years" (1964), "The Marburg Theology" (1964), "What is Metaphysics?" (1978), "Kant and the Hermeneutical Turn" (1975), "The Thinker Martin Heidegger" (1966), "The Language of Metaphysics" (1968), "Plato" (1976), "The Truth of the Work of Art" (1960), "Martin Heidegger—85 Years" (1974), "The Way in the Turn" (1979), "The Greeks" (1979), "The History of Philosophy" (1981), "The Religious Dimension" (1981), and "Being Spirit God" (1977).

1994   *Literature and Philosophy in Dialogue: Essays in German Literary Theory.* Translated by Robert H. Paslick. Edited by Dennis J. Schmidt. Albany, N.Y.: SUNY Press. 182pp. Abbrev.: *LPD*.

      Included Essays: Translator's introduction (pp. vii–xxiii), "Goethe and Philosophy" (1947), "Goethe and the Moral World" (1967), "On the Course of Human Spiritual Development: Studies of Goethe's Unfinished Writings" (1949), "Hölderlin and Antiquity" (1943), "Hölderlin and the Future" (1947), "Bach and Weimar" (1946), "The God of Most Intimate Feeling" (1961), "Poetry and Punctuation" (1961), "Rainer Maria Rilke's Interpretation of Existence: On the Book by Romano Guardini" (1955), and "Mythopoietic Reversal in Rilke's *Duino Elegies*" (1967).

1996   *The Enigma of Health: The Art of Healing in a Scientific Age.* Translated by Jason Gaiger and Nicholas Walker. Oxford: Polity Press; Stanford, Calif.: Stanford University Press. 160pp. Abbrev.: *EH*.

      Included Essays: "Theory, Technology, Praxis" (1972), "Apologia for the Art of Healing" (1966), "The Problem of Intelligence" (1966), "The Experience of Death" (1987), "Bodily Experience and the Limits of Objectification" (1986), "Between Nature and Art" (1987), "Philosophy and Practical Medicine" (1990), "On the Enigmatic Character of Health" (1991), "Authority and Critical Freedom" (1983), "Treatment and Dialogue" (1993), "Life and Soul" (1993), "Anxiety and Anxieties" (1993), "Hermeneutics and Psychiatrie" (1992).

C. Published Articles 1924–1996

1924

"Metaphysik der Erkenntnis: Zu dem gleichnamigen Buch von Nicolai Hartmann." *Logos* 12, no. 3 (1923/24): 340–59.

"Zur Systemidee in der Philosophie." In *Festschrift für Paul Natorp zum siebzigsten Geburtstage,* 55–75. Berlin: de Gruyter.

1928

"Der aristotelische Protreptikos und die entwicklungsgeschichtliche Betrachtung der Aristotelischen Ethik." *Hermes: Zeitschrift für klassische Philologie* 63: 138–64. (Reprinted in *Schriften zur aristotelischen Ethik,* edited by Christian Mueller-Goldingen, 1–27. Hildesheim: Olms, 1988.) *GW* 5: 164–86.

1930

"Praktisches Wissen." First appeared in an unpublished Festschrift for Paul Natorp's 70th birthday in this year. First formal publication was in *GW* 5: 230–48.

1933

"Wilhelm Dilthey zu seinem hundertsten Geburtstag am 19. November." *Literarische Rundschau* 3, no. 20: 1. *GW* 4: 425–28.

1936

"Antike Atomtheorie." *Zeitschrift für die gesamte Naturwissenschaft* 1, no. 2 (1935/36):81–95. (Reprinted in *Um die Begriffswelt der Vorsokratiker,* edited by Hans-Georg Gadamer, 512–33. Darmstadt: Wissenschaftliche Buchgesellschaft, 1968.) *GW* 5: 263–79.

"Kurt Riezler, *Parmenides* [a review article]." *Gnomon,* 12, no. 2 (Feb.): 77–86. Retitled "Kurt Riezlers Parmenidesdeutung: Das Lehrgedicht des Parmenides" in *GW* 6: 30–38.

1939

"Hegel und der geschichtliche Geist." *Zeitschrift für gesamte Staatswissenschaft* 100, nos. 1–2 (Nov.): 25–37. *GW* 4: 384–94.

"Zu Kants Begründung der Ästhetik und dem Sinn der Kunst." In *Festschrift für Richard Hamann,* 31–39. Burg bei Magdeburg: A. Hopfer.

1941

"Herder et ses théories sur l'histoire." In *Regards sur l'histoire,* by Hans-Georg Gadamer and others, 7–36. Paris: Ferdinand Sorlot. German: "Herder als Wegbereiter des 'historischen Bewußtseins.'" *Geist der Zeit* 19 (December): 661–70. Retitled "Herder und die geschichtliche Welt" in *GW* 4: 318–35.

1942

"Platos Staat der Erziehung." *Das neue Bild der Antike.* Vol. 1, "Hellas," edited by Helmut Berve, 317–33. Leipzig: Koehler und Amelang. *GW* 5: 249–62. Trans.: "Plato's Educational State." In *DD* (1980): 73–92.

1943

"Die Gottesfrage in der Philosophie." In *Festschrift für Karl Jaspers,* edited by Oskar Kammelbeck. (Unprinted typescript.) Retitled "Kant und die Gottesfrage." In *GW* 4: 349–60.

"Hölderlin und die Antike." In *Hölderlin: Gedenkschrift,* edited by P. Kluckhohn, 50–69. Tübingen: Mohr. *GW* 9: 1–19. Trans.: "Hölderlin and Antiquity." In *LPD* (1994): 67–86.

"Das Problem der Geschichte in der neueren deutschen Philosophie." *KS* 1 (1967): 1–10. First published in *KS* 1, but written during the war in 1943. *GW* 2: 27–36.

"Wissenschaft als Beruf: Über den Ruf und Beruf der Wissenschaft in unserer Zeit." *Leipziger Neueste Nachrichten und Handels-Zeitung* 270 (Sept. 27): 3. Also in *Deutsche Presse-Korrespondenz* 43 (Oct. 28): 4–6.

1944

"Was ist der Mensch?" *Illustrierte Zeitung Leipzig,* n.d. Special issue: *Der europäischen Mensch,* 31–34.

1946

"Die gemeinschaftsbildende Kraft der Kultur: Ein Beitrag zur Umformung deutschen Geisteslebens." *Göttinger Universitäts-Zeitung* 8 (Apr. 15, 1945/46): 4–6. Included as document 29 in Manfred Overesch's *Die Deutschen und die deutsche Frage 1945–1955,* edited by the Niedersächsischen Landeszentrale für politische Bildung, 89–91. Hannover, 1985.

"Leibniz' Philosophie und ihr geschichtliches Schicksal." His 1946 rectoral lecture published in typescript in 1946. *Studia Leibniziana [Stuttgart]* 22, no. 1 (1990): 1–10. *GW* 10: 295–307.

"Prometheus und die Tragödie der Kultur." Shorter versions appeared earlier in *Die Wandlung* 1, no. 7 (1945/46): 600–615, and *Anales de filologia clasica* 4 (1947–1949): 329–44. First full text: *Festschrift: Rudolf Bultmann,* 74–83. Stuttgart: Kohlhammer, 1949. *GW* 9: 150–61.

1947

"Hölderlin und das Zukünftige." In *Beiträge zur geistigen Überlieferung,* 53–85. Bad Godesberg: Helmut Küpper. *GW* 9: 20–38. Trans.: "Hölderlin and the Future." In *LPD* (1994): 87–108.

"Universität in unserer Zeit: Der Leipziger Rektor über den gesellschaftlichen Auftrag der Wissenschaft." *Göttinger Universitäts-Zeitung,* no. 11 (May 9): 10–11.

1948

"Die Bedeutung der Philosophie für die neue Erziehung." First of two lectures in his 1948 monograph, *Über die Ursprünglichkeit der Philosophie: Zwei Vorträge,* 5–14.

"Das Verhältnis der Philosophie zu Kunst und Wissenschaft." Second of two lectures in his 1948 monograph, *Über die Ursprünglichkeit der Philosophie: Zwei Votäge,* 15–28.

1949

"Die Bildung zum Menschen: Der Zauberflöte anderer Teil." In his 1949 monograph, *Vom geistigen Lauf des Menschen: Studien zu unvollendeten Dichtungen Goethes,* 28–55. *GW* 9: 80–111. Trans.: see section A above.

"Die Grenze des Titanischen: Prometheus, Pandora." In his 1949 monograph, *Vom geistigen Lauf des Menschen: Studien zu unvollendeten Dichtungen Goethes*, 9–27. *GW* 9: 80–111. Trans.: see section A above.

"Die Grenzen der historischen Vernunft." In *Actas del primer congreso nacional de filosofía, Mendoza*, edited by L. J. Guerrero, 2: 1025–29. Mendoza: National University of Cuyo. Enlarged in *KS* 1: 1–10. *GW* 10: 175–78.

"Karl Immermanns 'Chiliastische Sonette'." *Die Neue Rundschau* 60, no. 4: 487–502. Amsterdam: Bermann-Fischer. *GW* 9: 180–92.

1950

"Erich Frank, *Philosophical Understanding and Religious Truth* (1945)." A review article of this book in *Theologische Rundschau* 18, no. 3: 260–66. *GW* 10: 405–12.

"Zur Vorgeschichte der Metaphysik." In *Anteile: Martin Heidegger zum 60. Geburtstag*, 51–79. Frankfurt: Klostermann. *GW* 6: 9–29.

1951

"Die Philosophie in den letzten dreissig Jahren." *Ruperto-Carola* (Heidelberg) 5 (Dec.): 33–34. His inaugural lecture on being elected to the Heidelberg Academy of Sciences.

1952

"Gedenkrede auf Max Kommerell." In *Dichterische Welterfahrung: Essays*, 205–27. Frankfurt: Klostermann. Reprinted in *PL* (1977): 93–110, and translated in *PA* (1977): 93–110.

"Retraktionen zum Lehrgedicht des Parmenides." In *Varia variorum Festgabe für Karl Reinhardt*, 58–68. Münster: Böhlau. *GW* 6: 38–49.

1953

"Über die Autorität: Die Wahrheit in den Geisteswissenschaften." In *Bilder und Zeiten*, a supplement in *FAZ* 283 (Dec. 5): 4. *GW* 2: 37–43.

1954

"Mythos und Vernunft." In *Gegenwart im Geiste: Festschrift für Richard Benz*, edited by W. Bulst and A. Schneider, 64–71. Hamburg: C. Wegner. *GW* 8: 163–69.

"Über die Festlichkeit des Theaters: Walter F. Otto." In *Mannheimer Hefte* 3: 26–30. *GW* 8: 296–304. Trans.: "The Festive Character of Theater." In *RB* (1986): 57–65.

1955

"Bemerkungen über den Barock." In *Retorica e barocco*, edited by E. Castelli, 61–63. Roma: Fratelli Bocca Editori.

"Einleitung." In R. G. Collingwood, *Denken: Eine Autobiographie*, translated by H.-J. Finkeldei, v–xiv. Stuttgart: K. F. Koehler.

"Die Mythologie der Griechen: Zu dem Pastellwerk von Werner Scholz." *FAZ* 130 (June 7): 8.

"Die philosophische Bedeutung Paul Natorps." *Kant-Studien: Philosophische Zeitschrift* 46, no. 2 (1954–55): 129–34. Also in Paul Natorp, *Philosophische Systematik*, edited by Hans Natorp, xi–xvii. Hamburg: Meiner, 1958. Retitled "Paul Natorp." In *PL* (1977): 60–68. *GW* 10: 375–80. Trans.: "Paul Natorp." In *PA* (1985): 21–26.

"Rainer Maria Rilkes Deutung des Daseins: Eine Interpretation der Duineser Elegien." *PR* 2, nos. 1/2 (1954/55): 82–92. *GW* 9: 271–81. Trans.: "Rainer Maria Rilke's Interpretation of Existence: On the Book by Romano Guadini." In *LPD* (1994): 139–51.

1957

"Was ist Wahrheit?" *Zeitwende: Die neue Furche* 27, no. 4 (April): 226–37. *GW* 2: 44–46.

1958

"Aristophanes in Schwetzingen." *Die Gegenwart* 13, no. 12 (June 14): 372.

"Denken," "Geisteswissenschaften," "Geschichte und Geschichtsauffassung," "Geschichtlichkeit." In *Die Religion in Geschichte und Gegenwart*, 3d ed., edited by K. Galling, vol. 2, cols. 84–85, 1304–8, 1488–96, 1496–98. Tübingen: Mohr.

"Karl Reinhardt." *Die Neue Rundschau* 69, no. 1 (1958): 161–68. Retitled "Schein und Sein." In *GW* 6: 278–84. Not the same as the discussion of Reinhardt in *PL* (1977): 151–60.

"Symbol und Allegorie." *Archivio di Filosofia* 28, nos. 2/3: 23–28, edited by E. Castelli. See in *WM*: "Die Grenze der Erlebniskunst: Rehabilitierung der Allegorie." *GW* 1: 76–87.

"Zur Fragwürdigkeit des aesthetischen Bewußtseins." *Rivista di estetica* 3, no. 3 (Sept.–Dec.): 374–83. *GW* 8: 9–17. Trans.: "On the Problematic Character of Aesthetic Consciousness" by E. Kelley. *Graduate Faculty Philosophy Journal* [New School for Social Research] 9, no. 1 (1982): 31–40.

1959

"Historismus." In *Die Religion in Geschichte und Gegenwart*, 3d ed., edited by K. Galling, vol. 3, cols. 369–71. Tübingen: Mohr.

"Kausalität II: In der Geschichte." In *Die Religion in Geschichte und Gegenwart*, 3d ed., edited by K. Galling, vol. 3, cols. 1230–32. Tübingen: Mohr. See "Kausalität in die Geschichte?" (1965) below.

"Vom Zirkel des Verstehens." In *Martin Heidegger zum siebzigsten Geburtstag*, edited by G. Neske. See "Die hermeneutische Bedeutung des Zeitenabstandes" in *WM*: 251–54, 275–83. Also *GW* 1: 270–74, 296–305. See also "Vom Zirkel des Verstehens" in *GW* 2: 57–65. Trans.: "On the Circle of Understanding," in a volume by Gadamer, Specht, and Stegmüller, *Hermeneutics Versus Science?*, translated by J. M. Connolly and T. Keutner, 68–78. Notre Dame, Ind.: University of Notre Dame Press.

1960

"Nachwort." In Fritz Kaufmann, *Das Reich des Schönen: Bausteine zu einer Philosophie der Kunst*, 397–402. Stuttgart: Kohlhammer. *GW* 10: 426–32.

"Rede auf die Universität Leipzig des Professors Dr. phil. Hans-Georg Gadamer, ehemaliger Rektor der Universität Leipzig." *Ruperto Carola: Mitteilungen* 12th yr., vol. 27 (June): 203–13. See *PL* (1977): 136–38. Trans.: "University of Leipzig." In *PA* (1985): 114–15. Trans.: "The University of Leipzig, 1409–1959: A Former Rector Commemorates the 550th Anniversary of its Founding." In *EPH* (1992): 23–35.

"Zur Einführung." In M. Heidegger, *Der Ursprung des Kunstwerkes*, edited and introduced by H.-G. Gadamer, 102–25. Stuttgart: Reclam. Retitled "Die Wahrheit des Kunstwerks." In *HW* (1983): 81–93. *GW* 3: 249–61. Trans.: "Heidegger's Later Philosophy." In *PH* (1976): 213–28. Trans.: "The Truth of the Work of Art," by John Stanley. In *HWt* (1994): 95–109.

1961

"Dichten und Deuten." *Jahrbuch der Deutschen Akademie für Sprache und Dichtung* (Darmstadt), 13–21. *GW* 8: 18–24. Trans.: "Composition and Interpretation." In *RB* (1986): 66–73.

"Der Gott des innersten Gefühls." *Die Neue Rundschau* 72, no. 2: 340–49. *GW* 9: 162–70. Trans.: "The God of Most Intimate Feeling." In *LPD* (1994): 119–29.

"Hegel und die antike Dialektik." *Hegel-Studien* 1: 173–99. Also in *HD* (1971): 7–30 and *GW* 3: 3–28. Trans.: "Hegel and the Dialectic of the Ancient Philosophers." In *HDt* (1976): 5–34.

"Hegel und die Heidelberger Romantik." *Ruperto Carola* 13th yr., vol. 30 (Dec.): 97–103. In *HD*, 1st ed., 71–81; 2d ed., 87–97; but not translated in *HDt. GW* 4: 395–405.

"Hermeneutik und Historismus." *PR* 9, no. 4: 241–76. Included as an appendix in the second through fourth editions of *WM:* 477–512. *GW* 2: 387–424. Trans.: "Hermeneutics and Historicism." Supplement 1 in *TM*, rev. ed. (1989): 505–41.

"Die Philosophie." In *Die Juden und die Kultur: Eine Vortragsreihe des Bayerischen Rundfunks,* edited by L. Reinisch, 78–90. Stuttgart: Kohlhammer. Retitled "Die Philosophie und die Religion des Judentums." In *GW* 4: 68–77. Trans.: "The Philosophy and the Religion of Judaism." In *EPH* (1992): 155–64.

"Poesie und Interpunktion." *Die Neue Rundschau* 72, no. 1 (1961): 143–49. *GW* 9: 282–88. Trans.: "Poetry and Punctuation." In *LPD* (1994): 131–37.

1962

"Begriffene Malerei? Zu A. Gehlens *Zeit-Bilder.*" In *PR* 10: 21–30. *GW* 8: 305–14.

"Geleitwort." In *Einsichten: Festschrift für Gerhard Krüger,* edited by K. Oehler and R. Schaeffler, 7–10. Frankfurt: V. Klostermann. Trans.: "Gerard Krüger." In *PA* (1985): 61–67.

"Karl Löwith." *Stuttgarter Zeitung* 18, no. 5 (Jan. 8): 13. Trans.: "Karl Löwith." In *PA* 169–75.

"Die Natur der Sache und die Sprache der Dinge." In *Das Problem der Ordnung,* edited by F. Wiedmann and H. Kuhn, 26–36. Meisenheim: V. Anton. *GW* 2: 66–76. Trans.: "The Nature of Things and the Language of Things." In *PH* (1976): 69–81.

"Sprache, II. Philosophisch," "Tradition, I. Phänomenologisch," and "Verstehen." Entries in *Die Religion in Geschichte und Gehenwart,* 3d edition, edited by K. Galling, vol. 6, cols. 266–68, 966–67, and 1381–83. Tübingen: Mohr.

"Zur Problematik des Selbstverständnisses." In *Einsichten: Festschrift für Gerhard Krüger,* edited by K. Oehler and R. Schaeffler, 71–85. Klostermann: Main. *GW* 2: 121–32. Trans. "On the Problem of Self-Understanding." In *PH* (1976): 44–58.

1963

"Äesthetik und Hermeneutik." *Algemeen Nederlands Tijdschrift voor Wijsbegeerte en Psychologie* 56, no. 5 (Dec.): 240–46. *GW* 8: 1–8. Trans.: "Aesthetics and Hermeneutics." In *PH* (1976): 95–104.

"Einleitung." In Friedrich Oetinger, *Inquisitio in sensum communem et rationem* [1753], v–xxviii. Stuttgart: F. Frommann. Retitled "Oetinger als Philosoph." In *GW* 4: 306–17.

"Martin Heidegger." *Bilder und Zeiten* (*FAZ* supplement), no. 224 (Sept. 26), 2pp. Reprinted as "Martin Heidegger—75 Jahre." In *HW* (1983): 18–28. *GW* 3: 186–96. Trans.: "Martin Heidegger—75 Years." In *HWt* (1994): 15–27.

"Martin Heidegger." In *Zeit und Geschichte*, edited by Erich Dinkler. Tübingen: Mohr. pp. 479–90. Also, "Die Marburger Theologie." In *HW* (1983): 29–40. *GW* 3: 197–208. Trans.: "Martin Heidegger and Marburg Theology." In *PH* (1976): 198–212; "The Marburg Theology." In *HWt* (1994): 29–43.

"Nicolás de Cusa y la filosofia del presente." In *Folia humanística* 2, no. 23: 929–37. First German publication: "Nikolaus von Kues im modernen Denken." In *Nicolo Cusano agli inizi del mondo moderno*, 39–48. Florence: Sansoni, 1970. Retitled "Nikolaus Cusanus und die Gegenwart." In *GW* 4: 297–305.

"Die phänomenologische Bewegung." *PR* 11, nos. 1/2: 1–45. *GW* 3: 105–46. Trans.: "The Phenomenological Movement." In *PH* (1976): 130–81.

"Philosophische Bemerkungen zum Problem der Intelligenz." *Der Nervenarzt* 35, no. 7 (July): 281–86. *VG* (1993): 65–83. *GW* 4: 276–87. Trans.: "The Problem of Intelligence." In *EH* (1996): 45–60.

"Platon und die Vorsokratiker." In *Epimeleia*, edited by F. Wiedmann, 127–42. Munich : A. Pustet. *GW* 6: 58–70.

"Über die Möglichkeit einer philosophischen Ethik." In *Sein und Ethos*, edited by P. M. Engelhardt, 11–24. Mainz: Matthias-Grünwald. *GW* 4: 175–88.

"Zu Immermanns Epigonen-Roman." In *Auf gespaltenem Pfad*, edited by M. Schlösser, 254–73. Darmstadt: Erato-Presse. *GW* 9: 193–206.

1965

"Die Grundlagen des zwanzigsten Jahrhunderts." In *Aspekte der Modernität*, edited by H. Steffen, 77–100. Göttingen: Vandenhoeck und Ruprecht. Retitled "Die philosophischen Grundlagen des zwanzigsten Jahrhunderts" in *GW* 4: 3–22. Trans.: "The Philosophical Foundations of the Twentieth Century." In *PH* (1976): 107–29.

"Kausalität in der Geschichte?" In *Ideen und Formen*, edited by F. Schalk, 93–104. Frankfurt: Klostermann. *GW* 4: 107–16.

"Die Kontinuität der Geschichte und der Augenblick der Existenz." In *Geschichte— Element der Zukunft*, edited by R. Wittram, H.-G. Gadamer, and J. Moltmann, 33–49. Tübingen: Mohr. *GW* 2: 133–45. Trans.: "The Continuity of History and the Existential Moment." *Philosophy Today* 16, nos. 3/4 (1972): 230–40.

"Mensch und Sprache." *Muttersprache* 75, no. 9: 257–62. *GW* 2: 146–54. Trans.: "Man and Language." In *PH* (1976): 59–68.

"Vom Verstummen des Bildes." *Neue Zürcher Zeitung*, 186th year, no. 2223 (May 23): 6 (both sides). GW 8: 315–22. Trans.: "The Speechless Image." In *RB* (1986): 83–91.

"Vorwort." In *WM*, 1st ed. (1960) and 2d ed. (1965): xiii–xxiv. Also in 3d ed. (1972) and 4th ed. (1974/75): xv–xxvi. *GW* 2: 437–48. Trans.: "Foreword to the Second German Edition of *Truth and Method*." In *After Philosophy: End or Transformation?*, edited by K. Baynes, J. Bohman, and T. McCarthy, 339–50. Cambridge: MIT Press, 1987.

1966

"Apologie der Heilkunst." In *Physiotherapie in Einzeldarstellungen* (Festschrift for Paul Vogler), edited by D. G. R. Findeisen, 2: 227–34. Leipzig: Barth. *VG* (1993): 50–64. *GW* 4: 267–75. Trans.: "Apologia for the Art of Healing." In *EH* (1996): 31–44.

"Das Gedicht zwischen Autor und Leser." *Merkur* 20, 5, 218th issue (May): 431–42 (by H.-G. Gadamer: 440–42). Titled "Hilde Domin, Lied zur Ermutigung II" in *GW* 9: 320–22.

"Notes on Planning for the Future." *Daedalus* 95: 572–89. Also in *Conditions of World Order*, edited by S. Hoffmann, 324–41. Boston: Houghton Mifflin Co., 1968. German text: "Über die Planung der Zukunft." In *GW* 2: 155–73. Trans. also in *EPH* (1992): 165–80.

"Die Universalität des hermeneutischen Problems." *Philosophisches Jahrbuch* 73 (1965/66): 215–25. *GW* 2: 219–31. Trans.: "The Universality of the Hermeneutical Problem." In *PH* (1976): 3–17; also in *The Hermeneutic Tradition,* ed. by G. L. Ormiston and A. D. Schrift, 147–58. Albany, N.Y.: SUNY Press, 1990.

"Die verkehrte Welt." In *Hegel-Tage Royaumont 1964,* edited by H.-G. Gadamer, 135–54. Bonn: H. Bouvier. "Hegel—die verkehrte Welt" in *HD* (1971): 7–30. *GW* 3: 29–46. Trans.: "The Inverted World." *The Review of Metaphysics* 28, no. 3 (Mar. 1975): 401–22, and as "Hegel's 'Inverted World'" in *HDt* (1976): 35–53.

"Vorgestalten der Reflexion." In *Subjektivität und Metaphysik,* edited by Dieter Henrich and H. Wagner, 128–43. Frankfurt: Klostermann. *GW* 6: 116–28.

"Zum Gedenken an Karl Reinhardt." *Neue Zürcher Zeitung* 187, no. 1918 (May 1): 5. Retitled "Die Krise des Helden." In *GW* 6: 285–91. Trans.: "Karl Reinhardt." In *PA* (1985): 127–34.

1967

"Anmerkungen zu dem Thema 'Hegel und Heidegger'." In *Natur und Geschichte,* edited by H. Braun and M. Riedel, 123–31. Stuttgart: W. Kohlhammer, 1967. Retitled "Die Sprache der Metaphysik." In *HW* (1983): 61–69. *GW* 3: 229–37. Trans.: "Heidegger and the Language of Metaphysics." In *PH* (1976): 229–40. Trans.: "The Language of Metaphysics." In *HWt* (1994): 69–79.

"Bach und Weimar." In *KS* 2 (1967): 75–81. Published earlier as a monograph in 1946; see sec. A. *GW* 9: 142–49. Trans.: "Bach and Weimar." In *LPD* (1994): 109–17.

"Bild und Gebärde." In *KS* 2 (1967): 210–17. *GW* 8: 323–30. Trans.: "Image and Gesture." In *RB* (1986): 74–82.

"Das Faktum der Wissenschaft." *Sitzungsberichte der Wissenschaftlichen Gesellschaft zu Marburg* 88, 1: 11–20.

"Goethe und die Philosophie." In *KS* 2 (1967): 82–96. Originally published as a monograph in 1947. Trans.: "Goethe and Philosophy." In *LPD* (1994): 1–20.

"Goethe und die sittliche Welt." In *KS* 2: 97–104. Given as a lecture in 1949. *GW* 9: 72–79. Trans.: "Goethe and the Moral World." In *LPD* (1994): 21–30.

"Die Grenzen des Expertentums." In *Darmstädter Gespräch,* edited by Karl Schlechta, 160–68. Darmstadt: Neue Darmstadter Verlagsanstalt. Trans.: "The Limitations of the Expert." In *EPH* (1992): 181–92.

"Kunst und Nachahmung." In *KS* 2: 16–26. Delivered as a lecture in 1966. *GW* 8:25–36. Trans.: "Art and Imitation." In *RB* (1986): 92–104.

"Mythopoietische Umkehrung in Rilkes Duineser Elegien." In *KS* 2: 194–209. Delivered as a lecture in 1966. *GW* 9: 289–305. Trans.: "Mythopoetic Inversion in Rilke's Duino Elegies." In *Hermeneutics Versus Science?* by J. M. Connolly and Thomas Keutner, 79–101. Notre Dame and London: University of Notre Dame Press, 1988. Also: "Mythopoietic Reversal in Rilke's *Duino Elegies.*" In *LPD* (1994): 153–71.

"Rhetorik, Hermeneutik, und Ideologiekritik." In *Hermeneutik und Ideologiekritik.* Frankfurt: Suhrkamp (1971): 283–17. Translation retitled "On the Scope and Function of Hermeneutical Reflection" by R. E. Palmer and G. B. Hess. *Continuum* 7 (1970): 77–95, and *PH* (1976): 18–43. Also in *Hermeneutics and Modern Philosophy,* edited by Brice R. Wachterhauser, 277–99. Albany, N. Y.: State University of New York Press, 1986. Also: "Rhetoric, Hermeneutics, and the Critique of Ideology," translated by J. Dibble in *The Hermeneutics: Reader,* edited by Kurt Mueller-Vollmer, 274–92. Oxford: Blackwell, 1986.

"Die Stellung der Philosophie in der heutigen Gesellschaft." In *Das Problem der Sprache: VIII: Deutscher Kongress für Philosophie—Heidelberg 1966,* 9–17. Munich: W. Fink. *GW* 10: 308–16.

"Vom geistigen Lauf des Menschen: Studien zu unvollendeten Dichtungen Goethes." In *KS* 2 (1967): 105–35. Originally published as a monograph in 1949. *GW* 9: 80–111. Trans.: "On the Course of Human Spiritual Development: Studies of Goethe's Unfinished Writings." In *LPD* (1994): 31–66.

1968

"Amicus Plato magis amica veritas." In *PDE* (1968): 249–68. *GW* 6: 71–89. Trans.: "Amicus Plato Magis Amica Veritas." In *DD* (1980): 194–218.

"Der Dichter Stefan George." *Duitse Kroniek* 20, no. 4 (Dec.): 126–48. Also in *Ruperto Carola* 20, no. 45 (Dec.): 102–11 and in *GG* (1990): 12–38. *GW* 9: 211–28.

"Dialektik und Sophistik im siebenten platonischen Brief." In *PDE* (1968): 221–47. Originally published as a monograph in 1964. Trans.: In *DD* (1980): 93–123.

"Hölderlin und George." *Hölderlin-Jahrbuch* 15 (1967/68): 75–91. *GW* 9: 229–44. Trans.: "Hölderlin and George." In *EPH* (1992): 93–109.

"Lyrik als Paradigma der Moderne." *PR* 15, no. 4: 291–99. Retitled "Zu Poetik und Hermeneutik: Lyrik als Paradigma der Moderne." In *GW* 8: 58–64. A review article of *Immanente Ästhetische, Ästhetische Reflexion* (essays by members of the "Hermeneutik und Poetik Arbeitsgruppe"), edited by Wolfgang Iser, 543pp. Munich: W. Fink, 1966.

"Metaphysik im Zeitalter der Wissenschaft." *Akten des Internationalen Leibniz-Kongresses Hannover* 1: 1–12.

"Plato und die Dichter." In *PDE* (1968): 179–204. Originally published as a monograph in 1934. *GW* 5: 187–211. Trans.: "Plato and the Poets." In *DD* (1980): 39–72.

"Platons ungeschriebene Dialektik." In *Idee und Zahl*, edited by H.-G. Gadamer and W. Schadewaldt, 9–30. Heidelberg: Carl Winter. *GW* 6: 129–53. Trans.: "Plato's Unwritten Dialectic." In *DD* (1980): 124–55.

"Das Problem der Sprache in Schleiermachers Hermeneutik." *Zeitschrift für Theologie und Kirche* 65, no. 4 (Dec.): 445–58. *GW* 4: 361–73. Trans.: "The Problem of Language in Schleiermacher's Hermeneutic," by David E. Linge. In *Schleiermacher as Contemporary: Journal for Theology and the Church* 7, edited by Robert W. Funk, 68–84, subsequent discussion on 85–95. New York: Herder and Herder, 1970.

1969

"Der Denker Martin Heidegger." In *Die Frage Martin Heideggers,* edited by H.-G. Gadamer, 62–68. Heidelberg: Carl Winter. Reprinted in *HW* (1983): 55–60. *GW* 3: 223–28. Trans.: "The Thinker Martin Heidegger." In *HWt* (1994): 61–67.

"Hermeneutik." In *Contemporary Philosophy: A Survey.* Vol. 3, *Metaphysics, Phenomenology, Language, and Structure,* edited by R. Klibansky, 360–72. Florence: La Nuova Italia. *GW* 2: 425–36. A general survey of hermeneutics issues during the decade ending 1966. Not the same as his 1974 encyclopedia article by the same title.

"Karl Jaspers." *Ruperto Carola* 21, no. 46 (June): 50–56. In *PL* (1977): 199–209. Trans.: *PA* (1985): 159–67.

"Menschenbild und Lebensgestaltung." *Hessische Hochschulwochen für staatswissenschaftliche Fortbildung* 63: 133–49.

"Schleiermacher platonicien." *Archives de philosophie* 32, no. 1: 28–39. German title: "Schleiermacher als Platoniker." In *GW* 4: 374–83.

"Über die Macht der Vernunft." *Wissenschaft und Weltbild* 22, no. 1: 1–8. In *LT* (1983): 51–66. Trans.: "The Power of Reason." *Man and World* 3 (Feb. 1970): 5–15.

"Über leere und erfüllte Zeit." In *Die Frage Martin Heideggers,* edited by H.-G. Gadamer, 17–35. Heidelberg: Carl Winter. *GW* 4: 137–53. Trans.: "Concerning

Empty and Fulfilled Time." *The Southern Journal of Philosophy* 8, no. 4 (1970): 341–54.

1970

"Begriffsgeschichte als Philosophie." *Archiv für Begriffsgeschichte* 24, no. 1 (1970): 137–51. *GW* 2: 77–91.

"Nachwort." In *Parmenides,* translated, introduced, and interpreted by Kurt Riezler, 92–102. Frankfurt: V. Klostermann. Retitled "Das Lehrgedicht des Parmenides." In *GW* 6: 49–57. On Reizler's interpretation of Parmenides' poem.

"Signification de la *Logique* de Hegel." *Archives de philosophie* 33, no. 4 (Oct.–Dec.): 675–700. Retitled "Die Idee der Hegelschen Logik." In *HD* (1971): 49–69. *GW* 3: 65–86. Trans.: "The Idea of Hegel's Logic." In *HDt* (1976): 75–99.

"Sprache und Verstehen." *Zeitwende* 41, no. 6 (Nov.): 364–77. *GW* 2: 184–98.

"Über das Göttliche im frühen Denken der Griechen." In *Das Altertum und jedes neue Gute: Festschrift für Wolfgang Schadewaldt,* 397–414. Stuttgart: Kohlhammer. *GW* 6: 154–70.

"Vereinsamung als Symptom von Selbstentfremdung." *Wissenschaft und Praxis in Kirche und Gesellschaft* 59, no. 3: 85–93. *LT* (1983): 123–38.

"Verstummen die Dichter?" *Zeitwende* 41, no. 5 (Sept.): 344–52. *GW* 9: 362–66. Trans.: "Are the Poets Falling Silent?" In *EPH* (1992): 73–81.

"Wer bin ich und wer bist Du? Zu einem Gedicht von Paul Celan." In *Die Zeit Jesu,* edited by G. Bornkamm and K. Rahner, 306–12. Freiburg/Basel/Vienna: Herder. Expanded into a book on the *Atemkristall* cycle of poems, see *WW* (1973), and further expanded in 1986. *GW* 9: 383–451 (based on 1986 version).

1971

"Des Dichters wahres Wort." *Neue Zürcher Zeitung* 192, no. 25 (Jan. 17): 49–50. *WW,* 1st ed. (1973): 99–109, but without the title. Also in *WW,* 2nd ed. (1986): 101–6, 109–11. *GW* 9: 422–27.

"Hegel und Heidegger." In *HD,* 1st ed. (1971): 83–96, and 2d ed. (1980): 99–112. *GW* 3: 87–101. Trans.: "Hegel and Heidegger." In *HDt* (1976): 100–16.

"Hegel: Vollendung der abendländischen Metaphysik?" In *Hegel, Hölderlin, Heidegger,* edited by H. Gehrig, 11–23. Karlsruhe: Badenia.

"Die heutige Unfähigkeit zum Gespräch als philosophisches Problem." *Universitas* 26, no. 12 (Dec.): 1295–304. Retitled "Die Unfähigkeit zum Gespräch." In *GW* 2: 207–15.

"Hilde Domin, Dichterin der Rückkehr." In "Literatur und Kunst" section of the *Neue Zürcher Zeitung* 192, no. 364: 37–38. *GW* 9: 323–28. Trans.: "Hilde Domin, Poet of Return." *The Denver Quarterly* 6, no. 4 (Winter 1972): 7–17.

"Historicité." *Encyclopaedia universalis.* Paris: Encyclopaedia Universalis. 8: 452–55.

"Kramms Kafka—Zyklus" in *Wilibald Kramm 1891–1969: Gemälde und Zeichnungen aus 35 Jahren.* Heidelberg. In a privately printed exhibition booklet celebrating the painter's 80th birthday. Revised and enlarged in 1991; see "Kafka und Kramm" (1991). *GW* 9: 353–61.

"Die nicht mehr schönen Künste." *PR* 18: 58–62. A discussion of *Die nicht mehr schönen Künste: Grenzphänomene des Ästhetischen,* edited by H. R. Jauß. Retitled "Zu Poetik und Hermeneutik: Die nicht mehr schönen Künste." In *GW* 8: 65–69.

"Replik." In *Hermeneutik und Ideologiekritik,* 283–317. Frankfurt: Suhrkamp. *GW* 2: 251–75. Trans.: "Reply to My Critics." In *The Hermeneutic Tradition,* edited by Gayle L. Ormiston and A. D. Schrift, 273–97. Albany, N.Y.: SUNY Press, 1990.

"Semantik und Hermeneutik." *Akten des 14. Internationalen Kongresses für Philosophie* 6 (Vienna, 2–9 Sept. 1968): 259–64. Vienna: Herder. *GW* 2: 174–83. Trans.: "Semantics and Hermeneutics." In *PH* (1976): 82–94.

"Wahrheit und Dichtung." *Zeitwende* 42, no. 6 (Nov.): 402–10. Retitled "Über den Beitrag der Dichtkunst bei der Suche nach der Wahrheit." In *KS* 4: 218–27 and *GW* 8: 70–79. Trans.: "On the Contribution of Poetry to the Search for Truth." In *RB* (1986): 105–15.

1972

"Dichtung und Nachahmung." In the "Literatur und Kunst" section of the *Neue Zürcher Zeitung* 193rd year, no. 315 (July 9): 53. Retitled "Dichtung und Mimesis." In *KS* 4 (1977): 228–33 and in *GW* 8: 80–85. Trans.: "Poetry and Mimesis." In *RB* (1986): 116–22.

"Die Gegenwartsbedeutung der Griechischen Philosophie." *Praktika tis Akadimias Athinon* (Athens, Greece) 47(Nov. 7): 243–65.

"Hegels Philosophie und ihre Nachwirkungen bis heute." *Akademiker Information: Bulletin der Vereinigung Vorarlberger Akademiker* (Breganz, Austria) 3: 15–21. *VW* (1972): 32–53. Trans.: "Hegel's Philosophy and Its Aftereffects until Today." In *RAS* (1981): 21–37.

"Hermeneutik als praktische Philosophie." In *Rehabilitierung der praktischen Philosophie,* edited by M. Riedel, 325–44. Freiburg: Rombach. *VW* (1976): 78–109. Not in *GW*. Trans.: "Hermeneutics as Practical Philosophy." In *RAS* (1981): 88–112, and in *After Philosophy,* edited by K. Baynes, J. Bohman, and T. McCarthy, 325–38. Cambridge: MIT Press, 1987.

"Logos und Ergon im Platonischen 'Lysis'." In *KS* 3 (1972): 50–63. *GW* 6: 171–86. Trans.: "*Logos* and *Ergon* in Plato's *Lysis*." In *DD* (1980): 1–20.

"Nachwort." In *WM*, 3d ed., 513–41. *GW* 2: 449–78.

"Das ontologische Problem des Wertes." In *Human Sciences and the Problem of Values,* edited by K. Kuypers, 17–31. The Hague: Nijhoff. *GW* 4: 189–202.

"Poesie heute." *PR* 18, nos. 1/2: 54–62. A review of three books: Hilde Domin's *Wozu Lyrik heute?* (1968), *Doppelinterpretationen,* edited by Hilde Domin (1966), and *Die nicht mehr schönen Künste,* edited by H. R. Jauß (1968).

"The Science of the Life-World." *Analecta Husserliana,* edited by A.-T. Tymieniecka, 2: 173–85. German: "Die Wissenschaft von der Lebenswelt" in *GW* 3: 147–59. Trans.: *PH* (1976): 182–97.

"Theorie, Technik, Praxis." *Neue Anthropologie,* edited by H.-G. Gadamer and P. Vogler, 1: ix–xxxvii. Stuttgart: G. Thieme. *VG* (1993): 11–49. *GW* 4: 243–66. Trans.: "Theory, Technology, Practice," by Howard Brotz. *Social Research* 44, no. 3 (1977): 529–61. Also translated in *EH* (1996): 1–30.

"Über die Naturanlage des Menschen zur Philosophie." *Neue Zürcher Zeitung* 109 (5 Mar.): 49–50. Originally published as a monograph in 1971.

"Was muß der Leser wissen?" *Neue Zürcher Zeitung* 193, no. 517 (Nov. 5): 53. *GW* 9 (Appendix to *Wer bin Ich und wer bist Du?,* 1986 ed.): 383–451.

"Welt ohne Geschichte?" In *Truth and Historicity/ Vérité et Historicité,* edited by H.-G. Gadamer, 1–8. The Hague: Nijhoff. *GW* 10: 317–23.

"Wissenschaft als Instrument der Aufklärung." *Evangelische Kommentare* 5, no. 10 (Oct.): 584–88. *LT* (1983): 88–102.

1973

"Gibt es die Materie?" In *Convivium Cosmologicum,* edited by A. Giannarás, 93–109. Stuttgart: Birkhäuser. *GW* 6: 201–17.

"Hegels Dialektik des Selbstbewußtseins." In *Materialien zu Hegels "Phänomenologie des Geistes,"* edited by H. F. Fulda and D. Henrich, 217–42. Frankfurt: Suhrkamp. Retitled "Die Dialektik des Selbstbewußtseins" in *GW* 3: 47–86. Trans.: "Hegel's Dialectic of Self-Consciousness." In *HDt* (1976): 54–72.

"Jusqu' à quel point la langue préforme-t-elle la pensée?" *Archivio di filosofia* 41, nos. 2/3: 63–70. German: "Wie weit schreibt Sprache das Denken vor?" *Zeitwende* 44, no. 5 (Sept. 1973): 289–96. *GW* 2: 199–206. Trans.: "To What Extent Does Language Preform Thought?" Appendix to *TM* (1976), 491–98; 2d ed. (1989), 542–49.

"Marburger Erinnerungen I (Studentenjahre)." *Alma mater philippina* (University of Marburg Association) (summer semester): 23–27. Trans.: "Marburg." In *PA* (1985): 7–12.

"La morte come problema." *Giornale critico della folosofia italiana* 52, no. 2: 221–32. "Der Tod als Frage." In *GW* 4: 161–72.

"Die Unsterblichkeitsbeweise in Platons *Phaidon.*" In *Wirklichkeit und Reflexion,* edited by H. Gahrenbach, 145–61. Pfullingen: Günther Neske. *GW* 6: 187–200. Trans.: "The Proofs of Immortality in Plato's *Phaedo.*" In *DD* (1980): 21–38.

1974

"Hermeneutik." *Historisches Wörterbuch der Philosophie* 3, cols. 1061–73. Original, lengthened text, "Klassische und philosophische Hermeneutik" in *GW* 2: 92–117.

"Marburger Erinnerungen II (Studentenjahre)." *Alma mater philippina* (Publication of the University of Marburg Association) (winter semester 1973–1974): 19–24. Trans.: "Marburg." In *PA* (1985): 12–19.

"Marburger Erinnerungen III (Niemandsjahre)." *Alma mater philippina* (summer semester): 15–19. Trans.: "No One's Years." In *PA* (1985): 35–44.

"'Nur wer mitgeht weiß daß es ein Weg ist'." *Bilder und Zeiten* 225 (Sept. 28): 2. Trans.: "Martin Heidegger." In *PA* (1977): 210–21. Reprinted as "Martin Heidegger—85 Jahre." In *HW* (1983): 94–102. *GW* 3: 262–70. Trans.: "Martin Heidegger—85 Years." In *HWt* (1994): 111–20.

"Philosophie oder Wissenschaftstheorie?" In *Interdisziplinäre Arbeit und Wissenschaftstheorie,* part 1, edited by H. Holzhey, 89–104. Stuttgart: Schwabe and Co. Also in *VW* (1976): 125–49. Trans.: "Philosophy or Theory of Science?" In *RAS* (1981): 151–69.

"Vom Anfang bei Heraklit." In *Sein und Geschichtlichkeit: Karl-Heinz Volkmann-Schluck zum 60. Geburtstag,* edited by I. Schüßler and W. Janke, 3–14. Frankfurt: Klostermann. *GW* 6: 232–41.

"Was ist Praxis?" *Universitas* 29, no. 11 (Nov.): 1143–58. *VW* (1976): 54–77. *GW* 4: 216–28. Trans.: "What is Practice?" In *RAS* (1981): 69–87.

"Ziehen an Drähten, ziehen von Puppen." *Bilder und Zeiten* 195 (Aug. 24): 4. Trans.: "Max Scheler." In *PA* (1977): 27–34.

"Zusammenfassender Bericht." In *Vérité et vérification,* edited by H. L. van Breda, 210–23. The Hague: M. Nijhoff. Retitled "Zur Aktualität der Husserlschen Phänomenologie." In *GW* 3: 160–71.

1975

"Hermeneutics and Social Science." *Cultural Hermeneutics* 2, no. 2: 307–16.

"Introduction." To his "The Problem of Historical Consciousness," trans. H. Fantel. *Graduate Faculty Philosophy Journal* 5, no. 1: 2–7. See "Das Problem des historischen Bewußtseins" in *KS* 4 (1977): 142–47. Translated in *Interpretive Social Science,* edited by P. Ravinow and W. M. Sullivan, 103–9. Los Angeles: University of California Press, 1979. 2d ed. (1987): 82–88.

"Kant und die philosophische Hermeneutik." *Kant-Studien* 66, no. 4: 395–403. Retitled "Kant und die hermeneutische Wendung" in *HW* (1983): 45–54. *GW* 3: 213–22. Trans.: "Kant and the Hermeneutical Turn." In *HWt* (1994): 49–59.

"Kunst als Spiel, Symbol, und Fest" in *Kunst heute,* edited by A. Paus, 25–84. Cologne: Styria. Trans.: "The Relevance of the Beautiful." In *RB* (1986): 3–53.

"Marburger Erinnerungen IV (Dozentenjahre)." In *Alma mater philippina* (University of Marburg Association) (winter semester 1974/75): 21–24. Trans.: "Teaching Years." In *PA* (1985): 69–81.

"Sinn und Sinnverhüllung." *Zeitwende* 46, no. 6 (Nov.): 321–29. Retitled "Sinn und Sinnverhüllung bei Paul Celan." In *GW* 9: 452–60.

1976

"Einführung." In *Seminar: Philosophische Hermeneutik,* edited by H.-G. Gadamer and G. Boehm, 7–40. Frankfurt: Suhrkamp.

"L'herméneutique philosophique." *Sciences religieuses: Revue canadienne* 5, no. 1 (summer): 3–13. A 1974 lecture at the University of Montreal.

"Logik oder Rhetorik? Nochmals zur Frühgeschichte der Hermeneutik." In *Archiv für Begriffsgeschichte* (Bonn: Bouvier) 20: 7–16. *GW* 2: 292–300.

"Philosophie und Hermeneutik." In *Philosophische Selbstbetrachtungen,* vol. 2 (edited by André Mercier et al.): 33–41. *KS* 4: 256–61.

"Plato und Heidegger." In *Der Idealismus und seine Gegenwart,* edited by U. Guzzoni, G. Rang, and L. Siep, 166–75. Hamburg: F. Meiner. *HW* (1983): 70–80. *GW* 3: 238–48. Trans.: "Plato and Heidegger." In *The Question of Being,* edited by M. Sprung, 45–53. University Park, Pa.: Pennsylvania State University Press, 1978. Retitled "Plato." In *HWt* (1994): 81–93.

"Rilke nach 50 Jahren." In *Insel-Almanach auf das Jahr 1977: Rainer Maria Rilke 1875–1975: Eine Dokumentation,* 61–78. Frankfurt: Insel. "Rainer Maria Rilke nach fünfzig Jahren." In *GW* 9: 306–19.

"Über das Philosophische in den Wissenschaften und die Wissenschaftlichkeit der Philosophie." In *VW:* 7–31. Trans.: "On the Philosophic Element in the Sciences and the Scientific Character of Philosophy." In *RAS* (1981): 1–20.

"Das Vaterbild im griechischen Denken" in *Das Vaterbild im Mythos und Geschichte,* edited by H. Tellenbach, 102–15. Stuttgart: Kohlhammer. *GW* 6: 218–31.

"Vorwort." In Hans Lipps, *Werke,* 1: vii–xi. Frankfurt: Klostermann. Trans.: "Hans Lipps." In *PA* (1985): 89–92.

1977

"Das Blatt zwischen uns." *Bilder und Zeiten,* a section of *FAZ* 36 (Feb. 12): 4. Retitled "Ernst Meister, Gedenken V." In *GW* 9: 347–48.

"Erinnerungen an Richard Kroner." *Bilder und Zeiten,* a section of *FAZ* 281 (Dec. 3): 6. Trans.: "Richard Kroner." In *PA* (1985): 83–87.

"Hans-Georg Gadamer." In *Philosophie in Selbstdarstellungen,* vol. 3, edited by L. J. Pongratz. Hamburg: F. Meiner, 60–101. *GW* 2: 479–508. Trans.: "On the Origins of Philosophical Hermeneutics." In *PA* (1985): 177–93; revised and retranslated, it forms the first part of Gadamer's "Reflections on My Philosophical Journey" in this LLP volume.

"Herméneutique et théologie," *Revue des sciences religieuses* 51, no. 4 (Oct.): 384–97.

"Ich und du die selbe Seele" in *PC:* 69–76. *GG* 64–69. *GW* 9: 245–48.

"Die Kunst des Feierns." In *Was der Mensch braucht,* edited by H. J. Schultz, 61–70. Stuttgart: Kreuz.

"Philosophie und Poesie." In *Geist und Zeichen,* edited by H. Anton, B. Gajek, and P. Pfaff, 121–26. Heidelberg: Carl Winter. *GW* 8: 232–39. Trans.: "Philosophy and Poetry." In *RB* (1986): 131–39.

"Prefazione." In Heidegger, *Che cos'é metafisica?,* translated by H. Künkler, A. Martone, and G. Raio, vii–xiii. Napoli: Libreria Tullio Pironti. "[Heidegger's] *Was ist Metaphysik?*" In *HW* (1983): 41–44. *GW* 3: 209–12. Trans.: "What Is Metaphysics?" In *HWt* (1994): 45–59.

"Rudolf Bultmann." *Das Parlament: Die Woche im Bundeshaus* (Bonn) 27, no. 28 (July 16): 8–9. Trans.: "Rudolf Bultmann." In *PA* (1977): 55–60. GW 10: 387–92.

"Sein Geist Gott." In *Heidegger,* edited by Werner Marx, 43–62. Freiburg: K. Alber. *HW* (1983): 152–63. *GW* 3: 320–32. Trans.: "Being, Spirit, God." In *Heidegger: Memorial Lectures,* edited by W. Marx, 55–74. Pittsburgh: Duquesne University Press, 1955. Also in *HWt* (1994): 181–95.

"Das Spiel der Kunst." In *KS* 4: 234–40. *GW* 8: 86–93. Trans.: "The Play of Art." In *RB* (1986): 123–30.

"Wissenschaft und Öffenlichkeit." *Diagnostik* 10, no. 4 (Oct.): 770–74. Trans.: "Science and the Public." *Universitas* 23, no. 3 (1981): 161–68.

"Die Zeitanschauung des Abendlandes." In *KS* 4: 17–33. *GW* 4: 119–36. Trans.: "The Western View of the Inner Experience of Time and the Limits of Thought." In *Time and Philosophies,* 33–48. Paris: UNESCO, 1979.

1978

"Ästhetische und religiöse Erfahrung." *Nederlands Theologisch Tijdschrift* 32, no. 3 (July): 218–30. *GW* 8: 143–55. Trans.: "Aesthetic and Religious Experience." In *RB* (1986): 140–53.

"Emilio Betti und das idealistische Erbe." *Quaderni Fiorentini* 7: 5–11. *GW* 10: 432–37.

"Die griechische Philosophie und das moderne Denken." In *Festschrift für Franz Wieacker,* edited by O. Behrends and others, 361–65. Göttingen: Vandenhoeck und Ruprecht. *GW* 6: 3–8.

"Hermeneutik als theoretische und praktische Aufgabe." *Rechtstheorie* 9, no. 3: 257–74. *GW* 2: 301–18. Trans.: "Hermeneutics as a Theoretical and Practical Task." In *RAS* (1981): 113–38.

"Thrasybulos Gorgiades." *Das Parlament: Die Woche im Bundeshaus* 28, no. 29 (22 July): 7–8. *GW* 10: 423–26. Eulogy.

1979

"Die Ausdruckskraft der Sprache." *Jahrbuch der Deutschen Akademie für Sprache und Dichtung,* 45–55. Trans.: "The Expressive Power of Language." *PMLA (Publications of the Modern Language Association)* 107, no. 2 (Mar. 1992): 345–52.

"Das Erbe Hegels." In H.-G. Gadamer and J. Habermas, *Das Erbe Hegels,* 35–64 and 86–94 (additional notes). Frankfurt: Suhrkamp. *GW* 4: 463–74. Trans.: "The Heritage of Hegel." In *RAS* (1981): 38–68, but not in *VW*.

"Heidegger und die Griechen." *Verifiche* 8, no. 1: 4–32. "Die Griechen" in *HW* (1983): 117–28 and in *GW* 3: 285–96. Trans.: "The Greeks." In *HWt* (1994): 139–52.

"Heidegger's Paths." Translated by C. Kayser and G. Stack in *Philosophic Exchange* 2, no. 2 (summer): 80–91. First published in German as "Der Weg in die Kehre" in *HW* (1983): 103–16. *GW* 3: 271–84. Translated by John Stanley as "The Way in the Turn." In *HWt* (1994): 121–37.

"Hermeneutik und bildende Kunst." *Neue Zürcher Zeitung* 200, no. 220 (Sept. 22/23): 65–66. Retitled "Über das Lesen von Bauten und Bildern." In *GW* 8: 331–38.

"Historical Transformations of Reason." In *Proceedings of the International Symposium on 'Rationality Today' held at the University of Ottawa, October 27–30, 1977,* edited by T. F. Geraets, 3–14. Ottawa: The University of Ottawa Press. German: "Rationalität im Wandel der Zeiten." In *GW* 4: 23–36.

"Nachwort." In H.-G. Gadamer and J. Habermas, *Das Erbe Hegels,* 65–84 and 88–94 (additional notes). Frankfurt: Suhrkamp. *GW* 4: 474–83.

"*Die politische Ontologie Martin Heideggers.*" In *PR* 26: 143–49. *GW* 10: 46–53. A review article of the 1975 book by Pierre Bourdieu.

"Der Vers und das Ganze." In *Das Stefan George Seminar 1978 in Bingen am Rhein,* edited by P. L. Lehmann and R. Wolff, 32–39. Heidelberg: L. Stiehm. *GW* 9: 249–57. Trans.: "The Verse and the Whole." In *EPH* (1992): 83–91.

1980

"Anschauung und Anschaulichkeit." *Neue Hefte für Philosophie* 18/19: 1–13. *GW* 8: 189–205. Trans.: "Intuition and Vividness." In *RB* (1986): 157–70.

"A Classical Text—A Hermeneutic Challenge." Translated by Fred Lawrence in *Revue de l'Université d'Ottawa* 50, nos. 3/4 (July–Oct.): 637–42. Also appears in the book version of this anniversary issue, *Contemporary Literary Hermeneutics and Interpretation of Classical Texts,* edited by Stephanus Kresic, 327–32. Ottawa: University of Ottawa Press, 1981. No published German text.

"Denken als Erlösung: Plotin zwischen Platon und Augustinus." *Archivio di filosofia* 48, nos. 2/3: 171–80. *GW* 7: 407–17.

"The Eminent Text and Its Truth." *The Bulletin of the Midwest Modern Language Association* 13, no. 1 (Feb.): 3–10, 11–23 (discussion). German: "Der 'eminente' Text und seine Wahrheit" in *GW* 8: 286–95.

"Idea and Reality in Plato's *Timaios.*" In *DD* (1980): 156–93. Originally published as a monograph, *Idee und Wirklichkeit in Platos Timaios* (1974).

"Lob der Theorie." *Reden und Gedenkworte des Ordens pour le mérite für Wissenschaften und Künste* 16: 67–91. *LT* (1983): 26–50. *GW* 4: 37–51.

"Practical Philosophy as a Model of the Human Sciences." *Research in Phenomenology* 9: 74–85.

"Probleme der praktischen Vernunft." In *Sinn und Geschichtlichkeit,* edited by J. Derbolav, C. Menze, and F. Nicolin, 147–56. Stuttgart: Klett-Cotta. *GW* 2: 319–29. Retitled "Vom Ideal der praktischen Philosophie." In *LT* (1983): 67–76. Trans.: "The Ideal of Practical Philosophy." *Notes et documents: Pour une recherche personnaliste* 11, no. 14 (Apr.–June 1986): 40–45.

"Religious and Poetical Speaking." In *Myth, Symbol, and Reality,* edited by A. M. Olson, 86–98. Notre Dame: University of Notre Dame Press. Presented in English; no German text.

"Was ist Geschichte? Anmerkungen zu ihrer Bestimmung." *Neue Deutsche Hefte* 27, no. 3: 451–56.

1981

"Das Alte und das Neue: Rede zur Eröffnung der Salzburger Festspiele 1981." In the *Offizielles Programm der Salzburger Festspiele,* 19–23. Vienna: Residenz Verlag. *GW* 4: 154–60. Trans.: "The Old and the New: Opening Address of the Salzburg Festival 1981." In *Offizielles Programm der Salzburger Festspiele* (Official Program of the Festival) (1981), 24–28.

"Existentialismus und Existenzphilosophie." *Neue Deutsche Hefte* 28, no. 4: 675–88. *HW* (1983): 7–17. *GW* 3: 175–85. Trans.: "Existentialism and the Philosophy of Existence." In *HWt* (1994): 1–13.

"Heidegger und die Geschichte der Philosophie." *Monist* 64, no. 4 (Oct.): 423–33. Retitled "Die Geschichte der Philosophie" in *HW* (1983): 129–39. GW 3: 297–307.

Trans.: "Heidegger and the History of Philosophy." *Monist* 64: 434–44. Trans.: "The History of Philosophy." In *HWt* (1994): 153–65.

"Die Kultur und das Wort." In *Kultur als christlicher Auftrag heute,* edited by A. Paus, 11–23. Graz: Stylia. Trans.: "Culture and Words." *Universitas* 24, no. 3 (1982): 179–88. Also in *Hermeneutics and the Poetic Motion,* translated by D. J. Schmidt, 11–23. Center for Research in Translation, SUNY at Binghamton, 1990.

"Mythos und Wissenschaft." In *Christlicher Glaube in moderner Gesellschaft* 2: 5–42. Freiburg: Herder. Appears as "Mythos und Logos," "Mythologie und Offenbarungsreligion," and "Der Mythos im Zeitalter der Wissenschaft" in *GW* 8: 170–73, 174–79, 180–88.

"Philosophie und Literatur." In *Phänomenologische Forschungen,* no. 11: 18–45. Freiburg: K. Alber. *GW* 8: 240–57. Trans.: "Philosophy and Literature." *Man and World* 18 (1985): 241–59.

"Von hier und heute geht eine neue Epoche der Weltgeschichte aus'." *Neue Zürcher Zeitung* 202, no. 152 (4/5 July): 59–60. Retitled "Kants *Kritik der reinen Vernunft* nach 200 Jahren: 'von hier und heute geht eine neue Epoche der Weltgeschichte aus'" in *GW* 4: 336–48. Trans.: "A New Epoch in the History of the World Begins Here and Now." In *The Philosophy of Immanuel Kant,* edited by J. Donovan and R. Kennington, 1–14. Washington, D.C.: Catholic University of America Press, 1985.

1982

"Martin Heidegger: *Sein und Zeit.*" *Die Zeit* 37, no. 47 (Nov. 19): 51. Titled "*Sein und Zeit*" in *Die Heidegger Kontroverse,* edited by J. Altwegg, 11–13. Frankfurt: Athenäum, 1988.

"Mathematik und Dialektik bei Plato." In *Physik, Philosophie, und Politik,* edited by K. M. Meyer-Abich, 229–44. Munich: C. Hanser. *GW* 7: 290–312.

"Philosophie und Philologie." *Neue Zürcher Zeitung* 203, no. 211 (Sept. 11/12): 68. *GW* 6: 271–77.

"The Conflict of Interpretations" and "Discussion [with Paul Ricoeur]." In *Phenomenology,* edited by R. Bruzina and B. Wilshire, 299–304 and 213–30. Albany, N.Y.: SUNY Press.

"Die religiöse Dimension in Heidegger." In *L'héritage de Kant,* 271–86. Paris: Beauchesne. *GW* 3: 308–19. First published in Spanish in 1980. Trans.: "The Religious Dimension in Heidegger" by D. Looney. In *Transcendence and the Sacred,* 193–207. Notre Dame: University of Notre Dame Press, 1981. Also translated as "The Religious Dimension" in *HWt* (1994): 167–80.

"Wertethik und 'praktische Philosophie'." In *Nicolai Hartmann 1882–1982,* edited by A. J. Buch, 113–22. Bonn: Bouvier. *GW* 4: 203–15.

"Zwischen Ferne und Nähe." *Neue Zürcher Zeitung* 203, no. 66 (Mar. 20/21): 67–68. Retitled "Das Türmerlied in Goethes *Faust*" in *GW* 9: 122–27.

1983

"Die Aufgabe der Philosophie." *Neue Zürcher Zeitung* 204, no. 30 (Feb. 5/6): 65–66.

"Das Drama Zarathustras." In *The Great Year of Zarathustra 1881–1981,* edited by D. Goicochea, 339–69. Lanham: University Press of America. Retitled "Nietzsche— der Antipode" in *GW* 4: 448–62. Trans.: "The Drama of Zarathustra," by T. Heilke. In *Nietzsche's New Seas,* edited by M. A. Gillespie and T. B. Strong, 220–31. Chicago: University of Chicago Press.

"Die Gegenwärtigkeit Hölderlins." *Hölderlin Jahrbuch* 23 (1982/83): 178–81. *GW* 9: 39–41.

"Die Idee der praktischen Philosophie." In *Praktika Pankosmiou Synedriou "Aristoteles"* *Thessaloniki 7–14 Augustu 1978* (Proceedings of the World Congress on Aristotle, *Thessaloniki, August 7–14, 1978*) 4: 386–92. Athens: Ministry of Culture and Sciences. *GW* 10: 238–46.

"Die Idee der Toleranz 1782–1982." In *LT* (1983): 103–22.

"Der platonische *Parmenides* und seine Nachwirkung." *Archivio di Filosofia* 51, nos. 1–3: 39–51. *GW* 7: 313–27. Trans.: "Plato's *Parmenides* and Its Influence," by M. Kirby. In *Dionysius* (Halifax, Canada) 7 (Dec.): 3–16.

"Platos Denken in Utopien." *Gymnasium: Zeitschrift für Kultur der Antike und humanistische Bildung* 90, nos. 4/5 (Oct.): 434–55. *GW* 7: 270–89.

"Die religiöse Dimension." In *HW* (1983): 140–51. *GW* 3: 308–19. Trans.: "The Religious Dimension." In *HWt* (1994): 167–80.

"Über den Zusammenhang von Autorität und kritischer Freiheit." *Schweizer Archiv für Neurologie, Neurochirurgie, und Psychiatrie* 133, no. 1: 11–16. Retitled "Autorität und kritische Freiheit" in *VG* (1993): 149–58. Trans.: "Authority and Critical Freedom." In *EH* (1996): 117–24.

"Unterwegs zur Schrift?" In *Schrift und Gedächtnis,* edited by A. and J. Assmann and C. Hardmeier, 10–19. Munich: W. Fink. *GW* 7: 258–69.

"Der Unvollendete und das Unvollendbare." *Neue Zürcher Zeitung* 204, no. 271 (Nov. 19/20): 65–66. *GW* 4: 429–35.

"Wort und Verheissung." *Neue Zürcher Zeitung* 20 (25–26 June 1983): 68. Retitled "Schreiben und Reden" in *GW* 10: 354–55.

"Die Zukunft der europäischen Geisteswissenschaften." In *Europa: Horizonte der Hoffnung,* edited by Franz König und Karl Rahner, 243–61. Graz: Styria. Also in *EE* (1989): 35–62. Trans.: "The Future of the European Humanities." In *EPH* (1992): 193–208.

1984

"Articulating Transcendence." In *The Beginning and the Beyond: Papers from the Gadamer and Voegelin Conferences,* edited by F. Lawrence, 1–12 (with discussion). Chico, Calif.: Scholars Press.

"Gibt es auf Erden ein Maß? (W. Marx)." Review article in *PR* 31, nos. 3/4: 161–77. *GW* 3: 333–49.

"The Hermeneutics of Suspicion." In *Hermeneutics,* edited by G. Shapiro and A. Sica, 54–65. Amherst, Mass.: University of Massachusetts Press. Also "The Hermeneutics of Suspicion." *Man and World* 17, nos. 3/4: 313–23. No published German text.

"Hören—Sehen—Lesen." In *Antike Tradition und Neuere Philologien,* edited by H.-J. Zimmermann, 9–18. Heidelberg: C. Winter. *GW* 8: 271–78.

"Reflexionen über das Verhältnis von Religion und Wissenschaft." In *Rudolf Bultmanns Werke und Wirkung,* edited by G. Jaspert, 295–300. Darmstadt: Wissenschaftliche Buchgesellschaft. *GW* 8: 156–62.

"Text und Interpretation. In *Text und Interpretation,* edited by P. Forget, 24–55. Munich : W. Fink. *GW* 2: 330–60. Trans.: "Text and Interpretation." In *GDE* (1989): 21–51.

"Und dennoch: Macht des Guten Willens." In *Text und Interpretation,* edited by P. Forget, 59–61. Munich : W. Fink. Trans.: "Reply to Jacques Derrida." In *GDE* (1989): 55–57.

1985

"Auf schwankendem Boden." *Bilder und Zeiten,* supplement to *FAZ* 225 (Sept. 28): 4. Retitled "Vom Wandel in den Geisteswissenschaften" in *GW* 10: 179–84.

"'Bürger zweier Welten'." In *Der Mensch in den modernen Wissenschaften,* edited by K. Michalski, 185–99. Stuttgart: Klett-Cotta. Also *EE* (1989): 106–25. *GW* 10: 225–37. Trans.: "Citizen of Two Worlds." In *EPH* (1992): 209–19.

"Destruktion und Dekonstruktion." First German publication in *GW* 2: 361–72. Trans.: *"Destruktion* and Deconstruction," by G. Waite and R. E. Palmer. In *GDE* (1989): 102–13. Originally published in Italian.

"Dilthey und Ortega." First German publication in *GW* 4: 436–47. Originally published in Spanish.

"Ende der Kunst?" In *Ende der Kunst,* edited by Bayerischen Akademie der Schönen Künste, 16–33. Munich: Deutscher Kunstverlag. *EE* (1989): 63–86. *GW* 8: 206–20.

"Freundschaft und Selbsterkenntnis." In *Wissenschaft und Existenz,* edited by D. Bremer and A. Patzer, 25–33. Würzburg: F. Schöningh. *GW* 7: 396–406.

"Gibt es auf Erden ein Maß? II [Continuation]," *PR,* 32, nos. 1/2: 1–26. Retitled "Ethos und Ethik (MacIntyre u. a.)" in *GW* 3: 350–74. Discusses also Reiner Schürmann's *Heidegger on Being and Acting: From Principles to Anarchy,* translated by C. Gros. Bloomington; Ind.: Indiana University Press, 1986, 406pp.

"Grenzen der Sprache." In *Evolution und Sprache: Über Entstehung und Wesen der Sprache,* edited by W. Böhme, 89–99. Karlsruhe: Selbstveröffentlichung durch Verlagsdruckeri G. Tron, 1985. *GW* 8: 350–61.

"Der Kunstbegriff im Wandel." In *Künste unserer Zeit,* edited by the University of Heidelberg, 7–19. Heidelberg: Heidelberger Verlagsanstalt und Druckerei. Also in *Kunst ohne Geschichte?,* 88–103. Munich: Beck, 1995.

"Die Natürlichkeit von Goethes Sprache." In *Allerhand Goethe,* edited by D. Kimpel and J. Pompetzki, 45–57. Frankfurt: Peter Lang. *GW* 9: 128–41.

"Stefan George 1863–1933." In *Die Wirkung Stefan Georges auf die Wissenschaft,* edited by H.-J. Zimmermann, 39–49. Heidelberg: C. Winter. Retitled "Die Wirkung Stefan Georges auf die Wissenschaft." In *GW* 9: 258–70.

"Wilhelm Dilthey nach 150 Jahren." In *Dilthey und die Philosophie der Gegenwart,* edited by E. W. Orth, 157–82. Freiburg: Karl Alber. Retitled "Das Problem Diltheys." In *GW* 4: 406–24.

                                    1986

"Die dreifache Aufklärung." *Neue Deutsche Hefte* 33, no. 2: 227–33.

"Der eine Weg Martin Heideggers." *Jahresgabe der Martin Heidegger-Gesellschaft,* 5–25. Wuppertal: Published by the Heidegger-Gesellschaft. *GW* 3: 417–30. Trans.: "Martin Heidegger's One Path," by P. C. Smith in *Reading Heidegger from the Start: Essays in His Earliest Thought,* edited by T. Kisiel and J. van Buren, 19–35. Albany, N.Y.: SUNY Press, 1994.

"Einleitung in den philosophischen Teil." In *Karl Jaspers,* edited by J. Hersch, J. M. Lochmen, and R. Wiehl, 200–206. Munich: R. Piper.

"Erinnerungen an Heideggers Anfänge." *Itinerari* (edited by G. Moretti, Editrice Itinerari Lanciano) 25, nos. 1/2: 5–16. *GW* 10: 3–13.

"Geburt der modernen Wissenschaft." *Rhein-Neckar-Zeitung* 42, nos. 18/19 (Oct.): 57. Also published as "Zwischen Aufklärung und Romantic: Heidelberg und die Geburt der modernen Wissenschaft" in *Die Sechhundertjahrfeier der Ruprecht-Karls Universität Heidelberg,* edited by Eike Wolgast, 38–45. Heidelberg: Edition Braus Heidelberg. Also published as a monograph: *Die Universität Heidelberg und die Geburt der modernen Wissenschaft.* Berlin: Springer, 21pp. *VG* (1993): 95–110. *GW* 10: 336–45. Trans.: "The University of Heidelberg and the Birth of Modern Science." In *EPH* (1992): 37–46.

"Naturwissenschaft und Hermeneutik." In *Filosofi och Kultur,* edited by Philosophy Circle in Lund under the Direction of Arno Werner, 39–70. Lund: Filosoficierkeln. Retitled "Natur und Welt" in *GW* 7: 418–42. Trans.: "Natural Science and Hermeneutics." In *Proceedings of the Boston Area Colloquium in Ancient Philosophy,* edited by J. J. Cleary, 1: 39–52. Lanham, Md.: University Press of America. Translates only the first part of the essay.

"Religion and Religiosity in Socrates." Translated by R. Velkley in *Proceedings of the Boston Area Colloquium in Ancient Philosophy,* edited by J. J. Cleary, 1: 53–75. Lanham, Md.: University Press of America. Retitled in German: "Sokrates' Frömmigkeit des Nichtwissens." In *GW* 7: 83–117.

"Die Stellung der Poesie im System der Hegelschen Ästhetik und die Frage des Vergangenheitscharakters der Kunst." In *Welt und Wirkung von Hegels Ästhetik,* edited by A. Gethmann-Seifert and O. Pöggeler, 213–23. Bonn: Bouvier Verlag H. Grundmann. *GW* 8: 221–31.

"Tradition und Autorität." In *Was halten sie von Thomas Mann?,* edited by M. Reich-Ranicki, 85–88. Frankfurt: Fischer.

"Vernunft und praktische Philosophie." In *Vernunft und Kontingenz: Rationalität und Ethos in der Phänomenologie,* edited by E. W. Orth, 174–85. Freiburg: Alber, 1986. *GW* 10: 259–66.

"Von Lehrenden und Lernenden." *Rhein-Neckar-Zeitung* 42, no. 163 (19/20 July): 45. *EE* (1989): 158–65. *GW* 10: 331–35.

"Zwischen Phänomenologie und Dialektik: Versuch einer Selbstkritik." First published in *GW* 2: 3–23. Translated by R. E. Palmer as the final section of Gadamer's "Reflections on My Philosophical Journey" in this LLP volume.

1987

"Die anthropologischen Grundlagen der Freiheit des Menschen." In *Hanns Martin Schleyer-Preis 1986 and 1987,* 53–62. Cologne: J. P. Bachem. *EE* (1989): 126–35.

"Bild-Gedicht-Gespräch." Introduction to *Dieter Stöver 1922–1984,* edited by H.-G. Gadamer, 2–10. Bod Tölz: Kunstverein Bad Tölz.

"Bruno Snell." *Das Parlament: Die Woche im Bundeshaus* 37, nos. 30/31 (July 25–Aug. 30): 11–12. *GW* 10: 437–40.

"Celans Schlußgedicht." In *Argumentum e Silentio,* edited by A. D. Colin, 58–71. Berlin: W. de Gruyter. Retitled "Im Schatten des Nilhilismus." In *GW* 9: 367–82. Trans.: "Under the Shadow of Nihilism." In *EPH* (1992): 111–23.

"Die deutsche Philosophie zwischen den beiden Weltkriegen." *Neue Deutsche Hefte* 34, no. 3: 451–67. Retitled "Zur deutschen Philosophie im 20. Jahrhundert" in *Philosophisches Lesebuch,* edited by H.-G. Gadamer, 3: 360–80. Frankfurt: Fischer, 1989. *GW* 10: 356–72.

"Die Erfahrung des Todes." In *GW* 4: 288–94. *VG* (1993): 84–94. Trans.: "The Experience of Death." In *EH* (1996): 61–69.

"Erinnerungen an Heideggers Anfänge." *Dilthey Jahrbuch für Philosophie und Geschichte der Geisteswissenschaften* 4 (1986/87): 13–26. *GW* 10: 3–13.

"Frühromantik, Hermeneutik, Dekonstruktivismus." In *Die Aktualität der Frühromantik,* edited by E. Behler and J. Hörisch, 251–60. Paderborn: F. Schöningh. *GW* 10: 125–37. Trans.: "Hermeneutics and Logocentrism," by R. E. Palmer and D. P. Michelfelder. In *GDE* (1989): 114–25.

"Heideggers Rückgang auf die Griechen." In *Theorie der Subjektivität,* edited by K. Cramer et al., 397–424. Frankfurt: Suhrkamp. Retitled "Auf dem Rückgang zum Anfang" in *GW* 3: 394–416.

"Historik und Sprache: Eine Antwort." In *Hermeneutik und Historik,* edited by W. Wieland, 29–36. Heidelberg: C. Winter. *GW* 10: 324–30. (Answers R. Koselleck's "Historik und Hermeneutik.")

"Vom Anfang des Denkens." First published in *GW* 3: 375–93.

"Zwischen Natur und Kunst." In *Viktor von Weizsäcker,* edited by P. Hahn and W. Jacob, 45–50. Berlin: Springer. Also in *VG* (1993): 111–20. Trans.: "Between Nature and Art." In *EH* (1996): 83–91.

1988

"Dekonstruktion und Hermeneutik." In *Philosophie und Poesie,* edited by A. Gethmann-Siefert, 1: 3–15. Stuttgart: F. Frommann, Günther Holzboog. *GW* 10: 138–47. Trans.: "Letter to Dallmayr." In *GDE* (1989): 93–101.

"Die Höhe erreichen." *Neue Zürcher Zeitung* 209, no. 283 (Dec. 3/4): 69–70. *GW* 9: 329–34.

"Die Idee der Universität: gestern, heute, morgen." In *Die Idee der Universität: Versuch einer Standortbestimmung,* 1–22. Berlin: Springer. Not in *GW.* Trans.: "The Idea of the University—Yesterday, Today, Tomorrow." In *EPH* (1992): 47–59.

"Gedicht und Gespräch." In *Lyrik—Erlebnis und Kritik,* edited by L. Jordan, A. Marquardt, and W. Woesler, 314–26. Frankfurt: Fischer. *GW* 9: 335–46.

"Geschichte des Universums und Geschichtlichkeit des Menschen." In *Geisteswissenschaften—wozu?,* 267–81. Stuttgart: Franz Steiner. *GW* 10: 206–22.

"Hegel und Heraklit." First German publication in *GW* 7: 32–42. Originally published in Italian.

"Lesen ist wie Übersetzen." In *Michael Hamburger: Dichter und Übersetzer,* edited by W. Eckel and J. J. Köllhofer, 117–24. Frankfurt: P. Lang, 1989. *GW* 8: 279–85. Originally published in Italian.

"Oberflächlichkeit und Unkenntnis: Zur Veröffentlichung von Victor Farias [book on Heidegger]." In *Antwort: Martin Heidegger im Gespräch,* edited by G. Neske and E. Kettering, 152–56. Pfullingen: Neske. First published in French as "Comme Platon à Syracuse: 'Peut-être nous demande-t-on de renoncer définitivement à penser?'." *Le nouvel Observateur,* no. 1211 (22–28 January): 45. Trans.: "'Back From Syracuse?'." *Critical Inquiry* 15, no. 2 (1989): 427–30.

"Parmenides oder das Diesseits des Seins." *La parola del passato: Rivista di studi antichi* (Naples) 43: 143–76. *GW* 7: 3–31.

"Ein philosophisches Postskriptum." In *Wo Sprache aufhört . . . : Herbert von Karajan zum 5. April 1988,* edited by H. Götze und W. Simon, 149–53. Berlin: Springer. Retitled "Musik und Zeit: Ein philosophisches Postscriptum." In *GW* 8: 362–65.

"Reply to Nicholas P. White." In *Platonic Writings—Platonic Readings,* edited by C. L. Griswold Jr., 258–66, 299–300. London: Routledge. Answering White's paper, "Observations and Questions about H.-G. Gadamer's Interpretation of Plato." First published in German as "Zur platonischen 'Erkenntnistheorie'." In *GW* 7: 328–37.

"Das Sein und das Nichts." In *Sartre: Ein Kongreß,* edited by T. König, 37–52. Hamburg: Rowohlts Taschenbuch Verlag. GW 10: 110–24.

"Über die politische Inkompetenz der Philosophie." *Sinn und Form: Beiträge zur Literatur* 45, no. 1 (Jan.–Feb. 1993): 5–12. Originally published in Italian in 1988.

"Von der Wahrheit des Wortes." *Denken und Dichten bei Martin Heidegger: Fünf Vorträge,* 7–22. Published by the Heidegger Gesellschaft. Retitled "Dichten und Denken im Spiegel von Hölderlins 'Andenken'." In *GW* 9: 42–55. Trans.: "Poetizing and Thinking," by R. E. Palmer. In *Heidegger Towards the Turn: Essays on the Work of the 1930's,* edited by J. Risser. Albany, N.Y.: SUNY Press, 1996.

1989

"Anfang und Ende der Philosophie." In *Heideggers These vom Ende der Philosophie: Verhandlungen des Leidener Heidegger-Symposiums April 1984,* edited by M. F. Fresco and others, 7–19. Bonn: Bouvier. Trans.: "The Beginning and the End of Philosophy." In *Martin Heidegger: Critical Assessments,* edited by C. Macann, 16–28. London: Routledge.

"Ethos und Logos." In *ANOXOΣ: Festschrift für Helmut Kuhn,* edited by R. Hofmann, J. Jantzen, and H. Ottmann, 23–34. Weinheim: VCH Verlagsgesellschaft. Retitled "Aristoteles und die imperativische Ethik" in *GW* 7: 381–95.

"Gadamer über Gadamer: 'Platos dialektische Ethik'—Beim Wort genommen." *FAZ* 112 (May 17): 3N–4N. *GW* 7: 121–27. Trans.: "Gadamer on Gadamer." In *Gadamer and Hermeneutics: Science, Culture, Literature,* edited by H. J. Silverman, 13–19. New York: Routledge, 1991.

"Gesang Weylas." In *Verlust und Ursprung: Festschrift für Werner Weber,* edited by A. Maass and B. Heinser, 169–73. Zürich: Ammann Verlag. *GW* 9: 207–10.

"Die Grenzen des Experten." First published in *EE:* 136–57.

"Heidegger und die Griechen." In *Zur philosophischen Aktualität Heideggers,* edited by D. Papenfuss and O. Pöggeler, 1: 57–74. Frankfurt: Klostermann, 1991. *GW* 10: 31–45.

"Heidegger und die Sprache." In *Martin Heidegger—Faszination und Erschrecken: Die politische Dimension einer Philosophie,* edited by P. Kemper, 95–113. Frankfurt/New York: Campus Verlag. *GW* 10: 14–30.

"Heideggers 'theologische' Jugendschrift." *Dilthey Jahrbuch für Philosophie und Geschichte der Geisteswissenschaften* 6: 228–34. Introduces the document.

"Kultur und Medien." In *Kultur und Medien,* edited by H.-G. Gadamer and G. Pflug, 4–19. Hamburg: Freie Akademie der Künste. Trans.:"Culture and Media," by B. Fultner. In *Cultural-Political Interventions in the Unfinished Project of Enlightenment,* edited by A. Honneth, T. McCarthy, C. Offe, and A. Wellmer, translated by B. Fultner, 172–88. Cambridge: MIT Press, 1992.

"Der Mensch als Naturwesen und als Kulturträger." In *Mensch und Natur,* edited by G. Fuchs, 9–30. Frankfurt: Verlag J. Knecht.

"Die Vielfalt Europas: Erbe und Zukunft." In *EE* (1989): 7–34. Originally published as a monograph in 1985. Trans.: "The Diversity of Europe: Inheritance and Future." In *EPH* (1992): 221–36.

1990

"Denken im Gedicht." In Frank Bernhard, *Der Kopf: Zeichnungen,* edited by Erich Thies, 7–11. Stuttgart: Edition Cantz, 1990. *GW* 9: 349–52.

"Erinnerung." *Jahrbuch der Deutschen Schillergesellschaft,* 34: 464–68. (Of Heidegger.)

"Die Gegenwart der sokratischen Frage in Aristoteles." In *Zur Rekonstruktion der praktischen Philosophie: Gedenkschrift für Karl—Heinz Ilting,* edited by K. O. Apel and R. Pozzo, 17–25. Stuttgart: F. Frommann Verlag—G. Holzboog. Retitled "Die sokratische Frage und Aristoteles" in *GW* 7: 373–80.

"Heidegger und die Sprache." In *Martin Heidegger—Faszination und Erschrecken,* edited by P. Kemper, 95–113. Frankfurt: Campus Verlag. *GW* 10: 14–30.

"Das Philosophische und die praktische Medizin." *Internationale Allgemeinmedizin und Hochschule,* a supplement of the *Zeitschrift für Allgemeinmedizin* 21, no. 223 (April 30): 1511–14. Also "Philosophie und praktische Medizin." In *VG* (1993): 121–32. Trans.: "Philosophy and Practical Medicine." In *EH* (1996): 92–102.

1991

"Dialektik ist nicht Sophistik: Theätet lernt das im *Sophistes*." First publication in *GW* 7: 338–69.

"Geschichtlichkeit und Wahrheit: Zur versäumten Fortsetzung von Gesprächen in Walberberg." In *Versöhnung: Versuche zu ihrer Geschichte und Zukunft*, edited by T. Eggensperger, U. Engel, O. H. Pesch, 17–28. Mainz: Matthias Grünewald. *GW* 10: 247–58.

"Hegel und die Sprache der Metaphysik I and II." In *Sprache und Ethik im technologischen Zeitalter: Bamberger Hegelwoche 1990*, 11–23 and 25–38. Bamberg: Verlag Fränkischer Tag.

"Heraklit—Studien." First published in *GW* 7: 43–82. From a lecture given in 1984.

"Die Hermeneutik und die Diltheyschule." *PR* 38, no. 3: 161–77. *GW* 10: 185–205.

"Kramm und Kafka." In *Willibald Kramm: Kafka und die 50er Jahre*, edited by Riccardo Dottori, 26–32. Milan: Gabriele Mazzotta. *GW* 9: 353–61.

"Phänomenologischer und semantischer Zugang zu Celan?" In *Paul Celan "Atemwende": Materialien*, edited by G. Buhr and R. Reuß, 311–17. Würzburg: Königshausen und Neumann. *GW* 9: 461–69.

"Über die Verborgenheit der Gesundheit." *Erfahrungsheilkunde: Acta medica empirica* 40, no. 11 (Nov.): 804–8. Also in *VG* (1993): 133–48. Trans.: "On the Enigmatic Character of Health." In *EH* (1996): 103–16.

"Vergänglichkeit." In *Uraufführung Vergänglichkeit: Musik von Dieter Schnebel, Theater- und Bilderversionen von Achim Freyer* (Program for May 12 presentation in Hamburg), 11–16. Hamburg: Hamburgische Staatsoper. *GW* 9: 171–79.

"Die Vielfalt der Sprachen und das Verstehen der Welt." In *Sprache: Vorträge im Sommersemester 1990*, edited by the University of Heidelberg, 165–75. Heidelberg: Heidelberger Verlagsanstalt, 1990. *GW* 8: 339–49.

1992

"Hermeneutics and Psychiatry." Translated by Otto Dörr-Zegers in *Revista chilena de neuro-psiquiatria: Organo oficial de la Sociedad de Neurologia, Psiquiatria y Neurocirugia*, 46th year, 30 (July–Sept.): 189–92. First published in German as "Hermeneutik und Psychiatrie." In *VG* (1993): 201–13. Also translated in *EH* (1996): 163–73.

"Humanismus heute?" In *Die Wissenschaft und das Gewissen: Antike als Grundlage für Deutung und Bewältigung heutiger Probleme*, 57–70. Württemberg: Württembergischer Verein zur Förderung der humanistischen Bildung.

"Mozart und das Problem der Oper." In *Mozarts Opernfiguren: Grosse Herren, rasende Weiber—gefährliche Liebschaften* (Mozart's opera figures: great men, furious women—dangerous affairs), edited by Dieter Borchmeyer, 233–45. Bern: Verlag Paul Haupt. Retitled "Goethe und Mozart—das Problem Oper" in *GW* 9: 112–21.

"Rückkehr aus dem Exil." In *Grenzüberschreitungen: Baden—Württembergische Literaturtage in Karlsruhe*, edited by R. Kress-Fricke, 123–31. Karlsruhe: Edition G. Braun. Retitled "Heimat und Sprache." In *GW* 8: 366–72.

1993

"Angst und Ängste." A 1990 lecture first published in *VG* 189–200. Trans.: "Anxiety and Anxieties." In *EH* (1996): 152–62.

"Behandlung und Gespräch." A 1989 lecture first published in *VG* 159–75. Trans.: "Treatment and Dialogue." In *EH* (1996): 125–40.

"Europa und die Oikoumene." In *Europa und die Philosophe,* edited by Hans-Helmuth Gander, 67–86. Frankfurt: Klostermann, 1993. *GW* 10: 267–84.

"Leben und Seele." A 1986 lecture first published in *VG* 176–88. Trans.: "Life and Soul." In *EH* (1996): 141–51.

"Leiberfahrung und Objektivierbarkeit." In *Festschrift aus Anlaß der Verleihung des Dr. Margit Egnér Preises 1986 zum Thema "Das Problem des Leibes,"* 33–43. *VG,* 95–110. Trans.: "Bodily Experience and the Limits of Objectification." In *EH* (1996): 70–82.

"Paul Friedländer." *Eikasmos* 4: 179–81. *GW* 10: 403–5. A recollection.

"Philosophizing in Opposition: Stauss and Voegelin on Communication and Science." In *Faith and Political Philosophy: The Correspondence between Leo Strauss and Eric Voegelin 1934–1964,* edited and translated by P. Emberley and B. Cooper, 249–59. University Park: Pennsylvania State University Press.

"Stimme und Sprache." First published in *GW* 8: 258–70. A 1981 lecture to the Romanistics Seminar at the University of Heidelberg.

"Von der Wahrheit des Wortes." First published in *GW* 8: 37–57. From a 1971 presentation to a colloquium at the University of Toronto in Canada.

"Wahrheit und Methode: Der Anfang der Urfassung [ca. 1956]." Edited by Jean Grondin and Hans-Ulrich Lessing. *Dilthey Jahrbuch für Philosophie und Geschichte der Geisteswissenschaften* 8 (1992–1993): 131–42.

"Wort und Bild—'so wahr, so seiend'." First published in *GW* 8: 373–99.

"Zur Phänomenologie von Ritual und Sprache." First published in *GW* 8: 400–440.

1994

"Arbeiterstudium und Universität." *Kultur und Kritik: Leipziger philosophische Zeitschrift* 6 (Mar.): 112–22.

"Nausikaa." In *Der altsprachliche Unterricht.* Ernst Klett Schulbuchverlag, 2: 6–11.

1995

"A Conversation with Hans-Georg Gadamer [by Alfons Grieder]." *Journal of the British Society for Phenomenology* 26, no. 2 (May): 116–26.

"Denken und Dichten bei Heidegger und Hölderlin." First published in *GW* 10: 76–83. From a 1987 Heidegger-Gesellschaft presentation. Thematically related but not the same: "Von der Wahrheit des Wortes" (1988), *GW* 9: 42–55.

"Die Einheit der Welt und die Vielfalt der Kultur." *Akademie-Journal* (Mainz: Philipp von 'Zaserm) 1: 2, 4.

"Golden blüht der Baum der Gnaden." In *Drei Zeilen trage ich mit mir,* edited by Richard Riess, 187–91. Freiburg: Herder.

"Hans-Georg Gadamer: Interview with Christiane Gehron and Jonathan Rée." *Radical Philosophy* (Jan./Feb.): 27–35.

"Heidegger und die Soziologie: Bourdieu und Habermas." *GW* 10: 46–57. The discussion of Bourdieu originally appeared in 1979 as a review article in *PR* of Bourdieu's *Die politische Ontologie Martin Heideggers* (1975).

"Hermeneutik auf die Spur." First published in *GW* 10: 148–74. On Derrida. Written in 1994.

"Hermeneutik und ontologische Differenz." First published in *GW* 10: 58–70. (Written 1989.)

"Die Kehre des Weges." First published in *GW* 10: 71–75.

"Der Kunstbegriff im Wandel." In *Kunst ohne Geschichte?* edited by Anne M. Bonnet and Gabrielle Kopp-Schmidt, 88–103. Munich: Beck.

"Mit der Sprache denken." First published in *GW* 10: 345–53. A supplement to two previ-ous self-evaluations: first, the "Selbstdarstellung" of 1973 (see *GW* 2: 479–508) and "Zwischen Phänomenologie und Dialektik-Versuch einer Selbstkritik" written espe-cially for the 1986 publication of *WM* in *GW* (see *GW* 2: 3–23). This essay supple-ments these by dealing principally with the post-retirement period (after 1968), especially his experiences in America. With minor modifications, the three self-evaluations, translated, make up his "Reflections on My Philosophical Journey," pub-lished in this volume.

"Phänomenologie, Hermeneutik, Metaphysik." First German publication in *GW* 10: 100–109. Original publication was in Spanish in *Cuadernos de filosofia y letras* 6, nos. 1/2 (1983): 9–14.

"Subjektivität und Intersubjektivität: Subjekt und Person." First German publication in *GW* 10: 87–99. Based on a lecture in Dubrovnic in 1975.

"Vom Wort zum Begriff: Die Aufgabe der Hermeneutik als Philosophie." In *Menschliche Endlichkeit und Kompensation,* edited by Odo Marquard et al., 111–24. Bamberg: Fränkischer Tag Verlag. Subsequently in *MGV* (1996), 19–40. Not in *GW*.

1996

"Hermeneutik—Theorie und Praxis." In *Psychoanalyse heute und vor 70 Jahren,* edited by Heinz Weiss und Hermann Lang, 359–68. Tübingen: Diskord.

D. Published Interviews and Archival Tapes

Introduction to Published Interviews

Professor Gadamer has over the years engaged in interviews and conversations that have been recorded and subsequently published. Etsuro Makita's *Gadamer-Bibliographie: 1922–1994* (to be updated every ten years) lists over three dozen published interviews Gadamer has given. Since his retirement in 1968, Gadamer has also appeared on radio and television with increasing frequency. Tapes of these lectures and interviews generally exist in radio and TV archives; the section after the published interviews will be devoted to archival tapes of radio and TV interviews, lectures, and discussions. These have not been previously documented.

Interviews, either published or archivally tape-recorded, have a special importance in relation to Gadamer's philosophy for several reasons. First, they vividly embody the dia-logical openness he advocated and picture a man answering questions on many topics with engaging flexibility. Second, they are especially accessible because they are designed for a general rather than specialized audience and thus they help bridge the gap between a great philosopher immersed in his philosophy and the mundane world of non-philosophers. Third, they take us into the life history of Gadamer in a very vivid way. In interviews, for instance, Gadamer answers questions about the era of National Socialism, that oppressive chapter of German history he managed to survive.[1]

---

1. The information in these interviews becomes additionally important in light of Teresa Orozco's recent study, *Platonische Gewalt: Gadamers Politische Hermeneutik der NS-Zeit* (Hamburg: Argu-ment Verlag, 1995). Based on a very small number of his writings in the period, Orozco alleges that his two writings on Plato and one on Herder during this period demonstrate Gadamer's complicity with the Nazis. But Gadamer was specialized in Plato long before the Nazis, writing his doctoral and promotion theses on Plato already in 1922 and 1928, long before the era of National Socialism. Also,

Because the published interviews are so well documented in Makita's bibliography, the list presented below can be very short. When an entry below appears here and also in that bibliography—generally in much fuller detail—I have indicated this by placing an M after it. The few entries I have repeated here are ones that seemed of special interest either because of their topic or their availability in English or Spanish or French.

A Few of the Published Interviews

1981   "HGG et le pouvoir de la philosophie" (interview by Philippe Forget and Jacques le Rider). *Le Monde Dimanche,* 19 April 1981, xi–xii. An interview just before the symposium with Derrida and others which was published in 1984 as *Text und Interpretation,* edited by Philippe Forget. Cf. Gadamer's essay, "Text und Interpretation" (1984 and *GW* 2), and its English translation in *GDE* (1989). M

1988   "Interview with HGG" (by Roy Boyne)." *Theory, Culture, and Society* 5 (1988): 25–34. M

1989   "Dialogo con HGG" (on ethics). *Cuadernos de Etica: Asociacion argentina de investigaciones eticas,* 68–86. (Spanish.) M

Gadamer's essay on Herder did not endear him to the Nazis but actually put him at risk because the Nazis saw Herder as encouraging Panslav nationalism. Furthermore, the Nazis early lost interest in Plato when a prominent Platonist scholar proposed on the basis of Plato's *Republic* that under National Socialism interest not be charged on loans. An entirely independent review by Stefan Breuer in the *Frankfurter Allgemeine Zeitung* (Dec. 4, 1995)—titled "Mit Platon in den Führerstaat? Tersa Orozcos Analyse von Gadamers Wirken unter dem Nationalsozialismus überzeugt nicht"— found its argument "unpersuasive" *(überzeugt nicht).* I myself found the book a depressing exercise in character assassination that was more an imitation of Nazism than a cure for it. Interviews are one public place where Gadamer had openly discussed his experiences under National Socialism. On the other hand, his view is that direct reply to such preposterous allegations only gives them undeserved attention. In his memoir, *Philosophical Apprenticeships* (1977), in his shorter autobiographical sketch in this volume, and in published and archivally recorded interviews, he sufficiently discusses his relation to Heidegger's Nazism and his own basically liberal political views then and now. The facts are a matter of record. It is quite clear that Gadamer was taking refuge in Plato rather than seeking to please the Nazis.

Basically Gadamer's behavior in that era followed the pattern of those intellectuals opposed to Hitler who chose not to leave the country or commit pointless political suicide. Where refusal to go along would have meant immediate loss of his job or life, he went along, as when he signed a statement of solidarity along with many other nonparty educators. He avoided criticism of the Nazis in his public lectures, which in a police state would have been suicidal, and he was several times questioned by the Gestapo and only the intervention of friends saved him from probable liquidation. Gadamer is far from qualifying as one of the "Ideological Powers in German Fascism" (the name of the series in which Orozco published her study). Indeed, he was elected Rektor of Leipzig University immediately after the end of the war *because his noncomplicity with the Nazis was well known.* From the beginning, Gadamer privately had nothing but contempt for the Nazis, an attitude shared by his intellectual friends at Marburg. He never took a leadership role of any kind on behalf of National Socialism. He freely admits in interviews he underestimated the danger posed by the Nazis. The most one can reproach Gadamer with is that at a time when his Jewish friends were having to emigrate and were being deprived of their positions, he did not himself choose to emigrate in sympathy, or take actions that would have led to his immediate arrest. Rather, sensing himself to be under surveillance by the Gestapo, he made the compromises necessary to survive in a police state. By not taking action when it would probably have been suicidal, he outlived the defeat of Hitler. It is grotesque, however, to characterize Gadamer as "an ideological power in Fascism," and to do so is intellectually and morally irresponsible.

1990   "'Die wirklichen Nazis hatten doch gar kein Interesse an uns': HGG im Gespräch
        mit Dörte von Westerhagen." *Das Argument: Zeitschrift für Philosophie und
        Sozialwissenschaften* (Hamburg) issue 182, vol. 32, 4 (July–Aug.): 543–55. M

1991   "Gadamer: Un siglo de pensamiento." Interviewed by Isidoro Reguera. *Diario 16*
        (Madrid), 2 March, "Culturas" section.

1992   "Conversaciones con HGG" (by Fernando Zabala Caussin). *Revista Faro:
        Revista de Filosofía,* no. 2, 121–41. (Journal published by Universidad de
        Playa Ancha de Ciencias de la Educación, Valparaiso, Chile.)

1992   *Hans-Georg Gadamer on Education, Poetry, and History: Applied Hermeneutics.*
        EPH contains four interviews, including "The German University and German
        Politics: The Case of Heidegger" (1992) and "The 1920s, 1930s, and the Pres-
        ent: National Socialism, German History, and German Culture." M

1993   *Hermeneutik-Ästhetik-Praktische Philosophie: HGG in Gespräch.* 80pp. An
        excellent series of interviews on these three topics in HGG. M

1993   "Russen in Deutschland: HGG in Gespräch mit Vladimir Malachov." *Mesotes* 3,
        no. 1: 145–51.

1994   "Ein Kind, das Angst hat: Gespräch mit HGG über Sokrates und das Christen-
        tum" (with Rüdiger Offergeld). *Lutherische Monatshefte* 12: 24–26.

1995   "A Conversation with HGG (by Alfons Grieder)." *Journal of the British Society
        for Phenomenology* 26, no. 2 (May): 116–26.

1995   "HGG: 'Without poets there is no philosophy.'" Interview with Christiane
        Gehron and Jonathan Rée. *Radical Philosophy* (Jan./Feb.): 27–35. Discusses
        Marxism, democracy, and German politics.

1995   "An der Sklavenkette: Hans-Georg Gadamer, Nestor der deutschen Philosophie,
        über die Gefahren der Fernsehgesellschaft." *Die Woche,* 11 Feb.

1995   "Nein, das letzte Wort will ich gar nicht haben: Ein Gespräch mit dem
        Philosophen HGG über die gewaltlose Macht der Sprache." *Frankfurter Rund-
        schau,* 11 Feb., feuilleton, p. 8.

Introduction to Archival Radio and Television Tapes

In addition to his university lectures, which were often tape-recorded, many individual
public lectures Gadamer gave were recorded, transcribed, and revised for publication.[2]

---

2. Gadamer gave lectures all over the world, especially in Europe, the U.S., and Canada after his
retirement, and these were often recorded and later published. I have not attempted to track these
down. Indeed, Gadamer is regarded as something of a celebrity in Italy, so when he visits he is very
often featured on television (he speaks Italian). I have also not listed Italian broadcasts, except the
impressive series of philosophy multimedia discussions on RAI in 1993, which in the future will
include a lecture by Gadamer on his own philosophy. A set of twenty lectures (in German) done in

Tapes and often transcripts of lectures, discussions, and interviews on German radio and television are archived in a number of the over twenty radio/television archives in Germany. These tapes are in general available for scholarly use, although a small fee is usually charged for copying from their archival reel-to-reel tapes to a cassette, which is loaned for scholarly use and to be returned. In many cases, a transcript of the broadcast is also available for scholarly use (with appropriate copying fee), but permission for public rebroadcast or republication requires a substantial fee. Inquiries about either scholarly use or public rebroadcasting/republication fees should be directed to the individual broadcasting agencies listed below.[3] In the listing of Gadamer's radio and television broadcasts, the following abbreviations will be used to indicate the archival sources.

List of Archives

BR   — Bayerischer Rundfunk, Rundfunkplatz 1, D-80335 München.
DLR and DLF — DeutschlandRadio Köln, Raderberggürtel 40, D-50968 Köln.
DRA   — Deutsches Rundfunkarchiv Frankfurt, 8 Bertramstr., D-60320 Frankfurt am M. 1.
HR   — Hessischer Rundfunk, Bertramstr. 8, D-60320 Frankfurt am M.
NDR   — Norddeutscher Rundfunk, Fernsehstudio Lokstedt, Gazellenkamp 57, D-22504 Hamburg.
RAI   — Radiotelevision Italiana, Enciclopedia multimediale delle Scienze Filosofiche, Redazione Mondo 3, Via Salaria 1033, 00138 Roma, Italy.
SDR   — Süddeutscher Rundfunk, Neckarstr. 230aD, Postfach 10 60 40, D-70049 Stuttgart.
SWF   — Südwestfunk, Hans-Bredow-Straße, D, Postfach 8 20, 76485 Baden-Baden.
UHML   — Uni-Heidelberg Media Library (also: Archiv), Plöck 107, D-69117 Heidelberg.
WDR   — Westdeutscher Rundfunk, Appellhofplatz 1, D-50667 Köln
ZDF/3sat   — Zweites Deutsches Fernsehen/3sat Zentralredaktion, Postfach 40 40, D-55100 Mainz.

The Order of Listing within the Entry

The following list is in chronological order. The first item in each listing is the year and *month of take* (not date of broadcast unless date of take is not available), followed by an

---

Italy will be edited down to eight lectures on the history of philosophy and is scheduled for broadcast late in 1996 (see below).

3. A list of current archive director names, addresses, and phone or fax numbers for the over twenty German tape-archives may be obtained from DRA in Frankfurt. I want to thank archivist Walter Roller of the DRA Frankfurt, as well as producer Ulrich Boehm of WDR in Cologne, and archivists Ulf Scharlau and Brigitte Grimm of SDR in Stuttgart, and Wolfgang Hempel, Klemens Helmholz, and Klaus Schäfer of SWF for indispensable help in providing the data for this list. I also thank Markus Nikel of RAI Rome, for valuable information and support. In the case of TV broadcasts, the archival tape may be in beta, VHS, or 16 mm film, or all of these, so you need to inquire about what form is available of the particular broadcast you wish to view. Also, European tapes may not be compatible with some American cassette equipment.

abbreviation indicating the *genre* (RL=radio lecture, TVD=TV discussion; see list of abbreviations below). Next is the title of the lecture, interview, or discussion, then the name of the interviewer (abbreviated "Int.") or director/producer (abbreviated "Dir."), if relevant; then the name of the series, date of broadcast (if available, following the abbreviation "db" and using the European order of day, month, year, to avoid transcribing errors), then the length of broadcast (in minutes and seconds), and finally the archival source, along with the archival reference number when known. When information would appear to be missing by accident, the abbreviation "na" will indicate "not available." When two archival sources are given, the first as owner of copyright will be the best reference.

Abbreviations of Types of Presentation

RI=Radio Interview
RL=Radio Lecture
RD=Radio Discussion with others
RR=Radio Report featuring Gadamer

TVI=TV Interview
TVL=TV Lecture
TVD=TV Discussion
TVR=TV Report featuring Gadamer

Beginning List of Archival Broadcast Tapes, 1950–1996

1950, 7—RD—"Über Nietzsche und uns: Zum 50. Todestag des Philosophen." With Max Horkheimer and Theodor Adorno. 28 min. HR: 84 285. Recently published in Horkheimer's *Gesammelte Schriften,* edited by G. S. Noerr, 13:111–20. Frankfurt: S. Fischer, 1989.

1951, 9—RL—"Über Martin Heidegger." 57.30 min. BR: 31608-31611.

1952, 6—RI—"Aufgaben der Philosophie in der Gegenwart." 3 min. DLR Berlin: 65-268.

1956, 6—RI—"Zehn Jahre 'Studium generale' in Heidelberg." *Zeitfunk am Mittag* program. db: 30.6.56. 7.17 min. SDR: 6900506.

1964, 1—RL—"Kausalität in der Geschichte—1." db: 5.4.64. 22.52 min. SWF: 577–6505.

1964, 2—RL—"Kausalität in der Geschichte—2." db: 12.4.64. 26.31 min. SWF: 577–6506.

1967, 1—RL—"Grenzen des Expertentums." *Welt von Morgen* series. 28.10 min. SWF: 577–7987.

1967, 2—TVL—"Die Stellung der Philosophie in der modernen Gesellschaft." SWF.

1968, 2—TVD—"Was ist der Mensch? Dialogische Existenz und Sprache." A discussion with Kurt Steinbuch. *Horizont* series. db: 28.2.68. 30 min. WDR.

1968, 3—RL—"Die Unfähigkeit zum Gespräch." 30.50 min. SDR: 92–02 904. Cf. 1971, 3.

1968, 4—TVL—"Tradition und Person." Take: 19.4.68, Alte Aula. SWF-Fernseh.

1968, 4—TVL—"Die Einmaligkeit der Person." Take: 19.4.68, Alte Aula. SWF-Fernseh.

1968, 10—RL—"Semantik und Hermeneutik." One of four lectures featured from the 1968 Vienna Congress for Philosophy. Part of 58.46 min. db: 15.10.68. WDR: 2990/2.

1970, 3—RL—"Sprache und Verstehen." 58.35 min. SWF: 577/9463–64.

1971, 3—RL—"Die Unfähigkeit zum Gespräch." *Wissenschaft im Gespräch* series. A shortened version. 30.50 min. Repeated on Feb. 9, 1985 celebrating his 85th birthday. SDR-HW 10 283.

1971, 4—RL—"Wahrheit und Dichtung." db:18.4.71. 29.15 min. SWF: 536 1752 000.

1973, 2—RL—"Wie weit schreibt Sprache das Denken vor?" db: 18.2.73. 29 min. SWF: 015 0878.

1974, 8—RL+RI—"Spiel, Symbol, und Fest: Initiatoren und Mediatoren der Kunst." 42.50 min. (32.05 min.110.45 min. disc.) Int.: Bernd Stappert. db: 7.9.74. SDR: 60–18691.

1975, 2—RL—"Spiel und Spieler: Der wahre Schein der Kunst." 27.40 min. SDR: WR 5468.

1975, 4—RI—"Die vergessene Lust am Dialog." 3 parts, 98.35 min. *Zeit zum Zuhören* series. HGG in part 3 w/ a 15 min. int.: B. Stappert. db: 3.5.75. SDR: 60-12 188/III.

1975, 6—RI—"Das Du wurde zum Problem: Ein Dialog über den Dialog." Int.: B. Stappert. 27.45 min. SDR: W 10820.

1975, 6—RR—"Das Philosophische in den Wissenschaften und die Wissenschaftlichkeit der Philosophie." Cuts also from D. Henrich, W. Schultz, N. Luhmann, J. Habermas, A. Schmidt. Dir.: Marlis Gerhardt. 1975 Hegelkongress. 43.25 min. db.: 30.6.75. SDR: 60–12 083.

1976, 9—RD—"Martin Heidegger, Ein Unzeitgemäßer und seine Zeit: Dokumentation zu Leben und Werk." (3 mos. after his death.) With H. Buhr, W. Schulz, A. Schwan. db: 18.9.76. 96.40 min. SDR: W 10802–4.

1976, 12—RL—"Die Kunst des Feierns." db. 5.12.76. 30 min. SDR. KW 61830.

1976, 12—RI—"Mehr als die Schale eines Edamerkäses: Vorkriegs- und Zwischenkriegseindrücke." *Zeitgeschichte in Lebensgeschichten* series (1). Int.: Bernd Stappert. db: 14.1.77. 28 min. 1+2 repeated 22 and 29.6.79. 28+28=56.35 min. SDR: 6018692/100.

1976, 12—RI—"'Philosophische Liebesmüh': Hochschullehrerzeiten." *Zeitgeschichte in Lebensgeschichten* series (2). Int.: Bernd Stappert. db: 14.1.77. 28.50 min. SDR: 6018692/200.

1977, 5—RD—"Die Erbe der Antike." With Golo Mann, Friedrich Heer. Dir: L. Reinisch. *Sonntag um sechs* series. Typed ms. 35pp. BR.

1978, 4—RL—"Der Mensch ohne Hand." *Die Aktualität sinnlicher Bildung* series. 27.10 min. DLR: 5008636.

1979, 6—RI—"Ist die klassische Philosophie in die Ecke gedrängt?" Awarding of the 4th Hegel Prize to Prof. Gadamer, laudatio by Jürgen Habermas. Int.:Teja Fiedler. db: na. 6.30 min. SDR: 60–11 884/0 05.

1979, 6—RL—"Hegelpreisverleihung der Stadt Stuttgart 1979." *Der Rede wert* series. db: 15.6.79. 38.25 min. SDR: KW067781.

1980, 2—RI—"Interview mit HGG an läßlich seines 80. Geburtstages." Int.: Klaus Haller. db: 11.2.80. 10.15 min. WDR: 2091/2.

1980, 8—RL—"Die Kultur und das Wort." Salzburg lecture. db.: 26.9.80. 51 min. SDR: 60–16 124.

1981, 7—RL—"Das Alte und das Neue." Lecture opening the Salzburg Festival. db: 31.7.81. 30.17 min. SDR: 60–12 479.

1981, 8—RD—"Naturgesetz und Freiheit: Zur Aktualität Kant'schen Denkens." With Werner Marx and Klaus Werry. 23.05 min. DLR: 5016724.

1981, 9—RL—"Hegel, die französische Revolution und der Idealismus der Freiheit." Lecture celebrating the 150th anniversary of Hegel's death. 25.9.81. 53.55 min. SDR: 60–12 526/I–II.

1981, 11—RI—"Hegels Bedeutung heute, I: Gespräch mit HGG." Int.: Klaus Werry. DLR Köln.

1982, 2—RL—"Goethe lesend: Das Lied des Türmers [in act 5, *Faust* II]." db: 21.3.82. 27.15 min. DLR: 5 012 989.

1983, 7—RL—"Vom Fest zur Fete." 17.35 min. SDR: 9 202 322.

1983, 10—RL—"Wandlung des Todesbildes: Tod und Sterben: die verdrängte Wirklichkeit." *Das Heidelberger Studio* series. db: 10.10.83. 28 min. SDR: 9202393.

1984, 2—RL—"Über das Spezialistentum in der Wissenschaft und die Universalität der Bildung." *Der Rede wert* series. 41.05 min. SDR: 92–02 908.

1984, 4—RI—"Was tun die Philosophen?" Int.: Florian Sattler. 28 min. BR: 84/21536.

1984, 5—RL—"Ende der Kunst, Zukunft der Kunst." Joint presentation with Hans-Egon Holthusen and Peter Sloterdijk for the Bavarian Academy of Fine Arts in Munich. db: 26.9.84. Gadamer: 16.20 min.; total broadcast: 57 min. BR: 84/21840.

1984, 9—TVI—"Das Selbstverständliche ist das Rätselhafte: Ergänzungen zur Zeit." Int.: Erwin Koller. 60.40 min. Schweizer Fernsehen, Zurich. DRA: 84 U 2545/14 (sound track).

1985, 2—RI—"Die Unfähigkeit zum Gespräch." Int.: Jörg Tröger, celebrating G's 85th birthday. See 1968 and 1971 lecture of same title. 43.40 min. SDR: 92–02 903.

1985, 3—RI—"1945: Wie sollte es weiter gehen?" Remaining data missing.

1985, 12—RI—"HGG im Gespräch." Int.: Cord Barkhausen. Two tapes: 29.40 min./ 29.50 min. SWF: 016 6682 100/200.

1986, 1—RL—"Die Idee der Universität gestern, heute, morgen." Lecture celebrating the 600th anniversary of the founding of the University of Heidelberg. db: 24.1.86. 51.35 min. SDR: 92-03 365.

1986, 1—TVR—"HGG: Ein Leben für die Philosophie." *Zeitgenossen* series. Film by Arndt Breustedt. Dir: J. Kritz. db: 19.1.86. 38 min. HR and UHML: 82VA304.

1986, 2—RI—"Leonhard Reinisch im Gespräch mit HGG." *Europäische Lebensläufe* series. Nachtstudio. db: na. 54.35 min. BR: 89/21 858–59.

1986, 6—RL—"Verleihung des Karl-Jaspers Preises." date of event: 15.6.86. Mayor R. Zundel of Heidelberg and Gadamer. 26 min. SDR: 92–03 520.

1986, 7—RL—"Grenzen der Experten." 52.45 min. BR: 86/23187/88.

1986, 7—RI—"Gespräch mit HGG." Int.: Günter Verdin. *Von zehn bis zwölf* series. 120 min. Gespräch mit Musik. Südfunk 3. db:25.7.86. SDR: 6700156.

1986, 10—TVI—"HGG in Gespräch mit Kurt Stenzel." *Im Gespräch* series. db: 3.10.86. 72 min. SDR. (Fernsehmitschnitt: S3, 2.13.95.) FS/1 Plus (3SAT). UHML: two tapes, on one, conclusion is missing. Audio: DRA: 89 U 4989/4. Date of take unclear.

1987, 2—TVR—"HGG erinnert sich." *Bilder der Geschichte* series. Int.: A. Mayer-Papenberg. Dir: G. Felsberg. db: 18.2.87. 43 min. SWF. Retitled in UHML: "Annette Mayer-Papenberg in Gespräch mit HGG, dem deutschen Philosophen;" S3 18.2.87. 42.35 min. SWF: 7062. UHML: 87VA21LSA (VHS).

1987, 5—RI—"Die anthropologischen Grundlagen der Freiheit des Menschen." Hanns-Martin-Schleyer Prize acceptance speech. db: 15.5.87. 29 min. SDR: 60–16 383[200].

1987, 8—RI—"Gadamer: Dialogo filosofico." Int.: Nino Molinu. ms. 35pp., trans. Istituto di filosofia della facoltà di lettere e filosofia. U. di Cagliari, 09123 Cagliari, Italy.

1987, 10—TVD—"Auf der Suche nach einer neuen Ethik." Contains only a few statements by HGG, as there were many other participants. Dir.: H. Glaesgen. 45 min. NDR.

1988, 2—RD—"Die Welt des Geistes eine Geisterwelt?/Hermeneutik oder die Wut des Verstehens." Conversation with Jochen Hoerisch and interviewer Cord Barkhausen. db: 12.5.88. Two tapes: 33.55 min./19.55 min. SWF: 017 0314 100/200.

1988, 2—TVI—"Streit um Martin Heidegger." Dir. B. Runge. *Kulturszene* series. db: 19.2.88. 5 min. SDR.

1988, 3—RD—"Martin Heidegger: Die philosophische und politische Dimension seines Denkens." Excerpts from the discussion of 5 February 1988, in Heidelberg. With Jacques Derrida, Philippe Lacoue-Labarthe, and Reiner Wiehl. The discussion, in French, was translated by Philipp Rippel. db: 30.3.88. 58.20 min. HR: 3–257 410 100/200. (WDR has an unedited and unbroadcast archival videotape of the conference. Access is tightly controlled, but under some circumstances, such as a specific scholarly use, access might be allowed. Contact Ulrich Boehm, WDR.)

1988, 3—TVR—"'Lieb ist mir Platon, aber noch lieber die Wahrheit': Der Philosoph HGG." Film Portrait by Al Lauder. db: 28.3.88. 45 min. *Philosophie Heute* series. Producer: Ulrich Boehm. WDR. (Also in UHML).

1989, 4—RD—"Bedarf moderne Kunst der Kommentierung? Der Zusammenhang von Werk, Kritik, und Kommentar." Leader: Jochen Hoerisch. Other discussants W. Hofmann and J. Immendorf. *Aktuelle Kultur* series. Two tapes: 27.20 min./26.15 min. SWF: 017 2263 101/201.

1989, 10—RL—"Heideggers Sprachverständnis in philosophiegeschichtlicher Perspektive." db: 28.11.89. 58.58 min. HR: 259 583 100/200.

1989, 10—RD—"Wo aber Gefahr ist, wächst das Rettende auch: Heideggers Begriff von Freiheit im Zeitalter planetarischer Technik." Larger theme of Symposium: "Martin Heidegger: Faszination und Erschrecken: Die politische Dimension einer Philosophie." From an international Heidegger Symposium in Marburg, October 1989. Dir. Peter Kemper. Other participants: P. Aubenque, H. Ebeling, O. Pöggeler, A. Schmidt, H.-M. Schönherr. db: 9.1.90. 88.31 min. HR: 249 595 100/200/300.

1989, 12—RI—"Die Zeit ist ein Fluß ohne Ufer: Kairos, Ein Diskurs über die Gunst des Augenblicks und das weise Maß." Int.: Bernd Stappert. db: 29.12.89. 53.25 min. SDR 0016893.

1990, 1—TVL—"Philosophische Geschichten: Der Fall Martin Heidegger." Dir: J. Kritz. db: 4.1.90. 68 min. HR.

1990, 1—TVL—"Der Fall Martin Heidegger." db: 6.1.90. 29.05 min. (end missing). HR3 and DRA: 90 U 5045/3. Copyright HR.

1990, 2—RI—"Gespräch mit dem deutschen Philosophen HGG anlässlich seines 90. Geburtstags." Int.: R. Offergelt. *Kulturjournal* program. Topic: Heidegger. db: 11.2.90. 4.50 min. BR: 90/20506.

1990, 2—RR—"'Wahrheit und Methode'—Der Philosoph HGG wird 90." Int. Frank Nieß. *Südfunk aktuell* midday news program. 4.24 min. SDR.

1990, 4—RI—"Leipzig, die Hermeneutik, Martin Heidegger, und die Zukunft: Rüdiger Offergeld im Gespräch mit dem Philosophen HGG." *Zeitfragen/Streifragen* series. 29 min. WDR: 32142960. Also HR.

1990, 4—RI—"Rüdiger Offergeld im Gespräch mit dem Philosophen." Take date: 15.4.90. 29 min. WDR: 32142960. Same record # as preceding entry.

1990, 4—TVD—"Der letzte Traum—Auf dem Weg zur ewigen Jugend." Gadamer addresses the social consequences of prolonging life. Dir. P. Schlecht. With ten other interviewees, including Paul Segal and Linus Pauling, Gadamer's participation was quite brief. db: 29.6.90. Whole program 41.17 min. SWF: 0022643.

1990, 7—TVL—"Die Vielfalt der Sprachen und das Verstehen der Welt." *Tele-Akademie* series. A lecture given at the University of Heidelberg. Dir: Werner-Otto Feißt. db: 23.12.90. 45.24 min. SWF: 0024020. Also DRA: 90 U 5188/2.

1991, 3—TVD—"Was den Menschen fehlt: Frage und Antworten der Philosophie." Discussion with Dieter Henrich and Jochen Hoerisch. *Philosophie Heute* series, prod. by Ulrich Boehm. db: 30.3.1991. 45 min. WDR.

1991, 10—RI—"Eine private Plauderei mit dem 91-jährigen Philosophen HGG." R. Offergeld. *Kulturjournal* program. db: 20.10.91. 10.25 min. BR: 91/23936–38.

1992, na—RL—"Postmoderne und das Ende der Neuzeit." Vortrag 1992. Ref. #2055. *Autobahnuniversität* series. Audiotape published by Carl-Auer-Systeme Verlag, Weberstrasse 2, 69120 Heidelberg.

1992, 12—RR—"HGG [über sein Buch] *Gedicht und Gespräch* (Insel Verlag)." *Buchzeit* program. db: 6.1.93. 12.30 min. SWF: 017 6783 002.

1993—Multimedia (TV/book)—*Enciclopedia Multimediale della scienze Filosofiche.* Gadamer lectures/discusses in five volumes of a handsome initial ten-volume set, titled *Le radici del pensiero filosofico.* Eventually to be translated into other languages. Publisher: Istituto della Enciclopedia Italiana, Piazza Enciclopedia Italiana 4, 00186 Roma; tel. 39–6–689840. Ten volume price ca. 1,800,000L. The five volumes in which Gadamer participated are: 1. *La nascita della filosofia,* 53 min.; 3. *Parmenide,* 46 min.; 4. *Eraclito,* 52 min.; 5. *I Sofisti,* 56 min.; and 8. *Platone: La Politica,* 57 min.

1993, 2—RI—"'Wenn die Schwäne singen . . .': HGG—Sokrates, der Philosoph, das Schöne und der Tod." (Co-production with Rüdiger Offergeld; Regie: A. Kenntemich). 55 min. (Transcript 29pp.) BR.

1993, 6—RI—"HGG: [on his book:] *Über die Verborgenheit der Gesundheit* (Suhrkamp)." Ints.: C. Lachnicht and K.-R. Menke. *Bücherzeit* program. db: 14.6.93. 6.10 min. SWF: 017 7648 004.

1993, 7—TVI—"Über die Verborgenheit der Gesundheit." *Wortwechsel* series. Int.: M. -J. Schulz. db: 11.7.93. FS/S3 43.47 min. SWF: 29556. Audio: DRA: 93 U 5545/1.

1993, 10—RD—"Altwerden: Erfahrungen von Theologen, Philosophen, und Schriftstellern." With Franz König, Romano Guardini, Gertrud Fussenegger, Hans Jonas, Karl Popper, and Karl Rahner. 28.45 min. BR: 93/23815. Brief appearance of HGG.

1993, 10—RL—"Wandlungen des Todesbildes." 28 min. SDR; DRA: K 881.

1994, 1—RD—"Über den Tag hinaus, Erfahrungen mit dem Älterwerden, Aus dem Leben des Philosophen HGG." Dir. U. Schwarzer. With H. Roloff, L. Bardischewski. Take: 10.1.94. db: 10.2.94. 29 min. BR: 94/20456.

1994, 2—RI—"Der Philosoph HGG [Wort, Musik, Gespräch]." Int.: Claus Canisius. 81.47 min. SDR (Karlsruhe): KM 007003.

1994, 3—RL—"Die Unhintergehbarkeit der Kunst." *Das Kunstwerk im Zeitalter seiner ästhetischen Kommunizierbarkeit* series, no. 1. Take: 30.3.94. db: 1.4.94. 29 min. SWF: 017 8651.

1994, 5—RI—"Stefan-George-Gesellschaft und die Gesellschaft zur Förderung der Stefan-George-Gedenkstätte vereinigt." *Kultur regional* series-brief interview with a founding member. db: 16.5.94. 5 min. SWF: 716 9254 002.

1994, 8—RL—"Herder und die geschichtliche Welt: Zum 250. Geburtstag des Kulturphilosophen." *Aktuelle Kultur* series. db: 26.8.94. Two tapes: 24.55 and 28.56 min. SWF: 017 9136 100 and 201.

1994, 9—TVL—"Kunst im Zeitalter der Technik." *Tele-Akademie* series. Dir.: W. -O. Feißt. db: 4.9.94. 44 min. SWF: 33557.

1994, 10—RL—"Rätsel, das mich martert: HGG über das Verstehen von Musik." *Literatur regional* series. db: 11.2.95. 34.31 min. SDR: KWL93405.

1994, 11—RI—"HGG im Gespräch mit Ursula Schwarzer." 55 min. Note: Gadamer's voice slightly distorted on the tape. NDR: X100, R001246. DRA: L628891 (sound only).

1994, 12—RL—"Erziehung in der industriellen Revolution." *Der Rede wert* series. db: 12.2.95. 49.10 min. SDR: 6023222.

1995, 2—TVR—"Hans-Georg Gadamer." *Kultra* series. Dir.: Teresa Corceiro. 5 min. ZDF/3sat.

1995, 2—RI—"Das Gespräch: Der Philosoph HGG." Int.: Ralph Ludwig. *Die neue Lust am Radio* series. db: 9.2.95. ca. 45 min. NDR.

1995, 3—RI—"Memoiren: Carlos Oliveira im Gespräch mit dem Philosophen HGG." *Zeitgenossen berichten aus Leben und Werk* series. db: 30.3.95. 53.10 min. BR: 95/21188–89.

1995, na—RL—"Ist Ethik lehrbar?" Vortrag 1995. Audiotape. 21.80DM. *Tele-Akademie* series. Published by Carl-Auer-Systeme, Heidelberg. See 1992, na, "Postmoderne . . ." above.

1995, 10—TVL—"Philosophische Exkursionen mit HGG, von Christian-Michael Doermer." Lecture. Take date: na. Sat/1 (private TV producer). db: 9.10.95. 30 min. Published by Cene-Dokument-Films, Isabellestrasse 28, D-80796 Munich.

1996, 9—TVR—"Die Kunst des Verstehens: HGG und die Hermeneutik." Film by Rüdiger Safranski and Konstanze Brill. *Philosophie Heute* series, prod. by Ulrich Boehm. db: 15.9.96. 45 min. WDR.

1996, 12—TVL—"HGG erzählt die Geschichte der Philosophie." Original produktion: Istituto Italiano per gli Studi Filosofici Neapel and RAI Rom, but in German. Producer: Ulrich Boehm. 8 installments of 45 min., selected by R. Safranski. WDR.

1996, 3—TVI—"Mythos Heidelberg." Int.: Sebastian Krueger. *Suedwestfunk/Arte* series. Take date: 29.3.96. db: 20.4.96. A ca. 8 min. segment in a longer program. SWF.

1997, summer—TVI—"L'Enquéte sur l'architecture proche." Interviewer: Catherine Hueurzeler. Producer: Centre Pompidou, Paris, in cooperation with Ann Maria Productions. db.: summer, 1997. An interview of 1.5 hours will be edited down to less than ten minutes of interview as part of a broadcast on contemporary architecture. For information write C. Huerzeler, Hebelstr. 11, CH-4056 Basel, Switzerland.

E. Secondary Sources

This bibliography cannot for reasons of space list articles, but it will offer a selection of the following:

1. Bibliographical Resources
2. Book-Length Studies
3. Collections of Essays

1. Bibliographical Resources

Etsuro Makita's definitive 350-page *Gadamer Bibliographie* lists only writings *by Gadamer* and no secondary sources. In seeking recent book-length studies, one can scan the subject listings under "Hermeneutics" in the *National Union Catalog* on microfiche since 1985. For articles, consult the bibliographies listed below. *Dissertation Abstracts* is a good reference for dissertations on Gadamer and hermeneutics. The bibliographies in book-length studies are often quite extensive, listing articles as well as books. In those listed below, we have specified the extent of bibliography. For surveys of new hermeneutic literature, consult Jean Greisch's annual review of research listed below.

Bibliographies

Aguirre-Ora, José Maria. "Bibliografia de y sobre Hans-Georg Gadamer." (Gadamer Bibliography), *Scriptorium Victoriense* 39 (1992): 300–45.
Bibliographie de la philosophie. Institut International de Philosophie. Paris: Vrin. An annual bibliography since 1954.

Greisch, Jean. "Bulletins de philosophie herméneutique," *Revue des sciences philosophique et théologiques* 75 (1991): 97–128; 76 (1992): 281–310; 77 (1993): 255–88; etc.

Henrichs, Norbert. *Bibliographie der Hermeneutik und ihrer Auswendungsbereiche seit Schleiermacher.* Düsseldorf, 1968.

International Philosophical Bibliography/Répertoire bibliographique de la philosophie. Louvain: Éditions de l'Institut Superieur de Philosophie, Université Catholique de Louvain, Belgium. An annual bibliography since 1949 with comprehensive index of terms in titles.

Petit, Jean-Claude. *Répertoire Bibliographique sur l'Herméneutique: avec une section consacrée a H.-G. Gadamer.* Montreal: University of Quebec at Montreal, Department of Philosophy, 1984. 79pp. (Available from National Library of Canada and University of Iowa Libraries.)

The Philosopher's Index. Philosophy Documentation Center, Bowling Green, Ohio. Cumulative index back to 1940. Available on CD-ROM from Digital Library Systems since 1985.

Volat-Shapiro, Hélène. "Gadamer and Hermeneutics: A Bibliography." In *Gadamer and Hermeneutics,* edited by Hugh J. Silverman, pp. 311–27. London: Routledge, 1991.

2. Book-Length Studies

a. In English

Bernstein, Richard. *Beyond Objectivism and Relativism: Science, Hermeneutics, and Praxis.* Philadelphia: University of Pennsylvania Press, 1983. 284pp., bibliog. 267–76.

Bleicher, Josef. *Contemporary Hermeneutics. Hermeneutics as Method, Philosophy, and Critique.* London: Routledge and Kegan Paul, 1980. 288pp., bibliog. 272–80. 2nd ed. 1990.

Derksen, Louise Dorothea. *On Universal Hermeneutics: A Study in the Philosophy of Hans-Georg Gadamer.* Amsterdam: VU Boekhandel/Usitgeverij, 1983. 316pp., bibliog. 293–316.

DiCenso, James. *Hermeneutics and the Disclosure of Truth: A Study in the Work of Heidegger, Gadamer, and Ricoeur.* Charlottesville: University Press of Virginia, 1990. 183pp., bibliog. 173–79.

Gallagher, Shaun. *Hermeneutics and Education.* Albany, N.Y.: SUNY Press, 1994. 402pp., bibliog. 353–87.

Grondin, Jean. *Introduction to Philosophical Hermeneutics.* New Haven: Yale University Press, 1994. 208pp.; valuable general bibliog. of hermeneutics, pp. 169–228; bibliog. on Gadamer, 198–208.

Hirsch, E.D., Jr. *Validity in Interpretation.* New Haven: Yale University Press, 1967. 287pp., footnote refs., but no bibliog.

Howard, Roy J. *Three Faces of Hermeneutics: An Introduction to Current Theories of Understanding.* Berkeley: University of California Press, 1982. 182pp., bibliog. 177–84.

Hoy, David Couzens. *The Critical Circle: Literature, History, and Philosophical Hermeneutics.* Berkeley: University of California Press, 1978. 182pp., bibliog. refs.

Kusch, Martin. *Language as Calculus vs. Language as Universal Medium: A Study in Husserl, Heidegger, and Gadamer.* Boston: Kluwer, ca. 1989. 362pp., bibliog. 315–42.

Madison, Gary B. *The Hermeneutics of Postmodernity: Figures and Themes.* Bloomington, Ind.: Indiana University Press, 1988. 206pp., bibliog. refs.

Palmer, Richard E. *Hermeneutics: Interpretation Theory in Schleiermacher, Dilthey, Heidegger, and Gadamer.* Evanston, Ill.: Northwestern University Press, 1969. 282pp., bibliog. 254–74.

Ricoeur, Paul. *Hermeneutics and Human Sciences.* Trans. John B. Thompson. New York: Cambridge University Press, 1981. 314pp., bibliog. 306–8.

Schmidt, Lawrence K. *The Epistemology of Hans-Georg Gadamer.* Frankfurt: Peter Lang, 1985. 251pp., bibliog. 252–61.

Smith, P. Christopher. *Hermeneutics and Human Finitude: Toward a Theory of Ethical Understanding.* New York: Fordham Press, 1991. 286pp., bibliog. 283–86.

Sullivan, Robert. *Political Hermeneutics: The Early Thinking of Hans-Georg Gadamer.* University Park: Penn State University Press, 1990. 203pp., bibliog. refs.

Thiselton, Anthony C. *The Two Horizons. New Testament Hermeneutics and Philosophical Description with Special Reference to Heidegger, Bultmann, Gadamer, and Wittgenstein.* Grand Rapids, Mich.: W. B. Eerdmans, 1980. 484pp., bibliog. 447–66.

Warnke, Georgia. *Gadamer: Hermeneutics, Tradition, and Reason.* Stanford: Stanford University Press, 1987. 197pp., footnote refs. 175–97, no separate bibliog.

Weinsheimer, Joel. *Gadamer's Hermeneutics: A Reading of "Truth and Method."* New Haven: Yale University Press, 1985. 259pp., bibliog. 261–71.

b. In Other Languages

Albert, Hans. *Kritik der reinen Hermeneutik: der Antirealismus und das Problem des Verstehens.* Tübingen: Mohr, 1994. 265pp., no bibliog. The naturalistic critique of hermeneutics.

Bettendorf, Thomas. *Hermeneutik und Dialog: Eine Auseinandersetzung mit dem Denken Hans-Georg Gadamers.* Frankfurt: Haag und Herchen, ca. 1984. 232pp., bibliog. 218–32.

Betti, Emilio. *Die Hermeneutik als allgemeine Methodik der Geisteswissenschaften.* Tübingen: Mohr, 1962. 64pp., no bibliog.

Bronk, Andrzej. *Rozumienie Dzieje Jezyk: Filozoficzna hermeneutyka H.-G. Gadamera.* Lublin: Redakcja Wydawnictw Kul, 1988. 408pp., ext. bibliog. 355–99. English summary, 401–8.

Dockhorn, Claus von. "Hans-Georg Gadamer, *Wahrheit und Methode.*" *Göttingsche Gelehrte Anzeigen* 218 (1966): 169–206. Trans.: *Philosophy and Rhetoric* 13 (1980): 160–80. Excellent article-length critical discussion of *Truth and Method.*

Dutt, Carsten. *Hans-Georg Gadamer: Eine Einführung.* Heidelberg: Munatius Verlag, 1996. Footnotes, no bibliog.

Ferraris, Maurizio. *Storia della'ermeneutica.* Milano: Bompiani, 1988. 478pp., bibliog. 451–78. The history of hermeneutics in Ferraris's account begins in ancient times.

Fruchon, Pierre. *L'herméneutique de Gadamer: Platonisme et modernité, tradition et interprétation.* Paris: Cerf, 1994. 534pp., references, no bibliog.

Gerigk, Horst Jürgen. *Unterwegs zur Interpretation: Hinweise zu einer Theorie der Literatur in Auseinandersetzung mit Gadamer's Wahrheit und Methode.* Hurtgenwald: Pressler, 1989. 228pp., bibliog. refs., no bibliog.

Grondin, Jean. *Hermeneutische Wahrheit? Zum Wahrheitsbegriff Hans-Georg Gadamers.* Königstein: Forum academicum, 1982. 210pp., bibliog. 198–210. 2nd ed. 1994.

Hilberath, Bernd Jochen. *Theologie zwischen Tradition und Kritik: Die philosophische Hermeneutik Hans-Georg Gadamers als Herausforderung des theologischen Selbstverständnisses.* Düsseldorf: Patmos, 1978. 344pp., bibliog. 330–42.

Jakob, Samuel. *Zwischen Gespräch und Diskurs: Untersuchungen zur sozialhermeneutischen Begründung der Agogik anhand einer Gegenüberstellung von Hans-Georg Gadamer und Jürgen Habermas.* Bern/Stuttgart: Paul Haupt, 1985. 312pp., bibliog. 288–312.

Lang, Peter Christian. *Hermeneutik, Ideologiekritik, Aesthetik: über Gadamer und Adorno sowie Fragen einer aktuellen Ästhetik.* Königstein, Ts.: Forum Academicum, Hain and others, 1981. 207pp., bibliog. 197–207.

Pöggeler, Otto. *Schritte zu einer hermeneutischen Philosophie.* Freiburg: Alber, 1994. 508pp., extensive notes, no bibliog. Extensive coverage of hermeneutics prior to Gadamer.

Teichert, Dieter. *Erfahrung, Erinnerung, Erkenntnis: Untersuchungen zum Wahrheitsbegriff der Hermeneutik Gadamers.* Stuttgart: J. B. Metzler, 1991. 213pp., bibliog. 200–207.

3. Collections of Essays

Apel, Karl-Otto, Gadamer, Habermas, Bubner, and others. *Hermeneutik und Ideologiekritik.* Frankfurt: Suhrkamp, 1971. 317pp., no bibliog. Basic to the Gadamer-Habermas debate.

Dialogue and Deconstruction: The Gadamer-Derrida Encounter. Edited and translated by Diane P. Michelfelder and Richard E. Palmer, with an introduction. Albany, N.Y.: SUNY Press, 1989. 316pp., bibliog. 284–91, bibliog. refs. 295–316. Brief question-and-answer encounter at a conference on text and interpretation in Paris, April 1981. A dozen expert essays, plus four by Gadamer, interpret the encounter.

Festivals of Interpretation: Essays on Hans-Georg Gadamer's Work. Edited by Kathleen Wright. Albany, N.Y.: SUNY Press, 1990. 248pp., footnotes, but no bibliog.

Gadamer and Hermeneutics. Edited by Hugh J. Silverman. New York: Routledge, 1991. 309pp., bibliog. of books in English by Hélène Volat-Shapiro, 311–27.

Hermeneutical Inquiry. Edited by D. E. Klemm. Vol. 1, *The Interpretation of Texts.* 285pp. Vol. 2, *The Interpretation of Existence.* 323pp. Atlanta: Scholars Press, 1986. Bibliog. in vol. 2, 273–323. An anthology of texts by Schleiermacher, Dilthey, Heidegger, Gadamer, Bultmann, Tillich, etc. Primarily for theological students.

Hermeneutics and Modern Philosophy. Edited by Brice R. Wachterhauser. Albany, N.Y.: SUNY Press, 1986. 506pp., bibliog. 487–502.

Hermeneutics and Praxis. Edited by Robert Hollinger. Notre Dame, Ind.: University of Notre Dame Press, 1985. 296pp., no bibliog.

Hermeneutics and Truth. Edited by Brice R. Wachterhauser. Albany, N.Y.: SUNY Press, 1994. 255pp., bibliog. 229–55.

Hermeneutics: Questions and Prospects. Edited by Gary Shapiro and Alan Sica. Amherst, Mass.: University of Massachusetts Press, 1984. 307pp., bibliog. 292–307.

The Hermeneutic Tradition: From Ast to Ricoeur. Edited by Gayle Ormiston and Alan Schrift. Albany, N.Y.: SUNY Press, 1989. 380pp., bibliog. 335–65.

The Specter of Relativism: Truth, Dialogue, and Phronesis in Philosophical Hermeneutics. Edited by Lawrence K. Schmidt. Evanston, Ill.: Northwestern University Press, 1995. 295pp., bibliog. 271–91.

INDEX

Ab-wesenheit, as lightness, 405–6, 408–10
Achilles, 408–9
Adorno, Theodor, 17
Adrastus, 407–8
Aeschylus, 262, 332
  Agamemnon, 331, 342
Akiva, story of, 182–83, 185
Alain,
  Système des beaux-arts, 409
alētheia, 333
  and Aristotle, 321, 550
  and art, 450–53, 540
  and Gadamer, 68, 71–73, 77, 319, 321, 325,
    332, 447, 450–53, 542–43
  Heidegger's use of, 68, 71–73, 311–13, 321,
    332, 450–53, 549
  and Plato, 542
  and Plato's cave parable, 312–13
Alt, Karin, 482
Anaximander, 183, 190, 299, 553
Anaxagoras, 510
An-wesenheit,
  as heaviness, 405–6, 408, 412
  as *sum-phore,* 407–8
Anz, Heinrich, 47
Apel, Karl-Otto, 32, 120, 137, 202
  *Die Idee der Sprache in der Tradition des
    Humanismus von Dante bis Vico,* 67,
    95
Aquinas, Thomas, 15, 24, 183, 392
Arendt, Hannah, 502
  Eichmann in Jerusalem, 506
  The Origins of Totalitarianism, 506
  Rahel Varhhagen, 506
Aristotelianism, 20
Aristotle, 24, 25, 183, 184, 230, 434, 535, 552
  on art, 542
  and Christianity, 19
  De Anima, 140, 295
  on *energeia,* 543, 553, 554
  on *eros,* 333
  and *ēthos,* 88, 172
  on friendship, 337–38, 339, 527
  Gadamer on (*see* Gadamer: on Aristotle)
  and the Good, 57, 338
  Heidegger on (*see* Heidegger: on Aristotle)
  on Heraclitus, 220
  on language, 25
  on logos, 25, 172
  Metaphysics, 16, 48, 313, 322, 549, 550, 553
  metaphysics of, 48, 49
  Nicomachean Ethics, 9, 12, 56, 294, 297,
    337, 519
  On Interpretation, 394
  philosophy of nature, 30
  Physics, 49, 291, 475, 553
  and Plato, 270, 429
    similarities between, 9, 10, 11, 48, 263,
      274, 290, 293, 295–96, 302, 308, 309,
      553
  on Plato, 232, 422, 435
    criticisms of, 34, 291, 296, 297, 553
  Politics, 337
  and practical knowledge/reason (*phronēsis*),
    31, 97, 143, 298, 301, 338, 366, 513,
    527
  "practical philosophy" of, 31, 56, 526
  on reason, 380, 387
  Rhetoric, 291
  and science, 56
  on Socrates, 268
  on *theoria,* 387
  on truth, 313, 321
Arrau, Claudio, 213
art (*see also* Gadamer: on art; Heidegger: on
    art)
  being and meaning in, 178
  interpretation of, 209–10, 214–15, 217, 218,
    220
  and relativism, 97

truth claims of, 80–81, 322
understanding of, 209–10, 214
Augustine, 15, 34, 183, 392, 496, 520
   Confessions, 341
   The Trinity, 395
Auschwitz, 158
Austin, J. L.
   How to Do Things with Words, 530

Bach, J. S., 212
Badura-Skoda, Paul, 213
Baldassari, John, 450
Barth, Karl
   Commentary on the Letter to the Romans, 5
Bartók, Bela, 214
Bartuschat, Wolfgang, 17
Bauer, Ferdinand Christian
   Gnosis, 526
Baumgarten, Alexander Gottlieb, 30, 39
Beaufret, Jean, 158, 159
Beck, Lewis White, 354
Beethoven, Ludwig van, 7, 209, 213–15, 216,
   458
   Hammerklavier sonata, 210, 212, 213–14,
     215, 216
being
   "forgetfulness" of, 34–35 (*see also*
     Heidegger: on Being, forgetfulness of)
   and meaning, distinction between, 177,
     180–81, 185
   recollection of, 35
Benjamin, Walter, 488, 490, 546
Bergson, Henri, 133, 184
Bernasconi, Robert, 529
Bernstein, Richard, 86, 261, 356, 357, 370, 385
Bertram, Ernst, 5
Betti, Emilio, 113, 142, 261
Berve, Helmut, 14
Boeckh, August, 29
Bolzano, Bernard, 99, 105
Brahms, Johannes, 212
Brentano, Franz, 21, 32, 99, 105, 106, 109
Buber, Martin, 46, 327, 509, 510, 511
Bubner, Rudiger, 17
Bultmann, Rudolf, 179–80, 184, 190, 520–21,
   522

Calvinists, 240
Carnap, Rudolf, 184
Carter, Elliot, 213

Cartesianism
   as contrasted to
     continental philosophy, 111
     Davidson, 114, 121
     Gadamer, 114, 121, 317, 328, 358, 465,
       467
     Heidegger, 114, 121
     historicism, 379, 459, 465
     Vico, 139
   and Dilthey, 358, 465
   on logic, 146
   on the mind, 114, 466–67
   ontology of meaning in, 463
   and Spinoza, 314
   and subjectivism, 121–22, 459
Cassirer, Ernst, 23, 132, 138
   Philosophy of Symbolic, 138
Celan, Paul, 40, 50, 458, 537
Cézanne, Paul, 132
Cherniss, Harold F., 422
Christensen, Darrel E., xvi
Christian theology/thought. *See* theology:
   Christian; *see also* Christianity
Christianity
   early, 335
   as historical religion, 179–80, 184, 186
Cicero, 139, 183
Cohen, Hermann, 440, 458
Cohn, Jonas, 458
Collingwood, R. G., 43, 83, 138, 146, 155, 372,
   386
   Autobiography, 146
community, 333, 335–36, 338, 342
   in Dewey, 324
   in Gadamer, 248, 323, 330–31, 457
   in Royce, 340–41
Conquest, Robert, 227, 228
Cramer, Konrad, 17
Cratylus, 483 (*see also* Plato: *Cratylus*)
critical theory, theorists, 350–52, 356, 506 (*see
   also* Frankfurt School)
Croce, Benedetto, 138
Croesus, 407
Curtius, Ernst Robert, 458

Danto, Arthur, 176
Davidson, Donald
   on belief patterns, 120
   and Gadamer
     differences between, 430, 431, 433–34

similarities between, 111, 112, 114–19,
121, 123, 124, 125–26, 129, 421, 430,
431, 433
and Heidegger, similarities between, 12–22
and hermeneutics, 111, 114, 119
holism of, 117, 118, 121
intentionalism, rejection of, 118
on the *Philebus,* 422–30 (*see also* Plato:
Philebus)
principle of charity, 119, 120, 122–23,
124–25
"radical interpretation" of, 112, 115, 116,
118, 121, 124
and realism, 122
on "triangulation," 116, 432
deconstruction
and art, 44, 215
charity in hermeneutics, opposed to,
124–25
Gadamer on, 44, 50, 129, 171, 235, 326
and hermeneutics, 351, 390, 395
comparison between, 228–29, 329
democracy, 342, 357
Democritus, 11, 183
Derrida, Jacques, 87, 129, 352, 404
critique of phonocentrism, 390
deconstruction, use of, 44, 50, 124, 171
on *différance,* 87
and Gadamer, 123–24, 228, 329, 347, 392,
396, 398, 403, 404, 506, 535
Glas, 216
on Heidegger, 47, 171
on Husserl, 50
on Nietzsche, 47–48
on Plato's *Phaedrus,* 391, 394, 397
privileging of texts, 117
on writing, 397, 535
Descartes, René, 105–6, 149, 183, 223, 379
and Eros, 339
and Gadamer, 375
Heidegger on, 70
on reason, 380
and Spinoza, on idea, 314
Vico on, 143, 154
Dewey, John, 324, 339, 340, 346, 347
and Gadamer, similarities between, 323–26,
328, 332–33, 340, 342
"reconstruction" in, 342
dialectic, nature of, 33–34
Dilthey, Wilhelm, 5, 76–77, 247, 369, 458

and Gadamer, 45, 70, 76, 81, 83, 105, 139,
148, 205, 347, 358, 460, 465, 472, 511
and Heidegger, 22–23, 142
hermeneutics of, 26, 68, 71, 358
Outline of the History of Philosophy, 16
on understanding and explanation, 358, 367
Dingler, Hugo, 70
Dirlmeier, F., 522
discourse ethics, 88, 96
Donnellan, Keith, 74
Dostal, Robert, 165
Dostoyevsky, Fyodor, 6, 7, 458, 520
The Brothers Karamazov, 191
Douglas, 213
Dreyfus, Hubert, 120
Droysen, Johann Gustav, 71, 76, 369

Ebbinghaus, Harmann, 17
Ebert, Theo, 17
Ebner, Friedrich, 46
Echo (mythical), 398
Eckhart, Meister, 7, 34
Einsteinian theory of relativity, 4
Eliot, T. S., 19, 225
empiricists, 104
Engels, Frederick, 251
Enlightenment, the, 158, 227, 275–78, 281–84,
460, 526, 527 (*see also* Gadamer: and
the Enlightenment)
ontology and practice of, distinction between,
275, 282–85
Epicureans, 142, 143, 145, 147
Epicurus, 183
Ernst, Paul
*Der Zusammenbruch des deutschen
Idealismus,* 4
Eros, *eros,* 324, 333–34, 339, 340
three phases of Eros
agape, 334–37, 339
eros, 333–34, 337, 339
philia, 337–39
Evnine, Simon, 122
existentialism, 6
experience. *See* Gadamer: philosophical
hermeneutics of, and experience
expressionism, 4
Euclidean geometry, 70

Farías, Victor, 443
fascism, 240

Feuerbach, Ludwig
  Essence of Christianity, 241
Feyerabend, Paul, 89
Fichte, Johann Gottlieb, 49, 69, 274, 287
Finley, John, 422
Flack, Audrey, 505
Foucault, Michel, 123
Frank, Erich, 457
Frank, Manfred, 47
Frankfurt School, 350–51, 355, 356, 357, 366
Frege, Gottlob, 21, 74
Freud, Sigmund, 7, 178, 324, 326, 531
  Civilization and Its Discontents, 241
  on the unconscious, 241
Friedländer, Paul, 8, 10, 32, 245
Friedmann, Heinrich, 32–33
Fulda, Friedrich, 17
fusion of horizons, 211–14, 216, 218, 219, 337
  (*see also* Gadamer: fusion of horizons
  [*Horizontverschmelzung*], doctrine of)

Gadamer, Hans-Georg
  on aesthetic consciousness, 248, 249, 251,
    257
  on aesthetics, history of, 441
  on Aristotle, 56, 97, 106, 109, 131, 190, 223,
    226, 236, 260 297, 309, 338, 429,
    513–14, 522, 526, 530, 536–37, 538,
    542, 543, 552
    proximity of, to Plato, 9, 10, 48, 263, 274,
      290, 293, 295–96, 302, 308, 309, 553
  on art, 131–34, 135, 176, 209, 219–21, 223,
    250, 257, 308, 322, 347, 446, 449–51,
    453, 510, 541–42, 545
  absoluteness of, 545–47
  "Aesthetics and Hermeneutics," 446, 449,
    451
  and dialectic of question and answer, 43
  distance of, 447
  and *energeia,* 533–34
  as a game, 43
  and hermeneutics, 26, 29, 43–44, 100, 171,
    176–77, 195, 449, 452
  history of, unified, 450–52
  as personal, 448
  priority of, 546
  reading, as experience of, 51
  relevance of, to philosophy, 5–6
  "The Relevance of the Beautiful," 449–50,
    452, 529–30
  religious/spiritual dimension of, 131, 134
  and reproduction, 51
  "rightness" of, 542–43, 547
  surprise of, 447
  symbol in, 132–33
  tarrying with, 44, 300, 301, 541, 543–44
  timelessness of, 452, 545
  and truth, 310, 315–16, 319, 322, 450,
    536, 540, 543–44, 546–47
  "Word and Picture" ("Wort und Bild"),
    529, 536–37, 541
  autobiographical writings of, critique of,
    499–506
  on beauty, 101, 131, 135, 332–33, 450,
    536–37, 541–42, 545
    and *energeia,* 543
    and good, distinction between, 539–40
    and rightness, 539
    and truth, 323, 536, 540
  on community, 248, 323, 330–31, 457
  on consciousness, 27–28, 41, 47
    historical, 197
  critics of, 261
  and Davidson
    differences between, 430, 431, 433–34
    similarities between, 111, 112, 114–19,
      121, 123, 124, 125–26, 129, 421, 430,
      431, 433
  and Derrida (*see* Derrida: and Gadamer)
  and Dewey, similarities between, 323–26,
    328, 332–33, 340, 342
  dialogic thought in, 265–67, 269–71, 323,
    326
  and Dilthey, 70, 76, 81, 105, 139, 148, 205,
    347, 358, 460, 465, 472, 511
  and the Enlightenment, 275, 278–84, 287,
    317
    affinities with, 275, 280–85
  on festival, 133–34, 530, 531, 533, 534
  on freedom, 265, 270–71, 274
  on fusion of horizons
    (*Horizontverschmelzung*), doctrine of,
    209, 210–11, 218, 318, 323, 326, 328–29,
    330, 332, 375, 376, 462, 464, 468
  German idealism, critique of, 27, 134
  Gesammelte Werke, 529, 536
  on "good will," importance of, 329, 332
  on Greek culture, 530
  Greek philosophy in, xvii, 97, 109, 219, 297,
    308, 347, 534

and Habermas, 29–30, 32, 55, 123–24, 125, 201
debate between, 350–52, 356, 366, 506
and Hegel, 15, 16, 40, 44–45, 69, 80, 131, 146, 155, 163, 223, 235, 260, 267–68, 270, 301, 318–19, 356, 453, 516, 530, 537, 545
and Heidegger, xvii, 46, 133, 161, 223, 235, 260, 340
    differences between, 48, 68, 137, 142, 157, 262, 298, 300, 301, 319, 331, 373, 510, 514–17, 519, 521, 532; on humanism, 160–61, 163–65, 171; on Plato, 48–49, 166, 232, 289–90, 295–98, 301, 308, 549, 552
    influence of, 7–9, 12, 15, 21, 46–47, 68, 70, 71–73, 76, 82, 95, 109, 132, 142, 161, 167, 171, 208, 226, 260–61, 267–68, 289, 291, 299, 300, 301, 315, 316, 319, 330, 332, 370, 373, 377, 421, 422, 433, 437, 469, 496, 510, 530, 532; on art, 438, 445, 447, 448, 450–51, 458, 512–13, 536, 541
    similarities between, 80–81, 105, 147, 157, 280, 317, 371, 484, 518
on Heidegger, 501, 512
    critique of, on art, 451–53
    introduction to *Der Ursprung des Kunstwerkes,* 438–45, 453
    philosophical justification of, on art, 440–41
    politics of, 445–46, 448–49, 452, 454, 457–58
Heidegger's Ways (Heidegger's Paths), 46, 161
historicism, history in, 205–6, 208, 316, 322, 373–74, 411–12, 464, 468, 473
on human nature, 245
on humanism, 157, 161–64, 166–67
on humanities, 206, 257
and Husserl, 12, 15, 105, 109, 462
on the I-Thou encounter, 510
The Idea of the Good in Platonic-Aristotelian Philosophy, 263, 289, 290, 298, 300, 309
on intentionality, critique of, 460
on interpretation, 111, 114, 116–18, 120, 125–26, 176, 210, 219–21, 227, 317–18, 463–65, 469
    difference between correct and false, 472

on jurisprudence, 513
on justice, 242, 243, 244, 249–50
and Kant, 68, 69, 84, 105–6, 109, 135, 140, 141, 161–62, 223
    influence of, xvii, 56, 103, 131, 154–55, 235, 274, 287
on language, linguisticality, 22, 28, 269, 322, 328, 360, 386, 431, 469, 472, 473
    anthropological basis for, 530
    and art, 39
    and community, 248, 339
    as dialogue, 37, 165, 264–65, 269, 271, 325–26, 333
    as disclosure (*alētheia*), 319
    distinction prior to, 531
    as embodying, 250
    and existence, 261
    and experience, 28, 29
    and lifeworld, 531–33, 534, 536
    as a game, 41–43
    and hermeneutics, 25, 29, 37, 39, 42–43
    and naming, 533
    neediness of, 484, 491, 496
    openness of, 37, 266, 326
    and philosophy, 25, 38
    and relativism, 29
    and the unsayable, 496
    and the word, 22, 487, 496
    and writing, 487 (*see also* Gadamer: on writing)
life of, 3–4, 14–15, 223–24
    critique of, in relation to politics, 499–506
Lutheran influence on, 519, 521, 522–23, 527
on meaning, constitution of, 464
on meaning- and truth-happening, 80, 83, 89
metaphorical thought of, 259, 269–70
and metaphysics, 48, 310, 319
ontological thought of, 259, 260–62, 264–68
on the other, 325, 327–30, 339
People and History in the Thinking of Herder, 14
phenomenology in, 530
Philosophical Apprenticeships, 499–501, 503, 508
philosophical hermeneutics of, 26–28, 40–57, 73, 99, 123, 149, 165, 194, 201, 410, 503 (*see also* hermeneutic philosophy, hermeneutics)
and *agape,* 334

and art, role of, 26, 29, 43–44, 100, 171, 176–77, 195, 449, 452 (*see also* Gadamer: on art)
and authority, 198–99, 205
and charity, 124
circle in, 113 (*see also* hermeneutic circle)
and community, 323 (*see also* Gadamer: on community)
and concept of "earth," 442
and consciousness, 27, 41, 373
and conversation, 36, 45, 225–26, 297
as critique of reason, 372
and deconstruction, contrast with, 228–29
and democracy, 343
and desire, 396–97, 403
and distance, role of, 45–46
and experience, 28, 29, 36, 101, 102, 104–6, 176–77, 195, 198, 199, 226, 231, 235, 279, 375, 473
and game playing, 42, 225
and *Geisteswissenschaften* (humanities), 20, 40, 71, 100, 130, 137, 161, 194, 195, 197, 198, 199–200, 202, 326, 366
hierarchical structure in, 199
and historicism, history, 148, 369–70, 373–75, 444; finitude of, 373, 376, 377–78
as insular, 506
and interpretation, 119, 125–26, 372, 459 (*see also* Gadamer: on interpretation; interpretation); failure of, 230–31
and language, 40–43, 165, 195, 228, 249, 352–53, 375, 377–78, 389, 393, 502 (*see also* Gadamer: on language, linguisticality)
and literature, 50
logic of question and answer in, 372–73, 375, 386
and the natural sciences, 28, 40–41, 73, 76, 99
nonessentialism of, 349
as ontological, 208, 461
and otherness, 41, 396
phases of, 99–103
as phenomenological, 358
and philosophy's history, 173
as practical philosophy, xvii, 176, 298, 300, 357

and prejudice (*Vorurteil*), 227, 374–75 (*see also* Gadamer: on prejudice)
and relativism, contrast with, 228–30
and science, 71, 76, 357 (*see also* Gadamer: on science)
and Socratic dialogue, 28
and textuality, 353
and traditional philosophy, use of, 47, 375
and truth, 99–101, 225, 314, 321–22
and understanding, 70, 77, 80, 225, 351, 357, 371–73, 397, 437, 444 (*see also* Gadamer: on understanding)
universality of, 71, 75, 79–80, 111, 114, 270, 301, 349, 350, 353, 370, 373, 386
and the voice, 389–90, 392–99
on philosophy, 244, 246–47, 248, 251, 263, 453–54
and the question, role of, 244
and politics, 508
on *phronēsis* (*see phronēsis:* and Gadamer)
on Plato, xvii, 7, 12, 40, 56, 223, 224, 229, 235–36, 245, 249, 251, 257, 260, 290, 300, 458, 530
anamnēsis, concept of, 299
and Aristotle, proximity between, 9, 10, 11, 48, 263, 274, 290, 293, 295–96, 302, 308, 309, 553
and art, 134, 536–37
and beauty, 131, 332, 539–40, 545
Cratylus, 487, 496
dialogue of, 32, 37, 38, 250, 421
and doctrine of Ideas, 294
as the father of humanism, 166
and the Good, 294, 297, 539, 540, 542–43
influence of, 12, 32, 37, 38, 48, 97, 129, 166
and metaphysics, 32, 232, 545
on the One and the Indeterminate Dyad (Two), 231–33, 549, 550
on the one and the many, 295–96
on participation in the idea, 296
Phaedrus, 394–95, 450
Philebus, 421–24, 428–31, 433–35, 487, 490, 542–43, 549
"Plato and the Poets" ("Plato und die Dichter"), 13, 14, 239, 241–43, 245–46, 250, 256
"Plato's Educational State," 13, 14
recovery of, 292

on the soul, 295
Sophist, 549
Statesman, 542
Timaeus, 475–76
Plato im Dialog, 219, 274
Plato's Dialectical Ethics (Platos dialektis-che Ethik), 246, 249, 290, 292, 421, 424, 428, 433
on play (games), 27, 41, 249–51, 262, 366, 473, 530
political hermeneutics/themes of, 239, 243–44, 247, 248, 249–53, 309, 356, 357
on primacy of past, 69, 95
on practical philosophy, 55–56
on prejudice, 237, 278–80, 281–82, 317, 318, 332, 338, 460–61, 463
on progress, 78, 96
on prudence, 226–27, 235
psychological hermeneutics, critique of, 464
on the question, importance of, 358, 460, 468
and relativism, 81, 125, 221, 262
rejection of, 281, 282
The Relevance of the Beautiful, 332, 529, 530, 536–37
on ritual, 529, 530, 533, 534, 535, 536
and conversation, 531, 532
and rightness, 533–34
showing and naming in, 532
and Schleiermacher, differences between, 68, 69, 70
on science, 57, 77, 139, 147, 161, 193, 194–96, 205, 226, 366
on *sensus communis,* 137, 141, 144, 146, 257
(*see also sensus communis*)
and Socrates, 155, 166, 219, 257, 259–60, 262, 265, 267, 269–71, 274, 297, 300, 301, 309, 429
on songs of praise, 248, 249
on subjectivism, 472
critique of, 462, 464, 466, 469, 499
as a teacher, 509–10
"Thou," use of, 327, 330–32
on tradition, 239, 278, 281–82, 285, 317, 322, 331
and traditional hermeneutics, replacing of, 68
on truth, 71, 72, 76, 99–101, 135, 198, 261–62, 264, 266, 269–70, 285, 325, 332

Truth and Method (Wahrheit und Methode), 16, 19, 26, 40–57, 124, 129, 135, 149, 171, 227, 244, 289, 297, 347, 356
on aesthetic consciousness and art, 247–48, 251, 512, 536, 538, 540–41
on the beautiful, 537–40
on conversation, 237, 239
critique of, 251–53
on dialogue, 396
on experience, 36, 262
on fusion of horizons (*Horizontverschmelzung*), 177, 237, 238, 247
on *Geisteswissenschaften* (humanities), 161, 207
on Heidegger, 511
hermeneutics in, 67–68, 102, 237, 238, 538
on historical consciousness, 47, 239
on the historical, historicism, history, 53–54, 197–98, 200–202, 219, 369; and the claim to truth, 198
on humanism, 137, 162–63
on humanities, 238
on the I-Thou encounter, 516–18, 521, 522, 523
on language, 41, 45, 238, 239, 260, 483, 490, 512, 537–38
on otherness, 45, 237
on play, 41, 50, 261, 530
on prejudice, 237
on science, 40, 161–62, 193–96, 237–38, 356
sensus communis in, 251
starting point of, 45
on the 'Thou', 116, 195–98
on tradition, 239
on truth, 237–38, 261, 310, 315–19, 540
on understanding, 80, 178, 207 (*see also* Gadamer: on understanding)
on the word, 486
on writing, 394
and Vico, 138–39, 141 (*see also* Gadamer: Vico's influence on)
on understanding (*Verstehen*), 70, 71, 74–77, 80–81, 84, 95–96, 111, 113, 115, 116–17, 118, 178, 184, 207–8, 210, 221, 317–18, 461–62 (*see also* understanding)
anti-Cartesian account of, 467
and application, 463

and changes in world, 473
and community, 323
conditions of the possibility of, 68, 78, 80,
    81, 114, 460
conditions of the possibility of the inter-
    subjective validity of, 68
as dialectic, dialogic, 323, 326, 329, 340,
    379, 389, 468, 518
and Enlightenment principles, 279–80,
    283–85
and experience, role of, 279, 280
and explanation, 358
and historicity, history, 207, 208, 374, 464,
    466
as linguistic, 28
openness of, to other, 326, 332, 333, 339,
    340
and overcoming of distance, 463
as reaching out, 460
Vico's influence on, 138, 140, 142, 143,
    145–46, 154
Wer bin ich, Wer bist du, 537
on writing, relationship of, to speech,
    389–94, 398, 403, 485, 486, 487, 535,
    536
Gadamer-Lekebusch, Käte, 18, 502
Gaiser, K., 236
Galileo, 11, 28, 144, 386
Geertz, Clifford, 353, 354
Geisteswissenschaften (humanities), 27, 45, 46,
    76, 137
and hermeneutics, 20, 40, 71, 79 (*see also*
    Gadamer: philosophical hermeneutics
    of, and *Geisteswissenschaften*)
George, Stefan, 5, 32, 50, 245
George circle, 5, 458
German idealist philosophy, 8, 11, 21, 23, 27,
    29, 32, 36, 106
German romantics, romanticism, 6, 22, 23, 26
Goethe, Johann Wolfgang von, 13, 15, 50, 158,
    160, 256, 503
Gogarten, Friedrich, 46
the Good, transcendental status of, 310 (*see*
    also Plato: and the Good)
Grandy, Richard, 122, 123
Grumach, 293
Gundolf, Friedrich, 5
Gutenberg, Johann, 403

Habermas, Jürgen, 17

concept of reflection in, 32
discourse philosophy of, 79
and Gadamer, 29–30, 32, 55, 119–20,
    123–24, 125, 201, 261
    debate between, 350–52, 366, 506
and hermeneutics, 29, 350–51, 355–56, 358,
    360
Hermeneutik und Ideologiekritik, 79
Hacking, Ian, 122, 123
Haecker, Theodore, 46
Hamann, Richard, 458
Hamerow, Theodore S., 227
Hartmann, Nicolai, 7, 8
Metaphysik der Erkenntnis, 8
Haydn, Franz Joseph, 212
Hayek, F. A., 354, 355, 366
Hazard, Paul, 142
Hegel, G. W. F., 7, 173, 184, 191, 240, 270,
    372, 403, 472, 490, 526, 530
on art, 134, 176, 441–42, 453, 537, 545
on Battle of Jena, 216–17
beyond subjectivity, 37
concept of mind, 70
on desire, 396
dialectic of, 32, 37, 38, 45, 83, 244, 267, 389,
    516, 535
on the end of history, 35
on freedom, 35
and Gadamer (*see* Gadamer: and Hegel)
and Greek philosophy, 32, 36
and Heidegger, 36–37, 220, 453
and historicism, 370, 375, 385
history of philosophy of, 35
and Kant, 274
Kierkegaard on, 6, 7, 46
on language, 491
Lectures on the History of Philosophy, 9
Logic, 9
and metaphysics, 385, 387
and morality, 88
Outline of a Logic, 21
Phenomenology, 163, 238, 373, 382, 396,
    488
and Platonism, 34
and reason, 380
Science of Logic, 37
on Spirit (absolute spirit), 76, 268, 377, 545
on spirit and time, 80
and understanding, 81
Hegelian logic, 23

Heidegger, Martin, 19, 28, 95, 142, 178, 183, 190, 221, 270, 324, 327, 346, 501, 509, 523
  on *alētheia,* 68, 71–73, 311–13, 321, 332, 441, 450–53, 520, 549
  on Aristotle, 9–10, 23–24, 28, 38, 49, 268, 290–93, 296, 299, 302, 308, 437, 458, 514, 521, 549–50, 552, 553
  on art, 439–44, 448–49, 453, 458, 491
    and "the people," 443–44, 448, 449
  Basic Problems, 298
  on Being, 68, 80, 90, 160–61, 175, 180, 292, 512, 517, 519, 521
    forgetfulness, withdrawal, of, 34, 68, 159
    opening of, 72, 74–75
    "being" and "meaning," conflation of, 177, 185
  Being and Time (Sein und Zeit), 9, 11, 27, 46, 68, 72, 74, 109, 112, 117, 171, 210, 296, 298, 299, 313, 385, 439, 440, 443, 509, 511, 514, 515
  Biblical underpinnings of, 519–20
  on conscience, 514, 521
  on conversation, 297–98
  on *Dasein,* 11, 45, 46, 117, 261, 299, 376, 377, 440, 511
  Derrida on, 47
  Destruktion, concept of, 8, 21, 22, 24, 37, 291, 535
  dogmatism of, 291–93, 302
  early, 21, 22, 23, 109, 261, 526
  on "earth," 440–42, 448
  fragmentary quality of works, 224
  and Gadamer (*see* Gadamer: and Heidegger)
  "Gnosticism" in, 510, 511, 514, 519, 521, 526
  on Greek philosophy, 8–11, 32, 34, 36, 70, 135, 296, 519, 520, 549
  and Hegel, closeness to, 453
  and hermeneutics, 49, 113, 118, 484
    "hermeneutics of facticity," 511
  historicism of, 513
  on Hölderlin (*see* Hölderlin: and Heidegger)
  on humanism, 157, 158–61, 163–64, 166
  and Husserl, 22, 23, 72, 511, 514
  on information, 484
  on interpretation, 114, 120
    Auslegung, 112–13, 217
    Interpretierung, 112–13
  and Kant, 68, 122, 302

  and Kierkegaard, 509, 511
  and language, 37, 38, 165, 472, 483–84, 496
    neediness of, 484
    in the poem, 484
    and translation, 484
  later, 46, 47, 90, 458, 496, 517, 518
  Letter on Humanism, 137, 142, 159, 163–64, 521
  on meaning, 121
  on metaphysics, 8, 36, 37, 46, 48, 68, 159, 161, 163, 171, 289, 311–12, 389, 535, 550, 552
  ontic and ontological, distinction between, 371
  The Origin of the Work of Art (Der Ursprung des Kunstwerkes), 47, 536, 544
  on Parmenides, 489
  phenomenology in, 21, 22
  on philosophy
    the beginnings of, 24
    Plato as example, 38
    the task of, 22
  and phronēsis, 521, 526
  on Plato, 10, 34, 38, 68, 159, 166, 289–96, 299, 302, 308, 311–12, 458, 521, 549–50, 552, 553
  Plato's Doctrine of Truth, 159, 311
  politics of, 438, 443, 448, 449, 452, 454, 457–58, 503
  as seeker after God, 458, 521
  and Staiger, controversy between, 220
  on temporality, 511–12
  on the Thou, 514–15
  on truth, 35, 37, 72–73, 118, 121, 299, 311–13
    alētheia and *orthotes,* contrast between, 311–13, 321
  on understanding (*Verstehen*), 84, 85–86
    existential structure of, 26–27, 101
    lack of progress in, 26–27, 75
  violence in, 514, 521, 527
  What Is Called Thinking?, 297
  on the work of art, 37
  on world, 122, 440
  on writing, 485, 489, 491
Heinze, Richard, 8
Hempel, Carl, 357
Henkel, Arthur, 13
Henrich, Dieter, 17

Heraclitus, 29, 183, 220, 437
Herder, Johann Gottfried, 14, 162, 163
"hermeneutic circle," 90, 113, 118, 119, 121,
      148, 149, 373
hermeneutic economics, 353–55
hermeneutic philosophy, hermeneutics, 146, 190
      (*see also* Gadamer: philosophical
      hermeneutics of)
   application of, to politics and power, 355–56
   and art, 442
   "being" and "meaning," conflation of, 177,
      179, 180
   Cartesianism, critique of, 468
   and community, 342
   as critique, 355, 356, 358
   and Davidson, 111
   and distance, role of, 45–46
   dualism, rejection of, 358
   in early Christian theology, 99
   on explanation, 358–60
   and *Geisteswissenschaften* (humanities), 20,
      40, 71, 79 (*see also* Gadamer: philo-
      sophical hermeneutics of, and
      Geisteswissenschaften)
   and Greek philosophy, 25 (*see also* philoso-
      phy: Greek)
   and historicity, history, 405, 413–14, 459,
      468
   and humanism, 167 (*see also* humanism)
   and intention of author, role of, 52–53
   and interpretation, 111–12, 114, 116, 119,
      185, 358 (*see also* interpretation)
   and language, 25, 29, 37, 39, 40–43, 75, 112,
      352, 483
      and being, relation between, 483
      and need for words, 483
   and law, 180
   and modern science, 30
   and philosophy, relation between, 30, 31, 99,
      102, 183, 185
   pluralism of, 357, 360
   and poetry, 39–40
   and pragmatism, 325, 343
   primacy of practical in, 355–57
   and providence, 147
   and psychologism, 52
   and the question, sense of, 146, 358 (*see also*
      Gadamer: on the question, importance
      of)
   radical interpretation in, 112

   and reading, 51–52, 486
   and reflection, 147–49
   and relativism, 177
      contrast between, 228–30
   and rhetoric, 30, 55
   and science, 29–30, 40–41, 56, 357
   subjectivism, critique of, 459, 465
   transcendental (as distinct from philosophi-
      cal), 69, 70, 73, 81, 82, 87, 90
   and understanding, 50, 52–53, 56, 57, 69, 70
      finitude of, 483
      intersubjective, 73
   universality of, 10, 25, 28, 29, 40, 73–74,
      119, 349, 353, 360
      nonessentialist, 357, 360
      paradox of, 111, 115, 119
   and unmasking critique, 79
   and the voice, 486 (*see also* Gadamer: philo-
      sophical hermeneutics of, and the voice)
   and writing, 486 (*see also* Gadamer: on writ-
      ing)
"hermeneutics of suspicion," "method of suspi-
      cion," 81, 326
Hermogenes, 487
Herodotus, 407
Hesiod, 333
Hesiodic verse, 25
Hesse, Hermann, 4
Hildebrandt, Kurt, 33
Hindemith, Paul
   Ludus Tonalis, 214
Hirsch, E. D., 113, 261
historical relativism, 5, 6, 8, 16, 385–86 (*see
      also* historicism)
the "Historical School," 23
historicism, historicists, 379–80, 382, 385, 410,
      460 (*see also* historical relativism)
   and critique of reason, 369, 379–80
   first-degree, 369, 385
   philosophical form of, 369–70
   second-degree, 369–70, 385
history
   and *Ausgangspunkt,* 412–13
   of concepts, 18
   and consciousness, 500
   definitions of, 410–11, 412
   as distinct from philology, 54–55
   and lightness, 408–9, 410, 412
   of metaphysics, 34
   philosophical creation of, 405

reconstruction of, 88–89, 90, 405–6, 408, 410, 412–13
Hitler, Adolf, 13, 256, 503, 504
Hobbes, Thomas, 240, 241
Hölderlin, Friedrich, 10, 15, 50, 133, 223, 408,
and Heidegger, 37, 46, 165, 298, 302, 439, 444, 458, 484, 496
Homer, Homeric verse, 24, 25, 335, 391, 393
  Iliad, 408–9
Hönigswald, Richard, 4, 109
Horkheimer, Max, 17
humanism, 160, 162–64, 167
  forms of, 158
Humboldt, Wilhelm von, 5, 223, 252, 253, 318
Hume, David, 104, 141, 196
  Dialogues Concerning Natural Religion, 241
Husserl, Edmund
  concept of horizon, 462
  Derrida's critique of, 50
  fragmentary quality of works, 224
  and Gadamer, 12, 15, 105, 109, 235
  and Heidegger, 22, 23, 72, 511, 514
  Ideas, 50, 109
  on ideality, 229
  influence of, 5
  language of, 38
  Logical Investigations, 49, 50
  as Neo-Kantian, 7
  phenomenology of, 12, 19, 21, 22
    and time-consciousness, 49
  on vagueness, 230
Hutcheson, Francis, 141

Ikhnaton, King, 215, 216
Ingarden, Roman, 52, 109
intentionality, externalist account of, 459
interpretation, 51, 53, 176, 183, 218, 219–21
  in Davidson, 112, 114–18, 121, 125
  in Gadamer, 111, 114, 116–18, 120, 125–26
  in Heidegger, 112–13, 114
  in hermeneutics, 111–12, 114, 116, 119, 178, 185
  as historical, 469
  in psychoanalysis, 178, 190
  and subjectivity, 459, 465, 469
  types of, 112–13, 114, 116, 119
  and understanding (*see* understanding: and interpretation)
intersubjective validity of norms, 78
Isocrates, 360

Jaeger, Werner, 8, 158, 245, 433
  Paideia, 15
James, William, 100, 329, 346
Jaspers, Karl, 16, 158, 409
Jauß, Hans-Robert, 44
Judaism. *See* rabbinical Judaism

Kafka, Franz
  The Trial, 191
Kahler, Erich von, 5
Kant Immanuel, 21, 34, 39, 70, 78, 133, 142, 173, 216, 380, 537
  on art, 247, 441
  critique of the antinomies, 37
  Critique of Judgment, xvii, 11, 44, 238, 274
  Critique of Pure Reason, 103–4, 314, 322, 385, 472
  on the Enlightenment, 276, 277, 287
  Foundation for a Metaphysics of Morals, 56
  and Gadamer (*see* Gadamer: and Kant)
  and Heidegger, 68, 122, 302
  language of, 38
  and Plato, 48, 299
  practical philosophy of, 472
  Prolegomena, 23
  regulative ideal in, 69
  and science, 161, 287, 379, 460
  Third Critique, 141
  on truth, 314
Kantian "history of problems," 6
Kantians, 17, 23
Keats, John, 334
Kempff, Wilhelm, 213
Kiefer, Anselm, 450
Kierkegaard, Søren, 6, 7, 180, 380, 385, 409, 512, 520, 521, 522, 527, 545
  Either-Or, 6
  and historicism, 380
  influence of
    on Gadamer, 7, 46, 56
    on Heidegger, 21, 509, 511, 526
  Kierkegaardian absurdist paradox, 179
Kimmerle, Heinz, 17
Klein, Jakob, 13, 219, 236, 501
Kleist, Heinrich von, 50
Kline, George, xvi, 173, 178, 179
Kripke, Saul, 74
Kristallnacht, 257
Krüger, Gerhard, 274
Kuhn, Helmut, 18, 224

Kuhn, Thomas, 28, 75, 89, 123
Künne, Wolfgang, 17

Lacan, Jacques, 403
Lacoue-Labarthe, Philippe, 446
Lakatos, Imre, 89–90
Langer, Susanne K., 132
language, linguisticality, 360 (*see also*
    Gadamer: on language, linguisticality;
    philosophy: and language)
  and desire, 395
  and hermeneutics, 75, 112
  and meaning, 75
  neediness of, 485
  and poetry, 484–85
  and the voice, 392
  and words, 485
    and image, relation between, 487, 491, 496
  and writing (script), 488–91, 496
Lask, Emil, 346
Leibniz, G. W., 34, 488
Leisegang, Hans, 12
Lenin, V. I., 251
Lessing, Theodor, 158
  Europa und Asien, 4
Levin, Harry, 422
Levinas, Emmanuel, 327, 483, 491
'Liberal-Communitarian' Debate, 240
liberalism, 240, 252–53
"life-philosophy," 5
lifeworld (*Lebenswelt*), 75, 80, 84, 85, 346, 413
  of animals, 531
  Gadamer on, 85, 96, 176, 531–33, 534
Linge, David, 464
Lipps, Hans, 346
Litt, Theodor, 15, 29
Lledo, Emilio, 17
Locke, John, 143, 240, 252
logical positivism. *See* positivism
Lorenzen, Paul, 70
Löwith, Karl, 17, 48, 298, 509
Lukács, Georg, 251, 346, 458
Luke (biblical), 519
Lukes, Steven, 122
Luther, Martin, 519, 520, 522–23
Lütkehermölle, Matthias; xvi
Lyotard, Jean-Francois, 86

MacDonald, Graham, 122
Mach, Ernst, 104

MacIntyre, Alasdair, 84, 86, 173, 228, 240, 370,
    385
Maimon, Moshe ben, 183
Mallarmé, Stéphane, 537
Mann, Thomas, 4
Mannheim, Karl, 369
Marburg school, of philosophy, 7, 23
Margolis, Joseph, 360
Marty, Anton, 99
Marx, Karl, 7, 326
  Das Kapital, 251
McDowell, John, 466
McGinn, Colin, 466
Mead, George Herbert, 328
Meinecke, Friedrich, 369
Meinong, Alexius, 21, 99, 101, 103, 109
  On Emotional Presentation, 101
mens auctoris (mind of the author), 52, 463,
    473
the mental, mind,
  conceptions of, 466–67
    externalist, 467, 468–69
    relationalist, 467
  and dualism, 466
Merleau-Ponty, Maurice, 158, 397, 410
metaphysical tradition, 310–11, 313, 321–22
Michelangelo, 1
Mill, John Stuart, 240, 252
modern political philosophy/theory, 240, 242,
    248, 252
Modica, Giuseppe, 140
Mona Lisa, 210
Mondrian, Piet, 442
Monet, Claude, 174–75, 177, 190
Mörike, Eduard, 220
Mosaic code, 181
Moses (biblical), 182–83
Mozart, Wolfgang Amadeus, 212
  The Magic Flute, 223
Musil, Robert, 14

Nagel, Thomas, 101
Napoleon I, 217
Narcissus (mythical), 398
National Socialism, 13, 438, 445, 457–58
Natorp, Paul, 7, 8, 49, 291, 346, 437, 458
Natural Science Ideal, 354
Nazi party (the Party), 14, 15, 158, 239, 241,
    242, 257, 458, 500, 503, 504
Neo-Aristotelian ethics, 88

Neo-Kantianism, 4, 5, 6, 8, 21, 23, 36, 37, 38, 76, 109, 247, 290–91, 346, 526
   on aesthetics, 441, 442
   on the "history of problems," 7, 8, 23
Neopositivists, 36
Neo-Scholastics, 290
Neo-Thomism, 291
Neville, Robert, 173
New Testament, 516, 521
Newman, Barnett, 450
Newton, Isaac, 89, 133
Newtonian physics, 70
Nicholas of Cusa, 34, 223
Nietzsche, Friedrich, 79, 302, 319, 326, 527, 553
   and death of god, 240, 257
   Derrida on, 47–48
   and fascism, 241
   influence of, 5, 6, 7, 15, 32, 83, 218
   and Gadamer, 5, 6, 7, 15, 32, 82, 531
   on interpretation, 221
   and liberalism, 253
   on *Redlichkeit* (honesty), 221
nominalism, 20

Oakeshott, Michael, 226, 227, 230
   On Human Conduct, 224
Odysseus, 391
Ogden, C. K., 118
Onians, Richard, 391
ontic and ontological, distinction between, 371–72
Operation Rescue, 502
Ordinary Language Analysis, 308
Osenburg, 13
Osenburg-action, 14

Palmer, Richard E., xvi
Parmenides, 80, 183, 292, 377, 553
Pascal, Blaise, 191
Peirce, C. S., 69, 70, 73, 97, 120
Perelman, Chaim, 30
Pflaumer, Ruprecht, 17
phenomenology, 21, 229, 358 (*see also* Husserl: phenomenology of)
Phidias, 6
philology, as distinct from history, 54–55
philosophical hermeneutics. *See* Gadamer: philosophical hermeneutics of; hermeneutic philosophy, hermeneutics
Philosophische Rundschau, 18, 224, 502

philosophy, 16, 20, 24, 39
   American, 83, 97, 99, 323, 346, 347
   analytic, 19, 23
   Anglo-Saxon, 19, 83
   and art, 177
   and being, recollection of, 35
   continental, 19, 111
   dialogue in, 379
   first, 224–25
   Gadamer on (*see* Gadamer: on philosophy)
   German, 20, 21, 22, 23
   Greek, 7, 9, 19, 20, 25
   and hermeneutics, 30, 39
   and historicism, 7
   and history, 183–86
   history of, 70, 146, 173
   and interpretation, 177
   and language, 20, 21–22, 25, 30, 37–38, 48, 112
   and material life, relation between, 505–6
   and normative presuppositions of, 86–87, 88
   and the question, priority of, 244
   and reason, 381
   and reflection, 85, 146
   and relativism, 177
   and Socratic method, 244
phronēsis
   in Aristotle, 31, 298, 301, 338, 366, 514
   and *ēthos,* inseparability of, 97
   and Gadamer, 9, 298, 301, 310, 326, 338, 366, 514, 521
   and Heidegger, 9, 513
   and hermeneutics, 338, 356, 357
   Vico's use of, 143
Pindar, 10, 135
Plato, 80, 171, 183, 216, 262–63, 270, 376, 530
   Apology, 262, 266
   and Aristotle, similarities between, 9, 10, 11, 48, 263, 274, 293, 295, 308, 553 (*see also* Aristotle: on Plato)
   on art, 542
   on beauty, 332, 539–40, 542
   on care of the soul, 259, 266
   Charmides, 33, 295
   Clitophon, 434
   Cratylus, 487–88, 490, 491, 496
   dialectic in, 33, 34, 421, 425–26, 428, 430, 435
   dialogues of, 9, 24, 32, 34, 235, 434
      relationship of, to each other, 421

and the doctrine of Ideas, 32, 33, 34, 263,
    268, 294, 299
on *eros,* 324, 333
esoteric teaching of, 232
Euthyphro, 428
Gadamer on (*see* Gadamer: on Plato)
and the Good, 57, 263, 294, 309–10, 321,
    539, 542–43)
Gorgias, 292
Heidegger on (*see* Heidegger: on Plato)
Hippias Major, 232
Ion, 542
Laches, 33, 309, 428
Lysis, 33
the One and the Indeterminate Dyad (Two),
    231–33, 549, 550
Parmenides, 33, 232, 293, 427, 435
Phaedo, 30, 298, 434, 435, 510
Phaedrus (Phaidros), 292, 296, 298, 427,
    429, 450, 487, 535
    on writing, 485–86, 490, 496; and speak-
    ing, difference between, 390–91,
    394–95, 397–98, 403
Philebus, 12, 232, 290, 292, 293–94, 297,
    540, 542–43, 549
    on collection and division, 424–27
    elenctic method in, 423–25, 427, 428
    the Forms in, 422, 429, 435
    on the human good and virtue, 423,
    424–25, 426–27, 429, 430, 433
    relation of, to other dialogues, 422, 423,
    424–30, 434,
    on writing, 487, 490
Politicus, 422, 424, 425
and Protestantism, 19
on reason, 380, 382
Republic, 13, 172, 174, 232, 294, 295, 427,
    428, 429, 434, 478, 508, 542
    the Divided Line, 311, 313
    on the Good, 309–10
    the ideas as generative, 427
    parable of the cave, 311, 312–13
and science, 11, 31
Seventh Letter (Seventh Epistle), 24, 33–39,
    49, 230, 434, 496, 535, 552
and Socrates (*see* Socrates: and Plato)
Sophist, 10, 232, 291, 292, 293, 422, 424,
    425, 426, 549
Statesman, 293, 294, 542
Symposium, 166, 296, 332, 333–34

Theaetetus, 293, 294–96, 424
Timaeus (Timaios), 30
    on beginnings, 476, 480, 482
    discourses in, 476–77; choric, 479–80;
        memorial, 476, 478, 480, 482; narrative,
        478, 482
    mathematics, in, 482
    on truth, 310–13
    on word and icon, relation between, 487–88
    on writing, 390–91, 394–95, 397–98, 403,
        485, 489, 497
Platonism, 20, 34, 44, 379
Plotinus, 7, 34, 135, 183, 526, 545
poetry, 39–40, 484–85
Polanyi, Michael, 36
Pollini, Maurizio, 213
Popper, Karl, xvi, 41
positivism, 6, 357, 358
postmodernism, 79, 177, 215, 349, 355
poststructuralism, 79, 352, 506
pragmatism, pragmatists, 83, 84, 323–25, 341,
    343, 346–47
pre-Socratics, xvii, 183, 292, 302
Prokofiev, Sergei, 216
psychē, 391
Putnam, Hilary, 74
Pythagoreans, 294

Quakers, 7
"quest for the historical Jesus," 179
Quine, W. V. O., 112, 115

rabbinical Judaism, 181, 185
radical interpretation. *See* Davidson, Donald:
    "radical interpretation" of
Rambach, J. J., 113
Ramberg, Bjørn, 120–21, 122, 124
Ranke, Otto, 55, 206, 369
Ravel, Maurice, 213
Rawls, John, 119, 120, 240, 252
reading
    as center of hermeneutics, 51–52
    nature of, 52–53
realism (Scholastic), 20
reason, adequacy of, 381–82
reception-aesthetics, 44
recollection of being. *See* being: recollection of
Reich, Klaus, 17
Reichenbach, Hans, 184
Reid, Thomas, 102

Reinhardt, Karl, 13
relativism, 228–29, 281, 282 (*see also* historical
    relativism)
Renaissance, the, 158, 160, 162
reproduction
    as interpretation, 51
    nature of, 52–53
rhetoric, 30
Richards, I. A., 118
Rickert, Heinrich, 83
Ricoeur, Paul, 82, 351, 353, 366, 389
Rilke, Rainer Maria, xvii, 15, 50, 132, 223, 519
Rorty, Richard, 84, 86, 173, 176, 349, 370, 385
Rosen, Stanley, 173, 177, 355
Rosenzweig, Franz, 46
Rousseau, Jean-Jacques, 147, 287
Royce, Josiah, 69, 97, 340–41
    The Problem of Christianity, 340
Rushd, Ibn, 183
Russell, Bertrand, 74

Sachs, Eva, 482
Salin, 5
Sappho, 334
Sartre, Jean-Paul, 158, 327
Schaeffer, John, 140
Scheler, Max, 7, 102, 346, 501
Schelling, Friedrich Wilhelm Joseph von, 134,
    486
Schiller, F. C. S., vii, ix, x, 131, 158, 160, 238,
    244, 247, 252
Schilpp, Paul Arthur, vii
Schlegel, Friedrich, 124
Schleiermacher, Friedrich, 18, 23, 411, 420, 475
    and Gadamer, 465
    differences between, 68, 69, 70
    hermeneutics of, 26, 29, 68, 118, 367
    on interpretation, 53, 221
Schlick, Moritz, 41
Schmidt, Dennis J., xvi
Schnabel, Artur, 213
Schneewind, Jerome, 173
Schnittke, Alfred, 212
Schoenberg, Arnold, 213, 214
Scholasticism, 20, 38, 291, 302, 496, 535
Schulz, Walter, 13
Schütz, Alfred, 102, 109
Schweitzer, Albert, 178
science(s), 20, 148, 386
    and experience, 36

Gadamer on, 57, 77, 96, 139, 147, 161–62,
    193, 194–96, 206, 226, 356, 357, 366
Greek, 11, 56
and hermeneutics, 29–30, 40–41, 99, 224
history of, 70
of history, 193, 195, 200–202, 205
and humanism, 164
and Kant, 161, 287, 379, 460
and language, 22, 25, 29, 224
and learning processes, 75
method of, 196
modern, 11, 20, 30, 32, 37, 56, 224, 226
natural, 28, 30, 40–41, 73, 77, 78, 99, 102,
    147–48, 149, 202, 205, 238, 357, 358,
    366, 367, 382, 472
and rationality, reason, 31
the spread of, 23–24
and understanding, 96
Scriabin, Alexander, 213, 216
Seebohm, Thomas, 47, 148–49
sensus communis, 240, 241, 242, 248 (*see also*
    Gadamer: on *sensus communis;* Vico:
    sensus communis of)
Serkin, Rudolf, 213
Shaftesbury, Third Earl of, 137, 138, 141, 155
Shakespeare, William, 6, 32, 209
    Hamlet, 209, 331
Shostakovich, Dmitri, 213
Simmel, Georg, 458
Sina, Ibn, 183
Singer, Kurt, 33
Smith, John, 173
Smith, P. Christopher, 297
Snell, Bruno, 391
Sociobiology, 357
Socrates, 146, 183, 190, 266, 268, 373, 387,
    535
    on care of the soul, 253, 263, 265
    and the discipline of dialogue, 267
    elenctic of, 422, 423, 430
    and the Good, 30, 31, 57, 312
    and Gadamer, 155, 166, 219, 257, 259, 262,
        265, 267, 269–71, 274, 297, 300, 301,
        309, 429
    and human wisdom, 30, 31
    and humanism, 158
    and irony, 32
    and Plato, 10, 259, 262, 270, 434
    and science, 30
Socratic dialogue, dialectic, 28, 33, 271, 373, 376

Socratic ignorance, 553
Socratic wisdom, xvii
Solon, 407, 408
Sommermeier, Ralf, xvi
Sophists, the, 242
Sophocles, 6, 13, 32
Spencer, Theodore, 422
Spengler, Oswald
 The Decline of the West, 4
Spinoza, Baruch, 314, 317, 322
 Ethics, 314
 on history, 411
 Tractatus theologico-politicus (Theologico-Political Treatise), 241, 314
Spitzer, M., 220
St. Paul (biblical), 333, 335, 522
Staiger, Emil, 220
Stalin, Joseph, 251
Stenzel, Julius, 9, 435
Stevens, Wallace, 19
Stoics, Stoicism, 142, 143, 145, 147, 335
Strauss, Leo, 33, 209, 219, 224, 232, 236
subject, subjectivity, 470, 472
 conceptions of, 459, 466
 non-Cartesian, 469
Sullivan, Robert, 500, 508
Swift, Jonathan, 13

Tagore, Rabindranath, 7
Talmud, the, 182, 190
Tarski, Alfred, 119, 121
textualism and actionalism, comparison
 between, 465–66
theology
 Christian, 8, 19, 20, 179–80
 and Greek metaphysics, 8, 19
theory of signs, 21
Theuth, 426, 487, 490
Thucydides, 209
Torah, the, 181–82, 184, 190
totality, 37
transcendental hermeneutics. *See* hermeneutic
 philosophy, hermeneutics: transcendental (as distinct from philosophical)
Trede, J. H., 17
Troeltsch, Ernst, 5, 369
truth (*see also* Gadamer: on truth; Heidegger: on truth)

dual principles of, 313–14, 321
 transcendental status of, 310
Tugendhat, Ernst, 71–72
Twardowski, Kazimierz, 99

understanding
 as context dependent, 71, 75, 81–82, 83–84, 113, 118
 and dialogue, 432
 and explanation, opposition between, 358
 Gadamer on (*see* Gadamer: on understanding)
 Heidegger on, 26–27, 84, 85–86
 and hermeneutics, 31, 50, 52, 57, 69, 70, 75
 in the humanities, 70, 75
 and intention of author, 52–53
 and interpretation, 53, 113, 115, 221, 432, 465
  difference between, 211–12, 214–15
 and intersubjective validity, 81, 83
 linguisticality of, 28
 as ontic and ontological, 371
 progress in, possibility of, 75
 as reading, 51
 and reflection, 69–70, 81, 83
 regulative idea of, 71
 and science, 96
 temporal ontology of, 69
 universal norms for, 84, 87–88
"Unified Science" movement, 357

van Gogh, Vincent, 6
Valéry, Paul, 316, 322
Vattimo, Gianni, 17
Verra, Valerio, 17
Vico, Giambattista, 30, 137–49, 155
 on a common mental dictionary, 144–45, 149
 on the cycle of history, 142–43, 149
 and humanism, 138, 142, 146
 New Science, 138, 139, 140, 146, 149
 on reflection, 140–41, 144, 147, 149, 154
 On the Study Methods of Our Time, 139, 146
 sensus communis of, 138, 140–41, 143–46, 149
Vienna Circle, 104
Vietnamese War, 217
Vlastos, Gregory, 423, 428
the voice. *See* Gadamer: philosophical
 hermeneutics of, and the voice
Volkmann-Schluck, Karlheinz, 13, 15

Wagner, Hans, 5
Warnke, Georgia, 261
Weber, Max, 5, 77
  Protestant Ethic and the Spirit of Capitalism,
    241
Webern, Anton von, 212
Weimar Republic, 256–57
Weizsäcker, Viktor von, 46
Western civilization, unfreedom of, 35
Whitehead, Alfred North, 173
Wiehl, Reiner, 17
Wieland, Wolfgang, 17
Wilamowitz-Moellendorf, Ulrich von, 245–46
Winch, Peter, 358

Winckelmann, Johann Joachim, 158
Wittgenstein, Ludwig, 83, 86, 431, 473
  and Gadamer, connection between, 19, 22,
    39, 84, 85, 97 224, 235
  late, 41, 42, 85
  Tractatus, 39
Wolters, Friedrich, 5, 458
World War I, 3–4, 346, 500
World War II, 158, 256, 504

Yeats, William Butler, 19

Zimmerman, Robert, 99, 105